DATE DUE

THE FIRST
PRESIDENTIAL CONTEST

American Presidential Elections

MICHAEL NELSON

JOHN M. MCCARDELL, JR.

THE FIRST
PRESIDENTIAL CONTEST

1796 AND THE
FOUNDING OF
AMERICAN DEMOCRACY

JEFFREY L. PASLEY

1796

UNIVERSITY PRESS OF KANSAS

Published
by the
University
Press of Kansas
(Lawrence,
Kansas 66045),
which was
organized by the
Kansas Board of
Regents and is
operated and
funded by
Emporia State
University,
Fort Hays State
University,
Kansas State
University,
Pittsburg State
University,
the University
of Kansas, and
Wichita State
University

© 2013 by the University Press of Kansas

Library of Congress Cataloging-in-Publication Data

Pasley, Jeffrey L., 1964–
    The first presidential contest : 1796 and the founding of
American democracy / Jeffrey L. Pasley.
        pages cm. —(American presidential elections)
        ISBN 978-0-7006-1907-8 (cloth : alk. paper) 1. Presidents—
United States—Election—1796. 2. Democracy—United
States—History—18th century. 3. United States—Politics
and government—1789-1809. 4. Adams, John, 1735-1826.
5. Jefferson, Thomas, 1743-1826. I. Title.
    E320.P37 2013
    324.973'041—dc23
                                                    2012049238

British Library Cataloguing-in-Publication Data is available.

Printed in the United States of America

10 9 8 7 6 5 4 3 2 1

The paper used in this publication is recycled and contains
30 percent postconsumer waste. It is acid free and meets the
minimum requirements of the American National Standard
for Permanence of Paper for Printed Library Materials
Z39.48-1992.

CONTENTS

The 1790s was America's true "crucial decade." The bold republican experiment represented, as its currency proclaimed, a *novus ordo saeclorum*, or "new order of the ages." As the first decade of nationhood commenced under a new constitution, every action set a precedent.

"Experience must be our only guide," noted Pennsylvania statesman John Dickinson at the Constitutional Convention. Lessons learned, especially from recent experience, seemed to many of the Founders vivid and fresh. Concentrations of power inevitably corrupted. Executive authority, which could too easily degenerate into tyranny, must be severely circumscribed; yet legislatures, unchecked, could also behave tyrannically. Party and republicanism were antithetical; party could easily become faction, and faction could quickly upset the delicate balances that allowed representative government to function. Distance posed risk; the larger a political entity became, the greater the challenge of preserving the local and familiar against the anonymity of the large and consolidated. Nothing less than the virtue of the public, a prerequisite for just and effective government, was at stake. Leadership must be strong, but it, and the public it served, must also be ever vigilant.

And so, with a mixture of hope and fear, a fragile republic was born. Its first eight years, under the presidency of George Washington, did little to persuade Old World skeptics that the experiment would succeed. Moreover, the Founders themselves discovered many of their most fundamental assumptions challenged. Indeed, almost immediately, and probably inevitably, serious dispute arose. Is the new constitution permissive—if it does not specifically prohibit an action, then is that action allowed? Or is it restrictive—if it does not specifically authorize an action, then is that action proscribed? At what point does permissible dissent become impermissible disloyalty? How extensive ought a president's powers to be? What is the role of the cabinet? Should government play an active role in the development of the economy? Or does any such role risk unnatural outcomes and attendant corruption?

Because of Washington's stature, these vexing questions could be contained, often by a mere presidential utterance. But as his second term came to an end, and contenders vied for succession, the country found itself in an unfamiliar and threatening place. The election of 1796, the first truly contested election in American history, would test the ability of the new republic, and those charged with its preservation and protection, to allow legitimate political debate to occur and political power to transfer peaceably.

Jeffrey L. Pasley tells the story of this election, which he correctly identifies as an "absolutely seminal" event in American political history, with clarity, perspicacity, and wit. To a world descending into yet another round of armed conflict, and forcing neutrals to choose sides, the American experiment appeared to be short-lived. To an electorate schooled to believe that organized parties, even though primitive by today's standards, threatened the health of the republic, a campaign of what Pasley calls "metaphors and morality tales" did not bode well. To a people steeped in republican ideology, the choice posed a challenge to the virtue of the citizenry. To a founding generation that so carefully designed its electoral system to diffuse influence and thwart factionalism, the unintended consequences of their elaborate planning would cause alarm. And to readers accustomed to thinking that the election of 1800 was the first to pose an either-or challenge to voters, Pasley's story will reframe a familiar narrative.

What follows, then, is a careful, gripping story of an often overlooked political moment. Few of the vexing issues would be resolved. Further tests would follow. Many linger still. But the Constitution, and the republican experiment it sought to codify, have proved remarkably resilient, a testimony to the wisdom of the Founders and, not incidentally, for contemporary readers a reminder that lamentations over the present state of politics, in whatever present one may find oneself, are neither as new nor as distracting nor as ominous as might be believed. For these insights, and for a tale filled with colorful personalities and uninhibited rhetoric, readers will relish this lively new work.

ACKNOWLEDGMENTS

This book began its career as a minor side project that instead took over the nonteaching parts of my life for a number of years. I did not find it easy to write, to say the least, and accumulated many debts to the family and colleagues who helped out. My wonderful wife, Karen Kunkel Pasley—as patient with me as she is not with the ills of the world and misusers of the English language—kept me going through some difficult times. Our sons Isaac and Owen have managed to remain, or appear to remain, pleasantly oblivious to the emotional roller coaster that their father was riding. Our life together has not been without its worries, but the love and support and stability and freedom to be ourselves that we have in our little family are things to treasure.

More directly germane to this project, Karen once again acted as my copyeditor and indexer of first resort, and Isaac, who seems to have inherited his father's affinity for dusty library stacks and microfilm rooms, has grown up to be a crack research assistant, quotation checker, and book toter. (Those heavy volumes of Founders' papers do not carry themselves home to my study or back again to be renewed.) I should also ask my family's forgiveness for any neglect they suffered as I was chained to my desk in the basement. My graduate students of the past few years, Steve Smith, Jonathan Jones, Mike Marden, Bill Lewis, and Kris Maulden, probably suffered a little of that, too, while remaining valued comrades and, I hope, learning something. At the same time, the progress of their predecessors Lawrence Hatter and Eric Schlereth through the profession were extremely heartening.

This book would not exist, at least with me as the author, without the implacable, unflappable support of University Press of Kansas director Fred Woodward. Fred and his emails just would not go away, and he maintained confidence in me long after I would have fired myself from the project if I were in his position. I also appreciate the flexibility that he and the American Presidential Elections series editors, Michael Nelson and John McCardell, showed regarding the form and length of the book. It is quite different from the other volumes in the series, but it was the only one on the election of 1796 that I could write, and I am thankful that they saw the value in that uniqueness. The manuscript was much improved by the various comments and corrections and encouragements I received over the course of the editorial and production process, and in addition to the editors and UPK staff, my gratitude goes out to David Waldstreicher, Jack Rakove, Alan Taylor, Sean Wilentz, and Richard Matthews. At other stages, I benefited greatly from the comments of Andrew Burstein, Andrew W. Robertson, David Houpt, and of my University of Missouri colleague Jonathan Sperber.

The astounding Philip J. Lampi of the American Antiquarian Society and its New Nation Votes project were an irreplaceable resource and, in many ways, the source of the thought that a person could do a whole book on the mixed-up election of 1796. Phil's source tips, fact-checks, and shared documents saved me on many occasions, and I can only hope I have not grossly misused any of his hard-earned data. New Nation Votes advisory board meetings and other events with Phil, Andy Robertson, Rosemarie Zagarri, John Brooke, and the rest of our colleagues were always enjoyable and enlightening events. Meanwhile, some of the research that found its way into this book was conducted at the Antiquarian Society's wonderful library during a summer research fellowship in Worcester. My thanks to John Hench and Caroline Sloat for their hospitality during that stay.

Many of those mentioned above are also regulars at my favorite thing about the historical profession, the annual meeting of the Society for Historians of the Early American Republic. The atmosphere of openness, helpfulness, and friendship at SHEAR has always made it puzzling to me when people complain about the "conference circuit." I expect some interesting discussions there in the future about the contents of this book, with Nancy Isenberg, Reeve Huston, Bill Shade, Bill Rorabaugh, Dan Feller, and others already mentioned. To John Quist, Craig Hammond, and the rest of the SHEAR Anti-Temperance Society, I raise a craft-brewed local ale. Literally. Without the inspiration and encouragement of Richard R. John, I would never have gone to SHEAR or most anywhere else I have gotten to go in the profession.

At a very critical moment, Richard B. Bernstein generously helped me find a way into the mystery of John Adams during a dinner in Chattanooga after we had spent the day talking to high school teachers and driving over a mountain. He may not agree with everything in this book, but I hope he will see that I took his suggestions to heart. Bernard Bailyn has not heard much from me in recent years, but I am still coming to grips with his enormous intellectual (and literary) influence. Peter

Onuf has always been a good and generous friend to my work despite my occasional cantankerousness. Commenting on a paper by Washington University in St. Louis graduate student Nathan Green, who was pursuing a different interpretation of some of the same material, helped crystallize my thoughts on the election of 1796. I am grateful to Nate and his adviser, David Konig, for the invitation.

At the University of Missouri, in addition to other colleagues already acknowledged, Russ Zguta, John Wigger, Robert Collins, John Bullion, Steve Watts, Robert Weems, Melinda Lockwood, and Nancy Taube had kind words or deeds for me at times when they were badly needed, and the fellowship of Robert Smale, Michael Bednar, Catherine Rymph, Michelle Morris, Ian Worthington, Mark Carroll, and A. Mark Smith, though not all at the same time, was greatly appreciated. A research leave funded by the University of Missouri Research Council helped to enable the completion of the manuscript.

Finally, let me offer my sincere thanks to Joseph Adelman, Benjamin Carp, and another pseudonymous writer for their contributions to "my" blog "Publick Occurrences 2.0" at *Common-Place* (http://www.common -place.org/pasley) while the writing of this book kept me offline, and to editor Cathy Kelly for tolerating the blog's sporadic nature. It was a relief to have that commitment not be completely neglected. Readers of the blog, the *Common-Place* columns that preceded it, and the 2008 *Common-Place* special politics issue I coedited will probably be able to trace back the germ of this book. Therefore, previous *Common-Place* editors Jill Lepore, Jane Kamensky, and Edward Gray have to share some of the responsibility for pushing me in this direction. Joe Adelman, without whom I would never have learned to tweet properly, also became my guide to the brave new world of digital historical scholarship. Many of the scholars cited in this book have Joe to thank for giving me a much-needed introduction to the use of Zotero (http://www.zotero.org), an online citation management tool that—now that I understand it—I can highly recommend. Another online research tool this work benefited from was the America's Historical Newspapers database, a resource which I have enjoyed working with Remmel Nunn and his colleagues at Readex-Newsbank to improve.

Having said all this, and with hope that I have not forgotten too many other people and institutions that helped along the way, let me paraphrase the usual statement and affirm that any remaining errors and eccentricities are my responsibility alone.

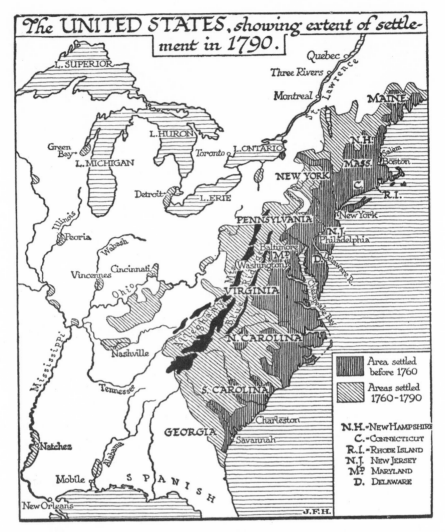

The following are labels visible on the map:

The UNITED STATES, showing extent of settlement in 1790.

L. SUPERIOR

Quebec

Three Rivers

Montreal

MAINE

L. HURON

N.H.

Green Bay

Toronto — L. ONTARIO

Salem

L. MICHIGAN

Detroit

L. ERIE

MASS. Boston

NEW YORK

C.

R.I.

Illinois

Peoria

PENNSYLVANIA

New York

Wabash

N.J.

Philadelphia

Vincennes Cincinnati

Baltimore

M.

Washington

D. Delaware R.

Ohio

VIRGINIA

Mississippi

Nashville

N. CAROLINA

Tennessee

S. CAROLINA

| | Area settled before 1760 |
| | Areas settled 1760-1790 |

N.H. = New Hampshire
C. = Connecticut
R.I. = Rhode Island
N.J. = New Jersey
M. = Maryland
D. = Delaware

Charleston

GEORGIA

Savannah

Natchez

Alabama

Mobile

S   P   A   N   I   S   H

New Orleans

J.F.H.

The New Republic in 1790: When the Constitution went into effect, the area of United States–controlled settlement had crossed the Appalachians in only a few places, and even much of the territory of the first sixteen states was still in Native American hands or near a frontier with European colonies. American politics took shape in this circumscribed yet transnational context. (Note that Washington, D.C., was as yet only a site, with Alexandria, Virginia, the largest town in that location.) (Map courtesy of the Florida Center for Instructional Technology.)

INTRODUCTION
THE UNINTENTIONAL CAMPAIGN

Few presidential elections turn out as expected, but the 1796 presidential campaign was never supposed to happen at all.

The varied group of revolutionary heroes Americans now call the Founders differed on many topics, but all agreed on their detestation of political parties and their fear of organized political competition.[1] "I never submitted the whole system of my opinions to the creed of any party," Thomas Jefferson wrote. "Such an addiction is the last degradation of a free and moral agent." John Adams pronounced the development of an enduring party conflict, the kind of thing we have to come to call a party system, "the greatest political evil" he could imagine. "There is nothing which I dread so much as a division of the republic into two great parties, each arranged under its leader, and concerting measures in opposition to each other." Adams opposed even holding presidential contests. Competitive elections for offices that were "great objects of Ambition, I look at with terror." As the Founders saw it, the fragile young republic would be unlikely to survive the strain of constant battles for power, and good, trustworthy leaders would never want to engage in those battles. More than just an elite prejudice, opposition to parties was the conventional wisdom of the era. A teenage orator in York, Pennsylvania, warned his classmates against "the odious distinction of party names."[2]

More than just conventional wisdom, antipartyism was a basic part of the Founders' political philosophy.

One of the top authors on the bookshelves of Adams, Jefferson, James Madison, and many others was Henry St. John, Viscount Bolingbroke. Adams read his famous treatise, *The Idea of a Patriot King*, five times, and Jefferson commended Bolingbroke to students (along with Tom Paine) as one of the two best political writers in English. Back in the early eighteenth century, Bolingbroke and many others had denounced the British parliamentary system for allowing a "prime" minister, the leader of the majority in Parliament, to act also as chief executive. As Bolingbroke saw it, to allow a party to control a government like this was to do nothing less than corrupt the morals of the whole nation. A patriotic head of state needed to rise virtuously above self-interest and personal belief and seek "the greatest good of [his] people" as a whole. His mission was "to defend and maintain the freedom" of the national constitution, and to do that he had to "defeat the designs, and break the spirit of faction, instead of partaking in one, and assuming the other." George Washington based his whole political career on this model of leadership, especially as presented in his favorite play, Joseph Addison's *Cato*, in which a Roman general kills himself rather than join Julius Caesar's party. The U.S. presidency, with its independence from any faction-laden legislative assembly, was to some degree designed for Washington so he could embody these sternly ascetic notions of leadership.[3]

Probably the Founders would not have been so interested in Bolingbroke if their reality had always measured up to his prescriptions. In fact, they had already experienced a great deal of party conflict during the Revolutionary era, especially in the new state legislatures where voting rights had been expanded and less august men with less elevated minds had found their way into office. Ordinary farmers and ambitious local politicians seemed more inclined to pursue their own interests and team up or pander to win votes than they were to model classical heroes or think of the national interest. One widely accepted interpretation is that the movement to create a stronger Federal government was motivated largely by the desire to move key decisions, especially economic ones, out of the reach of such parochial, party-mongering hands. The Framers of the Constitution developed the presidency as a kind of temporary elective monarchy that could fulfill the role of the Patriot King, selected by the people, but only indirectly, and wielding authority that could trump the national legislature.[4]

The voting system we now call the Electoral College was an ad hoc compromise rather than a careful design, but it was another layer in a constitutional structure the Framers hoped would prevent the development of political parties or any other kind of organized competition for control of the national government. The president was to be chosen by men who were elected in their own states, by any method the state chose, and picked from no set list of candidates. They could vote any way they chose and never meet together as a national body. How could any party possibly manage to control a body so fleeting and evanescent? The size and diversity of the country, and the complexity of the multilayered structure that the Framers had created, would make nationwide party organization almost impossible. Their hope was that George Washington or a patriotic executive much like him could lead, and enlightened gentlemen like themselves would come to the national capital and deliberate in peace, making wise, well-reasoned decisions for the good of all, without the need to compete for public favor or toe party lines. Their certainty about the lack of serious contention for the presidency extended to the provision that would prove so awkward after the resolution of the 1796 election—namely, that the vice presidency would go to the second-place finisher in the electoral vote. This meant that under normal circumstances, a president's major competitor would automatically be his understudy, a thinkable notion only in the absence of fundamental disagreements and dueling parties.[5]

Of course, this was not the way events played out at all. Despite the opposition to political parties, political divisions quickly developed after 1789 that would cause parties to form. The choices facing the young nation were simply too momentous to be contained by the relatively flimsy electoral framework that had been devised at the Philadelphia Convention. Having acknowledged that "we the people" were the ultimate source of all authority in a republican government, the Framers tried to blunt the force of popular opinion only to have to reach out for it themselves when faced with what seemed a battle for the soul of the new nation. However, it was a long way even from that concurrent decision, made shortly after the Constitution took effect, to a seriously contested presidential election. Thus, while 1796 was probably the shortest and least expensive *campaign* in the history of the presidency, the situation that produced it was many years in the making.

While avoiding the strong temptation to write a history of the whole postrevolutionary period, I have tried to trace out the long process that led to the campaign in the pages below, following the way the division manifested itself in increasingly expansive political battles over policy issues, especially foreign relations with Great Britain and France, that finally gave rise to a presidential contest. To paraphrase Clausewitz, I see the presidential campaign as the continuation of earlier policy debates (and broader ideological conflicts) by other means.

It might seem that there is little left to say about such a frequently covered event as the election of 1796. After all, there have been thousands of books published over the years on Thomas Jefferson, John Adams, the rise of political parties, the development of the presidency, and related topics, and most of them have had to address the first "real" presidential election in one way or another. However, there has not been a book published directly on the subject since the 1950s, and neither of those studies, one by political scientist Manning Dauer and the other by historian Stephen Kurtz, actually take 1796 as their sole focus. Instead, Dauer and Kurtz both deal with 1796 as only one episode in a story defined by the more easily intelligible Adams-Jefferson rematch of 1800.[6]

In researching the election, it has been easy to see why it has remained a relatively unpopular topic of study despite being mentioned so often. It lacks most elements of the familiar presidential election narrative that has proved so sturdy for journalists and historians: no formal party organizations, no nominations, no conventions, no speaking tours, no debates, not even a national vote or candidates who actually participated in the campaign. But historiographically, the problems run deeper than the lack of a familiar story. In many respects, the unfamiliar forms taken by the 1796 contest have come to dominate the interpretation of it, with scholars using the strange-looking package as an excuse to skate over the election or dismiss its significance, especially its popular and partisan aspects. (Many works on the politics of the Founding Era now take the Founders at their word and eschew the discussion of party labels or popular politics almost entirely.) The election of 1796 shows up as a fuzzy precursor to presidential politics, a disruption in the personal relationships among the major Founding Fathers, or, in many of the most ambitious and systematic political histories, as not much of anything at all.

Using a working definition of party politics drawn from mid-twentieth-century social science and the industrial democracies that spawned it, the political science–influenced "new political historians" who dominated political history through the 1980s generally looked for *institutionalized* parties: freestanding organizations that had openly identified personnel, commanded voter loyalties, fielded candidates for public office, and dispensed of patronage when they won power. This whole conception of political parties treated parties largely as devices for collecting votes, and thus tended "to empty party politics of its social, cultural and ideological content."[7]

Obviously, the institutionalized party is a tough standard to apply to an environment like the early United States, where parties were constitutionally unrecognized and so thoroughly disapproved of that it was a source of scandal for any public official suspected of participating in one. In America, the first private citizens to even approximate the organization of a political party, the members of the Democratic-Republican Societies of 1793–1794, got themselves denounced as revolutionists by no less a personage than George Washington, though all they had done was express opinions.

The institutionalized party may also be a false standard. The institutionalized party as defined by classic social science barely exists in present-day America either. Party labels do organize most twenty-first-century elections in the United States, but the parties still lack key aspects that institutional parties have in the rest of the world. The major U.S. political parties do not have "card-carrying" members, for instance, and in most states do not directly or formally control either initial candidate selection or final placement of candidates on the general election ballot. Modern candidates select themselves by filing the proper forms with the government and put themselves on the general election ballot by winning state primary elections or delegates at state party caucuses. American parties have voters who typically side with them and perhaps some campaign money to give out, but the political process is in the hands of candidates, their staffs, fundraisers, and consultants, in conjunction with the news media and the public agencies that actually conduct elections.[8]

Yet we could hardly argue there are no parties in 2012, when eighteen Republican primary debates were televised before the election year even began. By many measures, the early twenty-first century has been one of most intensely partisan and polarized eras in U.S. history, a time when one's choice of discount store or fast-food restaurant can be imbued with partisan meaning and minor lifestyle questions like what sort of lightbulb to use have been politicized. It has also been a period in which formal party institutions such as central committees and national conventions have declined sharply in importance. Political scientists have observed that modern parties have to some extent returned to their uninstitutionalized early national condition, but without losing any of their significance, and probably gaining some, as communities of opinion and networks of activists rather than centralized formal organizations.[9]

My own opinion is that when thinking of parties, political scholars (and journalists) are far too transfixed by visions of cigar-chomping party bosses running centralized, militantly nonideological organizations based on political patronage. The problem is that these images really only apply very well to the specific period and place they come from, that is, roughly the first two-thirds of the twentieth century (give or take a few decades), during the heyday of such canonical urban machines as Daley in Chicago, Tammany in New York, and Pendergast in Kansas City. This also happens to be when the academic discipline of political science, and hence most scholarly conceptions of the political party, were developed. This image and conception has little application to the parties of the Early American Republic.[10]

The real importance of parties in the time of the Founders is as rather loose but intense communities of political ideology, emotion, and action that took form among politicians, political writers, and their audiences, especially but by no means limited to the adult white males who could actually vote. One might drop Benedict Anderson's often-dropped phrase "imagined communities" to describe this concept, but a less pretentious term such as "affinities" or "affiliations" might also suffice.[11] These kinds of parties could be loathed or ignored as formal institutions, to the extent that they could even change form and media when necessary, but still inspire passionate followings that reached deep into society. The New England writer Catharine Maria Sedgwick's lightly fictionalized story "A Reminiscence of Federalism" gives us a glimpse of the feelings that a partisan community could generate, the intensity that was possible even in the absence of formal organizations: "I now look back, almost unbelieving of my own recollections, at the general diffusion of the political prejudices of those times. No age nor sex was exempt from them," despite the fact that neither women, children, nor poor men, in this age of property requirements for voting, could directly participate in elections. Party affiliation was not a matter of membership or private choice, but an all-encompassing cultural stance. "For myself, having been bred, according to the strictest sect of my political religion, a federalist, I regarded Mr. Jefferson . . . as embodying in his own person whatever was impracticable, heretical and corrupt in politics, religion and morals." In her western Massachusetts hometown, Sedgwick remembered, "All qualities and relations were merged in the political attribute. I have often heard, when the bell tolled the knell of a departed neighbour, the most kind hearted person say, 'we' or 'they have lost a vote!' " We might surmise that these early party affiliations actually thrived on the fact that parties of the Early Republic were not separate entities but only aspects of real people living their real lives.[12]

While the tendency among historians has been to downplay the significance, coherence, and even existence of parties in the early years of the Early Republic, my long immersion in the politics of this period, especially the partisan newspapers, has convinced me that "Federalist" and "Republican" were deeply meaningful and highly coherent categories for the politicians and citizens of the 1790s, even if the names could be inconsistent and the institutional presence lacking. While I try to be as precise as possible when a figure's or text's party affiliation is unclear or nonexistent, I freely use party labels in these pages, including "Democratic-Republican," a formulation rarely employed at the time that nevertheless captures both the ancestor relationship of Thomas Jefferson's party with the modern Democratic Party and the fact that all of the Early Republic's serious democrats affiliated themselves with the group then most often called the Republicans. "Democrat" was applied by many Federalists as an insulting term for a dangerous radical, just like "Jacobin." For intelligibility, I have also followed the modern practice of capitalizing party labels when discussing groups of politicians, though quotations have been rendered as found whenever possible. In the 1790s, standard English capitalization and punctuation was a work in progress, regarding political language and everything else.

It may be useful to make my position clear on the issue of party lineages, a concept that has sustained a good deal of collateral damage from historians battling over which political movements and what institutions should be considered as truly democratic and why.[13] I do believe that the histories, cultures, and symbolism of the current major American parties are only intelligible if we considered them, as their more historically aware leaders and thinkers have considered themselves, as descended from earlier parties on the "left" and "right." Hence the modern Republican Party had Abraham Lincoln and Theodore Roosevelt among its earlier icons, and those two considered themselves devotees of the Whig Henry Clay and the Federalist Alexander Hamilton, respectively. The lineage is even clearer with the Democrats, whose partisans once regularly attended Jefferson-Jackson Day dinners and got Thomas Jefferson enshrined on the Tidal Basin during the New Deal era. While it is true that some Jeffersonian Republicans became Whigs instead of Democrats during the Jacksonian era, and that some Federalists crossed party lines in the other direction, the later Democratic Party's strident embrace of their heritage as the party of Jefferson and Jackson seals this issue for me.[14]

Of course, none of the major parties has ever had a monopoly on democracy or goodness as genuine values, and the configuration of the major parties has undergone periodic changes as particular social groups and regions changed predominant party affiliations. One of the most striking of these shifts has been the exchange of African American and white Southerners between the major parties that has taken place since the national Democrats embraced civil rights legislation under Presidents Kennedy and Johnson in the 1960s. Yet the ideological and symbolic lineages remain even if the bipartisan embrace of the Mount Rushmore–level icons has confused matters a bit. Most importantly, the descent of particular politicians and families and regions and groups and ideas and policy preferences can be easily traced from era to era even if some of them have traveled significant distances and across party lines over the long run.[15]

By writing of parties and using their names, I do not mean to implicitly oversell the existence of early American political parties as freestanding institutions. Most politicians and observers of the time knew which major politicians, which newspapers, and which ideas belonged with each side ("federal" or "republican" were the most common terms), but the parties of 1796 were undeniably patchy and almost completely informal, inspiring grave doubts even in Noble Cunningham, the 1796 election's greatest enthusiast among prominent historians of the Founding Era. Among other issues, Cunningham worried about the "lack of party control" over most elections, as evidenced by the large number of candidates receiving votes in various congressional races: fourteen for one Massachusetts congressional seat, forty-six for another in New Jersey. The picture does not get much more impressive even when drawing on the American Antiquarian Society's New Nation Votes database of voting statistics, which only became available in the twenty-first century. In many jurisdictions, little seems to have happened during the election of 1796 at all, or at least not enough to leave much documentary trace. According to the New Nation Votes records, New Jersey's seven elector races were either uncontested or no one bothered to record the opponents' names if there were contests. Likewise, no known opposition candidate is listed for ten of the twenty-one Virginia electoral districts, with all of those unopposed winners reputed to be supporters of the Old Dominion's favorite son, Thomas Jefferson.[16]

My purpose here is not to argue what stage of "party development" the Early Republic had achieved by 1796 or to claim that "real" parties existed then. A rather semantic and truly academic debate on this topic took place back in the 1960s and 1970s and ended in more or less abject defeat for defenders of the so-called first party system. As long as the political party is defined in the modern institutional terms described above, the answer to whether the Federalists and Democratic-Republicans, the parties of Alexander Hamilton and Thomas Jefferson, are "real" parties is always going to be "no." Back in the 1980s, when scholars were working to establish the date for the full development of mass democracy and the party system, the moment seemed to be continually pushed forward in time, settling in the middle of the nineteenth century well after even the strenuously fought campaigns involving Andrew Jackson.[17]

However, the unintentional result of this victory of careful social science over democratic mythology has created a problem for our understanding of early American politics that I hope to rectify. It has turned the first contested presidential election into a relatively uninteresting bit of political juvenilia, the only presidential election since Washington stepped down that it is permissible to write about almost without mentioning voters, policy issues, or party ideologies. Hence the most prominent recent scholarly interpretation of the election focuses on elite machinations alone, confirming the tendency of popular "presidential historians" to describe politics largely in terms of leaders and personalities. The major candidates' habit of holding themselves above the fray and the evolving, inconsistently termed nature of party identifications as parties were just developing gets read as the essential nature of politics in this period. "It is this remarkable instability of political ties that best characterizes the presidential election of 1796," writes Joanne B. Freeman, and it was the "very personal and transient nature of politics in the early republic" that accounts for "the prevailing anxiety and high emotion" rather than any principles, issues, or interests that might have been at stake. In fact, there was a shaking out, and a few loose cannons, but not that much instability, especially at the aggregate level. The partisan images of Jefferson and Adams in 1796 were clear and starkly polarized, even though many individual politicians stuck to the old, less accountable, nonpartisan ways as long as they could. It was far more convenient not to be pinned down. There were some attempts to game the constitutional electoral system's lack of attention to the possibility of party tickets and running mates, but that mostly concerned vice presidential candidates. Such attempted exploits turned out to be futile anyway, as the two candidates with demonstrable popular support and clear party identities came in first and second. It was the Constitution's failure to recognize parties that produced the quirky result of both major candidates winning office, not necessarily any lack of partisan polarity.[18]

In my view, the rush to dispense with parties in writing about the 1790s is a mistake born of an excessive focus on what seems to interest twenty-first-century publishers and popular readers about early American political history—the personal interactions of famous personalities. If we look chiefly for what the Founders were doing about the election of 1796, then we will find that many of them, especially the candidates, were not doing much, as the political mores of the time dictated. As James Roger Sharp puts it, neither Jefferson nor Adams "campaigned or as much as lifted a finger to win the election." Abigail Adams congratulated her anxious husband on having been "an inactive spectator" to the events that decided his political fate.[19]

However, if we think a bit more broadly about the cultural structures of American presidential politics, then this first contested election was absolutely seminal. It set the geographic pattern of New England competing with the South at the two extremes of American politics with the geographically intermediate states deciding between them. It established the basic ideological dynamic of a democratic, rights-spreading American "left" arrayed against a conservative, social order–protecting "right," each with its own competing model of leadership. One can even detect the creation of what linguist and political commentator George Lakoff calls the essential "conceptual metaphors" of American political life, government as "strict father" or "nurturant parent," but it is not necessary to go that far. Historian Alan Taylor has described a similar idea as the competing political "personas" of Federalists and Democratic-Republicans: "fathers" versus "friends" of the people. It was the Federalists, especially, who got the battle of metaphors started with their efforts to emasculate the image of Thomas Jefferson, but the opposition redressed the balance with a vengeance in the attacks they mounted on the allegedly monarchical, tyrannical tendencies of George

Washington and "Daddy Vice," as Vice President John Adams referred to himself.[20]

Even with their patchiness, the two campaigns of 1796 managed to construct remarkably coherent images of the two candidates that connected clearly to the policy issues and cultural tensions of the day, especially those raised by the French Revolution. The young United States found its government severely pressured to choose sides in the world war that spun out of that revolution, and its politics were roiled by the democratic enthusiasms it spawned. Keynoted by congressman and pamphleteer William Loughton Smith of South Carolina, with some inspiration from Edmund Burke and guidance from Alexander Hamilton, the Federalist attacks of 1796 wrapped their caricature of Jefferson in a powerful conservative critique of French revolutionary radicalism, the Enlightenment, and post-Christian morals. With the Sally Hemings revelations still in the future, the critics focused chiefly on Jefferson's lack of manly qualities, as evidenced especially by his interest in science and technology. According to the Federalists, here quoted in a sort of dual biography of the two candidates published in Boston, the "timid and wavering" Jefferson was not cut out to be a "statesman, still less . . . a patriot." Woe betide America if "her liberties depended upon the depth of *his* political knowledge, the strength of *his* virtue, or the vigour of *his* mind." Jefferson's inability to "act the man" would invite foreign aggression and lead to national ruin: "our national honour forfeited; war probably ensue, our commerce be destroyed, our towns pillaged." Better to opt for the "security" of the "resplendent abilities," "faithful services," "inflexible patriotism," and "undeviating firmness" of John Adams, who would have the wisdom and strength to stand against "mad democracy" and "the wiles of ambition." The basic images of liberalism and conservatism in American politics have never strayed very far from this original Federalist template.[21]

The politics of the 1790s was not a primitive (or sophisticated) competition of personality cults, or at least not any more primitive than our own. In fact, the "informed voter" model of party politics touted in civics lessons and journalism schools, where the media provide information that allows voters to select the candidate who best matches their own policy preferences from a list of issues, has rarely been more than an aspiration in American politics. By taking a small leaf from the work of George Lakoff and other scholars of modern political culture, we can proceed on the premise that even with fully developed party politics, partisanship not only can be but may be *most effectively* expressed in terms of metaphors and morality tales rather than platforms and arguments. This seems to be particularly true under the conditions that the ends of the eighteenth and twentieth centuries had in common: newly potent institutions of political communication—newspapers then, cable news and the Internet now—and a popular aversion to the concept of party loyalty. In both eras, lofty sentiments praising political rationality, individualism, and independence coincided with bitter partisan invective and manipulative emotional appeals. One can cite no less an authority on this point than Federalist mastermind Alexander Hamilton: "Nothing is more fallacious than to expect to produce any valuable or permanent results, in political projects, by relying merely on the reason of men. Men are rather reasoning than reasonable animals," Hamilton counseled fellow Federalists. "For the most part" people were "governed by the impulse of passion," and successful politicians had to understand that.[22]

Infusing but also restraining some of the passion of 1796 was the fact that the election partly involved the country's halting search for new, more republican conceptual metaphors than the main one that underpinned the only form of government any American knew before the Revolution, namely, monarchy. Monarchy rested on what Lynn Hunt has called "the family model of politics," in which the king stood as father to his people. The family model fell into crisis in France, as the French people passionately rejected and killed parents who came to seem threatening and abusive, but it had been kept going in America by the presence of George Washington. The "nation as family" metaphor would return to American life by the era of "Father Abraham" Lincoln (at the latest) and would become the dominant conceptual metaphor in recent American politics, at least according to Lakoff. But it was troubled in 1796.[23]

Federalists wished devoutly to keep the model going. They begged Americans to remain "dutiful children to the *Father* and *Saviour* of his Country," George Washington, and follow his legatees. The Federalist poet and presidential elector St. John Honeywood rendered the question of the election directly into the language of the family model: "Whom hail we next as FATHER of the STATE?" Yet neither Jefferson nor Adams filled this role very well, metaphorically or actually. Jefferson did not seek it, and many of his supporters actively opposed it, complaining bitterly about Washington's paternal stance and accusing both Washington and Adams of trying to make themselves kings. Portly little John Adams hardly measured up to the tall, regal Washington as a father figure to look up to, but his status as a real father with a family full of sons raised serious questions for the future of the country, at least for the more radical Democratic-Republicans. This metaphorical tension was fodder not only for the first presidential campaign, but for what might also be thought of as the first "culture war" in American national politics, 1796 launched a long if intermittent tradition of presidential campaigns mixing the personal and the political in sometimes maddening but often revealing ways.[24]

It may reassure some readers to learn that such speculations do not take up the bulk of the pages that follow. Neither long-term continuities nor a politics conducted in terms of cultural metaphors have been very popular ideas with most American political historians, who are rightly concerned about oversimplifying and flattening the past to make it more comparable to the present. Without rejecting those concerns at all, this book tries to illuminate some familiar events and figures by taking a different approach, treating the politics of 1796 as a revealing rough draft of what came later rather than mere juvenilia or a dispatch from some distant political planet.[25]

One other note about my approach in these pages seems in order. Unlike almost every other recent study that covers presidential politics in the mid-1790s, this book tries to take seriously the well-accepted historical fact that the candidates were completely uninvolved in the 1796 campaign, and that the other frontline Founders (except Alexander Hamilton) were only slightly more involved than the candidates. Because the Founders are such compelling and bankable personalities, almost everything written about politics or political thought in the 1790s seems to become another entry in the vast corpus of Founder Studies. As coeditor of the book and manifesto *Beyond the Founders*, calling for new and less narrow approaches to early American political history, my intention here is not to pen yet another Founder tome. There are literally hundreds of works that tell the story of 1796 from the Founders' perspective. Most of these are quite effective as far they go, but unsurprisingly, they tend to leave the event a little murky *because their primary characters were uninvolved* or only involved from a great distance. While Washington, Adams, Jefferson, Madison, and Hamilton do stalk the pages below, I have tried to be truer to what was new and significant about the presidential campaign of 1796, a moment when national political competition (i.e., competition among candidates) had to reach out in public, to the voters, for the first time. Thus I focus as much as possible on the external, on the public images of the candidates that were created for public consumption, by friends and especially enemies, through the means of the press (newspapers, pamphlets, and handbills). If the candidates appear to be ciphers at times, that is just an accurate reflection of how the election of 1796 played out for ordinary citizens and even most of the direct participants in the campaign, who operated in local communities and never saw or heard a presidential candidate. Since the subject here is how the American presidential campaign came to be (or started at any rate), I also try to stay closer to the figures who were most directly involved in creating and organizing the campaign, an angle of vision that highlights the relatively unknown, midlevel figures who are the lifeblood of any major political effort, especially national ones. For the late eighteenth century, this means that newspaper editors, minor officials, now forgotten congressmen, and individual elector candidates all take a leading role in the story. What I have tried to practice is not so much a populist "history from the bottom up" that pumps up the agency of the masses as a more practically minded "history from the middle out" that means to show how politics actually works, how high and low (or "grass roots") politics are connected.[26]

Though limited by the only half-popular nature of the 1796 presidential voting and even more by the relative paucity of information available on it, I try to emphasize popular politics as much as possible in these pages. What can be documented is the fact that the first contested presidential election came about as a result of popular politics, broadly conceived, even if parties and elections themselves were not yet highly participatory. Elite disagreements played their role in the original sparks of the party conflict, but by 1796 those original disputes had long since spilled out of the cabinet and into the newspapers, streets, and polling places, as the rise of opposition to the Washington administration and its policies took on a life of its own, fueled by the democratic enthusiasm unleashed across the Atlantic by the French Revolution. Through an unpredictable series of events that will be detailed below, the constitutional system envisioned by the Framers was effectively rewritten to include competitive elections, and rather than insulating national policymaking from local majorities, the new system simply nationalized local elections in locations that were relatively diverse and divided. The Electoral College was rendered little more than a troublesome apportionment device the first time it was actually used to decide a presidential contest. The rudiments of a national democracy took shape without the benefit of a basic electoral infrastructure to support it (quite the opposite) and with only the beginnings of mass participation, at least outside of a few major cities. Yet take shape they most assuredly did. The rise of an unexpectedly popular presidential politics is the legacy of 1796 and the larger subject of this book.

A NEW REPUBLIC AND
ITS DISCONTENTS

In 1789, the United States was a new republic in more ways than one. It was the first attempt at a continental republic in the history of the world. Most of the others had been city-states like Athens, Rome, and Venice, and the sorry fate of liberty even in those small republics filled many Americans with anxiety for the future. Fearing the consequences of division and hoping for an economic revival, the supporters of the new Constitution had approved a new central government that was designed to be both above the state-on-state bickering and competition that plagued the Continental Congress and resistant to the development of national political parties.

Economically, socially, and politically, it was an elite group who framed the Constitution. Twenty-nine of the fifty-five Framers were college graduates in a time when almost no one went to college and the same number (though not the same people) had legal training. Almost all the Framers were wealthy attorneys, investors, merchants, or planters, or some combination of those, and twenty-five were slaveholders. Thirty of the fifty-five Framers were people the Confederation government owed money to. Forty-two had served in the old Congress, and a great many had been high-ranking state officials or military officers. From the vantage point of this "assembly of demi-gods," newly enfranchised voters and lax constitutional arrangements had brought too many locally minded provincial politicians to power in the states, eager to pander to their constituents' worst instincts, especially when it came to property. The new layers of government were supposed to create a situation where "individuals of extended views, and of national pride" could filter to the top and make better policy. The elite of the elite who filled the first administration and First Congress should have filled that bill nicely.[1]

THE FIRST MAGISTRATES: THE PATRIOT KING AND THE DEBATING TITAN

Accordingly, when choosing the first occupant of the new presidency, the members of the first Electoral College committed themselves to political unity by lining up almost unanimously behind the country's best-known and most universally beloved public figure, Revolutionary War commander-in-chief George Washington of Virginia. Washington had been the only and obvious choice for a position of national leadership since before the Constitution was written, and indeed, if he had not been sitting there as chair of the Federal Convention in 1787, such a powerful office as the presidency would almost certainly never have been approved. He had almost designed himself to be a republican version of the Patriot King.[2]

Connected by marriage to two of Virginia's wealthiest and most aristocratic families—including the colony's only resident nobleman, Lord Fairfax—Washington had found himself at the forefront of American and world events since young adulthood. As a twenty-two-year-old Virginia militia officer, he ordered the first shots of the French and Indian War and then led the heroic retreat of the surviving troops from the devastating British defeat at the Monongahela the next year in 1755. Striving for honor and position, Washington hoped for a commission in the British army, but settled down instead to the life of a Virginia tobacco planter, becoming of one largest landowners and slaveholders in the colony. Washington also became a politician: he served fifteen years in the Virginia House of Burgesses, and then, after British authority collapsed in 1774, helped organize a revolutionary government and personally bankroll one of America's first independent military forces in Fairfax County. Sent as a delegate to the Continental Congress, he happened to be one of the few experienced military officers on the scene when the new nation suddenly needed a general to lead its armies in 1775. As many of his colleagues recorded, George Washington of Virginia looked the part. The only delegate who showed up to the Congress in uniform, Washington stood at the then-towering height of over six

George Washington, Embodiment of the Nation: President Washington's centrality to the identity and very existence of the United States under the new federal government is rendered very literally in this print, where his gleaming profile is surrounded by linked seals of all the states. (Amos Doolittle, Display of the United States of America, *1794, Library of Congress.)*

feet tall, and carried himself, whether in front of a room or on top of a horse, as though he were already modeling for a monument. Even for an eighteenth-century gentleman, Washington was notably meticulous about his personal deportment and appearance and the messages they sent: the congressional uniform was his own design. While not always terribly effective as a field commander—he lost most of his battles—Washington's sheer gravitas, undergirded by genuine integrity and aided by iron control of his public demeanor and image, inspired enough confidence to carry the army and the country through the end of the war.[3]

It was at the end of the war, off the battlefield, that Washington forged his greatest military and political legacy and probably punched his ticket to the future presidency: he did it by stepping away from politics. Luckily for the young United States, the experience of founding a new nation had raised Washington's sights from mere honor and power to his place in the historical pantheon. Would he earn "fame" or infamy? With the Continental Army in its final encampment at Newburgh, New York, in early 1783, a group of officers circulated a memorial threatening to take up arms against the civilian government if it refused to deliver on promised pay and pensions. The officers were encouraged by a group of nationalist politicians looking to coerce the states into allowing the Articles of Confederation government to lay taxes. The conspirators called a meeting of all the officers and hoped General Washington would at least tacitly support them. He had been as angry as anyone about the incompetence and ingratitude of Congress. Instead, Washington appeared at the meeting by surprise and gave his one and only speech ever to his troops, urging them to set an example for posterity and go home quietly.[4]

Though not an original thinker or a highly learned man, Washington had considered the fate of past republics as seriously as any of the Founders, accessing that history especially through popular English renditions of ancient history like Joseph Addison's play *Cato*, a drama that the general had staged at Valley Forge to kill time and educate his men. History's great crime, in this classical republican tradition, was Julius Caesar returning from war and seizing power in Rome, destroying the republic and bringing on the empire. Addison's hero Cato the Younger was a Roman statesman who chose suicide over Caesar. Another favorite figure from ancient Rome was the mythical general Cincinnatus, a farmer called "from his plough" to save the republic on the battlefield. Given dictatorial power for six months to meet the emergency, Cincinnatus finished the job in six weeks and returned to his farm. Washington had committed himself to living this ideal of leadership in real life, so he not only quashed the conspiracy at Newburgh but soon after resigned his command, went home to Mount Vernon, and kept himself out of politics for a few years. Thus, said Thomas Jefferson, Washington had "prevented this revolution from being closed as most others have by a subversion of that liberty it was intended to establish." King George III found the story hard to credit, but he had no doubt that, if true, it would make Washington "the greatest man in the world."[5]

The King's was an excellent prediction. Washington probably really had saved the republic and did what he did in all sincerity, but his approach served his political ambitions very well, if he could admit to having any. Washington's approach also proved a better long-term strategy for achieving the 1783 conspirators' goal of a stronger central government. Ex-General Washington became such a sacrosanct, universally trusted figure that his presence could soothe fears about the 1787 Constitutional Convention even though it met behind closed, guarded doors with members pledged to secrecy. (Washington was no mere vessel or stalking horse for the plans of the nationalists either: the initial meeting to plan the campaign for a new government took place at his house.) The fact that Washington, who had already given up power once, was available to take the job allowed the Framers to create and sell to the people a chief magistracy that fell just short of an elective monarchy, but still ranked as the most powerful office in its sphere of any that had existed in the Anglo-American world since the seventeenth century. King George in Great Britain could not veto laws created by his people's representatives in Parliament, but President George would be able to do that.[6]

For his understudy, the vice president, the electors chose the best-known leader from the other end of the thirteen colonies, John Adams of Massachusetts, best remembered as the "giant in debate" who pushed independence through the Continental Congress in 1776 and a tough diplomat who helped negotiate peace with the British in 1783. An intellectual bulldog of a man, Adams had remained abroad to take on the rather thankless task of defending U.S. interests at the court of its former ruler and had just returned home from London in 1788. Like Washington's retirement on his farm, Adams's long tenure as a diplomat took him technically out of politics, preventing any imputation of being personally ambitious for power and thus making him considerably more eligible for office.[7]

The Lawgiver: Vice President John Adams as he appeared in the treatise on political theory that became a major issue during the first presidential campaign. (Frontispiece of A Defence of the Constitutions of Government of the United States of America, *rev. ed. [London: John Stockdale, 1794].)*

John Adams was almost unique among the major Founders in coming from a somewhat typical colonial American background. Like most eighteenth-century Americans, he grew up on a family farm where every person on the property had to contribute their labor from early childhood on. The Adamses had lived in much the same way in roughly the same place, the rural village of Braintree south of Boston, since the time the Puritans settled the colony 150 years before. His father, Deacon John

Adams, was a respected local official in Braintree, Massachusetts, but he was also an ordinary farmer who, like many of his compatriots in hardscrabble New England, had to practice a trade on the side—shoemaking in Adams's case—to make ends meet. Luckily for young John, the Adams family had a tradition of sending one son per generation away from the farm for formal education and a professional career. John was given rare opportunities—he was sent to Latin School and Harvard College and to apprentice in a law office—but at the same time was placed under tremendous pressure to work unrelentingly, excel at everything, and do right by his family and the Lord. However high he rose and far away he traveled, John Adams bore the marks of this background. Adams would never acquire the polished manners or dazzling conversational skills of many of his colleagues at the bar and among the Founders. Rather, he was a prodigious autodidact who preferred reading and writing about history, law, and politics to most other activities and often won simply by outworking his opponents, overwhelming them with erudition and the sheer unrelenting force and mass of his verbiage. Grinding study and pugnaciousness took Adams a long way from Braintree.[8]

These qualities made him a Founder *sui generis*, a powerful asset to the cause who was too unpredictable to be a reliable member of any faction or party. He and his cousin Sam Adams were on the ground floor of the Revolution, helping organizing the protests against the Stamp Act and other British taxes back in the 1760s. Though seen from outside as one of Boston's leading troublemakers, John Adams, like Washington, had early raised his sights to history, intervening repeatedly when he thought the Revolution was spinning out of control. He successfully defended the British soldiers accused of cold-bloodedly murdering civilians in the Boston Massacre in 1770. Then, just as his cherished drive for independence was succeeding, Adams took time out from the tumultuous affairs of 1776 to write a rebuttal to Thomas Paine's best-selling tract *Common Sense*, a pamphlet credited with doing more than anything else to shift American opinion toward independence and a break with monarchy. Adams had little respect for Paine, a working-class Englishman who had tried his hand at the staymaking (lady's underwear) trade and tax collecting before fleeing to America because of his radical politics. "A Star of Disaster," Adams called him. Adams's own modest beginnings left him the opposite of sympathetic to working folk who meddled in politics without his idea of proper training. While supportive of Paine's independence message, the rest he thought was a work of "simple

Ignorance," citing only the Old Testament in its argument against monarchy. Far worse, *Common Sense* proposed a unicameral model of government for the new nation, in which all power would be centered in a single democratically elected assembly without an executive branch or an "upper house." A devoted reader of republican political theorists who preached that only governments balanced between the cardinal types of monarchy, aristocracy, and democracy could be stable and successful, Adams was disgusted with the simple-mindedness of Paine's proposal. "His plan was so democratical, without any restraint or even an Attempt at any Equilibrium or Counterpoise" that it would surely produce "confusion [anarchy] and every Evil Work."[9]

What John Adams really prided himself on was being a self-taught expert on political philosophy and history, and this indeed was where he made his strongest imprint on American history. Adams enjoyed lecturing all comers on his favorite topics, but unlike most of the academic and journalistic lecturers who admire him today, Adams got to apply his knowledge in real life. He felt blessed that he and his generation had been "sent into life at a time when the greatest lawgivers of antiquity would have wished to live. How few of the human race have ever enjoyed an opportunity" of creating a government "for themselves or their children." Adams's pamphlet in response to Paine, *Thoughts on Government*, laid out a plan for what became the normative model for American governments, with different institutional branches checking and balancing each other: a bicameral legislature, a governor armed with veto power, and an independent judiciary. Nine states including Virginia adopted it in their state constitutions, with Adams himself installing it in the Massachusetts Constitution of 1780, which he designed on a break from his diplomatic tours abroad. The Massachusetts document became in turn the most immediate model for the Federal Constitution.[10]

The Adams model of American government was the product of both then-modern political science and some profoundly conservative impulses. He defended the fundamental worth of British institutions as he understood them and wanted to preserve contact with the accumulated wisdom of the past. The unwritten British constitution may have been corrupted in the eighteenth century and abused in the colonies, but it was still the freest in the world. At a famous dinner-table discussion among President Washington's three principal deputies, Adams had declared of the British form of government, "purge that constitution of its corruption, and give to its popular branch equality of representation, and it would be the most perfect constitution ever devised by the wit of man." For Adams, what the accumulated wisdom of the ancients and the Britons taught was that the only stable form of republican government was a balanced one where the different orders in society—the rulers, the landed elites, and the common people—were held in equilibrium and kept from dominating each other, as in the King, Lords, and Commons in Britain or the Governor, Council, and Assembly of the typical British American colonial government.[11]

For Adams, the ignorance of Tom Paine's Pennsylvania Constitution of 1776 lay precisely in its total break from the past. "Nothing is more certain from the history of nations and nature of man than that some forms of government are better fitted for being well administered than others," Adams wrote in *Thoughts on Government*, and while he thought of his checked-and-balanced model as a product of scientific reasoning, his purpose was restraining revolutionary impulses and preserving the existing state of late colonial society. If fundamental questions of political and social equality were raised in constructing new governments, there would be "no end of it. New claims will arise; women will demand a vote" (as his wife Abigail had, in a famous letter that set his teeth on edge), children would demand that their rights be respected, "and every man who has not a farthing will demand an equal voice with any other in all acts of state." This was madness, Adams believed; it would tend to "confound and destroy all distinctions and prostrate ranks to one common level."[12]

John Adams had the defects of his virtues. It was his boundless, loquacious energy that finally got Congress to approve the independence resolution, on July 2, 1776 (a key point in Adams lore), and kept the executive-free national government running in its early years, before Adams rotated out of it in 1777. Yet his dogged honesty and penchant for windy speeches severely hampered the long diplomatic career that began the following year, when he was sent to France to join the team of negotiators working out the rebel nation's military alliance with its mother country's old foe. Indeed, it would be hard to conceive of a less diplomatic diplomat than John Adams. Much against the wishes of his fellow American commissioner to France, Benjamin Franklin, Adams constantly and abrasively pushed at French officials to do more for their American allies, so annoying the French foreign minister, Comte de Vergennes, that he asked to have Adams called home or supplied with a "colleague capable of containing him," which the relaxed Franklin would not. Adams was temporarily sent home in semi-disgrace in 1779 and then packed off to Amsterdam during his second overseas tour.

If upward mobility and heavy parental expectations made Adams work harder than others and aim to be one of the lawgivers of history, it also made him obsessively status-conscious, suspicious, and jealous. His diplomatic years were embittered by the feeling that he was disrespected by the host nations and unjustly overshadowed by his colleagues, especially Benjamin Franklin, whose celebrity in France and bohemian ways enraged Adams with a fire that still burned brightly decades later. If the French knew the name Adams, they often mistook John for his more exciting cousin Sam. When Adams wanted to work—often to draft another hectoring missive to Vergennes—Franklin would be receiving visits from his French fans; in the evenings John read, wrote, and sulked, while Ben took up his nightly dinner invitations.[13]

Over time, Adams's festering jealousy and hatred toward Franklin seemed to color even his thought, pushing him away from the French Enlightenment culture that lionized his colleague and darkening his views on the social mobility and egalitarianism that the Philadelphia printer turned statesman and scientist personified to the elites of Europe. Adams particularly loathed the hypocrisy of the urbane "Dr." Franklin's habitual costume in France: a plain brown homespun suit, the better to play of the role of the humble son of liberty. Adams was a frugal man himself, but he was proud of his rise in the world and resented the idea of pretending poverty for political benefit. He got along much better with Franklin's replacement as minister to France, Thomas Jefferson, a good listener who deferred to older colleagues but was willing to engage Adam's intellectual disquisitions at their own level.

The aspect of John Adams best known to modern readers is his family, a topic touched on only occasionally in these pages but still crucial to understanding his point of departure. As prickly, overbearing, and maddeningly status-conscious as he could be, the strikingly egalitarian, starchily tender relationship John Adams had with the remarkable Abigail Smith Adams tells a different story about the private Duke of Braintree than did his often overbearing public persona. Abigail Adams has become a much more prominent figure to later generations than she was in her own time. She lived apart from John during much of his pre-presidential career, but ever since her vast corpus of letters began to be published, she has emerged as the most compelling member of the Adams family. Perforce less learned than John but his intellectual equal, she was the financial brains of the family and a much better administrator than her husband, a woman whose intelligence, energy, and eloquence would certainly have garnered her a political career of her own if she had lived in a later era. Politically, Abigail's biggest role was probably reinforcing John's growing conservatism, in one case provoking him to reaction with a famous letter that only half-joked that the new American lawgivers should "remember the ladies" when they were divvying up the political rights, but in most others just cheering him on. The Adams children had perhaps a more direct political role to play than Abigail, especially the three expectation-burdened sons who became an issue in the 1796 campaign, and most especially the eldest, John Quincy Adams, who went to France with his father as a child and then followed in his footsteps in so many other roles.[14]

John Adams felt an immense sense of vindication when he emerged as the leading choice for vice president, over other northern possibilities such as Governor George Clinton of New York and his and Sam's in-state rival John Hancock. But his joy was to be short-lived. By 1789, it had dawned on the organizers of the new government that there was a severe "defect" in the electoral system that had been devised by the Framers of the Constitution. Each elector was to vote for two men without designating which office he was voting for: the highest vote-getter became president, his runner-up vice president. Parties were not considered in this procedure, but the problem was actually much more basic. Even if the electors were unanimous, the resulting tie would send the election to Congress to be decided. Alexander Hamilton feared that this might open the way for the "machinations of Antifederal malignity" to sneak an opponent of the Constitution (like Governor Clinton) into the vice presidency or even deny the top prize to Washington. A few electors would need to vote for someone else besides John Adams, but they overdid it. When the votes were counted, half of Adams's support had disappeared: he ended up with thirty-four electoral votes to Washington's sixty-nine, including no votes at all from Georgia, Delaware, Maryland, and South Carolina, and only one of six from New Jersey. Adams bitterly fumed to his friend Dr. Benjamin Rush that "the scurvy manner" in which he was treated made the election, and national elections in general, seem "a curse rather than a Blessing. Is there Gratitude? is there Justice? . . . Is it not an indelible stain on our Country Countrymen and Constitution?" That was the mortification talking, but it was not a good start to what was destined to be a difficult vice presidency.[15]

LOCKED IN THE FIRST CABINET

In staffing the first edition of the new federal government, Washington strove for unity, collecting a matched set of officials who covered most of the regional bases while also including two of his closest wartime colleagues. From New England, there was Henry Knox of Massachusetts as secretary of war. A corpulent Boston bookseller who had become one of the most loyal and effective members of Washington's wartime general staff, Knox idolized his boss but also served both him and the country well. In 1783, Knox had angrily rejected the nationalist conspirators, vowing to keep "the reputation of the American Army as one of the most immaculate things on earth" and suggesting that they take their proposals to the people rather than trying to stir up mutiny at Newburgh. Knox also provided continuity with the outgoing government, having managed military and Indian affairs in the final years under the Articles of Confederation.[16]

Representing New York, but not really representing any locality, was General Washington's former military aide, attorney Alexander Hamilton, as secretary of the treasury. Not yet thirty-five years old when the Washington administration began, two decades younger than John Adams and a decade younger than Thomas Jefferson, Hamilton was an administrative wunderkind who had more or less run the army as a mere youth, and his new job was the result of a decade-long mission to make the U.S. national government into a more powerful and effective institution than the one he had dealt with during the war.

A native of the British Caribbean islands, where he conceived a sincere but inconsistently applied hatred of slavery, Hamilton was never steeped in any of the mainland colonies' local cultures and identified only with the new nation, giving his nationalism a depth and single-mindedness that none of the other major Founders had. Hamilton appreciated the relatively equal opportunities that America afforded and believed in republican government, but his youthful impressions of how the world worked had not taught him to expect a level playing field or a naturally, progressively improving future. He was the son of a downwardly mobile Scottish aristocrat and a French mother who had fled one husband and been abandoned by the other. Though commonly presented to readers today as a self-made man of humble origins, it would be more accurate to say that Hamilton was an unmade boy who spent his life aggressively trying to get his own back, not in terms of wealth necessarily but distinction. Orphaned at age eleven, young Hamilton was put to work as a clerk in a mercantile firm's office. He hated the "grov'ling . . . condition of a clerk," and longed for not only higher status but also power and fame in the grand historical sense that so many of the Founders did. Even at this young age, Hamilton was already displaying his great talent and passion for making and executing long-range plans. "I mean to prepare the way for futurity," the fourteen-year-old Hamilton told a friend in his earliest extant letter, and even though at the time it seemed a castle in the air to even imagine getting off the island of St. Croix, he consoled himself that even the most far-fetched and ambitious schemes could be realized "when the Projector is Constant."[17]

Constant, even aggressive projection of himself and his plans became the hallmark of Hamilton's meteoric rise. Starting as a teenage clerk, Hamilton developed a knack for finding benefactors and then leveraging every opportunity he got. A visiting Presbyterian minister took Hamilton back to the mainland to go to school in New Jersey, and then a year later he talked his way into King's College (Columbia University) in New York City, working a deal with the college president to allow him to move through the curriculum "with as much rapidity as his exertions would enable him to do." Before graduation, the Revolutionary War had started. Young Hamilton saved his Tory college from a Patriot mob, then joined the army and in no time was at General Washington's side. In his military job, Hamilton got dismal firsthand experience of a poorly funded, poorly organized government. With no executive branch, the operations of the early United States' government had to be directed by congressional committees, and as an unelected body with no power to lay taxes, the Continental Congress only had what money it could beg from the states or issue as currency. The result was "feeble indecisive and improvident" leadership and management that put the army through much unnecessary suffering, including starvation and poverty, that destroyed morale and hamstrung the war effort.[18]

After leaving Washington's staff, Hamilton became a lawyer and politician back in New York, gaining a huge leg up by romancing and marrying Elizabeth Schuyler, daughter of General Philip Schuyler, perhaps the richest of the Hudson Valley "manor lords," who controlled thousands of acres of land worked by tenant farmers (not unlike a European landed estate). Schuyler was also a slaveholder and a major force on the conservative side of New York state politics, opposed to populist Governor George Clinton and his popular policy of seizing and redistributing the property of wealthy Loyalists. Hamilton quickly assumed leadership of Schuyler's faction and soon ended up in the Continental Congress, determined to reform the place. There he fell in with the nationalist faction under the leadership of "Financier" Robert Morris, the first real executive official that the U.S. government had ever employed. Hamilton would follow Morris's approach to building a sounder financial base for the national government rather closely as secretary of the treasury. The richest man in the country, Morris founded the Bank of North America and used his personal credit to finance the war effort at times while lobbying Congress and the states ferociously to change the Articles of Confederation and allow a federal "impost" (import tax). Every state had to agree, and Rhode Island did not, so the measure failed, despite Morris's encouragement of the unrest and threatened mutiny in the army encampment at Newburgh. Alexander Hamilton and his fellow congressman Gouverneur Morris (no relation to Robert—he was part of a landed family out of New York) were in the forefront of the group trying to exploit the crisis to force reform of the Articles by politicizing the army enough either to coerce Congress and the states directly or better yet to simply scare them into doing the right thing: "The claims of the army urged with moderation, but with firmness, may operate on those weak minds which are influenced by their apprehensions more than their judgments," Hamilton urged Washington, especially if the latter were to "take the direction of them."[19]

Probably it was while working with Morris that Hamilton conceived the idea that nation-building would be his path to historical fame. He wanted a national state powerful and efficient enough to let the United States "assume an attitude correspondent with its great destinies: majestic efficient, and operative of great things." As the example of the British Empire had shown, an example that Robert Morris and French statesman Jacques Necker had tried to follow, sound public finance with ample credit and the revenues to support it was the indispensable base for an "energetic" government, to use a bodily metaphor that Hamilton favored. It was not simply about amassing power. The wartime experience had concentrated Hamilton's mind on the dangers that America's republican experiment faced from the threats posed by its enemies and most especially by the misguided impulses of its own people, who were too prone to being misled by "little demagogues" or big ones like Governor Clinton. "The vigour of government is essential to the security of liberty," he wrote in the first *Federalist* essay, a statement that reflected the fundamentally republican but often misinterpreted motives behind his statecraft.[20]

The brinksmanship of Robert Morris, sidling up to the edge of a military coup, had failed, so in the middle 1780s, Hamilton turned to less drastic, more long-range methods of strengthening the national government. Like many of the "young men of the Revolution," members of the educated political elite who had come of age during the war, Hamilton was deeply concerned with the "excess of democracy" he saw in the state governments, where narrow but popular local politicians showed too little respect for property and refused to cooperate in measures for the national good. He teamed with his congressional colleague James Madison of Virginia to create a quiet movement among the political elite first to revise and then (without telling all the participants) to completely replace the Articles of Confederation. When it came time for Hamilton to present his own ideas about the new national government, he revealed just how conservative his thinking had become about the new nation's political possibilities—its economic potential was another matter entirely. Supported by the "opinions of so many of the wise & the good," he had concluded that the British government offered "the best model the world ever produced" and "doubted much whether anything short of it would do in America." The British system, with its monarch, its House of Lords, and its powerful state apparatus that most of the propertied elite were invested in or personally benefited from, recognized the principle that to be secure and stable, government had to give due weight to the weighty members of society: "All communities divide themselves into the few and the many. The first are the rich and well born, the other the mass of the people. The voice of the people has been said to be the voice of God; and however generally this maxim has been quoted and believed, it is not true in fact. The people are turbulent and changing; they seldom judge or determine right." Hamilton's proposal for the new Constitution was a slight modification of the British constitutional monarchy. The executive would be chosen by state-appointed electors and serve for life, so as to be "above temptation." The executive would be buttressed by an upper house (senate) that would also serve for life. The executive could veto any laws that were passed, and any state laws that conflicted with the national government's dictates would be "absolutely void."[21]

As Hamilton expected, the convention largely ignored his plan, but his speech outlined the thinking behind his approach to the new government. The common people only respected the government out of mental habit or coercion. The elites would only be moved by what benefited their interests. Under the Articles of Confederation, it was the state governments that buttered their bread, most specifically in the form of securities that had been issued to fund the war. One of the fundamental purposes of the financial system that Hamilton proposed soon after the new government launched was getting the federal government into business with the "rich and well born" and winning their allegiance away from the states or potentially from foreign governments. In the British system that Hamilton admired so much, the prime ministers centered power in Parliament and held their vote majorities there stable by spreading offices, salaries, honors, and opportunities for personal profit widely among the social and financial elites, and most particularly among the members of Parliament. The empire, the military, the Church of England, and the Bank of England were all part of the system British radicals called "Old Corruption." Hamilton's enemies saw his proposals as corruption, too, and direct and candid man that he was, Hamilton more or less agreed. In the famous conversation with Adams cited above, Hamilton's reply to Adams's formulation had been that if one were to "purge [the British government] of its corruption, and give to its popular branch equality of representation, . . . it would become an *impracticable* government: as it stands at present, with all its supposed defects, it is the most perfect government which ever existed." To Hamilton, it was only such realistic thinking that could allow a fragile young nation to survive in a dangerous world and to realize his hopes for it.[22]

Hamilton found the Constitution as written far too weak but was willing to work for and with it. He was more concerned with results than maintaining republican purity or keeping himself out of the fray on his Patriot King perch. Partly because he was younger and not a candidate for high office, but mostly because of his inclination toward direct action, Hamilton plunged into campaigning personally, giving speeches and writing hundreds of thousands of words for the newspapers, under a wide array of pseudonyms. (The famous "Federalist" essays by "Publius," defending the Constitution in 1787, were just a fraction of his output.) Hamilton wrote and wrote in the public press throughout his life despite severe doubts about the people's judgment or the advisability of popular politics as a way to direct government policy. His competitive and public spirit seemed to overwhelm his antidemocratic philosophy.[23]

Unknowingly sharing the cabinet with Hamilton and this mighty agenda were two men from President Washington's beloved home state of Virginia: Governor Edmund Randolph was named attorney general, and the nation's other chief diplomat abroad, minister to France Thomas Jefferson, was chosen to oversee foreign affairs and the administration of the government itself as secretary of state. As the subject of so much of the campaign discourse in 1796, Jefferson will not get the full biographical treatment here, but it is worth reviewing some salient facts. Tall and slender where Washington was imposing and Adams and Hamilton were mini-dynamos of differing thickness and temperament, Jefferson offered a stark personal contrast to the others. A rather retiring man who did not dominate a room with his physical presence or verbal onslaught, Jefferson instead drew allies into his orbit with quiet conversation and luminous written prose.

To say that Thomas Jefferson was full of contradictions is now a well-established cliché in American historical writing. To begin with, he was an urbane sophisticate who idealized rural life, a humble farmer who ransacked the shops of Paris, London, New York, and Philadelphia for rare books, exotic foods, and luxurious furnishings to consume in the backwoods palace he called Monticello. In politics, Jefferson encouraged others to take up the rhetorical cudgels but shied away from confrontations himself, loved newspapers but never wrote for them, celebrated democracy and equality while carefully limiting his close personal associations and government appointments to the educated and the brilliant. He denounced slavery in soaring terms but never acted against it in office and depended on enslaved people for his livelihood (and sex) for most of his life. Jefferson praised the frugality of the yeoman farmer and condemned public debt as a tax on future generations but left his daughter such a mountain of debt that Jefferson's mountain home and most of his slaves had to be sold out of the family after his death.[24]

But while Jefferson was called out as a hypocrite by critics in his own time, and continues to be assailed in those terms today, the accusations miss the meaning of Jefferson among the Founders. He could be a tremendously effective politician and statesman, but his primary role was to be the Great Articulator, the man who could put America's highest ideals into words that were broad and eloquent enough to set them reverberating through the minds of his fellow citizens, and through history and around the world, taking on lives of their own. The famous sentence from the Declaration of Independence—"We hold these truths

The Prime Minister: Treasury Secretary Alexander Hamilton reprised his wartime role as Washington's chief aide during his first administration, and acted as primary leader and strategist of the Federalist party. (Portrait by John Trumbull, 1832, Yale University Art Gallery.)

to be self-evident, that all men are created equal, that they are endowed by their Creator with certain unalienable Rights, that among these are Life, Liberty and the pursuit of Happiness"[25]—was by far the most consequential, but it was not the only one. As historian Gordon Wood has suggested, it was not the originality of Jefferson's arguments or political courage that made Jefferson matter, but the quality and austere grandeur of his language. As Jefferson wrote of the Declaration, admittedly in long hindsight, his object was

> not to find out new principles, or new arguments, never before thought of, not merely to say things which had never been said before; but to place before mankind the common sense of the subject, in terms so plain and firm as to command their assent. . . . it was intended to be an expression of the American mind, and to give to that expression the proper tone and spirit called for by the occasion.[26]

Born in 1743, Thomas Jefferson was considerably younger than Washington or Adams but much older than Hamilton, a fact that partly explains the differing levels of respect he accorded to all of them. To the manor born, after a fashion, Jefferson grew up in comfort on his father Peter's plantation in the Virginia Piedmont but experienced a certain condescension from his mother's lineage-proud Tidewater relatives, the Randolphs, that left him resentful of unearned aristocratic pretensions. The Randolphs' airs and the rustic, pleasantly frontier-like nature of his home region, still accessible only by horseback and lacking any significant towns until relatively late in his life, seem to have planted in Jefferson a sense of sympathy and identification with the ordinary American farmer that was his unique bailiwick among the major Founders.[27]

Despite this minor inferiority complex, Jefferson led a life of leisure and privilege. He was sent to the College of William and Mary, a school that impressed him so little he started his own college a few years later, but where he came under the influence of several mentors and teachers who introduced him to the Enlightenment culture and thought that came to dominate his life. For Jefferson, the Enlightenment was a broad cultural movement that meant "pushing back . . . the boundaries of darkness" by "the spreading of light and knowledge." It also meant simply being up to date, participating in the most progressive intellectual and cultural currents of his day. So Jefferson filled his life with reason, harmony, beauty, and what he thought was modernity. "We shall never understand the young Jefferson," writes Gordon Wood, "until we appreciate the intensity and earnestness of his desire to become the most cosmopolitan, the most liberal, the most genteel, and the most enlightened gentleman in all America." He was "eager to discover" and implement "just what was the best . . . in the world of the eighteenth century." Anyone who has visited Jefferson's hilltop estate, Monticello, a tourist site even in his day, can attest that no man took living the Enlightenment more seriously than Jefferson. He collected books, learned music, corresponded with European intellectuals, and took up science as a very serious hobby, traveling with scientific instruments that let him record the weather and measure distance. Monticello filled up with examples of art and design and technology that reflected the best Enlightenment principles, including numerous devices of Jefferson's own invention that were intended to make life and work more rational, efficient, and harmonious: revolving bookcases, swivel chairs, whole-house wall clocks, and so on. "Fortune has cast my lot in a country" that was in "a state of deplorable barbarism," Jefferson wrote to an Italian friend, and he devoted many of his efforts to pulling his fellow Virginians and Americans out of barbarism, aesthetically and politically. He learned what was then cutting-edge modern architecture, the symmetrical Palladian style adapted from ancient Greek and Roman temples and villas, and applied it to his own home, the Virginia capital, and everywhere else he could, fixing domes and columns and pediments as the signature motifs of American public architecture.[28]

In politics, Jefferson took the same approach of trying to raise his country and countrymen up to enlightened standards. Though not without a melancholy and disappointed side as time wore on, Jefferson was essentially a liberal and an optimist. Human beings and human society could change and be improved. "I am among those who think well of the human character generally" and who think the human "mind is perfectible to a degree of which we cannot as yet form any conception," he wrote in the face of criticism later. Determined resistance to improvements puzzled Jefferson and, once he had been pilloried in the 1796 campaign and afterward for his Enlightenment commitments, came to seem sinister: "This is precisely the doctrine which the present despots of the earth are inculcating, & their friends here re-echoing; & applying especially to religion & politics; 'that it is not probable that any thing better will be discovered than what was known to our fathers.' We are to look backwards then & not forwards for the improvement of science,

& to find it amidst feudal barbarisms and the fires of Spital-fields." This was not Thomas Jefferson's approach.[29]

Acceding to the House of Burgesses almost automatically, as was typical among the Virginia gentry, Jefferson became involved in revolutionary politics and found his métier in penning some of the key documents of the Revolution, including *A Summary View of the Rights of British America*, written as the Virginia delegation's instructions for the first Continental Congress in 1774. Then of course while cooperating with John Adams in the drive for independence, he got the chance to write the document that became America's mission statement and, at least ideologically and rhetorically, its first step toward a democratic form of government. With a young family and an unhealthy wife, Jefferson refused some of the same overseas posts that John Adams accepted, returning to concentrate on domestic matters both private and public. As a Virginia legislator, Jefferson worked on a comprehensive program (some 120 bills) to modernize the state's laws according to Enlightenment principles, making the language more transparent, eliminating such aristocratic restrictions on fee simple land tenure such as primogeniture and entail, and restricting the use of capital and corporal punishment. His efforts to reform slavery, create an educational system, and separate church and state were more heavily resisted and cut short by an unhappy stint as a wartime governor that became an issue in the 1796 presidential campaign.

After his wife Martha's early death in 1782, Jefferson returned to the Continental Congress, where he devised or helped devise the basics of the western land system that he believed would determine the future of the country. Western lands would be regularly surveyed and sold, and perhaps most crucially new states would be formed out of them that would join the Union on an equal basis with the original thirteen. The idea was expansion rather than colonization. Jefferson also wanted to keep slavery out of all the western lands, but congressional action limited the ban to the western territory north of the Ohio River, disastrously extending the dividing line between slavery and freedom into the future.

In 1784, Jefferson finally accepted a diplomatic posting, as the new nation's emissary to its wartime ally, France. Jefferson became close friends with John and Abigail Adams in Europe, but his diplomatic experience was far more enjoyable than theirs. It was as though he had been named ambassador to his favorite intellectual and cultural movement: he hobnobbed with *philosophes*, soaked up design ideas, and shopped for furnishings to improve Monticello. The extremes of wealth and poverty in Europe disturbed Jefferson, as did the questionable morals and assertive women he encountered, but in general he had a grand time that shaped the rest of his career. He traveled the continent, had a fling with an actress, and witnessed the beginnings of a revolution in France that seemed to be a continuation of and compliment to the American one. He was even asked to help with the new French Constitution. Jefferson went home looking forward to a bright future in which America and France continued to work together for the cause of liberty. He arrived back in Virginia sounding as though he could have sacked the Bastille himself. Republicanism was "the only form of Government . . . not eternally at open or secret war with the rights of mankind," he told the people of Alexandria, Virginia, in 1789, and it was "an animating thought" that America should stay in the vanguard of political progress: "While we are securing the rights of ourselves and our posterity, we are pointing out the way to struggling Nations, who wish, like us, to emerge from their tyrannies also."[30]

A major player who had no chance for the cabinet ahead of so many more senior Virginians was Jefferson's good friend and ally James Madison Jr. Madison had less literary flair than Jefferson, but he was even more incisive as a writer and much comfortable with public disputation and legislative wrangling. Unlike the others, Madison's role in the Revolution had been exclusively political; he was a major force in the Virginia legislature, the Continental Congress, various constitutional conventions, and the press, but the young Madison was never an army officer or diplomat. As the coarchitect (with Hamilton) of the movement for a new Constitution, Madison enjoyed enough confidence from President Washington to be asked to contribute drafts for many of his key first-term speeches, but he just barely made it into any office under the new government at all. Virginia political baron Patrick Henry held Madison in open enmity, denouncing him as "unworthy" and predicting "rivulets of blood" if he should end up in high office. Henry's political muscle prevented Madison from being selected by the state legislature for the prestigious new Senate, so he was forced to compete for a seat in the relatively lowly House of Representatives. Triumphing in his race over fellow future president James Monroe, Madison went to Philadelphia expecting to be one of the principal leaders in the House and work closely with the new administration. The first expectation came true, but Madison was in for a rude awakening regarding the second. Only

John Adams seemed to realize how much trouble was in the offing. "My Country appears to me I assure you in great danger of fatal Divisions," Adams wrote Dr. Benjamin Rush. "I scarcely know of two Persons who think, speak and act alike in matters of Government."[31]

CONFLICTING VISIONS AND "MONARCHICAL PRETTINESSES"

The assembled Founders discovered soon enough that a commitment to unity only goes so far in the presence of fundamental disagreements. The problem was that the question of what kind of nation the United States would become was completely open, and it turned out that American political leaders had dramatically different answers to it. Take the two states that considered themselves the coleaders of the new nation and that supplied all its presidents up through 1828—Massachusetts and Virginia. New England's economy was diverse, but its population was not: there had been little new immigration since the Puritan "Great Migration" of the seventeenth century. Virginia was the state with the largest population, with not only a racial divide but also, especially in its backcountry, an increasingly rich mix of ethnicities (Germans and Scots-Irish especially) and dissenting Protestant denominations such as the Baptists, Methodists, and Quakers. Much of its population was on the move to better farmland in Virginia's west, and its port towns were just beginning to develop.

If colonial Massachusetts and Virginia were different to begin with, the American Revolution had rendered their societies even more divergent. While almost none of the tax protestors who started the dispute with the British back in 1765 had set out to reform American society, the "contagion of liberty" had spread from issues of taxation and representation to basic social institutions such as property and religion, to the chagrin or annoyance of more socially conservative Founders such as Washington, Adams, and Patrick Henry. As Americans of all classes, creeds, and colors applied the principles of the Revolution to their own situations, fundamental changes began. There really was no end to it, as John Adams had predicted.[32]

The end of slavery in the northern half of the new nation was the most momentous and immediate change. The institution had existed in every colony, but it was well understood how badly it contradicted the American Revolution's stated principle that "all men were created equal." It also created problems attracting the international support, and funding, that American diplomats such as Franklin, Adams, and Jefferson were desperately seeking. So in the more northerly climes where slave labor was less economically important, slavery began to vanish rapidly. By the time the Constitution was written, it had been destroyed in New England and weakened everywhere except Georgia and South Carolina. Slaves petitioning for their own freedom triggered a court ruling against slavery in Massachusetts, while other New England states eliminated it by statute or in their constitutions, and Pennsylvania began to implement a gradual emancipation plan. With the old slavery-based tobacco economy declining and a larger slave population than planters could profitably sustain, the Upper South states (especially Virginia) considered emancipation but ultimately only liberalized the laws governing manumission, making it easier for planters who wanted out to free their slaves, and supported an end to the international slave trade.[33]

Virginia and Massachusetts and their regions also grew apart in their religious cultures and institutions where once they had much in common. Except in Pennsylvania and Rhode Island, both founded as islands of religious tolerance, the colonies had all maintained religious "establishments" in which taxes on the whole population supported the local majority Christian church, usually the Church of England in the South and the Congregational churches in New England. Almost all of the colonies and even many of the early states (early on) also imposed religious tests and oaths that effectively banned anyone who was not an orthodox Protestant from holding public office. At the same time, the Enlightenment had been eating away at religious enthusiasm for decades, and the educated elites of all regions, including almost all of the Founders, tended to espouse a cool, intellectualized faith and live largely secular lives.[34]

But the regions reacted very differently to the revolutionary impulse to sweep away orthodoxies and downgrade the place of religious institutions in public life. There had always been some marked differences between the regional religious cultures. Every village in Puritan-founded Massachusetts and Connecticut was centered on its Congregational church, with the minister guiding the people's political choices and personal lives as well as their souls. The clergy did not hold office directly, but some minister gave an "election sermon" to each new legislature, and in Connecticut, the Congregational clergy met as a group beforehand to determine whom the legislature would select as governor, lieutenant governor, and council. By contrast, Anglican churches in Virginia were much rarer animals: there was no church in Thomas Jefferson's Charlottesville near Monticello until Jefferson designed and paid for one himself near the end of his life. The planters firmly controlled the local vestries and often treated the priests as expensive pests. One of Virginia's and Patrick Henry's first challenges to the British government in the 1760s involved cutting the clergy's tobacco-based salaries.[35]

Over the course of the Revolution, however, the regional religious contrasts yawned wider as the southern states largely abandoned their church establishments, led by North Carolina and Virginia. North Carolina's 1776 constitution forbade religious taxes and made contributing to or attending church a purely private and voluntary act. In Virginia, Thomas Jefferson's revision of Virginia's laws included "A Bill for Establishing Religious Freedom" that declared religious taxes "sinful and tyrannical" and guaranteed that no man would be "restrained, molested, or burthened in his body or goods, nor shall otherwise suffer, on account of his religious opinions or belief." The bill failed to pass during the war, but the Anglican establishment largely lapsed anyway in the face of both wartime chaos and the opposition of dissenting sects such as the Baptists, Presbyterians, and Methodists. After the war, the increasingly conservative Patrick Henry raised the alarm about creeping "moral decay" and promoted bills to reimpose religious taxes and fund a new and improved church establishment, but James Madison, who had returned to Virginia from the Continental Congress, led the charge against the idea and finally got Jefferson's bill passed in 1786. Jefferson later listed the "Statute of Virginia for Religious Freedom" as one of his three greatest, tombstone-worthy accomplishments, and Madison's cousin, the Reverend James Madison, preached in a sermon that Virginia thus marked "the first glorious instance, wherein religion and polity are no longer connected." Other southern states followed suit soon thereafter. In New England, by contrast, the "Standing Order" of Congregational clergy and officeholders circled the wagons and maintained taxpayer funding of their religious institutions for another generation or more, and in Massachusetts until 1833. Protestant dissenters (primarily Baptists and Methodists) were grudgingly allowed to file for exemptions papers from Congregational taxes, but only if they could prove membership in another legally recognized Christian church. A long-term conflict was set up between Virginians (and Pennsylvanians) inveighing against New England "bigots" and "Popes" with their "holy laws," and

New Englanders responding in kind with warnings against the infidels, atheists, and libertines who ruled down south.[36]

Taken as a whole, the Revolution had replaced the separate colonies governed by relatively uniform British colonial institutions with a single but potentially divided nation: a self-consciously Christian, newly "free" northeast suddenly faced a newly secularized, self-consciously "slave" South (although there were guilty feelings about slavery in some quarters of the South), with the mid-Atlantic states working out their own places in between. Cultural differences that were not so obvious before became inescapably prominent, and because they overlapped with increasingly divergent economic systems, the differences immediately found their way into politics. The influence of the Lower South saw to it that the Constitution did nothing about slavery except protect it, with always ultra-proslavery South Carolina forming the keystone of several compromises that allowed the Constitutional Convention to complete its work. In South Carolina and Georgia, the plantation economy (focused on rice, indigo, and cotton rather than tobacco) was still growing, and whites ruled over a black majority population they feared to lose any degree of control over. The protections they won included partial representation of the slave population for apportioning seats in Congress and the Electoral College, and a twenty-year ban on the only type of national antislavery legislation that anyone could imagine, the abolition of the international slave trade. Under those restrictions, slavery could poke its head up only occasionally as an issue during the early years of the new government, but the peculiar institution's shadow was obvious in the regional divisions it outlined. In the battles of the 1790s, Upper South planter liberals and Yankee preacher conservatives would be two of the major political antagonists, with the two largest states in each respective region supplying the leading combatants.[37]

However, neither Virginia nor Massachusetts could boast of being the chief regional influence over the new federal government's policies. That honor went to New York and Alexander Hamilton, who acted not just as minister of finance but de facto prime minister to President Washington. In the eyes of Hamilton's visionary nationalism, America was "a Hercules in the cradle," the raw material out of which they could build an urban, ocean-going commercial empire like Great Britain's, with the financial and administrative wherewithal to develop itself rapidly and project a credible military force to the rest of the world. Cities full of counting houses, factories, and fine homes would grow up, and the United States would take its place among the world's great nations. "A noble career lies before it," Hamilton wrote.[38]

Love his urban capitalist future or hate it, Hamilton was several leagues ahead of most of his colleagues in the first federal government, who were far more concerned with political questions than economic development and had no long-range policy schemes they were itching to implement. Though Vice President John Adams usually acted with Hamilton and his allies in the politics of the Washington administration, when he was called on to act at all, his economic views were much closer to Jefferson's. Both were farmers at heart, distrusting cities and the financial institutions that drove them. Adams had no particular vision of the future he wanted to pursue; though he sometimes complained of its narrowness, Adams tended to idealize the colonial Massachusetts of his youth, where he believed good republican principles had "been felt if not understood . . . from the Beginning" despite or perhaps because of the established church, religious tests for political rights, and social homogeneity. As his star turn in revolutionary politics receded into the past, and he cast his eyes on the increasingly chaotic course of events in Europe and America, Adams's conservatism grew as he dwelled on the long odds against preserving liberty and republicanism from the base urges of the people, the ambitions of their rulers, and the craftiness of the propertied elites. Beginning during his diplomatic service, Adams turned to writing progressively darker versions of his *Thoughts on Government*, most notably in his three-volume work *Defence of the American Constitutions*, published in 1787 but a campaign issue in 1796 that we will deal with extensively below. Trapped in a do-nothing job that he pronounced the most insignificant ever conceived, Vice President Adams pursued no visions; he broke tie votes and obsessed over procedure and protocol.[39]

Thomas Jefferson and James Madison idealized their rural society, too, but in a different, much more expansive way. Jefferson and Madison hoped the new republic would become a reformed and enlightened version of their imagined colonial Virginia, gradually purged of ignorance, slavery, and the grossest inequalities. For Jefferson and Madison, a landscape of independent, landowning farmers—inevitably white, according to their racially restricted views—was the key to maintaining a healthy republic. Following from this vision, their main policy goals were expanding the nation's land base and the available markets for its agricultural produce, though only by methods consistent with republican

Locked in the Cabinet: Thomas Jefferson as he appeared while serving as Washington's secretary of state and battling Hamilton behind the scenes over policy. (Portrait by Charles Willson Peale, 1791, Independence National Historical Park.)

principles. That meant no permanent armies or large navies that might threaten popular rule and require heavy taxes for their support. Instead, they wanted to promote free trade, not by military force but by withholding or curbing access to American markets and crops if a foreign nation, especially Great Britain, imposed restrictions on American commerce. Making such a unified "commercial discrimination" policy possible had been one of Madison's primary motivations for creating a new federal government in the first place, and he was more than dismayed when Hamilton's supporters in the First Congress swiftly rejected it.[40]

The Founders' diverging visions of the future were predicated on different roles for the American state and different policies. With Hamilton ensconced as Washington's right hand, his option got the first trial. Working on the assumption that ample revenues and stable credit were the "sinews of power," Hamilton worked directly with Congress to set up a British-style system of public finance. Under his funding and assumption scheme, the federal government would assume the Revolutionary War debts of the states and redeem all the many millions in heavily depreciated debt certificates still outstanding—the paper that been had printed to pay for war without adequate tax revenues—into new securities that were payable at face value and earn interest for their holders. This would not only restore the battered credit of the United States, but also create an immense amount of wealth overnight as nearly worthless debt certificates suddenly shot up in value. To support the structure and get the people in the habit of obeying the federal government, Hamilton moved to immediately use the federal government's new power to impose internal taxes, in the form of an excise tax on distilled spirits. Most controversially of all, Hamilton successfully proposed the creation of a Bank of the United States that would loan the government money and hold its funds but be a privately controlled, profit-making enterprise. The final plank of Hamilton's financial system was never implemented: a system of federal subsidies to manufacturing start-ups, a visionary idea that was economically premature. Wages were so high and farmland so plentiful in America that women and children were likely to be the only available factory workers.[41]

Along with many other observers, Jefferson and Madison were aghast at the windfall profits that "funding and assumption" meant for investors in the coastal cities and Europe. The old debt certificates handed out for military pay and supplies had mostly been sold off for a fraction of their value by soldiers and farmers who desperately needed the cash to live. Speculators had sent agents out into the southern countryside in advance of Hamilton's proposals to buy up seemingly worthless paper from veterans and farmers who did not know any better. New York and Philadelphia investors and investor politicians who were privy to the plans did and acted on their knowledge, including several close colleagues of Hamilton going back to the days of the Continental Congress. Hamilton was not concerned, since his intention all along had been to bind the "rich and well-born" to the new federal government by showing it could profit them. When Madison proposed that only the original holders of the debt certificates be able to redeem them for full value, Hamilton and his congressional supporters crushed the idea. Making the U.S. government a more attractive investment, and hence a better-funded and more "energetic" institution, was for them a main purpose behind the creation of the new Constitution. Lacking any very keen understanding of or sympathy with the world of finance, Jefferson and Madison saw the debt and banking proposals as "poison & corruption." They considered any paper wealth thus generated as no better than gambling winnings, money that would be withdrawn from productive use and would nourish "in our citizens habits of vice and idleness instead of industry & morality," in addition to widening the chasm between rich and poor. Their fears seemed to be confirmed by the swashbuckling and irrationally exuberant atmosphere of speculation that swirled around the new financial institutions. The initial stock offering for the Bank of the United States sold out in a single hour, and seemingly everyone who had voted for Hamilton's financial plans ended up as an investor in the bank, the debt, or both. It looked worse when Hamilton's chief deputy, William Duer, resigned his office and then speculated so heavily it caused a credit crisis, the Panic of 1792, in which the treasury secretary was forced to intervene and bail out the New York banks with public money.[42]

Jefferson and Madison also saw a political threat. The accumulation or prospect of paper wealth would in effect buy permanent congressional support for Hamilton's program and, worse, ensure the shift toward a more imperial federal government or even the British-style constitutional monarchy that Hamilton, Adams, and their "sect" seemed to be aiming for. This was just the sort of tactic that the British prime ministers had used to gain control of Parliament and unbalance the British Constitution. Jefferson's thinking was revealed in the interim names he gave the two parties while trying to explain them to President Washington in a long letter written in May 1792. Almost all the capital's politicians were putative supporters of the Constitution ("federalists" in the language of 1787–1788), but as Jefferson now saw it, the two groups had radically divergent purposes: Hamilton's group consisted of

"Monarchical federalists," while he and Madison and their allies were "republican federalists." Soon one-half of each label transferred exclusively to each set of competitors.[43]

Last but not least, Jefferson and Madison bristled at the freedom from constitutional restraint with which Hamilton acted—there was no constitutional provision authorizing a national bank or even the creation of corporations. Hamilton's relaxed reading of the Constitution's "necessary and proper" clause as allowing any government action that was conducive to its general purposes horrified Jefferson and Madison, who considered it tantamount to no constitutional limitations at all. In May 1792, Secretary of State Jefferson wrote a long letter to Washington setting out his constitutional objections to Hamilton's Bank of the United States proposal. "All powers not delegated to the United States by the Constitution" were supposed to "be reserved to the States or to the people," Jefferson quoted, and "to take a single step beyond the boundaries thus specially drawn . . . is to take possession of a boundless field of power, no longer susceptible of any definition." Jefferson had become convinced that Hamilton and his "Monarchical federalists" must have been insincere about the new government all along, pointing out to Washington that loose constructions like Hamilton's had been loudly abjured before the people during the ratification debate, by Hamilton himself and many others, only to be pulled back out again once the government was in place.[44]

While recent historians have generally concluded that Hamilton did accept the validity of at least some constitutional limitations, he did his reputation on this score no favors by submitting a rebuttal to Jefferson's objections that fueled his opponents' fires by being far too lawyerly and thorough in its effort to utterly demolish the constitutional case against the Bank. Pushing the "loose construction" argument to the furthest possible extent, Hamilton sent the message that the new Constitution existed only to strengthen the central government, not to place any functional constraints on it at all. In his "Opinion on the Constitutionality of a National Bank," addressed to Washington and the rest of the cabinet, Hamilton took the view that the United States enjoyed full sovereignty, and hence complete freedom of action, in any area the Constitution had granted it power over, including interstate commerce, public finance, foreign trade, and national defense. The Constitution did not explicitly prohibit national banks or corporations, so it must be assumed their creation was permissible if done for a constitutional purpose. Constitutional limitations that hampered or prevented necessary government actions would furnish "the singular spectacle of a *political society without sovereignty, or of a people governed without government.*" Then Hamilton decided to almost lampoon Jefferson's strict definition of "necessary," spinning out a long list of preferred synonyms that made his impatience with the idea of strict functional limits a little too clear. By the rules of grammar and habits of colloquial speech, "*necessary* often means no more than *needful, requisite, incidental, useful,* or *conducive to.* It is a common mode of expression to say that it is *necessary* for a government or a person to do this or that thing, when nothing more is intended or understood, than that the interests of the government require, or will be promoted by, the doing of this or that thing." Elsewhere in the document, "convenience" was invoked as a possible justification. The functionally unshackled government Hamilton's rhetoric envisioned reminded Jefferson and Madison of the type of unlimited government Americans had recently rejected, monarchy.[45]

Hamilton, for his part, was thunderstruck that seemingly serious men could believe that a strong, stable government could ever operate in an environment where its every move could be fundamentally challenged on grounds of overstepping a malleable paper document. He explained to the future Federalist presidential candidate Charles Cotesworth Pinckney, a fellow military man, that he formerly had great esteem for Jefferson but now regarded him as "a man of sublimated and paradoxical imagination—entertaining & propagating notions inconsistent with dignified and orderly Government."[46]

Hamilton was primarily concerned to have a government that could vigorously execute its policies, but many of his allies, including George Washington, fretted about the presidency itself. How could its prestige be built up? How could they be assured that the American populace and foreign governments would respect it? In constructing the protocols and rhetoric of the new presidency, they borrowed heavily from European monarchies. Their view was that a touch of divine right was needed, at least symbolically and emotionally, to keep the people in order. The president, and by extension all officials at their appropriate levels, should be raised above other men. As Oliver Ellsworth of Connecticut argued: "The Sentence in the Primer of *Fear God and honor the King* was of great importance; . . . kings were of divine appointment; . . . head and shoulders taller than the rest of the people." The "monarchical prettinesses" built up around President Washington included official birthday tributes, a magnificent coach and mansion, and the restriction of access to the presidential person to official "levees" at which guests were forbidden the democratic gesture of shaking Washington's hand. Those observers not awed were horrified. "It is a wretched and mad opinion that some high flying republicans maintain," the newspaper satirist Philip Freneau imagined a Federalist thinking, "that officers of the government ought to deport themselves as the *equals* of the people."[47]

Though he sulked about attending levees and riding around in expensive carriages, Vice President Adams went into his only official duty, presiding over the Senate, bent on installing as many monarchical formalities as possible. His years of dealing with the French and British monarchies and reading up on the history of government had planted plenty of ideas about the importance of hierarchies and the best ways of maintaining them. Since returning, Adams had grown frustrated at how "miserably bewildered" his fellow Americans seemed to have become. They were born and bred under the British "limited monarchy" but seemed to have forgotten the need for some regal authority to balance and stabilize their popular sovereignty: "There is not a more ridiculous Spectacle in the Universe than the Politicks of our Country exhibits: bawling about Republicanism which they understand not."[48]

So Adams decided to teach his countrymen, or at least the Congress, about the monarchical element that a republic needed to have if it did not want to devolve into a rampant, uncontrollable democracy. Making a "ridiculous spectacle" of himself, the new vice president assumed the Senate chair wearing a regal outfit of his own invention, including a wig, formal military coat, and ceremonial sword. To Pennsylvania senator William Maclay, Adams looked like "a Monkey just put into Breeches" sitting up on the dais in his strange quasi-uniform. The vice president harangued friends and senators repeatedly about the need to adopt royal-esque titles when addressing high U.S. officials. Privately Adams thought only "Majesty" was good enough for the president and vice president. Having not been present at the Federal Convention, he thought the name chosen for the office was weak tea—it "put him in mind that there were presidents of fire companies and cricket clubs. . . . What will the common people of foreign countries, what will the sailors and soldiers say, 'George Washington, President of the United States'? They will despise him *to all eternity*." Eventually a Senate committee came up with the option "His Highness the President of the United States and Protector of the Rights of the Same," but the House of Representatives rejected the whole idea. The episode embarrassed Washington, as Virginia tongues began to wag about the "pomp & parade" at the capital. Adams soon found himself held at arm's length, attending only two or three cabinet meetings for the next eight years. When the 1792 election came around, abortive efforts were made on both sides to ease him out of the heir apparent spot. Governor George Clinton of New York failed with fifty electoral votes. The damage was done, however, as Adams came to symbolize the more undemocratic and inegalitarian impulses of those who guided the new federal government, impulses summed up at the time by the idea of monarchy.[49]

Adams made matters worse by using his ample vice-presidential spare time to write a series of newspaper essays expanding on his ideas in the form of a commentary on the Italian historian Davila (which was also the projected fourth volume of his *Defence of the American Constitutions*) that was simply chock-full of statements that cast Adams's views in an almost sinister light. Though chiefly an intellectual exercise, much of what Adams churned out read as "a fervent defense of hereditary succession," according to admiring historian Zoltán Haraszti. Particularly damning was the attitude he expressed toward the common American. The "laboring part of the people can never be learned," Adams wrote, and they would always envy the more fortunate. Merely asking "the people to respect property will be regarded no more than the warbles of the songsters of the forest. The great art of lawgiving consists in balancing the poor against the rich," especially by giving the rich their own branch of government (the Senate) and special laws to protect themselves. Many Federalists concurred in these sentiments, but it was highly characteristic of Adams that he was willing to publish openly in newspapers what others only whispered in private.[50]

As he battled Hamilton within the administration over a host of issues, Thomas Jefferson was horrified by his old colleague Adams's startling departures from what he had assumed to be their shared egalitarian republican faith, which seemed to connect ominously to so many other disturbing developments. One of Jefferson's connections to the street and tavern circles of radical Philadelphia was House of Representatives Clerk John Beckley, who was eager to get Jefferson more publicly and directly involved in the opposition. When Beckley received a copy of Tom Paine's defense of the French Revolution, *The Rights of Man*, which he was arranging to have published in America, he lent the book to the secretary of state. Jefferson's cover note returning the volume proved too great a temptation for Beckley, who had it published as the preface to the American edition of *The Rights of Man*, without permission. Soon the letter had been propagated as a reprinted newspaper item throughout the American press. Writing to Beckley's publisher but inadvertently to the world, Jefferson expressed delight "that something would at length be publicly said against the political heresies which have sprung up among us. I have no doubt our citizens will *rally* a second time round the *standard* of COMMON SENSE." The incumbent secretary of state was thus outed as a critic of both the vice president and the administration they both served.[51]

Adams and Jefferson had been close friends and allies in revolutionary politics and diplomacy, which added personal pain to the gaffe. An open rupture was avoided, but the reaction was immediate. The vice president's son, young John Quincy Adams, launched a series of articles under the signature "Publicola" that acidly wondered what "this very respectable gentleman" had meant by *"political heresies"* and turned the phrase around to forge a link between democracy and hostility to Christianity that opponents would use against Jefferson for the rest of his political career. Did Jefferson consider *The Rights of Man* "the canonical book of political scripture"? His words seemed, young Adams wrote, "like the *Arabian* prophet, to call upon all true believers in the *Islam* of democracy, to draw their swords, and, in the fervour of their devotion, to compel all their countrymen to cry out, 'There is but one Goddess of Liberty, and Common Sense is her prophet.'" This association of democracy with foreign irrationality and violence would return again in the 1796 and 1800 campaigns. The inversion tactic—the claim that progressive, open-minded thought was actually regressive and rigid— would have a long career, too.[52]

By the summer of 1791, Thomas Jefferson and John Adams found themselves the unwilling figureheads of a controversy between the supporters and opponents of democracy and revolution. Jefferson had yet to write more than a few lines in favor of democracy, and Adams only wanted to use some monarchical tools to save democracy from itself, but it was too late. The party conflict had begun, and it would only get worse as 1791 wore on and the parties began to take more concrete form. Adams Sr. was blamed for the "unmanly" attacks on Jefferson, while the latter's very movements became fodder for political suspicion. When Jefferson and Madison set off on a previously planned vacation trip together in May, "botanizing" their way through New York and New

England where neither had ever traveled before, it was a matter of public comment. Representative Madison was hailed in Albany as the *"Charles Fox* of America," after the leader of the British parliamentary opposition, while Hamilton and his allies assumed that the trip's real purpose was not ecotourism but the building of alliances with disaffected politicians in the North. In fact, there is little evidence of any such activity on the trip. Though some of the Federalists found Jefferson's and Madison's hobbies as goofy as their politics, amateur scientific observation was a genuine vogue among enlightened gentlemen like Jefferson and Madison. They collected more specimens than supporters during the trip, and the main result was a new type of tree (sugar maples) at Monticello. Yet nothing either side did looked innocent or apolitical to the other anymore.[53]

REACH OUT, PUBLIC OPINION WILL BE THERE

Jefferson's *Rights of Man* "preface" was a premature eruption of something Jefferson and Madison had already been contemplating: taking the debate to a new level, where they would begin to actively reach out to the public for support against the forces they believed had suborned and corrupted the new government. Back when he had helped Hamilton create the Constitution, James Madison had been keen to limit such active public supervision, especially the kind that emanated from local communities. Local public opinion was incorrigibly narrow and self-interested, he had argued before the Constitutional Convention of 1787: "Is it to be imagined that an ordinary citizen or even Assemblyman of Rhode Island" would ever seriously consider how a policy decision "would be viewed in France or Holland; or even in Massachusetts or Connecticut?" No, they would not, as long as it was popular in their own area. Then, too, "the honest but unenlightened" were prone to become "the dupe of a favorite leader" who might not have the interests of the nation at heart. In the now-famous tenth *Federalist* essay, Madison had argued that the sheer size and careful layering of the new union provided "a Republican remedy" for the democratic "diseases most incident to Republican Government," giving enlightened elites room to breathe and make broader, less pressured decisions.[54]

Long distance from France, Thomas Jefferson had maintained his optimism about American public opinion. Indeed, Jefferson was prone to a touch of utopianism about the people and the available means of reaching them. To Jefferson, public opinion was an overwhelming but benign force, and the "good sense of the people will always be found to be the best army," even in times of unrest. "They may be led astray for a moment, but will soon correct themselves," Jefferson wrote home at the time of Shays' Rebellion in 1787. "The people are the only censors of their governors: and even their errors will tend to keep these to the true principles of their institution." It was crucial, however, that the people be kept fully and accurately informed. Jefferson's panacea for improving and managing public opinion was newspapers. "The way to prevent these irregular interpositions of the people is to give them full information of their affairs thro' the channel of the public papers, & to contrive that those papers should penetrate the whole mass of the people. The basis of our governments being the opinion of the people, the very first object should be to keep that right." Print was the only form of mass communication available, and newspapers were the most effective format yet devised for regular delivery of information and political messages to a wide audience. Jefferson, and John Adams too, were among the many American revolutionaries who felt that the press had been a crucial weapon in their political struggle against the British Empire.[55]

During the 1790s, Jefferson drew strength from and tried to encourage others with his conviction that the people at large would have no truck with the Federalists' monarchical departures. He assured Thomas Paine that while there might be "a sect preaching up . . . an English Constitution of king, lords, and commons. . . . our people, my good friend, are firm and unanimous in their principles of republicanism, and there is no better proof of it than that they love what you write and read it with delight." The Federalists would "find themselves all head and no body" when the people were able to choose.[56]

Confronted with Hamilton's policies and Jefferson's encouragement, James Madison turned his mind to undoing some of his own constitutional work. He still believed his *Federalist* 10 analysis that a large-scale republic tended to strengthen the central government by reducing each citizen's sense of political efficacy: "the more extensive a country, the more insignificant each individual is in his own eyes." But where this had been the whole point in 1787–1788, by 1791 Madison had concluded that this situation might be "unfavorable to liberty" after all. Rapid development of the press and other forms of communication offered a way to bridge the geographic gaps in the new federal system. "Whatever facilitates a general intercourse of sentiments," such as "a free press, and particularly *a circulation of newspapers through the entire body of the people*," would "be equivalent to a contraction of territorial limits" and "favorable to liberty." National public opinion might be harder to discern or express, but once it was discerned, it would be all the more powerful than the small-minded local variety. "The sentiments of the people" would become "the real sovereign" as it ought to be in "every free" government.[57]

While newspapers seemed to be the solution to their problems, the political mores the Founders worked under did not permit Jefferson and Madison to sponsor them openly or write for them in their own names. Almost all political opinion in the newspapers was published anonymously or under pseudonyms in the eighteenth century, and Jefferson refused to write for the press even pseudonymously, though he constantly urged Madison to do so. The British government's heavy use of the press, including the official *London Gazette* and extensive payments to individual journalists, was considered one of its corruptions. Corruption of the press was also one of Jefferson and Madison's complaints against Hamilton. Quite accurately, they considered the one existing newspaper devoted to covering the national government, the sycophantic *Gazette of the United States*, to be under Hamilton's influence. The *GUS* was the handiwork of John Fenno, a Boston businessman who had come to New York specifically intending to glorify the new government and profit from the resulting subsidies and printing contracts.

Especially if they were to continue to influence federal government policy from the inside, Jefferson and Madison needed a surrogate, and so Madison turned to Philip Freneau, his college roommate, who was a poet, sea captain, and former newspaper editor, as the man. Freneau was offered a job translating French documents in the office of fluent French speaker Jefferson and told rather winkingly that he could pursue whatever activities he wanted in his spare time. Meanwhile, an arrangement was made with New York printer Francis Childs to bring out a new, nationally circulating newspaper, the *National Gazette*, under Freneau's editorship. The plan was to circulate the paper throughout the nation by mail, removing the local advertisements newspapers usually carried and addressing itself to a national audience of concerned citizens. Jefferson and Madison and their friends began recruiting subscribers, who were to be the new journal's main source of income.[58]

With its subscriber list comprising a national network of budding partisans, the *National Gazette* became the first physical and institutional manifestation of the opposition party, usually considered the world's first. Freneau's satirical complaints about the corrupt, aristocratic political culture that had developed at the seat of government were put into the same pages as Madison and Jefferson's complaints about Hamilton's financial policies and cavalier approach to the Constitution, along with documents that reflected a different, less Anglocentric view of world affairs than was allowed into the *Gazette of the United States.* Quite intentionally, the pages of Freneau's newspaper became a community of political ideas, facts, and, more subtly, politicians that readers could hold in their hands and not even have to imagine. In time, the movement that these ideas and people formed together was given a name, the Republicans. (Like most party labels, this was a tendentious choice: Hamilton and Adams's followers also supported a republican form of government, and the opposition's arrogation of that term to themselves was another way of making the monarchism charge. By the same token, the other side grabbed the name "Federalists" to imply that their competitors were actually opponents of the Constitution.) "Republican" was first used as a party label in connection with Jefferson and his followers in Freneau's April 1792 essay "Sentiments of a Republican." In an era and a country where parties were agglomerations of opinion rather than membership organizations—there were no registered voters or "card-carrying" members—the *National Gazette* and the thousands of party newspapers that followed in its footsteps over the next century defined what party members believed, and especially in the early years, became themselves almost the only concrete form of party "membership" available.[59]

James Madison himself anonymously contributed several litanies and dialogues that aimed to define the opposition party as he and Jefferson chose, including "The Union: Who are Its Real Friends?" in March 1792 and "A Candid State of Parties" in September of that year. Madison tried to abstract the issues being debated at the seat of government into stark terms that could be made compelling and intelligible to readers across the country. Madison took complex matters of governing style, foreign policy, constitutional law, and public finance and boiled them all down to a conflict between the people and the aristocracy, or, more properly, between the friends of the people and those who sought to build a new hereditary elite in America. Self-servingly, Madison divided American politicians into "republicans," who believed "mankind are capable of governing themselves," and "anti-republicans," who disagreed on that key point and "were openly or secretly attached to monarchy and aristocracy" as a result. Most American leaders who had supported the Federal Constitution did so out of a desire to secure "republican liberty," but others "hoped to make the constitution a cradle" for new "hereditary establishments." Madison and Jefferson's more democratically oriented group "hated hereditary power as an insult to reason and an outrage to the rights of man," while their opponents, the present rulers, had "debauched" their revolutionary principles and come to believe that "government can be carried on only by the pageantry of rank, the influence of money, . . . and the terror of military force." (These dividing lines have run through American politics ever since.) By the end of 1792, the question that entitled one of Madison's last essays, "Who Are the Best Keepers of the People's Liberties?," almost answered itself.[60]

Of course, party-building was probably not done best through systematic political philosophy, incisive commentary, or literary elegance. Madison's essays stopped after a time, and it was Freneau's histrionic satires and doggerel poetry that more emotionally framed the party struggle in Philadelphia as a desperately compelling one for every American, a battle between "the general mass of the people, attached to their republican government and republican interests, and the chosen band devoted to monarchy and mammon." While a truly popular national political party was a long way off, Freneau's goal was getting readers into a *"phrenzy of thinking for themselves,"* and the *National Gazette* marked out the themes and tone that would be required to accomplish that goal. This tone was admittedly a rather hysterical, almost paranoid one, but embedded within Freneau's barrages was an acute political analysis of the unexpectedly hierarchical turn that the young republic seemed to be taking and the strategies being used to push it in that direction.[61]

Perhaps the most influential and prescient document the *National Gazette* ever produced was "Rules for Changing a Limited Republican Government into an Unlimited Hereditary One," a satire that was still being circulated in the early twenty-first century on the Internet, if sometimes in strangely mutated forms. One of the major "rules" was "Divide and Govern," which applied not only to the workings of the Electoral College, but also to what we now call interest group politics, in which legislative majorities are amassed by buying off various economic interests. Likewise the fear, inattention, and confusion of ordinary working Americans were to be exploited. Constitutional limitations were to be quietly "explained away" until precedents were set. Critics of the government's policies were to have their loyalty questioned and be deluged with countercharges "till at least such confusion and uncertainty be produced, that the people, being not able to find out where the truth lies," threw up their hands and "withdrew their attention." "Every occasion of external danger" should be seized on to expand the government's powers and the size of its military forces, so that even "a military defeat will become a political victory."[62]

Most of all, Freneau confronted the elective quasi-monarchy that, it seemed to him and other Republicans, the presidency had almost immediately started to become after 1789. The editor railed against the overpowering influence of "great names" like George Washington "over the human mind." Freneau recognized that personifying the government, putting on it a face and name people liked and respected, was a good way to distract even sincerely republican citizens from the potentially unrepublican policies and values of that government. Once the officer and the office were thoroughly conflated, popular veneration of the great personage would make criticism of the government seem churlish and almost treasonous.

The *National Gazette*'s heyday was brief. Freneau was a terrible manager, and Jefferson's idea of a national circulating newspaper sent strictly through the mail to subscribers never worked out well. What this experience and many others showed was that financially stable newspapers had to draw on their local communities for support: through advertising sales and job printing, and the sale of local subscriptions delivered by carrier in addition to those that were mailed. Articles and ideas traveled more quickly and widely by being copied and reprinted from one local newspaper to another rather than by a single national paper circulating everywhere. The hand-operated printing presses of the time could never have produced enough copies for that anyway. This decentralized system was facilitated by the long-standing postal policy of allowing printers to exchange newspapers with each other through the mail without charge. Freneau's paper folded in 1793, but its mantle was taken up by a growing network of locally based journals, with prominent outlets in Philadelphia, New York, and Boston to start. The *National Gazette*'s business model may have been a failure, but its political model of building a political party around a newspaper would be followed by American parties throughout the nineteenth century.[63]

In terms of presidential politics, the simple existence of the *National Gazette* may have pushed matters ahead more than anything Freneau or

Madison wrote. The presidency was hardly discussed in the *National Gazette*, except to criticize Washington's practice of it, but Alexander Hamilton made sure that Thomas Jefferson's connection with the newspaper became a scandal, the first presidential election year imbroglio in American history, in only the second presidential election (1792). Correctly divining how the news would irritate President Washington's sensitivities about his reputation and the loyalty of his subordinates, and plenty steamed himself, Hamilton saw an opportunity for final victory in his struggle with Jefferson for the administration's policy soul. Hints began dropping in the *Gazette of the United States* about the true nature of Freneau's job in Jefferson's office, and the situation spiraled from there. By the late summer of 1792, Hamilton was personally emitting a stream of essays in the *GUS*, under multiple pseudonyms, detailing the "*indelicate and unfit*" relationship between Jefferson and the *National Gazette* and emphasizing the way it undercut the opposition's high-minded stance as "the best keepers of the People's liberties." The underhanded setup was "inconsistent with those pretensions to extraordinary republican purity, of which so suspicious a parade" had been made, Hamilton wrote as "An American." In another essay, he compared Freneau to a "Viper" that Jefferson had tried to secret away in the "bosom" of his country. Even more devastating as far as George Washington was concerned, Hamilton's essays exposed Jefferson as the would-be "head of a party."[64]

In fact, Hamilton was projecting a bit of his own proactive personality: he imagined that Freneau's job and one local Philadelphia congressional campaign were part of "a vigorous and general effort . . . by factious men to introduce every where and in every department persons unfriendly to the measures, if the not the constitution, of the National Government." Certainly that described what was going to happen as American political parties developed, but the evidence is scant that Jefferson's and Madison's thinking or activities had progressed that far. Meanwhile, Hamilton was actively recruiting southern allies on the basis of the need to counter the opposition party and doing a fairly thorough job of ensuring that all of the federal government's local officials were ideologically committed to his program. In addition to providing the Federalist press with far more copy than any major opposition figure did for their newspapers, Hamilton and his allies were also heavily supporting Fenno's *Gazette of the United States* with government printing contracts and mercantile advertisements, making it a far more sustainable enterprise than Freneau's. According to the mimetic principle that seems to drive political innovation in America, Hamilton began strenuously party-building because he thought the other guys were doing it.[65]

In fact, the debate over Jefferson's political character in 1792 was remarkably one-sided. Freneau angrily defended his own independence, which was quite real, and Madison and James Monroe contributed a sort of legal brief that tried to exculpate Jefferson on the grounds that he did not technically control the *National Gazette*. Yet no amount of logic-chopping could change how the thing appeared. Freneau's advocacy for Jefferson himself was limited to Madison's brief, reprinted from *Dunlap's American Daily Advertiser* and given the dry title "Defence of Mr. Jefferson's Political Character." Too demure to actually review Jefferson's career "for the sake of applause," Madison took up much of the essay's running time reprinting some of Jefferson's letters from Paris on the Constitution, showing both how supportive he had been of it and how concerned he had always been about the problems that contested presidential elections might cause, especially if the officer could be reelected. Hamilton responded almost hysterically as "Metellus," with a variation on the perennial conservative theme of the liberal leader as an object of irrational, idolatrous worship. He complained that in the "votaries of Mr. Jefferson . . . devotion for their idol kindles at every form, in which he deigns to present himself," a swipe at Hinduism.[66]

Meanwhile, the scandal greatly reduced Jefferson's influence in the Washington administration and contributed mightily to his decision to retire from office and most all political involvement at the end of 1793. Hamilton left Washington's cabinet not long after, but he maintained close contact with his former assistant and successor, Oliver Wolcott Jr., and indeed enjoyed more unchallenged influence over administration policy remotely than he had while actually in office, as he no longer had to contend with Jefferson's objections.

Winning the power struggle over policy may have come at a steep cost, however. Hamilton had hurt Jefferson with Washington by naming the secretary of state as opposition leader, but he had also greatly increased Jefferson's public prominence. Hamilton and his most avid congressional lieutenant, William Loughton Smith of South Carolina, introduced and practically promoted the idea that Jefferson was scheming to get the presidency for himself, that the whole opposition aimed only to gain power for its own sake. This was a good way to subtract Patriot King points, but it also thrust a mantle upon Jefferson that he was uniquely suited to wear but reluctant to accept. Though radicals like

John Beckley and admirers like James Madison believed Jefferson was the only man who could adequately fulfill the role of opposition chief, they found Jefferson resistant; but here was Hamilton doing their work for them. Thus, in a sense, one of the 1796 nominations, Thomas Jefferson's, was made by the *Gazette of the United States* in 1792.[67]

Hamilton's harassment also helped provide motivation for a new approach to party that helped Jefferson around some of his scruples and would later power some important innovations in party politics and the defense of the press against Federalist reprisals. In one of the few tough passages from his "Defence of Mr. Jefferson's Political Character," Madison argued that Hamilton's real beef was not with Jefferson but with opposition itself—that is, with the idea that there might be serious, ongoing criticism and political resistance to the government's policies. "This attack has obviously something further in view, than simply to wound the fame of one deserving citizen. It is leveled at that free and manly spirit of enquiry, which has lately . . . demonstrated the mischievous tendency of some of the measures of the government." Hamilton and his allies sought to "crush" that "spirit of enquiry" by discrediting the person they blamed for it, who also happened to be the biggest name "in the republican list." If they were allowed to do that, the Republican "cause would be humbled, and the friends of monarchy [would] triumph."[68]

POPULAR POLITICS IN A POSTCOLONIAL NATION

The conflict at the seat of government over finance, constitutionalism, and style of governance might or might not have produced on its own a full-fledged party conflict involving the voters and a national contest for power. What the historical records show, however, is that it did not happen that way. Surprising as it may be from the inward-looking modern American perspective, the catalyst for full-scale party conflict actually came from outside the republic's borders and across the ocean.

IN THE HANDS OF THE POWERS

To understand this, we need to consider that the early United States was also a new nation in the global order of its era, not a world power but the kind of place that would be called a developing nation in later centuries. Like the new postcolonial nations of the post–World War II era, the United States was small, weak, and subject to harsh buffeting by political, economic, and cultural winds coming from the more developed world. Politics in excolonies commonly revolve around debates over the new nation's relationship with the parent country, debates often manipulated by outside forces with agendas of their own. The United States was no exception to this rule. Britain, France, Spain, and other European powers had been scrambling to control, exploit, and influence North America for centuries. Often they did by manipulating intermediaries and clients, such as the American Indian peoples that the European empires recruited as military allies and trading partners and the various quasi-independent colonial governments whose money and troops had to be coaxed rather than demanded. There was no reason to assume that a fledgling independent republic stretched along one coast was going to change this long-standing pattern. The Revolutionary War had only been won after military intervention by France, which was exacting revenge for the loss of their mainland colonies to the British at the end of the Seven Years' War in 1763. Looking on from Paris in 1787, American diplomat Thomas Jefferson had predicted that elections for the new presidency would entice France and Britain to "interfere with money & with arms" to see that a "Galloman or an Angloman," respectively, took charge of a valuable and potentially strategic territory.[1]

Great Britain's postwar policy toward the United States did much to exacerbate America's postcolonial anxieties. In the years after the Treaty of Paris, the British had tried to maintain America's colonial status as much as possible and contain both the economic development and geographic expansion of the United States. Just as the peace was signed, the influential British politician and trade theorist Lord Sheffield published his *Observations on American Commerce*, which seemed to guide the British government's attitude. Taking a pessimistic view of American economic potential that rankled on the other side of the ocean, Sheffield argued that the United States was a "now foreign and independent nation" and deserved no special privileges in the empire it had rejected despite the immense business British and American merchants and ships had done with each other before the war. Great Britain was the world's richest and most powerful nation, with the most prolific and efficient manufacturers and an overwhelmingly superior navy. The United States was still a captive market for British manufacturing, dependent on British credit and naval protection. According to Sheffield, the Americans would become even more dependent if they were kept out of the British Caribbean islands that had been so important to their prewar trade, and if U.S. ships were not allowed to carry British goods, the American shipping and shipbuilding industries would be stunted as well. The United States would have to accept trade on British terms if it wanted any possibility of prosperity or growth.[2]

Even more flagrant was the approach that the European powers took to U.S. ambitions on the American continent itself. With the United States unable to fulfill some of its treaty obligations, especially compelling its citizens to pay all prewar British debts, the British left in place their military installations on the new nation's western border, on land acknowledged as U.S. territory by the treaty, at Detroit, Niagara, and other locations. The threat here went far beyond the British army. British forts were centers of the fur trade and crucial sources of supply and organization for Native Americans inclined toward resistance to U.S. encroachments. Especially west of the Appalachians, the native forces during the Revolutionary War had lost no major battles and held their boundary with white settlements at the Ohio River. Skipping only a few beats, the British Indian Department resumed its prewar goal of fostering Indian-dominated buffer territories along the frontier; its field representatives south of the Great Lakes encouraged the growth of a pantribal resistance movement centered among the Miami, Shawnee, and Lenape (Delaware) peoples living in present-day Ohio. The civil and military authorities in Canada joined in eagerly, as both they and the Indians shared a desire to deter U.S.-based settlers and land speculators from muscling in on their land. Attempts by War Secretary Henry Knox and Northwest Territory governor Arthur St. Clair to simply declare the northwestern Indians to be conquered peoples only inflamed the situation further. Once the cash-strapped Articles of Confederation government had shrunk the military forces to nearly nothing, the conditions were created for two of the most humiliating setbacks the U.S. Army has ever experienced. In present-day northwest Ohio, two successive expeditions against the Indian resistance were surprised and routed. The second of these expeditions, in 1791 under Arthur St. Clair, was surprised in camp by warriors fighting under Miami chief Little Turtle. In what was termed at the time a "bloody Indian battle, perhaps the most shocking that has happened in America since its first Discovery," St. Clair's hapless, surrounded troops suffered some nine hundred casualties. That was more than any other engagement in the whole history of the U.S.-Indian wars and a figure larger than the total strength of the regular army at the time. (Most of the troops were frontier militiamen.) Whites sold Indian leadership short when they blamed the disaster on British meddling, but British support was unquestionably a major factor in the northwestern Indian confederacy's progress.[3]

Though a Revolutionary War ally of the United States, Spain now joined the British in trying to restrain its expansion. Worried about their lucrative colony in Mexico, the Spaniards had suddenly closed the Mississippi River to U.S. commerce after the war and began offering land on the Spanish side of the river to both Indians and U.S. citizens in exchange for loyalty to the Spanish crown. (A number of settlements in Missouri got started this way, mostly obviously New Madrid in the Bootheel region.) Prominent westerners were bribed to become Spanish spies and allowed to bypass the trade restrictions if they signed secret loyalty oaths. Others agreed to become Spanish officials. Recipients of such favors included the elderly Daniel Boone and the young Andrew Jackson.[4]

Inevitably American leaders were divided over how best to respond to these pressures. Respecting Great Britain's wealth and power and admiring many aspects of its system, Hamilton and the Federalists generally favored reestablishing a close economic relationship with the British, or at least wanted to avoid antagonizing the empire until such time (in the distant future) as the United States might be able to challenge the British in military and industrial capacity. Most Democratic-Republicans wanted to forge some new status in the world that would be completely independent of the British Empire and would stake the country's claim on new, more enlightened principles of free trade, national equality, and political transparency. They hoped that mutual benefit and understanding rather than force and fraud would guide relations among the world's new republics.

ROILED BY THE FRENCH REVOLUTION

The outbreak and later radicalization of the French Revolution unleashed a whole new set of external forces on American politics, forces whose impact was increased by the fact that the French Revolution seemed to engage the emotions of the American populace much more than the details of postwar trade policy. In popular politics, the winning argument for the Constitution had been the promise that greater stability would bring prosperity. World revolution and war invoked fundamental social values and hopes for the future that seemed to make political feeling much more intense. The first popular overthrow of a major European monarchy, the French Revolution reverberated all over the world, but perhaps especially in the young republic that French revolutionaries believed they were imitating, the United States. European fashions, wars, and depressions all made strong impressions on an American population that was still well informed about and deeply engaged with its mother continent. After 1789, most American newspapers often contained as much information about French affairs as they did about America, helping spread to American shores a wave of "popular cosmopolitanism" that was sweeping the Atlantic world.[5]

The great political upheavals of Europe during the 1790s not only raised tremendous passions in America, but also reached out inexorably to influence American political events, especially in the form of a long, grinding war between revolutionary France and the monarchies of Europe, led by Great Britain. One of the great dangers that had plagued earlier republics was foreign intervention, often invited by competing factions within the republic. The republics of Venice and Poland had both run tragically afoul of this problem. The United States would not be immune to the fear or (in a limited form) the reality of it, in an atmosphere of tension and suspicion created by the ideological disagreements between left and right that the French Revolution spawned all over the European world.[6]

American politics in the 1790s is impossible to understand without some knowledge of the basic chronology of the French Revolution. Before 1789, France had what was, within its own territory, a much more powerful monarchy and aristocracy than Great Britain's. It was an absolute monarchy in which the King was not limited by a constitution— even an unwritten one—or a powerful Parliament. There was a national legislative assembly called the Estates-General, but it had not met from 1614 until 1789, when financial crisis forced Louis XVI to finally call it into session. The poverty and powerlessness of the peasantry and the urban lower classes in France was also much worse than in Britain, and the political and social position of the middle, commercial classes (the *bourgeoisie*) much weaker. The nobility and the clergy controlled most of the property, were immune to conventional forms of taxation and prosecution, and monopolized the ranks of civil and military officials.

When Parisian crowds sacked the Bastille fortress in July and forced the monarchy to share power, liberal political thinkers and Enlightenment enthusiasts all over the Atlantic world hailed it as the greatest event in history. The *Declaration of the Rights of Man and the Citizen* was issued in August 1789, just in time for outgoing American envoy Thomas Jefferson to provide feedback on several drafts of the document. It was far more sweeping than Jefferson's own declaration but ignored his advice to leave the word "property" and various hedges for aristocratic privilege out of the list: "Men are born and remain free and equal in rights. Social distinctions may be founded only upon the general good. The aim

CALENDRIER REPUBLICAIN
—
POUR L'AN V.
De la Republique Francaise,
ET LE XXIme
DE L'INDEPENDANCE AMERICAINE.

———

Embelli de deux gravures des Costumes des Fonctionaires de la Republique.

—

ET CONTENANT

Le Décadaire et ses rapports avec l'ere vulgaire.
Lever et coucher du soleil. Age de la lune.
Analise de la Constitution Française.
Description des Costumes des Fonctionaires en Fr.
Epoques remarquables dans les Revol. Fr. et Amer.
Tableau des Departments et Population, de la Fr.
Etat des Flottes des Republiques de France et de Hollande.
Anecdotes frappantes tirées de l'histoire de France.
Fêtes Nationales de l'an V.
Noms de villes changés depuis la Revolution Fr.
Forces militaires de la Republique Française.
Routes des Etats Unis.
Valeur des Exportations des Etats Unis.
Monnoye des Etats Unis.
Valeur des Monnoyes étrangères dans les E. U.
Depart et arrivée des Postes.
Reglemens des Banques.
Marche des Marseillois, &c. &c. &c.

PHILADELPHIE,
De l'imprimerie de BENJ. FRANKLIN BACHE,
N°. 112, rue du Marche.

---

*Francomania: The enthusiasm in America for the French Revolution
is suggested by the publication in Philadelphia of this French-language
almanac using the revised French Revolutionary Calendar, with new, more
rational months and days and a dating system that began time anew with
the creation of the French Republic. It was one of the "Political Novelties" for
sale in the bookstore attached to the Philadelphia Aurora office. (Title page,*
Calendrier Republicain pour l'an V. de la Republique Francaise, et le
XXIme de l'independence Americaine *[Philadelphia: Benjamin Franklin
Bache, 1796].)*

of all political association is the preservation of the natural and impre-
scriptible rights of man. These rights are liberty, property, security, and
resistance to oppression."[7]

Americans were almost universally thrilled at first, and why not?
The French Revolution seemed to be modeled on (and inspired by) the
American one, and it even had a true American hero, the Marquis de la
Fayette, as one of its primary leaders. In command of the Paris National
Guard, Lafayette had the remains of the Bastille demolished and sent
the keys to George Washington as a symbol of the inspiration America
had provided. A National Constituent Assembly was created, a constitution was written, feudalism was abolished, and the most unfair aspects
of the *ancien régime* were reformed, especially the special privileges of
the aristocracy and church. France became a constitutional monarchy,
with King Louis left on his throne but now answerable to the people's
representatives. Though the American clergy would later wax hysterical
about the French Revolution's threat to Christianity, little complaint was
made in Christian America at the early moves to curb religious institutions under the constitutional monarchy, not even at the fairly shocking
step of seizing the Catholic Church's property and converting priests to
public employees. It helped that the people of the Early Republic's Bible
Belt, New England, were strongly anti-Catholic.[8]

The French Revolution became more divisive in America as it grew
steadily more radical and violent, fueled by a much more virulent version of the "contagion of liberty" that metastasized in the streets of
Paris. It was worsened by economic privation and the intransigence of
the Revolution's enemies. Important in speeding up the process of radicalization were the networks of debating societies that sprang up once
political participation was opened to commoners, especially the Jacobin
Clubs. The Jacobins became a kind of political party, a much more hierarchical and tightly organized one than any that ever developed in the
United States.

Events took a turn for the worse when the royal family disguised
themselves and tried to escape France in June 1791, hoping to enlist the
aid of Europe's other monarchies, especially Austria, where the queen
of France's brother was emperor. They were caught at Varennes and
brought back to Paris as suspected traitors to the constitutional monarchy they had professed to support. The radicalism of the Revolution
leaped forward in response. Sentiment flared in Paris for dispensing
with the monarchy entirely, and Lafayette found himself falling out of

favor with French patriots after he ordered the National Guard to fire on a threatening crowd in the Champs de Mars on July 17, 1791. He resigned command of the National Guard not long after and lost his influence over national policy.

Meanwhile, relations with the rest of Europe spiraled. In August, Marie-Antoinette and Louis XVI's brothers joined the king of Prussia at Pilnitz Castle near Dresden to issue a statement that it was the "common concern" of all Europe's monarchs to see the French king restored to his throne with full powers, preparing the ground for an invasion. In America, angry Republicans, including Philip Freneau of the *National Gazette*, denounced the Pilnitz Declaration as "the Death Warrant" for the meddling monarchs. Pilnitz pushed the French revolutionaries into violent action against their external enemies, before they had time to strike. In April 1792, France declared war on Austria, and soon Austria and Prussia declared war back, beginning a series of conflicts between revolutionary France and most of the rest of Europe—as well as Great Britain, which took over after the Austrians and Prussians failed—that would not end until Napoleon Bonaparte's final defeat in 1815.[9]

The French revolutionaries and their supporters welcomed the war as a way to test the mettle of "liberty, equality, and fraternity." The American diplomat Joel Barlow wrote a poem describing the conflict as *The Conspiracy of Kings* against "Justice" and "Freedom" and "the rights of Nature." War only made the revolutionary cause that much more popular in America—and "those prolific monsters, courts and kings," seem that much more odious, "vampires nurs'd on nature's spoils"—among those already concerned about creeping monarchy. Other American supporters called the monarchies arrayed against France the "league of despots," while Jefferson tried on "the confederacy of princes against human liberty." There was no question about which side had the hearts of those Americans who felt passionately about the continued progress of their own revolution.

The struggle between European empires also tugged on more than American feelings. The French expected the United States to keep faith with the old Revolutionary War alliance, not so much by actively supplying troops or formally joining the war as by keeping its ports, ships, and produce available to France in its time of need. This was perfectly consistent with neutrality as Jefferson and Madison understood it, but not at all acceptable to the other side of the conflict, the British. Britain refused to treat American trade as neutral if they suspected it was being conducted with their enemy. Both sides periodically retaliated against American shipping for trading with the other and sought to push American policy in the desired direction.[10]

The drive toward war was led by a political faction called the Girondins, relatively moderate, middle-to-upper-class revolutionaries who were France's most ardent admirers of America and greatest optimists, in the sense of expecting that liberty would sweep the world. The name came from the region on the southwestern coast of France, near Bordeaux, where many of the party leaders originated. Coming from outside Paris, the Girondins were somewhat distrustful of the Parisian crowds and their leaders. Several of Thomas Jefferson's friends from his diplomatic tour in France were leading Girondins, as was Thomas Paine, then living in France. One important way in which they followed the American example was in favoring relative lenience toward political enemies within France, including the king. The Girondins mostly had control of France from spring 1792 to spring 1793, but were doomed to be outdone and overthrown by the more stringent Jacobins, who initially did not want the war, believing that France was too weak. The Jacobins had middle-class leaders such as attorney Maximilien Robespierre, but their base was in the streets of Paris, among the hardest-bitten, barricade-manning laborers and artisans. While the factional differences could be read about in American newspapers, Federalists took to calling all American sympathizers of the French Revolution, and eventually all the Democratic-Republican opposition, "Jacobins," despite the fact that any real-life connections that existed were with the Girondins. (The actual French Jacobins preferred dealing with the Federalists.)[11]

The war with the "league of despots" sparked the end of the French monarchy, a Jacobin takeover, and tremendous bloodshed inside France. At first the revolutionary armies were easily defeated, and many regiments even went over to the enemy. The commander of the allied forces announced that he intended to put Louis XVI back on the throne and threatened to destroy Paris if the royal family was harmed. Naturally, this resulted in the royal family being harmed, and much more. In the summer of 1792, all hell broke loose. An August uprising in Paris, fomented by the Jacobin Clubs, seized control of the city; the king was imprisoned and all his guards and servants killed in the process. General Lafayette, who had earlier risked his life by publicly denouncing the Jacobins, tried to bring his troops to save the king, and failing that, fled to Belgium with a few of his officers. A few weeks later, with Prussian armies marching on Paris, more than a thousand political prisoners, including hundreds of nobles and priests, were slaughtered in the so-called September Massacres. Then, just when things seemed darkest, the threatened Revolution was miraculously vindicated by the surprise defeat of the Prussian army at Valmy. The very next day, September 21, 1792, the new National Convention formally abolished the monarchy and declared France a republic.

Jefferson and other officials received a steady stream of melancholy reports on all this from American diplomats in France, but the folks at home loved it. Bells rang out when news of the Prussian and Austrian retreat reached Philadelphia, and the September Massacres were over-looked during the holiday season of 1792 as towns across the United States celebrated the French Republic, the first wave of many such cel-ebrations over the next several years. The courthouse windows in the rural county seat of Carlisle, Pennsylvania, were illuminated with the transparent letters "LET MAN BE FREE," while Philadelphia's Germans raised their glasses in hopes that France's "arms and example" might "exterminate tyranny and inequality." In January 1793, Boston held a "Civic Feast" to celebrate the French Republic that was one of the most impressive in the city's history. Breakfast was served out on State Street with eight hundred loaves of bread, hogsheads of punch, and a spec-tacular roast ox that had one horn decorated with the French tricolor and the other with the American stars and stripes. Each child in atten-dance received a "civic cake" with the legend "Liberty and Equality" on it. In the afternoon, "Citizen Samuel Adams," the vice president's cousin and governor of Massachusetts but also an enthusiastic "Jacobin," pre-sided over a formal banquet, and in the evening there were bonfires and fireworks. The celebrations were general and outwardly unified, but not without an undercurrent of tension. Abigail Adams reported to her husband that "men of reflection" and "men of property" in Boston had "found the Cry of Equality . . . not so pleasing" but went along with the feast and helped pay for it "for fear of being stiled aristocrats."[12]

As is well known, Thomas Jefferson counted himself among the country's most enthusiastic fans of the French Republic, warts, guillo-tines, and all. When a friend with the embassy in Paris wrote him in late 1792 that the streets were red with blood, Jefferson snapped back that he ought not to be so squeamish: "The liberty of the whole earth was depending . . . on the [outcome of the French Revolution], and was ever such a prize won with so little innocent blood? . . . Rather than it should have failed, I would have seen half the earth desolated. Were there but an Adam & Eve left in every country, & left free, it would be better than it now is." Kept private at the time, this statement and others would be widely quoted by his later detractors as evidence that Jefferson was a blood-thirsty incipient Stalin figure, but in fact his were fairly common American sentiments at the time that he just happened to put far more eloquently than most.[13]

While a debate over the French Revolution had already been taking place, spinning out of the transatlantic one between Thomas Paine and Edmund Burke, one of the first signs of serious popular disquiet in America—or perhaps more accurately, of American conservatives trying to generate popular disquiet—was the newspaper items that appeared in response to the next major French news event, the trial and execution of Louis XVI and Marie Antoinette in January 1793. These dwelled heavily on the French revolutionaries' favored method of execution. The guillotine was originally a reform, introduced at the very beginning of the Revolution to make executions more humane and egalitarian. Previously, capital punishment varied by class: aristocrats could die quickly by the sword, but their inferiors were slowly strangled with ropes (hanging) or beaten to death (breaking on the wheel). The rather moving London newspaper accounts of Louis's death—"CITIZENS, I FORGIVE MY ENEMIES, AND I DIE INNOCENT!"—circulated widely along with a chillingly clinical description of the device used to kill him. The *National Gazette* and other opposition newspapers felt the need to counter this with a satirical item claiming that Marie Antoinette had been in the habit of having a toy guillotine brought in every night after dinner and chopping the heads off little pastry figures of revolutionary leaders, so that the ladies of the court could see how sweet was the blood of the patriots. This was mashed up (in the typical fashion of the press at this time) with a more serious item pointing out that King Louis himself had inspected and improved the guillotine, and that the Prussian general, the Duke of Brunswick, had planned to use it liberally in purging the rebels once he captured Paris. "What a *change* is here! LOUIS dug a pit for *tens of thousands*—and by the direction, no doubt, of the *unerring hand of God*—HE ALONE, *fell into it!* Where, reader, is your *horror* now! *Change it into the other scale*—cries the still voice of conscience—turn your face *from* MONARCHS—support THE RIGHTS OF MAN and of human nature."[14]

Little was said officially, but Washington, Adams, Hamilton, and their fellow Federalists increasingly recoiled from a close relationship with this new French Republic. Hamilton's long-range vision for the country was impossible without British trade and capital, and lacking much sympathy for French egalitarian ideals in the first place, he had readily concluded, long before the end of the monarchy, that it was not realistic to honor the old alliance. To believe otherwise, Hamilton argued in good conservative fashion, was to be irrational and emotional and unfit for the manly pursuits of politics and diplomacy. Among his long litany of complaints against Jefferson and Madison was that they had a "womanish attachment to France and a womanish resentment against Great Britain." President Washington was more inclined to loyalty, but much less so after his old patron Louis XVI was killed and his surrogate son Lafayette was forced into exile.[15]

On the streets and lanes of the American Republic, the regicide actually seemed to fan rather than dampen the popularity of the French Revolution, and when Great Britain entered the war shortly thereafter, hoping to prevent the further spread of royal decapitations, pro-French passions were doubly inflamed by renewed resentment of the British. At one Philadelphia dinner, a severed pig's head was part of the feast, and some diner got the idea of hailing the decapitated hog as the king, allowing each member of the company to put the liberty cap on the beast's head, call it "tyrant," and stab it a few times with their steely knives.[16]

So little did the bloody turn reduce enthusiasm for the French Republic that even the now extreme-seeming acts of cultural reconstruction that came in with the French Republic found many American supporters. In 1792, French revolutionaries called for "Citoyen" or "Citoyenne" to become the only acceptable appellations in polite society. Even the ordinary terms "Monsieur" and "Madame" originated with the honorifics "my lord" and "my lady," so they were banned. For a time some Americans adopted the same practice, using only "Citizen" or "Citizeness." Officially addressing King Louis XVI as "Citoyen" had been part of the process that led to his overthrow and death, but at least one New Hampshire gathering in February 1793 seemed to have perfectly friendly intentions when they gathered to celebrate "Citizen Washington's Birth-Day."[17]

Even the fall of the Girondins and the beginnings of the Jacobin "Reign of Terror" in April 1793 made a surprisingly small dent in the popularity of America's sister republic. Revolutionary violence and terror became a major theme for the Federalists only later, when the actual

Reign of Terror was already years into the past. What seemed to hurt the French revolutionaries more with the Federalists than their violence was the fact that when they reached out to their sister republic for help, the French found the American people more ready to respond than their government.

POLITICAL PARTYING WITH CITIZEN GENET

The next wave of love for France came with the dramatic arrival of Edmond Charles Genet, the first diplomatic envoy from the French Republic, in April 1793. The Girondist government had sent Genet aboard the frigate *L'Embuscade*, and the original plan was that he be accompanied by King Louis and the royal family as they moved into exile. Tom Paine's scheme to spare the French royals failed, but Genet went anyway, leaving Paris secretly on the very night of the execution. With the Jacobins taking power and sympathy for the royal family a treasonable offense, the dashing young diplomat would never be able to return home safely, but he soldiered on to carry out his romantically conceived mission.[18]

According to his official instructions, Genet's job in America was to declare that with the "vile henchmen of despotism" out of the way, it was now time for a new era of frank, open, straightforward relations between republics, a new diplomacy that would be "diametrically opposed to the tortuous paths in which their predecessors had crawled." Genet was to propose "a national pact in which the two peoples would join [*confondroient*] their commercial and political interests and establish an intimate concert, which would promote the extension of the Empire of Liberty, guarantee the sovereignty of all peoples, and punish those powers" (Great Britain) that still tried to maintain colonial systems. If the U.S. government did not go for that grand scheme, then Genet was still to do everything he could to make the "principles of liberty and independence . . . germinate" in the western territories of Kentucky and Louisiana, where the French might make or supply expeditions against the colonies of Britain and Spain. (Attacking each other's colonies was standard procedure in eighteenth-century imperial warfare.) As a minimum fallback position, Genet was to insist on France's rights under the 1778 treaties, which included operating privateers out of American ports and preventing any nations France was at war with from doing the same. To make good on all that, the minister was empowered to

Emissary of Revolution: The arrival of "Citizen" Edmond Genet, the first diplomat sent by the infant French Republic, sparked the foundation of the Democratic-Republican Societies and hence the beginning of the Democratic party. (Engraving from Harper's Encyclopedia of United States History *[New York: Harper & Brothers, 1905], 4:42.)*

commission officers and outfit privateers himself and encouraged to influence American public opinion if he could.[19]

Genet's mission was doomed from start. Guided by Hamilton, President Washington had already decided that the United States would remain firmly, coldly neutral in the French Revolutionary War. A proclamation reflecting this position was issued before the French Republic's emissary had even reached America. While the United States did not formally abrogate the old treaty of alliance with France, the Washington administration and its partisan Federalist supporters took the position that the French Republic was a new government; the treaty had been signed with the deposed *ancien régime*. Not even Thomas Jefferson was truly interested in so close a partnership as Genet was supposed to set up, not if it meant war.[20]

Bad weather forced Genet's ship to land not in Philadelphia but in Charleston, South Carolina, where a huge crowd and the local French consul awaited him on the pier. Escorted directly to the governor's mansion, Genet got busy carrying out his orders despite having not yet contacted the government with which he was supposed to be conducting relations. Four captured British ships were converted to French privateers, with largely American crews, and local recruiting was begun for an attack on British Florida. After a week of this, word finally arrived that the federal government had forbidden all such activities, and a hasty announcement was published in the Charleston newspaper that "all houses of rendezvous for volunteers in the French service" were to be immediately shut up. Undeterred, Genet finally set out for Philadelphia on April 19, traveling overland and stopping regularly for banquets in his honor at the towns along the way. He wanted to see the country and stir up some fervor for the French cause.[21]

At this last task, Genet was tremendously successful. With charisma to spare and a powerful singing voice, Genet was more than prepared to be the life of whatever parties were thrown up around him, charming even the suspicious with his enthusiasm and informality. The parties seemed to get bigger as he moved north. Besides the speeches and dinners, farmers and merchants offered Genet huge quantities of provisions for the war effort, including six hundred thousand barrels of flour, at fraternally discounted prices. (Or so Philip Freneau claimed.) Philadelphia was determined to have the biggest reception yet. A notice appeared in the *National Gazette* suggesting that "the true republicans of this country" should prepare a hero's welcome for Genet: militia companies should march, fire cannons, and "hoist the three-colored flag" in salute and women should wear "patriotic" (tricolored) ribbons in their hair. Genet sent *L'Embuscade* ahead of him as a herald. It sailed up the Delaware into Philadelphia and fired fifteen of its forty guns in salute. The ship was impossibly decked out in revolutionary swag. "Liberty caps" perched on the figurehead and atop the mast, and mottos were emblazoned all over it: "Enemies of equality, reform or tremble!" across the foremast, "Freemen! Behold we are your friends and brethren" on the main mast, and "We are armed to defend the rights of man" on the mizzen.[22]

When Genet arrived in person two weeks later, *L'Embuscade* fired its guns again three times so that the people of Philadelphia could come out to watch the ambassador enter the city. An even more elaborate greeting was planned for a town meeting in the backyard of Independence Hall (then still the Pennsylvania State House) the next day. The welcoming committee was heavy with the city's most prominent Republican-leaning citizens, including many who would later be major participants in or financial backers of the campaign that would carry the state for Jefferson in 1796. They were a cross section of upwardly mobile men who felt excluded from the elite circles of power in the city because of their ethnicity, immigrant status, or simply their beliefs. They were sincere democrats, but their main goal was not a completely equal society so much as one where the social barriers among whites were weak and porous. "A vision of classlessness," historian Joyce Appleby has called this Democratic-Republican approach to class warfare. What outraged them was the idea that others might claim exclusive, aristocratic privileges or permanent, hereditary advantages in American society or government. Among those welcoming Genet were *General Advertiser* editor Benjamin Franklin Bache, hatter and militia leader John Smith, Irish-born tobacco dealer Thomas Leiper, and tavernkeeper Israel Israel (who was technically not Jewish but the target of anti-Semitic slurs from Federalist bigots just the same). Then there were colleagues of Jefferson's in the Philadelphia-based national scientific organization, the American Philosophical Society, along with local political figures of moment who were considered sympathetic to Jefferson and the congressional opposition, including Secretary of the Commonwealth Alexander J. Dallas (originally from Jamaica), dandified merchant-poet and newly elected state legislator John Swanwick, and the man who had gotten him elected, Scottish physician James Hutchinson.[23]

Encouraged by Hamilton, Philadelphia's established merchants had just issued a statement thanking President Washington for the neutrality proclamation, and the Genet welcoming committee was intent on answering. They offered Genet their "wishes and prayers" that even though America could not enter the war, it could still "demonstrate the sincerity of her friendship, by affording every useful assistance to the citizens of her sister republic." An "immense body of citizens, walking three a-breast" then conducted Genet to the nearby City Tavern, where his extemporaneous reply brought such acclaim he was asked to repeat it for the crowd gathered outside. Genet told the audience that he was glad to see and hear that the fighting French would "be treated as brothers in danger and distress" by the American people. When they learned of Genet's reception, the people of France would "consider this day as one of the happiest of their infant Republic." There would be "no secrets, no intrigue" between republics.[24]

Already thrilled with the French as the star players for republicanism's team, the Philadelphians swooned under Genet's amorous overtures. What the French Republic seemed to be seeking, Jefferson summarized, was a kind of perfect modern relationship—transparent, egalitarian, and free of coercion: "We see in you the only persons on earth who can love us sincerely and merit to be so loved."[25]

A couple of days later, a banquet was held, the first of a long series that continued throughout the summer. One hundred "French-American citizens," including Citizens DuPonceau and Freneau, gathered at Oeller's Hotel to dine with Genet, the officers of *L'Embuscade*, and other local French citizen-dignitaries. After dinner there were fifteen toasts, all elaborately published afterward in the *National Gazette* and the *General Advertiser*, and a concert. On the program were a French ode to the United States, which Freneau was commissioned to translate; the French revolutionary anthem with two extra naval stanzas penned; and finally a number from Citizen Genet himself: "Tyrants beware! Your tott'ring thrones must fall; / One int'rest links the free together, / And Freedom's sons are Frenchmen all."[26]

The *"fêtes perpetuelles"* (nonstop parties) that Genet boasted of were highly convivial and quite sincere as pure joy and fun, but they also carried distinct, finely crafted political messages. In this case, the messages were American popular support for a strong relationship between the two republics and the rhetorical construction of a French revolutionary cause that was continuous with both the old alliance and the vanguard of a new world revolution that defined the progress of liberty, equality, and democracy in their struggle with despotism. If American politicians or citizens professed to support those things, the celebrations argued, they needed to join with the French, at least in sympathy.[27]

The mode in which Philadelphia's and New York's French-sympathizing Republicans were working is what historians have labeled "celebratory politics." They built on a tradition of nationalist celebrations that stretched back before the Revolutionary War and had reached an early crescendo during the "Grand Federal Processions" of the constitutional ratification campaign. Fraternal associations were organized; banquets and community feasts were held; parades, illumination of buildings, and fireworks were organized; elaborate toasts and songs were drunk and sung. By staging such community events to observe a political moment (e.g., a military victory, the ratification of the Constitution, the Fourth of July) and then publishing the proceedings in the newspapers, promoters of American national identity built what we might now call an involvement device that pulled whole communities—including their nonvoters and ethnic subcultures—into a closer imaginative relationship with the young American Republic. Though sometimes used in controversial situations, celebrations and clubs before those for Genet had usually been aimed at unifying communities and ending disputes if they had any specific purpose. For instance, the "Grand Federal Processions" of 1788 had aimed to bring Americans together behind the new Constitution. Festive politics had an almost automatically democratizing element in that such events invited at least the vicarious support and participation of a wider public who merely witnessed them in the streets or read about them in the newspapers. Even the most "elegant entertainment," once it was held in a public place and an account of it was published for all to read, offered at least the idea of joining in political activity or forming a political opinion to an unpredictably wider circle of people.[28]

The unusually intense celebrations surrounding Genet were the beginning of a new phase of festive politics, in which the celebrations began to splinter and become more pointed in their political messages. While the events still tried to attract unity and community support, their organizers were now well aware that they were promoting sentiments that not everyone was prepared to accept. In the space of a few months, celebrations and their toasts and songs suddenly became the most important weapons in the arsenal of the Republican opposition, with government supporters returning fire in kind. Preexisting patriotic clubs like the Society of the Cincinnati and the Tammany Society became politicized one way or the other. The Cincinnati, a hereditary order of former Continental Army officers, naturally went Federalist. Tammany died in some cities but turned vociferously Democratic-Republican in Philadelphia and New York.[29]

After Genet's arrival, the Fourth of July celebrations showed signs of trouble immediately after celebrating America in overtly Francophilic ways and toasting some sweepingly progressive visions of the future and subversive ideas of the present. In Philadelphia, the *"sans-culottes"* (without breeches) of France were compared with the *"sans-souliers"* (without shoes) of Valley Forge, and another round was downed in honor of "true democrats throughout the world." In New York, glasses were raised to "Science: may this powerful foe of despotism annihilate her adversary and become Empress of the world." A militia regiment toasted President Washington as usual while implicitly criticizing his policies: "may his conduct in the *cabinet* be as meritorious as it was in the *field*." By the next year, Federalists and Republicans were having separate celebrations and competing to expand their feast day calendars to dates that better favored their respective points of view.[30]

Diplomatically, the soaring public response to Genet was too much too late, confusing the envoy about the strength and nature of his position. The in-between relationship that France's U.S. sympathizers wanted was never going to happen on Alexander Hamilton's watch— he was convinced the British would never tolerate it, that they would declare war immediately—but Citoyen Genet quickly made things impossible even for his allies inside the government. Outraged at the administration's rejection of all French treaty rights and dazzled by his seeming popularity, Genet proceeded to act fully and immediately on his instructions, handing out commissions for Kentuckians to attack Spanish Louisiana and outfitting the captured British ship *Little Sarah* as a privateer renamed *La Petite Démocrate*, right under the federal government's nose and against its wishes. Convinced that the American people loved France and the Rights of Man more than their own temporarily elected officials, the envoy dared the Washington administration to try enforcing its own rules against armed French ships. When local officials in Philadelphia arrested two sailors who had enlisted in Charleston for violating the neutrality proclamation, the jury acquitted the first to come to trial—there was no actual statute against foreign military recruitment on U.S. soil—and Genet threw the man a dinner party.

Secretary of State Jefferson was quickly pushed to his wit's end. He had resisted the precipitous neutrality proclamation earlier in the spring, and continued to press for "manly neutrality, claiming the liberal rights ascribed to that condition," such as freely trading with all comers, rather than "a mere English one" that honored British trade restrictions.

Hamilton and his allies were too afraid of war with Great Britain and too willing to provoke one with France, Jefferson believed, and had put the United States in the position of tacitly abetting "the conspirators against human liberty" to a degree that was "unjustifiable in principle, in interest, and in respect to the wishes of our constituents." But Genet seemed intent on making this position untenable. Matters came to a head in July, when, after another round of fulsome celebrations, the French minister rejected the administration's order—and Jefferson's personal request—to stop *La Petite Démocrate* from going to sea until President Washington returned from Mount Vernon and reviewed the issue. Misunderstanding the presidential system and assuming that a republic must have a sovereign assembly of representatives like the French National Convention, Genet refused "in a very high tone" and ranted that he would appeal Washington's expected negative decision to Congress or the people themselves. He seemed to imagine rallying the crowds in Philadelphia as the revolutionaries had done in Paris.

When Jefferson tried to explain the three-branch construction of the U.S. government, and how the executive branch really was authorized to make foreign policy decisions, Genet bowed sarcastically and said he could not make Jefferson any compliments on such a constitution. In writing, Genet declared that the treaties with France were "considered by the American People as the most sacred laws," and that thus "when treaties speak, the agents of nations" (be they local customs officials or the president himself) "have but to obey." Jefferson was shaken by both Genet's disregard for American sovereignty and the egregiousness of his political miscalculation. Edmond Genet's had been the most "calamitous" appointment in the history of diplomacy, Secretary Jefferson decided. It was all Jefferson could do to head off a proposal that would have started a war with France immediately: placing cannon in position to fire on *La Petite Démocrate* if it tried to leave the harbor and thus pitting the world's two genuine national republics against each other in a way only a conspiracy of kings could love. It was high time to ask for Genet's recall and retire back to Monticello as soon as possible.[31]

In terms of predicting what the European powers would do, Jefferson turned out to be a better judge than Hamilton. *La Petite Démocrate* sailed without harassment, and became one of France's best privateers, but the British decided not to hold the U.S. responsible. They hardly needed a new American war when they had one to deal with in Europe already. Out in Ohio, the American Indian rebels that the British had been encouraging were soon abandoned to their fate on the same grounds: the gates of the new Fort Miamis were locked when defeated warriors tried to retreat to it after the Battle of Fallen Timbers in 1794.

Despite Genet's catastrophic failure as a diplomat, his mission was hugely significant in its impact on American politics, bringing politics out of the newspapers and into the streets and meeting halls where the actual political parties would be created. From the *La Petite Démocrate* crisis on, France versus Britain became the preeminent issue, fueling the widening and deepening of the party conflict like no other. What can get lost in our shock at the willingness of Americans to take sides in a foreign war is the way that the French revolutionary wars provided a metaphorical keystone for the two budding party ideologies. Neither side was proposing entry into the war or a real alliance with either side, but the two warring powers and their opposing political systems became stand-ins for differing visions of American society and the way that it ought to relate to the U.S. government: an active, diverse, questioning democracy versus a loyal, homogeneous, affirming nation. The French revolutionary war issue and its local avatar, Edmond Genet, were also spectacular enough to bring out Americans in mass numbers, ready to be mobilized for political, even revolutionary, purposes. According to John Adams, many in Philadelphia's Quaker elite believed, not very charitably, that only the yellow fever epidemic of fall 1793—which emptied the city and killed several members of Genet's welcoming committee along with ten to fifteen percent of the city's population—ended the "Terrorism" and saved the country from "a total Revolution of Government." The yellow fever epidemic revealed how deep the partisan divide opened up by the French Revolution was already becoming. In diagnosing and treating the yellow fever victims, doctors divided along party lines, with the Federalists certain that the disease was alien in origin, imported by one of the French ships and Democratic-Republicans blaming it on problems in American society itself, namely, the poor living conditions in the city.[32]

There was no French-style revolution in the offing, but Genet and the French had clearly sparked something new in America: democracy that was not just an element in the mix or a theory of popular sovereignty, but a daily, living thing. While some were working in the name of democracy and others against it, all sides in the Genet crisis were appealing to the people "out of doors" (public opinion outside the government) in some fashion. Genet said so in as many words, and despite his chagrin at the French minister's hubris, Jefferson had been gratified to see the people physically rejecting the administration policies he himself questioned: "Our constituents seeing that the government does not express their mind, perhaps rather leans the other way, are coming forward to express it themselves," he reported to Madison after Genet's reception in Philadelphia. Ham-fisted as he was, Genet offered a more robust kind of democracy than Jefferson was initially ready for. A shocked Jefferson had first rejected the idea of appealing a foreign policy decision beyond where the Constitution seemed to settle it, with a president and senate thoroughly insulated from popular elections, but as we will see below, that was exactly the position he and Madison would take two and a half years later, led by their Philadelphia supporters. Contesting the election of 1796 was another kind of final appeal to the people, and likewise one not envisioned in the Constitution. The French example, and direct French influence, pulled and pushed the United States in democratic directions all throughout the process, even long after France had ceased to be a democracy itself.

Ironically, American opponents of democracy played a role in promoting it in their response to Genet, rallying the people for support outside the government. Though frightened and angry about the "French frenzy," Hamilton and the Federalists saw Genet's dealings with the administration as a way to turn things around on the opposition and expose them as dupes and ingrates. Before they took action, only Genet's romantic speeches and dramatic gestures were public knowledge. Having already thoroughly beaten Jefferson in the cabinet infighting over neutrality and having started the process of having Genet removed as minister, Hamilton pushed repeatedly for a public release of the French minister's offensive correspondence with the administration, hoping to keep the Genet issue alive. When it was finally clear that the controversy-averse Washington would not agree to this, partisan Federalists forced the disclosure themselves.

A round of town meetings was organized in support of neutrality, including one overseen by future Chief Justice John Marshall in Richmond. Then the relentless Hamilton launched another wave of newspaper essays, again under multiple pseudonyms, that leaked the word of Genet's defiance and goaded Genet into documenting it. The leaks began with an essay signed "No Jacobin" that got right to the point, essentially quoting Jefferson's arguments with Genet over *La Petite Démocrate* under the thin pretext that it was "publicly rumored in this city that the minister of the French republic has *threatened to appeal from the President of the United States to the people.*" Heaping on further accusations, some accurate and some not, Hamilton soon got the rise out of Genet he was hoping for: the envoy released his confidential letters to the administration himself. This soon lost Genet many of his Republican sympathizers, who had believed his promises of transparency and assurances that he did not intend to force America into the war. Already on his way out of office and condemned by the Jacobins back home, Genet shifted his attention to a romance with New York Governor George Clinton's daughter Cornelia, his most ardent fan, but Federalists kept his name constantly in the papers for months and years afterward, a watchword for Jacobin terror and treason despite the fact that he had never been a literal Jacobin.[33]

JOINING THE CLUBS

The most momentous political development inspired by the French Revolution—and the one that moved the opposition closest to the status of a party organization that could contest elections—was the emergence of a network of political clubs that historians have grouped together as the Democratic-Republican Societies. (The individual clubs used "Republican" or more often "Democratic" in their names, but not usually both.) Voluntary associations were nothing new and even something of a fad in the late eighteenth-century Atlantic world; freemasonry was at its height, and there seemed to be almost nothing that upwardly young American men considered more fun than organizing a group away from family and church, devising some rules and rituals for it, and then holding lengthy meetings. Yet the appearance of popular political societies in Britain and America, in conjunction with the French Revolution, was treated in many quarters as a potential thunderclap of doom. Edmund Burke had begun his *Reflections on the Revolution in France* by denouncing a group called the Revolution Society, and once the war broke out, the British government viciously repressed the London Corresponding Society, the Society for Constitutional Information, and other popular associations that appeared to promote parliamentary reform. In America, much smaller political clubs would get the honor of becoming President Washington's personal scapegoat for the disorders that he thought plagued the country.[34]

Though inspired by the French Republic and to some degree by the increasingly infamous Jacobins, the American popular societies were both more and less than branches of the "Jacobin Club of Paris," as one New York Federalist charged. The most basic purpose of the Democratic-Republican Societies was not to aid the French war effort but to provide the active democratic counterbalance that the Constitution left out by promoting an ethic of and a vehicle for ongoing popular political expression and participation. Through a sequence of events we will get to shortly, the clubs themselves would quickly become a relic of the eighteenth century, but they laid the foundations for the creation of an opposition political party that could compete for hearts, minds, and votes with those who controlled the government.[35]

What is generally accepted as the first of the American clubs, the German Republican Society of Philadelphia, was launched while the city was waiting for Genet to arrive. The previous July 4, the *National Gazette* had published a suggestion that Americans follow the example of Londoners and form a society "for the discussion of Political Knowledge called THE FRIENDS OF THE PEOPLE," but no one seems to have followed up until after the French Republic was declared. The German Republican Society was headed up by two Philadelphia politicians who were German with good English skills, Dr. Michael Leib and paper manufacturer Henry (Heinrich) Kammerer, a member of the state legislature. They presented their group partly as an educational endeavor. According to them, much of Pennsylvania's large German population was "wholly ignorant of the English language, and therefore ignorant of the most essential transactions of our government." One practical effect was that Germans tended to not participate very much in American political debates or contests and to side with the established authorities when they did. Or so democratically inclined, bilingual Germans like Leib and Kammerer believed. Apparently initiated in German and among the Germans only, the group provoked a "hue and cry," so "to shut the mouths of *snarlers*," its organizers went public and English in the *National Gazette*, calling for "political societies" like theirs to be established everywhere for everybody: "They would prove powerful instruments in support of the present system of equality, and formidable enemies to aristocracy in whatever shape it might present itself—May the example of the German Republican Society prove a spur to the friends of equality throughout the United States!"[36]

By the time of Genet's arrival, English-speaking Philadelphians were ready to follow suit, drawing up the *Principles, Articles, and Regulations* (bylaws, in essence) for a club of their own and publishing them on May 30, 1793. According to tradition, Citizen Genet himself suggested naming the organization the Democratic Society of Pennsylvania, instead of the "Sons of Liberty." The German Republican Society provided a bit more than a spur to the new club's creation: Dr. Michael Leib was a member and leader of both. The Democratic Society of Pennsylvania was not shy about the world-historical context in which it placed its activities, declaring that the "successive Revolutions of America and France" had "clearly developed" in the world an understanding of "the RIGHTS OF MAN" and "the genuine objects of Society" and had "withdrawn the veil which concealed the dignity and happiness of the human race, and . . . taught us, no longer dazzled . . . or awed, . . . to erect the Temple of LIBERTY on the ruins of *Palaces* and *Thrones*."[37]

Intellectual historian Jonathan Israel has identified what seems to be a crucial source of the ideas and convictions that powered the Democratic Societies and undergirded their case for political expression and participation as positive goods. This was what Israel calls the Radical Enlightenment, developed by Denis Diderot and the French Encyclopedists and typified by Thomas Paine among English speakers. Israel distinguishes these radicals from the much less daring and more religious "mainstream" of Enlightenment thought that took in most other English-language republican thinkers, including most of the Founders. According to Israel, Radical Enlightenment thinkers saw representative democracy as the crux of a "General Revolution" that would eradicate hereditary distinctions in every form and help create a new world operating on the principle that "every person's needs and views are of equal weight." A "revolution of mind" would help revolutionize everything else, without undue violence and coercion, while also creating leaders, thinkers, and ordinary citizens unafraid to face down determined resistance by the forces of chaos and reaction. Continuous popular political participation, through reading, writing, speaking, listening, and voting, would be the way to smooth out or avoid the cycles of revolution and reaction that had plagued republics and doomed democracies in the past. Mainstream Enlightenment thought, meanwhile, was more pessimistic about social or mental revolutions and the possibilities of democracy, feeling the need to leave some traditional institutions like the aristocracy and the church in place to moderate those cycles and protect property and order. The Enlightenment political thinkers most influential among the Founders, such as Montesquieu, tended to advocate some kind of balanced system that preserved such historic oligarchies as counterweights to the despotism of kings and the potentially frightening power of a roused people.[38]

Besides Leib, one of the Democratic Society of Pennsylvania's major writers and ideologists was "Lightning Rod, Jr.," Benjamin Franklin Bache, grandson of Benjamin Franklin and editor of the Philadelphia *General Advertiser* (later called the *Aurora*). Bache had spent his childhood in Europe accompanying his grandfather and arrived back in Philadelphia as a young adult and, in effect, an immigrant from France. Having imbibed Radical Enlightenment thought directly from its sources, he was much more firmly connected to the international currents of democratic radicalism than to existing American traditions. Bache and his newspaper were major forces pushing the opposition forward, first in defending France and then in mounting election campaigns against the Federalists.[39]

On a more practical level, the Democratic-Republican Societies cultivated the political habits necessary to sustain a democratic system. For instance, the clubs promoted the ethic of mass political participation that became such an ideal in American political culture, prizing high levels of citizen engagement and voter turnout.[40] The key argument for political clubs that met and made public statements regularly was the need for ongoing, continuous popular supervision of the government, between elections and in response to events as they transpired. "In a republican government it is a duty incumbent on every citizen to afford his assistance," announced Leib and Kammerer's German Republicans; "either by taking a part in its immediate administration, or by [the citizen's] advice and watchfulness . . . the spirit of liberty, like every virtue of the mind, is to be kept alive only by constant action." Nor was mere thought or expression sufficient. It had to be effective expression and therefore collective and organized: "Objects of general concern seldom meet with the individual attention they merit . . . [and] individual exertion seldom produces a general effect," so "in a free government" political associations were needed so "that a joint operation may be produced."[41]

Finally, the clubs did not limit themselves to mere expressions of patriotic resolve or comments on policies, but insisted on their right and duty to evaluate public men as well. The societies were predicated on the idea that it was the duty of ordinary citizens to be jealous of their rights and vigilantly "guard . . . against every encroachment on the equality of freemen." Consequently, when the New York Democratic Society was criticized for countenancing remarks critical of President Washington and becoming involved in local campaigns, it argued that this was only consistent "with the independence and firmness which ever character- ize PATRIOTS" and that clubs should be able to "constantly express our sentiments as well of our PUBLIC OFFICERS, as their MEASURES."[42]

As critics pointed out, all this was party-like behavior that looked even more so when, by design, similar clubs popped up in other cities and the original clubs began communicating with them. The Democratic Society of Pennsylvania became the epicenter and "mother club" of the movement and the controversy over it. The two Philadelphia clubs even- tually had at least forty imitators in every state except Rhode Island and New Hampshire, with the West (Kentucky and western Pennsylvania) quickest to respond but the port cities developing the most active out- lets. The craze for toasting and resolving had swept the nation.[43]

We are now so accustomed to the idea of citizens and outside groups commenting on government affairs and trying to influence government policy as to make it hard to grasp how threatening and illegitimate this seemed to Washington, Hamilton, and the Federalists. In their view, the United States already had a government of the people, and they were in charge of it. If the elections were valid, then it was constitutional of- ficials and legislators who had the right to speak and act for the people, not some body of unknown men who presumed to arrogate that right for themselves. Why should the president and his secretaries or the Congress accept guidance or criticism from private individuals with no standing to give it? As the first self-identified practitioners of democracy in American politics, the popular societies faced some serious backlash from those above. They were accused of fomenting violent revolution and acting as agents of a foreign power. Most crucially, they were de- nounced as "self-creators," nobodies who had appointed themselves "in- termediary guides betwixt [the people] and the constituted authorities," a role that neither prevailing theories of government nor the U.S. Con- stitution recognized. Under orthodox Lockean theory, if the people were not actively seeking to invoke their right of revolution and change their form of government, then private individuals should keep quiet until the next appointed time to speak. If some loud-mouthed, presumptu- ous individuals continued to complain, suspicion should fall on them for representing not the community or the people but their interested selves. The argument boiled down to the question of whether common Americans had the right to any significant input and influence over government between elections (other than petitioning for favors), and astonishing as it might seem today, the answer the Federalists gave was "no." The Revolution was over.[44]

The members of the Democratic clubs, in contrast, saw the Revolution as an ongoing process rather than one that was complete and safely relegated to the past. They were self-conscious about the need for their generation to maintain and advance the gains made by the Revolution of 1776: "The patriotic mind will naturally be solicitous, by every proper precaution, to preserve and perpetuate the Blessings which Providence hath bestowed upon our Country: For, in reviewing the history of Nations, we find occasion to lament, that the vigilance of the People has been too easily absorbed in victory; and that the prize which has been achieved by the wisdom and valor of one generation, has too often been lost by the ignorance and supineness of another."[45]

The Federalists, for their part, were concerned about a completely different kind of supineness. We Americans like to boast to the rest of the world about our peaceful transfers of power. The popularity of George Washington had eliminated any serious contention in 1788–1789, but in 1794 it looked very much to Washington and Hamilton and their closest allies like there were people out there, within and without the country, with unpeaceful designs on power.

POPULAR POLITICS VS. POPULAR VIOLENCE: THE DEMOCRATIC SOCIETY OF PENNSYLVANIA CONFRONTS THE WHISKEY REBELLION

For the Federalists, one particularly worrisome aspect of the Republic's youth was its lack of opportunity to prove itself, meaning its ability to project force like a proper state should be able to do. Edmund Randolph, Jefferson's indecisive replacement as secretary of state, was shaken to hear one of his fellow cabinet members, most likely Hamilton, lay down the principle that "a government can never be said to be established, until some signal display has manifested its power of military coercion."

Though many of the Founders worried about the dangers to liberty posed by taxes and "standing armies," for Hamilton and the Federalists one of the major advantages of the new government's firmer financial footing was the newfound ability to pay for a stronger military. In Hamilton's last year as treasury secretary, 1794, he finally got to flex the "sinews of power." Thomas Jefferson was back in Virginia and out of the way, but the government's other challengers still waited to be taken down. The Indians got it first. The early humiliations at the hands of a confederacy of Miami, Shawnee, and Lenape warriors were avenged by General Anthony Wayne's sleekly outfitted United States Legion at the Battle of Fallen Timbers, near present-day Toledo, Ohio, on August 20, 1794. A humiliating peace was imposed following the battle that forced the northwestern Indians to accept U.S. sovereignty and occupation north of the Ohio River. Next on the agenda were the white "savages" who refused to accept the federal government's policies. A few weeks after Fallen Timbers, Hamilton and Washington returned to the saddle and personally led the largest force ever assembled in North America until that time against lightly armed insurgents in western Pennsylvania.[46]

The specific occasion for this last exploit was putting down resistance to the much-resented revenue plank of Hamilton's financial system, the excise tax on distilled spirits. This was the first tax the federal government ever levied on the internal U.S. economy, and it proved even less popular than many of the later ones. Considered to fall unfairly and disproportionately on frontier farmers who had few other ways to market their grain than turning it into whiskey, the excise had been protested and sporadically resisted throughout the West since before its enactment in 1791, but there had been a recent flare-up in the Pittsburgh area over the activities of tough-talking federal revenue collector General John Neville. A Virginian and former military underling of Washington's, Neville was a plantation owner and distiller many of the Pennsylvanians considered corrupt because he had opposed the excise himself before getting a job collecting it and changing his opinion.[47]

"Whiskey Rebellion" has always been a grandiose term for the mess that developed on Neville's watch. There were, to be sure, some real acts and fairly serious threats of violence committed against federal officials in western Pennsylvania. The mail was robbed, a revenue collector's home was marched on, and the collection of the excise was deemed physically impossible in the four western Pennsylvania counties. Yet chiefly these actions were of the type that social historians have labeled "rough music": ritualistic forms of community intimidation like tarring and feathering and forcible haircuts, along with occasional property destruction. As Pauline Maier, Paul Gilje, and many other historians have noted, this type of limited political violence was part of a long tradition in Pennsylvania and the rest of Anglo-America. Always carefully targeted at specific laws and the officials charged with enforcing them, it was a familiar form of protest that posed little threat to the underlying social order.[48]

Washington, Hamilton, and the Federalists saw these activities as the spear point of a Jacobin revolution that flowed from Paris and was being locally organized by the Democratic-Republican Societies. Yet rough music against tax collectors was nothing any rural American had to copy from a French Jacobin or from a city debating club. These were the tactics that had rendered the Stamp Act unenforceable and set the thirteen colonies on the road to independence. The western Pennsylvania tax protesters thought they had got the idea from the American Revolution, not the French one.[49]

The Whiskey Rebellion proper began on July 15, 1794, when armed men near Pittsburgh fired in the general direction of John Neville as he tried to serve papers on a local farmer, William Miller. The only true gun battles of the rebellion occurred when Neville fired into the angry crowd that besieged his "Bower Hill" plantation the next morning, and then again troops were brought from Fort Pitt to protect the revenue collector's house. In both cases, the only dead were among the protesters. The reaction of Pittsburgh-area Federalists to the deaths at Bower Hill was to "lament that so few of the insurgents fell." The Pittsburgh landowner and commercial distiller Isaac Craig was certain that "such disorders can only be cured by copious bleedings." The high point of the insurrection was an assembly of several thousand people at Braddock's Field in early August, but this was more of a meeting about a possible rebellion than the actual thing—the armed men who gathered decided not to attack Pittsburgh that day after all.[50]

Luckily for the Whiskey rebels, somewhat cooler heads prevailed, but the use of force and threats of violence became central features of the Federalist approach to governing. When Washington and his cabinet conferred with Pennsylvania state officials over how to respond in August 1794, Hamilton startled his cabinet colleagues by wishing that the rebels had gone ahead and burned Pittsburgh, so as to more clearly authorize the massive military response he thought was required on general principles: "The crisis was arrived when it must be determined whether the Government can maintain itself," Hamilton said for the official record.[51] Later, Hamilton's longtime congressional ally Robert Goodloe Harper of South Carolina elevated this approach to the status of a Federalist mission statement. Federalists knew, Harper wrote, that "force displayed in due season, . . . with energy and promptness" was the best way of dealing with opposition: "When you are known to be strong you may pardon; if thought to be weak you are compelled to punish." So against the Pennsylvania farmers, the Federalists sent "a force so great as to preclude all hope of successful resistance."[52]

The "Watermelon Army" sent into western Pennsylvania to put down the largely dispersed Whiskey rebels numbered some twelve thousand men, much larger than previous military responses to domestic insurrections that were far more serious threats. (Watermelons were used for military target practice at the time, and the nickname was the equivalent of calling the army "paper tigers": powerful-looking but fragile.)[53] The British Empire itself had managed to field no force so large in America before or during the Revolutionary War. Shays' Rebellion in 1786 had threatened a federal arsenal but attracted only a fraction of the response. The Shaysites had even gotten some of their demands met, to boot.[54]

Of course, the circumstance that inspired the Federalists to fully implement their belief in forceful government was neither the French Revolution nor the western Pennsylvania disturbances. Instead, it was the conjunction of both of these with the preexisting condition of an organized opposition to the government in the form of the Democratic-Republican Societies. Peaceful groups of citizens gathering to express their opinions about government policy were treated as the moral equivalent of armed men preventing the execution of existing laws, and both were seen as the inevitable precursors to full-scale revolution.

When violence broke out in the west, Federalists almost instinctively blamed it on the Democratic Societies and further assumed that the ultimate intention of both the societies and the rebels was seizing power. Washington immediately saw the rebellion as the "first *ripe fruit* of the Democratic Societies," with a bountiful crop of murder and pillage yet to come. In his valedictory for Federalist policy, Robert Goodloe Harper blandly asserted that the Pennsylvania tax protest "undoubtedly [had] for its secret object the overthrow of the government." If you believed that, only one course of action was open to the president. As Johann Neem has argued, "Washington's decision to use force was intended not only to put down the rioters, but to eliminate organized opposition altogether." The winning argument at the Washington administration meetings over how to respond to the Whiskey Rebellion had been that just rounding up a few ringleaders of the recent disturbances would not be enough. Critics and resisters of government would scatter into the woodwork and then crawl back out again later. The threats to would-be rebels and critics needed to be made frightening enough to deter *all* future resistance.[55]

Contrary to the Federalists' (and seemingly many historians') expectations, America's most heated "Jacobins" actually condemned rather than justified popular violence and joined the Federalists in seeking to suppress it. Radical Democratic-Republicans in the eastern cities were trying to vindicate a new model of politics that comes closer to the condition "democracy" that modern nations work toward: a constitutional order in which public opinion is consulted and freely expressed all the time, at elections but also in between them, in print and in public gatherings and organizations, but in which violence and other forms of physical and economic coercion are strictly forbidden. When decisions are made through a fair and democratic process, the person or policy that emerges with the most votes wins. While remaining free to criticize the winners and influence public opinion all they want, the losers must respect the results until the next vote, especially by obeying constitutionally sanctioned laws and refraining from physical resistance. This kind of democracy was an alternative to popular violence rather than the origin of it. To put it another way, violence was a different, less democratic path rather than some ultimate extension of the democratic process. Over the long term, the democratization of the 1790s opened the door for mass political participation and fundamental changes that simply would not have occurred—that *did not* occur—in the older system where rulers could only be checked by periodic uprisings when the people just couldn't take it any more.

Popular violence was anathema to the particular variety of Radical Enlightenment thought that influenced the Democratic-Republican Societies. Outside of a context where power had completely repressed the ability to freely speak, write, and vote, the resort to violence was seen as an irrational, retrograde path. (In France, the Girondins had lost ground to the Jacobins partly because of their reluctance to go along with the 1792 massacres and subsequent execution of the king and queen.) For the Radical Enlightenment thinkers depicted by Jonathan Israel, whose description seems to fit Bache, Leib, and company so well, backwoods violence was an example of the kind of "simple," direct democracy that would never be sustainable for long. Violent uprisings usually played into the hands of despots and reactionaries by fostering anarchy that evoked and justified authoritarian responses. The radicals firmly rejected "mixed" constitutions in favor of fully democratic polities like the unicameral design Paine had suggested for Pennsylvania's original state constitution of 1776. But they also recognized the justice of political theorists' long-standing observation, going back to ancient times and the experiences of the Greek city-states, that simple democracies inevitably decline into bloody dysfunction and get replaced by monarchies and aristocracies. It was impossible for entire populations, even for the entire subset of propertied men, to govern themselves directly, especially when they were accustomed to defending their rights and views with fists, swords, and guns. The Paineite version of Radical Enlightenment thought favored in the Democratic Society of Pennsylvania reasoned that a system based on lively but rational debates resolved by popular voting had the best chance of avoiding such cycles of rebellion and reaction; it would foster a permanent, egalitarian "revolution of the mind" instead. The people would be educated through their participation in a broad political process: reading the newspapers, attending the celebrations, discussing politics in clubs and social gatherings, and for adult white men (though not all of them) voting in frequent elections.[56]

The issue for the Philadelphia radicals was whether their new political culture of celebrations, newspapers, and popular associations was going to become the norm, or whether the older colonial (monarchical) one—in which an inarticulate people periodically rose in violent anger—would prevail. Even the Democratic-Republican side of the new nation's political elite tended to straddle the fence. Though clearly members of the opposition and French sympathizers, more conventional Pennsylvania leaders such as Representative Albert Gallatin, Governor Thomas Mifflin, Chief Justice Thomas McKean, and Secretary of the Commonwealth Alexander J. Dallas responded to the Whiskey Rebellion in a way that was consistent with the state's existing institutions and political culture, including its tradition of occasional popular recourse to vigilantism. One of the more infamous instances had been the Paxton Boys uprising in 1763, when some rural Pennsylvanians took up arms to protest the Quaker-controlled colonial government's perceived lenience toward Indians. Benjamin Franklin had helped defuse that situation, limiting the damage to "only" the Conestoga Massacre of a few peaceful Indians, but preventing a threatened overthrow of the colonial government. In relying on the educated gentleman lawyers of western Pennsylvania to co-opt the tax protests and wind them down, the state's top Republican politicians followed the accepted formula for elites responding to outbreaks of popular mayhem. Something not unlike this had occurred in the wake of the popular disturbances over the Stamp Act and the quartering of British troops in Boston and New York before the Revolution: the savage Stamp Act riots gave way to the carefully controlled, nearly nonviolent Boston Tea Party a decade later.[57]

The new, democratic political culture was instead created in the streets, taverns, and print shops of Philadelphia and other cities, especially by the various members and fellow travelers of the Democratic Society of Pennsylvania. While great admirers of the French Revolution and not unwilling to defend some of its excesses, Bache and his allies marked out a decidedly different path for France's American sympathizers. They started from the belief that, unlike the French, Americans (a term they conflated with white American men) had already secured their basic rights as republican citizens. "In this country we have fortunately no yoke to shake off; we have neither the king's power to fear, nor the oppression of an hereditary aristocracy," declared the *General Advertiser*'s July 26 editorial column. Where the Democratic Society of Pennsylvania differed from Washington and Hamilton was in believing, just as its name implied, that the United States was and should operate as an active democracy. It is important not to get too starry-eyed about this. Though Democratic Society members referred to each other as "Citizen" and tended to favor egalitarian social reforms such as public education and the abolition of slavery, the group used the word "democracy" in a typically American and more narrowly procedural sense, denoting a polity where leaders are guided by public opinion and policies are chosen by a majority vote according to constitutional rules. "In a Democracy, a majority ought in all cases to govern; . . . and where a Constitution exists, which emanated from the People, the remedies pointed out by it against unjust and oppressive laws and bad measures, ought to be resorted to."[58]

The excise tax was one of the Democratic Society of Pennsylvania's many targets of complaint, just as it had been for the *National Gazette* and the congressional opposition before that. The *General Advertiser* had mounted elaborate arguments against the partiality of "indirect taxes" that were levied only on certain industries or regions or classes of people, comparing the excise on western whiskey levied by easterners to Great Britain's efforts to tax the colonies before the Revolution. Yet there the analogy ended. Instead of revolution, the *General Advertiser* declared the situation a golden opportunity to deploy its chosen strategy of political association: "The feeble hand of an individual or any class of citizens contemplated to the objects of oppression will have little power to stop the progress of this destructive monster." The Philadelphia radicals therefore called on the citizens of the nation "in general, and the Democratic Societies in particular to come forward and oppose by legal measures every attempt" to use this form of taxation.[59]

Like all the Democratic Societies and most of the opposition press, the Philadelphians vigorously defended themselves from the criticisms of President Washington, upholding "out of doors" political expression and organization as the very essence of republican citizenship. One of the Federalist arguments they denied most vehemently was that by trying to turn public opinion against the administration, the Democratic-Republican Societies were committing an inherently revolutionary act aimed at overthrowing the government and Constitution rather than just influencing the operation of them. Contrary to Federalist fears that the societies might "*over-awe*" the government, the radicals emphasized the mismatch in a confrontation between a private body of relatively ordinary men like themselves and the institutions and officers of the state. To pretend that the Democratic Societies were so overwhelming a force was to suppose "our governors . . . a set of idiots." The modern term would be "crybabies."[60]

The outbreak of violence in western Pennsylvania came as most "disagreeable intelligence" to Bache and the Democratic Society radicals. It made a mockery of the sort of peaceful opposition through association and argument they were trying to promote, and undermined the claim that the republic at large had nothing to fear from such associations. The whole world was watching, and it was crucial "to demonstrate that . . . the genuine principles of democracy were perfectly compatible with the principles of social order."[61]

As soon as the *General Advertiser* had printed its first reports of the Pittsburgh disturbances, Bache issued a stern plea that citizens engage only in political activity that followed democratic norms and constitutional rules. The excise "was odious in many parts of the Union," he admitted, and the executive should have tried harder to persuade the western people of its benefits and not tried to enforce it so rigorously. Nonetheless, the tax had "received every constitutional sanction" and so stood as legitimate law. Opposing its execution by force was an act "hostile to liberty and good government"—and democracy. In a sentiment that connected Bache forward to Abraham Lincoln, the *General Advertiser*'s editorial condemned the rebellion primarily as an attack on the principle of majority rule. The electoral and legislative processes had to be able to settle important questions and be obeyed: "It is the right of regulating their internal concerns by the voice of a majority" that is "the standard which in republican governments we must abide by." It was "to be lamented" that "freemen should so far lose sight of their duty, as by force of arms to infringe on the rights of their fellow-citizens, by counter-acting the will of a majority."[62]

Rather than simply denounce the rebels as Washington and the Federalists had done, the *General Advertiser* set out to educate them on the proper means of expressing their grievances in the new political culture that the Philadelphians were trying to create. The newspaper explained that there were plenty of other, more appropriate avenues western Pennsylvanians might have chosen to pursue before tarring-and-feathering tax collectors, and especially before marching on John Neville's house: "If a law is obnoxious to any part of the country, let the citizens there petition for its repeal, expose its defects, or injustice through the medium of the press; let them change their representation, put into their legislature men they know will be active to procure its repeal."[63]

The Philadelphia radicals themselves pushed the idea of changing the political complexion of the federal government, especially by electing a more democratically minded and French-friendly Congress. Gearing up for a local congressional election in which it was backing Democratic Society member John Swanwick's challenge to Federalist Representative Thomas Fitzsimons, the *General Advertiser* suggested that excise tax haters redirect their energies toward more productive ends: "You have a constitutional mode of doing yourselves justice, and should this not be exerted, no resort to other means can be pardoned or excused." Swanwick went on to win in what is generally thought to be the first successful unseating of a congressional incumbent based on national issues. The *General Advertiser*'s optimism about what a lone off-year congressional election might mean almost brings a chuckle today, but Bache and friends were pioneering a new institution at the time—the opposition party—and their idealism was heartfelt: "Let the men of your choice be the friends of justice, the enemies of inequality, the patrons of the rights of man, and the lovers of freedom, and America will become a land of promise where tranquility and contentment shall inhabit."[64]

Philadelphia's 1794 congressional election probably seemed more important to the political activists of Philadelphia than it did to western farmers, and Bache admitted that his recommended strategy might not be successful against the excise tax. But after a certain point, that was just too bad. Democratic citizens needed to accept that fundamental policies would not and should not change until a majority of voters were convinced they should, and further, they needed to understand that democratic politics was an ongoing process. If their views could not win the day in this current election or Congress, the campaign could be renewed in the next one. Even if the excise opponents' persuasive efforts ultimately met with no success, "they should rest satisfied, that other parts of the nation do not view the law in the same light, that a majority of their fellow-citizens conceive it necessary or proper." It then became even the opponents' duty "to bear its burdens, not however without continuing their remonstrances and legal endeavours to have it removed." In other words, citizens did not lose their freedom just because they had to pay a tax they disagreed with, nor did they lose their right to speak and write and organize against it. If opponents considered the law fundamentally illegitimate, they had the more extreme—yet still peaceful and legal—remedy of trying to have the Constitution amended.[65]

To go further would be to reverse the enlightened political progress that Bache and the Democratic-Republican Societies constantly celebrated and tried to practice. A Democratic Society of Pennsylvania resolution lamented that "passion instead of reason had assumed direction of [the western counties'] affairs" and that "disorder and disunion were the consequences." To allow a return to revolutionary-era tactics would be to reverse the course of history, though perhaps not quite as far as Bache argued in the *General Advertiser*: "If every portion of the republic rises in arms to prevent the execution of laws obnoxious to them we revert to a state of anarchy and barbarism" and "forfeit every advantage of organized society." A few days after the original editorial, "A Democrat" developed the same thought in a more partisan direction by suggesting that violent opposition to "the establishment or enforcement of a republican government" was not only a retrograde but also an *aristocratic* act, even if it was done in the name of the people:

> The first principle of democracy is that government is instituted for the happiness of the many. The first step of aristocracy is to throw it into the hands of the few. . . . Have not those citizens who oppose the execution of a law of the union by force of arms endeavored to introduce this aristocratic principle into action? If the minority in a republic think themselves oppressed the only just mode of redress is . . . by

reason to get the majority on their side; if they fail it is their duty to submit; but if they appeal to arms, the majority must make the same appeal, and the minority must either introduce an aristocracy or undergo the punishment due to their unjust attempt.[66]

The threat at the end of "A Democrat's" statement, and several others that appeared in the *General Advertiser*, was unmistakable. Bache, Leib, and company were not pacifists, but it is important to note that chastisement was threatened explicitly to vindicate the possibility of peaceful politics. The Federalist interpretation of the Whiskey Rebellion was precisely that a regression to revolutionary violence was the natural consequence even of supposedly peaceful opposition activities like the Democratic-Republican Societies. The clubs' behavior in response to the rebels aimed to prove that "however they may be disposed to watch over the conduct of the servants of the people, they are at the same time enemies to every principle of anarchy."

This belligerence for peace was far from universally accepted within the Democratic Society of Pennsylvania, and the Bache-Leib radical faction's insistence on it would eventually help tear the club apart. Initially it held together, but with evident signs of tension. A "considerable and respectable part" of the group argued for keeping completely silent about the western tax protests, but soon after the first reports of the disturbances, the society passed a brief set of resolutions that echoed the *General Advertiser*'s editorials: "Every other appeal but to the Constitution itself, except in cases of extremity, is improper & dangerous." At the same time, an admonishing letter was drafted to the Democratic Society in Washington County, Pennsylvania, which was suspected of being a hotbed of the insurrection apparently even by the brethren in Philadelphia.[67]

Secretary of the Commonwealth Alexander J. Dallas and Governor Thomas Mifflin had already taken the position that Pennsylvania could deal with the problem itself through its own justice system, without federal intervention or military action. Their official letter to President Washington had explicitly linked their preference for "this lenient course" to their experience running the state of Pennsylvania. Rural Pennsylvanians had a habit of expressing their approval or disapproval of their rulers through the direct and practical means of following them or not. The potential for violence was a fact of political life. There had been "riots" many times before, but the courts had handled them when necessary. Mifflin (with Dallas writing) had warned President Washington that Pennsylvanians would need to be convinced to go along with the enforcement of a law they disagreed with, especially if militia service was involved: "Their general character does not authorize me to promise a passive obedience to the mandates of government. . . . [A]s freemen, they would inquire into the cause and nature of the service proposed to them; and I believe that their alacrity in performing, as well as in accepting it, would essentially depend on their opinion of its justice and necessity." Mifflin and Dallas wanted to avoid the embarrassment they would suffer if the Democratic Society took a tougher position against the rebels than they had, but they were also working within the older political paradigm that incorporated physical resistance to government as a live option for democratic expression, not the *ultimate* expression of democracy in the event of popular revolution, but one that would be resorted to with some frequency. This venerable idea did not die out easily, and the United States would suffer flare-ups of violent popular political expression throughout the nineteenth century. But the Radical Enlightenment ideologues in the Democratic Society of Pennsylvania, led by Bache and Leib, made a crucial early stand for a rational and truly democratic means of conducting politics. It was one of the many reasons the Philadelphia radicals ended up as the masterminds of the most crucial state contest of the 1796 presidential campaign, while Dallas largely sat out.[68]

Matters came to a head in the early fall of 1794 as the state and federal governments made their final moves. In early September, the people of the western counties rejected a settlement with peace commissioners who had been sent by the governor in hopes of calming things down without federal intervention. With the chances of a nonmilitary solution greatly reduced, a number of other Democratic-Republican Societies joined in the denunciations of the rebellion, including clubs in Baltimore, Maryland, and New York State. The Philadelphia club issued so stern a resolution against the violence that it became controversial among its own members for the way it seemed to read the western rebels out of the Democratic-Republican family, drawing a line between those who could and those who could not follow democratic norms: "The intemperance of the Western Citizens, in not accepting" the Governor's peace offers "augurs an enmity to the genuine principles of freedom, and . . . such an outrage upon order and democracy, so far from entitling them to the Patronage of Democrats, will merit the proscription of every friend to equal liberty" and "exhibit a rank aristocratic feature." This turn of phrase reflected the Radical Enlightenment idea that any relic of the unenlightened past, such as a resort to popular violence, partook of this past's larger "aristocratic" or "monarchical" character. A group of Democratic Society moderates led by wealthy ex-Quaker dilettante Dr. George Logan stormed out rather than vote for a statement that insulted and "proscribed" their friends in the state government. This left Benjamin Franklin Bache in the chair but the Democratic Society of Pennsylvania in organizational ruins.[69]

The radicals carried their point home to its conclusion when, with some fanfare, they rallied the democrats of Philadelphia to join Hamilton and Washington's march west against the rebels en masse. Dr. Michael Leib, his brother, and numerous other Democratic Society members enlisted in the campaign. Henry Kammerer of the German Republican Society bragged that his group's "brethren, the Democratic Society of Pennsylvania, could have made a quorum in the field." Dyed-in-the-wool city folk all—Leib had never slept in a tent before—they were relieved to find no rain and no armed rebels during the whole of their western jaunt.[70]

While the Philadelphia radicals were the most loquacious on the subject, and their club the best documented, other Democratic-Republican Societies responded to the rebellion similarly or even more strongly. The Baltimore Republican Society unanimously passed a resolution condemning forcible resistance to law as "dangerous to freedom, and highly unbecoming good citizens." Then, after Alexander Hamilton sent warning of an alleged rebel attack on the Maryland state arsenal at Frederick, an estimated 90 percent of the Republican Society's members marched west with a force hastily assembled by militia General Samuel Smith. (Samuel Smith was also a congressman, just beginning on a forty-year career as a Democratic-Republican pillar, and perhaps even boss, that would last through the Jackson presidency.) According to Smith's fellow Maryland congressman Gabriel Christie, the Baltimore Republican Society members had tried to show themselves to be "the friends of peace and order, and not the disorganizers" that presidential and congressional denunciation had depicted. But they also wanted to proclaim themselves enemies to monarchy and to the British, "the present lawless disturbers of the world" Baltimore had helped "drive from the soil of America" during the Revolutionary War, or so Christie claimed. The assault on the Frederick arsenal turned out to be a figment of Hamilton's imagination, but the Baltimoreans had made their point.[71]

After returning home from their western outings, Democratic-Republican Society members found themselves not lauded, but attacked even more severely than before and eventually from the mouth of George Washington himself. The president took the occasion of his Sixth Annual Message to Congress, given in November 1794, to drop the hammer on the clubs for good, blaming the insurrection on "certain self-created societies" acting "in formal concert" against the excise. Federalists in Congress then expanded on the theme and made the charges more specific in their official response to the president, setting off a debate that brought out many defenders of the clubs but overall seems to have damaged their political viability by making them too controversial for sober-minded citizens with jobs and careers to be associated with.[72]

The Democratic-Republican Societies seemed to go into decline after the presidential speech and the congressional debate, but not before most of them put out lengthy rebuttals to the charges from on high. The Democratic Society of Pennsylvania was operating without its elected officers and most socially prominent members, but Bache and Leib were able to produce a magnificent statement defending the clubs against Washington's accusations and touting the role their particular society had played in helping preserve the young republic's governing authority. Reminding readers how many Democratic Society members had marched west, they praised "those Citizen-soldiers, who by their readiness to take the field, have probably saved this country much bloodshed, and given this important lesson to the world, that the spirit of Republicans, and their knowledge of the principles of civil liberty, give to their Government all the energy required to secure a due subordination to the laws." Thomas Jefferson would echo this same sentiment in his inaugural address in 1801, likely thinking of the response to the Whiskey Rebellion. Despite the fact that American citizens were free to criticize their government, Jefferson believed his democratic version of the United States to be "the strongest Government on earth. . . . the only one where every man, at the call of the law, would fly to the standard of the law, and would meet invasions of the public order as his own personal concern." So the Democratic-Republican Societies had. The cessation of partisanship was only temporary in any case. Subordination to the laws of the United States in 1794 just laid the groundwork for an all-out drive to peacefully change them, and the person who signed them, in the following years.[73]

THE JAY TREATY CRISIS AND THE ORIGINS OF THE 1796 CAMPAIGN

The issue that led most directly to national electoral competition between parties was the so-called Jay Treaty with Great Britain, ratified by the Senate in 1795. While historians have long debated exactly when and how political parties first emerged, there has never been any question about what the politicians of the Early Republic regarded as the point of no return. While ideological cleavages and some electoral competition had already developed in Philadelphia, inspired by the French Revolution and a range of other issues, it was the Jay Treaty that came to encapsulate them all, deepening the conflict and taking it national. The treaty issue connected the elite policy debates in Philadelphia with the popular movement represented by the Democratic-Republican Societies. This conjunction formed the beginnings of a national opposition party that almost denied the presidency to George Washington's anointed successor. The intense partisan and patriotic emotions unleashed by the treaty debate, and stoked by the two competing foreign governments, were another factor all their own. The opposition felt they were doing nothing less than refighting the revolutionary battle for independence from Great Britain. Their refusal to give up this fight exposed some notable gaps in the constitutional system, and led to a situation where contesting a presidential election seemed the only outlet available for releasing the building political tension and for expressing what the opposition believed was the will of the people.[1]

The Jay Treaty was the Washington administration's final answer to the vexed question of how the United States should respond to the pressures of the European war resulting from the French Revolution. For such a young nation, there were no good answers available. The world's greatest military power, especially because of its vast navy, Great Britain took a hard line against any American activities it considered helpful to revolutionary France. The republic of France, for its part, believed the French nation was owed American cooperation despite its changes in the form of government because of the alliance of 1778. Unilaterally asserting a right to prevent the United States from trading with France or its colonies, the British government in November 1793 issued "Orders in Council" stipulating that all American ships engaged in such trade were to be seized. Two hundred and fifty vessels were swept up in a few weeks, costing American merchants millions of dollars and consigning numerous American sailors to harsh service in the British Navy.[2]

The deeper issues over policy toward Great Britain revolved around the nation's fledgling sense of national identity. The Orders in Council were just the most recent humiliating reminder of the new nation's status as a weak state barely emerged from colonialism, and they made the British failure to honor the peace treaty and evacuate the western forts seem doubly galling and ominous. A writer in the *Pittsburgh Gazette* put many Americans' feelings succinctly: "It was not enough, for ten years, to deny us the use of our own territory, line our frontiers with an armed force, and instigate the Indians to cut our throats. . . . Our independence must be destroyed, and we must again become a colony of Great Britain." To many, the British actions were little but a continuation of the Revolutionary War and the corrupt, unfair policies that had led to it.[3]

Just as important as national pride for many Americans was the sense that the British were enemies not only to American independence, but also to the egalitarian and democratic political values of the American Revolution. "Despotism like a roaring lion has pursued man in all his steps," local orator Phinehas Hedges told the Republican Society in Ulster County, New York, and the British Empire was its modern avatar, "eager to throw every obstacle in the way" of America and democratic liberty. A public meeting in Halifax County, North Carolina, combined the themes of national pride and ideological outrage in terms salty enough to burn the eyes of the London diplomats who would eventually read them: "That imperious and cruel wretch" King George "would, if he could, beggar and enslave the human race. Men purchasing their freedom as we have, with the blood of our heroes, a freedom endeared to us by the fruits of a virtuous and equal government . . . feel an abhorrence at the idea of being carried back to those chains we manfully broke asunder."[4]

The uproar over the Orders in Council was deepened by what appeared to be serious British aggression on the northwestern frontier. In late March 1794, word reached Philadelphia that governor-general Lord Dorchester had sent a message to the Indians of Lower Canada predicting immediate war with the United States and advising his "children" that when the war did come, the hazy border between Indian lands and the U.S. settlements "must then be drawn by the warriors." Within days, Dorchester's deputy, lieutenant governor John Graves Simcoe, was at the rapids of the Maumee River, in undisputed U.S. territory on the site of present-day Toledo, directing the construction of a new and powerful British military installation.[5]

To many Americans, this British aggression in the northwest already provided ample justification for retaliatory action, including war. Backing down in the face of such insults would be an act of cowardice and, some said, a direct contradiction of the *"popular* voice." Congress was urged to "oppose the overbearing spirit of imperious aristocrats and to pay due respect to the sentiments of the American people." Conditions became inflamed enough for James Madison to finally win congressional approval for his pet foreign policy measure, trade sanctions against Great Britain. Though Madison's trade proposals had last been rejected only days earlier, the news of the British seizures and Dorchester's message to the Indians spurred Congress to quickly approve a one-month embargo on foreign trade.[6]

As far as many Republican oppositionists were concerned, the embargo was only the beginning. They proposed harsher measures such as the sequestration of British debts, and military action seemed to hold no terrors, though few Republicans believed the British would fight the United States while they were facing off with the French. "Would a ten year's open war with [Britain] have deprived us of as much of our shipping, as they have filched from us during these few months past, of *peace?*" asked Benjamin Franklin Bache's *General Advertiser*. "An invasion of our states would be an attempt worse than Quixotic."[7]

To the administration's supporters, the city of Philadelphia seemed to be gripped with a war fever, raising the fears of an illegitimate, coercive irrationality that haunted both sides of the decade's political debate. For Federalists, this danger lurked in the mean streets and frontier hovels inhabited by common laborers and farmers, whose loud voices and strong arms could be deployed for the cost of a few drinks and a little crude oratory. On Monday, April 14, a mob of unemployed sailors paraded to Congress Hall "colours flying" and huzzahed three times under the windows as Congress debated further trade sanctions. According to one report, the sailors "demanded a month's wages, or a declaration of war against England." The city mobilized its defenses and brought out the cannon in anticipation of violence that never materialized.[8]

Inside Congress Hall, the mood was anxious as members defensively counseled each other to ignore the pressure they were feeling from the streets outside. Samuel Dexter of Massachusetts lamented that "passion is called American feeling" and that "noise and declamation" were mistaken for "fortitude and patriotism." Dexter urged his colleagues to ignore the "tumultuous minority" who liked to "hallo loud and often," assuring them that a silent, "peaceful majority" dominated the country beyond Philadelphia. As the sailors bellowed, a member from Maryland (probably Federalist William Vans Murray) jumped up to respond more directly, in a moment sadly left out of the published *Annals of Congress*: "It was high time the Legislature sought for a place, where no Democratic Societies, and no mobs should attempt to rule their decisions." (Of course, a new capital was just then being prepared along the Potomac in the wilds of rural Maryland.) As with the Whiskey Rebellion, the sailors' visit to Congress was not a simple case of Republicans speaking for the common people and Federalists denouncing them. The leading opposition newspaper, soon to be renamed the *Aurora*, disavowed support of the unruly street protesters. As *Aurora* editor Benjamin Franklin Bache saw it, presaging his response to the Whiskey Rebellion, political influence was more properly exerted through institutions like elections and the Democratic-Republican Societies: "Republicans place more reliance on the effects of those institutions, than on mobs."[9]

Washington administration policy makers refused to take their cues from the stridently anti-British feeling in the streets and looked instead to the men they thought of as the true stakeholders in the issue. The mercantile elites who were Hamilton's and the Federalists' greatest supporters and sponsors saw the British depredations with cooler businessmen's eyes. A few seizures and impressments could be written off as the costs of doing business. Federalists noted the fact that merchants were rarely present at the anti-British demonstrations of 1794–1795, claiming that the crowds were made up of "strangers, sailors, country people, and boys" scarcely qualified to judge the commercial situation. A New Englander visiting Philadelphia "did not see four merchants or traders, and few steady mechanics" at the April 1794 town meeting, and yet, he scoffed, this motley group believed its "pompous . . . resolutions" would be "a guide to Congress, and a terror to Great Britain." Benjamin Russell's Boston *Columbian Centinel,* the voice of New England Federalism and the Boston mercantile community, noted that "the roaring advocates for coercive measures . . . do not include one out of an hundred of the American sufferers." Hamilton's deputy Oliver Wolcott regarded the opposition's professed concern for American commerce as rank hypocrisy and the trade war approach as indicative of their fundamentally uneconomic attitudes toward commerce and finance. According to "the Virginians," Wolcott fumed, "we must trade, not simply with a view to profit, but to display certain romantic affections and gratify resentments." Hamilton more calmly and cogently pointed out to Washington that Madison's proposed cures, which included total nonintercourse with Britain, would be worse than the disease; stringent trade sanctions against the British would disrupt the economy far more than the British depredations had done, and probably bring on further British attacks to boot.[10]

At the same time, Hamilton's allies were not without their own affections and resentments. Most established merchants were also social conservatives who greatly feared the popular movement that had sprung up in sympathy with the French Revolution and dreaded the possibility that war would radicalize and empower the street politicians at home just as it had in France. Far worse than losing a little money in the short run was the likelihood that further conflict with Great Britain would push the United States closer to the French. British policies were playing hell with "our maritime commerce," admitted Boston merchant and Massachusetts senator George Cabot, but anything was better than the social ills threatened by further contact with the French, which was "more to be dreaded, in a moral view, than a thousand yellow fevers in a physical." Oliver Wolcott admitted that he would rather see the United States "erased from existence than infected with the French principles."[11]

Hamilton and Washington realized that neither the Orders in

Council nor American public opinion could go completely unanswered. To head off the rising anti-British feeling and any further concessions to Madison's trade war approach, they decided to send the chief justice of the Supreme Court, John Jay, on a special mission to negotiate with the British. This was a less strange choice than it might seem to modern readers: Jay was an experienced diplomat of high integrity, and the Supreme Court was as yet a rather underutilized institution. Jay's name also added a great deal of fuel to the opposition's fire. While one of the few credible candidates for the mission that Hamilton and his closest allies felt they could trust, Jay the diplomat was reviled in many other (especially southern and western) quarters as a weak negotiator with strong biases in favor of northeastern merchants. In an infamous 1786 treaty with Spain, Jay had given up U.S. rights to the Mississippi River in exchange for commercial concessions.[12]

The Jay appointment brought howls of outrage in the streets of Philadelphia and in local communities across the country, especially in the West. Critics suspected a sell-out. The Democratic Society of Pennsylvania protested that "it was a sacrifice of the interests and peace of the United States to commit a negociation to him . . . [and that] at stake was the blood of our fellow citizens on the frontiers." There were also constitutional objections: the theory went that deputizing the head of the judicial branch to perform an executive task that would create a law (a treaty) united the functions of the three branches of government in one person. The Democratic Society's resolutions declared the Jay mission "the most unconstitutional and dangerous measure in the annals of the United States." In Kentucky, Jay was remembered as "the evil genius of Western America" and his effigy stuffed with gunpowder, beheaded, and then blown to bits. James Madison hoped that the administration had overreached by appointing Jay and made themselves "severely vulnerable."[13]

After the initial outrage faded, however, the "hocus pocus embassy"— as an opposition newspaper termed the Jay mission—seemed to pay off. The pressure for action against the British went away, and political attention turned elsewhere: 1794 was the eventful year of the Whiskey Rebellion, General Anthony Wayne's campaign against the Indians, and the controversy over the Democratic Societies. As Hamilton prepared to hand over his Treasury Department duties to Oliver Wolcott and return to his law practice in early 1795, Washington's prime minister was feeling good about the country's political direction. "All is well with the public," he assured his sister-in-law Angelica Church. "Our insurrection is most happily terminated. Government has gained by its reputation and strength."[14]

Published Fourth of July toasts were a good barometer of political sentiments throughout this period, and the 1794 editions show a remarkable level of unanimity. Most of the reported gatherings wished the French well in their war with the monarchies, and patiently awaited a favorable outcome to Jay's mission. In New York City, the merchants who dined at the Tontine Coffee House on Wall Street hoped Jay would "preserve the honor and peace of the United States," while the mechanics and tradesmen who celebrated at Mr. Amory's tavern urged Jay, with perhaps a touch of skepticism, to conduct himself "with that manly firmness and persevering integrity as shall be satisfactory to the people." The militiamen of Bucks County, Pennsylvania, gave Jay some less reassuring encouragement when they followed up their salute to his negotiations with a bloody image of the fate that might await an official whose actions the people found unsatisfactory: "May the guillotine of freedom lop off the oppression of tyranny." In fact, not everyone was waiting patiently, at least not in the neighborhoods where Jay was most loudly reviled. A thunderstorm calmed the streets of Philadelphia on the Fourth of July, 1794, but just a few days earlier, an effigy of Jay had been placed in the pillory on Market Street, then decapitated with a homemade guillotine, and blown up. In Boston, mobs replayed scenes from the 1765 Stamp Act riots and entered homes in the North End to vandalize some and destroy others.[15]

Unfortunately for George Washington's peace of mind, the results of the Jay negotiations seemed to vindicate the initial outrage against Jay. Though fears of corruption and bad faith on Jay's part were unfounded, the "Treaty of Amity, Commerce, and Navigation" he brought back included no concessions that the British had not already decided on themselves. Chiefly His Majesty's government agreed, again, to abandon its military bases on the western frontier of the United States. In return, Jay agreed to have the United States forswear retaliatory measures while accepting most British regulations on its trade and leaving the issue of impressed sailors to the discretion of the Royal Navy. The agreement was a blow to the already-wounded pride of Americans who still considered the British their old colonial oppressor. Historian Henry Adams, John

Adams's great-grandson and no lover of Jefferson or the French, judged the Jay Treaty so bad that there was no time after 1810 when the United States would not have preferred war to such a humiliating peace.[16]

While critical of Jay's "nervous anxiety" and the "unnecessarily humiliating" language he allowed to stay in the final document, Samuel Flagg Bemis and most other diplomatic historians have deemed it unlikely that anyone else could have extracted a fundamentally better deal from the British, given the situation in which Jay was placed. Among many other limitations, the British secret service had broken the code American diplomats were using. Even worse, Alexander Hamilton gave away one of the few bargaining chips his negotiator possessed by privately assuring British ambassador George Hammond that the Washington administration's "settled policy" was "to avoid entangling itself with European connexions." This was a reference not just to the rejected French alliance, but also to the far more realistic possibility of the United States accepting an invitation to join Sweden and Denmark in a league of armed neutrality. Once British foreign minister George Grenville had his ambassador's dispatch in hand, Bemis argues, he was assured "there was no danger of what he most feared" and "no longer was there any reason why he should even listen to [further] recital of Jay's propositions" for better treatment of American commerce.[17]

The slow pace of transatlantic communications in wartime meant that the results of the negotiations did not reach America until March 1795, a full year after Jay was sent on his mission. By that time, patience had already expired. A report reached Philadelphia in February that a group of London merchants trading with North America had given Jay a lavish dinner, and that the American envoy had saluted his hosts with the toast, "An honorable peace to the Belligerent powers of Europe." Sharply contrasting with the antimonarchical tenor of most American toasts at the time, Jay's expression of apolitical, amoral neutrality regarding the European revolutionary wars suggested to the Republican opposition that the fix was in: France was to be betrayed, the United States was to be Great Britain's "spaniel," and the apparent wishes of the American people were to be disregarded. These suspicions intensified when almost the same toast was given at the president's official birthday celebration in Philadelphia on February 23. They were just about confirmed when the text of the treaty finally landed on March 7, and Washington immediately sealed its contents pending a Senate debate scheduled for June.[18]

SEARCHING FOR DEMOCRACY ON THE EVE OF THE JAY TREATY CRISIS

The arrival of the Jay Treaty in Philadelphia brought on a looming crisis, and inspired a determination to challenge the document with words and votes rather than violence.

The leading Republican printer-editors seemed to sense that a turning point was at hand and retooled their papers for the more frankly partisan battle ahead. In New York, old Antifederalist warhorse Thomas Greenleaf launched a new daily paper called the *Argus* after the hundred-eyed giant of Greek myth who could penetrate "the most tenebrous shades . . . with his fifty *wakeful* eyes." The *Argus* made journalism history by becoming perhaps the first American newspaper to frankly embrace its role as a party organ from its inception. In the *Argus*'s "address" to readers, an editorial mission statement that was a standard feature of just-launched newspapers, Greenleaf argued that his partisan stance showed his independence rather than compromising it. "Parties, say some, are abominable; they destroy the peace of society, &c.," Greenleaf wrote, yet the secular patron saint of American printers, "the great Franklin, and many eminent men before and after him, have established as a principle, that *liberty*, without parties, can never be maintained."[19] The opposition's journalistic point man in Philadelphia at the time of the Jay Treaty was Benjamin Franklin Bache. Bache rechristened his *General Advertiser* the *Aurora* in late 1794, building the paper's political and educational mission into the title: "The AURORA, as far as the editor's exertions extend, shall diffuse light within the sphere of its influence,—dispel the shades of ignorance, and gloom of error and thus tend to strengthen the fair fabric of freedom on its surest foundation, publicity and information."[20]

In early 1795, the *Aurora* got busy setting up what would become the opposition press's favorite frame for explaining the foreign policy crisis. Instead of being merely a question of Britain versus France, Democratic-Republican newspapers treated the debate as a matter of monarchy, privilege, backwardness, corruption, and groveling submission versus republicanism, democracy, enlightenment, virtue, and self-respecting independence. Only sycophantic wannabe aristocrats would be willing to bow before some pretended superior just to gain some pecuniary benefit. Such an impulse was beneath the dignity of a democratic American citizen. "Some gentlemen think that *even the name* of a treaty with Great Britain is honourable and beneficial," the *Aurora* theorized, "as some

General ✦ Advertiser.

SURGO UT PROSIM.

Published *(DAILY)* by BENJ. FRANKLIN BACHE, No. 112, Market, between Third and Fourth Streets, *PHILADELPHIA.*

Eight Dollars *per ann.*)   F R I D A Y, September 30, 1796.   (*No.* 1799,

Avatar of Democracy: The Aurora *was the focus of the Democratic-Republican newspaper network that attacked the Jay Treaty and George Washington and then supported Thomas Jefferson for president in 1796. It was edited by Benjamin Franklin's grandson, and featured the contributions of numerous refugee radicals. (Philadelphia* Aurora General Advertiser, *Nameplate, 30 September 1796.)*

men claim a merit from an acquaintance with noblemen, even at the expense of their own personal consequence. Let such enjoy the feast, it will prove less savoury to the vulgar palates of the people."[21]

The most straightforward element of this frame was democracy; simply put, the issue was whether the assumed state of popular opinion was going to be respected by the government or not. The most important statement of this theme ran in the *Aurora* but actually originated with the other major Republican paper in the capital, Eleazer Oswald's old Antifederalist (against the Constitution rather than the Federalist party) journal, the *Independent Gazetteer*. This was a series of essays signed "Franklin" that came from the pen of an unidentified member of the Democratic Society. Rambling, repetitive, and often maddeningly abstract though they often were, pseudonymous newspaper essay series were one of the primary forms of political expression in the Early Republic. Madison, Hamilton, and Jay's "Federalist" series, now known as *The Federalist Papers,* is the most famous example of the genre today, but they were a standard feature of the American political press throughout the partisan era. Bache and Oswald both ran the fourteen-part "Franklin" series from March to June, and then Oswald republished it as a pamphlet with some additional comments.[22]

The "Franklin" letters made up for their lack of detail on the yet-to-be-released treaty by grounding the likely opposition to it in the democratic assumptions and patriotic feelings of ordinary Americans, particularly within Philadelphia's artisan community. In his introduction to the published edition, editor Oswald expressed puzzlement at the apparent gap between popular opinion and administration policy; he expected that some way to link the two would emerge: "There certainly cannot exist so wide a difference between the Government and the People, as to render the former regardless of the opinions of the latter.—Public functionaries ought to pay some attention to the opinions of those who constituted them." "Franklin" himself made a stronger claim, namely, that popular influence even over foreign policy was already embedded in the constitutional system:

> It may be said, that President and Senate are alone the constitutional organs to make and determine on Treaties; but if they are derived from *the People*, and do not imagine themselves *independent* of them, the voice of the Body, from which they ought to be but emanations, will have an influence on their decisions. . . . "*We the People*" made the Constitution, and the Officers under it, "*We the People*," it is to be expected, will have some influence on the laws which are to be made to bind us.[23]

"Franklin's" assertion reflected a widespread popular belief about how the U.S. Constitution, or indeed any republican government, was supposed to operate: democracy, in the form of popular opinion, should be felt in all the government's activities. As popular constitutionalists like "Franklin" saw it, the true state of affairs was captured in the Preamble's "We, the People," which they read without much reference to its original context. The Preamble had been crafted by the self-consciously aristocratic Gouverneur Morris, a scion of the New York manors: he had also argued in the Constitutional Convention that only property owners should be able to vote in federal elections. Replacing a list of individual states with "the People," Morris's rewrite of the Preamble had shifted the rhetorical authorship of the Constitution from the state governments to the population of the United States as a whole. It was a nationalist move that had nothing to do with promoting democracy.[24]

Yet Morris's words also baldly stated the premise that the people were sovereign in a way that radical democrats and the common people themselves could interpret according to their own hopes and convictions. According to what historian Lance Banning has described as the established pattern of Anglo-American constitutional thinking, critics "required an ancient constitution against which [they] could measure the degeneration of the present day." They made the brand-new Constitution old in their minds and rhetoric, and found settled doctrine in it that the Framers probably never intended to put there. What

Democratic Society radicals like Bache and "Franklin" found embedded in the Constitution was a full-throated national democracy that they were surprised to see thwarted and that they constantly looked for ways to operationalize.[25]

While everyone understood the concept of organizing an election campaign to remove an obnoxious official, especially on the local level, doing it to influence policy was less familiar, and not even the most ardent democrats in Philadelphia were ready to try it nationally right away. The Jay Treaty crisis launched the opposition into the first stages of a process that would only lead to a presidential campaign more than a year later. The opposition spent the first half of 1795 groping toward a mobilization of public opinion whose form was yet unknown. In the early stages, opponents like "Franklin" still held out hope that President Washington and the Senate could be brought to their senses through rational discussion. From a Democratic Society point of view, it seemed almost impossible that democratically expressed popular opinion could really be barred from the process of formulating foreign policy. Yet this is what seemed to be happening. "Is this to be the effect of the boasted checks and balances in our government," asked "Sidney" in the *Aurora*. "Is the Executive determined thus to declare an open war with the legislature and the People?"[26]

With no specifics to attack, opposition writers prepared the ground between March and June by highlighting the "excessive secrecy" with which the administration and its Senate supporters had handled the treaty. Secrecy was corrupt, unrepublican, and monarchical, they argued. "*Monarchs* . . . make a trade of secrecy," an *Aurora* correspondent wrote. The Senate was considering the treaty in the "darkness of a conclave or a seraglio," declared another, invoking two favorite symbols of the decadent Old World politics thought to be the "antipodes" of republicanism, one Catholic and one Muslim. Secrecy also subverted the people's rightful role in democratically supervising what was supposed to be their government. The treaty had been kept secret upon no known "constitutional or republican principle," and "yet it is said that 'We the People' are the sovereign."[27]

On a more tactical level, it was pointed out many times that the secrecy regarding the treaty seemed to be part of a deliberate political strategy to avoid any sort of democratic decision on it. First the administration had played bait and switch with the Jay mission itself, telling the public that Jay was being sent to avert war with Great Britain and redress

American grievances. "Scarcely a person in this country supposed that anything short of complete indemnification for our losses would be accepted," declared one Republican writer, "and not one in ten thousand, I believe had any idea" of a full-scale commercial treaty. Surprise at what Jay had done curdled quickly into the darkest of suspicions. "A deception of such magnitude must leave permanent impressions," argued the "Franklin" letters, "it must lead to a suspicion of the candor of every subsequent measure, and awaken opinions, that there is a greater sensibility for *Kings and Thrones,* than for *the People and Republicanism.*" To many it seemed that only conspiracy or corruption could explain the decision to conciliate a "desperate, haughty" enemy rather than a "gallant" ally: "Can any *honorable* reason be given, why the United States have *courted* a treaty with great Britain, and have *neglected* the overtures from France?" Now, critics feared, the administration hoped to make Jay's shameful capitulation a *fait accompli.*[28]

Although historians have cleared Washington, Hamilton, and Jay of corruption and conspiracy, the opposition was not too far wrong in their appraisal of Federalist strategy. While never doubting their choice of Britain rather than France as the European power to appease, Washington, Hamilton, and many other Federalists were deeply embarrassed by Jay's treaty, especially Article 12's limitations on the exportation even of certain American-grown crops in American ships, and were not eager to trumpet its contents. Yet there was also little chance that the administration and its allies would admit defeat or give any comfort to the French or to the domestic opposition.[29]

Another factor in the Washington administration's handling of the treaty was a phenomenon that has become depressingly familiar since 1795: a presidential conviction that the chief magistrate and his advisors, and not the Congress or public opinion or any other democratic body, should possess autonomous authority over the conduct of foreign policy and warfare and have no duty to share detailed information about such weighty matters of state with legislators or the public. Washington came to this position rather hesitantly, but concluded by July that he would pay little attention to the public debate and listen only to "dispassionate men, who have knowledge of the subject, and abilities to judge of it." Washington would stick with this conclusion to the bitter end of his administration, denying all further congressional requests for information about Jay's negotiations. Neither Washington nor Hamilton believed that public opinion should or could be ignored completely in a republic, but they notably lacked any instinct for, or interest in, the sort of broadly consultative democratic leadership that the opposition advocated. "The man of the People has a sensibility for their feelings, and commits his conduct and transactions to their inspection," lectured the Democratic Society member who wrote the "Franklin" letters. "It is the mind only which feels itself a Sovereign, that enshrouds itself in mystery."[30]

Deeply convinced that the people at large felt as they did about the British and the treaty, the Republicans still faced a serious problem in finding some way to put those sentiments into action and actually affect the government's policies and personnel. John Swanwick's victory in highly politicized Philadelphia notwithstanding, the link between national government policy disputes and electoral politics in the states was far from automatic. In most places, local oligarchies continued to get by on voters' deference to prominent names without much reference to policy or ideology. At first the anxiety over the treaty did not even hurt Jay himself politically. The Federalists were confident enough in Jay's popularity to run him for governor of New York in the spring of 1795, in absentia; the main Republican campaign statement raised Jay's diplomatic career only to make the rather mild-mannered point that he had been away from New York for a long time and did not know very much about its government anymore.[31]

Instead of elections, the battle against the Jay Treaty was first carried on in the familiar modes of early American politics, on the streets and in the taverns, with many drinks at hand. Toasts and other forms of convivial celebration were highly developed arts in the eighteenth century and a basic part of public politics in this time when other, more formal party institutions were nascent or suspicious. In the absence of party platforms and campaign rallies, accounts of public occasions organized by groups of local partisans were frequently published in the newspapers and treated as informal platforms.[32]

As the date for the June Senate debate on the treaty neared, the political atmosphere in the seaport towns heated up along with the weather. Despite Jay's concessions, a grain shortage in Europe and bread riots in England had prompted the British to start seizing American ships again, under a new, secret Order in Council. Crowds in Norfolk and Boston denounced the British as pirates and acted out their feelings. Posing as the "Leather Medal Society," the Norfolk demonstrators limited themselves to satire, holding a mock banquet for King George III's birthday where the "utmost hilarity" included toasts to Caligula, Blackbeard, "despotism throughout the world," and fourteen other evils.[33]

In Boston, a less hilarious demonstration broke out when a hand-bill spread word that a notorious privateer out of Bermuda was docked at Long Wharf. The handbill reminded "CITIZENS!" that almost three hundred American ships had been taken, their crews and owners receiving "the most barbarous treatment from those *Damn'd* PIRATES!!!" Those Bostonians who felt "the spirit of resentment, or revenge, kindling in [their] breasts" were invited to spend Saturday night down at the wharf. The "enraged multitude" drove the captain and crew off without injury, then visited extreme property damage on their ship. "Exasperated" at finding weapons on the ship along with a cargo of fish, potatoes, and flour, the rioters cut down the masts and rigging, threw the "warlike implements" overboard, towed the vessel into the harbor, and set it on fire. The blazing hulk drifted with the tide far enough to nearly burn Charles Town across the harbor. (Unfortunately the ship was not the "Bermudian privateer" but the sloop *Speedwell*, an apparently innocent merchant vessel based in Halifax.)[34] A few tension-filled and violent days later, a new handbill appeared suggesting an attack on some British vessels at Goldsbury's Wharf. Another, larger riot seemed likely until Governor Samuel Adams called out the militia. Boston Federalists tried to blame the disturbances on the local Democratic-Republican newspaper, the *Independent Chronicle*. In fact, the men of the *Chronicle* office took the same dim view of violent political protest that the *Aurora* had during the Whiskey Rebellion, as something that undermined the opposition's efforts to build a democratic movement that worked through legal and political means. A selectmen's investigation showed that the handbills actually came from a Federalist-leaning print shop.[35]

Things were only superficially calmer in Philadelphia, where, gratuitously meeting in secret, the Senate carried on a bitter debate but ratified the Jay Treaty by a close vote on June 24, 1795, suspending only the offensive Article 12 in which Jay had allowed the British to dictate, in certain cases, what American produce American ships could carry. "This imp of darkness, illegitimately begotten, commanded but the bare constitutional number required for ratification," the *Aurora* raged, toting up the populations of the states whose senators voted for and against the treaty. Through secrecy, the Senate majority had "passed an act more binding than the constitution, and more influential than any law" and revealed the democratic deficiencies of the constitution: "Such is the effect of the glorious system of checks and balances." Exasperatingly, the Federalist majority in the Senate also voted to keep the treaty's text secret still, with little explanation and no real justification other than the political embarrassment it would cause if revealed. The Philadelphia *Independent Gazetteer* argued correctly that the habit of government secrecy for political convenience augured open repression down the road, starting with the newspapers and printers that had annoyed the Federalists so much during the treaty debate and its prequels:

> The next attempt that we may anticipate will be upon the freedom of the Press; for a conduct so repugnant to every sense of propriety as that of the Administration, cannot bear the order of the Press, and it must endeavor to shelter itself by imposing silence upon the only voice that can speak daggers to injustice, and awaken the public mind to tyranny. . . . Methinks . . . that the patriotic and virtuous Editor of the AURORA is to be the first victim!

When the Federalists finally got a strong congressional majority again, in 1797–1798, Benjamin Franklin Bache would indeed be the first target of the new Sedition Act.[36]

The needless provocation of secrecy helped inflame the already incendiary situation, but it also provided the street-level Democratic-Republicans with their greatest political opportunity ever. As the opposition saw it, it would be an "act of patriotism" for someone in the Senate to expose the "dark transaction" that had just occurred. Hoping to spark a groundswell of public opinion that might yet convince President Washington to scrap the treaty, Virginia senator Stevens T. Mason provided Bache with an article-by-article summary, which appeared in the *Aurora* on June 29. Unfortunately this act of patriotism may have been initiated or facilitated by a foreign source. The newly arrived French minister Pierre Adet claimed to his superiors that he bought a copy of the secret document from Mason and arranged for it to fall into Bache's hands.[37]

Bache then immediately set his grandfather's state-of-the-art printing facility to the task of making the treaty into a pamphlet and turned his newspaper's office into the command center of a national effort to spread the news of the outrageous document. Recruiting fellow members of the Democratic Society to help, Bache left his wife Margaret and colleague Dr. Michael Leib in charge of the *Aurora* and set out northward along the eastern seaboard with thousands of copies of the pamphlet. At the same time, another Democratic Society leader, hatter and militia officer John Smith, set out on a similar mission to the South. As the news hit, the opposition deployed celebratory politics on a scale not seen since Genet's visit, marking a turning point in the history of that phenomenon. From 1795 on, published toasts were both far more numerous and almost always identifiably partisan in one orientation or another.[38]

Traveling north, Bache missed out on perhaps Philadelphia's most tumultuous Fourth of July celebration ever.[39] The "only political Sabbath of freedom" in Philadelphia began with people crowding into the *Aurora* office (and the Bache/Franklin home) on Market Street, seeking copies of the paper and the treaty pamphlet. This posed a challenge for Mrs. Bache and Dr. Leib; with half the printers in the shop out drinking and parading against the treaty with the rest of the city's artisans, they had to cut the newspaper's usual four pages down to two. Down the street the like-minded *Independent Gazetteer* carried a half-facetious death notice for "Mrs. Liberty," the "consort of America," poisoned to death by "his gracious majesty . . . to quiet this turbulent jade that has so often thwarted his ambition."[40]

A toast calling for the people to stand up for their rights seemed to signal a major demonstration that was planned for the evening of the Fourth. For several days prior, members of the Democratic Society and other leaders of the city's working-class districts had been working on an elaborate illuminated display. Such "illuminations" had become standard fare on patriotic holidays, but the 1795 edition would be politically pointed. The centerpiece of the display was a giant "transparency"—really a bigger than life-sized political cartoon lighted from behind—of John Jay, acting out a popular conspiracy theory about how the treaty had been negotiated. The figure of Jay held a pair of scales in his right hand, with "American Liberty and Independence" on one side but tipping toward "British gold" on the other side; in his left hand was the treaty, "extended to a group of senators . . . grinning with pleasure and grasping." A word balloon issuing from Jay's mouth carried the words, "Come up to my price, and I will sell you my country."[41]

A procession was planned in which the lighted transparency would be taken through the streets and burned in front of Vice President Adams's house. It was scheduled for 11 o'clock at night to avoid a possible clash with the militia, which had been called out to march before the president and governor earlier in the day. The Democratic Society was still eager to prove that democrats could be politically aggressive but nonviolent, and there was some expectation that the Federalists who commanded the city's upper-class militia companies would try to stop any political demonstrations in their vicinity.[42]

The militia had long been a political tool and occasional political football in Philadelphia, and it would become even more so over the course of the 1790s. Several Democratic Society members and *Aurora* staff members helped organize and lead special Republican militia companies charged with protecting Republicans and their businesses as well as the city. The 1795 Fourth of July celebrations marked an early stage of these divisions. In the same *Aurora* issue that carried the orders to march on the Fourth, "A Militia-Man" urged the citizen-soldiers to ignore orders aimed at using the militiamen as props in a spectacle glorifying the administration and its policies: "Are you, fellow citizens, a *praetorian band* . . . liable to be called upon . . . to minister to the vanity of others, and exhibit yourselves to public view, for the gratification of ambition . . . as if you were a band of hirelings, at the disposal of your cashier?"[43]

There is no way of knowing how many militiamen boycotted the holiday parade, but it is clear that the split was on full display during the late-night demonstration. A crowd of some five hundred men, a number of ship carpenters and sailors among them, set out from the working-class and immigrant district of Kensington northeast of Philadelphia City, moved down Front Street along the Delaware River, then on to the heart of the city via Callowhill, Second, and Market Streets. All the reports of the march agree that the marchers and spectators alike were remarkably silent, in keeping with the "mourning for liberty" motif, at least until the procession reached Vine Street. At that point, a witness recalled, the marchers seemed to think they had evaded the possibility of militia interference and gave out three cheers. The cry of "to horse, to horse" rang out down the street, and the procession retreated swiftly back to Kensington, with one Captain Morell and a few members of his light-horse company in pursuit. When the horsemen caught up and rode in among the marchers, a short but furious melee broke out, the crowd pummeling Morell and his men with stones and clubs, knocking one man off his horse, and forcing the company to flee Kensington for their lives. The battle won, the marchers and a neighborhood audience several hundred strong burned the image of Jay with great ceremony and then dispersed. At the spot where the marchers had fought the city cavalry, a sign appeared reading, "Morell's defeat / Jay burnt in effigy, 4th July, 1795."[44]

The Fourth was relatively peaceful elsewhere, but the sentiments expressed were much the same. In frequently violent Baltimore, tempers were amazingly calm; sailors were in short supply on the streets just then, with more than fifty Baltimore ships sailing as French privateers. The town's shipowners were expecting to make some money out of the crisis. Baltimore's rather well-heeled Republican Society "sat down to an elegant entertainment" with both Governor John H. Stone (a Federalist) and the French consul in attendance. President Washington was toasted warmly in "remembrance of his services," but the governor walked out after "The People of France" was added to the list. The Baltimoreans then urged the current government to model the behavior of the revolutionary one they were celebrating: "The Congress of 1776, who in a time of weakness, and actual war, defied the power which bullied the world." In Wilmington, Delaware, two hundred revelers consumed a "Republican Repast" and finished their after-dinner toasts with an angry salute to "His Excellency, John Jay, Esq. . . . *may he and his treaty be, for ever politically d____d.*" Contrarily, Thomas Jefferson, "the Scientific and Republican Statesman," was toasted from the floor. This was one of the few public mentions of the soon-to-be opposition candidate in the press of 1795.[45]

The leading sentiment at Wilmington and most of the other published gatherings was that scuttling the treaty was a matter of democratic imperative. The people overwhelmingly opposed the treaty, Democratic-Republicans believed, and their public servants were duty-bound to follow their constituents' wishes. "The Sovereignty of the People," they drank in Baltimore, "May every knee bow to it, and every tongue confess it supreme."[46]

In New York, Benjamin Franklin Bache dropped off his bundles of treaty pamphlets the day before the celebrations and received a nice testimonial in a toast that praised his role in stoking the opposition: "May our country never be in want of the patriotism and pen of the modern FRANKLIN." Bache's gift helped spark one of the most remarkable displays of unity in the history of New York City Democratic politics as the Democratic Society, the Tammany Society, the General Society of Mechanics and Tradesmen, and various local militia companies held a joint procession and fireworks display, with a series of dinners in between. All of New York's many mutually hostile Republican-oriented factions were involved or praised, including the Livingston family, Aaron Burr, and former Governor George Clinton (and all their respective followers), in gatherings set up by the artisans and middle-class radicals in the city's self-created societies. Newly elected congressman Edward Livingston led off the joint celebration with a reading of the Declaration of Independence, followed by the Reverend Samuel Miller's oration, and an "Ode to Freedom" that showed little diminution in the Democratic-Republican Societies' revolutionary zeal: "But ranc'rous kings must die, / For Freedom's reign's begun / And lords and despots, trembling, fly / Before this glorious Sun!"[47]

New York's Democratic-Republicans still held out hope that Washington could be induced to abandon what they perceived as Alexander Hamilton's policies. One of the displays was a giant transparency of the president draped over one of the government buildings. Perhaps the most striking toasts of the day saluted Washington but busted him down to the status of "citizen" and placed him on a level with various Founders who had gravitated to the Republicans, including Jefferson, Madison, and George Clinton. Across the river in New Jersey, celebrants at "Citizen Christie's tavern" wished for "Citizen Washington" to be as brave and patriotic in directing government policy as he was "brave in the field." The possible fate of a leader lacking in commitment to patriotism, liberty, and equality was included a few toasts later: "The guillotine—May it maintain its empire till all crowned heads are laid in the dust."[48]

On his northern trip, Benjamin Franklin Bache also had an unexpected encounter with the strange compound of political insight and myopia that was the eventual Federalist presidential candidate. The Fourth of July found Bache in Connecticut, trying to get his pamphlets to Boston. Cadging a pass from the mayor of Hartford that would let him travel on Sunday in Connecticut despite the blue laws, Bache caught up with and spent the night in the same building as none other than Vice President and Mrs. John Adams in the "very pretty town" of Worcester, Massachusetts. At breakfast, Adams cross-examined Bache about the treaty—specifically whether word of it was out yet in Philadelphia and, one imagines, what the *Aurora*'s editor was doing in Worcester. Bache "told him a little" and Adams dismissively "assured [him] that the generality of the people would like [the treaty] very well after a trial of a few months." In about a year, Adams would be proved correct as to the treaty. His implication that political quiet would follow turned out to be more wishful than accurate.[49]

KICKING THE TREATY TO HELL

Boston had a quiet Fourth as the local Republicans waited for the treaty's text to arrive—quiet, at least, by the standards of the summer of 1795. "Civic testimonials" were held at the Old South Meeting House, and the Republican activist George Blake gave a corking patriotic oration, the best since Hancock's in 1773, said the *Boston Gazette*. Blake compared Parliament to "the den of the Cyclops" and Great Britain as a whole to Beelzebub, who, "stung by the tortures of disgrace . . . in the abyss of infamy, still broods on mischief, and meditates our destruction." The speech ended with a near-recruiting pitch for the French revolutionary armies, whose "cause is half our own." Blake compared the Revolutionary War unfavorably to what the French now faced and opined that Americans should not "dwell with uncommon anguish" on Louis XVI's violent demise, despite his role in the American events being celebrated. It was an index of the febrile tenor of that political moment that even the arch-Federalist, anti-Jacobin *Columbian Centinel* mustered only the mild comment that Blake's speech was a bit "too strongly tinctured of party-spirit."[50]

Benjamin Franklin Bache hit Boston on Monday, July 6, and spent the next few days conferring with "the principal Demos" in town, especially Dr. Charles Jarvis and renegade merchant Benjamin Austin Jr., both habitués of the offices of the Boston *Independent Chronicle* and prolific contributors to its pages. The editor was also invited to meet with the patron saint of Democratic-Republicanism in Boston, Governor Samuel Adams. Despite what most of New England's congressmen and other newspapers said, Jarvis and Austin assured Bache that the treaty was "as much disliked" in Boston as it was in Philadelphia and New York. Convinced that the vast majority of ordinary Americans shared their feelings and still hoping that President Washington might not give his final approval to the treaty, the three newspapermen and other Democratic-Republican activists considered what they might do to bring about that result. Their working assumption was that public opinion would matter to the president if he could be shown, unmistakably and incontrovertibly, just where it stood on the treaty: "If the People make good use of the present moment of enthusiasm. I think it yet in their power to prevent its finally becoming the Supreme law of the land, and this only by a vigorous expression of their Sentiments."[51]

The problem was that such expressions rarely occurred spontaneously or speedily, nor was there any obvious means of gauging mass opinion in this age before polling or even national elections. Toasts and newspaper essays were useful, but they clearly came from particular individuals and groups. The solution that Bache and the Bostonians hit upon resulted in the largest series of mass meetings the country had yet seen and a push toward the democratization of American political culture that the Federalists eventually had to meet rather than merely condemn. Both spontaneously and by careful design, public hatred for the treaty was expressed in the streets throughout the country during the summer of 1795.

Drawing on the long Massachusetts tradition of democratic local government, which had been used to powerful political effect in the run-up to the Revolution, the Boston "demos" planned to hold "a regular town meeting" on the treaty that would begin a process of officially expressing the people's voice on a national scale. This would not be just a political rally; in Boston, it was possible to call a legal town meeting that the authorities could not shut down or denounce as "self-created" if a certain number of citizens signed a petition. If the Boston meeting voted against the treaty, and if that measure was "backed by the voice of the citizens of New York and Philadelphia, expressed in the same manner"—by similar town meetings that the Democratic-Republicans would organize, in other words—President Washington might find it "prudent to suspend, at least, the ratification" of the treaty.[52]

A day or two after Bache's and the treaty's arrival in the city, even Federalist leader Fisher Ames had to admit that Boston was "in a very inflammatory state . . . [and that] the Jacobins have been successful in prejudicing the multitude." The *Independent Chronicle* staff distributed the necessary petitions and delivered them to the town selectmen, who duly called a meeting for Friday, July 10. Alarmed by the shifting of the political ground under their feet, and feeling little enthusiasm for the treaty themselves, the major Federalists responded by once again attacking the legitimacy of citizens organizing to criticize or influence government policy. "A Real Republican" in the *Columbian Centinel* pretended that it was both unconstitutional and unprecedented in world history for a town to express its opinion on a treaty; in fact Boston had held a similar town meeting on the treaty ending the Revolutionary War in 1783. Despite its manifest legality, the writer denounced the new meeting as "the frightful brat of disorganizing Jacobinism." Particularly telling was the way the Federalist writer accurately described the meeting's purpose but treated it as a scandal. "The avowed intention of the projectors of this measure is," the *Centinel* writer huffed, "to influence the President of the United States."[53]

When the Boston antitreaty meeting convened, some fifteen hundred people crowded into Faneuil Hall, with Benjamin Franklin Bache in attendance but many of the leading Federalists absent by their own design. After the assembled citizens elected a relatively neutral moderator, architect and state legislator Thomas Dawes, Dr. Jarvis opened the meeting with a speech condemning the Jay Treaty as ruinous to American commerce, lacking in any sort of reciprocity, and intended by the British to damage America's old allies the French and possibly to provoke a U.S.-French War. The few Federalists present responded only with requests for delay or questions about "the propriety and constitutionality" of having the meeting at all. A Mr. J. Hall asked whether a town successfully influencing the president might not amount to "unsenatorizing the Senate"; this possibility was actually rather attractive for the *Independent Chronicle* crowd. In response to Hall, Dr. Jarvis and the other Republican activists grandstanded for the people's right "to assemble to express their sentiments on all matters in which their interest was concerned." The question of whether the town approved the treaty was then put to a vote, and not one hand went up. A committee of fifteen was appointed to draft resolutions against the treaty that were approved at another meeting on Monday, paragraph by paragraph. The resulting memorial was referred back to the selectmen with instructions that they send it to President Washington immediately.[54]

The Boston meeting and its sequels were a high point in the campaign by the Democratic Societies and their allied newspapers to vindicate democracy as the basis of the American constitutional system and also to model democratic behavior. As writers of this period often did when depicting favorably disposed crowds, Benjamin Franklin Bache fell back on the specialized language of sensibility in his account of the meeting, searching for specific mental-emotional reactions that would show on people's faces: "I watched the countenance of the citizens assembled . . . [and] not one instance of that stupid gaze was seen, so often to be observed among a people less enlightened, all appeared intelligent and to feel the force of every argument that was used. . . . I was highly delighted . . . by the orderly and spirited manner in which the business was conducted." In fact, it was a delicate balancing act that Bache described, between the bourgeois public sphere's vision of politics as rational, disembodied argument and a more practical understanding of democratic politics as a real-life activity that had to be practiced on flesh-and-blood human beings whose intellects were best approached through their emotions. It would prove quite difficult to maintain the Jay Treaty opponents' balance of emotional fervor and principled democratic arguments over the long run.[55]

In the meantime, the town meeting bug spread up and down the country. With the Boston Federalists writing to Philadelphia that the local meeting was just a "Jacobin measure" that did not reflect popular sentiment, the memorial itself was unlikely to have much impact. Instead, it was the wide publicity the Boston meeting received that made it important, and treaty opponents in other cities became eager to repeat the process in their own localities, despite the fact that most places outside New England lacked Boston's convenient town meeting laws. Portsmouth (New Hampshire), Elizabethtown (New Jersey), Charleston (South Carolina), Norfolk (Virginia), and several other communities would eventually get into the act, but the New York and Philadelphia meetings directly followed the Boston example.[56]

With handbills and newspaper notices, the New York meeting was called for Saturday, July 12, at noon, a time when the city's laborers and artisans, most of them vociferously opposed to the treaty, would be able to attend. Federalists, of course, actually complained about the timing for exactly the same reason: too many workers would be present. There had not been a mass political meeting of this scale in the city since the beginning of the Revolution, and plebeian New Yorkers turned out in force, "the hod men and the ash men and the clam men" as well as the "respectable mechanics." A Federalist sniffed that there was "not a whole coat amongst all those who voted against the treaty," which was the vast majority of the crowd; only the wealthy would have possessed coats. Alexander Hamilton and other local Federalist leaders were thrown into a panic. They met with some merchants the night before the meeting to plan strategy and quickly decided that Federalists would have to attend the meeting instead of boycotting it as they had in Boston. The only strategy they could think of was Hamilton himself;

the former treasury secretary would simply try to hijack the meeting by force of personality and rhetoric.[57]

The result was perhaps the most humiliating day of Hamilton's political career, and one he was lucky to physically survive. Some five thousand New Yorkers gathered outside Federal Hall, and the intended moderator for the day, Colonel William S. Smith, planned a dignified meeting following parliamentary procedure like the one in Boston. Hamilton appeared with a small posse of friends, mounted some steps, and then, just as the bells tolled noon, began to harangue the crowd. Someone called, "Let us have a chairman," and Smith was duly elected and took his place on the balcony of Federal Hall. Republican Peter R. Livingston asked for the floor, but Hamilton demanded it for himself and started talking again. The crowd erupted with hisses, and Smith gave the floor to Livingston, whose appointed role was to take the sense of the crowd. He suggested that those who favored the treaty should move to the left, those opposed to the right. Almost no one moved left. Meanwhile Hamilton tried to keep talking, complaining that there should be a full discussion before there was any vote, but another wave of hisses, coughs, and catcalls swamped the former treasury secretary's voice. Brockholst Livingston bellowed that there was no need for further discussion; everyone knew where they stood, and at any rate a real debate would not be possible in such a gathering. Edward Livingston warned the crowd to "take care, or that man [Hamilton] will ruin you," and at that point Hamilton was said to have been physically dragged from his stoop. Several hundred people who had moved right according to Peter Livingston's call headed down to the Battery and burned a copy of the treaty, a step without which few gatherings seem to have been complete in the summer of 1795.

While the treaty roasted, Hamilton tried to take the meeting over one more time, pulling out a written resolution to the effect that there was no need or right for the people or the town to give any opinion on the treaty, and that "the wisdom and virtue of the President" could simply be trusted to make the right decision. The remaining crowd erupted again with shouts of "we'll hear no more of it" and "tear it up," and the Republicans rammed through a proposal to appoint a committee of fifteen to report back with resolutions on Monday, again following the Boston example. Hamilton then rather pathetically submitted his resolutions to a vote of his little crew of supporters, got a smattering of "ayes," and fled, dodging a couple of rocks that legend turned into a hail of stones that the Federalist chieftain braved with witty put-downs, blood streaming down his face.[58]

The afternoon went no better for Hamilton, for whom even strolling around the city with friends became a perilous activity. A chance encounter with a group of Republican leaders led to a shouting match that ended with Hamilton's challenging Commodore James Nicholson, one of the local Democratic Society's more prominent members, to a duel. (Nicholson had earlier accused Hamilton of having suspicious British investments, and muttered that he was "an abetter of Tories" during the argument in the street.) Only minutes later, one of Hamilton's more hotheaded cohorts, state assemblyman Josiah Hoffman, got into another spat in front of Republican congressman Edward Livingston's house. Seeing a number of the morning meeting's organizers present—most of them members of the Livingston family, rival manor lords to his father-in-law Philip Schuyler—Hamilton could not contain his fury and burst out "that he would fight the whole party one by one, . . . the whole detestable faction." Maturin Livingston volunteered to be first in line, and Hamilton acquired his second duel of the afternoon. Fortunately neither of those affairs proceeded as far as actual shots fired. To add insult to insult, a group of Revolutionary War veterans reenacted the Philadelphia Fourth of July scene by parading with the American and French flags over a reversed British flag and burning yet another image of John Jay (now the state's sitting governor) selling his country for British gold.[59]

Benjamin Franklin Bache returned from a weekend at the former Citizen Genet's country estate on Long Island in time for the even larger Monday meeting. With no interference from Hamilton this time, Brockholst Livingston read the resolutions against the treaty that had been framed over the weekend, and the crowd unanimously voted to approve them one by one. The calm decorum of the Monday meeting contrasted sharply with the "tumult" of Saturday, allowing the *Argus* to jeer how remarkable it was that the day should have been so harmonious when " 'the *friends of good order*' were absent!!!"[60]

Hamilton and many other Federalists spent the next few days in a state of shock. Attempts at counterdemonstrations and protreaty meetings failed. The Chamber of Commerce was convened, and even in that Federalist bastion, a significant number of attendees opposed the treaty. The Chamber's treaty supporters produced a resolution that basically apologized for it. On a more threatening note, an *Argus* writer signing himself "Hypocrite" reported that a list was being drawn up of just who was for and against the treaty in town, along with their home addresses and what side they had taken during the Revolutionary War. New York had been occupied by the British for much of the war, and many New Yorkers had remained behind the lines and had willingly done business with the enemy, including twenty-five of the merchants who had supported the Jay Treaty at the Chamber of Commerce meeting.[61]

After writing out his will in anticipation of the ultimately aborted duel with Nicholson, Hamilton worked himself into an apocalyptic mood, fearing "Jacobin" plots against "certain Individuals" (presumably himself and other Federalist leaders). Worried that the local militia was infested with Democratic Society types who could not "be depended on," Hamilton wrote Oliver Wolcott to ask if federal troops could be stationed near the city, "as a resource in a sudden emergency," as though some bloody Parisian-style massacre was in the offing.[62]

Hamilton was understandably traumatized by his experiences in the Jay Treaty protests, but the "Jacobins" he feared so much were too intent on celebrating the peaceable and rational nature of their protests to plan any seriously violent reprisals. A Philadelphia Republican leader bragged to a New York counterpart that "perhaps no occasion of an equal assemblage of people ever presented so orderly, peaceful and dignified a Conduct." It was not social revolution but a strong sense of democratic responsiveness that they sought, a quality they thought of themselves as restoring to American constitutionalism (and increasingly equated with free government) despite the Framers' express disinterest in any such thing. "While it ought to be imprinted in our hearts, that obedience to law (for nothing unconstitutional can be law) is the glory of a Republican," wrote one of New York printer Thomas Greenleaf's most pugnacious contributors, "it should be remembered with equal energy, that in a free government, the voice of the people, when unequivocally expressed, ought and must be regarded."[63]

Bache returned to Philadelphia in time for its own town meetings, which were not quite so chaotic as New York's but more rollicking and frightening for Federalists than the ones in Boston. Philadelphia's gatherings followed the now-established two-stage format. The first meeting was called for Thursday, July 23, at 5 o'clock in the evening in the garden behind the Pennsylvania State House, now known as Independence Hall. A group of Philadelphia radicals that included much of the

Aurora staff and many veterans of the Democratic Society, along with Clerk of the House John Beckley, organized the meetings; their handbill calling the meeting put the question of democratic constitutionalism front and center, and in the most highly colored terms possible. Citizens were called "to discuss the Momentous Question, viz: Are the People the Legitimate Fountain of Government? There is creeping into your Constitution an Insidious SERPENT whose venom, once infused, will exterminate every remaining spark of Gratitude and National Faith! *Attend!* Your rights are invaded!" America's "avowed Friend" France was to be betrayed in favor of Great Britain, "the universal Foe of *Liberty*" that had made the American people "the guiltless victims of her Infernal malice."[64]

At the meeting itself, racing a thunderstorm and dealing with a crowd so large it was said that it would have required a "voice of thunder" for everyone to hear, the organizers were ready with resolutions that stated the handbill's ideas a bit more simply and calmly. The resolutions asserted that it was "the constitutional right and patriotic duty of the Citizens of the United States, to express on every important occasion, the public sense of public measures" and that "the citizens of Philadelphia *in judgment and in feeling*, disapprove the Treaty, and are desirous . . . to prevent its becoming the supreme law of the land." With Dr. William Shippen in the chair, the crowd of some five thousand people was observed to approve the resolutions and "utterly condemn" the treaty with "one Voice and one Mind," John Beckley reported to De Witt Clinton in New York. Then a committee of fifteen—the same number as in Boston and New York—was appointed to craft a more specific memorial against the treaty to be considered at a second meeting in the same place on Saturday, July 25. The committee included a number of prominent Republican and Republican-sympathizing gentlemen, including two congressmen, Pennsylvania Chief Justice Thomas McKean, Secretary of the Commonwealth (and Democratic Society veteran) Alexander J. Dallas, and the city's richest man, Stephen Girard. Perhaps having learned from Hamilton's experiences the previous weekend, Federalists stayed away from the Philadelphia meetings.[65]

The Saturday town meeting was even larger than the first. Bache hoped in the morning *Aurora* that the "whole business will be conducted . . . with the order and decency which ought always to attend the deliberations of the enlightened citizens of the Metropolis of America" (Philadelphia, that is). Whether that was the case would be a matter of great controversy in the weeks to come. Shippen led the huge crowd through the memorial paragraph by paragraph, asking for shows of hands; when one or two men voted against the propositions and the bulk of the crowd, the *Aurora* reported approvingly, "not the least violence was attempted to be offered to this dissenting citizen." Then there were three cheers for Senator Mason, the source of the leaked treaty text, and three more for the Irish patriot Archibald Hamilton Rowan, at that point a refugee living in Philadelphia. Rowan had been introduced by Democratic Society president and fellow Irishman Blair McClenachan, who kept the floor long enough to make another remark that was left out of the official minutes of the meeting published in the *Aurora*. Waving a copy of the treaty in the air, McClenachan declared that he had "one more motion to make to my fellow countrymen, and that is, that you kick this damned treaty to hell." (In other accounts, the line was, "What a damn treaty! I make a motion that every good citizen . . . kick this damn treaty to hell.") With that he threw the copy into the crowd. Some of them later marched through the city with copies of the treaties on poles, and then burned them outside the houses of British envoys George Hammond and Phineas Bond and the mansion of wealthy merchant William Bingham. A disputed number of windows were broken as well.[66]

The Irish presence represented by Rowan and McClenachan was accorded a sinister significance by Federalist observers of the meeting. Federalists deployed some faulty, xenophobic math to calculate that the State House yard could only hold fifteen hundred people, so therefore the crowd must have been composed largely of immigrants fresh off the boat and herded in for the occasion. The attendees were not true Philadelphians at all, they claimed, just the contents of the last two ships to arrive from Ireland, "interspersed with about 50 French Emigrants." Bache disputed the attendance figures, and most other sources agree that the number was more likely over five thousand. The debate over the attendance at the meeting quickly descended into mind-numbing detail, but the serious issue at hand was what the meetings actually showed about the state of public opinion on the treaty. John Fenno and other Federalist editors were eager to show that the attendance at the meeting meant little, especially about what *real* Americans thought, meaning native-born property-owning men, not immigrants or craftsman or laborers or women or children.[67]

Privately several Federalists indicated that they did not actually believe this analysis, but also that they did not necessarily care where popular opinion stood on the treaty. What did concern many Federalists was the threat that a rampant democracy was beginning to pose to their favored government policies and the political power that suited their self-image as "the wise and the good," the country's natural and best possible rulers. For some of the more conservative and depressive Federalists, it seemed like time to throw in the towel on the present form of republicanism altogether. "After all, where is the boasted advantage of a representative system over the turbulent mobocracy of Athens, if the resort to popular meetings is necessary?" George Cabot asked Rufus King. "Faction, and especially the Faction of great towns, always the most powerful, will be too strong for our mild and feeble government."[68]

Most Federalists, however, felt that they and the president still had the people's confidence deep down, that the treaty's popularity might be salvaged to a degree if the progovernment forces could counteract the impressions made by the July demonstrations. Even Cabot was as upset about the "supineness" of the government's friends as he was about the opposition itself. It was generally agreed that the protests had to be answered in some fashion. As a New York Federalist wrote to Massachusetts leader Theodore Sedgwick, the people needed to be "impressed with right notions. The antis will be indefatigable in spreading every thing that may tend to militate against the Government—if so the friends to it ought to be, at least, as industrious to communicate facts to counteract the poison." The push-back would begin immediately, making two political groups actively court the people in the streets, a huge step toward popular party politics.[69]

Now that the bold statement had been made, treaty opponents faced the problem of how to translate the apparently overwhelming public sentiment against the administration's policy into a political force that could actually change it. The treaty had been kicked, but how could the Republicans get it to stay down? For a time, it seemed that the president really might bow to the people's wishes: with the British again seizing American ships, Washington delayed the final ratification of the treaty for much of the summer, considering whether to make a new condition that the ship seizures stop before he signed. Even the most extreme Democratic-Republicans genuinely seemed to hope that Washington would not in the end put himself above public opinion and sign the treaty. "It is not a painful reflection," John Beckley wrote, "that the machinations and intrigues of a British faction in our Country, should place our good old president in the distressing situation of singly opposing himself to the almost unanimous voice of his fellow Citizens . . . and of . . . destroying his own tranquility, peace of mind, good name, and fame? I trust in heaven to enlighten his mind and give him wisdom and firmness to turn away the evil cup."[70]

Such hopes were dashed in early August, partly through timely British interference. Supplied with ambiguous, translated letters from a captured ship, the two most partisan Federalists in the cabinet, Oliver Wolcott and war secretary Timothy Pickering, confronted President Washington with dubious evidence that his new secretary of state Edmund Randolph had requested money from the French for some allegedly sinister purpose. Randolph happened to be the cabinet's last treaty skeptic and last holdout from the party conflict. Though Randolph's guilt was far from conclusively proved, there was enough criticism of the administration in the captured correspondence to prick Washington's thin skin. The president announced he would sign the treaty without conditions and Randolph was forced to resign and try to clear his name. As far as the Washington administration was concerned, the issue was dead. The opposition was not so sure.[71]

FROM MEASURES TO "THAT MAN"
TOWARD THE PRESIDENTIAL
OPTION FOR POLITICAL CHANGE

The Constitution's unfilled blanks allowed the battle against the Jay Treaty to continue even beyond this point of official acceptance. In the minds of treaty opponents, at stake were not only the foreign policy questions, but more importantly the whole popular constitutional tradition to which they thought Americans were heirs. Democratic governance had to be vindicated, public opinion and government policy realigned. "The constitution supposes," declared the Philadelphia *Aurora*, "that the voice of the people ought to govern." If "that voice was competent to decide upon a form of government," then surely it had equal ability to determine how that government operated. This was of course a leap that the real-life Framers had not made, relegating "We the People" to their rhetorical formulation about the source of the authority to establish a Constitution, in the Preamble rather than the main text. Even that was a late, largely undiscussed refinement that was probably aimed more at diminishing the role of the states rather than enhancing the power or participation of the people at large. When the president and Senate were granted power over treaties, "can it be supposed, that it contemplated a treaty which would be ratified by them in opposition to the almost unanimous voice of America!" It could not. That would be "a libel upon the constitution, and upon the people who received it."[1]

On the basis of this reinvented Constitution, the antitreaty campaign proceeded, along two tracks: one in Congress among high Republican officeholders like

James Madison and another "out of doors" in the streets, taverns, and newspapers. The latter track began earlier chronologically and applied more directly to the presidential contest of 1796, so we will turn to it first. The more radical Democratic-Republican activists in Philadelphia, spearheaded by the *Aurora* and its circle, decided that it was high time to take on the man they now considered the chief obstacle to their political hopes, none other than George Washington himself. Expressing and demonstrating public opinion was not going to be enough. They were going to have to change the men if they wanted to change the measures.[2]

THE DEMOCRATIC-REPUBLICAN ATTACK ON THE WASHINGTON CULT

While the upcoming election was still rarely mentioned in the fall of 1795, publicly or privately, the *Aurora*'s attack on Washington's reputation was the real beginning of the presidential campaign. In a number of crucial respects, everything was frozen in place as long as Washington continued occupying his exalted position. Once he had signed the Jay Treaty and purged Edmund Randolph from his cabinet, getting Washington out of the way, physically and politically, became the required first step in fundamentally changing the government's personnel and policy. While there was a general assumption in Philadelphia political circles that the president would retire after his second term, there was no constitutional limitation on the president's stay in office.[3]

The people at large certainly had no idea of Washington quitting, and Federalists aimed to keep it that way as long as possible. Deep into what would be the lame-duck phase of most later presidencies, Washington's friends and political supporters publicly spoke of his administration as an ongoing concern, denying its increasingly divisive, partisan nature and expressing hope that it would continue to guide the nation and the world for many years to come. In the early phases of the Jay Treaty battle, elite Bostonians held an ideologically fence-straddling "Feast of Reason" for Washington's retired secretary of war and long-time aide Henry Knox. Hoping that "republican principles, and federal affections" would continue to distinguish their state, they also toasted their hopes for Washington's continued popularity with the voters: "Perpetual verdure to the true laurel which encircles his brow—THE LOVE OF THE PEOPLE." Nothing could be done openly for any other candidate as long as such sentiments dominated the land. Any potential alternative chief magistrates would be lost against the "perpetual verdure" of Washington's prestige with the people and politicians of the United States. Something had to be done to brown it up a bit.[4]

While the turn against Washington personally was new and noticeable in late August 1795, it built on what had come before. Some of Washington's revolutionary colleagues, especially the jealous John Adams, had worried since the 1780s that the extreme public veneration for the general might someday result in his emergence as a despotic force independent of the people or their legislators. For a whole host of reasons, not least the role that relatively ordinary men like themselves played in politics, Democratic-Republican Society radicals wanted a politics based on ideas rather than leaders—"principles, not men," as the phrase went. Following a particular man was the essence of monarchy, and it was only in a polity where decisions were made by discussion and debate among the people at large, rather than simply within the halls of government and over the dining tables of the wealthy, that self-government could truly be said to exist. Nevertheless, even though the opposition press had already been critical enough to upset the touchy Washington, before late summer 1795 the complaints had largely been limited to satires and oblique comments that dwelled on the monarchical trappings surrounding the president or the possibility that Washington was too easily manipulated by advisors like Hamilton.

The *Aurora* announced that this was about to change in the local leader of its edition for Friday, August 21. (Early American newspapers usually place the material that originated with the editors of that particular journal in a column beginning on page two or three that was labeled with the city and date.) There was no more pretending that Washington was not ultimately responsible for the treaty, and thus had put his own judgment above "the happiness, the liberties, the independence of the people of the United States," argued a piece signed "Hancock." Criticism of the president would now be direct and substantive, even if some considered it "sacrilegious" or "treasonable": "I can no longer persuade myself that any man in a free country . . . is above the strictures of a freeman. We have been guilty of idolatry too long . . . it is high time that we should have no other Gods than one."[5]

The religious language was invective, but not solely. Quite accurately, the radicals felt that Washington's reputation as savior and patriarch of the nation, and the public reverence toward the president that went along with this reputation, were being used to deflect and demonize legitimate criticism of his policies. By exalting Washington's name and exaggerating his role in the Revolution, both the active Federalists and the culture at large made it difficult for anyone to oppose the administration on any issue without seeming unpatriotic and narrowly partisan. Alexander Hamilton indicated the role that Washington's image played in Federalist politics when he later lamented the loss of an "aegis," or shield, that had been "very essential" to his career and agenda. On this, Hamilton actually agreed with his Democratic-Republican critics, one of whom wrote that "the impenetrable shield of Presidential inviolability has been held up to cover [Federalists] from attack." While Washington would have to die before he was actually pictured with choirs of angels, his cult was already well established during his presidency, with his supporters quick to sense a divine presence in all the actions of the man they considered quite literally as God's gift to the country, "THAT MAN, whom God hath honored to be the instrument of countless blessings to this land; whose name will live, whose memory will be recovered, when the blighting eye of malignity is sealed in darkness."[6]

More than florid overpraise, such statements demanded that citizens adopt a reverent and obedient attitude, toward not only Washington but all constituted authority. Crafting their own doctrine of the Divine Right of Presidents, Federalists asserted that God's legatee on Earth, President Washington, would not be mocked or flouted. On the occasion of the day of national thanksgiving that Washington proclaimed for a few days after his birthday in 1795, Harvard divinity professor David Tappan explained to Jedidiah Morse's Charles Town congregation that "Christian thankfulness" contradicted democratic self-assertion. When "the thankful Christian . . . regards and exalts God, he proportionably abases himself. Those persons who do not feel their own dependence, meanness and guilt, but proudly imagine themselves important and meritorious beings, cannot properly see and acknowledge their obligations to the divine bounty." Submission to the "wholesome authority both of God and man" was necessary to restrain Americans from "pursuing the splendid phantom of an undefined, romantic liberty and equality." Luckily, as Tappan saw it, the voters had shown few signs of straying in the elections for "federal rulers" thus far.[7] The Reverend Samuel Stanhope Smith's Thanksgiving and birthday sermon was actually one of the more measured statements of Washington's transcendence, but it still struck the keynote of deference to divine authority, linking Washington's image directly to a rejection of democratic political pressures: "I confess,

The Washington Cult: The Federalists used the public veneration of George Washington to deflect Democratic-Republican criticism of their policies, but after Washington's death, images like this made the veneration literal. (John James Barrelet, Apotheosis of Washington, etching and engraving, 1800–1802, Metropolitan Museum of Art.)

I recognize in this illustrious citizen the immediate hand of heaven." Among Washington's "fortunate assemblage" of traits were "love of the people, yet superiority to popular clamour."[8]

Federalists sincerely believed that theirs was the more Christian party, but the cult of Washington was less about religion than politics, both of the nation-building and the partisan kind. Obedience to God's will and veneration for Washington were all well and good, but what Federalist elites really desired was unquestioning deference to their judgments. Religion itself was optional, at least for nonclerical Federalists. "Reverence and obey, is the maxim now laboured to be established on the public mind," one opposition writer observed accurately. A sentimental sketch published in numerous New England newspapers featured an elderly revolutionary veteran asking the gentleman narrator to explain to him "the reason why we hear so much complaint from *Boston*, and other great towns." In the sketch, the old man fails to understand his interlocutor's brief explanation of the Jay Treaty controversy, but then asks, "eyes swimming with tears of gratitude,"

> "*Is General WASHINGTON in favor of it?*" He is, my friend, cried I.—
> He was again silent for a moment, when putting his hand on mine he said, "If I could revisit earth after I had been dead for years, and should hear any public question agitated, which involved the great interests of my country, the first question I should ask, would be, "Is GEORGE WASHINGTON alive? If he was, I would next inquire if he approved it; and if he did, I should retire in peace to my grave."

This trusting old codger was the Federalists' idea of a perfect citizen, embodying precisely the submissive attitude that the Washington cult sought to instill.[9]

The Philadelphia *Aurora* and its writers tried to encourage a different approach. The Washington cult had helped make the treaty issue hang "in awful suspence, on the will of ONE MAN," and once his decision was made, sought to "hurry us to the brink of despair" about what further the people could do. "Despair! *Shall Freemen despair?*" a writer calling himself "Valerius" thundered. The message was that they should not. Dire things awaited any individual who tried to put his personal will over a whole people or nation. Any one man, no matter how well respected, would find his voice "lost in the tempest of popular fury" if he tried to raise it too high. "Believe me, sir, your fellow citizens are not mere moulds of wax, calculated to receive any impression which the *dicta* of a magistrate may attempt to make upon them," promised "Belisarius." The people were roused now, and it was impossible "for the American people to unthink what they have thought, to unlearn what they have learnt, or to recede from the principles of freedom."[10]

The key news peg of the early attacks was the dismissive way Washington had replied to the antitreaty resolutions that were generated by the July town meetings. Addressing a short reply to the Boston committee and then simply forwarding the same letter to the other cities, Washington had refused to engage any of the protestors' arguments and flatly asserted his and the Senate's constitutional right to make the decision, without being influenced by "the opinions of others, or [seeking] truth through any channel but that of a temperate and well-informed investigation." The president asked citizens angry over the treaty to simply trust in his wisdom and commitment to the common good: "In every act of my administration, I have sought the happiness of my fellow citizens. My system for the attainment of this object has uniformly been to overlook all personal, local, and partial considerations; to contemplate the United States as one great whole; to confide, that sudden impressions, when erroneous, would yield to candid reflection; and to consult only the substantial and permanent interests of our country." Washington's ostentatiously above-politics pose contained a backhanded political message, "insinuating" to the petitioners, observed the *Aurora*, that *they* had consulted only their narrow and fleeting interests rather than the substantial and permanent ones of their country. The suggestion was that critics were not concerned citizens but predatory political enemies who were owed no explanations.[11]

Finally unleashed, Democratic-Republicans spared few words or metaphors in retaliating for Washington's dismissive attitude. Reaching for the rhetoric of orientalism and sexual degradation that early Americans so often used to express their fears of political dependence or submission, *Aurora* writers claimed Washington had conducted himself as if he "was the omnipotent director of a seraglio" rather than "first magistrate of a free people": instead of being seen "as the father of his country, we behold in [Washington] a master," or perhaps just a very bad, threatening father. "Pittachus," reversing the usual metaphor, wondered if Americans had not "spoiled their president, as a too indulgent parent spoils its child."[12]

The bad father, the oriental despot, the lustful demigod, the "Roman Church," and virtually every other metaphor for autocracy available was deployed in small items and lengthy essay series—actually a series of series, under different pseudonyms—that launched over that late August weekend and would continue with varying degrees of intensity until slightly after Washington left office in 1797. Besides the nationally circulating *Aurora*, the main venue for these critiques was the small network of newspapers around the country that copied from it, and vice versa. The plan was to desanctify Washington's hallowed name: "As he has treated us with disrespect, he must expect to be no longer viewed as a saint, as he has spoken daggers to [our] feelings, he must no longer expect a blind devotion to his will." It was not easy for even pseudonymous writers to face down a god. They had to continually reassure readers and likely themselves that doubting Washington was permissible. The essays built up rather gingerly toward serious questioning of competence and character, devoting much more space to standard arguments against the Jay Treaty and repetitious complaints that Washington was simply bent on betraying the French alliance.[13]

One purpose of the welter of pseudonyms attached to the anti-Washington essays, besides giving the impression that they came from a legion of different writers, was an attempt to give them distinct themes based on the particular pseudonym used. Several of the more interesting and prominent series tried to reclaim the high ground of patriotism by invoking other figures from classical antiquity, or the literary version of it Americans knew in the 1790s, that might counteract Cincinnatus. "Valerius" was a reference to Publius Valerius Publicola, also the source of the *Federalist Papers*' pseudonym, Publius. General Valerius helped found the Roman Republic, but afterward took the advice that the Democratic-Republicans were urging on Washington and gave up his quasi-monarchical prerogatives in the face of public opinion. Criticized for building a fortress-like palace on a Roman hill, Valerius had the building torn down as a sign "that the majesty and power of the people were greater than that of the consul."[14]

Another prominent series was named after the great Byzantine general Belisarius. At the end of his life, Belisarius had supposedly been reduced to beggary, his eyes put out by an ungrateful emperor, but stayed loyal to Roman ideals despite it all. The legend of Belisarius was retold many times in eighteenth-century literature, including in one of Thomas Jefferson's favorite novels, *Bélisaire*, by the French historian and Encyclopedist Jean Francois Marmontel, and in a tragedy by Margaretta V. Faugeres that had just been published in New York. Marmontel's version had the blind but still patriotic Belisarius inspiring his listeners with political maxims that were highly applicable to the politics of the 1790s, such as: "There is no absolute power except that of the laws, and he who aims at despotism enslaves himself."[15]

In keeping with this sentiment, "Belisarius" the newspaper writer expatiated on Washington's perceived devotion to "the odious principle of a distinction between the people and their Executive servants, as manifested in the mock pageantry of monarchy, and the apish mimickry of Kingship." The series began with an "index" of Washington's top twenty policy missteps and constitutional infractions, all revolving around this theme. From there the series moved to other examples of the Washington administration's "moral and political turpitude." The first "Belisarius" article amounted to one of the earliest presidential campaign statements to ask voters whether they were better off than they were four or eight years earlier. The writer's conclusion was a bit tougher than a modern campaign commercial: "The stern . . . unerring voice of posterity, will not fail to render the just sentence of condemnation on the man who has entailed upon his country deep and incurable public evils." Clearly "the name of Washington" would inexorably "descend . . . to oblivion."[16]

Over time the attacks moved past Washington's presidency to include his revolutionary record. A writer calling himself "Portius" applied some rather sound historical reasoning to the question of whether it was right to give Washington so much credit for the Americans' success during the war. "Portius" explained the way that Washington had come to symbolize the "protecting providence" Americans believed had allowed their new nation to survive the war. Washington was the country's good luck charm, in effect, and his name became suffused with the gratitude Americans felt about their victory, to the point that many believed that it was to Washington "alone that they were indebted for liberty." Testing that hypothesis, "Portius" reviewed the key events and factors that allowed the United States to gain its independence and asked, "how many were the immediate consequences of your abilities and exertions?" The capture of Burgoyne's army at Saratoga, the diplomacy that brought about the French alliance and forced the British to open other fronts overseas, Nathaniel Greene's southern campaigns, the role of the militia (which Washington famously detested)—Washington was peripheral or uninvolved in all of these. Even the one major battlefield victory for which he was commander, Yorktown, could never have happened without the French fleet. (Other writers later expanded these relatively measured arguments into more generalized questions about Washington's competence as a military leader.) The careful historical argumentation in the "Portius" essays was eclipsed, however, by what became one of the anti-Washington campaign's most infamous pull quotes, in which Washington was asked "to point out ONE SINGLE ACT which *unequivocally* proves you a FRIEND to the INDEPENDENCE OF AMERICA."[17]

Such rhetoric was perhaps too outrageous and counterintuitive to be very effective. Even some newspapers generally sympathetic to the opposition, such as the *New-Jersey Journal*, objected. While the attacks on Washington brought the expected howls of outrage from the Federalist press, high Federalist leaders like Alexander Hamilton did not seem to regard them as a serious threat until the charges took a less sweeping and more concrete form. This happened with the debut of the "Calm Observer" series in late October 1795, as the *Aurora*'s campaign was moving into its third month.[18]

The series was written by John Beckley, a longtime Virginia follower of Jefferson, Madison, and Edmund Randolph who had been brought up from Richmond to administer the House of Representatives (as its clerk) when the new government started in 1789. A poor London boy sent to Virginia as an indentured servant just before the Revolution, Beckley found the lively, egalitarian atmosphere of Philadelphia's streets and taverns exhilarating after rural, class-bound Virginia and became deeply embroiled in transatlantic radical politics. While not a formal member of the Democratic Society of Pennsylvania, he was a close personal and ideological associate of its leaders in all their political projects and one of the main conduits between the street-level radicals, the opposition leaders in Congress, and Thomas Jefferson himself. Beckley employed the resources of his office to aid the antiadministration forces whenever possible, cataloguing the bank stockholders and financial speculators who voted for Hamilton's program in Congress and keeping copies of a secret congressional investigation of Hamilton to use at a later time. (Based partly on Beckley's discoveries, a committee made up of James Monroe and two other members looked into allegations that Hamilton was illicitly paying an agent, James Reynolds, to buy up government securities based on inside information. Hamilton admitted to the committee that he was paying Reynolds, but for blackmail rather than inside information; the treasury secretary was sleeping with Reynolds's wife. The committee agreed to seal Hamilton's "precious confessions," a deal Beckley honored until Federalists voted him out as House clerk in 1797.)[19]

The "Calm Observer" put Beckley's inside knowledge to the service of his radicalism. Fervently believing that "equal liberty is our birthright," and, with Paine, that the Revolution had allowed Americans to be the first common people on Earth to claim that birth-right, Beckley was thoroughly disgusted with the Federalist project of raising Washington and the presidency above all other citizens and public officials. Like other members of the opposition, Beckley wanted to puncture the president's façade of Roman virtue, but he had better sources than most others and managed to catch the fastidious president in a financial scandal. As part of his Cincinnatian stance, Washington had very publicly refused to accept his presidential salary, asking only to be reimbursed for his official expenses. In the treasury accounts, Beckley discovered that in fact Washington had been allowed to overdraw the amount of his salary by more than $6,000, and even get advances on it, in the name of paying his expenses. In other words, Washington was doing better than he would have if he *had* accepted a salary. Elaborately documenting this revelation was the essence of the "Calm Observer" series. It is hard to begrudge Washington these funds from a modern perspective—he was actually paying many of his own presidential expenses—but it did bring his high-flown reputation back a little closer to earth.[20]

While factually presented, the tone of the essays did not always live up to the "Calm" pseudonym. Beckley predicted that "in vain will be all future precautions of the Legislature . . . if one man can exalt himself above the law and . . . disregard those high restraints which the people have ordained." In particular the clerk condemned the special allowances made for Washington for their unfairness, not only to the people, but also to other public servants: "Is there any other man in the government of the United States who would have dared to ask, or to whom [Hamilton and his successor Oliver Wolcott] would have presumed to grant the like favour?" The most incendiary line was saved for the closing of the opening essay. It placed the Father of the Country in the same sentence with two great villains of republican thought: "Will not the world be led to conclude that the mask of political hypocrisy has been alike worn by a CESAR, a CROMWELL, and a WASHINGTON?"[21]

Whether because the charge was new or so thoroughly proved or because it involved his own integrity, Alexander Hamilton and his followers in Washington's cabinet reacted immediately to the "Calm Observer."

For the first time since the *Aurora* attacks began, they went into damage control mode and prepared direct responses. Angry and worried over "the villany [*sic*] of the suggestion against the President," Treasury Secretary Oliver Wolcott Jr. pumped out two replies in three days, both of which the *Aurora* published with further rejoinders from Beckley. Wolcott took the lawyerly position that the president's private secretaries had made the requests, making the president "merely accountable in a pecuniary view for the act of his agent; as a matter affecting personal character he is in no manner concerned." Wolcott denied any illegal disbursements but took "responsibility for whatever is complained of" on himself, in the now time-honored fashion of presidential aides.[22]

Thrown back on their heels by the addition of real data to the Republican attack on Washington, Federalist editors were unable to do much more than impugn the putative source of the charges, or make the inaccurate claim that all high officials got salary advances. Noah Webster of the New York *Minerva* was rattled, opening his attempted reply with an admission that the "Calm Observer's" charges were "of a high nature and demand notice," while privately warning Wolcott that merely "*being* upright" was not enough: administration officials needed to follow the law so strictly "as to prevent even spurious accusations," that is, to avoid even the appearance of wrongdoing. Major Russell of the *Columbian Centinel* was reduced to reexaggerating the Washington cult, reminding readers that the "Calm Observer" had assaulted "their beloved WASHINGTON— a Man, who for 21 years has scarcely known what money was."[23]

Once again, Alexander Hamilton tried riding to the rescue of the Federalist press and his old administration. He wrote to Washington as soon as he saw Beckley's first essay, advising that an explanation was required and saying, "I mean to give one with my name." The rare act of signing a major statesman's own name to a newspaper publication suggests the gravity he attached to the accusation. To Wolcott, Hamilton sent three notes in three days, requesting documents "*as soon as possible*" to assist the project. Two weeks later, in between the twenty-second and twenty-third installments of his sprawling, pseudonymous series on the Jay Treaty ("The Defence"), the energetic Hamilton published an "Explanation" of Washington's expense account in the New York *Daily Advertiser* that runs twenty-six closely printed pages in the modern edition of Hamilton's writings. While clearing the president of intentional wrongdoing and working the figures to show that the government actually owed Washington $846 at that moment, Hamilton and Wolcott could not disprove what the records clearly showed: large advances for most of Washington's presidency.[24]

Having finally drawn some visible blood, the *Aurora* rolled the attacks on Washington into the larger critique of his administration's policies and succinctly summarized it all in a widely reprinted item entitled the "Political Creed of 1795." The creed first appeared on November 23. Its fifteen numbered points covered everything from Hamilton's excise tax and bank to the Jay Treaty debates, depicting it all as an effort to create a "kingly government" if not a literal monarchy:

1. I believe in God Almighty as the only Being infallible. . . .
3. I believe that national Banks are . . . dangerous in a free country. . . .
6. I believe that a little smiling, flattering adventurer [Hamilton], was once placed at the head of a Treasury, because he had contended for a monarchy over a free people. . . .
11. I believe that honest government requires no secrets, and that secret proceedings [like the Senate debates on the Jay Treaty] are secret attempts to cheat the governed. . . .
13. I believe it the duty of every freeman to watch over the conduct of every man who is entrusted with his freedom.
14. I believe that a blind confidence in any men who have done services to their country, has enslaved, and ever will enslave, all the nations of the earth.
15. I believe that a good joiner may be a clumsy watch-maker; that an able carpenter may be a blundering taylor; and that a good General may be a most miserable politician.[25]

Political parties barely existed on an institutional level, but here was the Democratic-Republican opposition's basic belief system, as applied to current issues, put into a catechistic form that would help readers memorize the key points or keep them in their pocket. Eighteenth-century partisans groping toward the notion of party ideologies and platforms not infrequently adapted devices borrowed from religious teaching: catechisms, creeds, dialogues, and parables. Theology may have been the closest thing to party ideology that partisans could find at this early stage of political development. Bache seems to have picked up the idea from Federalist satires criticizing "Jacobin" extremism, part of the continual back and forth in which each side tried to associate the other with despotism and bigotry. The natural way for Enlightenment-influenced

Protestants to do this was in terms of religious language and imagery, especially of the caricatured Catholic variety.[26]

Though many readers then and since have recoiled from the *Aurora's* anti-Washington rhetoric and wondered how Bache could possibly have believed that such tactics would be effective, the appearance of the "Political Creed of 1795" just in time for the presidential election year suggests the practical political purpose of the attacks: trying to drive the proud but sensitive Washington out of office by making it too painful to stay on the public scene. A late entrant in the pseudonymous barrage, "Scipio," suggested that only an "immediate resignation" could save both the country and Washington's reputation: "The heavy charges of vanity, ambition, and intrigue, might then lose some proportion of their force—your friends might say, behold the man . . . he no longer wishes to govern others, but is among the governed." Immediate resignation was never going to happen, but the criticism had some of its intended effect. "The Turpitude of the Jacobins touches him more nearly than he owns in Words," Vice President John Adams believed. When the president finally made his retirement decision the following spring, the wounds given by the *Aurora* and other newspapers were among the factors he cited.[27]

The more immediate impact of the attacks was the way they emboldened his congressional opponents. In the wake of the *Aurora* assaults, Republicans in Congress found presidential prestige a less forbidding obstacle to voting their consciences than they had in the past. In February 1795, only thirteen members of the House had dared to oppose the traditional half-hour recess in honor of the president's birthday, but in 1796 the motion was defeated, fifty votes to thirty-eight.[28]

HOUSE OF CARDS: THE POPULAR BRANCH CHALLENGES THE TREATY POWER

The focus of opposition efforts moved to another track, congressional action in the House of Representatives, when the Fourth Congress finally convened in December. It had been a long time politically since the tax unrest of late 1794, when the last congressional elections were held—during the eighteenth and nineteenth centuries, a new Congress convened a full year after its election—but Republicans hoped that the seemingly strong House majority elected back then would continue to stand firm against the Jay Treaty. (Without official party labels or formal party organization in Congress, there was always a little uncertainty until floor votes began.) Convinced that the tide of public opinion was with them, the more radical and rambunctious elements of the opposition were spoiling to show their strength. Casting the House of Representatives as the all-powerful voice of the people because it alone was popularly elected, an *Aurora* writer warned President Washington that if he tried to oppose the House majority on "the serious question, as to the powers of Congress to regulate our Commerce," it would "consume" his political standing, which would "then be buried on Mount Vernon."[29]

The opposition's de facto leader in the House of Representatives, James Madison, was not nearly as certain of himself as some of his allies in the press. Morally and politically, there were serious arguments to be made against the insulation of the treaty power from the people's direct representatives, but constitutionally, the ground was much softer. "There is pretty certainly a majority agst. the Treaty on its merits," Madison mused to Jefferson, but "there is a real obscurity in the constitutional part of the question, and a diversity of sincere opinions about it." As one of the primary Framers of the Constitution, Madison knew from direct experience that the document did not give the House of Representatives any clear role in the treaty-making process. Indeed, according to the existing record of the Philadelphia Convention's debates, the question there was whether even the *Senate* ought get a role in treaty-making, with many of Madison's then allies arguing that that power should belong to the president alone. Genuine popular influence over foreign policy was not even on the table. Hence there was some cognitive dissonance for Madison that probably reduced his effectiveness as opposition floor leader of the House. These later stages of the Jay Treaty debate tied Madison in intellectual knots that saw him "reconsider fundamental premises of his theory of government," as constitutional historian Jack Rakove puts it. Ridiculed for his reticence to talk about the Philadelphia Convention's debates, Madison was reduced to claiming that die-hard Antifederalist critics of the Constitution actually provided the best evidence of the document's original intent, even though, as Rakove drily notes, "the opposite inference was more logical." Madison's logic was that the Constitution's original meaning was best expressed by the elected conventions that ratified it, because they represented the people who were the document's true authors, in a broad, philosophical sense. ("Authorizers" might capture the people's relationship with the constitutional process a little more accurately.) This move allowed the citation of material from the ratification debates that supported some role in foreign policy for the popular branch of government, though awkwardly much of that material came from opponents of the document.[30]

The hook for any effort to stop the Jay Treaty in the House lay in that body's constitutional power to originate money bills. To set up certain commissions required by the treaty, $90,000 in appropriations was needed, so theoretically the House could block the treaty by refusing to fund its implementation. This was a fragile reed made more fragile by the fact that the strategy could not be fully employed until after the president actually requested the necessary appropriations. Thus Washington and his advisors were able to keep the antitreaty forces off balance throughout the winter of 1795–1796 through simple inaction. By holding off on any formal presentation of the ratified treaty to Congress until all the necessary papers arrived from Great Britain, the administration put the House Democratic-Republicans in the position of having to make any early response to the treaty in the form of some direct remonstrance to the president. Far from comfortable with *Aurora*'s approach, Madison quailed at this step of bringing Washington "personally into the question," and looked desperately for ways of "disentangling" the treaty question from Washington's personal prestige. "The situation is truly perplexing," he fretted to Jefferson. After an abortive attempt to respond to the president's speech at the opening of Congress, Madison settled into a pattern of making excuses to his allies and waiting for the formal treaty to be presented.[31]

Younger Republicans emboldened by the *Aurora* attacks grew increasingly impatient, however, and eventually shook off Madison's restraints. New York freshman Edward Livingston was the first congressman to publicly pick the fight. "Beau Ned" was the baby brother in an illustrious political family that owned a vast estate in the Hudson Valley. It was Ned and his brothers who had scrapped with Alexander Hamilton during the New York Jay Treaty demonstrations. Though the Livingstons came as close to embodying a genuine aristocracy as any set of politicians in the United States, they had recently made common cause with the Democratic-Republicans because of their rivalry with the competing manorial family headed by Hamilton's father-in-law, Philip Schuyler. A flamboyant dresser and speaker, Edward Livingston had had little success in politics until he joined up with the artisans and middle-class activists of the New York City Democratic and Tammany Societies. As their "uniform assertor of the Rights of Man," Livingston had been swept into Congress during the tumult of 1794, but because of the slow-moving congressional schedule of this period, he had not yet been able to do anything with his office until the new Congress met in December 1795. By that time, he was already facing reelection in a few months. In February 1796, Livingston successfully pushed legislation to aid American seamen impressed into British service, an effort that garnered him significant exposure in newspapers across the country. Still, he chafed at the "lukewarm patriotism" and indecisiveness of Madison's leadership on the supreme issue of the day, the Jay Treaty.[32]

When Washington announced that the treaty was in effect on March 1, without asking for the appropriations, Edward Livingston was more than ready. He rose on the floor March 2 without Madison's permission and proposed resolutions demanding that President Washington turn over copies of John Jay's diplomatic instructions and other correspondence and documents related to the negotiations. Treaty opponents had long intimated that there was something corrupt in the negotiations. Madison reeled at Beau Ned's rashness and promised Jefferson he would get the resolutions dropped. On the floor the next day, Livingston expressed the "highest respect" for Madison's opinions, but would only "meet [his] suggestions" by softening the resolution slightly to exempt any sensitive papers related to pending negotiations.[33]

With Livingston's resolutions on the floor, a month-long debate broke out that went to the heart of critical but unanswered constitutional questions about the relationship of the executive and legislative branches. If they had succeeded, Livingston and his supporters would have effectively rewritten the Constitution, or rather, filled in the Constitution's blanks very differently, establishing a degree of popular control over foreign policy. Printed widely in the newspapers, the debates were an education for many observers. A New Jersey newspaper commented that Americans should study them, "as they tend to explain the constitution, and accurately mark out the powers of the different branches of government." Unfortunately, the discoveries were not always happy ones.[34]

It is crucial to understand that Americans of the 1790s not only disagreed about what the Constitution meant, but also differed on its most basic operations. In particular, there was no agreement on the means of constitutional interpretation and enforcement. This has become more or less the exclusive province of the federal judiciary, especially the Supreme Court, but the options were still wide open in the 1790s. Many of the major Founders, including the man credited as the Father of the

Constitution, James Madison, assumed that constitutional interpretation would be performed by the Congress, the states, and the people as well as the courts. Any of these bodies could and should act if its rights and prerogatives were infringed or if the federal government grossly violated the Constitution's provisions in any other way. This view accorded well with the larger British constitutional tradition, in which the constitution was an unwritten set of customary rules and procedures that had evolved out of the political process itself and could change in the face of new historical pressures and trends. With no written text, the British constitution could more easily embrace a much wider variety of political activities than the written American one could. In the unreformed British system with only virtual representation and almost no avenue for formal input from the people themselves, riots and other forms of political violence could, in effect, be seen as the people's constitutional voice.[35]

Following the pattern set by Hamilton in the earliest days of the new government, Federalists moved aggressively to establish their more top-down view of constitutionalism as soon as the House's move against the Jay Treaty started to materialize. House Federalists voted in caucus for a full-court press against Livingston's resolution and pushed the debate immediately onto constitutional grounds, before the Republicans had even begun to mount a constitutional argument of their own. Following the debate from Connecticut, Treasury Secretary Wolcott's father was like many conservative Federalists in welcoming the test of the House's constitutional powers, but fearing the consequences:

I hope that the session of Congress will be continued until it shall be indubitably ascertained whether there is a latent constitutional power in some part of Congress, which can defeat a national treaty made by a power especially constituted for the purpose. . . . and which has also become the supreme law of the land. The full discovery of such a lurking power, if any such exists, will be a desideratum which the publick have a right to be gratified with the full view of it; and indeed the nations of the world have a right to know . . . of such a rare curiosity, that . . . they may govern themselves accordingly.[36]

The unknown factor was just what response this constitutional debate would meet in the broader spectrum of opinion, among politicians and the voters at large. The Federalists' relatively narrow, executive-centered vision of constitutional enforcement was not the one that most Americans had known or practiced so far.

Edward Livingston and the bolder spirits among the House Republicans were convinced that their more democratic vision of the Constitution was the one that would naturally win wider support. As the people's only elected representatives in the federal government, the House had the right to request whatever information it needed that "would tend to elucidate the conduct of the [government's officers]." It was by the same theory that the power to impeach rested with the House: "The House were on every occasion, the guardians of their country's rights. They are, by the Constitution, the accusing organ of the officers employed. The information called for they ought to possess." There was also some reason to hope that, if there really was nothing suspicious in the papers, that Washington might actually release them. No clear precedents had yet been set on the issue of what would later be called "executive privilege." Congress had already investigated the executive branch on several occasions, and Washington had already shared information, but in the previous cases, most of the details had been worked out informally.[37]

Instead, much to the shock of James Madison, the Federalists took a strong stand in favor of autonomous, unitary executive authority. Congressional Federalists denied that the House, or by extension the people, had the sort of supervisory relationship with the presidency that the Republicans envisioned except in the most rare and extreme circumstances. Unless there were an actual impeachment proceeding, Federalists contended, it was improper for the House to demand any information from the president that he did not want to share voluntarily. Arguing against the president's initial inclination to go along with the request, Alexander Hamilton (still Washington's most trusted adviser even as a private citizen practicing law in New York), along with the more partisan members of the cabinet, convinced Washington to stonewall the House request completely, for fear of making the administration look weak and submissive toward the British and the opposition both. Hamilton and the new secretary of state, Timothy Pickering, among others, wrote long memos that shaped the intransigent response to the House Washington eventually made.[38]

Washington's official statement, dated March 30, refused to provide any documents or give a substantive explanation for not supplying them. Instead, Washington asserted his total discretion to provide the House with only such information as he, the president, deemed appropriate. While Hamilton, Pickering, and Washington justified this in terms of protecting the president and Senate's exclusive jurisdiction over foreign policy, their statement made the far more sweeping claim, necessary to support total rejection of the House's request, that the executive branch was to be the only judge of its own actions and limitations in any case short of a full impeachment process. The people's representatives simply could not be trusted with sensitive information, even though the president's *former* cabinet secretaries apparently could. The executive's double standard regarding supposed state secrets was revealed when Washington decided unilaterally to violate the agreement made at the Federal Convention in 1787 and quote from that body's still-sequestered records to buttress his constitutional arguments. Presaging future presidential claims to near-absolute authority over information about all the executive's deliberations and operations, even in areas clearly shared with the legislative branch, Washington cast his refusal to share the treaty records as a simple matter of preserving "the boundaries fixed by the constitution between the different departments." The popular branch had no right to even ask for information about treaties, much less approve them.[39]

Though the Framer in him still harbored real concerns that the House might be infringing on the constitutional powers of the presidency, Madison was genuinely surprised at Washington's flat rejection of the House request. It "was as unexpected, as the tone & tenor of the message, are improper & indelicate," he sputtered to Jefferson. Indeed, Washington's dismissive attitude presented more serious constitutional problems for Madison than withholding a few documents, since it more than implied that the government's one popularly elected body was not only not coequal, but possibly subordinate to the other, indirectly elected ones. The House oppositionists had really only expected partial compliance, Madison informed James Monroe, who was in France, but Washington "not only ran into the extreme of an absolute refusal, but assigned reasons worse than the refusal itself." Finally galvanized into action by this bald assertion of presidential prerogative, Madison (likely with John Beckley's help) called together a historic meeting of the Democratic-Republican members of Congress that took place on the evening of April 2, the opposition party's first formal caucus. Though presidential politics may have been discussed on the sidelines, the major thrust of the meeting was planning a united strategy against the treaty in the wake of Washington's noncooperation. While no record of the discussions was kept, the caucus voted to block the treaty appropriations, and Thomas Blount of North Carolina introduced resolutions on

April 6 that embodied the decision and became the basis for the rest of the debates. "I *fear* that the B[ritish] Treaty will be carried into effect," wrote John Beckley, vowing that it would "not, however, without some vote asserting the Constitutional power of the House."[40]

The presidential election only peeked around the edges of the treaty debate. Both sides were sincerely focused on the treaty and the larger issues it raised, but each suspected the other side of having more sordid and small-minded political schemes afoot aimed chiefly at grabbing national power for themselves. To the Virginians leading the congressional opposition, Washington's response to the House was a last desperate stroke to keep power. James Madison was certain that the refusal had been "contrived in New York" and conjectured self-servingly that Hamilton "had seen that if the rising force of the republicans was not crushed it must speedily crush the British party and that the only hope of success lay in forcing an open rupture with the president." In fact, Hamilton was much more absorbed with vindicating his own policies and theories than winning votes for a party or candidate.[41] For their part, many Federalists were convinced that everything the opposition did evinced "their electioneering zeal for Jefferson." But while Madison and his close allies were indeed planning to "push" Jefferson forward for president at some point, the bulk of their efforts in April 1796 were bent toward winning the grand congressional war that was just reaching its climax.[42]

SEIZING THE PUBLIC OPINION: THE FEDERALIST COUNTERATTACK

As it turned out, the great constitutional stand that Madison and Beckley expected would never quite be made. The force of more ordinary political concerns threw it off balance. Then an extraordinary Federalist counterattack, orchestrated by Alexander Hamilton in one of his few successful forays into popular politics, knocked the opposition flat. In close contact with Senator Rufus King and other Federalists at the seat of government, Hamilton swung into action as soon as he learned of the April 2 Republican caucus. "A most important crisis ensues. Great evils may result unless good men play their cards well & with great promptitude and decision," he wrote King, laying out a strategy. Part of Hamilton's plan concerned the moves that could be made to save the treaty even if the House vote was lost. More importantly for our purposes, he suggested a highly public campaign in which Federalists would generate support for the treaty outside of Congress, or at least evidence of support: "For we must seize and carry along with us the public opinion." The key was to build on the Federalists' strong base among wealthy merchants and financiers in the cities and towns of the Northeast. Merchants were "to meet in the Cities & second by their resolutions the measures of the President & Senate" and ask their "fellow Citizens to cooperate with them." Speed and "an imposing attitude" were "indispensable" to the success of the plan, the former treasury secretary lectured. Though not always at his best in the popular political arena, Hamilton traded in his policy memos, legal briefs, and philosophical essays for a remarkably terse and effective political message in these last weeks of April 1796, framing the issue as a stark choice facing both politicians and the people: "The truth most assuredly is, Fellow Citizens, that the CONSTITUTION and PEACE are in one scale—the overthrow of the CONSTITUTION and WAR in the other," he wrote in a short address that keyed the Federalist counterattack. "Which do you prefer?"[43]

More and more, it was this prediction of war and an accompanying economic collapse that became the Federalists' most crucial and devastating argument. The conceit was that if the Jay Treaty was rejected, Great Britain would go to war in retaliation, keeping the western forts and sending waves of Indian allies in to raid the American settlements.

On a more practical level, Federalists engineered a sudden barrage of petitions in favor of the treaty, designed to show that public opinion had decisively shifted and crush the resolve of wavering Republicans who had voted for the Livingston resolution. Federalists had been occasionally holding meetings and signing counterpetitions in favor of the treaty since the late summer of 1795, but there had been nothing like the frenetic activity of April 1796. On the same day Hamilton's letter was written, the "Merchants and Traders" of Philadelphia gathered at the city's elite Coffee House and drew up a memorial asking the House of Representatives to preserve "the faith, the honor, and the interest of the nation" as well as the "peace, on which the prosperity of this country depends," by approving the Jay Treaty appropriations. A committee of correspondence was then formed to transmit the memorial to the merchants of other towns.[44]

The Philadelphia committee was led by recently defeated Federalist congressman Thomas Fitzsimons, a merchant who also was a bank director, an insurance company head, and the Chamber of Commerce president. Men like Fitzsimons necessarily had extensive networks of business contacts, many of whom were dependent or heavily involved with them financially. Through these networks, along with other city institutions that merchants and financiers tended to control, it was a simple matter to call public meetings, have the petitions drawn up, and then collect large numbers of signatures from people who wanted to maintain the instigators' commercial goodwill.

The Philadelphia committee used its business contacts to spread the memorial up and down the United States. Merchants in Frederick-Town, Maryland, called a similar meeting at Fitzsimons's request the following week, pressuring an otherwise opposition-sympathizing Republican congressman, Thomas Sprigg, to support them. Printed copies of the Philadelphia memorial with blanks for the town name and signers turned up as far away as Boston, making the Philadelphia committee's effort an early version of the modern political practice known as "astroturfing," in which a welling of grassroots support is simulated by means of preprinted cards and letters to be sent to Congress from distant locations. A Rhode Island Federalist wrote home with a report of the Philadelphia merchants' meeting, and by the time his letter was printed a week later, Providence merchants had already had a similar meeting of their own.[45]

In another Philadelphia sally south across the Mason-Dixon, war secretary, Baltimore merchant, and budding Hamilton factotum James McHenry followed his chief's instructions and sent a draft petition to his allies back home. McHenry and Hamilton's draft not only supported the treaty but also formally instructed Republican merchant-congressman Samuel Smith to vote for it. McHenry suggested that the petition be circulated secretly so that Smith, who had a large, rough-hewn following among the city's sailors, laborers, and artisans, would not have time to counteract it. Baltimore Federalists neglected the secrecy suggestion and advertised their protreaty petition in the newspapers. Made available at the offices of a local insurance concern, it attracted six hundred signatures in a few days. Only then did Baltimore merchants dare to hold their meeting. It turned out to be surprisingly well attended, especially compared to a countermeeting of Baltimore's "Manufacturers and Mechanics" (Republican-leaning followers of Samuel Smith) the next day. Though hyped by the Republicans as prospectively the largest political gathering ever held in the city, the antitreaty meeting turned out to be sparsely attended, by a largely uncommitted crowd. Meeting turnouts were about the hardest evidence of the state of public opinion that anyone had in 1796, so with "Washington & Peace" being the slogan "in every Street of the Town," even the indefatigable Smith gave in to the pressure and changed his vote.[46]

By April 25, the Philadelphia Federalist plan was in operation even in Richmond, Virginia, the capital of Jefferson's commonwealth. Local Federalist leader John Marshall, the future chief justice, debated Alexander Campbell on the treaty, "concluding every third sentence with the horrors of war," according to an observer. The meeting concluded with the crowd narrowly approving a protreaty resolution. A minority of the meeting immediately drew up a counterresolution, but it was an impressive Federalist showing for a landlocked town where many of the leading citizens were vociferous Republicans.[47]

Naturally, Hamilton and the Federalists were particularly aggressive in the mastermind's own swing-state backyard. On April 19, New York's merchants met at the Tontine Coffee House and decried, in words that Hamilton probably wrote, the "very extensive and complicated evils" that would result from rejecting the treaty. As in Philadelphia, "unexampled unanimity" was the order of the day. Hundreds of copies were printed and circulated, and within a few days the New York petition had 3,200 signatures, only a little short of the highest vote total ever recorded in the city, "*on both sides*," Hamilton claimed. Republicans organized an outdoor countermeeting of disputed size, but many of the more prominent artisans seem to have stayed away. Hamilton himself may have helped curb the turnout with a blistering preemptive broadside that appealed to fear, pride, and greed all at once, with a regional accent: "Do not second the ambition of a VIRGINIAN FACTION . . . sacrificing very essential Interests of the State of New York." The sentiment was widely enough shared that treaty archfoe Edward Livingston, who represented the city, felt constrained to present the House with two conflicting sets of resolutions from his constituents.[48]

The protreaty forces made an even stronger showing upstate. In Albany, General Philip Schuyler, one of the state's richest men, waited for word from the city, then convened forty citizens, approved a nearly identical petition, had copies printed, and sent them each with a signed cover letter to town clerks in the surrounding communities. These public officials were asked to help gather signatures, and apparently they did, Republicans signing along with Federalists. Further west in Otsego County, would-be land baron and Federalist congressman William Cooper reportedly gathered more than five thousand signatures in favor of the treaty, with only ten men willing to stand against it. That number of signers seems exaggerated, but there was no doubt that the New York frontier, with the British army and the Iroquois next door, wanted the treaty to go through.[49]

Undoubtedly the most strenuous protreaty efforts were made in Massachusetts, the most partisan Federalist state and not incidentally the one most tied to trade with the British Empire. Irritated by the loud but outnumbered Republican opposition based around the *Independent Chronicle* newspaper, Boston Federalists went all out. They gathered 1,323 signatures to the Philadelphia memorial and gained a 30-to-1 vote in favor of it at what Benjamin Russell's *Columbian Centinel* claimed was the largest "Town-Meeting" ever held in Massachusetts, with "not less than 2,500 voters present" (a thousand more than the previous year's antitreaty town meeting) on Monday, April 25, at Faneuil Hall. The crowd was so large the meeting had to be moved to the Old South meetinghouse. New blank petition forms were then issued for distribution at the Commonwealth's churches the following Sunday, asking whether citizens preferred "HAPPINESS and SAFETY" or "WAR! Horrid WAR!"[50]

By Thursday, April 28, the *Centinel* was able to publish an extra edition, emblazoned "THE CRISIS!!"; it recapped the Boston meeting and catalogued further town meetings and memorials organized over the intervening days in the coastal towns of Salem, Marblehead, Newburyport, Newbury, Lynn, Hingham, and Gloucester. One of the few Federalist editors capable of a certain sort of populism, the *Centinel's* Russell, tried to stir the old Puritan colony's ample xenophobia and regional chauvinism by highlighting the role of the "assuming foreigner," Swiss-born Pennsylvania congressman Albert Gallatin, in leading the House Democratic-Republicans. The rest of the American people "will no doubt side with faction and declare for anarchy," sniffed the *Centinel* extra. "But the citizens of *Massachusetts*—the enlightened Yeomen, Merchants, Professional men, and Mechanicks of a free State, are too wise, and too happy to commit a POLITICAL SUICIDE." This turn to reactionary populism intended to rile the feelings of native-born northeastern Protestants would increasingly characterize the Federalists throughout their history as a national political force. (Later the same mantle would be taken up by the Whigs and Republicans.) In New York, the treaty opponents were depicted as "negro representatives [southerners], . . . fraudulent bankrupts . . . french *partizans*, imported Scots, Irish, English malcontents etc."[51]

Historians have commonly seen this last big push for the Jay Treaty as a crucial departure from previous Federalist behavior, or even as the start of a transformation of American political culture toward a popularly based politics. (This argument is often intended to take some of the credit for the rise of democracy away from the Democratic-Republicans.) At the very least, it is an indication that the Federalists' often-stated aversion to democratic tactics and "out of doors" public opinion should not be taken entirely at face value. "The voice of the People, will now be emphatically the Voice of God," thundered Ben Russell after reporting on the Boston town meetings, though he was far from sanguine about the godliness of the people's voice outside the holy precincts of eastern Massachusetts. For Alexander Hamilton's part, it is superficially hard to square his strenuous efforts in April 1796 with his November 1794 declaration to President Washington that he had "long since learnt to hold popular opinion of no value." In point of fact, Hamilton had long kept close watch on public opinion, writing frequently for the press and expertly managing Washington's reputation as a way to maintain support for Federalist policy initiatives. But Hamilton truly did not "value" public opinion in the democratic sense of seeing the people's will as something government officials had a duty to follow. He had even less use for "popular" opinion as it might boil up from the streets, taverns, countryside, and opposition newspapers. Instead, for Hamilton and most of his allies, public opinion remained a wild thing that good men needed to tame and direct.[52]

This attitude accounts for one of the rhetorical oddities in the pro-treaty petitions that strikes a modern reader: the petitions constantly apologize for themselves, laboring to make this occasion for "out of doors" politics into a singular exception to the Washingtonian rule against the self-creation of political groups in society. New York's merchants assured readers that the House threat to the treaty provided "just cause of anxiety and alarm" sufficient to warrant "a respectful Address" to the government. "We view the period as important and alarming, and cannot avoid expressing our earnest wishes," insisted the Hartford petitioners. Likewise the Philadelphia Merchants and Traders' memorial declared, more in sorrow than in anger, "that they should deem themselves wanting in that spirit and independence which ought ever to characterize freemen, if they forbore, on so interesting an occasion as the present, to express their wishes and expectations." Republican writers were quick to point out that only weeks or days earlier, "these very men considered all meetings as improper and disorderly . . . but now they are the first to stir up tumult, they are the first to talk of '*spirited remonstrances*' to the Representatives of the people!"[53]

In fact the Federalists were quite fearful of anything resembling tumult, and were themselves at pains to distinguish their gatherings from the sort of "unlawful meeting without doors" that the Republicans had convened against the treaty. Instead, their petitioners claimed a special right to speak on this issue based on their commercial expertise and the financial interests they had at stake in foreign trade. The original Philadelphia memorial dwelt heavily on the value of the property the signers had lost to the British—"upon a moderate computation, five million of dollars"—and pinned their hopes of restitution on the treaty. It was they, the merchants and traders, who would be "materially affected" by the sinking of the treaty, and so they were the ones whose opinions mattered and should be listened to. Tellingly, Massachusetts Federalists looking to broadcast the Philadelphia memorial across their state changed the wording to suggest that "independent" of the five million, the "interest of the Farmer, and every other class of Citizens, [would] be materially injured" if the United States refused to make good on its commitments, materially changing the meaning of the word "materially." The protreaty petitions less directly tied to mercantile interests still spoke in the tones of established community leaders, substantial men who knew the "REAL wishes of the people" who counted in their towns.[54]

In fact, petitions were not in much tension with Federalist opposition to democratic politics, because they departed so little from the traditional business politics merchants had practiced since colonial times. Before the imperial reforms of the 1760s, petitions drawn up by local bigwigs and routed through well-connected lobbyists were the established means colonists had of requesting favors and policy changes from the British crown and parliament. Petitions were also an important form of local representation that could be used to transmit grievances without stirring the larger political waters. In at least one colony, petitions and lobbying had almost wholly substituted for the sort of electoral competition that drove representation in other colonies. Before, during, and after the Revolution, merchants and manufacturers freely exempted themselves from the classical republican prohibition on political campaigning when it came to their business interests. Even before the new Congress had officially opened in 1789, the government had been inundated with petitions and memorials from businessmen and trade groups asking for this or that favor. Most of the petitions that came to the first Congress addressed these sorts of narrow economic concerns.[55]

In short, the Federalists gravitated to petitioning in the case of the Jay Treaty precisely because there was nothing innovative or potentially disruptive or especially democratic about it.

In Massachusetts, the town meetings that so stoked the partisan flames of the Boston *Columbian Centinel*'s Benjamin Russell constituted an even more established means of avoiding "outdoor" political upheavals. While the exact status of the protreaty gatherings is not clear, they were presented as official bodies coterminous or closely related to the basic unit of local government in New England, also called the town meeting. Open to the participation of most adult males in theory, New England town meetings had a long-standing pattern of being more often passive vehicles for the expression of community consensus, under the guidance of leading men, than true forums for discussion or debate. The democratic forms legitimated a fundamentally conformist and hierarchical political order that New England's Federalist leaders took great pride in. The meeting in politically divided Boston indeed featured some ferocious debate—four speakers on each side, including *Independent Chronicle* principals Benjamin Austin Jr. and Charles Jarvis against the memorial. "LANGUAGE displayed new powers, and ORATORY exhibited new beauties," reported the *Massachusetts Mercury*, though that Federalist journal could not approve what a lively display of democratic discussion the meeting turned out to be. "Less exultation" would have been preferable: "Clapping, Huzzaing, &c. are not intirely consistent with the regularity which ought to be observed in deliberative bodies." There were fewer unseemly demonstrations around the rest of the Commonwealth. Russell's correspondent at the Gloucester town meeting sang hosannas to its unanimity: "NOT ONE DISSENTING VOICE!" was heard.[56]

Along with the great care that the Federalists took to see that protreaty meetings did not set a precedent for willy-nilly expressions of popular political sentiment, they made more than good on Hamilton's suggestion that an "imposing attitude" might be necessary for the campaign to succeed. In particular, Federalist business owners made use of their extensive economic power. Two bank presidents in Philadelphia hinted to people who needed loans that their chances would improve if they signed. "Under such circumstances, a Bank Director soliciting subscriptions is like a Highwayman with pistol demanding the purse," Madison wrote Jefferson.[57]

More pervasive and broadly threatening was a sudden, seemingly intentional economic slowdown that was directly linked to the House debates. International commerce depended heavily on credit and insurance. The Federalist *Gazette of the United States* printed a letter from a "gentleman of good information" stating that payments for neutral cargo had stopped, but that if the House "should discuss the subject of the Treaty, temperately and finally resolve to carry it into effect," the purse strings would be loosened again and American merchants and farmers would see "the most advantageous neutrality that a nation ever enjoyed." As the debate continued, the word went out that the uncertainty had put the economy in a "state of suspense" because of the war with Great Britain that the majority of the House was allegedly seeking to start. Then Hamilton engineered some very concrete and immediate economic pressure by manipulating the insurance industry. At his urging, marine insurers in New York and Philadelphia announced that they could no longer insure American vessels or cargos as long as "the present critical and alarming situation of Public Affairs" continued. Word filtered back to Providence merchants that the underwriters were waiting until they knew "whether to ask a War or Peace Premium." Vessels could not sail and cargo could not be shipped without insurance, so commerce was brought to a temporary halt, sending shivers of alarm through the port towns and their hinterlands.[58]

It is difficult to gauge the extent to which panic had genuinely set in among the commercial community and what was merely ginned up for political purposes. The timing of the underwriters' announcements certainly suggested politics was at work. The announcements came as the antitreaty forces were obviously faltering and dovetailed a little too exactly with points that Federalist speakers were making in Congress. What is perfectly clear is how forcefully the business slowdown brought home the Federalists' warnings, giving just a taste of what was to come if the administration did not get its way. From Portsmouth, New Hampshire, Senator John Langdon summed up the treaty supporters' devastating closing argument: "The Cry is war, war, no Insurance to be had, Vessells hauled up, no employment for the people; they modestly declare that the Treaty is a very bad one . . . but our Situation is such that we must take it." Small wonder that even many who sincerely opposed the treaty came to feel that their livelihoods might well depend on letting it go through.[59]

The opposition press thoroughly exposed the merchant influence behind the petition campaign and tried hard to debunk it as a real indicator of public opinion. The Federalists' ever more certain and melodramatic warnings were correctly labeled as political theater. "On Friday and Saturday last," wrote a New York satirist signing himself "Dramaticus," "the citizens of New-York were presented with a new political drama, entitled *war with Britain*, in which each of the principal performers of the *royal* company of comedians bore a conspicuous part."[60] Such dismissals do not seem to have been terribly effective, however. While we have no way of knowing how much the war fears affected public support for the treaty, much of the House Republican majority was clearly rattled by them, their once burgeoning political self-confidence severely shaken.

As a matter of historical fact, scoffers like "Dramaticus" had the stronger argument regarding the possibility of a new war with Great Britain if the Jay Treaty failed. Despite the warnings of their compatriots to the contrary, Washington administration officials seemed to proceed on the assumption that the chances of such an eventuality were low. For instance, they made few moves to secure a frontier that was allegedly about to explode. War Secretary Timothy Pickering proposed withdrawing General Anthony Wayne's troops back to the Ohio River in the fall of 1795 and had to be convinced that to leave the frontier totally exposed until the British departure was finalized. In truth, the threat level was minimal. Though the northwestern frontier buzzed with baseless rumors of a reversal and a new war, just as it had when the French were leaving in 1763, His Majesty's government had conceded the western posts because they wanted to get rid of them. London policymakers saw no reason to sink any more British prestige or treasure in that quarter of the world, not when they had the French Revolution and its supporters to deal with in Europe. With barely enough resources to keep the border forts minimally staffed, much less ready for all-out war, Canadian officials and their Indian allies had feared a British military withdrawal long before the Jay Treaty was even negotiated. Far from poising to retaliate against a potential rejection of the treaty, Whitehall could not even get its instructions through to Simcoe and Dorchester, who often had to learn about British policy in 1795 and 1796 by reading the U.S. newspapers. General Anthony Wayne ruled as the virtual viceroy in the northwest, with Little Turtle and other leaders of the formerly rebellious Indian confederacy flocking to support him out of disgust with the British and a lack of alternatives. The true situation on the northwestern frontier was so far from dire that General Wayne asked for and received leave to spend the winter of 1795–1796 on holiday back east, where the only campaign he mounted was a search for a wife.[61]

THE SPEECH: ROASTING THE WRETCHES WITH CONGRESSMAN FISHER AMES

Despite its unlikelihood, war on the frontier was the theme of the Federalists' last and perhaps most devastating blow in the Jay Treaty fight, a celebrated speech by Representative Fisher Ames of Massachusetts. The Boston area's congressman since the launch of the new government, Ames was one of the most noted conservatives of his day, a reader of Edmund Burke whose anti-Jacobinism had been fired by bitter challenges in the elections of 1792 and 1794 from members of the *Independent Chronicle* circle, most recently Dr. Charles Jarvis.[62] Ames's speech drew an extra charge from playing on Americans' racial fears, on an almost gothic fascination with savage warfare and whites in Indian captivity that was only becoming more intense as frontier life became more of an abstraction for eastern readers and politicians. Though fear and loathing of the native population had long been a populist cause in America and would later be a hallmark of the Democratic Party's politics in the Jacksonian era, in the 1790s it was the more conservative Federalists who seemed to deal most often in this article. Along with French revolutionaries, American Jacobins, and "wild Irish" immigrants, Native Americans were one more source of the primitive, atavistic violence that Federalists saw constantly threatening to erupt through the crust of civilization and destroy their well-ordered commercial society. For Federalists, human life outside of established social and political forms was, to borrow a phrase from the literary scholar W. M. Verhoeven, "a tale of wanton human evil and depravity . . . over which republican reason and understanding have no power whatsoever." The fullest expression of the linkage between Indian war and these conservative fears was probably Charles Brockden Brown's frontier novel *Edgar Huntly*, published in 1799 and written during the French war scare that brought on the Alien

The Orator: Massachusetts congressman Fisher Ames, one of the most eloquently conservative of Federalists, gave the bloodcurdling speech that saved the Jay Treaty. (Miniature portrait by John Trumbull, 1792, Yale University Art Gallery.)

and Sedition Acts. An earlier and far more politically effective version of the Federalist race war nightmare was Fisher Ames's speech on the Jay Treaty appropriations.[63]

Though widely considered the Federalists' finest orator, Fisher Ames had been sick all spring and unable or unwilling to give a floor speech, much to the consternation of his colleagues. Finally in the last week of April, the word went out that Mr. Ames, "one of those extraordinary characters . . . a beneficent Providence calls into existence, to instruct, delight, and astonish mankind," would speak at last. The "flower of Philadelphia" society flocked to Congress Hall to hear him. While Congress's lobby was a popular gathering place throughout the time that Philadelphia was the capital—this is where the political term "lobby" first arose in America—Ames's speech, by many accounts, drew the biggest congressional crowd ever. The ladies and gentlemen of the city were joined by high officials from the other branches of government, including Vice President Adams and Supreme Court Justice James Iredell.[64]

Though still haggard and perhaps a bit theatrically hushed as he began, Ames did not disappoint his audience, uncorking a speech for which no Federalist could find superlatives vaulting enough to contain their admiration. "Bless my stars I never heard any thing so great since I was born!" gushed James Iredell. "Divine," replied John Adams, reporting that there was literally not a dry eye in the house. The best thing since Cicero, opined a writer for the Federalist literary journal, the Port-Folio, with "more of the irresistible sway, the soul-subduing influence of ancient eloquence, than anything heard since." For another witness, it was merely the "most splendid" speech ever given in Congress to that point.[65]

Even without the partisan exaggeration, Ames's speech was by any measure a remarkable performance, running as many as fifty-nine pages in the five published editions that were issued in Philadelphia and Boston after it was given. Despite coming from an articulate opponent of democracy in principle, it was also one of the more innovative examples of democratic politicking to be found in 1796.[66]

Ames began with a long exordium reviewing the treaty debate thus far, rather abstractly, in terms of the rhetorical and psychological theories of the time. Federalists had often criticized the administration's opponents for the heated, passionate nature of their arguments, which seemed to violate enlightened standards of public decorum and rational debate. In their essays and speeches, including several occasions during the Jay Treaty debate, eighteenth-century gentlemen often admonished each other that legitimate political ideas and decisions could only be produced through the dispassionate use of reason. Though often violated in practice, this was one of the basic tenets of Anglo-American liberalism and a primary rule of behavior in what philosopher Jürgen Habermas later dubbed the bourgeois public sphere, the idealized space in which an enlightened political debate was supposed to take place and true public opinion was to be formed.[67]

Ames dismissed this concern by invoking psychological theories of "sensibility," from a different branch of Enlightenment thought and literature that was just then developing toward what would be known as Romanticism: "Let us not affect to deny the existence and the intrusion of some portion of prejudice and feeling into the debate, when, from the very structure of our nature, we ought to anticipate [it] . . . as a probability." It was useless to scold each other that "no influence should be felt but that of duty, and no guide respected but that of the understanding" when the country's passions had already been so deeply engaged.[68]

The theory of sensibility taught that human beings were naturally receptive and emotionally responsive to the impressions brought by their senses. While overresponsiveness was considered an illness, the belief had emerged that some outward displays of emotion, even to works of art or scenery, were natural and beneficial in persons of keen and perceptive intelligence. Hence it had become acceptable and even a bit fashionable for a gentleman to be a "man of sentiment" who openly expressed the upwellings of his heart and shed a few tears now and then. On a broader and more serious level, sensibility and the sentimentalism that came with it were forging a place for emotion and imagination in the notoriously rationalistic and materialistic culture of the Enlightenment.[69]

In political rhetoric, sensibility opened the possibility of a style of speaking and writing that might touch audiences on a more emotional, less rational, and thus potentially more powerful level. The opposition press had made effective use of impassioned, so-called hortatory rhetoric in trying to rouse popular opinion against the administration and the treaty, building on the tradition of Thomas Paine.[70] On this occasion, Ames's speech did them one better by bringing the meaning of the Jay Treaty down to a starkly personal level. Sensibility was a common language that crossed the ideological lines in the Early Republic, but Ames was able to draw on a Gothic strain of violent nightmare that was more often wielded in the 1790s by conservative critics of the Enlightenment and the French Revolution: Edmund Burke on the death of Marie Antoinette, the antiliberal horror novels of Charles Brockden Brown, and any number of Federalists on the dangers of Jacobinism and Illuminism.[71]

Understanding that his elite congressional audience might recoil from too blunt and crass an emotional appeal, Ames carefully justified his approach in the early section of the speech. "Our understandings have been addressed . . . with ability and effect; but, I demand, has any corner of the heart been left unexplored?" Ames asked his audience. Though Ames and most other Federalists were bitterly resentful of newspaper criticism and would soon support silencing opposition newspapers, on this occasion he praised passionate rhetoric as the engine of what we could call a successful democratic politics, and also of the will of God: "The only constant agents in political affairs are the passions of men—shall we complain of our nature? . . . It is right already, because He, from whom we derive our nature, ordained it so; and because thus made, and thus acting, the cause of truth and the public good is the more surely promoted."[72]

Though he began with this justification of partisan bombast, Ames constructed the speech in a much more subtle fashion, upholding one kind of political passion while delegitimating another. The first substantive section of the speech chided the antitreaty forces for their own emotional appeals, specifically the appeal to the "self-love" of House members who expressed a "jealous and repulsive fear" that their rights and status were not being respected by the Senate and the administration: "We hear it said that this is a struggle for liberty, a manly resistance against . . . a scheme of coercion and terror, to force the Treaty down our throats, though we loathe it, and in spite of the clearest convictions of duty and conscience." This was a pretty decent summary of how treaty opponents in the House and around the country felt; constitutionally they very much did believe that the administration's interpretation of the treaty-making power was intended to make the popularly elected branch of Congress a nonentity in the government. According to Ames, however, "suggestions of this kind" were "unfair in their very texture and fabric, and pernicious in their influences": "They oppose an obstacle in the path of inquiry, not simply discouraging, but absolutely insurmountable. They will not yield to argument; for, as they were not reasoned up, they cannot be reasoned down. They are higher than a Chinese wall in truth's way, and built of materials that are indestructible."[73]

Having issued this clarion call for rational debate, Ames next made a move that left the Republican members of his audience fuming. "He artfully stated his intention to be an appeal to the understanding of the members, and disclaimed every idea of addressing their passions," one Republican wrote in the New York *Argus*, "yet with astonishing inconsistency he totally abandoned the field of argument" for "nothing but an address to the fears and feelings of his audience."[74]

While these opponents could probably be forgiven for thinking otherwise, more than simple hypocrisy was at work in Ames's speech. At stake was just what sort of emotions were going to be dominant in the new nation's public culture. The opposition had successfully challenged the Washington administration and its supporters with passionate attacks on their allegedly monarchical political principles and pro-British policies. Yet for Ames and the Federalists, it was precisely the tendency to inspire these sorts of *political* passions that made "Jacobinism" of the French or Jeffersonian type so dangerous. The "destroying rage" of "Jacobin phrenzy" threatened to rend apart society itself with its thoughtless, jealous, relentless application and reapplication of democratic and egalitarian principles. While the Federalists' most apocalyptic rhetoric about the democratic threat to society would not fully emerge until their grip on power started to loosen after 1798, the association of democracy with dangerously overheated emotionalism was in place from the beginning of the party conflict. On different occasions, Ames had described democracy as "a volcano that contained within its bowels the fiery materials of its own destruction," and worried that the oppositionists would "inflame" public opinion. Another Federalist who poetized on the Jay Treaty debate praised the diplomat for floating above the "party rage" directed at his work. Another version of the Federalist warning against political passion was the commonplace comparison, made by John Adams and others, of democracy to the rake character in every sentimental novel of the time, who seduced an innocent girl (the citizenry) by stoking up her desires and fantasies and then left her ruined, pregnant, and suicidal.[75]

One way of understanding the root of Federalist party ideology, and a common theme of conservatism more generally, is the primacy of society—existing social relations and their attendant, established cultural traditions, especially religion—over politics and philosophy as the proper source of basic values and motivations. From Ames's point of view, the only safe and decent place for strong emotion was the private realm of family and social friendship, and even there it needed to be strictly limited. If passion was to appear in public at all, it could only be in expression or defense of those private emotional commitments.

While today we somewhat grudgingly accept the notion that "private," personal values and behavior are appropriate or at least inevitable subjects of political conflict, this was far from the case in 1796. The decaying classical republican commitment to a politics of virtuous non-partisanship had placed a premium on the character of public figures, but linking policy issues such as a treaty to personal values was a new departure. The advantage rhetorically was that family feelings were not publicly debatable or negotiable. You could not argue against a man's love for his wife and children any more than you could debate the Father of Your Country. Ames's goal was not so much winning the debate on the merits of his arguments as ending it on a point of order. In a country still just beginning to think in terms of democratic partisan politics, Ames knew that most of his listeners and hearers could be counted on to regard the personal and religious feelings he invoked as far more fundamental than Jacobin or Jeffersonian dreams of a democratic republic.

Ames began to turn his speech toward personal values and emotions while still discussing the treaty's legal and economic aspects. He expatiated at some length on the moral dangers to the American people if the nation were to "break our faith" and renege on the commitments John Jay had made to the British. Could any action, he asked, "mark upon a people more turpitude and debasement? . . . It would not merely demoralize mankind, it tends to break all the ligaments of society, . . . and to inspire in its stead a repulsive sense of shame and disgust." Invoking the old monarchical image of the nation as a patriarchal family, Ames doubted that a "good citizen" would be able "to look with affection and veneration to such a country [one that had broken its faith] as his parent." Stretching for a suggestion of blasphemy, Ames complained that the House might as well "repeal . . . the Ten Commandments" themselves.[76]

Having stirred up the audience's moral and religious feelings, Ames saved his most overpowering sentimental appeal for last, dealing with the issue of the western posts that the British might not give up if the Jay Treaty were disowned and the role the forts might play in the war that Federalists were predicting as the inevitable sequel. The specter Ames raised was not just war, but Indian war, and here there was plenty of history to back him up: while there was much reason to question whether the British would bother fighting over the failure of the Jay Treaty, there was no question that any war with the British that did come would also involve the Indians. There was a long tradition in North America of natives joining the European empires in their battles with each other, seeking to fight their own enemies with Europeans paying for the food and ammunition or to maintain the European trade ties they had come to depend on for many of the necessities of life. Indian war typically took a particularly fearsome form as well, involving raids on outlying settlements and attacks on exposed travelers, situations in which noncombatants were frequently killed or taken into captivity. Since the goal was often pushing back the enemy's settlements, the terroristic aspect of native tactics suited European war aims quite well. Most tribes had fought with the French against the British in the colonial wars, and during the Revolutionary War, with the British against the United States, gravitating to the white group that planned the fewest settlements. European forts doubled as trading centers for the natives, so they easily became staging points for raids.[77]

Drawing on a deep well of racial hostility as well as human sympathy, Ames captured his listeners' imaginations and recruited their personal emotions to his cause with what was, for the time, an unusually vivid and even gory word picture of just what a new wave of British-inspired Indian raids might mean for western families. "On this theme my emotions are unutterable," he began, rather misleadingly:

> If I could find words for them—if my powers bore any proportion of my zeal—I would swell my voice to such a note of remonstrance it should reach every log-house beyond the mountains. I would say to the inhabitants, Wake from your false security; your cruel dangers, your more cruel apprehensions are soon to be renewed; the wounds, yet unhealed, are to be torn open again. In the daytime your path through the woods will be ambushed; the darkness of midnight will glitter with the blaze of your dwellings. You are a father—the blood of your sons shall fatten your cornfield; you are a mother—the war-whoop shall wake the sleep of the cradle!

> On this subject you need not suspect any deception on your feelings. It is a spectacle of horror which can not be overdrawn. If you have nature in your hearts, it will speak a language compared with which all I have said or can say will be poor and frigid. . . .

> It is no great effort of the imagination to conceive, that events so near are already begun. I can fancy that I listen to the yells of savage vengeance and the shrieks of torture. Already they seem to sigh in the West wind; already they mingle with every echo from the mountains.[78]

Whatever emotional state Ames claimed to have worked himself into, he made sure that his listeners got the message that Jay Treaty opponents should be held personally responsible for any blood the Indians spilled. Indeed, in a deft bit of rhetoric that nested the Federalist policy argument inside their deeper cultural fears about the threats to civilization and family posed by revolution and democracy, Ames cast the Republican opposition as the savages: "By rejecting the posts, we light the savage fires—we bind the victims. This day we undertake to render account to the widows and orphans whom our decision will make; to the wretches that will be roasted at the stake . . . while one hand is held up to reject this treaty, the other grasps a tomahawk."[79]

Here in its purest form was Ames's strategy: removing the issue from the sphere of rational, democratic political debate in which it was possible to oppose the treaty and moving it into a realm of emotional necessity full of roasted constituents and wailing children screaming to be saved. If "reflections of this kind" were going to be the basis of such of an important decision, a New York *Argus* writer mused darkly, "then indeed we are ripe for any government short of republican." According to John Adams, some of the Republicans present at the speech tried to show their contempt by mirthlessly laughing at Ames's emotionalism, "but their Vissages grinn'd horrible ghastly smiles" that must have made the "savage" role that Ames had cast them in seem all the more accurate. There was really no decent response available.[80]

To the great discomfiture of these resistant Republicans, the effect of Ames's speech was quite literally sensational. "Friends and foes . . . were equally melted—and I speak within bounds when I say hundreds who heard him, were unable to suppress their tears," a New Hampshire congressman wrote back to a home state newspaper. Political audiences were apparently unaccustomed to having their imaginations stirred by a congressional speech, and it was the novelistic flourishes, especially the little scenes of frontier melodrama, that caused the most comment. "Such a blending of argument, fancy, and feeling, has very rarely indeed been seen," the *Gazette of the United States* enthused, spinning a weirdly mercantile fancy of its own in trying to express its admiration: "[Ames] was a fine ship, on a summer sea, decorated with her colours, and bearing a rich cargo of spices before a fair wind." However, it was clearly not so much the elegance of Ames's diction as the raw emotionalism of his imagery that proved so devastating. Then as now, nothing moved an audience like dead children, to the point that even those in the audience who were not refined men of sentiment could not help but be overwhelmed. "Notwithstanding my insensibility," the New Hampshire congressman admitted, when Ames warned that the "innocent *slumbers of the cradle* must again be disturbed by the War Whoop of Indians,—my imagination painted my little child lying tommyhawked on the pillow, and his mother running frantic in the woods; I became as weak as the rest, and paid a plentiful tribute of tears to the powers of his eloquence." As some Republicans pointed out, sympathy for the prospective victims of projected Indian raids completely overwhelmed calmer, nobler feelings like national dignity, making Ames's speech, in effect, a "MANIFESTO of American debility and pusillanimity."[81]

If Ames really did intend his speech as a discussion ender, he succeeded. After the Yankee orator finished, the Virginian Abraham Venable got up woozily to stop the question from being taken immediately, admitting that "there were mischievous effects staring them in the face" whatever the House decided about the treaty appropriations. The best this associate of the Philadelphia radicals and former bitter opponent of the treaty could ask for was a cooling-off period.[82] The next day only treaty supporters were heard, including a political weathervane, New Jersey's Jonathan Dayton. A onetime ally of Republican leaders and fellow Princetonians Aaron Burr and James Madison, Dayton confessed that Madison's indictment of the treaty had once been "strongly impressed upon his mind" but that he now had come to see the other side, convinced in no small degree by "a gentleman from Massachusetts, in a strain of eloquence never exceeded in that House, which affected every one who heard." In the next Congress, Dayton would become the first partisan speaker of the House, an out-and-out Federalist.[83]

After Dayton spoke, Republican floor leaders James Madison and Albert Gallatin watched the mushy remnants of their majority cave in. The wavering New York and western swing votes were long gone, and others soon followed. Maryland Republican Gabriel Christie complained that the warnings about the consequences of not implementing the treaty were "something like the tale of 'Rawhead and Bloodybones,' to frighten children," yet because his own constituents seemed to fall for it, Christie "found himself bound to lay aside his own opinion" and vote for the treaty. When the question was called immediately after, one of the most partisan Republicans in the House, William Findley of western Pennsylvania, was nowhere to be found, leaving the vote on the treaty appropriations tied 49–49. (Findley claimed he had been out arranging to have a trunk sent home to his family, a lame excuse that supposedly led some erstwhile supporters to wish that the trunk had been his coffin.)

That left it for another erstwhile opponent from Pennsylvania, Speaker of the House Frederick A. C. Muhlenberg, to break the tie in the treaty's favor.[84]

Muhlenberg had been subject to excruciating pressure even beyond the speeches and petitions. His son's prospective father-in-law, a Philadelphia merchant, had made it clear that if the speaker did not give the Federalists his "vote, your son shall not have my Polly." Adding injury to insult, Muhlenberg was almost stabbed to death two days after the vote by Bernard Schaeffer, an unstable brother-in-law who was a bit steadier than Muhlenberg in his political leanings.[85]

According to their own testimony, the motives of the various Republican defectors should be put down to democracy rather than political cowardice. Even beyond the fact that the treaty opponents had been identifying themselves as defenders of the people's rights since the beginning of the party conflict, the essence of their constitutional argument in the Jay Treaty appropriations debate was that the treaty-making power should be answerable to the popular majorities represented in the House. This made the signs of a shift in public opinion almost impossible for truly democratic Republicans to ignore. Actually believing in the will of the people made it much harder to win political battles in which the will of the people seemed to have turned against them. Like Christie and Venable, Philip Van Cortlandt pled *vox populi* in explaining his vote in favor of the treaty despite his own reservations. "From memorials and other sources of information," Van Cortlandt wrote apologetically to his constituents, "it appeared . . . to be the general wish of the people of the northern and eastern states, that it ought to be carried into effect."[86]

ALL OVER BEFORE THE SHOUTING: THE JAY TREATY AND THE FEDERALIST VICTORY IN NEW YORK STATE

Nowhere was this more the case than in Van Cortlandt's home state of New York, where the Jay Treaty debate and the British war scare collided directly with the presidential election of 1796. One of the many oddities of the nascent electoral process in this first contested presidential election year was the fact that a key state contest was already decided before a single candidate had been publicly named. Article II, Section 1 of the Constitution allowed each individual state to determine how it would "appoint" its presidential electors, and the default option in 1796, or at least the one most states chose, was to have their state legislature do it. (For the schedule of elections, and the methods used, state by state, see table 1 at the end of chapter 8.) State legislative elections were also typically held in the spring, and the combination of these factors—method and timing—meant that a major prize, New York, was on the line within days of the final Jay Treaty vote.

Even the most optimistic estimate of the opposition's potential electoral base, in which it carried every vote from every state south and west of the Potomac, left it eighteen votes short of an Electoral College majority. As we will see in the following chapter, Thomas Jefferson's candidacy was still just a rumor, but those who had the project in mind realized that he would need to carry one or more of the mid-Atlantic states (New York, Pennsylvania, New Jersey, or Maryland) to have any chance of winning. In the spring of 1796, John Beckley and James Madison were deeply absorbed in the Jay Treaty battle, and seemed quite startled to realize that the presidential election might be on the line before the campaign had even begun. As a kind of afterthought, Beckley wrote in mid-April to remind an old acquaintance, young New York City legislative candidate De Witt Clinton, that the "future choice of a president" might well depend on their legislative elections, hoping that the stakes would "call forth all the energies of patriotism" among the local New York Republicans. As a motivator, Beckley reported on dubious authority that President Washington had "publicly declared at his own house, that he will not serve again," making it possible to openly campaign for a successor. With some prescience, Beckley predicted that Republicans would do well in the states where presidential electors were chosen by popular vote, but only as long as the elections were not held too soon. Opposition campaigners needed time to prepare and to let the British war scare dissipate. In New York, the "friends of republicanism" were not going to have either benefit and simply had to "redouble their exertions to counteract their opponents."[87]

New York was an extremely slender branch for the Republicans to hang their national hopes on. The nascent opposition party there was riven by factional rivalry between two family "interests" led by former Governor George Clinton and Chancellor (chief judicial officer) Robert R. Livingston, with Senator Aaron Burr navigating in between and hated by both. The rivals were frequently more concerned with supremacy over each other than building a national coalition. The more serious problem was that there was no state where the Federalist framing of the

Jay Treaty debate, as a matter of peace or war with Great Britain, bit deeper than it did in New York State, because there was no location in the country more directly affected by the possible consequences of a new war with Britain. With its major urban center just a growing town, New York in 1796 was still very much a part of the frontier, not only abutting but actually overlapping potentially hostile British and Indian territory. There were British military installations on New York soil at Niagara and Oswego, and west of the Hudson, much of the state was still officially in Iroquois hands. For New Yorkers, the major benefit that the Jay Treaty offered, the evacuation of the British forts, was much more than the pitiful sop it seemed to the radicals in Philadelphia and Boston; if U.S.-British relations were to spiral into conflict because of the treaty's rejection, New York state would be on the front lines, just as it had been during the French and Indian War and the Revolutionary War.[88]

Fisher Ames's heavily reprinted speech must have met a receptive audience in upstate New York. Federalism was surprisingly strong there, and the area had also been the scene of a relatively recent and particularly bloody episode of Indian war in the raids conducted by Joseph Brant's Mohawks and other Iroquois during the Revolutionary War, working with the British army and white Loyalists. The last raids had taken place only fifteen years earlier. Even those who were never touched by violence themselves may have had a friend or relative who was, and most upstate New Yorkers who had lived before 1781 certainly had some memory of displacement; whole regions of white settlers would flee if the word went out that Indian forces were coming. By 1796 neither the Mohawks nor the other Iroquois nations were any longer in a position to threaten the United States, but Brant was still active and the Mohawks were still numerous in Canada. It was feared that any new conflict with the British would bring down a new wave of Indian attacks on upstate New York settlements, many of them rebuilt since the Revolution.[89]

Under the influence of these fears, the New York delegation emerged early as a weak spot in the treaty opposition, to a degree that few of the House Republicans, even point man "Beau Ned" Livingston of New York City, had anticipated. It had already lost one member when upstate congressman John Williams got up to answer his city colleague Livingston's call for Washington's papers. Williams was an avowed "anti-Federalist" who agreed with the Republicans' constitutional position and even supported an amendment to democratize the treaty-making power by letting the House have a say. In a lengthy and incisive speech, Williams tried to inject some realism into the debate, from a Democratic-Republican perspective. He explained to the House that the people of New York State were "peculiarly situated with respect to . . . Canada" and that the failure to get the British out of the posts would be "more detrimental to them than any other part of the Union." Williams bristled at the cavalier attitude that out-of-state Republicans such as Madison of Virginia and John Swanwick of Philadelphia had displayed toward the possibility of war. "Confusion and wretchedness will be the consequence" in New York, he declared. Frontier settlers would "fly from their habitations" at the first sign of trouble with the Indians. He wished that his city colleagues "had been with him in the late war, when he marched seventy miles before the enemy, forty of which with his family in the greatest distress."[90]

Probably even more pressing to Williams and other New Yorkers than the possibility of physical or emotional harm was the degree to which the British posts and attendant Indian war fears were arresting the state's economic development. Well-laid plans were afoot, involving an international cast of financiers, land speculators, and politicians, to carve up the vast Iroquois lands of western New York and sell them to the settlers. Schemes were also already moving forward to fully exploit the trade route from the Hudson to the Great Lakes that was to become the most lucrative in American history, the route of the Erie Canal that would spark the rise of New York City to metropolitan status. Representatives of New York State, led by Alexander Hamilton's father-in-law, General Philip Schuyler, spent the mid-1790s negotiating a series of treaties with the various Iroquois nations that were highly dubious from a moral and legal viewpoint, but bore the economic hopes of many powerful (and not-so-powerful) whites. The same state legislature that would cast the crucial electoral votes was being lobbied to grant the Dutch bankers who owned the Holland Land Company full rights to sell their holdings in the far west of the state. It would all come to nothing if the British held on to their forts and frightened off the speculators' potential customers. Just a year and a half before the House debate, Lieutenant Governor Simcoe in Upper Canada had sent a British officer to warn out a settlement at Sodus on the south side of Lake Ontario. Whites in western New York claimed they could not travel in the area of the forts without fear of being detained by the Iroquois as British deserters if they could not show a pass from the British commander.[91]

By the time of John Williams's speech, April 10, it was clear that three other New York Republicans (Theodorus Bailey, Jonathan Havens, and Philip Van Cortlandt) might "want the necessary stamina" to persevere against the treaty, as John Beckley put it, because of what they were hearing from their constituents. Williams deftly reframed this apparent waffling as a matter of democracy, the duty of the people's representatives to respond to shifts in public opinion. He hoped that "the will of the people . . . would be obeyed," even when their will seemed to change. When Williams left for Philadelphia in December, "three fourths" of his constituents "were against the Treaty, but now, by letters he had received, a very large majority wished it to be carried into effect." This was only reasonable, Williams believed. In his district, "hundreds of industrious families, some with six or eight children a-piece, lived in log huts" exposed in the woods and "defenceless" against whatever "weapon of death" the "savage" might send in the event of a new war: "Gentlemen who live surrounded by luxuries in a city do not think of the situation of this class of their citizens, who were nevertheless worthy of their consideration."[92]

Believing that only their nationally oriented viewpoint constituted the popular democratic side of the treaty fight, John Beckley and the other Philadelphia ringleaders gave the wavering New Yorkers' actions a less charitable reading. As the Philadelphians saw it, Williams, Bailey, and the others were from closely contested districts and simply afraid of not being reelected. "So often and so fatally my friend do personal supersede public considerations," Beckley lamented. In fact, the issue was not personal versus public, but local popular opinion versus the would-be national party line. With respect to another aspect of Democratic-Republican ideology—government according to the will of the people—the New Yorkers could claim solid ground for going soft.[93]

During the last week of April, just as the last stages of the Jay Treaty debate unfolded, New Yorkers went to the polls to elect a new legislature. The timing could not have been worse for the Republicans. Not only was the treaty issue blowing back on them as described above, but a huge distraction from national issues had developed that prevented any marshaling of "patriotic energies" behind a potential new president that Beckley had hoped for.

The distraction was a serious political and social upheaval on the streets of New York City that turned the spring 1796 elections into "in the view of the common people a question between the Rich &

the Poor." Two Irish ferry workers, Thomas Burk and Timothy Crady, had been jailed and one flogged for insulting a city alderman, Gabriel Furman, after an argument on the trip over from Brooklyn. Federalist mayor Richard Varick wanted to make an example of the two ferrymen to encourage more submissive attitudes among city workers (and improve ferry service) in the wake of the earlier antitreaty disturbances. The ferrymen soon escaped from Bridewell Prison, but they became the center of a *cause célèbre* when young Republican lawyer William Keteltas took up their case in the press. Beginning with a caustic account of Burk and Crady's trial signed "One of the People," Keteltas's letters framed the case not so much as the rich oppressing the poor as the well-placed abusing their official authority to establish an unearned superiority over the less-privileged. The ferrymen had been humiliated, he wrote, to "gratify the pride, the ambition, and the insolence of men in office." In retaliation, Federalists hauled Keteltas before the state assembly, then meeting in the city, and turned him into an overnight folk hero of the New York docks, streets, and taverns. Some two thousand supporters, by far the largest audience that had ever gathered to watch a session of the New York state assembly, showed up to support Keteltas at the hearing. Struggling to be heard over the cheering throng, the legislators ordered the young lawyer to jail, for breach of privileges (contempt), and he was conveyed to his cell in a large armchair carried aloft through the streets by the crowd. Soon after, John Jay himself, now governor of New York, appeared in military uniform, ready to put down an uprising.[94]

Alexander Hamilton complained bitterly about the way the "vile affair" of the ferrymen and William Keteltas was handled, believing it had "embarrassed & jeoparded" the Federalist cause, but in many ways it actually helped.[95] Amid the local sound and fury of the legislative campaign that began soon after the old assembly adjourned and William Keteltas was released from jail, New Yorkers largely ignored the presidential question. Though the pages of the local Republican sheet, Thomas Greenleaf's New York *Argus*, overflowed with political material on both national and local issues, John Beckley's clarion call for redoubled presidential exertions seems to have gotten through to its readers exactly twice. With a barrage of exclamation points, an essay over the signature "UNITE AND CONQUER" tried out what might have been the formula for a Jefferson win in New York given different timing and circumstances. That formula was to tie the presidential election to an aggressively nationalistic posture on the Jay Treaty issue that cast the question in terms of the ordinary American man's self-respect as a democratic citizen:

> This! this! is the very time which calls for your *utmost exertions*—NOW OR NEVER! The ensuing session of the Legislature will perhaps be the most important session held since the ever memorable 1776. The Legislature, whom you are now to elect, will have the choosing of . . . your ELECTORS FOR PRESIDENT AND VICE-PRESIDENT of the United States. It may, nay, it is probable *it will* depend on . . . this election, whether we are to have GENUINE PATRIOTS at the head of our government, or . . . *venal slaves to a despotic and foreign King*, . . . who are seeking once more to fix on you the galling fetters of an ignominious bondage! . . . Let me conjure you, I say, to exercise your own judgements [*sic*]; pin not your faith upon the sleeve of an imperious landlord, or time-serving flatterers! Remember! . . . You are now perhaps to decide on the FATE OF YOUR COUNTRY! You are now to determine whether countless millions, yet unborn, are to bless or curse you![96]

The word "unite" was especially aimed at bringing together the many competing factions among New York's opposition sympathizers. "A Republican Whig" slate for the city's legislative seats was constructed featuring a member of each rival family "interest," Peter R. Livingston and De Witt Clinton. At the head of the ticket was outgoing U.S. Senator Aaron Burr, standing for state senate while positioning himself for the vice presidency. They were joined by two other assembly candidates put there to play to the popular unrest of recent months: William Keteltas himself, plus another aspiring tribune of the local common man, the Democratic Society secretary Tunis Wortman.[97]

The statement announcing the ticket was the second of two to actually mention the national implications of the New York state elections, but it was much more absorbed with keeping the resentments of the Keteltas affair boiling. "Is this a free country, where *poverty* is already treated as a *crime*," the Republicans asked, "where to be *poor* is, in other words, to be considered as a *vagrant*?" The minirecession that the Federalists had engineered through the financial community to bring pressure for the ratification of the Jay Treaty was dismissed with a denial that there were any common interests between the financiers and ordinary city voters: "The gentleman insurers have refused to underwrite vessels forsooth! What is that to us plain men?" Only at the end of a very long document was it mentioned, tentatively, that the new legislature would choose presidential electors: "If the President is willing to serve again, he will be rechosen; Should he decline, and the Republicans prevail, then *Jefferson*, the man of *public liberty*, the *man of the people*, will succeed him." That was both a frank summary of the situation and one of the earlier expressions of just what Thomas Jefferson meant, or would come to mean, to the northern city Republicans who would be decisive to his national prospects.[98]

Perhaps the presidential election came up more in the extensive street-level politicking that occurred over the days the polls were open. As was typical in New York City, partisans speechified in the street and hounded voters throughout the time the polls were open, and wagered each other over the outcome. Thomas Greenleaf seemed relieved to report on May 3 that the "electioneering campaign" had "closed for the season without any bloodshed . . . although the conflict has been great." The excitement succeeded in energizing the city's voters. More citizens went to the polls than ever before, including five hundred more Democratic-Republican voters, cutting the Federalist majority from the previous year and making inroads into the city council for the first time.[99]

Unfortunately for the Democratic-Republicans, the "question between rich and poor" seems to have energized property owners and ferry users just as much as the laborers and mechanics, and the Federalists had a built-in electoral advantage. Many less prosperous New Yorkers, including a number of young Republican politicians, could not vote for the higher offices under New York's graduated suffrage laws. To vote for the lower house of the state legislature, New York citizens needed to own real property worth £40 or pay rent of at least 40 shillings. To vote for any higher office, including the state senate, the property requirement increased to £100. Some two-thirds of the city's Democratic-Republican voters in 1796 could only qualify as renters. With the property qualification depressing the downscale vote, the Federalist vote increase over the previous year's legislative election was even greater than the Republicans', especially outside Manhattan. Running in a wider district under the higher property qualification, Aaron Burr and the state senate ticket went down by an almost 2-to-1 margin, including a 280–8 drubbing on rural Staten Island.[100]

Once ballots were cast in New York State, the process of counting them all took weeks. A joint committee of the legislature had to canvass the votes, with the Mayor, Recorder, and Aldermen doing the same job in New York City. The results of the 1796 canvass were not released until early June, and they were a stunning disappointment for the Democratic-Republicans. A letter from New York announced gleefully to the Boston *Columbian Centinel* that the New York elections had "terminated federally," and it let slip one of the earliest recorded public mentions of what the ultimate consequence might be: "You may rely on the genuineness of our Legislature and Executive, and may safely count on twelve votes for your worthy fellow-citizen JOHN ADAMS . . . in case the PRESIDENT is not a candidate." Among the local Democratic-Republicans, blame for the losses was deflected onto the state's recent reapportionment, which had just created a number of new legislative districts in western New York where worries about the British forts and the Indians were strongest. Combined with the property requirement, the new western seats had given the Federalists a "prodigious preponderance" in the state senate particularly.[101]

Already reeling from the failure of his strategy for stopping the Jay Treaty in the House of Representatives, James Madison was terribly rattled by the bad news out of New York. "A crisis which ought to have been so managed as to fortify the Republican cause, has left it in a very crippled condition," he noted. The electoral prospects had seemed favorable but now had "taken a wrong turn under the impressions of the moment." The New York Democratic-Republicans had laid some important groundwork for their future victories by bonding with the city's working classes, but for the national strategists the future looked a little dark. Three other state legislatures had been elected that spring that seemed equally Federalist.[102]

Federalists celebrated their victories in the late spring and early summer of 1796, saluting Fisher Ames and congratulating each other for their victory. Ames's speech might have been the start of a powerful new democratic direction in Federalist political culture, one that would have made full use of the sentimental, reactionary populism Ames had modeled. Instead, many Federalists seemed more relieved that the crisis was over and inclined to treat their strenuous efforts to marshal public opinion behind the treaty as a one-off that could be left behind now that the nation had returned to its senses. The once-Francophilic planter elite in South Carolina seemed to be embarrassed by their earlier attitudes. William Loughton Smith reported to Rufus King from Charleston: "The Treaty-phobia is completely cured here, and federal politics, when they engage the attention, excite general approbation. Those who made such a ridiculous clamor last summer seem ashamed of themselves and are glad to throw a veil over what has passed." It had all been just a big mistake.[103]

The long-term impact of the Federalists' victory in the Jay Treaty matter was quite different from what they must have expected. Hoping that the clamor of popular politics was safely in the past, they looked forward to a quiet presidential selection process that required only a little string-pulling behind the scenes, and perhaps not even that if Washington could be convinced to stand again. Instead, underestimating the opposition's intensity and tenacity, the Federalists had only forced the Democratic-Republicans' efforts onto the hitherto relatively undisturbed plane of national electoral competition. Moreover, the Federalists would have to compete chiefly in states where the presidential electors would be chosen by popular vote. Thus the Jay Treaty's final victory was more a beginning than the end, because in some degree it called the American presidential election campaign into being.

5

THE LONG GOODBYE
FINDING CANDIDATES IN THE SHADOW OF WASHINGTON

The end of the Jay Treaty fight signaled the beginning of the first presidential campaign, and certain key state elections with presidential implications occurred immediately. There was only one problem: a total lack of any publicly acknowledged candidates. Most accounts of American presidential campaigns begin with the battle for the major party nominations, but this was a notion as yet unconceived in 1796. Instead of candidates planning their presidential ascent for years in advance, the possibility that there might be candidacies at all was regarded as a rather scandalous thing, to be kept hidden at all costs.

Despite all the policy battles and partisan feelings, little had changed in terms of the general feeling toward parties and aggressive politicking, especially when it came to the matter of national leadership. When a stranger in town wandered into a Boston celebration and gave the following toast, it made the newspaper as a commonplace sentiment: "May the *canker worm* of *faction* never ascend the stem, nor blast the fruit of the tree of Liberty." No gentleman of national reputation was going to risk comparison with a canker worm, so there were no public candidates, especially when it was not yet completely clear that the job was even open.[1]

WAITING FOR GEORGE

The main practical obstacle was the deliberate uncertainty surrounding the future plans of an incumbent against whom no challenger could hope to stand. Though his reputation had been battered by the opposition press, George Washington was still the young republic's greatest national symbol and most popular man. There were no presidential term limits, and no word came from the administration or any of its supporters indicating that the president intended to step down.

The conventional wisdom inside the 1796 beltway was that Washington would retire at the end of his second term if not sooner. Yet the prevailing political culture forbade anyone from speaking or writing openly of the possibility, reducing the whole notion to gossip with remarkably little information or activity connected to it. Rather hopefully, Vice President John Adams contended that the retirement was "well known to every body in public Life, but is talked of by nobody." Outside Philadelphia, his rather disappointed future First Lady reported, the possibility that Washington might soon be replaced was unknown and unremarked. The election and succession was "not thought of, or contemplated any more than if it could not happen."[2]

Conventional wisdom had some foundation, but from the outside it was impossible to tell exactly what the president would do. Washington had made talk of old age and retirements something of a fetish over the years, since long before his presidency. It was part of his Cincinnatian pose, and also sowed confusion and uncertainty about his plans among enemies and competitors. While General Washington's willingness to step away from power at the end of the Revolutionary War was undoubtedly one of his greatest contributions to the cause of liberty, 1783 was one of many occasions when he rolled out well-honed paeans to "a Retirement, for which I have never ceased to sigh . . . and in which (remote from the noise and trouble of the World) I meditate to pass the remainder of life in a state of undisturbed repose." Though a hearty if dentally impaired man of just over fifty at the end of the war, Washington had moved the audience to tears in his big speech at Newburgh by fumbling theatrically with his glasses and remarking how he had "grown gray" in the service of his country and "now found himself growing blind." This was all very sincere—his health was suffering from army life— but it was also brilliant politics, defusing the army's tense standoff with Congress and burnishing his own image. Four years later, Washington came out of retirement with some aplomb to begin a career in national politics in which he was a nigh-unstoppable force.[3]

As president, Washington had been talking of retirement since not all that long after taking the job, alluding to the possibility as early as April 1791. Profoundly irritated by the public criticism and contentiousness that came with the presidency, the aging general was quite sincere in these later rounds of retirement talk. A little less than a year before his first term ended, Washington had made concrete plans to step down before the election of 1792. Using his standard line about his "ardent wishes to spend the remainder of my days (which I cannot expect will be many) in ease & tranquility," the president solicited advice about how and when to announce his retirement, as well as a draft of his prospective Farewell Address, from none other than James Madison. As it happened, Washington did not retire in 1792. Seeing that his own presence in office was preventing the partisanship he abhorred from rising to the level of the chief magistracy, Washington left himself the ready out that he would not leave if it "would involve the Country in serious disputes" over his replacement. With policy disputes aplenty and no other George Washingtons emerging, this condition was easily met, and the Father of His Country stayed on the job.[4]

By 1796, there was better reason to believe that Washington was committed to retiring this time. He was sixty-four years old, and the old age talk was more than talk. A third term was his for the taking, but neither the election nor the service promised to be quiet or pleasant. There might not have been anyone to run against him, but clearly the *Aurora* and the rest of the Democratic-Republican press were not going to let him stand again completely unmolested. Washington himself seemed to agree with one of the bitterest statements against his administration, the *Kentucky Gazette*'s "Political Creed of a Western American," which said that he was in "political dotage" and in need of "a "transfer . . . from the chair of state to the chair of domestic ease.'"[5] Yet the president's specific intentions, especially as to the timing and manner of retirement, were a mystery even to those quite close to the situation. By early January, Vice President John Adams was convinced he was being groomed to take over. He was "quite a favourite," Adams told his wife, having been asked to dine with the president three times in three weeks, a change from the indifference of earlier years. Daddy Vice was feeling a little giddy about being "Heir Apparent," but a close reading of his letters to Abigail indicates that Adams had little firsthand knowledge on which to base this hope: "Every Person I meet believes The P. is determined unequivocally to retire," but The P. himself had not said anything. The election was not even "a subject of Conversation as yet."[6] Aching for promotion, the vice president kept himself on tenterhooks as numerous insulting rumors swirled through the city, many suggesting that he, Adams, might stay on as vice president under whoever might be elected to replace Washington, be it Thomas Jefferson or the man favored by many devoted Hamiltonians, Chief Justice John Jay. Highly status-conscious, John and Abigail Adams both resolved that he would "be Second under no Man but Washington."[7]

Inquiring Federalists had more on their minds than torturing Adams with possible slights. In response to the House treaty debate and the Republican newspaper attacks, they had set themselves to elevating Washington's reputation even higher than before, putting on the most elaborate birthday celebrations yet. Literal hymns of praise "raise[d] the note of rapture high," inviting the nation to *"hail the morn,* A WASHINGTON for you was born" and the angels, "those Patriots from the spangled sky," to "applaud our gratitude and love." Parades and dinners were held, salutes were fired, and in a uniquely Federalist twist on festive politics, the students at Harvard went to bed early. "Saying to each other, it would be disgraceful to pretend to honor WASHINGTON with riot and disorder," the young men were in their rooms, lights out by 9 o'clock, and let others do the drinking for a change. The celebrations were intended to show the president, and his opponents, that the people still loved him best. According to John Adams, the Federalists hoped "to counterballance Abuses by Compliments" and perhaps persuade the president not to resign after all. Every day's mail, the Boston editor Benjamin Russell was convinced, would "bring fresh recitals of the joy of the day"; since the opposition had declared "the voice of the people" to be "the Voice of Heaven," they would have to stop their "endeavors to estrange the affections of the People from the Man who unites all hearts." Amid the pealing paeans, Washington invited Adams to the theater with him and Martha to reassure his understudy about his retirement plans and quiet the talk (or so it has been surmised), but prominent Federalists continued to hold out hope for a third term into the late summer.[8]

They were left free to hope because Washington continued to withhold a definitive announcement of his retirement. Still advising the president long distance from New York, Alexander Hamilton was well aware that Washington truly wanted to resign: he visited Philadelphia in February and learned of the president's renewed decision directly. During the visit, Washington asked his old amanuensis to work on a new, updated draft of the Farewell Address that Madison had penned four years earlier. Hamilton and others expertly managed the general's ample pride and habitual caution, continually urging delay and suggesting excuses to stay in office no matter what people expected: "You have an obvious justification in the state of things. If a storm gathers, how can you retreat?" The president originally planned to announce his resignation and publish his valedictory remarks at the end of the congressional session, thinking correctly that this option would leave the least room for the complaint that he was trying to unfairly influence the election: "It would have removed doubts from the minds of *all*, and left the field clear for *all*." Talked out of that plan by Hamilton, who did not want to leave the field clear and was keen to delay the announcement by any means possible, Washington was reduced to asking his former secretary the "*next* best time" to break the news. He was loath to appear as though he was leaving office because of "fallen popularity, and despair of being reelected." Hamilton counseled silence and expressed his hope that Washington would reconsider, even as they worked out the final text of the Farewell Address late in the summer.[9]

The other parties to Washington's retirement decision were the British and the French governments. The outbreak of war, especially with France, was the main eventuality that could have kept the general in the game for a third term; but while French envoy Pierre Adet and his Paris superiors were bitterly hostile to Washington's administration and their official policy was intrigue against it, Adet also believed that the best chance for restoring the old U.S.-France alliance was a new president. His advice to the officials back home was to avoid for a while the kinds of provocative statements and actions that might inspire Washington to remain in office. French foreign minister Charles Delacroix wanted to foster "*l'heureuse Révolution*" in the United States and get Washington ousted as soon as possible, but his government also premised its actions on the idea that "friends of France" were many among the American leadership and the population at large. Thomas Jefferson was only one of many names mentioned in the French correspondence as a more congenial alternative to Washington and Hamilton. These friends could get the job done and, perhaps with a little help *de leurs amis*, make America "the Holland of the New World" (a reference to a recent French-inspired revolution in the Netherlands). One of the friends, James Monroe, represented the United States in Paris, and he assured Delacroix that "left to ourselves, everything will I think be satisfactorily arranged and *perhaps in the course of the present year*."[10]

Monroe's last remark seemed to refer to the possible change of presidents, but he may or may not have been aware how little had actually been done about the upcoming election in the middle of the Jay Treaty battle. In response to Monroe's inquiries, and indirectly to the French government's, James Madison penned a letter of reassurance that has become our earliest confirmation that an opposition candidate had been agreed upon, though not nominated in any formal or public sense. "The republicans knowing that Jefferson alone can be started with hope of success," Madison wrote, "mean to push him." While this missive has been taken as evidence that the campaign had already been launched, in reality it meant something like the opposite. Don't worry, we're ready, Madison was letting interested parties in Paris know; but in fact he and the other leading Republicans in Philadelphia were too preoccupied just then with the constitutional crisis over the Jay Treaty appropriations to take much action on the presidential question.[11]

NOMINATION: THE PROCESS THAT DARE NOT SPEAK ITS NAME

It was one of the ironies of the Washington-era republic's political culture that meddling foreign governments were more interested in fostering American democracy than most American officeholders were. French foreign policy was to "raise up the people" of the United States so they could seek a new president, but locals had barely mentioned the issue to the people or anyone else. While both parties believed the majority of the people were ultimately on their side, and appealed to public opinion in promoting their preferred policies, they showed remarkably little interest in the part of the presidential election process that now goes on the longest, the identification and selection of candidates.[12]

On one level, this was a reflection of the convictions about national leadership discussed at the beginning of this book. Patriot Kings were selected by the hand of God and social consensus, not floated like trial balloons. Washington had simply emerged as the country's most virtuous gentlemen, and hence as the man most eligible to become national leader and stand-in monarch. Anyone who seemed more aggressively or self-interestedly ambitious was unworthy of the post and a danger to liberty.[13] While not without elements of calculation and even hypocrisy, this ethic was not merely a cynical stance. It really did govern the leading contenders' personal behavior. Of all the eventual leading candidates, only New York's Aaron Burr did anything overtly on his own behalf, and he caused problems for himself and Jefferson by doing so. Burr's visit to Monticello in the fall of 1795 became an issue in the fall of 1796, especially in the one Virginia elector race where Jefferson actually lost a vote. Even more tellingly, only John Adams ever committed to paper the idea that he might be interested in the presidency, and then only within his own family, though over and over and over again. Living in the political hothouse of Philadelphia while serving as vice president, Adams claimed that he remained silent when someone brought up the presidency in his presence. Partly it was just embarrassing to expose oneself to the potential failure of one's ambitions. "I have no very ardent desire to be the Butt of Party Malevolence," admitted Adams. "Having tasted of that Cup I found it bitter, nauseous and unwholesome."[14]

Of course, a more practical reason for the lack of a public nomination process was the seeming lack of need for one. The Founders all had extensive networks of correspondents that circulated certain kinds of political information well enough, along with a stream of rumors and predictions that often turned out to be accurate. Private letters and word of mouth had been adequate to concentrate the 1789 and 1792 electoral votes on Washington and Adams, and Jefferson and Madison had made heavy use of private correspondence in recruiting like-minded members of the political elite to oppose the policies of Hamilton, long before the creation of the *National Gazette*. As the source notes of this study indicate, private letters were a crucial channel between the politicians of 1796. At the same time, the inadequacies of the private mode of conducting high politics showed in the many stratagems, deceptions, and misunderstandings surrounding the question of running mates. As we will see below, these included multiple plays designed to substitute an obvious running mate for the man widely understood to be the presidential candidate, accidentally on purpose, by gaming the original rules of the Electoral College.[15]

Unquestionably, the first candidate to be "selected" for the 1796 presidential election was the Democratic-Republican champion, Thomas Jefferson. Alexander Hamilton and his minions had been accusing Jefferson of presidential ambitions since 1792, and by mid-November 1795 the assumption was widespread enough for New York Republican leader Robert R. Livingston to write Madison suggesting that with the House Jay Treaty fight looming, "public attention should be turned as soon as possible on Mr. Jefferson." In Livingston's mind, matters had already progressed to the point where it was time to maneuver for the vice presidency. But perhaps the New Yorkers, as per usual, were a bit aggressive in their ambitions. Other than Madison's occasional reassurances to outsiders, there is little evidence of serious activity toward a Jefferson campaign before the late spring of 1796, in the press or in private.[16]

What we can say for certain is that whatever was happening, Thomas Jefferson himself was not involved. Back home farming since the end of 1793, Jefferson himself did nothing to bring his candidacy about. Even if Jefferson was the shifty mastermind painted by his rivals, remotely managing his own presidential campaign from Monticello was out of the question. The mountains of Albemarle County, Virginia, were still a remote place in 1796, and Jefferson claimed to be enjoying the soft pillow of ignorance as to current events in Philadelphia. He could keep up a furious rate of correspondence, but that rate declined noticeably during the years after his resignation as secretary of state. He admitted to John Adams that he was not keeping up his usual twelve-a-day pace. The notoriously comprehensive *Papers of Thomas Jefferson* series, which took half a century and twenty-seven volumes to get Jefferson through 1793, knocks out the interregnum between his tours as secretary of state and vice president, 1794–1796, in a mere volume and a half.[17]

While Jefferson exaggerated his isolation from national political currents, there is ample evidence that he really was focusing his attentions elsewhere in this period. Much of this evidence can be found around Monticello itself. Many of the key renovations that brought the mansion to its present form were performed in this period, which also saw Jefferson launch a nail-making business (using slave labor, of course) and work on a number of agricultural improvements, including his famous mould-board plow. He and his family sometimes lived in temporary quarters while construction work was going on, occasionally without a roof. Not surprisingly, Jefferson was frequently in ill-health during his agricultural and architectural interregnum.[18]

Another domestic matter that may have distracted the master of Monticello from politics around this time was his slave Sally Hemings. Long before extrapolations based on descendants' DNA were thought of, the best evidence for a sexual relationship between Jefferson and Sally (his late wife's half-sister) was the fact that all of Sally's known children were conceived at times when she and Jefferson were occupying the same location. She was with him in France as a teenager, and gave birth for the first time in 1790 just after they returned. Jefferson lived away from Monticello during most of his time serving as secretary of state, and despite being in her prime childbearing years, Sally did not become pregnant again until after his retirement from that post. The oldest of her children to survive infancy, a girl named Harriet, was born in 1795 right in the middle of Jefferson's long preelection sojourn at home. Not coincidentally, Jefferson freed Sally's brothers James and Robert in the same period. Harriet died in 1797, but there would be other children who became the progenitors of a large extended family of African Americans who knew they were descendants of Thomas Jefferson.[19]

Much like his colleagues Washington, Adams, and Madison, Jefferson also had a complex relationship with his own political ambitions, a topic almost never raised in his voluminous correspondence covering every other conceivable subject. Jefferson's only recorded remarks about his presidential candidacy concerned the possibility of announcing his refusal to stand for the office and the superior qualifications of others, including Madison. Of course, providing some fodder for those who see Jefferson as maddeningly coy and hypocritical, the Sage also never took the definitive step of publishing a letter abjuring the presidency. However, he did repeatedly disavow any further political ambitions to Madison and other friends, in full knowledge that his private letters had a way of ending up in the press without his consent. Madison worried about the impact of his candidate's disavowals becoming public knowledge. "I fear much that he will mar the project" and ensure a Federalist win, Madison wrote nervously to James Monroe, "by a peremptory and public protest" against any interest in the presidency. Worried about what his candidate might say, Madison avoided contact and correspondence with his neighbor and best friend for much of 1796 so as not to give Jefferson any opportunity to mess things up permanently.[20]

Though it was not publicly expressed during the election year, one thing we know Jefferson did not lack in 1796, at least until the election's confused aftermath, was emotional and ideological commitment to the opposition party. Though he still caviled at the idea of being run for president and continued to play the "mute tribune," Jefferson no longer had any patience with a definition of patriotism that demanded staying above or trying to steer between the two parties. Principles were at stake, not just power and money, and that made all the difference. By the end of 1795, Jefferson was defending partisanship from his Virginia mountaintop in a vein that would not have been out of place in the pages of the *Aurora* or a Tammany Society meeting: "Were parties here divided merely by a greediness for office, as in England, to take a part with either would be unworthy of a reasonable or moral man. But where the principle of difference is as substantial and as strongly pronounced as between the republicans and the Monocrats of our country I hold it as honorable to take a firm and decided part, and as immoral to pursue a middle line, as between the parties of Honest men, and Rogues, into which every country is divided." Private letters were often shown around in early American politics, so undoubtedly such sentiments filtered out to Jefferson's supporters around the country, emboldening some of them with the impression that their standard-bearer sat with them, even if he could not yet stand. In that sense, even such a private letter was an act of campaigning.[21]

It would be wrong, however, to think of passionate expressions like this as only or primarily calculated. Much more than James Madison, Thomas Jefferson was privately in profound agreement with the views of even the most radical elements of Democratic-Republican politics in Philadelphia, including the turn against President Washington. Observing the final battle over the Jay Treaty from afar in April 1796, Jefferson fired off a cri de coeur that he certainly did not expect anyone in American politics to read. It was attached to a business letter to one of his European intellectual friends, Phillip Mazzei, an Italian wine merchant who had once lived in Virginia (where he tried to start a vineyard) but returned back across the Atlantic in 1785. Jefferson reported to Mazzei that things had fallen apart woefully in the nation that had once been such a beacon to Old World liberals like himself: "The aspect of our politics has wonderfully changed since you left us. In place of that noble love of liberty and republican government which carried us triumphantly thro' the war, an Anglican, monarchical and aristocratical party has sprung up, whose avowed object is to draw over us the substance as they have already done the forms of the British government." Then Jefferson uncorked some near-poetic invective that he would come to regret putting in the mail. "It would give you a fever," he told Mazzei, "were I to name to you the apostates who have gone over to these heresies, men who were Samsons in the field and Solomons in the council, but who have had their heads shorn by the harlot England." Thus Jefferson accused his senior revolutionary colleagues George Washington and John Adams of being little more than British stooges, it mattered not whether by corruption or gullibility. The "Mazzei letter" became a kind of historical gaffe that followed Jefferson through the centuries, but it did not become public until after the 1796 election was resolved. For our purposes, it is more important for revealing that Jefferson's heart was resolved to reenter the lists and carry on the campaign against the Federalists even though his head told him to stay out of the public presidential campaign of 1796: "In short we are likely to preserve the liberty we have obtained only by unremitting labors and perils."[22]

The pretzels of denial that Jefferson and most of the other early presidential candidates twisted themselves into are not without their darkly comic aspects. Printer and Aaron Burr henchman Matthew Livingston Davis was flabbergasted at the "unexampled hypocrisy" and "base abandonment of all principle" on display in Jefferson's comments about the 1796 election, upon getting to read his letters when they were first published many years later. "In relation to office," wrote Davis, Jefferson "was very jesuitical, always disclaiming any wish to fill public stations, yet always ready to accept them." Jefferson's rivals commonly complained about this tendency to achieve his ends through "stratagem, manoeuvre, finesse, and deception" rather than open confrontation, but he was not at all unique among the founding generation in terms of operating quietly and indirectly through "friends."[23]

This was indeed *standard* operating procedure. Friends were considered the most appropriate way for an elite man to have his interests promoted, a practice that provided society with some degree of protection by theoretically showing that a candidate could be trusted, because others trusted him and would take responsibility for his character and actions. Among the gentry, friends carried each other's letters, guaranteed each other's debts, and adjudicated each other's disputes—under the code of honor, the arrangements for a duel (or an apology) had to be handled by the parties' friends until the actual shooting started. Friends certainly handled much campaigning for office, or at least it looked better if they did. A large network of friends indicated influence and popularity.[24]

Normal as it was, this personalistic system ran into problems when applied to a position of national leadership like the presidency, especially one that required the support of the voters at large. Trust networks did not work among people who did not trust each other, like the Virginia and New York Republicans, and face-to-face contacts could only stretch so far. Even networks extended by private letters could do little to win broader public support, at least not directly. (Letters that fed into some public forum like a newspaper were a different story.) New kinds of campaigning quickly emerged, but for the rest of the eighteenth and most of the nineteenth century, it would almost never involve campaigning by the presidential candidates themselves. They had to sit still and silent, and be auditioned for the role: British historian Michael Heale dubbed this stance "The Mute Tribune." The experiments with speaking tours by William Henry Harrison in 1836 and 1840, Winfield Scott in 1852, and Stephen Douglas in 1860 were controversial exceptions, put down by traditionalists as the desperate acts of tyros and losers. In the 1880s, presidential candidates normalized the practice of speaking regularly to voters by doing so from their front porches, but only after the William Jennings Bryan stump-speaking campaigns of 1896 and 1900 would critics stop complaining and candidates be expected to tour the country.[25]

The seemingly passive and monarchical stance of the early presidential candidates did not necessarily exclude the idea of democracy, of the national leader as the people's choice. Americans wanted to have their mystical, patriotic unanimity and their democracy too, without the messy arguments. The unwilled nature of Washington's elevation to the presidency was adduced as both the ultimate evidence and a continuing cause of his popular support. To the arch-Federalist Boston *Columbian Centinel*, the birthday celebrations and legislative victories of early 1796 proved that Washington was still the "man of the people," using a phrase that would be much more commonly applied to Thomas Jefferson. The *Centinel* seemed to approve "man of the people" status in Washington's case, even as it denounced "democrats" and their ideas in almost every other. John Adams hoped fervently that the election would be a noncompetitive, monarchy-like process: he habitually referred to it as "the succession." Yet at the same time, he claimed to bow before the power of democracy: "I have a pious and a philosophical Resignation to the Voice of the People in this Case which is the Voice of God." The Federalist version of *vox populi* had the particular character of speaking rarely, giving voice to what it imagined to be society as a whole and only in cases of extreme danger. This usually silent majority was omnipotent when roused against mere "factions" that threatened the community with division and evil. In the case of the Jay Treaty, "Had [the people] been silent, our country was *ruined.*—FACTION has fallen! Fallen, like LUCIFER, never more to rise!"[26]

One reason that the "man of the people" mantle could settle on

Thomas Jefferson was that his candidacy, like Washington's, had the advantage of seeming to emerge on its own, gaining the support of a wide variety of politicians in various parts of the country without anyone seeming to promote it very heavily or even write each other about it. One of the very few public mentions of Jefferson that can be found during the years of his retirement was a toast raised by Philadelphia County's militia officers for the Fourth of July 1795 that did not even mention the former secretary of state by name. The Philadelphians raised their glasses to the "Congress of 1776," and issued a rather oblique call for a Jefferson presidency: "May the illustrious framer of the declaration of American independence . . . be called from his retirement, and by his virtues, his patriotism, and his wisdom save us from the calamities which threaten us."[27]

John Adams's home state supporters somewhat belatedly tried to do something similar for him in conjunction with Washington's birthday in 1796. The Boston birthday toasts gave Adams a rather backhanded salute that actually highlighted his previous eight years of obscurity with occasional breaks for controversy over his philosophical writings: "The Vice President of the United States—May Americans never forget the blessings they owe to his firmness, nor the truths his talents have explored." Taking what she could get, Abigail Adams was glad the locals had "for once done justice" to her husband and hoped the toasts looked forward to "a future contemplated event." Unfortunately, the wanness of the efforts to boost the Adams image and the whole Adams family's tendency to obsess about John's candidacy, without feeling able to actively do or write anything about it, were factors that would hamper both of his presidential campaigns.[28]

The transition of Jefferson's candidacy from a consensus among officials and political activists to a public matter was actually effected by opponents seeking to reduce his credibility as a new Patriot King. In retrospect, we can see that what a national candidate needed to cut through the Electoral College's tiered system was name recognition, but the immorality of campaigning for the presidency loomed much larger in the minds of eighteenth-century politicians, especially the Federalists. So it was Alexander Hamilton and his close allies who took it upon themselves to publish the idea of Jefferson as a presidential candidate before Madison had breathed or written even a private word about it. Modern students of presidential nominations have written of the press's role as "The Great Mentioner," putting names into play at the beginning of the process. There was clearly a similar effect at work in the 1790s, but in many cases that effect was intended to be negative—the Great Mentioner in Reverse. By mentioning a candidate's name in the press, opponents could make him seem too designing and ambitious to be president.[29]

As we have seen, Hamilton and friends had been outing Jefferson as the opposition's prime mover since the very beginning of the party conflict. So naturally they claimed to see an "evident design" to promote his presidential candidacy in the 1795 Fourth of July toasts, despite the fact that almost every subject imaginable, including female education and the republic of Holland, were mentioned as much as, or far more than, Thomas Jefferson. Before Hamilton renewed his assault, it was only with hindsight and inside knowledge that one could even detect from the public prints that Jefferson was a major leader of the opposition. Not overwhelmingly famous to begin with, certainly not on the level of Washington or Franklin, Jefferson had been virtually invisible since the scandals over the *National Gazette* and Citizen Genet that had helped drive him from office. In the first installment of his "Camillus" essays in defense of the Jay Treaty, Hamilton advanced the dubious thesis that much of the hue and cry against the treaty amounted to a personal assault on Jay, intended to raise up Jefferson and Governor George Clinton in his place. Noah Webster agreed. The "real grounds" of the drive to stop the treaty in Congress was "that Jefferson, Madison, and Burr, itching for the high offices of our government, will leave untried no probable means of accomplishing their views."[30]

In one of those self-destructive gambits that marked his record in electoral politics (as opposed to policy or law or military strategy), Hamilton incorporated into his first "Camillus" essay one of the first open listings of the likely contenders for the presidential chair in the event that Washington retired; he put forward the names of two of his least favorite people, along with a third candidate who may have stood high in New York elite circles but elsewhere was more likely to be burned in effigy than bruited for high office: "There are three persons prominent in the public eye," Hamilton wrote, "Mr. Adams, Mr. Jay, Mr. Jefferson."[31]

Had there been such a person as a manager of Jefferson's primary campaign in 1795, he would have been very pleased to see his man anointed as a front-runner by his greatest enemy. Throughout his newspaper writings, during the Jay Treaty controversy but also going back to 1792, Hamilton periodically singled out Jefferson for attack, and in doing so inspired some early public defenses and promotions of the Sage of Monticello as national leader and tribune of the people. A writer in Newburgh, New York, departed from the usual Latinate pseudonyms and signed himself "Jefferson" under an essay emphasizing the need for every American "to think and to act for himself," not listening to high government officials or presumed social betters, at such an "awful crisis of our affairs." On one occasion, the Philadelphia *Aurora* probably dared too much in offering Jefferson as an alternative to Washington, and indeed as a key bulwark against the allegedly rising tide of monarchy. According to "Valerius," the attacks were nothing more than a plot designed to weaken an obstacle to Hamilton's evil plans: "[Jefferson's] popularity, it was expected, would become so universal, in a little time, as to make him emphatically the man of the people. He had already shewn himself the disciple of liberty. Such a name possessed by such a man might delay, by a century, the era of monarchy, it might destroy it forever. This reputation must therefore be blasted." Overdrawn and premature as this article was, it put its finger on the mentality that drove Hamilton to continually invoke Jefferson's name when the more effective strategy might have been to let it recede into the obscurity of the Virginia Piedmont. At any rate, partly because of the Federalist penchant for attacking Jefferson, by early 1796 Madison was clearly correct that his friend was the only viable Democratic-Republican candidate.[32]

Another figure who owed much of his national prominence to the Reverse Great Mentioner was Senator Aaron Burr of New York. The grandson of the famous New England preacher Jonathan Edwards, Burr had turned his back on the Christian faith and politics of his forebears and relatives, then stepped on toes and raised hackles with his rapid rise to political power in New York. Without a firm alignment to any major faction in New York politics, Burr was appointed by Governor George Clinton as state attorney general in 1789, and two years later surprised both observers and rivals by taking a Senate seat from Philip Schuyler, Hamilton's father-in-law and one of New York state's richest and most powerful men. With little hope of allying with his own Federalist relatives after that, Senator Burr emerged as one of the more effective congressional opponents of the Washington administration, becoming especially conspicuous in the Jay Treaty debate. He was the only senator from east of the Potomac to vote against John Jay's original appointment

The Candidate: New York senator Aaron Burr was the only 1796 candidate to campaign for himself, and there were many questions about what Burr was really after—to be Jefferson's running mate, to be president himself, or possibly something more. (Drawing after St. Memin, Library of Congress.)

and then became the leader of the "Patriotic Ten" senators who voted against the treaty.[33]

The legend of Burr was built especially by the Federalist press. By 1796, complaints about "a certain little senator" had been issuing from Federalist editors like Noah Webster for some time. During the Jay Treaty controversy, the leading literary men of the time, the so-called Connecticut Wits, made Burr a star villain of their satirical epic *The Democratiad*, published as a separate pamphlet and also as part of their ongoing newspaper series "The Echo." Two of the leading Wits, Theodore and Timothy Dwight, were cousins of Burr. "On Burr alone our hopes and wishes lay, / Burr was our spokesman, counsellor, and stay," the Wits made the congressional Republicans say. These were not compliments. In fact, the thrust of the poem was damning the "Jacobins" for getting in bed with a man like Burr: "Go search the records of intrigue, and find, / to what debasement sinks the human mind, / How far 'tis possible for man to go, / Where interest sways and passions urge the blow; / While pride and pleasures; haughtiness and scorn, / And mad ambition in his bosom burn."[34]

Why was allowing Burr to become an important leader such a terrible prospect? In short, no politician of the time seemed to contradict prevailing political and social mores more flagrantly. Even among blunt New Yorkers, Burr seems to have stood out in the nakedness of his ambition for political power and place and even more for his willingness to campaign openly, for causes and for himself. In a manner more common among the ambitious young senators of the twentieth and twenty-first centuries than the eighteenth, Burr set his eyes on higher office almost immediately after his arrival in Philadelphia. The Republican opposition needed a non-Virginian to stand on the deck of their flagship, if not actually to helm it, so why not a certain little senator? Burr first put himself in the running for vice president during the abortive 1792 effort to oust John Adams. New York rivals and prospective Virginia allies alike were shocked that someone so new "upon the public theatre" was being put forward, and Burr had to bow out late in favor of the baggage-laden Governor Clinton. By 1795, Clinton was ill and seemingly headed for retirement, so Burr went first for the governor's chair, touring all over New York State in the first of his several unsuccessful runs for that office. Beginning in the second half of 1795, Burr seemed to take aim at the vice presidency again, traveling up and down the country from New Hampshire to Virginia on errands that were widely interpreted as political in nature. In October 1795, Burr's extensive itinerary even included a day at Monticello, a fact that the normally secretive senator must have made known as he headed west from Richmond. A local editor's notice that Burr was on his way to see Jefferson and Madison "on business of importance" spread far and wide through the Republican and Federalist press. The latter came to treat the trip as evidence of a political conspiracy. At the same time, the publicity pushed Burr's name to the top of the list of potential opposition candidates not named Jefferson. As Hamilton put it, this was a man who was not afraid to be "industrious in his canvass."[35]

Burr's strenuous politicking earned him a fiercely loyal network of supporters, the "Little Band"; but even an impressive intellect and magnetic personal charm could not outweigh the distrust Burr inspired in other leading men of both major political persuasions. Aggressive campaigning in a man of his education and august family background seemed a suspicious sort of slumming, raising fears that he was grossly opportunistic and "unsettled in his politics." Few men on either side of the party conflict seemed to believe that Burr was sincere or truly committed in abandoning his Federalist family connections for Democratic-Republican political allies. Almost alone among the major leaders of his generation, Burr left almost no documents behind outlining any kind of political philosophy. Some of his congressional speeches were reported, but no substantive political essays or even letters have been identified, at least not between Burr and other politicians. (He wrote much more openly and philosophically to his wife and daughter.) On paper, Burr was all business and systematically enigmatic. Alexander Hamilton cordially hated the man, not only as a longtime professional rival going back to army days and continuing into their mutual legal careers, but also for private character flaws he never detailed for the record. Most of all, however, Hamilton feared Burr's combination of vaulting ambition and complete lack of discernible principle. "As a public man he is one of the worst sort—a friend to nothing but as it suits his interest and ambition," Hamilton had written privately at the time of Burr's first run for vice presidency. "In a word, if we have an embryo-Caesar in the United States 'tis Burr." On various occasions, Hamilton threw his support to some of his other least favorite politicians, including George Clinton and Thomas Jefferson, just to block Burr.[36]

Many of Burr's Democratic-Republican colleagues did not like him much better. The visit to Monticello may not have been welcome. Jefferson's only recorded reference to the event was a throwaway line making it clear to his neighbor Wilson Cary Nicholas that Burr had only been at his house for one day. Later, in response to Federalist charges of conspiracy, the word was put out that no other politicians had been present during the visit; Burr had only gotten the same Jefferson family dinner that hundreds of other travelers enjoyed. While the master of Monticello's capacity for secret transactions should never be underestimated, subsequent developments do not suggest that any clear-cut meeting of minds was reached. The Little Band believed that Jefferson and Madison betrayed their man by not securing Virginia's full electoral vote for him in 1796, but in truth it seems doubtful that Burr ever had their support to begin with, at least not unequivocally. Savvy as he was, Burr may have let himself be taken in by one of Jefferson's erudite and friendly but indirect dinner conversations. Table chat was one of his great gifts as a politician; Burr would not have been the only visitor to Monticello who came away with inflated ideas of his own relationship with the host.[37]

Jefferson later claimed he had never trusted Burr, and there is good evidence that the Virginians were extremely wary of him from the beginning. From Paris, James Monroe wrote that he considered Burr "a man to be shunned . . . an unprincipled adventurer . . . whom it is better to get rid of at once." Beyond the character issues, the Virginians saw Burr as a potential threat to Jefferson. The electoral system did not make a distinction between presidential and vice-presidential slots, so vice-presidential candidates could not be legally defined as such; the running mate or his supporters would have to defer, preferably by dropping a few electoral votes and trying to come in second. The New Yorker's basic purpose in visiting Jefferson was probably to assure him that no competition was intended by his campaigning, but few who dealt with Burr ever seemed completely sure what he was up to, and ambition *was* one of his few proven qualities.[38]

The true origin of the antipathy to Burr, or at least a possible explanation of its intensity, seems to be his private life. For many of his colleagues, Burr's willingness to transgress customary limits in his political activities dovetailed a little too well with what they knew or heard about his personal behavior. Simply put, Burr was a seducer, not only of the audiences he swayed with his speeches and the impressionable young politicians who became his followers, but also of women, apparently of all ages and conditions. He also probably paid a considerable number of women for their sexual services, a quite common and legal practice in this era, especially in New York City, where prostitutes made themselves openly available in the balconies of theaters and leading citizens invested in or rented property to brothels. However, Burr was characteristically more open about it than most men of his station. His second wife was "the leading prostitute in post-Revolutionary America," Eliza Bowen Jumel. (Jumel and Burr got together decades later; he was a recent widower during the 1796 campaign.) Of course, slave-owning men did not require the services of prostitutes, so it would have been hypocritical of the Virginians to be shocked by Burr's behavior, but there were plenty of northerners who seemed to feel the same way.[39]

Burr began his lifelong campaign of womanizing early and kept it up throughout a very long life, amassing and carefully preserving a collection of trophy letters from his conquests. The habit may or may not have been suspended during his seemingly happy marriage to Theodosia Bartow Prevost from 1782 to 1794, but even there Burr transgressed. Prevost was an attractive widow ten years his senior whose previous marriage Burr had invaded before her absent British officer husband's timely death. Modern historians have tended to skirt this aspect of Burr's life, perhaps because so much of the concrete evidence was deliberately destroyed, but a reputation for sexual libertinism seems to be one likely explanation for the veiled references that detractors commonly made to his private morality, often as the crowning argument against trusting Burr. It was over an (unrecorded) comment of this type that Burr would duel and kill Alexander Hamilton in 1804.[40]

The person who destroyed the evidence was more frank about this "strong and revolting trait" in Burr's character. Having proudly burned the love letter collection to save the reputations of several prominent families who had contacted him, the former vice president's long-time crony and literary executor Matthew Livingston Davis devoted two pages of his otherwise admiring book to a scathing if maddeningly vague denunciation of Burr's relations with the opposite sex: "For more than half a century," seducing women "seemed to absorb his whole thoughts. His intrigues were without number. His conduct most licentious. The sacred bonds of friendship were unhesitatingly violated when they operated as barriers to the indulgence of his passions." Davis did link his hero to the ruination of one specific woman, the fourteen-year-old daughter of a British officer, Major Moncrief, because she later had published her own story. In Davis's account, Burr comes off like the rake character in an early sentimental novel.[41]

His most scholarly biographer, Nancy Isenberg, takes the very different view that Burr was in fact an early feminist, based on the extremely progressive views on women's equality and child-rearing expressed in his letters to his wife and daughter (who was also named Theodosia). According to Isenberg, Burr was an enthusiastic reader of Mary Wollstonecraft's *Vindication of the Rights of Woman* who educated his daughter to transcend the gender limitations of the age: "His daughter's special calling was to prove that Wollstonecraft was right and that women were as capable as men of genius and reflection—that, indeed, 'women have souls.'" Isenberg makes a strong case; Burr did take a strikingly open, egalitarian tone in communicating with the two Theodosias. Yet both Davis and Isenberg might be right. Burr would hardly be the only cultural avant-gardist in history capable of abusing his advanced new morality to justify the gratification of his baser impulses. At the same time, any philosophical heterodoxies he expressed to other men on the subject of sex and gender would only have made his behavior more disturbing to the more socially traditional gentlemen he dealt with in politics. If anything, the sexual outlet provided by slavery probably only reinforced the narrow thinking of southern men like Jefferson, Madison, and Monroe where the sexuality of white women was concerned.[42]

Despite their distrust, Virginia's Democratic-Republican leaders found it impossible to follow Monroe's advice and get rid of Burr politically. It seemed crucial to balance Jefferson of Virginia with a northerner, especially from the mid-Atlantic, and Burr's name kept coming forward, pushed there by its owner *and* his many detractors. In the end, Burr's canvassing may have forced the first semiformal nomination activity in American presidential history. However, the event was far too fleeting and inconclusive to count as the beginning of the congressional caucus nominating system, an "institution" that never attained sufficient legitimacy to merit the attention that historians and textbooks have lavished on it.[43]

Here is what happened in 1796. Recognizing that some agreement was required on a vice-presidential candidate if the Federalists were to be shut out of the executive branch, and that the congressional session was the only occasion when national leaders could talk face-to-face, Democratic-Republican members of Congress held a meeting about the upcoming election at the very end of the House Jay Treaty debate. Or so rumor had it. The Federalists who provide our only evidence of this meeting called it a "caucus," a word connoting a secret conspiratorial cabal rather than just a gathering of legislative allies. If there really was such a nominating caucus, it failed to make a firm decision. James Madison did not report attending such a caucus. He was able to tell James Monroe what was "now generally understood" in Philadelphia, but the passive voice and vague language seem key. It was thought that the president would retire, Madison told Monroe, and that at the next election, "Jefferson [would be] the object on one side Adams apparently on the other." However, the "secondary objects" were "still unsettled." Aaron Burr would not have been pleased to learn that he was only a "secondary object" to Madison.[44]

The Federalists told each other much better stories. Representative William Loughton Smith and Secretary of the Senate Samuel A. Otis heard that Aaron Burr led the vote but not decisively. Too many Republicans were "afraid he would go over to the other side." John Langdon of New Hampshire and Burr's more senior New York rival, Robert R. Livingston, also received significant support, and South Carolina senator Pierce Butler left the meeting in a huff because he was not more heavily favored. The only objection to Butler was sectional balance: his "being a Southern man and as Jefferson is to be president, it won't do." The Virginians leaned toward Livingston, a jurist and country gentleman who contrasted well with Burr in that he operated politically in much more conventional manner, or at least more like Jefferson and Madison: reversing the Burr profile, Livingston's political ideas were down on paper and his political ambitions had been pursued with circumspection and indirection. At any rate, though this first nominating "caucus" is sometimes said to have blessed Burr's candidacy for vice president, in truth endorsement by such a shadowy meeting was the opposite of a blessing: it relegated the Burr candidacy to the status of failed backroom cabal that no elector was truly bound to respect. Later, many of them did not. The "caucus" does seem to have worked for Burr in Pennsylvania, a state that was more accustomed to parties and nominations than most. In early summer, the leading Pennsylvania Republicans were reported to be "decided in favor of Burr," apparently regarding him as the regular Republican candidate.[45]

On the Federalist side, there was no overt nomination activity at all while Washington still reigned—just rumors and whisperings. John Adams retired to *his* farm, too, at the end of the congressional session, and while he paid much more overt attention to politics than Jefferson, he did little about it except lap up scraps of rumor. Abigail Adams could truly say to her husband, when it was all over, that the whole election "had been a jugal [juggle], in which you have been an inactive spectator." Luckily for Adams, he had some home state supporters eager to promote the idea that he was a somewhat worthy successor to Washington. A letter from an anonymous Federalist congressman was published recounting the whole history of the French-British foreign policy dispute, granting Adams an unusually prominent role in breaking a tie vote in the Senate in 1793, which thereby defeated a Republican bill to impose trade sanctions on the British. "Thank heaven for giving us the man," the writer enthused. On the April state election day in Boston,

Colonel Elliott's Independent Cadets toasted the vice president's possible promotion while leaving him firmly in the incumbent's shadow: "When WASHINGTON recedes from upholding the New World, may this Atlas balance our sphere." In early June, Ben Russell of the Boston *Columbian Centinel* rushed into print with the news that the president was going to retire and coupled that with a partisan message, alerting readers to take care that "none but Federal electors be appointed at the next choice." "Your worthy fellow-citizen, JOHN ADAMS" would get those votes, Russell's readers learned, even though Adams himself was still not certain about the retirement weeks later.[46]

Other potential Federalist candidates lacked allies like Ben Russell, willing to move in public and openly appeal for popular support. Exploration of the other potential candidacies proceeded in great secrecy and with predatory intent against the heir apparent. Working through intermediaries, Federalist supreme leader Alexander Hamilton was actively seeking alternatives to John Adams. Hamilton had long harbored grave doubts about Adams's abilities as a statesman, questioning the "solidity of his understanding" when it came to questions of finance and administration, and wondering whether he was not "far less able in the practice, than in the theory of politics." Not inaccurately, Hamilton was suspicious that Adams was not fully on board with his financial system and was fearful that he was potentially soft on France. Determined to see his own policies remain in place permanently, Hamilton read Adams's independence from typical Federalist views as an incapacity for "the regular display of sound judgment" or "steady perseverance in a systematic plan of conduct." He also simply found Adams a ridiculous, "eccentric" figure, blinded by "a vanity without bounds" and such an "extreme egotism of the temper" that he could even resent playing second fiddle to George Washington himself. Perhaps it took an egotist to know one.[47]

Hamilton was looking especially for a southerner who might be able to take votes away from Jefferson. The Federalists have come to be thought of as a northern, antislavery party, but like any national coalition they had to win support in more than one region, and any lack of appeal in the South had not yet been demonstrated. George Washington was a southerner, after all, and Hamilton was not willing to simply concede the region just because Jefferson was the likely opposition. What was more, it made perfect sense that the Tidewater and Low Country planter elites of Virginia and South Carolina, some of the wealthiest and most status-conscious people in the country, would not all be rampaging democrats. At the same time, much of Pennsylvania appeared to be vociferously Republican, and becoming more so as the crisis over the Whiskey Rebellion faded, so the Federalists could not rely completely on northern states to carry the day.[48]

Hamilton's first southern choice was probably the biggest name from the Revolution who had not yet made it to the national leadership, the great Virginia orator Patrick Henry, of "give me liberty or give me death" fame. One of the Constitution's most prominent opponents, Henry's primary concern had long been to celebrate and defend Virginia's local status quo—he had also stood against Jefferson's Bill for Establishing Religious Freedom and most other reforms of the state government. A bitter rival of Jefferson and Madison in Virginia politics, Henry had even less use for the French revolutionary sympathizers with whom they allied themselves in the North during the 1790s. The Federalists had been courting him for years, with President Washington offering Henry any post he wanted in his administration, up to and including secretary of state. Yet Henry had always refused; he had done a stint as governor of Virginia and seems to have sensed himself that he was more of a talker than an administrator.[49]

This noninvolvement in the battles of the first administration actually made Patrick Henry a more appealing candidate. With his fame and lack of recent baggage, Henry was perhaps the only southern figure who might have been able to usurp Jefferson's southern and western support while not losing much with the northern mercantile elites who formed the backbone of the Federalist party. With fame from the Revolution that was actually greater than Jefferson's, Henry was one of the few figures with the potential to win something close to a Washington-like national consensus victory. Through his close co-conspirator, Senator Rufus King, and the direct agency of Virginia Federalist politician and future chief justice John Marshall, Hamilton offered to have his network of supporters run Henry for the presidency, but he could not get his potential candidate to agree. Marshall sounded out Henry in Richmond personally but found him "unwilling to embark on the business." Henry seems to have feared venturing out of the Virginia pond, where he had always been the biggest fish around. His relatively advanced age (sixty) and some festering ethical issues regarding public land purchases may have added to his "apprehension" about "the difficulties of those who shall fill high Executive offices."[50]

The secret Patrick Henry boomlet was only the beginning of the machinations by Hamilton and his friends. While there was no formal Federalist caucus on the presidential nomination, Rufus King was eager to get an "arrangement" settled while most of the Hamiltonian cabalists were still together at the congressional session in Philadelphia. It was time "to fix on another person [besides Adams to run] without delay." Pondering the reports on Henry's foot-dragging and attendant warnings from Marshall that as a strident opponent of the Constitution in 1788, Henry might not be a reliable follower of national Federalist positions, Hamilton experienced some sober second thoughts about pushing Henry or any other already-established national figure. He decided abruptly in early May that he would rather "be rid of P. H." so that his network would be "at full liberty" to take up a new possibility, Thomas Pinckney of South Carolina.[51]

Having spent most of the Washington administration in Europe as a diplomat, Thomas Pinckney was a cipher in the partisan politics of the 1790s and not particularly well known in the North, but looked eligible nonetheless. A war hero who had been wounded and captured at the Battle of Camden in 1780 and who later served as governor of South Carolina, Pinckney was a member of the same Low Country rice and indigo planting family that supplied two Framers of the Constitution and a later Federalist presidential candidate, Charles Cotesworth Pinckney. In 1796, Thomas Pinckney was just preparing to return home after negotiating a treaty with Spain that had secured access to the Mississippi River, an apparent diplomatic victory that contrasted very favorably with John Jay's humiliating work in Britain. Federalist leaders hoped that this achievement would make Thomas Pinckney play as well as Patrick Henry in the expansion-minded South and West. With a popular treaty to his name and no established positions on other issues, Pinckney might possibly attract some extra votes from electors who otherwise sympathized with the Republican opposition. Jefferson, Madison, and even the *Aurora* had nice things to say about him. Hamilton and King also seem to have hoped that Pinckney's inexperience in national politics might make him someone they could more easily guide than Adams or Henry.[52]

Many historians have treated Pinckney as a *vice*-presidential nominee, but it seems clear that he and Henry were being considered from the beginning as replacements for John Adams at the top of the ticket, at least by some of the sharper-dealing Federalist leaders. Federalist

The Shadow Candidate: War hero and diplomat Thomas Pinckney, of South Carolina, was touted as Adams's running mate, but Hamilton and other Federalist leaders schemed to make Pinckney president instead of John Adams. (Miniature portrait by John Trumbull, Yale University Art Gallery.)

congressman Robert Goodloe Harper wrote back home to South Carolina with assurances to "Major Pinckney" that "the intention of bringing him forward was to make him President, and that he will be supported with that view." The reality was a bit less clear-cut. Adams was still the primary Federalist candidate, but now Pinckney's name would be thrown into the mix with his. Since the electors cast two votes without specifying which was for president and which was for vice president, it would be left "to casual accessions of votes in favor of one or the other, to turn the scale between them." One potential source of votes for Pinckney was Republicans. In short, there was nothing casual at all about the threat this posed to the Adams "succession." By bringing in a second candidate they believed to have broader appeal than the lead, Alexander Hamilton and Rufus King were plotting against John Adams.[53]

The avid interest of Federalist strategists in Thomas Pinckney, owner of multiple plantations worked by slave labor, may come as a surprise to modern readers trained to think of the Federalists as northern abolitionists battling proslavery southern Jeffersonians. Pinckney not only owned slaves, but advocated that they be treated harshly if Charleston whites were to survive as a racial minority population. It is true that many Federalists, including Alexander Hamilton and Rufus King, manifested moderate antislavery convictions in other contexts, but in 1796 they were trying to hold on to their national power and eagerly sought to keep the slaveocracy in the Federalist fold. Slavery's great bastion, South Carolina, was one of their best southern states. At the end of the spring 1796 congressional session, William Loughton Smith went back home to Charleston deputed to find some other South Carolina leader who was willing to be on the Federalist ticket if Thomas Pinckney would not.[54]

The Pinckney plot would unfold more fully later in the year, but it always had the character of a backroom manipulation, and not a very successful one at that. (See table 2 at the end of chapter 8 for a rundown of the vice-presidential scenarios.) Hamilton grossly overestimated his ability to shove aside two heroes such as John Adams and Patrick Henry, and underestimated the degree to which popular opinion and "name identification" already mattered despite the antidemocratic features of the Electoral College system. Hamilton's too-clever tactics would do much to put his ideological opposite, Thomas Jefferson, in high office not once, but twice, in 1796 and 1800.

TENNESSEE STATEHOOD AND THE SELF-FULFILLING PROPHECY OF A JEFFERSONIAN SOUTHWEST

The unformed, completely state-driven electoral process of 1796 meant that the emergence of the nominations overlapped and in some cases actually came after a number of states had in effect already made their presidential decisions. As we saw in the previous chapter, the Federalists already knew they had won New York in its spring legislative elections. But while holding New York and most of New England in pocket, they almost simultaneously alienated another state, and possibly a whole region, by seeming to set themselves in opposition to the aspirations of the southwestern frontier, then no further away than present-day Tennessee.

A long-standing, largely unexamined assumption of early American political history is the idea that the early South and West were automatically Jeffersonian territory. This belief was a staple of the "frontier democracy" thesis that was current at the turn of the twentieth century, but it has survived thanks to twenty-twenty hindsight about later voting patterns and the close link between southern expansionism and slavery that flowered in the nineteenth century. In the currently popular view, the Democratic-Republicans were a southern-dominated, proslavery, and aggressively expansionist party hostile to the interference of the federal government, like the Civil War–era Democrats, from the very beginning of their existence. Hence, the story goes, Jefferson had an automatic lock on the early West, and Kentucky and Tennessee especially.[55]

Eastern Republican leaders may have hoped that they had the West locked up, but in reality, the Jeffersonianism of the southern frontier was a pattern not yet set in 1796. It was true that the Republicans had some advantages: most Kentuckians were ex-Virginians who still had Virginia ties and allegiances that helped Jefferson; Hamilton's whiskey tax and manner of enforcing it were not appreciated in the back country; John Jay's name was mud-like throughout the Mississippi watershed and stuck to the Federalists. Yet permanent western hostility to Federalist governance was not a foregone conclusion. Indeed, there were many factors suggesting the potential appeal of the Federalist approach on the frontier. Most of the leading Federalists were not opposed to expansion, they simply wanted to see it proceed in a controlled and orderly and elite-guided way. The energetic style of government installed by Alexander Hamilton had accomplished great things for the western frontier. It was Federalists who created the United States Legion and forcefully secured the Northwest Territory against Indian rebellion and British intervention in 1793–1794. (All three of Washington's war secretaries, Henry Knox, Timothy Pickering, and James McHenry, were committed Federalist partisans.) It was on the Federalist watch that Pinckney's Treaty with Spain reopening the Mississippi River and the port of New

Orleans was signed. As for the bad Federalist treaty negotiated by John Jay, frontier regions were its only immediate beneficiaries, and as we saw in the previous chapter, the protection of frontier settlers was the argument that seemed to win that battle for the protreaty forces. The trans-Appalachian states should have been a ready market for the Federalist party, especially with Thomas Pinckney as its figurehead. As historian François Furstenberg has suggested, "it could be argued that Federalists, far more than Republicans, were most responsive to the demands of western settlers."[56]

The problems occurred when the Federalist officials indulged their tendency to treat common whites as their enemies, but poor settlers were not necessarily the primary audience for Federalist appeals. The Old Southwest has become notorious in American history for entertaining expansionist and disunionist conspiracies, sometimes with and sometimes against European nations that had adjacent colonial possessions. Yet this image is bit misleading. Much of the complaining and conspiring by the elites in places like Kentucky and Tennessee arose not from hostility to a strong central government per se, but rather from the fact that the United States neglected to provide the strong government they needed. These were not the mythical pioneers moving west to seek absolute freedom and isolation. Instead, the men who dominated politics in the early West were merchants and land speculators and officials primarily concerned with acquiring wealth and making the frontier a stable and lucrative place to buy and sell property, including both land and slaves. Their interests were represented perfectly in the Federalist land law that Congress had just passed in the spring of 1796, which set the price and sale terms for public lands to suit large-scale developers rather than individual settlers: land would be sold only in lots of 640 acres and up, for the increased price of $2 an acre. Federalists wanted an expansion that would proceed under the direction of gentleman developers and maximize revenues for both them and the government. Squatters did not make money for anybody.

Many western officials were also tough old soldiers loyal to George Washington, and they were eager to help bring his far-flung domains under control. To say that such men were unsympathetic to idealistic French schemes for world revolution, including the abolition of slavery and the slave rebellion that French abolition had spawned in Haiti, would be a serious understatement. Toasts at a public banquet denounced the "murderers of Louis XVI," while the Southwest Territory's only newspaper drew links between revolutionary and Indian violence. The Knoxville *Gazette* juxtaposed accounts of local native raids with stories of the royal executions in France. Cherokee chief Doublehead was noted as having killed as many people "as any man (not a Jacobin) of the age."[57]

One of most prominent of these frontier Federalists was William Blount, governor of the Southwest Territory that was to become the state of Tennessee. Blount came from a wealthy merchant family in North Carolina, and he had early enlisted among the friends of order by helping put down the Regulator rebellion there on the eve of the Revolution. After extensive service as an officer during the war and as a delegate to the Constitutional Convention, Blount lobbied for the job of territorial governor, partly as a way of guarding and adding to his property holdings but also out of genuine Federalist convictions. Once in office, Governor Blount "strained every nerve" to support Federalist policy coming out of Philadelphia, even when that called for a major military offensive against the northwestern Indian confederacy on the distant shores of Lake Erie but provided little funding even for self-defense against the Chickamauga, Shawnee, and Creek warriors who were actively threatening the core settlements in Tennessee. With not a little hypocrisy considering that he himself was one of most aggressive land-grabbers of the founding generation, Blount also tried to enforce the hopeless federal treaty commitments to driving whites off of unceded Indian lands and arresting white murderers of Indians. Blount became infamous a year later for his involvement in a conspiracy to organize an illegal military expedition against Spanish territory along the Mississippi, but even this was motivated by basically conservative Federalist ideas. Blount and his cohorts' chief concern was that, without intervention, Spain would inevitably turn its lands over to "the sans-coulottes" (revolutionary France), who would destroy the social order and block their development plans. Who would stand up for the property values of large-scale speculators? If the United States could not or would not defend the southwestern frontier, Blount would get the British and their Indian allies to help him do it.[58]

It took Tennessee's experience with a statehood process distorted by presidential politics to finally push Blount away from his Federalist loyalties and toward treason. Despite a burgeoning white (and unwilling black) population, the Southwest Territory remained divided into two isolated zones, one in the Appalachias on the east end of the present state and the other along the Cumberland River in the middle, centered on the present-day Nashville and Clarksville areas. Surrounding the two settlement zones were huge tracts of Indian land that the Chicka-maugas, Creeks, and other tribes vigorously defended until after Major James Ore's raids in 1794 and Pinckney's Treaty. Even then, the continuing native possession of these hunting lands was a frustrating barrier to the development of the region, a problem that the late Washington administration seemed actively hostile to addressing. Washington's second secretary of war and last secretary of state, arch-Federalist Timothy Pickering of Massachusetts, was unusually fair-minded in his approach to the Indians (in contrast to his attitude toward the French and the American "Jacobins") and an opponent of southern expansion. Blount had dutifully worked to keep the peace with the southern Indians as instructed, but after years of "rascally Neglect" by Philadelphia, the governor decided that the only way to get the attention the Southwest Territory deserved was to push ahead with an application for statehood.[59]

Tennessee would be the first state to graduate from territorial status according to the process stipulated in the Ordinance of 1787—Kentucky and Vermont had been created from pieces of the original thirteen states—so there were no precedents to follow. Against his autocratic Federalist inclinations, Blount initiated the election of a territorial legislature in 1793, and the new body promptly sent Dr. James White as their agent to lobby Congress, originating the system of nonvoting territorial delegates to Congress. White found little inclination in Congress to proceed with statehood for the Southwest Territory on its own, but concluded (very wrongly) that the deepening partisan divisions would smooth the way. The delegate passed along advice he received from someone in Philadelphia that the territory itself should initiate the process by petitioning Congress for statehood and setting up a provisional state government. Senator Aaron Burr, looking southwest for a possible base for his own presidential ambitions, may have been the source of this advice. In June 1795, Blount called the territorial legislature into session three months early so that a constitutional convention and a census of the territory could be authorized—a population of sixty thousand was necessary to qualify for statehood. The census was taken immediately, and a state constitution was written in January 1796. A provisional state legislature was soon elected, and it naturally appointed William Blount as one of Tennessee's first two senators. The formal application for statehood arrived in Philadelphia in the thick of the Jay Treaty debate and was immediately ensnared in presidential politicking.[60]

Congressional Federalists recoiled from the Tennessee application on many grounds. First of all they perceived it as merely "one twig of the electioneering cabal for Mr. Jefferson" to which they needed to respond in partisan kind. Upon reflection, they decided that Tennessee's improvised statehood process was another bit of dangerous Jacobin innovation, of a piece with the Democratic Societies. Representative Chauncey Goodrich of Connecticut sneered that the Tennesseans had "self created" their new government in the name of "the rights of man," even though Blount had informed the administration every step of the way and the statehood application came recommended by President Washington. It was "a new kind of coin . . . counterfeited by rogues and rascals," wrote Goodrich. The state census was treated as fraudulent until proven otherwise. The New England Federalists were particularly hostile. They feared expansion as likely to reduce their political and cultural influence in the nation—antislavery feelings were only part of this—and disdained the western settlers as ignorant savages, even when they were actually blue-blooded Federalist gentlemen like William Blount.[61]

Federalist strategists did not have the votes to stop Tennessee statehood outright, especially not in the population-based House of Representatives where there was still a Republican majority, even if it had cracked over the Jay Treaty appropriations. Instead, they determined to drag their feet, taking so long to inspect the application and demanding so many revisions to the state constitution that Tennessee would miss having any of its votes counted in the presidential election. The more heavily Federalist Senate referred the matter to a committee comprising Federalists Jacob Read of South Carolina and John Rutherfurd of New Jersey, as well as Hamilton's intimate Rufus King, a Massachusetts native who lived in New York City. King's report found sweeping but technical reasons to turn back Tennessee's application. Two dense columns in the *Annals of Congress* are taken up by their efforts to establish the idea that the Ordinance of 1787 set the terms for new states entering the union, and that since that enactment packaged several state land cessions together as one territory, and Tennessee was only part of the territory south of the Ohio, it was therefore not qualified to become a state. In other words, because the Northwest Territory was supposedly required to come in as one giant state—which was not true—Tennessee would have to wait to come in with the rest of the Southwest, most of which was conveniently still in Indian or Spanish hands. To this tendentious, small-state, New England theory of the statehood process, King added a long chain of reasoning using the census provisions in Article I of the Constitution to invalidate Tennessee's state census, which was said to be unconstitutional because the federal government had not ordered it and the existing states had not approved it. Of course, the approval was just then being sought, and the pre-Constitution ordinance had not stipulated how the census was to be taken. In the middle of the Senate's consideration of the Tennessee application, Blount and his colleague William Cocke arrived in town expecting to take their seats as senators, only to be rudely dismissed. Secretary of the Senate Samuel A. Otis or some other supercilious Federalist inserted the event into the official record as the two Tennesseans presenting "a paper purporting to be" their appointment.[62]

Blount and Cocke wrote back to purported Tennessee governor John Sevier that the whole problem was due to the possibility of a contested presidential election and the assumption that Tennessee would identify with the South and the Republicans: "It is generally believed that the State of Tennessee would have experienced no difficulty in the admission of her Senators if it had not been understood that George Washington would not again accept the Presidency and that the State would throw its weight into the Southern scale against Mr. Adams whom it seems the Northern people mean to run at the approaching election." Even some of the Federalist press reported the congressional resistance to Tennessee's admission as a matter of New England sectional jealousy. The *Gazette of the United States* carried a letter from a North Carolina congressman who told his constituents that the admission of Tennessee was doubtful because "*the eastern states are afraid of the balance of power.*" Antislavery feelings were not an explicit factor in this concern for balance, but slavery was certainly the basis of the sectional difference that was being felt.[63]

When the House of Representatives finally began debating the issue in early May, ubiquitous Federalist apparatchik William Loughton Smith of South Carolina was up quickly with a laundry list of procedural objections to Tennessee's application, some similar to the King report's, some even more offensive. Addressing a region where many people felt that friends and relatives had died partly because of Congress's unwillingness to defend American citizens who happened to live on the Tennessee frontier, Smith declared in effect that the Tennesseans did not possess the full rights of American citizens, that their rights "and their claim to participation in the councils of the nation" came *only* in the Northwest Ordinance, from which they had extrapolated incorrectly. This cold, narrowly legalistic approach dominated the Federalist response. Other members questioned whether the two major settlement areas formed one or two communities, and how the boundaries were determined; almost all the Federalist speakers parsed the procedural correctness of the state census in some way, and many said or implied that it was somehow inflated or fraudulent. Smith and others complained about details of the Tennessee constitution, which admittedly had a quirk or two, such as the inclusion of a right to navigate the Mississippi in its bill of rights. Theodore Sedgwick of Massachusetts brought up the existence of slavery in the territory, but only to point out mistakes in the Tennessee application rather than to raise a moral issue. In fact, it was Sedgwick who was making the mistake. A separate Southwest Ordinance had specifically exempted the Southwest Territory from the Northwest Ordinance's prohibition against slavery, which was commonly observed in the breach even where it actually applied.[64]

Congressional Republicans made good use of the opportunity to win back any western affection they may have lost in trying to torpedo the Jay Treaty. Defenders of the Tennessee application had a relatively straightforward case to make. With no detailed procedures having been created, Tennesseans had met the basic requirements of establishing a substantial new community and providing it with a republican form of government. There was no substantive reason not to admit the new state just as Kentucky and Vermont had been admitted. James Madison made the quite trenchant point that the whole territorial system resembled the colonial status of prerevolutionary America and that it behooved Congress not to keep American citizens in this state any longer than absolutely necessary: "The inhabitants of [the Southwest Territory] were at present in a degraded situation—they were deprived of a right essential to freemen—the right of being represented in Congress. Laws were being made without their consent. . . . An exterior power had authority over their laws." In the Senate, Aaron Burr's role in defending the Tennessee application and managing its way through the process helped him emerge as the West's greatest eastern friend.[65]

The end result of the battle over Tennessee statehood was the worst of both worlds for Federalist hopes in the West. Having been thoroughly offended, Tennessee got its electoral votes anyway. The solidly Republican majority in the House that had crumbled in the drive to stop the Jay Treaty reasserted itself and voted for immediate admission despite the fiery debate. In the Senate, where the Federalists were stronger, Burr's parliamentary skills saved Tennessee statehood at the last minute. Having approved several amendments that added conditions and delayed Tennessee's admission, some Federalist senators left town before the issue was fully resolved at the end of session, including mastermind Rufus King, who had just been appointed U.S. minister to Great Britain. Burr got himself appointed to the conference committee to resolve the differences between the House and Senate bills and came out with a compromise measure that admitted Tennessee without requiring a new census but only gave the new state the minimum of one representative in the House, less than Tennessee leaders felt they deserved. Federalists Humphrey Marshall of Kentucky and Samuel Livermore of New Hampshire deserted the ranks on a final vote to delay the bill, and Tennessee was admitted to the union. Tennesseans were pleased to be in, but bitter about the treatment they had received, which "could not fail to excite discontent among a people, who knew and were attached to their rights." Soon a rankled William Blount would be seated as one of the state's first senators and immediately start working against his former Federalist allies. Word came east from Tennessee even before Washington had retired that Thomas Jefferson was favored as Washington's successor, because, among other qualities, he was taken to be "a friend to America in general," including the settlements of the western frontier. Blount took "a great agency" for Jefferson and Burr in the fall election. According to historian Mary-Jo Kline, the Federalists had "turned their fears of the state's Jeffersonian tendencies into a self-fulfilling prophecy."[66]

FAREWELL TO THE KING

By the standards of just about any later presidential election year, the summer of 1796 was deafeningly quiet. There was still no official announcement of Washington's retirement, but the rumors (and inside knowledge in certain political circles) had muted even the fulsome celebrations of the incumbent that had peaked during the late Jay Treaty debate. There seemed to be no hope of convincing Washington to stay on, but his southern fans, in particular, seemed unsure of where to turn.

The Fourth of July toasts that were printed everywhere and used as barometers of public opinion barely acknowledged the upcoming event, with one very notable exception. The Philadelphia ringleaders of the Jay Treaty protests signaled their plans to continue their campaign into the realm of building a national party, linking voters and officials from the presidency on down. As reported in the postholiday issue of the *Aurora*, the "Citizens" of Philadelphia raised their tenth drink of the afternoon to "The Election of 1796—May all the Officers of Government be cast in a pure Democratic Mould." The Philadelphians positioned the election as an extension of the American and French Revolutions and the work of the Democratic Societies ("all genuine Republican Societies thro' out the Globe, by whatever Name they may be called"), but significantly they did not mention Thomas Jefferson by name. This was not only to avoid the Great Mentioner in Reverse effect, but also to observe one of Benjamin Franklin Bache and company's bedrock Radical Enlightenment principles, that the "popularity of no Man render him dangerous to liberty."[67]

Several other less high-minded gatherings did use the name, showing or trying to show that Jefferson was emerging as a genuine contender for popular affection. The New York Tammany Society even dared to directly broach the idea of the former secretary of state making a political comeback: "May his integrity and talents again illumine the councils of his country." Across that city, Captain Snowden's artillery company drank to Jefferson as the author of the Declaration of Independence, "the cornerstone of our political creed."[68]

To Federalist chieftain Alexander Hamilton, hindering the process of selecting a potential successor was the chief *benefit* of delaying Washington's retirement announcement. Until the announcement was made, "the parties" would only be able to "electioneer conditionally" and thus not very effectively. Unhappy with the idea of an Adams presidency, Hamilton clearly would have welcomed some new foreign crisis that might impel his "aegis" to stay on. If a successor was to be chosen, Hamilton wanted it done as late, as quickly, and as quietly as possible, allowing maximum room for a choice by elite consultation and backroom maneuvering rather than popular opinion or democratic voting. In the end, Washington threw up his hands and let Hamilton set the date for making the retirement public knowledge and allowing the replacement process to begin. The ex-secretary opined that two months would "be sufficient" to take the next presidency from state secret and unprecedented world-historical event to *fait accompli*.[69]

Then there was the matter of the grand statement that Washington had long wanted to issue when he announced his departure. Even Alexander Hamilton could not string the Father of His Country along forever. Having sat on the project for most of the summer while nursing the Thomas Pinckney candidacy, Hamilton finally forwarded the requested draft of the Farewell Address to Washington in late July. It would become perhaps the most quoted presidential speech in American history, though it was never spoken, and one of the holy scriptures of the American political tradition. There should be no need to add here to the rushing rivers of ink that have been spilled parsing the Farewell Address for its foreign policy ideas and political thought. Both abstractly and with specific regard to the loose-cannon French government of the mid-1790s, Washington and Hamilton had some wise things to say about the need for a young nation to forge its own independent course. Felix Gilbert's Bancroft Prize–winning essay from the Kennedy era argues that Hamilton's ideas laid the foundations for America's (much) later emergence as a power player in world politics, and this argument would not seem to be without merit.[70] This foreign policy "realism" is one of the factors that made Hamilton a hero to some right-wing intellectuals and allowed him to finally gain a measure of popular acclaim in the early twenty-first century.[71]

What concerns us most here is the way that Hamilton managed to craft into the Farewell Address a biting campaign document along with all of its other qualities. It was not actually a speech at all but a special form of newspaper essay, highlighted by the fact that it emanated from a named person who was directly "addressing" readers. Most newspaper essays were pseudonymously or anonymously written and pitched to a more generalized realm of printed discourse. Only certain public persons got to make addresses: officials communicating with their constituents, men defending their reputations from scandal, and printers and editors, who commonly "addressed" readers at the launch of a new publication as a kind of mission statement.[72]

Though the Farewell Address incorporated both Madison's original draft and talking points approved by Washington, Hamilton shaped it into a partisan Federalist message, dovetailing precisely with all the themes and strategies he and others were using against the opposition generally and Thomas Jefferson in particular. While keeping the elements of Madison's work that Washington insisted on, Hamilton carefully excised any Democratic-Republican-sounding language and a mention of Madison's name from Washington's text. Washington had emphasized genuine advice to his countrymen and a substantive defense of his policies. He wanted to warn about the dangers of the "spirit of Faction" and "foreign intrigue" and urge the people to be patient and "cherish the actual government" rather than worrying about whether it had too much or too little power. He was extremely concerned about the development of regional antipathies and the likelihood that the party conflict would map onto those antipathies and threaten the union. Above all, Washington wanted to defend the neutralist foreign policy he had staked out in his second term, pointing to the April 1793 Proclamation of Neutrality as the "key to my plan." This neutralism was terribly one-sided, cutting only against the French and their Democratic-Republican sympathizers. Old alliances entangled, but new commercial treaties did not. Yet on the whole, Washington was much more concerned with vindicating his own reputation and policies than scoring points against the opposition.[73]

Hamilton's version covered all of Washington's points but surrounded them with material intended not just to defend the administration but also to delegitimize its critics and potential successors. The final Farewell Address questioned the patriotism of the administration's opponents and anyone who might think as they did in at least eight different passages. Critics were branded as disunionists and dupes of "the insidious wiles of foreign influence."[74]

The Farewell Address set Washington's tremendous prestige directly against all aspects of the emerging democratic methods that had allowed the Democratic-Republican opposition to gain a foothold. Famously the president warned his people "in the most solemn manner against the baneful effects of the spirit of party," but he also went much further than good government bromides: the Farewell Address equated all opposition to government and organized efforts to influence public opinion with conspiracy, riot, and authoritarian takeover. The earlier, ill-tempered denunciations of the Democratic-Republican Societies were elevated to an eternal principle: "all combinations and Associations . . . with the real design to direct, control, counteract or awe the regular deliberation and action of the Constituted authorities" had a "fatal tendency." In a classic case of Catch-22 logic, out of doors political activity was deemed to be only acceptable under regimes where it was not technically permitted: "In governments of a monarchical cast, patriotism may look with indulgence, if not with favor, upon the spirit of party. But in those of the popular character, in governments purely elective, it is a spirit not to be encouraged." This followed from a dim view of human nature that came more from Hamilton than Washington. Partisanship existed in all political societies, rooted "in the strongest passions of the human mind," but under more hierarchical and repressive forms of government, like monarchy, it was "more or less stifled, controlled, or repressed." It was under governments "of the popular form" like the United States and France that party spirit was "seen in its greatest rankness." The political judgments and desires of ordinary people were potentially dangerous and not to be trusted without strict guidance: "A fire not to be quenched, it demands a uniform vigilance to prevent its bursting into a flame, lest, instead of warming, it should consume."[75]

In a somewhat more specific vein, the Farewell Address laid important groundwork for the Alien and Sedition Acts by having Washington not just complain about the opposition press but suggest that it was a fundamentally dangerous, unpatriotic, foreign (French!) institution: "Real patriots who may resist the intrigues of the favorite are liable to become suspected and odious, while its tools and dupes usurp the applause and confidence of the people to surrender their interests." The outrage against the press was pure Washington, and Hamilton actually toned down Washington's language. But what for Washington was a man of honor's personal need to "notice" aspersions on his character, Hamilton turned into a general principle.[76]

The imprint of the partisan Federalist message perhaps shows most clearly in the way Hamilton salted the Farewell Address with little digs at Thomas Jefferson and a caricature of Enlightenment philosophy unlikely to have come from George Washington's pen or mouth uncoached. Since 1792, Hamilton and William Loughton Smith had been developing an anti-intellectual attack on Jefferson as a nutty professor, an airy theorist unfit for leadership. (See the following chapter for much more.) Hamilton the speechwriter managed to weave this theme throughout Washington's political testament. The "experience" of serious men operating unimpeded would cement the union and allow the constitutional system to mature. If there were a problem, "let experience solve it." Jefferson and Madison's constitutional arguments were mere hypotheses that would threaten "secure and tranquil enjoyment of the rights of person and property." In such a vulnerable position as the young nation found itself, the American people should look to old-fashioned fatherly wisdom rather than new-fangled philosophy: "To listen to mere speculation in such a case were criminal."[77]

Most striking was the way that Hamilton used the Farewell Address to introduce the idea of Jefferson as a threat to "religion and morality," before such cultural issues had ever been raised in a national political context. Jefferson had hardly dealt with Christianity as a public man since his days in Virginia state politics, and then it had been only to work for the disestablishment of the Anglican churches in Virginia. Even though no one in American politics had come out against religion and morality, Hamilton saw a political winner in using the fears of the more traditionally pious to color popular views of Jefferson and his allies on other positions.

Appealing to Christian piety was something new to Washington's political career when the Farewell Address introduced it. Personally Washington subscribed to the mild and rationalistic version of Christianity that was common among the Founding generation; he was known to pray but never took communion though he was a lifelong Anglican. Washington's presidential messages had only mentioned the Christian religion before in the context of a Thanksgiving proclamation and as something the Indians ought to learn. Now suddenly, with a presidential election at hand, he and Hamilton devoted several paragraphs to extolling the crucial role of religion and morality as "a necessary spring" in foreign policy, public finance, and basic social order, coupling it with oblique but heavy insinuations against unnamed other pretenders to high office. By implication, Thomas Jefferson's liberal views on religious toleration became a character flaw and a failure of leadership: "In vain would that man claim the tribute of Patriotism, who should labor to subvert these great pillars of human happiness." A "mere Politician" ought to be more cautious about disturbing what Hamilton revealingly called "these firmest props of the duties of men and citizens." But such misjudgments, he implied, were typical of a vaporous philosopher too callow to understand that the impulses of real men could only be restrained by firm rules and the fear of God. Reason alone might seem to suffice for "minds of peculiar structure" and "under the influence of refined education," but most people needed stronger stuff. Hamilton would promote the use of religion as a political weapon against Jefferson and the Democratic-Republicans for the rest of his career.[78]

The Farewell Address was part of an interlocking set of stratagems that Hamilton was working as the first presidential campaign opened. His language cut against John Adams almost as much as Jefferson. Adams was somewhat less heterodox in his religious views than Jefferson, but he was another avid political theorist and a "mere Politician" whose "experience" was all in legislative halls and diplomatic parlors. In the meantime, Hamilton and his allies carried on with their plot to sneak in someone who was more than a "mere politician" over Adams as the new Federalist president. Partly through Hamilton's agency Thomas Pinckney had been given permission to return home from his diplomatic position; the newspapers reported that "Major Pinckney" embarked from London around the time that the Farewell Address was published. As an old soldier and leader of men—a war hero who had done time as a British prisoner of war—Pinckney far more obviously fit the image of presidential leadership Hamilton was trying to project in the Farewell Address. Pinckney may have been no George Washington, but he was considerably closer than the portly, querulous attorney from Braintree.

With its appeal to southern manhood (and southern interests), the Pinckney plot struck a chord in the drawing rooms of Charleston, South Carolina. Carolina political baron Edward Rutledge, once slavery's great defender in the Continental Congress, realized that he might hold the balance of power in the upcoming election and determined that his close ally Pinckney should "fill the presidential chair" instead of his old antagonist John Adams. What was more, Rutledge planned to have South Carolina give its votes to Pinckney and Jefferson, hoping to shut the North entirely out of power. Thus it was Hamilton who, while so self-righteously decrying principled opposition as subversion of the union, stirred up a truly sectional monster when he tried to slip a South Carolinian past John Adams. Hamilton should have realized what would happen: the northern Federalists had very recently earned the Rutledge family's ire by first supporting the nomination of Edward's brother John as chief justice of the United States, and then voting against his confirmation after he made a speech against the Jay Treaty.[79]

Hamilton's suggested two-month window for open discussion of a replacement president was opened in mid-September. Washington revealed the final text to the cabinet on Thursday, September 15. Late that same day he called in David C. Claypoole, editor of the Philadelphia *American Daily Advertiser*, for a personal audience that was not often given to ordinary citizens. Claypoole was a special case, a newspaper editor Washington did not bitterly resent—he had been printer to the

Continental Congress back in the day, and Washington had long felt the *Daily Advertiser* to be one of the capital city's very few trustworthy newspapers. It was also much less politicized than the paper often considered Hamilton's mouthpiece, the *Gazette of the United States*, and hence much more trusted by Republicans and neutral parties as well. So Washington gave David Claypoole the honor of being "the channel of his communication with the people" on this occasion—copyediting, typesetting, and publishing the Farewell Address. Claypoole thus became the first person outside government, besides Hamilton, to be informed of Washington's retirement. The president and printer worked out the final details—Washington even specified the type size and font style to be used—and the *Daily Advertiser* then printed the Farewell Address in the Monday, September 19, issue. The *Gazette of the United States* got to reprint it the same day, while the hated *Aurora* had to wait twenty-four hours, publishing the document serially over its next few issues.[80]

Few opponents were taken in by the statement's above-party stance. Mortified that the text still contained language he had written with completely different ideas in mind, Madison marveled at the "inconsistency" of the Farewell Address and wrote Monroe in Paris that it showed that Washington had at last fallen "compleatly in the snares of the British faction" and adopted the full rancor of the most partisan Federalists. Even those who agreed with the address thought it a campaign document under the circumstances. Fisher Ames believed that the publication of the Farewell Address was the beginning of something loud, big, and awful. The speech "will serve as a signal, like dropping a hat, for the party racers to start, and I expect a great deal of noise, whipping, and spurring; money, it is very probable will be spent, some virtue and more tranquility lost; but I hope public order will be saved." Hence the famously nonpartisan Farewell Address did much more to stoke the flame of party spirit than snuff it out.[81]

6

THE FIRST CULTURE WAR
THEMES AND ISSUES OF THE
FEDERALIST CAMPAIGN AGAINST
THOMAS JEFFERSON

In point of fact, the hat Fisher Ames wrote of had been dropped even a little before the Farewell Address. At the start of the September week when Washington's valedictory was being finalized, the Philadelphia *Aurora*, the nation's most vehement opposition newspaper, announced that it was time to end the condition of political suspension in which the country found itself: "It is to be regretted that tho' [Washington's] determination [to retire] has long since been communicated to his confidential friends, the public generally should still be in the dark respecting it." The people needed to know what the *Aurora* could now confirm, that the president was stepping down. What was more, the newspaper announced what had hitherto been mostly whispered in elite circles: "It requires no talent at divination to decide who will be the candidates for the chair. Thomas Jefferson, and John Adams, will be the men." This made the nature of the coming election obvious, the newspaper claimed, at least in the eyes of the Democratic-Republican opposition. It was to be a clear choice, made as much as possible by the voters at large, and a culmination of all the political debates that had taken place since the early Washington administration. According to the *Aurora*, "Whether we shall have at the head of our executive a steadfast friend of the Rights of the People, or an advocate for hereditary power and distinctions, the People of the United States are soon to decide." This was a tendentious, one-sided view of history, but it was also effective partisanship, a framing of the election that the opposition stuck to consistently throughout the nation and through-out the rest of 1796. A vote for John Adams represented a confirmation or intensification of the pro-British, authoritarian policies of the Washington administration, while a vote for Thomas Jefferson represented a rejection of these supposedly monarchical tendencies and a return to the purportedly democratic core ideals of the Revolution.[1]

The clarity on display in the *Aurora* and most other public commentary during the 1796 election stands in remarkable contrast to much of what historians have had to say about it. Even historians willing to write about parties or "proto-parties" existing in the mid-1790s have tended to cluck over the supposed lack of true party conflict in the campaign of 1796, complaining that it was "merely" a sectional contest in which the only issue debated was "the characters of the two candidates," as though full-fledged parties with largely regional bases battling over character issues was unknown in later American history. The late 1990s, when a southern-dominated Republican Congress impeached a president over his personal behavior, beg to differ.[2]

Unquestionably, the historian looking for a formal platform of policy positions framed explicitly in terms of party ideology and linked directly to presidential choice finds slim pickings in the discourse of 1796, but we know from our own time that there is nothing mutually exclusive about a political discourse filled with character attacks and a "modern" political culture structured by party conflict and policy debates. Instead, we need to think of political campaigns, even the most primitive ones, as stories: competing public narratives that seek to explain the world to voters in a way that compels a particular choice. Policy positions and partisan identities are sublimated into, and summarized by, stories about the fundamental characters and basic values of the two candidates. In 1796, it was Jefferson's effete, egg-headed "want of firmness" versus the monarchical ambitions of "King Adams" with his suspicious brood of eligible sons. While the tendency has been to see these attacks as ad hominem smears or half-baked conspiracy theories, they are in fact among the most significant aspects of the 1796 campaign, more predictive of the future of American politics than anything else about it. Negative campaigning has always frustrated scholars and good government advocates, but it is also the oldest, most effective, and most informative kind of campaigning there is, if taken with proper proportions of salt and interpretation. More to the point, the predominance of character attacks in a historical political campaign tells us little about its stage in some timeline of political development. If the "character issue" circa 1796 tells us anything, it is that politics has not changed as much since the time of the Founders as we might like to believe. The basic policy options were clearly contained within the competing images of Jefferson and Adams that the campaigns produced: support or resistance to the spread of revolutionary radicalism; national defense through trade sanctions against Britain or military preparedness and rhetorical belligerence toward France; active popular influence over government or deference to an occasionally and indirectly elected leadership.[3]

Even more than in other sections of this book, readers should keep in mind that the following two chapters are a deliberately public and external account of the stories and arguments used in the 1796 campaign. While I do address the accuracy of the partisan claims made about Thomas Jefferson and John Adams, I largely ignore whatever personal responses or inner turmoil the two candidates may have had—little of this is recorded in any case—because truly following the dictates of eighteenth-century political culture, neither candidate had any substantial involvement in their own campaign. Attention *will* be paid to the more obscure men who actually did the campaigning, and even more to the images they projected onto the two candidates. I will have to beg the indulgence of readers looking for insights into the deep thoughts and true characters of their favorite Founders. What I am dealing with here are the products of a political campaign: the twisted thoughts and distorted characters of the competing Founders as spun out by their enemies and friends for the public.

THE ELEVATED MAN: JEFFERSON'S IMAGE IN THE EARLY YEARS

Understanding how the Federalist culture war developed first requires grappling with a surprisingly undercanvassed issue in the historiography of the Founders: Thomas Jefferson's reputation in the years before he became a presidential candidate. Public knowledge of Jefferson was not nearly as extensive as modern readers might assume, but nevertheless, a clear-cut image had formed among educated and politically informed readers. This image was, quite simply, of Jefferson as a national treasure, "an ornament to this his native country." Here was an enlightened American statesman who operated on a higher, more rarefied plane than the rest of us and made the country better just by being part of it—with the brilliance of his ideas, the eloquence of his words, and the beauty of his hopes for a more peaceful, just, and rational future. The mold was set by the Marquis de Chastellux's lyrical account of his visit to Monticello in 1782, as published in his *Travels in North America* and translated for the British press. Jefferson's friend Francis Hopkinson ran an edited version in Philadelphia's *Columbian Magazine* in 1787, and from there it seems to have found its way regularly into periodicals:

> Let us describe to you a man, not yet forty, tall, and with a mild and pleasing countenance, but whose mind and understanding are ample substitutes for every exterior grace. An American, who, without every having quitted his own country, is at once a musician, skilled in drawing, a geometrician, an astronomer, a natural philosopher, legislator and statesman; . . . in voluntary retirement, from the world and public business, because he loves the world, inasmuch only as he can flatter himself with being useful to mankind. . . . His knowledge indeed was universal. Sometimes natural philosophy, at others politics and the arts were the topics of our conversation. It seemed as if from his youth he had placed his mind, as he has done his house, upon an elevated situation, from which he might contemplate the universe.

The subject of this sketch told the author that he could not read the passage without "a continued blush from beginning to end," protesting that "it presented me a lively picture of what I wish to be, but am not." But what Jefferson did *not* deny was that the image Chastellux drew was exactly what he was going for. He could not have written it better himself. As the historian Andrew Burstein has written, when Jefferson received Chastellux's visit he had just "completed his self-construction" and was ready to present it the world.[4]

It was not only the French or southerners who loved the enlightened Jefferson. New England Yankees adored him, too. Receiving a visit, Yale president Rev. Ezra Stiles pronounced Jefferson "a most ingenuous . . . a truly scientific and learned Man" who was in "every way excellent." Among the achievements that Jefferson's northern admirers praised most was his book *Notes on the State of Virginia*, written as a corrective to French Enlightenment misconceptions about America and first published against the author's will in 1785. Though full of speculative opinions that would feature heavily in future Federalist lampoons (and modern vilifications) of Jefferson, the *Notes* were received warmly by polite literary circles in the first years after their publication and undoubtedly burnished Jefferson's luminous legend. In 1787, the *Connecticut Magazine*'s "Essay on American Genius" saluted Jefferson for refuting the French theories with "the urbanity of a gentleman, and the accuracy of a scholar, supported by the sound reasoning of a philosopher." Even Noah Webster, a Federalist newspaper editor and bitter Jefferson detractor in 1796, opined back in the day that the "sciences and his country" would "ever be indebted" to the "industry and talents" Jefferson showed in producing the *Notes*.[5]

One of the more surprising aspects of the early Jefferson image for modern readers may be the fact that, despite his southern origins and deep lifelong involvement with slavery, Thomas Jefferson was understood in the postrevolutionary era as a figure who was unambiguously hostile to human bondage. Jefferson freed relatively few of his own slaves, but he was almost the only major Founder who had gone personally and extensively on record against the institution of slavery, proposing legislation to reduce it in Virginia before the Revolution, trying to insert antislavery language in the Declaration of Independence, and successfully getting slavery officially barred from the Northwest Territory. (The Continental Congress came one vote short of banning it from all the western territories.) These were not crushing blows against the peculiar institution, and a bit hypocritical considering the source, but Jefferson's antislavery moves and statements were a sincere outgrowth of his Enlightenment ideals and also of his statesmanship. In close touch with the currents of European liberal thought, Jefferson was keenly aware of how important it was for the United States to be perceived abroad as a land of liberty if it wanted to attract international support for its independence, and of the image problem that slavery posed.[6]

As befitted a man whose greatest political asset was his writing, Jefferson denounced slavery in vivid language and lacerating insight that probably revealed more of his own life than he intended. His best-known material in this vein was contained in the *Notes on Virginia*, which, despite its ample helping of racist pseudoscience, was generally read as an abolitionist work. A reader of the *Massachusetts Magazine* submitted several passages from the *Notes*, suggesting that the editors "may perhaps aid the cause of humanity, by republishing the following." The extracts included Jefferson's famous discussion of the brutalizing, corrupting effects on both slave owners and slaves of the power and violence inherent in their relations: "The whole commerce between master and slave is a perpetual exercise of the most boisterous passions, the most unremitting despotism on the one part, and degrading submissions on the other," Jefferson observed, with participants in the institution "thus nursed, educated, and daily exercised in tyranny" and "stamped by it with odious peculiarities." Even more striking for many readers was Jefferson's stark admission that slavery was consistent with neither his young nation's stated liberal philosophy nor its long-term existence: "Can the liberties of a nation be thought secure when we have removed their only firm basis, a conviction in the minds of the people that these liberties are the gift of God? That they are not to be violated but with his wrath? Indeed I tremble for my country when I reflect that God is just: that his justice cannot sleep for ever." Recent scholars and journalists have often pointed out how poorly Jefferson practiced his antislavery preachings in his personal life and political career, but perhaps they do not sufficiently acknowledge the liberationist meaning of Jefferson to his contemporaries. In his time, Jefferson's tentative exploration of the possibility of black biological inferiority, which he entertained while never doubting that blacks were full humans deserving of universal human rights, helped set off a cottage industry in the antislavery community of finding and publicizing examples of black mental achievement to answer Jefferson's questions. That was just how important a figure Jefferson was to the antislavery reformers of his day.[7]

The Declaration of Independence was relatively less prominent in Jefferson's record than we might expect, and relatively unpolitical, before 1796. Jefferson's role in writing the Declaration had been public knowledge since at least 1783, but in the nation's early years, public discourse usually treated the Declaration as a simple announcement of separation rather than as the democratic manifesto and statement of American principles that it became later. The Declaration distinguished Jefferson as "among the earliest friends and advocates of American independence," but not necessarily as the apostle of equal rights.[8]

The problem that the enlightened Jefferson's image presented for his Federalist opponents was that it was far above normal politics, just as far in its own way as George Washington's. Even his emergence as a relatively strident supporter of the French Revolution, described in chapter 1, did not truly bring Jefferson down to earth. Jefferson supporters instead treated his politics as the self-evident result of applying enlightened thought to history and world affairs and Jefferson himself as simply the best-qualified man on the planet to hold any high office. Seen as a kind of expert in the science of politics, broadly understood,

Jefferson (along with his colleague James Madison) was held up as a model for modern youth. If a young man wanted to ascend to his "present preeminence of fame" and assume "the honours of a true statesman," wrote an essayist in the *Maryland Journal* in 1791, he needed to systematically enlighten himself as it was believed that Jefferson and Madison had. "Like them, you must devote your whole leisure to the most useful reading—Like them, you must dive into the depths of philosophy and government—Like them, you must examine, compare, and weigh every separate article in the various and discordant systems of political economy; . . . and like them, sedulously apply this mass of congregated and digested wisdom to the improvement and prosperity of your own country."[9]

All this adulation stuck deep in the craws of Alexander Hamilton and John Adams, both of whom were quite sure they had done far more of substantive merit for the Revolution than the showy Jefferson. Adams thought his qualifications were much better than Jefferson's, but he was far too wrapped up in his solitary statesman pose to do anything more about it than write to Abigail. Hamilton, however, set out immediately to pull Jefferson's reputation down out of the stratosphere to where enemies could get to it.

The basic outline of the Federalist culture war on Thomas Jefferson that dominated the 1796 campaign was actually sketched during the very first stirrings of presidential politics in 1792, almost prophylactically. The only serious electoral moves made back then had aimed to replace Vice President Adams with Governor George Clinton of New York, who had been the runner-up in the very first presidential election in 1789. Jefferson's Virginia allies were happy to cooperate with removing Adams after the title debate and the *Rights of Man* incident (as discussed in chapter 1), but the impetus for Clinton's candidacy came out of New York, from Governor George and his friends. With fellow New Yorker Aaron Burr also putting his name forward, confusion and embarrassment reigned in opposition circles, and there was no coordinated effort to inform voters or electors that John Adams had any opponent. Neither Thomas Jefferson nor his name entered into the 1792 veepstakes at all; he would have had no chance in any case because of the constitutional provision that forbade presidential electors from casting both of their two undifferentiated votes for a candidate from their own state. Virginia had the largest number of electoral votes, and as long as George Washington was standing, Virginia's second votes would be denied to Jefferson.[10]

Yet Hamilton saw Jeffersonian presidential ambitions behind everything, so he and his allies began their opposition research and campaign against him immediately. In the summer of 1792, Hamilton and his friends worked out the rough draft of the disparaging message that would follow Jefferson through the rest of his career. With few of the famous scandals yet known but that annoying image looming over them from the clouds, the anti-Jeffersonians tried to take their target at what seemed to be his strongest point, his Enlightenment credentials. The strategy was to bring popular anti-intellectualism and Christian piety into play against Jefferson. Instead of a national ornament, Jefferson would be made to seem an effete dilettante and annoying smarty-pants who lacked real-world experience and disrespected the basic Christian values and masculine code of behavior that the all-male electorate held dear.

WILLIAM LOUGHTON SMITH, EDMUND BURKE, AND THE DEVELOPMENT OF THE FEDERALIST MESSAGE

Not that Hamilton did it all himself. The energetic treasury secretary provided much of the raw material in a series of pseudonymous essays for the *Gazette of the United States* in the fall of 1792, but the first time it was gathered together was in *The Politicks and Views of a Certain Party, Displayed*, an anonymous pamphlet written by one of his most active congressional lieutenants, Representative William Loughton Smith of South Carolina. Smith also happens to be one of the more influential unknown figures in early American political history, a founder of American conservatism worth taking some time to sketch here.[11]

The key role of a Lower South stalwart like William Loughton Smith in the creation of the Federalist party's original message offers a caution to modern scholars who have accustomed their readers to the idea of the Federalists as a northern-dominated and antislavery party, the ideological and literal fathers and grandfathers of abolitionists, Conscience Whigs, and Radical Republicans.[12] The Federalists had an active southern, proslavery wing as well, and in South Carolina their political and personal bloodlines ran to the Nullifiers and fire-eating secessionists who later threatened the Union and found archenemies in the children

*The Pamphleteering Congressman: One of most aggressively partisan
Federalists in Congress, Representative William Loughton Smith of South
Carolina wrote pamphlets in 1792 and 1796 that keyed the presidential
campaign against Thomas Jefferson. In the pro-Jefferson Aurora, Smith was
dubbed "a snivelling cur from the southward" for his trouble. (Portrait by
Gilbert Stuart, 1795, Gibbes Museum of Art.)*

of northeastern Federalists who become abolitionists and antislavery politicians.[13]

Hamiltonian Federalism and slaveholding went perfectly well together. Federalists considered themselves the proper governing class and the "best people" in every region, and they presented themselves as the defenders of established social institutions and existing property relations in the South as well as the North. They also perceived the leveling impulse of democracy, as practiced by the American friends of the French Revolution, as a threat to slavery, or at least as a principle drawing from the same source of questionable ideas as abolitionism. Slave rebellion was just as fearful a prospect as other kinds of revolution, and the realistic possibility of it was suggested, especially to South Carolinians, by the stories of the numerous French refugees arriving in Charleston from the black revolution in Saint-Domingue (Haiti). A Virginia Federalist satirically celebrated the Democratic-Republican House majority's attempt to assert the popular branch's authority over foreign policy as a step on the way to the elimination of all social and economic distinctions and the coming of anarchy: "It is hoped they will still continue to persevere in the same principles of *Liberty and Equality*" and "without delay, pass a law, to make an equal distribution of property throughout the United States—and that our *black* brethren so unjustly held in slavery may be emancipated, and partake with us all in the general distribution—*No Government!—Huzza!*"[14]

Still developing its plantation economy in the revolutionary era, South Carolina was always the most oligarchic and militantly proslavery of the states, with its planter elite defending the institution aggressively from northerners and liberals in the Continental Congress, the Philadelphia Convention of 1787, and then in the new federal government.[15] This was no obstacle to the recruitment of South Carolina leaders by both of the contending national parties, but the Federalists were especially persistent in this regard. William Loughton Smith and Robert Goodloe Harper were two of the most active Federalist congressional leaders, two South Carolinians sat on Washington's Supreme Court, and two Federalist presidential candidates came from the Pinckney family of Charleston. While Smith's Federalist politics seem to have been primarily motivated by his admiration for Alexander Hamilton and personal investments in government securities, he was an adept user of the race card, which was already a factor in South Carolina politics by the 1790s. He first got elected to Congress by painting his opponent, Dr. David

Ramsay (an idealistic supporter and the first historian of the American Revolution), as an "enemy to slavery." In Congress, he frequently had a caustic remark for liberal thinkers willing to toy with the existing social order in the name of their personal moral enthusiasms. When the Philadelphia Quakers presented petitions asking for the abolition of the slave trade in 1790, Smith gave a vituperative speech asking, among other things, whether "any of them [had] ever married a Negro." The comment underlined Smith's essentially conservative social philosophy, which rejected any kind of social reform, and its consistency with Federalist thought more generally. It was fine to create buildings, plantations, and wealth, but social relations were basically a static thing that would change only at the will of the Almighty. "Why did they not leave that, which they call God's work," he asked of the Quaker abolitionists, "to be managed by Himself?" It was presumptuous of the present generation of mankind to meddle with the fundamental order of their fallen world. If slavery was "a moral evil, it is like many others which exist in all civilized countries, and which the world quietly submit to." Any attempts to reform or eliminate evil would only bring on what to Smith were far worse calamities, such as revolution and interracial marriage.[16]

Being a South Carolinian did not prevent William Loughton Smith from being a stereotypical Federalist in most other ways. He was wired into the worlds of commerce and finance and thus able to both understand and personally profit from the Hamiltonian policy agenda he supported, partial to monarchical Great Britain rather than revolutionary France, and brimming with self-conscious elitism. Federalists were commonly and often unfairly derided as "British merchants" or the creatures of British merchants, but that sobriquet applied fairly well to William Loughton Smith. Descended from one of the original West Indian planter families who had founded the colony of South Carolina, Smith's background was aristocratic enough that he could actually look down on comparative parvenus like the Piedmont Virginia farmers Thomas Jefferson and James Madison. (At least the leading Virginia Republicans looked like rude country folk in wealth and lifestyle when compared to the Low Country elite with their giant plantations and elegant Charleston town houses.) William Loughton Smith's family had become one of wealthiest in the colony through the commercial activities of his father, Benjamin Smith, who had acquired the London mercantile house of James Crokatt's Charleston importing franchise back in the

1730s. Besides becoming one of the major conduits for British luxury goods coming into Charleston and Carolina and for rice and indigo going out, Benjamin Smith took a major position in the still-burgeoning trade in slaves from Africa. Thanks to the elder Smith's resulting profits and British connections, William got to sit out the Revolutionary War (which included a long British occupation of Charleston) while obtaining a thorough but fun-filled European education, replete with tourism and debauchery, in London and Geneva.[17]

William Loughton Smith returned home in 1783 considerably anglicized in his manners and speech but ready to step into a career in the top echelon of his new state's elite. Marrying the daughter of continental congressman and diplomat Ralph Izard, Smith became what his admiring biographer calls South Carolina's "first corporation lawyer" and a prominent member of what might be described as the mercantile faction in South Carolina society and politics, fueled by money made before, during, and after the war in trade with Great Britain. As an investor, Smith put his money into development schemes such as the Santee Canal and into buying South Carolina state war debt, positioning himself for windfall profits once Hamilton's funding and assumption plans were passed. Some in Charleston society found Smith a little too dandified and mouthy—"priggish little Will" was complained about in poetry—and even his fellow Federalists came to feel Smith had "too great a bias to Britain & British politics." Yet he won a seat in First Congress anyway with the help of a slavery-baiting campaign (mentioned above) and held on to it for four controversial terms.[18]

Smith's London-honed refinement and gift for satirical invective made him a natural leader in the politics of Federalist Philadelphia, as he and his father-in-law, Senator Ralph Izard, emerged as two of the Hamiltonian program's key southern supporters. Smith spoke with a sharp tongue on nearly every issue and became, in effect, the Washington administration's congressional floor leader against James Madison for the opposition. He and Izard were particularly crucial in shepherding Hamilton's financial plans through Congress. Smith became a frequent guest of President Washington's, both in Philadelphia and at Mount Vernon, and in 1790 he and Izard embarked on a tour of the Federalist northeast, visiting the homes of such worthies as Representative Theodore Sedgwick of Massachusetts and Senator Oliver Ellsworth of Connecticut, as well as the manor houses of General Philip Schuyler and Stephen Van Rensselaer near Albany. All in all, Alexander Hamilton knew "no man whose loss from the House would be more severely felt by the good cause."[19]

The Politicks and Views of a Certain Party, Displayed was most immediately motivated by the way that some of the fire directed at Hamilton's financial system had deflected onto William Loughton Smith himself. In an atmosphere where administration critics were looking on in horror at the frenzy of government securities speculation and writing about it in the *National Gazette,* Smith like many other Federalist politicians was visibly in business with the new Bank of the United States. Smith won a few weeks' delay in its initial public offering in 1791 so he could personally travel to Charleston to make sure some of the stock was bought by the wealthy men of his home state. He was elected to the bank's first board of directors in October 1791 and heavily influenced the creation and staffing of a Charleston branch bank early in 1792. Smith spent much of that summer borrowing money, including $6,000 from the bank itself, to invest in U.S. public securities. Smith was hoping to cash in on the European war—he calculated that the French Revolution would make the United States look like a safer bet for foreign investors—and possibly retire back to Charleston with his winnings.

Convinced to change his mind and stay in Congress where he was needed, Smith found himself constrained to answer some of the "cruel reports" circulating in Philadelphia and at home that Federalist officials, including Alexander Hamilton and Smith himself, were corrupt speculators, using their inside knowledge of government finance to build their fortunes. Hamilton was largely innocent of such charges, but not of averting his eyes while political allies like Smith took full advantage. The attacks put Smith into a fighting mood—he saw nothing wrong with personally benefiting from policies that also benefited the nation and rather relished the opportunity for an argument. Not lacking self-confidence, Smith was the kind of man who, if he encountered someone reading the *National Gazette* while traveling, would linger to harangue the person about how misinformed they were and then ride off convinced he had made a convert.[20]

In his pioneering pamphlet, Smith went on the offensive, attacking Thomas Jefferson rather than trying to exculpate Hamilton or his financial speculator friends. Smith kept the text allusive rather than direct and relied on very limited materials: the *Notes on Virginia,* the bare facts of Jefferson's early public career, and his documented scientific interests. The target was mentioned only as "a certain Personage" (later, "the Generalissimo") who had recently arrived "from a foreign Country" and ruined American political discourse. Thanks to this "certain Personage," "a certain Gazette" now "teemed" with "intemperate abuse" of the new financial system, all originating in and "prosecuted in pursuance of . . . *private* and *party* purposes and not the public good." One of the pamphlet's primary concerns was proving that the opposition's "system of Detraction" was only personal in nature, the work of a "designing Competitor, who sickens with envy at the fame of others." Jefferson was just jealous of Hamilton, in other words, and the *National Gazette*, the memos to the president, and the congressional opposition were all just devious stratagems aimed at eliminating a superior competitor for "higher honors." While Smith was partly just settling Hamilton's old scores with former allies (especially Madison) who had betrayed him, treating the opposition's criticisms as a mere matter of personal competition was also a way of discounting and delegitimizing them by denying the existence of substantive, reasonable, patriotic grounds for disagreeing with administration policy.[21]

More importantly, Smith's pamphlet seems to mark the national debut of the Federalist turn against the culture and thought of the Enlightenment. In a shift from the revolutionary elite's almost universal embrace of Enlightenment rationalism, Federalist speakers and writers came to deem religious skepticism a mortal error and to treat an excessive devotion to reason and science in life and politics as fatuous and reckless if not downright subversive. The change was especially notable in the later 1790s and after, when the New England Federalist clergy took up the jeremiad against Enlightenment "infidelity" in reaction to Thomas Paine's *Age of Reason* and then promoted the Illuminati scare during the Quasi-War with France, fingering Thomas Jefferson and the Republican opposition as pawns of a world conspiracy against decent society and the Christian religion. Once Jefferson became president, attacks on the danger and stupidity of Enlightenment culture became a staple of even secular Federalist oratory and literature.[22]

However, the roots of the reaction actually go back even further, especially in the Federalists' New England heartland. The politically and culturally powerful ministers of New England had been feeling disquieted for years, long before Paine, over what they perceived as the declining piety of the postrevolutionary era and their concomitantly declining influence. Connecticut's Reverend Timothy Dwight published a mock-epic poem called *The Triumph of Infidelity* in 1788 that enlisted with Satan such major Enlightenment figures as David Hume, Voltaire, and the still-living scientist Joseph Priestley, who would be exiled from England to Pennsylvania in the 1790s and would become (as Dwight predicted) a French Revolution and Democratic-Republican sympathizer. A writer in the New York *Diary* on "The Present State of Religion" complained that Americans were abandoning the religious customs of "their forefathers," based "on the precepts and injunctions of the word of God," simply because they did "not suit the vitiated taste of this truly enlightened age."[23]

Conservative unease with the post-1789 world was set down in eloquent prose by Edmund Burke, Great Britain's chief critic of the French Revolution. Burke railed at "the petulant, assuming, short-sighted coxcombs of philosophy" that Enlightenment culture had produced. Their "shallow speculations" threatened to destabilize the most basic institutions of society, the church and the patriarchal family, along with hereditary forms of government, all bulwarks of each other "binding up the constitution of our country with our dearest domestic ties." Against the Enlightenment principle of applying reason in the quest for new knowledge and progressive improvement, Burke praised the English for their "prejudice" in favor of their own way, including (or so he hoped) hereditary rule. "In this enlightened age I am bold enough to confess that we are generally men of untaught feelings," taking one of the original "brave" conservative stands in defense of the status quo:

> We have not been . . . filled, like stuffed birds in a museum, with chaff and rags and paltry blurred shreds of paper about the rights of man. We preserve the whole of our feelings still native and entire, unsophisticated by pedantry and infidelity. We have real hearts of flesh and blood beating in our bosoms. We fear God; we look up with awe to kings, with affection to parliaments, with duty to magistrates, with reverence to priests, and with respect to nobility. Why? Because, when such ideas are brought before our minds, it is *natural* to be so affected; because all other feelings are false and spurious, and tend to corrupt our minds, to vitiate our primary morals.

Though much more was to come later, Federalist-sympathizing William Cobbett, one of the few conservative émigré journalists of the 1790s, gave blunt expression to these domestic anxieties in a pamphlet castigating the work of female playwright Susanna Rowson in 1796: "I have strange misgivings hanging about my mind, that the whole moral as well as political world is going to experience a revolution." The "Democrats and grog-shop politicians" might end up electing a House of Representatives full of women. Marriage would be ruined as men were forced to obey their wives or else sex would just forge ahead "in this enlightened age . . . whether people are married or not."[24]

Cobbett was far more frank than most American writers, but there was clearly an ambient sense of cultural disquiet that William Loughton Smith and Alexander Hamilton were plugging into when they brought the reaction against Enlightenment culture into presidential politics with the attacks on Thomas Jefferson in 1792 and 1796. They would hold Jefferson up to the world as one of Burke's philosophical coxcombs, as, in Hamilton's words, a "concealed voluptuary" and "intriguing incendiary" who only pretended to be a "quiet modest, retiring philosopher"—not that Federalists would have liked Jefferson any better as a leader if here really *were* a philosopher.[25]

Let me be clear that what I am giving here is an account of changing political rhetoric rather than intellectual history. The Federalist backlash against enlightened culture and philosophy was perhaps more a theme or a talking point than a fully formed intellectual position. All of the Founders were children of the Enlightenment in the broadest sense, and there would have been no American republic without the political science of John Locke. Like Burke, the Federalists' ire was directed more at the recent, radical, and French manifestations of the Enlightenment than at the more moderately liberal ideas that had informed the American Revolution, which the Federalists and Burke supported.[26]

Yet in the 1790s, both began to pull away from earlier commitments in reaction to the French Revolution and its sympathizers. Compared to Thomas Jefferson, to say nothing of the radicals in the Democratic Societies, the members of the Founding generation who ended up in the Federalist party evinced much less faith in human reason and much less optimism about human nature, especially as found in the mass of mankind. According to intellectual historian Darren Staloff, Hamilton's great Enlightenment influence was David Hume, a Scottish thinker on the political right of the movement whose skeptical turn of mind did not prevent him from being an enthusiastic royalist. Hume extended his skepticism to the liberal premises of most enlightened political thought and tunneled through it to the other side. The ideas of the state of nature and the social contract, which formed the theoretical basis for individual natural rights and the right of a people to change their government, Hume attacked as "mere philosophical fictions." Hamilton's hard-edged governing philosophy, trying to build up and utilize concentrations of wealth rather than condemning or protecting government against wealth's corruptions, was in one sense a fulfillment of Hume's enlightened realism, but it also set him against the Enlightenment's more idealistic American advocates. John Adams, Staloff argues, "transcended" the Enlightenment's political convictions even as he tirelessly employed the historical, comparative methods of its political science.[27]

To the Federalists of the 1790s, then, democracy seemed like a morally questionable principle, and the perfectibility of human society by reason alone a vain hope. Evincing a fundamentally conservative distrust of universalist humanitarian principles and self-consciously progressive thought, they reached instinctively for what political theorist Albert Hirschman calls the "rhetoric of reaction" and its perennial tropes of futility, perversity, and jeopardy. In Hirschman's account, conservative rhetoric continually returns to the message that progressive ideas are shallow, unrealistic, and, if implemented, likely to fail (futility); accomplish the opposite of what they intend (the perverse effect); or cause new dangers by undermining the established institutions that protect the very liberal values reformers think they are promoting (jeopardy). The three tropes work in synergy even though they frequently contradict each other: a proposal or movement or figure can be ridiculed for ineffectiveness and also decried for its sweeping revolutionary horrors. Over all its arguments, the rhetoric of reaction ladles a thick coating of condescending scorn, the reactionary author arrogating all worldly wisdom to himself like an exasperated father warning a particularly willful and stupid child.[28]

As part of its fascination with perversity, the rhetoric of reaction delights in almost automatic inversion, whereby increased liberty leads to slavery, open-mindedness is a form of fanaticism, and anticlericalism becomes a "political gospel," and so on. During the House debate on the Quaker slavery petitions, Wílliam Loughton Smith took great glee in pointing out that Father Bartolomé de las Casas's humanitarian campaign to improve the treatment of Indians in the Spanish Empire had resulted in a shift to African slaves; thus the attempted alleviation of one evil had led to an even worse and larger one. Smith read aloud from a history book to prove it. A corollary tactic to the perversity thesis was what might be called the authenticity test. Just as important as debunking the promised results of progressive or revolutionary ideals was impeaching their sources, to prove the insubstantiality and deceptiveness of the whole project of progressive reform or revolution. Why should anyone listen to the criticisms of reformers when they could not believe in their own ideas enough to practice them, if behind their professed love of freedom and equality were hidden designs to gain power, wealth, and privilege for themselves? This would be the burden of Hamilton's attacks on Jefferson.[29]

Not surprisingly, Hirschman identifies Edmund Burke as one of the originators of the rhetoric of reaction, specifically his great polemic, *Reflections on the Revolution in France*. Published in 1790 when the French Revolution was still in a moderate phase, the book somewhat uncannily predicted that the democratic dreams of the French revolutionaries would quickly curdle into a nightmare of mass murder and dictatorship. The new French state "affects to a pure democracy," Burke observed, but it appeared to be "in a direct train of becoming shortly a mischievous and ignoble oligarchy." The book was in many respects the father of all right-wing warnings of left-wing disaster, progenitor of a thousand hysterical screeds, but credit should be given where due. It was powerfully written and one of the most readable political books of the era; furthermore, Burke had the French dead to rights, at least as a prognosticator. Initially, the *Reflections* were poorly received in America on all sides. Its fulsome defense of monarchy, aristocracy, and hereditary rule was hard to take, and its harsh language redounded badly on other skeptics of the French Revolution. A Burke line referring to the common people as the "swinish multitude" was commonly thrown back at Federalists by opposition journals such as the *National Gazette* and *Aurora*. So Federalists did not openly cite Burke that often, and sometimes even denounced him, but there is no question that they were heavily influenced by his great reactionary tract or at least deeply sympathetic with it. John Adams thought Burke had gotten all his ideas from John Adams, especially in terms of his admonitions about France. Burke's analysis gained even more currency with American conservatives as his predictions came true in the subsequent history of the French Republic.[30]

Perhaps the aspect of Burke's book that influenced the Federalist campaigns most was his derision of the leading French revolutionaries as feckless intellectuals without the worldly experience to effectively or safely design or run a government. Burke was not only defending his country and system of government but also his profession—politician—

from the upstart *philosophes* across the channel. Trying to drive home his argument that the British constitutional monarchy was grounded in the solid wisdom of nature and the ages because it grew up gradually over time, Burke belabored France's ad hoc, changing, crisis-wracked efforts to develop a republican alternative to their crippled absolute monarchy on the spot. All the changes were rung on the terminology of anti-intellectualism: French revolutionary leaders (and their supporters abroad) were "theorists," "speculatists," "professors in universities," "literary caballers and intriguing philosophers, with political theologians and theological politicians," all obsessed with "metaphysical abstraction" rather than serious matters of morals and government. "This sort of people are so taken up with their theories about the rights of man, that they have totally forgotten his nature," Burke lectured, so instead of statesmen they had become "politicians of metaphysics, who have opened schools for sophistry, and made establishments for anarchy." Nearly coining a common bit of folk anti-intellectualism—those who can, do, those who can't, teach—Burke chided "professors of the rights of men" for being "so busy in teaching others, that they have not leisure to learn anything themselves." The attempts to create a just, stable, and effective government in France would not only be futile, but also perverse and dangerous, because the Enlightenment had sapped both the wisdom and the morals of the revolutionaries and filled them with impious arrogance: "The whole clan of the enlightened among us . . . have no respect for the wisdom of others; but they pay it off by a very full measure of confidence in their own. With them it is a sufficient motive to destroy an old scheme of things, because it is an old one." Their true intentions were the opposite of their stated humanitarian goals or rooted in opposite feelings; their Enlightenment learning and thought were no more than a quest to inflate themselves, their sympathy for the powerless masked an unquenchable lust for power, and so on. France had fallen victim to "the selfish enlargement of mind and the narrow liberality of sentiment of insidious men, which, commencing in close hypocrisy and fraud, have ended in open violence and rapine."[31]

William Loughton Smith's 1792 pamphlet and its 1796 follow-ups were among the first extended applications of the rhetoric of reaction to American politics. Smith took aim at Thomas Jefferson and James Madison, ridiculing each of their key policy suggestions as "a visionary scheme" or "a new-fangled Project." "Visionary" was no compliment in this period. It meant something more like a psychotic, a hallucinator, or a dreamer in modern usage: a psychologically unstable person who saw unreal things and pursued unrealistic plans. Resentment of the possibility that Jefferson rather than Hamilton might emerge as a popular leader and Washington's successor was channeled into scorn of Jefferson's alleged qualifications. The "certain Personage" at State was a lightweight compared to the heavy-hitter at Treasury. How could anyone compare the merits of the man who had spearheaded the constitutional movement and directed the Washington administration's policy program with the insubstantial "medley of heterogeneous qualities" that was Jefferson? How could Jefferson dare to "enter the lists" with such a thin record? Just being "Chairman of the Committee who drew up" the national divorce petition was nothing.[32]

The rest of Jefferson's medley of qualifications was frivolous or even negative, according to Smith, beginning with his interest in Enlightenment natural philosophy and political liberalism. Certain passages constitute an early example of what became a veritable Federalist genre, the satirical send-up of Jefferson the *philosophe*. For "evidence of [Jefferson's] Abilities, as a Statesman," there was only "the confusions in France," supposedly the "offspring" of political ideas fostered by Jefferson when he was minister to France, "certain theoretical Principles only fit for Utopia." Jefferson's alleged accomplishments as a scientist were evidenced only by the embarrassing racial speculations in the *Notes on Virginia* and "a knack at *Mechanics*." Thus sardonic quotations from the well-received *Notes* and ridicule of the inventions that so amaze present-day visitors to Monticello became staples of Federalist anti-Jefferson detraction. Despite the ridiculousness of "this certain Personage's" claims, Smith complained, "this philosophical Patriot, or patriotic Philosopher, is . . . cried up to the skies by his Party as the only person in America fit to fill the President's chair on the first vacancy."[33]

Jefferson had hardly been "cried up to the skies" in 1792, nor would he be in 1796, at least not by the standards of the Federalists' soaring panegyrics to George Washington. Yet it was a key component of the Federalist strategy to deflect attention from the substantive criticisms that the opposition was making by discounting them as hypocritical grabs for power. The "pretended outcry against Monarchy and Aristocracy" was meant to gull the "ignorant and unsuspecting," but "discerning citizens" knew that "under the assumed cloak of humility lurks the most ambitious spirit, the overweening pride and hauteur." Jefferson's commitment to egalitarian ideals was not to be taken seriously because it was inauthentic; he was an aristocratic man of education and taste who lived a luxurious life himself: "the *externals* of pure Democracy afford but a flimsy veil to the *internal* evidences of aristocratic splendor, sensuality, and Epicureanism." It seems to be a characteristic rightist assumption, across many places and eras, that social privilege and luxurious tastes are culpable only in political figures who are critical of wealth and privilege. Reformers' and revolutionaries' complaints about "the distinctions, and honours, and revenues" of the church and aristocracy Edmund Burke denounced as "the *patois* of fraud . . . the cant and gibberish of hypocrisy." Egalitarians could be taken as "honest enthusiasts" only "when we see them throwing their own goods into common, and submitting their own persons to the austere discipline of the early church." In any case, Thomas Jefferson was damned if he lived well and damned if he did not. Truly humble social origins would have made him all the more contemptible in Federalist eyes. Borrowing directly from a Hamilton essay over the signature "Catullus," Smith assailed the deception he perceived in Jefferson's well-known attempts to practice democratic informality in his social life and official interactions, dressing in "plain garb" (for the era) and greeting visitors casually. The pamphlet specifically took issue with Jefferson's habit of signing official documents and invitations with just his given name instead of using a title. "Stiling himself . . . plain Thomas, and similar frivolities" were naught but "a ridiculous affectation of simplicity." Such "little pitiful tricks" would surely "render the inventor of them contemptible in the eyes of discerning citizens."[34]

Smith's pamphlet also went out of its way to raise the issue of Jefferson's liberal religious views, the beginnings of a Federalist pattern that would grow more intense with the years. Most Federalist politicians, like most of the Founders, had relaxed, intellectualized religious views and habits similar to Jefferson's—Unitarianism was by and large their shared faith—but many disagreed with him on the public role of Christianity, seeing it as an essential basis for morality and social order, at least for the common man. (This was also one of the most strident and insistent themes in Burke's *Reflections on the Revolution in France*.) One of the few practical differences this made for governance in the 1790s was that Presidents Washington and Adams regularly proclaimed days of thanksgiving and prayer, while the opposition complained about the practice. Most Federalist commentary on the religious views of their opponents had far more to do with culture war than with any real debate over religious freedom or public Christianity. Jefferson's Virginia Statute for Religious Freedom, his real record on the issue, was largely avoided in favor of guilt by association with the deistic extremes of the French Revolution and snide efforts to "other" Jefferson with the American reading public.[35]

What Federalists truly saw in religion-baiting was a crucial political strategy against Democratic-Republican challengers. Convinced that the people were predominantly driven by their "vicious passions," Alexander Hamilton regretfully came to understand that the Federalists' trickle-down economic policies had little popular appeal, and advised his allies that if they hoped for success "in the competition for the passions of the people," they had to "contrive to take hold of & carry along with us some strong feelings of the mind." High dudgeon in defense of "the Christian religion," even if said religion was not really threatened, was the Federalists' best chance of this. After his ouster from power, Hamilton would go so far as to suggest the formation of an organized Christian right ("The Christian Constitutional Society," he called it), but in the early 1790s, he probably only urged an occasional rhetorical sally in this direction to Federalist writers like William Loughton Smith. Of course, inciting pious common folk against free thinkers was not an idea original to the Federalists. In England, "Church and King" mobs were fomented against deists and constitutional reformers like Dr. Joseph Priestley.[36]

For Federalist writers and strategists, religion was the most powerful way to turn Jefferson's Enlightenment positives into campaign negatives. Jefferson's freethinking religious views would tie the other character indictments together and give the anti-intellectualism moral heft. Here politics and conviction dovetailed nicely. Most Federalists genuinely subscribed to the idea, as expressed by Burke, that religion was "the basis of civil society" and that Christian morals were the only possible foundation of right behavior and good government. Christianity was where a man's politics, thought, and character connected. Social utopianism, luxurious living, and inappropriate ambition could be blamed on Jefferson's religious liberalism and made to seem much more blameworthy because of it. His "modern *Philosophy* was an overmatch" for his Christianity, and thus "the uncertain torments of a *future* State were of no avail to obstruct the *certain* pleasures of the *present*." There could be no true morality or self-control without religious faith and fear of God's punishment. The other forms of worldly misconduct and corruption that Jefferson and his allies complained of were trivial in comparison, while faithlessness opened the door to the worst crimes imaginable. So Smith contrasted what he considered the petty, jealous complaints of Jefferson, Madison, and the *National Gazette* with the far more momentous consequences of their theological laxity:

> If cheating the poor Soldiers (as it is called) plundering the industrious Farmer by an Excise Law, destroying the morals of the people by Custom House oaths, and similar acts, have stirred up the wrath of the National Gazette, that Scourge of immorality and promoter of virtue, how has it happened that it is the professed panegyrist of *Atheism* and *Infidelity* which have been in all Countries the *Sources* of Immorality, Fraud, Cruelty, and Rapine.[37]

Though not necessarily followed by either set of Founders in their own lives, this preference for an essentially private, religiously-based morality focused on personal behavior and divine sanction over a more public, politically-based morality guided by the abstract liberal principles of democracy, equality, and transparency has been an essential part of rightist political messaging in America nearly ever since. "Moral strength" is at the heart of the "strict father morality" that linguist George Lakoff has identified as the central metaphor in conservative politics. Lakoff was writing about late-twentieth-century politics, of course, but the same themes can be traced back through the ideologies of all the major rightist parties in American political history—the Federalists, Whigs, and the modern Republicans (GOP). In its day, each was the party of the business leaders and strivers, espousing a code of Christian middle-class behavior for all: self-denial, self-discipline, and suppression of the passions, qualities that workers, rivals, and society as a whole needed to display or have imposed on them. Each of those parties also attracted most wealthy Americans of its day, including (for the Federalists and Whigs), the largest-scale slave owners as well as the merchant princes, financial wizards, and industrial captains.[38]

"Strict father morality" also fits well with perhaps the most particularly American and devastating of Smith's strategies: impugning Jefferson's manhood, especially in terms of painting the Sage of Monticello as not the sort of man that most Americans would want to follow or personally know. This Jefferson fellow, he was arrogant, sneaky, and full of weird ideas he had gotten out of foreign books. He looked odd, too, "like a certain tall and awkward Bird which hides it head behind a Tree and supposes itself unseen." He had strange habits such as working in a "whirligig chair," a custom-built swivel desk chair that was one of Jefferson's many self-designed home office gadgets. Jefferson apparently commissioned the chair from New York cabinetmaker Thomas Burling and used it as secretary of state, a little touch of Monticello at the seat of government. Jefferson sang the chair's praises often enough for it to become a joke among the Federalists.[39]

What is worse, this Jefferson lacked the bodily skill and physical courage that were prized in American men, whether they aspired to the gentleman's code of honor or only the rougher, competitive physicality of the frontier or the docks. While Hamilton was "the intrepid Hero, the active and intelligent officer" who "hazarded his life in the field," Jefferson was a "quondam Governor" who had failed his only test as a "Warrior" with "his Exploits at *Monticelli*," an allusion that will be explored more fully below. Faced with a lion like Hamilton as a competitor, the weak Jefferson naturally had to rely on "stratagem . . . finesse and deception."[40]

Lurking behind all this from the Hamiltonian Federalist perspective was the fact that neither Jefferson nor Madison had ever served in the military or participated in the code of honor that American officers had picked up from their European counterparts during the war. (Neither did the two friends ever show much interest in such typical competitive pursuits of southern men as horse racing, gambling, and shooting.) Hamilton's political conflicts with other former officers, including Jefferson's allies James Monroe and Aaron Burr, were often adjudicated through the code of honor, in which actual duels fought by men with guns were always a possibility but not always the end result. Personal confrontations and formal letters of "explanation" or apology could often suffice to satisfy affronted honor. It was a source of great frustration to Hamilton that he could not fight Jefferson and Madison directly. Instead, the two Virginians insisted on carrying out their disputes with Hamilton largely through what later generations would call the political process, as though they were substantive (which many Federalists refused to believe), and much of the time by proxy through the press and other media of party politics. We can now recognize that Jefferson and Madison (and many of their followers) were pioneering a more modern, impersonal, and democratic style of politics, one that eventually defeated the Federalists but in these early years just irritated them.[41]

Not that Hamilton and Smith and the others were helpless themselves

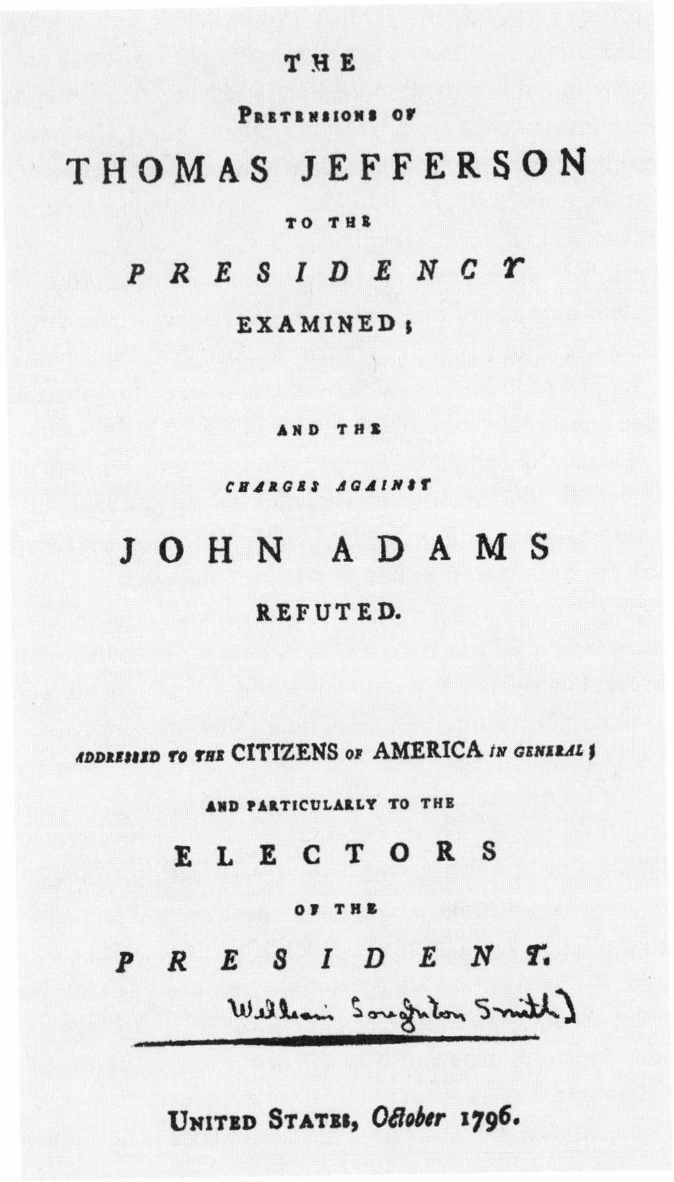

THE

PRETENSIONS OF

THOMAS JEFFERSON

TO THE

PRESIDENCY

EXAMINED;

AND THE

CHARGES AGAINST

JOHN ADAMS

REFUTED.

ADDRESSED TO THE CITIZENS *OF* AMERICA *IN GENERAL;*

AND PARTICULARLY TO THE

ELECTORS

OF THE

PRESIDENT.

William Soughton Smith)

UNITED STATES, *October* 1796.

The Pamphlet: William Loughton Smith sent Jefferson up as a weak-kneed, head-in-the-clouds intellectual dilettante, the prototype of the liberal "egghead" leader that American conservatives attacked in so many later campaigns. (The Pretensions of Thomas Jefferson to the Presidency Examined; and the Charges against John Adams Refuted, *part 1* [Philadelphia: John Fenno, 1796], *title page.*)

when it came to influencing public opinion. They could see that a "disappointed, envious and crafty Politician" might be spun into something that would appear remarkably weak, effeminate, and unattractive to the men who made up almost all of the electorate. Naturally the Federalist commitment to a hierarchical social order placed some limits on this: it was the Democratic-Republicans who later came to pitch their candidate as the "People's Friend," and the Federalists were certainly not about to claim that any of their figureheads—Washington, Hamilton, or John Adams—was the sort of man ordinary voters would want to quaff an ale with. Instead, Smith asked readers to consider whom they would feel more confident following onto a battlefield or trusting to protect their homes and families.[42]

The Politicks and Views of a Certain Party was premature when it was written in 1792. Few noninsider readers were likely influenced by a pamphlet that never mentioned its target by name and most likely barely circulated outside the city of Philadelphia. Then, of course, Jefferson retired to Monticello, rendering the whole issue Smith had written about temporarily moot. The strategy mapped out by Hamilton and Smith would be taken up again in 1796.

THE PRETENSIONS OF THOMAS JEFFERSON

In the years between presidential elections, Smith continued to distinguish himself in Congress as the sharpest of Federalist hatchet men, playing a prominent and sometimes overbearing role in the major debates. He also proved a stubborn survivor in South Carolina politics, withstanding the ire of both the street Jacobins of Charleston and rival Federalists in the planter oligarchy. Because of Smith's long absence from Charleston and stridently pro-British positions, Charles Cotesworth Pinckney backed Smith's challenger John Rutledge Jr. in the 1794 congressional race, a "decided Federalist" who still "prefers America to every foreign interest," unlike Smith, the Pinckneys had decided. Meanwhile the Republican Society of Charleston issued a resolution declaring that it was high time for the people to choose a representative who was not "offensive and injurious to American Republicanism," someone "whom they know and can trust." Smith all but thumbed his nose at the challenge, publishing a sarcastic response to the Republican Society that graciously tendered his "future labours to an ungrateful public" *again*, after "six years spent in arduous unceasing toil," despite "the base calumnies and unmerited indignities offered him by a poisoned, misjudging populace." In the oligarchic, malapportioned politics of South Carolina, Smith's standing in actual public opinion mattered but little. Employees of his father-in-law, Senator Ralph Izard, got busy and found ways to increase the Smith vote in the outlying parishes more than enough to outweigh what popularity the incumbent was losing in Charleston.[43]

Smith stuck to his guns throughout the Jay Treaty battle, without electoral consequences. In the summer of 1795, when news of the treaty arrived, a mob hung effigies of Satan, John Jay, John Adams, Secretary of State Timothy Pickering, and Little Will Smith on a gallows outside the Exchange building, and feelings continued high thereafter. Yet in a miracle of applied political science, Smith's margin at the election following was even bigger. In 1796, he was free to campaign for Adams all he pleased despite the charred candidate's seemingly doubtful prospects in his home state.[44]

It may seem strange that an arch-Hamiltonian and South Carolinian like William Loughton Smith would take up the cause of the Yankee John Adams just as Hamilton was undermining Adams with a South Carolina alternative (Thomas Pinckney). While building on Hamilton's themes, Smith was well motivated to not only stick with Adams but do more for him than almost any Federalist officeholder anywhere. Hamilton's favorites, the Pinckneys, were competitors of Smith and Izard inside South Carolina, while the Izards and Adamses were close friends from their diplomatic years abroad. Meanwhile Smith had higher ambitions that now seemed to be blocked by Hamilton's influence. There was extensive turnover in the late Washington administration cabinet, and Smith would have been a logical candidate to move up, with all the water he had carried in the House. Washington considered Smith for secretary of state, but Hamilton, who had a habit of undermining even friendly competitors for Washington's ear and for the highest rungs of Federalist leadership, argued that it would be a politically damaging appointment. Smith lacked the stature to be America's chief diplomat (he was "not of full size") and had played the heavy a little too well in Congress: Hamilton judged Smith to be "popular with no category of men, from a certain *hardness* of character" and an "uncomfortable temper." Almost certainly discerning Hamilton's attitude, Smith must have decided that fall 1796 would be a good time to perform some conspicuous services for a different leading Federalist, the likely incoming president

John Adams. The *Aurora* reported the gist without being very nice about it, announcing that "a snivelling cur from the southward" was now "laboring hard for Adams, that he may have his darling wishes [of higher office] gratified."[45]

Smith began his Adams move when he gave the Fourth of July address at St. Philip's Church in Charleston. The task was a bit awkward, given that one of the opposing candidate's major claims to fame was the exact object the holiday celebrated. Smith handled this partly by making John Adams's pet point that July 2 was the day that the Continental Congress voted for independence, while July 4 was merely the date that the announcement of the decision (Jefferson's Declaration of Independence) was released. More substantively, Smith shaped his torrent of soaring rhetoric (forty printed pages) into a conservative history of the Revolution that set up the fall campaign: "Our political emancipation" and the "founders of the revolution" were both saluted, but according to Smith only "the strong curb of rational government" had made America a nation worthy of survival.[46]

In the oration, Smith projected Edmund Burke's critical account of the *French* Revolution (picked up from French reactionaries who had long warned of a "literary cabal" sapping the foundations of society) onto American history using a fractured timeline that mashed up the events and issues of the 1780s with those of the 1790s. Back before the Constitution, the "unbraced government" of the immediate postrevolutionary period had allowed "a relaxed state of society" and let the new nation slip into "rapid decay" that put "all the miseries of anarchy before our eyes." This was an extreme interpretation, and Smith brought it into the realm of fiction by pushing the return of Thomas Jefferson and the advent of the Democratic-Republican Societies back a few years. Directly echoing the language of Edmund Burke, Smith alleged that the Constitution had been opposed by "political speculatists," deriving their naïve "ideas of government from abstract theorems." In real life, many of the young nation's most creative political thinkers had been present at the Federal Convention, including James Madison, James Wilson, Alexander Hamilton, and many more. At the same time, the leading opponents of the Constitution, such as Patrick Henry, George Clinton, and George Mason, were many things—old political warhorses for one—but far from "speculatists."[47]

Supposedly these wooly liberals had wanted "to erect an Utopian constitution, on a sandy basis" that would have allowed "the wild passions of demagogues, and . . . of restless and noisy zealots" to rage "unchecked and uncontroled." The nation "would have been minced up into ten thousand little clubs" and the government "swayed by the fluctuating caprices of a giddy throng." Had the "monstrous dreams of these Utopians been realized," Smith warned, "desolation and horror" would have been the result. "Sacred manes of our departed heroes!" he cried out to heaven. "Was it for this ye shed your precious blood?" Obviously not.[48]

Smith sailed back to Philadelphia in August with presumptive Federalist vice-presidential candidate Thomas Pinckney in tow. Smith was feeling good, believing not only that his own reelection was secure, but less accurately that the state as a whole was firmly in the Federalist column. What Smith did not realize was that despite the returning political calm, the state was hardly secure behind John Adams. While a wild card in partisan politics, Edward Rutledge had decided that he could not allow his friends and business partners the Pinckneys to become pawns of Hamilton's plot against Adams. Rutledge was also a correspondent of Jefferson's, sharing information on scientific agriculture and receiving some quiet encouragement to "come forward" and join the opposition. Rutledge proceeded with his own plot for an all-southern dream ticket that would include Jefferson on the top with Thomas Pinckney as his understudy. Thus, quietly and behind the scenes, Jefferson was outflanking South Carolina's loyal Federalists in the battle for the state's electoral votes.[49]

Smith's work would have much more impact nationally than in South Carolina. As he perused the materials openly promoting Jefferson for president that began to appear in the fall of 1796, Smith found the opposition standard-bearer praised in terms both contemptible (to him) and potentially vulnerable. Building on their candidate's established image, pro-Jeffersonians made Jefferson's intellectual credentials the leading element of his candidacy. "As a statesman," claimed a New York writer, "Mr. Jefferson is entitled to foremost rank," especially because of "a penetration and research that but few of his contemporaries can boast." A Tennessee politician (quoted in Virginia and Connecticut newspapers) cited Jefferson's reputation as an "enlightened statesman, warmly attached to the rights of man" as one of the traits that ought to be "so conspicuous in the character of the President." A poem published in *New York Magazine* celebrated Jefferson as foremost among the "sages" of the Revolution as Washington was among its "heroes."[50]

One particularly fulsome panegyric that caught Smith's wrathful eye was an essay out of Richmond, Virginia, over the pseudonym "Hampden." Not widely circulated outside its state of origin, "Hampden" started off obnoxiously by arguing that Virginia was so superior in terms of territory and population as to have permanent dibs ("the best claim") on the presidency. Then "Hampden" offered Thomas Jefferson as the best Virginian for the job, with all of his distinctly cerebral qualities catalogued. Jefferson merited the presidency, "Hampden" argued, because he was "an ornament to this his native country, whose merits as a philosopher, as a republican, and as a friend to the civil and religious rights of mankind, are universally known in America, and generally acknowledged in Europe." In addition to his "political sagacity," Jefferson blessed the country "with a disposition which continually impels his fertile genius to discoveries and improvements in the arts and sciences."[51]

William Loughton Smith sat down to puncture all of Jefferson's pretensions, to the presidency and otherwise, in the form of a reply to "Hampden" that was far lengthier and better distributed than its target. Entitled *The Pretensions of Thomas Jefferson to the Presidency Examined; and the Charges against John Adams Refuted. Addressed to the Citizens of America in General; and Particularly to the Electors of the President*, this was the seminal presidential election "hit piece." The Federalist printer John Fenno published Smith's assault in both of the available media: as a series of twenty-five widely disseminated newspaper essays signed "Phocion" (an old Hamilton pseudonym) that were simultaneously repackaged as two pamphlets, a sixty-four-page opus released in October, followed by another forty-one-page volume in November. Most major newspapers in the country reprinted the series, and other writers picked up on Phocion's themes.[52]

Smith's series expanded on his pamphlet from 1792, adding the "certain party's" actual name and as much detail as he could dredge up. Once again Smith's personal mission was to expose Jefferson as a malignant, hypocritical lightweight who had no business challenging serious men for the presidency, but this time his "rhetoric of reaction" was developed much more fully, deploying the perversity, futility, and jeopardy arguments. The strategy was to take what "Hampden" claimed was Jefferson's leading qualification for the presidency, his reputation for being America's greatest exponent of Enlightenment thought, and turn it into a *dis*qualification, while at the same time showing that even on his own terms, Jefferson was not in fact very enlightened or thoughtful. Here was a supposed scientist whose scientific discoveries amounted to no more than self-serving prejudice and laughable "Gim Krackery" like the "wonderful Whirligig Chair." This time out, Smith lampooned the Jeffersonian furniture in a Swiftian mode: "it had the miraculous quality of allowing the person seated in it to turn his head without moving his tail." Here was a supposed democratic radical who was really an aristocratic dilettante with ideas completely at odds with both the reality of his own slave-supported life and the requirements of mature national leadership. Smith thus set out to make Jefferson into the original model of that favorite conservative target, the effete liberal elitist whose squishysoft political sympathies revealed a naïveté of thought and cowardice of character that rendered him totally unfit for office.[53]

Even more strongly than before, Smith's keynote was anti-intellectualism. The first and longest section of his series took aim at Jefferson's first pretension to the presidency, as listed by "Hampden": "His merits as a *philosopher*." At the time, "philosophy" most often referred to "natural philosophy," or what we would call science, as it was practiced in the eighteenth century by gentleman amateurs such as Jefferson, Benjamin Franklin, Dr. Joseph Priestley, and many others in both America and Europe. In this time before professional scientific research, men like these were real scientists, making significant discoveries and amassing valuable data (especially samples and measurements) in addition to their political and literary pursuits. Priestley managed to discover oxygen while also promoting deism and constitutional reform. Smith derided the notion that such activities were suitable for men of affairs and launched what may be the first conservative attack on a left-wing intellectual (for it was thus that Jefferson was quite literally being depicted) in the annals of American politics: "It should seem that the active, anxious, and responsible station of president would illy suit the calm, retired and exploring views of a *natural philosopher*, his merits might entitle him to the professorship of a college, but they would be as incompatible with the . . . presidency as with the command of the Western army." Smith's South Carolina Federalist colleague Robert Goodloe Harper repeated the professor line in a letter to his constituents, and allowed that Jefferson might make a good "President of a Philosophical Society" or even a decent diplomat, "but certainly not the first magistrate of a great nation."[54]

While Smith was again following Edmund Burke in deriding intellectuals, it was a more uniquely American twist to simply sneer at the professors and eggheads the way Smith did. Burke's anti-intellectualism

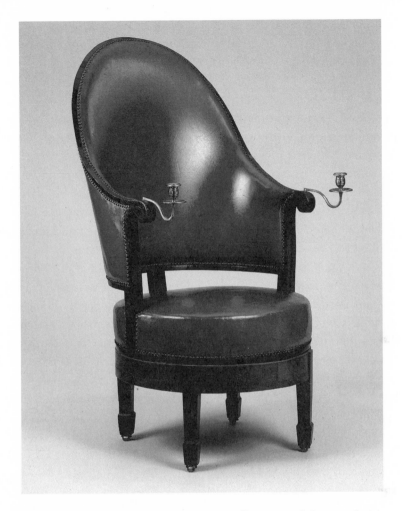

The "Wonderful Whirligig Chair": Thomas Jefferson's revolving armchair, made by Thomas Burling of Philadelphia, and made a campaign issue in William Loughton Smith's 1796 pamphlet. Ironically, the chair was a copy of one owned by George Washington. (Photo from Monticello collections.)

arose from a much more sophisticated Old World understanding of the intellectual and the artist's proper place in society: under the firm control (via patronage) of the nobility and the church who kept them fed and funded. The problem came when intellectuals tried to break free of their aristocratic sponsors and seek power and influence on their own. "Happy if learning, not debauched by ambition, had been satisfied to continue the instructor, and not aspired to be the master!" Burke cried. He was worried that when the revolutionary masses rose up and threw down the church and aristocracy, the intellectuals would become victims, too. "Along with its natural protectors, and guardians [the nobility and aristocracy], learning will be cast into the mire, and trodden down."[55]

The problem was, America really had no class of kept intellectuals. In American society, learning and political power largely coincided, in the Founders and their peers, and in groups that already enjoyed a powerful voice in American affairs such as the learned New England clergy and the legal profession. (Other intellectuals had to sell their work to the public in some way; there was no aristocratic patronage available.) When William Loughton Smith attacked Jefferson as a "professor" and a "theorist," he was tarring learning and intellect in general, in an effort to flatter the relative ignorance of the common people in just the way Burke had warned against, as one of the dangers of democracy. Looking to gain votes, leaders would "make themselves bidders at an auction of popularity," Burke wrote, and "become flatterers instead of legislators,—the instruments, not the guides of the people." In his original attacks on Jefferson, Alexander Hamilton had hoped that American citizens would be able to "distinguish the men who *serve* them, from those who only *flatter* them." Instead, William Loughton Smith had pioneered one of the most dangerous and damaging weapons in the arsenal of know-nothing demagoguery, and pushed the country down the road toward a type of democracy considerably less high-minded than what the Democratic Societies had in mind.[56]

THE CASE OF THE FRATERNIZING EPISTLE: A PROSLAVERY ATTACK ON JEFFERSON

The main source for Smith's attacks was Jefferson's book *Notes on the State of Virginia*, highly praised but full of so many loose speculations and high-flown pronouncements on so many miscellaneous subjects that it provided ample source material for book-length ridicule. Smith had a particularly sharp eye for the soft underbelly of Jefferson's book, the uncomfortable discussions of race and slavery. He had first targeted the *Notes* six years earlier during the House debate on the Quaker antislavery petitions, tweaking both Jefferson and the Quakers by reading out some of the more bigoted passages to show that even this noted detractor of slavery and "respectable author" found the social difficulties that emancipation would involve "insurmountable." In his pamphlet, Smith highlighted the contradiction between the Sage of Monticello's high-minded desire "to vindicate the liberty of the human race" by abolishing slavery and his conviction that the freed slaves should then immediately be removed from the state rather than be allowed to share a society with their former masters. This "colonization" policy would become the mainstream of American abolitionist thought in the early nineteenth century, winning such notable adherents as Henry Clay and Abraham Lincoln, but Smith zeroed in on its cruelty and absurdity, especially as presented by the speculative Jefferson. It was emblematic of Jefferson's "philosophical sagacity," Smith wrote, that "he hits on the notable expedient of emancipating all the slaves of Virginia, and then instantly *shipping them off*, like a herd of *black cattle*, the Lord knows where."[57]

Smith made the idea look especially cruel, even frivolous, by highlighting the fact that Jefferson's stated argument for colonization rested heavily on his aesthetic concerns about the impact of racial mixing on white physiognomy. Early on, Smith inserted a long quotation that contained some of the most grossly racist sentiments found anywhere in Jefferson's writings, including his attempt to show that blacks had "a less share of beauty" than whites, based on Jefferson's own skewed observations and weird pseudofacts that he had gleaned from his reading. For instance, Jefferson cited what he perceived as the "eternal monotony" of dark faces, "that immoveable veil of black which covers all the emotions," and discussed the alleged preference of black men for white over black women, which occurred "as uniformly," Jefferson claimed to know, as the orangutan's preference "for the black women over those of his own species." Emancipation in ancient Rome was easier, Jefferson thought, because "the slave when made free might mix *without staining the blood of his master*" (the emphasis is Smith's).[58]

Undoubtedly one of Smith's aims was to alienate Jefferson from the affections of northerners with a distaste for slavery, but his pamphlet should not be taken as an example of Federalist abolitionism or proto-abolitionism. He was from South Carolina Low Country, after all, home to some of the largest plantations in the country and a black majority population. What Smith hoped to do by playing the slavery card was prevent the South's votes from going to Jefferson simply by sectional default. Smith's intent in 1796 was not to condemn Jefferson for holding slaves or to take issue with his racial views per se, but instead to dramatize his main theme, which was Jefferson's inconstancy and shallowness as a leader and thinker: "The confusion of ideas which pervaded the understanding of our author through the whole of this very ingenious and learned dissertation must be manifest."[59]

The whole idea of abolishing slavery, even in some gradual or relatively unsatisfactory way, was to Smith "an extravagant project" formed by a ditzy pseudo-philosopher who could not make up his mind about how it should be accomplished or whether it was a good idea to begin with. Still more damning than the racial theories themselves for Smith was Jefferson's willingness to shift his position and his reckless disregard for social boundaries and hierarchies.[60]

To this end, Smith highlighted Jefferson's famous exchange of letters with the free black astronomer and surveyor Benjamin Banneker. The retired owner of a Maryland tobacco farm, Banneker sent Secretary of State Jefferson a copy of an almanac he had published with the avid encouragement of members of the Maryland and Pennsylvania Abolition Societies. Partly in response to the racism of *Notes on Virginia*, the antislavery movement discovered and publicized a spate of black mathematical prodigies in the early 1790s as evidence of black mental equality. Banneker was the best-documented and most celebrated case. The accuracy of his calculations was checked by Philadelphia scientist David Rittenhouse, a Democratic Society member who was also a revered colleague of Jefferson's in the American Philosophical Society. In the cover letter enclosing the 1792 edition of the almanac, Banneker appealed to Jefferson as a renowned liberal, "a man far less inflexible" than most whites and "measurably friendly and well disposed towards us" (or so Banneker had heard), offering his own work as contradiction to the "abuse and censure" the world had long directed toward his "race of Beings." Having read the *Notes on Virginia*, Banneker called on Jefferson to reconsider what he had written about black mental capacity, and even more boldly, challenged him on the hypocrisy of making strident calls for liberty while still keeping "by fraud and violence so numerous a part of my brethren under groaning captivity and cruel oppression." In one of the first recorded instances of a move often made against Jefferson in the years after, Banneker quoted the Declaration of Independence and asked its author to recall "a time when you clearly saw into the injustice of a State of Slavery" and wrote about it in language "worthy to be recorded and remember'd in all Succeeding ages." Banneker ended his letter humbly hoping that by exposure to examples like his, white hearts would "be enlarged with kindness and benevolence"; but what he had written was a daring provocation, similar in sentiment and strategy to the sallies of mid-nineteenth-century feminists and black abolitionists, who often challenged American politicians and American society by re-writing or requoting the Declaration.[61]

Despite the challenging tone, Jefferson sent Banneker an immediate, encouraging reply. The secretary of state stopped short of promising to work for the abolition of slavery but expressed gratitude for the counter-evidence Banneker's work provided against the theory of black biologi-cal inferiority. "No body wishes more than I do to see such proofs as you exhibit," Jefferson wrote, "that nature has given to our black brethren, talents equal to those of the other colours of men." Banneker and his editors then published his letter and Jefferson's reply in the next edition of the almanac, as a separate pamphlet, and in several other places. To-gether and apart, the Banneker almanac and the Banneker-Jefferson let-ters became popular texts of the worldwide antislavery movement. They were packaged with other antislavery materials and republished, cited on the floor of Parliament, and commented on throughout the transat-lantic press for decades.[62]

The correspondence with Banneker no longer impresses historians as it once did. On Jefferson's part, concrete steps against slavery were lacking, and he never really gave up the idea of black inferiority, holding Banneker's almanacs to be only one data set possibly counterbalanced by others. Yet Jefferson did not completely reject Banneker's evidence either, arranging for his correspondent to become Andrew Ellicott's technical assistant in the survey of the District of Columbia's bound-aries. However inadequate, the Banneker-Jefferson letters represented a moment of genuine scientific questioning and personal engagement between an American statesman and a free African American. This was a rare event in the Early Republic that the antislavery movement and the African American community of the time had good reason to celebrate.[63]

It was this tiny interracial opening that Phocion seized on. From the South Carolina Federalist perspective, even a fleeting moment of egalitarianism signaled grave danger, suggesting that Jefferson might be willing to throw away southern white wealth and lives on the spur of his enlightened enthusiasms of the moment. "Forgetting all his learned discoveries on the skin and scarf skin and kidneys of the unsavory Afri-cans," Smith wrote, Jefferson "sat down and wrote to brother Benjamin a fraternizing epistle in which 'he rejoiced that NATURE had given to his *black brethren* talents equal to those of *other colours.'*" According to Smith, this was "a *direct and flat contradiction*" of Jefferson's stated racial theories. Why had he cast them aside? Had he changed his mind about the natural inferiority of blacks? No, Jefferson's shift was that of a cheap, whorish politician, "a piece of gross hypocrisy, calculated to filch a little popularity with a few free Negroes" and abolitionists "at the expence of his own character and of the peace of his country." The word "fraternizing" was used deliberately, to invoke the French Revolution's credo "Liberty, Equality, and Fraternity" and call to mind the dangerous consequences that the French disruption of social hierarchies had already had for some slaveholders: the sparking of slave rebellions in Saint-Domingue (Haiti) and other French sugar islands. An anticipation of the racist jibes Federalists would make about Jefferson's relationship with his slave Sally Hemings when it was exposed during his presidency, Smith's real animus was against the capacity for slumming that the "fraternizing epistle" to Benjamin Banneker represented for those concerned with maintaining social order. It was exactly the kind of thing a careless armchair philosopher like Jefferson might do.[64]

Smith's discussion of the Banneker letter built into a full-scale, proslavery attack on Jefferson, aimed at alarming southern readers about the possible impact that the presidency of a noted egalitarian might have on their slave property:

> What shall we think of a *secretary of state* thus *fraternizing* with negroes, writing them complimentary epistles, stiling them *his black brethren*, congratulating them on the evidences of their *genius*, and assuring them good wishes for a speedy emancipation; What must the citizens of the *southern states*, particularly, whose slaves are guaranteed to them as *their property* by the constitution and laws of the United States, think of a secretary of the United States, (whose peculiar duty it was to watch over the interests of every part of the Union) who, at the hazard or primary interests of those states, promulgates his approbation of a speedy emancipation of their slaves?—What will they think of such a *candidate* for the office of President of the United States?—What will they say to the *Electors* of the *southern states* who shall be so *entirely regardless of the interests and future peace and tranquility of their country* as to vote for such a person?[65]

Jefferson's slumming and the Jeffersonian threat to slavery became Phocion's introduction into a wider linkage of Jefferson with the French

Revolution and the Enlightenment philosophy behind it, predicting that President Jefferson would bring disasters similar to what France had suffered. The main disaster Smith had in mind was a bloody slave rebellion on the American mainland, which southern Federalists saw as the likely result of the "epidemical contagion" spreading out of Paris and arriving on our shores in the body of Jefferson. Smith repeatedly mentioned Jefferson's promise, in the "fraternizing" letter, to share Banneker's almanac with his old Parisian associate the Marquis de Condorcet, an early leader of the French Revolution and prominent member of the abolitionist Société des Amis des Noirs. (Smith insinuated that this promise must have been disingenuous, but Jefferson actually did pass the almanac along to Condorcet and another old friend turned revolutionary leader, Jacque-Pierre Brissot de Warville.) Following a narrative popular among white refugees from the slave rebellions in France's Caribbean colonies and the French Revolution's detractors, Smith argued that Condorcet and his friends had "set up certain wild and mischievous theories of government" and that this had immediately resulted "of course, [in] the massacre of the whites, and the desolation of the colonies."[66]

In reality, of course, the events in the islands were initiated by the colonists and slaves, moved much too fast for anyone in Paris to control, and divided French revolutionary leaders in Paris over the appropriate response. But Condorcet and other old friends of Jefferson were among those leaders who rejected pressure from colonial interests to preserve slavery in contradiction of revolutionary principles. "What was *Philosopher Condorcet's* reply" to the defenders of French colonial slavery? Smith asked. "Attend to it, Citizens of the southern States!! He answered with true philosophic calmness, '*Perish all the colonists*, rather than that we should deviate one tittle from our principles.' This is the *enlightened* Condorcet, to whom his friend Jefferson, stimulated by a sympathetic philanthropy, sent Banneker's Almanac." With all the links in the chain of guilt by association laid out—Banneker to Jefferson to Condorcet to Haiti to "thousands of aged colonists and innocent women and children massacred"—Smith sketched the bloody picture of what a Jefferson presidency might mean for his southern readers.[67]

FRENCH FRYING A FOUNDER

Smith's pamphlet covered many other subjects but continually circled back to the mental and moral weakness engendered by Jefferson's devotion to a life of the mind. He was so flighty and impressionable that the time in prerevolutionary France had completely warped him. Smith noticed that even the apparent change in Jefferson's racial views between *Notes on Virginia* and the Banneker correspondence came "*soon after his return from France.*"[68]

The same was true, Smith argued, of Jefferson's views on religion. The "Hampden" essays had touted Jefferson's authorship of the Virginia Statute for Religious Freedom as showing his "attachment to the RE-LIGIOUS *rights* of mankind." The debate over disestablishing Christian churches, and Jefferson's position on the issue, went back to the beginning of the Revolution and long before he ever visited France, but here again Phocion claimed that Jefferson had been perverted by the French. The "men of letters and philosophers" he met over there "were generally *Atheists,*" Smith wrote, allowing Phocion to make the assumption that opponents of the separation of church and state commonly did: proponents of religious freedom were in fact enemies of Christianity, whether they admitted it or not. "*Religious freedom* and *freedom from religion*" were now equivalent terms "with most modern philosophers, particularly those who have been educated in the philosophical schools of France." To be sure, the French Revolution during the period of Jacobin domination had well earned its reputation as an enemy of Christianity, seizing churches and rededicating them to the Cult of the Supreme Being. But even this was deism rather than atheism, the substitution of a rationalistic civic religion for Catholicism. And none of it was relevant to the United States. Jefferson never advocated anything more than withdrawing state support from Christian churches. The assumptions of atheism on the part of the French and Jefferson extended longtime conservative suspicions and fears about the intentions behind the revolutionary movement for religious freedom and the impact of withdrawing government support from Christian churches. Smith and other Federalists, especially the avatars of New England's "Standing Order," firmly believed that complete religious toleration such as existed in Pennsylvania and as Jefferson brought to Virginia had "an immediate *tendency* to produce a total disregard to *public worship*" and "an absolute *indifference to all religion whatever.*" In the absence of coercion, they feared, Americans would drift away from Christianity and the church would wither.[69]

Federalist leaders also took up the militant defense of Christianity as an area of common ground with common Americans whose inclinations they feared in most other respects. Phocion almost cackled at the fact that the "Hampden" essays had dared to raise the issue of religion. "HAMPDEN would have acted more wisely . . . had he passed over this *tender* subject in silence. It was certainly indiscrete to mention *Thomas Jefferson* and *religion* in the same paragraph." In the tenth Phocion essay, Smith showed why, inserting one of the most indelible quotations from all of the *Notes*, "in discussing the subject of religious freedom, he makes this witty observation—'It does me no injury for my neighbour to say there are twenty gods, or *no god*; it neither picks my pocket nor breaks my leg.'" This was meant as damning evidence of Jefferson's hostility to Christianity, and for the most orthodox, downgrading religion to the status of a private opinion did indeed constitute hostility. Jefferson was Christian, and a church member, but one who followed Jesus as a moral teacher rather than a supernatural being. This was not a definition of the faith that some orthodox Christians could accept, but it was not uncommon among the Founding generation. Jefferson was willing to tolerate whatever Christian practices faithful citizens chose to follow, but he was critical of the Christian role in history and politics, and per usual, in *Notes on Virginia* he had written more publicly and eloquently on the topic than most other political figures.[70]

Beginning another chapter in the presidential campaign playbook, both sides of the 1796 election developed the tactic of exploiting the gaffe: encouraging citizens to angrily reject a candidate for making frank but relatively factual observations, often about their own views, that reflected unflatteringly on majority cultural affiliations. It was all about serving up moments of excessive candor, no matter how true or defensible, for readers to be outraged about. As we will see below, the Democratic-Republicans beat John Adams in Pennsylvania by publicizing various statements from his writings that seemed to traduce the people and celebrate the British Constitution. William Loughton Smith wanted pious Americans to burn against a would-be leader who held himself so arrogantly above the mainstream of American life as to insult Christianity: "How must it sink in our eyes the pretended philosopher, who could attempt to degrade the Christian religion by charging to it the murder of millions" or shrug at modern "innovations on the mild and simple religion of our forefathers?" Phocion also had red meat for biblical literalists. Like Tom Paine, this "Tom Jefferson" had questioned Noah's flood and wondered "whether the Almighty ever had a chosen people," a comment that exploited the exact wording of Jefferson's famous salute to farmers, "Those who labour in the earth are the chosen people of God, *if* ever he had a chosen people" (emphasis mine). Another Federalist newspaper writer chimed in with an anecdote about Jefferson's opposition to a national fast day when he was serving in the Continental Congress back in 1776. Supposedly Jefferson had attacked the idea "with Sneer and Ridicule," representing the proposal as "the Offspring of Ignorance or Superstition."[71]

Smith devoted even more space to tarring Jefferson by association with his old revolutionary colleague Thomas Paine. Though still a hero to many Americans, Paine had become a conservative target by becoming a participant, ardent defender, and then victim of the French Revolution, narrowly avoiding execution (as a Girondin) during the Reign of Terror. During his stint as a political prisoner in the repurposed Luxembourg Palace, Paine had begun the work that would push his notoriety over the top into infamy for many Americans, his two-part anti-Christian tract *The Age of Reason*. In late 1795, the second half of Paine's magnum opus appeared, a book-by-book critique of the Bible, sending up its many internal contradictions and unbelievable elements in a spirit of nasty, skeptical fun. British and American presses and pulpits teemed with responses, including some from fellow deists and revolutionary sympathizers such as Joseph Priestley and John Thelwall.[72]

It is not clear that there was truly a popular backlash against *The Age of Reason* in America. After *The Age of Reason*'s publication but before Paine's name began to crop up in the fall campaign (discussed below), the American press generally still treated the author of *Common Sense* as a serious, respectable thinker. His pamphlet against the British financial system, published in mid-1796, was widely discussed and cited. During the same period, prints of Paine's likeness were offered for sale, and British songs and even a joke book celebrating him were republished in America. In contrast, William Loughton Smith and other Federalist writers saw in *The Age of Reason* an opportunity for generating a backlash, and they could not resist the symbolism of a revolutionary firebrand almost killed by the instability he had foolishly helped cause by attacking the foundations of society. Paine provided concrete evidence for the link that Federalists wanted to make between religious freedom, deism, and Thomas Jefferson on the one hand, and French revolutionary hostility to Christianity on the other. Paine's "late impious and blasphemous works" had been "much applauded in France" and "very industriously circulated in the United States, by all *that class* of people, who are friendly to Mr. Jefferson's politics." Of course, Jefferson, Madison, and former minister to France James Monroe (who had gotten Paine out of prison and sheltered him for a time afterward) were indeed friendly to Paine, but his books were sold everywhere and republished by printers unaffiliated with the opposition.[73]

Nevertheless, Smith pictured a future America where Jefferson's countenance of Paine would make a mockery of the Christian nation that Washington had tried to create; Washington's Hamilton-written Farewell Address was quoted back as if it was only by coincidence that the speech had asked whether any man who questioned religion could lay claim to patriotism—a remark that Hamilton had aimed straight at Jefferson. "Should Mr. Jefferson be President, there is no doubt Tom would return to this country, and be a conspicuous figure at the President's table at Philadelphia, where this enlightened pair . . . would fraternize, and philosophize against the *christian religion*, and all *religious worship*." The result would be a nation of atheists, and the fabric of society would unravel from the top. "What? do I receive no injury, as a member of society, if I am surrounded by atheists," Phocion asked, "with whom I can have no social intercourse, on whom there are none of those . . . sacred ties, which restrain mankind from the perpetration of crimes, and without which ties civil society would soon degenerate into a wretched state of barbarism, and be stained with scenes of turpitude, and with every kind of atrocity?" The idea that the religious practices of the chief magistrate and father of the nation would set the behavioral standards for all of his children ran deep in Federalist thinking. Though Jefferson's church attendance record as a public official was actually better than that of George Washington or John Adams, Smith spread the smear, easily accepted by those who feared his politics, that no one had ever seen Jefferson in a "place of worship": "The man who can say he has seen such a *phenomenon*, is himself a much greater curiosity than the elephant now traveling through the southern states." The predictions that Jefferson's accession would bring the Illuminati to power, or some French Revolution–style ban of all churches, or even legislation against God himself, would get worse and worse as his electoral career proceeded. For 1796, Smith contented himself with charging that the ideas Paine and other atheistic *"new lights* are to be disseminated throughout America, under the *auspices* of the *Chief Magistrate of the Union*!!"[74]

"CUT AND RUN AS USUAL": INDICTING THE
WEAKNESS OF DEMOCRATIC LEADERSHIP

Obviously, not everything in William Loughton Smith's campaign against Jefferson had the staying power of Jesus on the guillotine. Much space was taken up by pet peeves of Hamilton against Jefferson that were too insiderish and technical even at the time. One constant theme in Smith and other Federalist writers of 1796 (and earlier) was the claim that critics of the Washington administration policy were in fact only disguised Antifederalists, enemies of the entire Constitution whose political lineage could be traced back to the original opponents of the document. This was both factually incorrect and somewhat irrelevant. James Madison had been one of the Constitution's creators, and Jefferson had supported it, while Patrick Henry, nearly the Federalist presidential candidate, had been the Constitution's most famous critic. Even as oppositionists, Jefferson and Madison and the rest of the Republicans had long ago learned to make their arguments in terms of defending the Constitution. Then there was Hamilton's obsession with rehearsing the secret origin of the *National Gazette*. It was a good story that made Jefferson look like a party man, but by 1796 it was old news about a long-defunct paper that had been replaced by many others, hardly worth the space Federalists devoted to it.[75]

Also originating in a Hamilton pet peeve but more promising were the efforts to develop the capitalist morality of the Protestant ethic into a weapon against Jefferson. Federalists regarded honoring debts as the sacred duty of any good Christian man or nation. "The faith of America" had been pledged to pay back the Revolutionary War debt, Hamilton had written in proposing the funding and assumption scheme; he had been appalled that supposedly serious men such as Jefferson and Madison could cavil at the "calls of justice" to the nation's creditors. For finance savants like Hamilton and Smith, the thought that some Americans entertained the idea of less than full payment on debts stirred up angry emotions, but it was tricky to use in a public campaign. For a long time, Hamilton and Smith's favorite illustration of Jefferson's "political *profligacy*" had been an item that Hamilton culled out of the diplomatic correspondence from his rival's later years as minister to France. Jefferson had approved a proposal that some of the American debt to France be sold off to Dutch speculators who were offering to buy it, even though default on the U.S. national debt seemed likely at the time. If there were to be losses, Jefferson observed, it was better for a third party to take them than our tottering French ally. Hamilton depicted this as an attempt to defraud the Dutch. Opening the second half of *Pretensions* with a new iteration of the charge, Smith tried to make the incident emblematic of the dishonorable, irresponsible approach that Jefferson and democrats took to money in general: in modern parlance, they were con artists, free-loaders, welshers. Combined with a Virginia rumor that Jefferson's major motive for supporting the Revolution was getting out from under his father-in-law's debts to British merchants, a theme Smith left largely to other writers, the Dutch debt story was intended to convert opposition to Hamilton's financial system from a policy difference into a character flaw: "Here is a plain question of *moral feeling*," Smith wrote, echoing Hamilton, but it was the kind felt mostly in counting houses. The debt transfer had never occurred, and at most Jefferson had been guilty of not caring that much whether some Dutch bankers made a poor investment. It was a nonevent that required a lot of explanation for not much political payoff.[76]

Seemingly more effective was the linkage Smith and numerous copy-cat writers made between Jefferson's soft "philosophic" character, his alleged weakness as a political leader, and the dangers this weakness might pose for the United States in a world full of more powerful and predatory states. More explicitly than in his pamphlet from 1792, Smith hammered on the message that only physical heroism really qualified a man for patriotic laurels, never mind that this standard excluded Federalist candidate John Adams as well: "Patriotism announces itself by DEEDS, not by words. . . . The proof of a steady attachment to the civil rights of one's fellow-citizens ought not to rest merely on *writings*; this attachment ought to be evinced by *public conduct*, by *action*, and in *times of danger*." Instead, according to Smith, it appeared "that Mr. Jefferson, has generally sacrificed the civil rights of his countrymen to his own personal safety."[77]

Lampooning a phrase from "Hampden's" praise of Jefferson, "Phocion" used forms of the word "retire" over and over again to convey a craven avoidance of direct confrontation and an unwillingness to openly compete, highlighting Jefferson's periodic returns to "philosophic retirement" at Monticello between his stints in public office: after he had been governor of Virginia, before and after his mission to France, and finally when he retired from the post of secretary of state at the end of 1793. Of course the pattern of periodic retirements was something Jefferson shared with George Washington (though not John Adams), and the most recent retirement was an event that Smith and Hamilton cheered at the time, but now Phocion strained nautical metaphor to the limit trying to express his outrage at Jefferson's desertion: "When the peace and tranquillity of the United States were in extraordinary peril, when it required the exertions and talents of the wisest and bravest statesmen to keep the federal ship from foundering on the rocks with which she was encompassed, he, when his aid was most essential, abandoned the old helmsman, and, with his wonted caution, sneaked away to a snug retreat, leaving others to buffet with the storm."[78]

The most damning example of Jeffersonian retreat, and the one that became perhaps the most discussed and damaging "scandal" of the 1796 campaign, was the troubled ending of his term as governor of Virginia in 1781. Citing the evidence of two northern Virginia pro-Adams electors who had published addresses decrying Jefferson's "want of firmness," Smith accused Governor Jefferson of having "shamefully abandoned his trust" and fled the British army when his bravery and patriotism "might have shone very conspicuously, by facing and averting the danger."[79]

Virginia in 1781 became a big enough issue in 1796 as to require a bit of explanation here. The Federalists exaggerated, but even Jefferson's most ardent scholarly defenders seem to agree that his tenure as war governor was one of the low points of his political career.[80] Still only in his late thirties, with a young family who included a wife in precarious health, Jefferson had been elected governor on a split vote of the Virginia legislature in June 1779, just as the American fortunes in the Revolutionary War and American government finances were spiraling downward. While his time as chief executive was not without accomplishments, including the state capital's move to Richmond, Jefferson was left little time or leeway for the reform projects that had been his signature as a legislator. Instead of revising the laws or promoting religious freedom, Governor Jefferson had to worry about mobilizing troops, collecting tax revenues, and securing Virginia's far western flank, which his predecessor Patrick Henry and adventurer George Rogers Clark had pushed all the way to the Mississippi.

Through it all, there was the vague but omnipresent possibility of some British attack on Virginia. For the first year and a half of Jefferson's term, the British were too busy ravaging the Carolinas and dealing with the French navy to bother the Old Dominion, but late in 1780, after Horatio Gates's defeat at the Battle of Camden, Jefferson's luck started to run out. A British fleet arrived off the coast, and General Benedict Arnold landed troops who promptly seized Portsmouth and the rest of the Virginia coastal area. Soon it became clear that Cornwallis and the main theater of the war would be moving north. A dream team of foreign generals was sent to help save Virginia, but Lafayette and the overrated Baron von Steuben could do little, with few troops available and the state of Virginia critically short of money. Governor Jefferson had done a much better job minimizing expenses and limiting militia call-ups than preparing defenses, but neither did he receive much cooperation from Virginia's counties or legislature. Steuben lost Petersburg in April, and Lafayette had to evacuate Richmond in May. The state government shifted operations a hundred miles west to Charlottesville, but faulty intelligence led Jefferson to store many of the state records in an iron foundry upriver from Richmond. This turned out to be one of Arnold's primary physical targets, because it was one of the few available: there were as yet no permanent public buildings in the new state capital to destroy. The loss of the Virginia state records would be placed high up on the list of Jefferson's crimes in the campaigns of 1796.

Jefferson had already decided not to seek reelection as governor, but his nightmare was not yet over. His term expired on Saturday, June 2, 1781, but the legislature sitting at Charlottesville, not realizing that there was any further trouble afoot, decided to wait until Monday to choose a successor. Jefferson continued to do the paperwork, but unbeknown to any of the Virginia officials, General Cornwallis had ordered a raid west to capture the Virginia state government. Acting Governor Jefferson only received warning of this late Sunday night, literally as British troops under Colonel Banastre Tarleton were approaching his neighborhood. He had time to send his family safely away and gather up a few papers before Tarleton arrived at the base of Monticello itself. Jefferson had little choice but to escape into the Carter's Mountain woods where an army would not be able to pass. (One has to be impressed with Jefferson's horsemanship and knowledge of his own terrain that he was able to get away and meet his family for dinner at a neighbor's home later that day, but perhaps those skills were too expected to be noticeable.) This was as close a call as any high American official suffered in the course of the Revolutionary War, and certainly it was part of a rebel governor's duty to stay out of enemy hands. Jefferson had every reason to flee, but the optics of the situation, politically, were not good.

Besides the general damage to Jefferson's image, this incident served as one crux of the Federalists' ideological indictment of Enlightenment-inspired democracy. By refusing to assume the role of father and protector of the people, the democratic leader revealed the ineffectuality and inauthenticity of his rationalistic beliefs. By acting like an ordinary man, who put protecting his own family and life at least slightly ahead of public duties and refused to commit himself to soaring codes of honor, Jefferson showed that he was not a true advocate even of the liberal ideas he had expressed so eloquently:

> Here would have been a fine opportunity for him to have displayed his public spirit in bravely *rallying* round the standard of liberty and civil rights; but, though in times of safety, he could *rally* round the standard of his friend, Tom Paine, yet when real danger appeared, the *governor of the ancient dominion* dwindled into the *poor, timid philosopher*, and instead of rallying his brave countrymen, he fled for safety from a few light-horsemen, and shamefully abandoned his trust!![81]

During the 1796 campaign, a Fredericksburg, Virginia, paper republished a letter from 1788 that framed the invasion story specifically as an exposure of the shallow unreliability of Chastellux's ethereal philosopher. After failing to defend the state, Jefferson had "stationed himself on Monticelli [sic], where," as Chastellux observed, "the sublimity of his mind seemed to sympathize with the sublimity" of the landscape. A manly, practical mind would have seen the military possibilities of such hilly, wooded terrain, but not Jefferson. "A baby in his cradle" could not have been more helpless, the Fredericksburg letter noted contemptuously. "Col. Tarleton being no respecter of his sublime excellency" had ridden seventy-five miles unopposed "thro' a most defensible country" and "drove his sublimity from his contemplations."[82]

Critics then and later were not without hypocrisy in suggesting that Jefferson had some more noble option than flight in this case. Perhaps he should have maintained some defensive force for himself despite the available troops being needed elsewhere, but under the circumstances, was he supposed to fight off a British patrol single-handedly? Wait for Tarleton to arrive at his door and make a patriotic speech before his arrest and execution? As Jefferson recalled sarcastically later, the "closet heroes" who wanted him to have "disdained the shelter of a wood" and make a Don Quixote–like stand against a whole troop forgot about his lack of superpowers: "I was not provided with the enchanted arms of the knight, nor even with the helmet of Mambrino." Through such inflated notions about the vainglorious acts of physical courage that service as war governor supposedly required, his critics had turned history into a "romance."[83]

Probably it was Jefferson's behavior right after his flight that was most damning. Reunited with his family, he took the attitude that his work as governor was done even though there was as yet no one else to do it. Virginia's government lapsed into a state of dubious legality that lasted for almost ten days until the legislature could gather again. Once the solons were back together, they further embarrassed Jefferson by passing a resolution to investigate his conduct before and during the invasion. Pushed by a faction of critics that included his predecessor, future Virginia Federalist leader Patrick Henry, and the Lee family, this procedure was agreed to by Jefferson's allies with the idea of exonerating him. It eventually did, but later the fact that an investigation had taken place became part of the scandal. The charges made by legislative critics were generally quite different and more practical than the ones the Federalists popularized later, revolving around the question of whether better military preparations or more effective resistance could have been made against Arnold's troops. Luckily for Jefferson, America's and Virginia's fortunes soon reversed for the better. With the war concluding successfully at Yorktown in October 1781, Virginians were feeling good, and the legislature belatedly issued the ex-governor a clean bill of health and a resolution of thanks in December.[84]

The whole affair received relatively little publicity and remained largely unknown outside Virginia until Jefferson emerged publicly as a presidential contender in September 1796. The vector by which the story spread will be covered in the next chapter. What concerns us here is how heavily circulated the charges were and the use the Federalist press made of the scandal.

Between Smith's lengthy "Phocion" series, the statements of the Virginia electors Smith cited as corroboration, and the reprints, quotations, and commentaries on all of them, a feedback loop was created where the name Jefferson and the qualities of weakness and inconstancy—or "want of firmness"—became almost synonymous for a few weeks in the fall of 1796. The repetition of themes and specific phrases across the Federalist press suggests a strong degree of coordination among individual newspapers, arranged either through leaders like Smith or by Federalist editors themselves. In one of the remarks most strikingly prescient of future American politics, a Reading, Pennsylvania, writer warned against Jefferson's unsteadiness in the face of trouble or danger: At "the Appearance of some black Cloud or a sudden Clap of Thunder . . . we may expect Mr. Jefferson to cut and run *as usual*."[85]

On one level, this was an attack on Jefferson's character that simply aimed to alienate him from the voter's affections by impugning his manhood; but it was also a deeper ideological indictment, condemning the whole idea that an Enlightenment intellectual and professor of democracy could ever be firm enough to be a strong, trustworthy national leader. In early American political discourse, the psychosexual qualities of hardness and manliness were closely related to the ideal of political virtue (derived from the same word as virility), the ability to be independent, to stand up to pressure. The erection of obelisks and liberty poles to memorialize a great leader or symbolize the nation were physical enactments of this core idea. The penis was "an emblem of liberty" that should be presented "in a posture of strong erection," wrote the poet Joel Barlow. Tom Paine argued that "a well constituted republic" would bring out the political virility in all its citizens: "The human faculties act with boldness, and acquire, under this form of government, a gigantic manliness." The frontispiece of the Continental Congress's journals featured an emblem of twelve hands all grasping a single long upthrust shaft. Thus, there was a subtext to the constant talk of "firmness" and "manliness" and size that was actually not terribly far below the surface. It was thought that the fragility of republics required an especially rugged brand of virtue, among leaders and citizens, to keep it pure and stable. Jefferson, however, had "dwindled" in the face of danger.[86]

The case against Jefferson's manhood was used to promote a lopsided debate about national security and the proper conduct of foreign policy, especially in light of the increasing French hostility toward the United States following the Jay Treaty. What should the response to French pressure be? Could Jefferson stand up to it, and would he even want to? Federalists argued that a democratic leader was inherently weak because he feared the gigantic manliness of his constituents, looking to his supporters for validation and direction: "The violent [are] for Jefferson because they can bend him to what measures they wish." What they wished, Federalists assumed, was social anarchy under the oversight of the French. Writing in a Virginia paper, "Bradford" pictured a Jacobin conspirator licking his chops at the "feeble and timid administration" that Jefferson would lead, immediately succumbing to the "Fraternal-hug" of France.[87]

William Loughton Smith brought it all home in the last number of his "Phocion" series, summarizing all of his earlier charges and predicting doom for the nation if such a "capricious and wavering . . . whimsical and visionary" man were elected to the chief magistracy: "His elevation to the Presidency must eventuate either in the *debasement* of the American name, by a whimsical, inconsistent, and feeble administration, or in the *prostration* of the United States at the *feet of France*, the *subversion* of our excellent *Constitution*, and the consequent *destruction* of our present *prosperity*."[88]

The charges of cowardice and incompetence and shrinkage must have stung more than others made in 1796, because the response to them is one of the few aspects of the campaign for which we have any evidence of Thomas Jefferson's active participation. As an avid record keeper who had invented several personal copying devices to more easily preserve documents for posterity, Jefferson particularly resented the Federalist accusation—their most frequent—that he had carelessly allowed Virginia's public records to be destroyed. In Jefferson's papers, editors found three depositions dated October 1796 from witnesses to the events of 1781; the witnesses testified that the governor had been "extremely active" or "extremely anxious and very active" in trying to secure the public records before Arnold's troops arrived and had done "every thing which the nature of the case and his situation would admit, for the Public Interest," including staying up until almost midnight one evening. There are no letters from Jefferson requesting the depositions, but he cared enough to keep them in his files. They do not seem to have been published, so perhaps Jefferson reserved them to show visitors.[89]

Whether or not they involved the letters in Jefferson's possession, there was a major effort by Democratic-Republicans to counter the charges made against their candidate, focusing especially on his Virginia record. Official documents were exhumed and published, with much emphasis on the official approbation Jefferson had received from the legislature, the terms and timing of which then became subjects of debate themselves. Virginians scrapped viciously in their local press over the issue, and on the national level House of Representatives clerk John Beckley, who had held the same position in the Virginia legislature in 1781, wrote his own account of the British invasion of Virginia and got it published (as "A Subscriber") in two widely circulating Philadelphia newspapers. Beckley's account featured a manly, decisive Governor

Jefferson who charged around "issuing his orders and using every exertion" but could do little with the militia troops committed elsewhere.[90]

Unsurprisingly, the charge of physical cowardice was most problematic for Jefferson in the South, as Smith and his allies doubtless intended. The invasion story received far more comment to the south of Philadelphia than it did to the north. Jefferson's more honest southern defenders were at pains to rescue their national treasure by defending the less aggressive, more intellectual brand of manhood that Jefferson represented. From William Loughton Smith's hometown of Charleston, "Z" chided "Phocion" for his "littleness" in stooping to ridicule a man of "universal talents" for lending some of his efforts to public service. "Z" questioned the destructive illogic of Smith's anti-intellectualism. Was it really a bad thing to have thoughtful men with broad interests in power? Should Benjamin Franklin have been disqualified from politics and diplomacy because he was a world-renowned scientist and writer? Was Frederick the Great a bad king because he was familiar with the intellectual currents of his time?[91]

Other Jefferson defenders went further in this pro-philosophy direction than may have been advisable. "Cassius" writing in the Petersburg *Intelligencer* implicitly praised Governor Jefferson's flight as a case of man knowing his own limitations: "Not educated amidst the din of arms, he had devoted his fine talents to the elegant pursuits of calm philosophy. It was laudable in him to retire from a station which a fiercer genius could fill better." Every man had a duty to his country and the world, but one suited his particular abilities, to "employ his talents in the form most likely to render them useful." Hence it was the duty of talented minds like Franklin and Jefferson "to avoid the battle," where they might be beaten by any "brutal soldier," and instead to employ themselves "in legislation and negociation, the sublime subjects of national concern." While "savage and cruel people" might regard "aversion to war" as "a crime which no genius nor worth can make an atonement," a "civilized and amiable people" like that of the United States was capable of appreciating finer and more benevolent qualities in their leaders.[92]

The battle in 1796 over the events of 1781 was only the first round of this particular Jefferson scandal. The controversy would be more thoroughly developed, on both sides, with each successive election that Jefferson was involved in, and would continue to haunt him through the annals of historiography.[93]

HIS ROTUNDITY
THEMES AND ISSUES OF THE
DEMOCRATIC-REPUBLICAN
CAMPAIGN AGAINST JOHN ADAMS

The strategy that the Federalists used against Jefferson—sublimating policy positions, political ideologies, and cultural values into character attacks—would have worked less well against John Adams, even if the Democratic-Republicans had bothered to try it. As vivid a character as John Adams becomes when a modern writer or HBO samples his private letters and diaries, the public Adams presented a far less definable and personal face to the world than Jefferson. There was no Monticello, no quirky inventions, no personal testaments like the *Notes on the State of Virginia* or luminous statements of high principle like the Declaration or the *Summary View of the Rights of British America*. To this day, despite David McCullough's best-selling biography, the television series based on it, and a boom in Adams studies, he lags far behind Jefferson, Washington, Hamilton, and even Madison in widely known symbols of his life and career: John Adams remains free of major monuments in Washington, D.C., major collegiate namesakes, and likenesses on the currency.[1]

It was not that different in 1796. Last elected to office in his own right before the Revolution, and buried in diplomatic posts or the vice presidency since, Adams was remembered as a hero of the political struggle for independence, but without many specifics. As he himself preferred, John Adams was a leader for the cognoscenti, a statesman whose greatest deeds were known chiefly by his peers and superiors, not the public at large. If Adams ever gets a monument in Washington,

D.C., the check-and-balanced Massachusetts Constitution of 1780 ought to be on it. Adams later became the toast of constitutional historians for this work, and thought so highly of it himself that he brought a copy to show around Paris when he went over to help negotiate the end of the Revolutionary War. Yet in 1796, his role in forging American constitutionalism was barely a rumor as far as the public was concerned.[2]

The lack of material on John Adams was a problem for panegyrists and critics alike. All a pro-Adams man had to work with were a few biographical facts, mostly concerning his diplomatic career, and a large and growing corpus of writings on political theory. The closest thing to an Adams campaign biography that 1796 produced was a thirty-one-page pamphlet reproducing a series over the pen name "Aurelius," which had appeared in the Boston *Columbian Centinel*. Written by one John Gardner, from Milton, Massachusetts, near Adams's hometown of Braintree, it was called *A Brief Consideration of the Important Services, and Distinguished Virtues and Talents which Recommend Mr. Adams for the Presidency of the United States*. The pamphlet, however, devoted only a few pages to its ostensible subjects; it quoted a few paragraphs from David Ramsay's history of the Revolution about Adams's work in the Continental Congress and the diplomatic corps, both quite technical topics apart from the great debates with John Dickinson over independence (later immortalized in the musical *1776*). Securing loans from the Dutch and diplomatic protection for the New England fisheries were good things, no doubt, but hardly the stuff to earn a passionate following. Gardner and other Federalist writers generally spent more effort trying to conjure an Adams who contrasted well with the Federalist caricature of Jefferson. Thus the campaign Adams had showed great "firmness" and remained "unintimidated by the risk of dungeons and of death" in accepting the wartime overseas mission that Jefferson declined. While the rhetoric required to turn a pear-shaped little attorney into a righteous badass can induce chuckles today, political courage and blunt personal honesty were indeed primary Adams qualities. Gardner's best passages captured something of what Adams had really meant to the independence movement: "Perhaps a man of more political intrepidity never took a part in public affairs. Those timid politicians who wished well to their country, but trembled at every step, often found in his energetic counsels, an antidote to their doubts and fears; and our enemies saw in him the developer of their darkest schemes." At the same time, being at the forefront of the independence movement offered no real contrast with the author of the Declaration of Independence: Jefferson had the 1776 vote nailed down.[3]

For the most part Federalists were content to play offense against Jefferson and bring up Adams the man only when absolutely necessary. Surprisingly, perhaps, the Republican side of the campaign showed even more reluctance to focus on Adam's character or résumé, which they mostly admired. The *Aurora* attacks on President Washington notwithstanding, Republicans were much less comfortable (than the Federalists who attacked Jefferson) with metaphors and personalities. They tried to stick to directly political arguments: what political philosophy did Adams profess to believe in? To Virginia elector candidate Daniel Carroll Brent, it was "disagreeable and offensive to assail the character, or detract from the merit of one, who has so long served his country on important and critical occasions," and Brent refused to do it. He took issue only with the distasteful political sentiments that Adams was in the habit of signing his name to.[4]

THROWING THE BOOKS

What Republicans did instead of assailing Adams's character was try to read his books and take the man at his very voluminous word. For many of Adams's writings were eye-opening reading indeed. A writer signing himself "Sidney" explained that his "favourable opinion" of Adams had been "so completely changed" by reading his books as to suggest it should be "a constitutional law of any commonwealth, that every man who aspired at filling the first offices of state should publish his political creed as Mr. Adams has done."[5]

The critics' chief target was Adams's book *Defence of the American Constitutions*, first published in 1787 but reissued in a London edition in 1794 that reached America just in time to become a political issue. (The edition opened with a portrait and a biographical sketch that sealed the book's association with the sitting vice president.)[6] By Adam's own admission, the *Defence* was in the strictest sense a reactionary text, reacting against the "pernicious, destructive, and fatal schemes" of those who favored more purely democratic forms of government. When Adams had arrived in Paris with his Massachusetts convention report in hand, he had been surprised to find that his ideas about balanced government were not at all welcome among French liberals such as the Duc de la Rochefoucauld and Marquis de Condorcet. Benjamin Franklin was already firmly ensconced on the French scene, lending his prestige to Thomas Paine's unicameral model suggested in *Common Sense* and adopted in the Pennsylvania Constitution of 1776, with a single-house legislature elected under near-universal white male suffrage and a weak, veto-less governor. Adams was infuriated when the French thinkers "reprobated" his model in favor of Paine's; this reprobation was capped by a letter from the respected statesman Baron Turgot criticizing American state constitutions and the Articles of Confederation for their division of authority among different levels and branches of government. (Competing power centers had doomed Turgot's attempted reforms of the *ancien régime*.) As the French thinkers saw it, the extra institutions were a waste of effort and money in a free republic like the United States, where there was no nobility or royalty or priesthood, and political authority was grounded on the consent and the basic social equality of all citizens. Why bother to represent three estates (in France, nobles, priesthood, and common people) if there was really only one? Instead, power needed to be gathered by the whole people into one central institution where it could be wielded for the good of all.[7]

Reposted to London, Adams stewed on the "Ignorance of Government and History" entailed in this "gross Ideology" of "simple Democracy" that the French insisted on following. He claimed to have started writing the *Defence* in response to the first stirrings of the French Revolution and the news of unrest back home in Massachusetts (Shays' Rebellion). Rochefoucauld and Condorcet emerged as leaders of the late efforts to reform the French monarchy, and Adams just knew that they "would establish a government in one assembly" that "would involve France and all Europe in all the horrors we have seen; carnage and desolation, for fifty, perhaps for a hundred years." Perpetually torn between taking credit for the American Revolution and lecturing it for its mistakes, Adams wanted to make it perfectly clear that *his* revolutionary principles were not to blame in France or at home. The people of the world were going mad with democracy, with Tom Paine and Ben Franklin on their lips, but he, Adams, had always aimed at the creation of a properly balanced government that had monarchic and aristocratic elements to restrain the democratic ones and keep everything in equilibrium. As Adams remembered later, he "was determined to wash my hands of the blood that was about to be shed in France, Europe, and America, and show to the world that neither my sentiments nor my actions should have any share in countenancing or encouraging" the mistakes that led to it. So John Adams sat down with his giant collection of European books to school the world on the science of free government.[8]

The *Defence* became a kind of mirror image of Jefferson's *Notes on the State of Virginia*. Both books were written abroad in response to French thinkers at around the same time: a famous pair of diplomatic portraits features the two bewigged friends actually holding a copy of each other's book. Both books were full of candid remarks that were then turned against their author in the campaign.[9]

In form, however, the two controversial works did not mirror each other at all. In contrast to Jefferson's elegant personal testament, Adams produced a kind of constitutional history mixtape that was almost impossible to read, and which was certainly the most unlikely book to ever become a presidential campaign sensation. Brilliantly incisive at times but also endlessly repetitive, the work stretched over three volumes. Only a handful of the work's critics and defenders in 1796 ever seem to have made it past the first volume. Seeking to deliver the sledgehammer edition of his long-time political message about the need for a balanced government, Adams marched the reader through capsule descriptions of the governing systems in some fifty republics, modern and ancient, "democratical," "aristocratical," and "monarchical"; over and over again, the stories demonstrated to Adams's satisfaction the empirical truth of his maxim that "without three orders, and an effectual balance between them, in every American constitution, it must be destined to frequent unavoidable revolutions: if they are delayed a few years, they must come in time." Interspersed with the summaries were the constitutional theories of other historians and philosophers with Adams's rebuttals. It was all capped by a comprehensive, volume-length commentary on the writings of the seventeenth-century English journalist and theorist Marchamont Nedham.[10]

In addition to its unwieldiness, the *Defence* had the problem of being heavily plagiarized, even by the loose standards of eighteenth-century publishing. It was not that Adams had really intended to deceive anyone. Working rapidly in the off hours of his diplomatic day job, Adams more or less published his reading notes, incorporating reams of not-well-indicated quotations and paraphrases from the rare European volumes he used as sources. Some Italian chronicles went into Adams's manuscript whole, along with some one hundred pages of Machiavelli's *Florentine Histories*. One scholar has estimated that 80 percent of the book consists of quotations, most of them unmarked, poorly marked, or lightly paraphrased. Adams tried to justify his unusual methods ex post facto by presenting the *Defence* as a sourcebook, "a Looking Glass for Monarchists, Aristocrats and Democrats" that merely sought to provide primary materials about the history of government for his fellow Americans to study. Plagiarism was not raised as an issue against Adams in 1796, but the borrowing did create a serious problem for him: by failing to mark or digest so many unfamiliar quotations from such disparate authors, many of them with political views anathema to most Americans, Adams laid himself open to having everything in the *Defence* received and reviled as his own ideas. And so it was.[11]

The response to the *Defence* was generally cordial when it was originally published in 1787. British reviewers hated it, but Lafayette claimed to be a "constant reader" and Dr. Benjamin Rush promised to make it his school-age sons' "almanac" on government. Like Rush, Thomas Jefferson disagreed with some of Adams's ideas but thought the book should be "an institute for our politicians, old as well as young." The tendency was to treat the *Defence* as a kind of political science textbook, which is exactly what it became when the University of North Carolina was first founded. In that context, the excessive quotation and superabundance of political trivia only made Adams's scholarship seem more impressive, inspiring some newspapers to call him "Dr. Adams" for a few years, which the title-loving Adams must have enjoyed. The Federalist press even promoted the work for a time early in the 1796 campaign, touting its educational value and accidentally positioning it as the opposition's primary text for the campaign against Adams.[12]

Yet if the *Defence* went down smoothly as a sourcebook, it was much harder for many Americans to digest as an argument, especially once the edition of 1794 arrived on American shores in the midst of the controversy over the French Revolution, foreign policy, and the alleged creeping monarchism of the Washington-Hamilton administration. The balanced government message alone might have been fine: Americans had already mostly accepted Adamsian governments of executives, houses, and senates. Paine's Pennsylvania Constitution of 1776 had been thrown out in favor of a more orthodox model. It was Adams's balanced arguments for balanced government that got him in trouble.[13]

Most immediately striking was Adams's insistence on Great Britain as the fount of all America's constitutional wisdom. This was a consistent aspect of his political thought and a historically defensible position, but right in its opening pages, the language of the *Defence* went way over the top in making the point. Adams heartily disliked Great Britain as a place to live and explicitly denounced the idea that monarchy was the right system for the United States, but he filled his book with what read very much like extravagant praise of both Britain and monarchical government. For instance, in what became a much-lampooned turn of phrase, Adams contended that the unwritten British constitution—not despite but *because* of its constitutional monarchy and its representation for the aristocracy—was "in theory, the most stupendous fabric of human invention." Nothing, Adams continued and Democratic-Republicans quoted, "does more honour to the human understanding than this system of government," and it was to his "mortification" that Americans had not copied the British system more accurately. This was by no means an isolated instance. Adams capped his account of ancient Thebes with a giddy speculation about an alternate universe where the Theban leader Epaminondas had lived to "display his talents as a legislator." If so, "the world might possibly have been blessed with something like an English constitution" two thousand or three thousand years early, Adam gushed. This was not language that many Americans who fought or lost loved ones in the Revolutionary War relished reading, to say nothing of the many who resented the way Britain seemed to set itself against American and French aspirations in the present. Probably it was relished even less by those Americans who only heard about the book or read a few extracted phrases.[14]

The edition of 1794 seems to have made its political debut during the protests against the Jay mission to Great Britain: Kentucky demonstrators prepared two effigies, one of Jay and one of Adams. They tied a "*Hempen* string" (a noose) around the Adams doll's neck with a package that included a copy of the *Defence*, labeled "gold bade me write." Public discussion of the book then quieted, apparently, until the beginning of the campaign proper, when it began to be offered up as the main piece of evidence against John Adam's candidacy. A notice in late September 1796 out of Boston alerted citizens to the "Eulogium of Monarchy and the British Constitution" that the potential successor to George Washington had penned "whilst Minister at the Court of London." Appending a sort of reading guide to the *Defence* with paraphrased passages and page references, "Americanus" submitted that Adams had "apostatized from all his former sentiments in favor of American liberty and independence" and hence was no longer "a fit person to be elected

President of the United States." This notice became the template for the majority of the campaign literature against Adams that was published in the fall of 1796. Some of the specific paraphrases and page references even found their way onto the voter tickets that were distributed all over the state of Pennsylvania. (See chapter 9.) Virtually every newspaper that published any political essays at all that fall featured some exegesis of Adams's *Defence*, some pro, in the opposition press overwhelmingly con.[15]

"Americanus" was able to pull a substantial list of damning, partly paraphrased quotations just from the first volume of Adams's magnum opus:

VOL. I.

p. 8.　A limited Monarchy may be justly denominated a Republic.

p. 110.　Wealth, Birth, Family Pride respected by all people.

p. 116.　Wealth, Birth and Virtue, form the best men.

p. 159.　A Commonwealth can no more consist of a people without *gentry*, than of a gentry without people.

p. 206. *Kingly* government best, Tyranny worst: No city is more wretched than that under Tyranny, nor any more happy than that under *regal* power.

p. 294. If the power of negotiation and of treaty be in one man, there can be no intrigue.

p. 321.　Had Epaminandos lived to display his talents as a Legislator, the world might have been blessed with an *English* Constitution, two or three thousand years sooner than it was.

p. 324. Limited *Monarchy* the best government; superior to Republicanism.

p. 360. Distinctions of Poor and Rich, as necessary as labor and good government: Poor are destined to labor; the Rich, by advantages of education, independence and leisure, to superior stations.

p. 373.　Men of property and family, fittest for public service.

p. 375.　*Rich, well born, well educated*, must be preferred to OFFICE, otherwise the people themselves will despise them.

p. 379. Ministers of the Executive, only ought to be responsible.[16]

With a few gradual additions and revisions, this became the list that circulated throughout the opposition press and served as a rough index of where the would-be president differed from his fellow Americans in social and political philosophy, at least according to his Democratic-Republican opponents.

Many aspects of John Adams's thought got distorted and misunderstood during the 1796 campaign, but one part that Democratic-Republicans perceived quite accurately was the vice president's sincere abhorrence of the active democracy that they advocated. Adams knew that the American people would never accept a government in which they were not sovereign in some broad sense, but he wanted to see their legislative power diffused by competing institutions and curtailed by strong authority from above. "If the people should ever aim at more, they will defeat themselves," he wrote in the introduction to the *Defence*. He was willing to tolerate the idea of choosing the national government by popular election, but only if the electorate was consulted as "soberly" and infrequently as possible. Electing high officials was a "hazardous experiment," and if it caused any kind of social disturbance, the only way for "the evil" to be "lessened and postponed" was by lengthening the terms of the chief magistrate and senators gradually "till they become for life." A president who served for life, perhaps by being automatically reelected until his death, seemed like the safest option. Such published speculations became a little inconvenient for Adams in the context of a presidential election.[17]

Toying with the idea of a presidency-for-life was not the same as being a monarchist. Adams, like Alexander Hamilton, thought a stable ruler insulated from democratic pressures was the only way to keep the fractious republic from tearing itself apart. He was even willing to let the people participate more actively, as long it was "by gentle means, and by gradual advances" achieved by improvements in education. Yet Adams's language was easy to misunderstand. One of the *Defence*'s more unfortunate rhetorical devices, perceptually speaking, was Adams's loose construction of the words "monarchy," "republic," and "democracy," categories he blurred to the point that any of these could be the others and Great Britain could be all of them. The campaign reading guides to the *Defence* usually listed this as the second outrageous statement, from page 22 (though it was all over the book): "A limited Monarchy may be justly denominated a Republic." (The original "Americanus" piece put that statement first, but gave the incorrect page.) Adams really did make this argument in almost those exact words. Even a simple monarchy, with no representative body at all, "might justly be denominated a republic" as long as it was "a government of laws" in the sense that the monarch actually followed the laws. Anything short of the most absolute, despotic monarchy counted as at least somewhat republican. A "limited monarchy," on the other hand, where there were other independent branches of government present, as in Great Britain, might be called a republic under Adams's strictest definition of the term, which was in fact one of the loosest ever applied. All he seemed to require was that citizens were represented or governed by consent in some theoretical sense, and not subject 100 percent to the will of a single man. A monarchy could be a democracy, too, if its people (the enfranchised nation, however small and infrequently consulted this group might be) were broadly acknowledged as sovereign. Thus Adams could see eighteenth-century Great Britain, with its king and grossly unrepresentative, only partially elected Parliament, as Europe's only significant surviving democracy: "The English have, in reality, blended together the feudal institutions with those of the Greeks and Romans" and from those materials had made their own "noble composition, which avoids the inconveniences, and retain[s] the advantages, of both." It was an "immortal honour" to the people of England that they had done so well.[18]

The English people may have deserved their honors, but the distance between Adams's view of the British government and that of the world's democrats, who now saw the British as the sworn archenemy of republican liberty and popular government, could not have been more extreme. The American Republicans, from Jefferson on down, concluded that Adams must have been corrupted or seduced while serving in London as a diplomat. Even "Solomons in the council," Jefferson lamented to Mazzei, had "had their heads shorn by the harlot England."[19]

The British had not bought Adams off with money or harlots, but his long diplomatic residence in England and the occupational requirement of socializing with the British aristocracy had clearly colored his thought. He was deeply impressed by the wealth, power, and social deference that European aristocrats enjoyed, and combining this impression with observations from his own life, Adams concluded that aristocracy was forever: elites were an ineluctable force in human society that designers of political institutions could not stop, but only try to contain: "The rich, the well-born, and the able, acquire an influence among the people that will soon be too much for simple honesty and plain sense" in a democratic political institution such as a house of representatives and so "the most illustrious of them must therefore be separated from the mass, and placed by themselves" in a body of their own. This was Adams's conception of a senate, as a containment vessel for the aristocratic forces in society.[20]

In an emphasis that seems unique to him, Adams believed the genius of the British system lay in the little-loved and declining House of Lords, which he liked for the way he thought it quarantined the British aristocracy from the lesser members of society and limited their influence. The prestige of elevation to an upper house would be irresistible for elites, but according to Adams it was "to all honest and useful intents, an ostracism," not a promotion to power at all. On a certain level, Adams had a point about the House of Lords, which did become increasingly removed from the levers of British political power—but only because the British system had lost its checks and balances, and centralized power in the House of Commons became the increasingly dominant part of "the King-in-Parliament." Perhaps the U.S. Senate as it originally operated, elected by legislators and meeting in secret, might have become an "ostracizing" body, but given the fact that senators had also been given longer terms and direct, exclusive influence over government appointments and foreign policy, this was unlikely.[21]

The notion that powerful men would be so bewitched by a title that they would ostracize themselves out of power spoke volumes about just how much store the status-conscious Adams himself set on such outward forms. The title campaign of 1789 was not forgotten in 1796. The *Aurora* got off one of its better and longest-lasting shots at Adams with "A Pleasant Anecdote" before the election, recalling the ridiculous regal getup Adams had worn to the Senate in the early days, including an ornamental sword and fancy coat buttoned below the waist. With his "considerable sesquipedality of belly," Adams had inspired a southern senator to suggest that he be styled "His Rotundity." This famous quip seems to have first become public knowledge during the 1796 campaign. While some of Adams's friends agreed with him about presidential titles, no one but the author of the *Defence* would have taken that on as a pet project.[22]

As Adams explained more clearly in his letters and notes than he did in the book, he was far more worried about the threat posed by aristocratic elites than he was about monarchy. While American students of constitutional history more typically saw the English aristocracy as a buffer against the tyranny of ambitious monarchs—the thinking behind the Magna Carta's fame—Adams saw the danger coming from the other direction. His reading of European history, especially the history of the city republics he catalogued in the *Defence*, convinced him that it was the nobility and other elites who most often threatened the liberty and stability of republics, and misgoverned generally, rather than kings. Single authorities like kings Adams felt rather good about. As he saw it, kings tended to rule less greedily and often allied with the people against the aristocracy. And the people needed a strong protector to keep away the wolves: "A balance can never be established between two orders in society without a third to aid the weakest." Adams summed up his lesser-evil view of monarchical power to Jefferson after the *Defence* was first published: "You are afraid of the one—I, of the few. We agree perfectly that the many should have a full fair and perfect Representation.—You are Apprehensive of the Monarchy, I, of Aristocracy." Newspaper critics would have blanched at Adams's further flourish: if the president ended up in office for life, "so much the better it appears to me" than the dangers posed by competitive elections.[23]

While clarifying that the containment of aristocracy was Adams's central concern may clear up the monarchy charge, at least in the long view, the critics of 1796 devoted as much attention to the pessimistic view of human possibility that underlay his argument for balanced government. He had decided that only one factor, throughout recorded history, had ever allowed a great people to retain a shred of their "democratical authority"—"the balance, and that only." What needed to be balanced? The "three powers" of division and discord that were eternally "strong in every tribe" from the ancient Germans and Greeks to modern Indians and Italians: the one, the few, and the many who each sought domination for their own group in the form of rampant monarchy, oligarchy, or democracy.[24]

This was a realistic outlook, but not one that comported well with the American dreams of social mobility and ever-increasing prosperity that much of the population harbored even in 1796. Against the hopeful "vision of classlessness" that the Democratic-Republicans projected, Adams offered the dim prospect of inevitable inequality, put forth so obsessively and with such conviction that many readers detected more than a hint of admiration and vindication. Around half the page references typically cited in the Jeffersonian guides to the *Defence* highlighted sweeping statements, sometimes the ones unwisely copied from Adams's sources without clear attribution, about the impossibility (and undesirability) of social equality. Pages 110 and 116 of volume 1 were cited in all the guides, paraphrasing two passages that tried to explain the political deference of common people to their social betters as a natural outcome of inexorable forces: "Wealth, Birth, Family Pride respected by all people" and "Wealth, Birth and Virtue form the best men." Page 360 was another common citation, one that more nearly quoted the exact statement that Adams had put in his book. It was a bucket of icy cold water poured on the hopes of many ordinary citizens and Founding Fathers alike: "The distinctions of poor and rich are as necessary, in states of considerable extent, as labour and good government. The poor are destined to labour; and the rich, by the advantages—of education, independence, and leisure, are qualified for superior stations." This is what drew the real outrage. "Here is an undisguised blow at equal rights," wrote "Sidney" in the *Aurora*, connecting Adams's social theory to his suggestion that senates in American governments ought to have property requirements or some other prerequisite that would make them socially exclusive: "The *mass* of the people must be satisfied with a representation in the *lower* house; but *riches* and *family* as well as talents are to be the qualifications for a seat in the *illustrious* Senate." The Republican address distributed on a leaflet with the Adams quotations in Pennsylvania struck a more elemental note, casting the competition as one between hope and fear about the success of the American experiment. The leaflet contrasted Jefferson's optimistic message "that all men are *born equal*" with the thesis of John Adams's book: "*John Adams* says this is all a farce and a falsehood; that some men should be born Kings, and some should be born Nobles."[25]

John Adams did not say that this *should* be the case, exactly; but if anything, the paraphrases did not do justice to the darkness of his message. Adams delighted in bitter truths and gave no quarter to anyone's foolish illusions and aspirations. Pages 110 and 116 were part of a chapter attacking Benjamin Franklin's reputed preference for a single legislative body and, less openly, Franklin's cultural meaning as the icon of American social mobility, the proof that a poor manual laborer could rise to become a world-famous politician and philosopher. "Dr. Franklin" inspired Adams to a long discourse on the overwhelming power conferred by "birth, fortune, and fame." Was the reader shocked at his introducing the idea of class distinctions by birth into a discussion of American society? "Let the page in history be quoted, where any nation, ancient or modern, civilized or savage" existed "among whom no difference was made between citizens on account of their extraction."

Veneration for famous names, distinguished ancestors, and "splendid wealth" were natural human tendencies, and their role in the creation of hereditary elites was reinforced by the superior qualifications received by children of the elite, in addition to the automatic advantages they carried based on their names alone: "The children of illustrious families, have generally greater advantages of education, and earlier opportunities to be acquainted with public characters, and informed of public affairs, than those of meaner ones, or even those in middle life." Adams was certainly onto something here, despite an unbecoming tone of prejustifying his hopes for his own children. His great proof was the existence of the long-standing colonial elites that had produced most of the Founders, which had developed notwithstanding a relatively egalitarian atmosphere: "Know thyself is as useful a precept to nations as to men. Go into every village in New England, and you will find that the office of justice of the peace, and even the place of representative, which has ever depended only on the freest election of the people, have generally descended from generation to generation, in three or four families at most."[26]

Even if one is inclined to give Adams due credit for an observation that matches the conclusions of dozens of New England town studies by professional historians, we should note that he took this point far beyond merely observing it into the realm of seeming to celebrate a phenomenon that other Founders regretted or hoped to see reformed, as in Jefferson's plans for a public educational system. Adams and Jefferson (and many other Founders) shared the belief that there was a "natural aristocracy" of talent and intellect among mankind, that they were both part of it, and that such persons were the best qualified to serve in government. But more idealistic republicans like Jefferson wanted to open the elite to new members through education and "rotation in office," and to counteract elitism, where they could. One way to do that was by not officially recognizing its boundaries in setting the qualifications for elected office and by reducing the social protocols with which Washington had surrounded the presidency and Adams was seemingly so determined to expand. Where Adams differed from Jefferson and most other American writers (except for certain other Federalists) was in insisting that this "natural aristocracy" needed to be treated like a real one, with its members' status factored into the construction of the government, by property qualifications or lifetime service: "This natural aristocracy among mankind, has been dilated on, because it is a fact essential to be considered in the institution of a government. It is a body of men which contains the greatest collection of virtues and abilities in a free government; it is the brightest ornament and glory of the nation; and may always be made the greatest blessing of society, if it be judiciously managed." As expressed in the sharpest of the Republican reading guides to Adams in 1796, by "A Friend to Equal Rights," Adams regarded "this superior order of beings" as "the very *life* and *soul*" of a republic, or it would be if his magic formulas for balance were followed.[27]

In stark contrast to Jefferson's optimism about the possibility of expanding the educated elite, or reducing its privileges, Adams saw social inequality as too fundamental to ever imagine successfully changing it: "These sources of inequality, which are common to every people . . . can never be altered by any, because they are founded in the constitution of nature." Indeed, Adams found elites, the formation of elites, and deference to elites such universal traditions as to suggest that they had what we would call genetic roots. Throwing in a disclaimer that "no man" should be presumed good or bad "merely" because his father was, Adams argued that, actually, you probably could assume that:

> Wise men beget fools, and honest men knaves; but these instances, although they may be frequent, are not general. If there is often a likeness in feature and figure, there is generally more in mind and heart. . . . In all countries it has been observed, that vices, as well as virtues, run down in families, very often, from age to age. Any man may run over in his thoughts the circle of his acquaintance, and he will probably recollect instances of a disposition to mischief, malice, and revenge, descending, in certain breeds, from grandfather to father and son.

This superficially reasonable view looked much less so when Adams illustrated it with a tragic anecdote about the crushed psyche of a downtrodden person that he thought was about biology rather than society. He had read about a young woman in Paris, about to be hanged for stealing, who refused a pardon on the grounds that her grandfather, father, and brother had been hanged for stealing, so she might as well get it over with: "It runs in the blood of our family to steal, and be hanged; if I am pardoned now, I shall steal again in a few months more inexcuseably: and therefore I will be hanged now." Even Adams admitted that "an hereditary passion" to become the victim of capital punishment was unlikely to be a common problem, "but something like it too often descends, in certain breeds, from generation to generation." In other words, poverty and criminality were genetic conditions.[28]

While "breeds" seems more offensive today, a number of critics called attention to Adams's repeated use of the term "orders" to describe the men who made up and would be represented in the three balanced parts of the government. Occasionally Adams seemed to be referring only to different roles in government that might be played, but more often he seemed to advocate the representation of permanent, perhaps legally defined social divisions that would appear in American society or ought to be created even if they did not yet exist: perhaps a titled nobility, landed gentry, and commoners, with a king lording over them all, as in Great Britain. Adams was transfixed by the idea that properly balanced governments had to balance social groups in their different institutions and that this was the essence of the American constitutions he was defending. This was a mistake in addition to being offensive to many readers. The society of the United States was riven by distinctions of race, gender, and class, but there were no titled aristocrats. Since free white men held all the offices in any case, the separation of powers in America had always been of governmental functions—executive, legislative, and judicial rather than monarchy, democracy, and aristocracy. As a "Communication" in the Philadelphia *New World* put it, "This worthy citizen [Adams] frequently falls into the dangerous mistake, that accurate and effectual separation of the different powers of government involve[s] the necessity of three 'orders' among the members of society. The American people generally asserted and practiced these three divisions of governmental powers long before the commencement of Mr. Adams's work, and to this day there are no 'orders' among the American people." Indeed, one of the practical issues that neither Adams nor the relatively few like-minded men at the Philadelphia Constitutional Convention ever worked out was exactly what social distinction an upper house like the Senate could be based on when there was no titled aristocracy. Wealth was considered, but a minimally different age requirement for representatives, senators, and the president was all that remained in the final Federal Constitution. As eventually in almost all American constitutions, Adams's balanced structure was followed, but the logic that underpinned it not so much.[29]

The sad part for Adams's reputation during his lifetime was that he sincerely believed that he was the doughtiest and most perceptive defender of free government around, and even of such democracy as he was willing to see exist. The burden of the defense of the *Defence* mounted by Federalist defenders was more or less that John Adams got a lifetime pass. He had proved his republican bona fides in the years leading up to 1776, and so anything he wrote must have been written in the service of republicanism, no matter how it read. Many historians have taken more or less the same line. Adams himself signaled the strategy by pausing regularly for disclaimers: "It would be better for America, it is neverthe-less agreed, to ring all the changes with the whole set of bells . . . rather than establish an absolute monarchy," he wrote in the preface, but he could not help adding an undisclaimer, "notwithstanding all the great and real improvements made in that kind of government."[30]

"KING ADAMS" AS POLITICAL REALITY
AND METAPHOR

Once the *Defence* came to be more widely read in the fall of 1796, one could almost hear the jaws dropping and pens scribbling from Provi-dence to Pittsburgh, New York to Charleston, as Adams made new opponents and old opponents took notes. How could an American rev-olutionary have written such a book? All of these passages and many more made it into the reading guides that Jefferson supporters spread far and wide. A great many Americans were simply not ready to hear that there was anything to admire or emulate about their recently es-caped monarchical oppressor, much less that it had history's greatest form of government, most honorable people, should be considered a democratic republic, and so on. It would have been a red-letter day in the annals of postcolonial nationalism if such language did not upset some readers. As "Sidney" in the Philadelphia *Aurora* put it, Adams had become "a great admirer and warm panegyrist of that political monster the British form of government" and ought to get "a star and garter from every monarchy and aristocracy on the face of the globe." His book was "not a *defence* but in fact a libel on our constitutions . . . and a satire upon the people." Clearly no man who held such views was a safe choice to "preside in our general government unless, indeed, the people are tired of self government." If the voters prized "their liberties and their constitution let their votes be given to men [electors] who will not give their support to the deadliest foe to both."[31]

It was but a short leap to the conclusion that a man who had such nice things to say about the British monarchy must be some sort of monarchist himself. "What the Vice President *was* is not the question, but what he *is* ought to be the criterion. He *was a Republican*, but he *is* in favor of Monarchy." Besides directly praising life terms of office, Adams had provided easy access to the idea of his monarchism through his loose terminology. "Sidney" suggested that readers should support Adams if they wished "to exchange their elective republic for a republic according to Mr. Adams's understanding of the word, that is, *a limited monarchy*."[32]

Not every anti-Adams writer made the monarchism charge outright, but most of the shorter-form campaign materials highlighted the idea, and some of the most bitter and bluntly partisan items carried the accusation a step further, suggesting that Adams hankered after a dynasty himself. Almost the only personal characteristic of John Adams ever mentioned in the Republican press, besides the one reference to his weight, was the fact that he had "Sons who might aim to succeed their father." (Jefferson was safer because he had "daughters only.") As noted by one of the most cynical Adams critics, "Safety" out of Boston, the Adams sons had already been "placed in high office, and are no doubt understood to be what he calls *the well-born*," the sort of people Adams spent much of the *Defence* demonstrating would always come to the fore, even in a supposedly egalitarian society. In parts of the book, Adams seemed to be almost subconsciously answering charges of nepotism that largely went unmade, perhaps out of a guilty conscience. Supremely talented as future legacy president John Quincy Adams was, there was no doubt that he and his brothers and brother-in-law had been able to jump the queue of preferment. Not yet thirty in 1796, John Quincy had already held two of the five major foreign posts available in the early U.S. diplomatic corps, what we would call ambassadorships, to the Netherlands and Portugal, with more jobs on the way. "Following his own principles," wrote "Safety," Adams's sons might in time "become the Siegneurs and Lords of this country." They were unofficial princes already.[33]

Historians have rightly scoffed at the notion that John Adams was looking to settle John Quincy on the throne, and he was certainly not the "avowed monarchist" of the Democratic-Republican campaign literature. Defenders such as John Gardner and William Loughton Smith argued that the offending passages were taken out of context and that Adams's intention had always been to defend republicanism and America from the dangers that beset them. Gardner chalked up some of the edgier passages to the vice president's "deep researches" and "daring spirit of investigation," excuses that had the advantage of being fairly accurate. Even some Jefferson supporters were embarrassed by the more extreme abuses of Adams's writings. Yet clearly Adams had arrived at a place philosophically and personally where he was fairly open to or even eager to accede to what the editor of the Adams Family Papers calls a "republican monarchy," in which the chief executive might be elected but otherwise would be largely free of any close supervision from below. Adams's republican monarchy was meant to shore up republicanism rather than destroy it, but for those concerned with political democracy and social equality, Adams's version of republicanism was so narrow as to destroy most of the system's progressive potential.[34]

Even if John Adams did not deserve the suspicions about his yen for a crown, there was no Founder more committed to hierarchical government than Adams. As explained in the *Defence* and practically demonstrated in his 1789 title campaign, Adams's theory of governance relied on underlying social hierarchies and traditions of deference to gain the allegiance of the populace. The *Defence* shifted from page to page and source to source on the question of whether America already had social orders of some kind, but Adams was unswerving in his contention that wide class distinctions were crucial to maintaining the stability of a free government. It was the social orders that had to be balanced in the different branches of government, and only if the people's rulers were social betters that they could look up to would the people quietly obey. In another oft-cited passage, Adams declared flatly that all important officials needed to come from the upper social strata: "The army, the navy, revenue, excise, customs, police, justice, and all foreign ministers, must be gentlemen, that is to say, friends and connections of the rich, well-born and well-educated members of the house; or, if they are not, the community will be filled with slander, suspicion, and ridicule against them, as ill-bred, ignorant, and in all respects unqualified for their trusts; and the plebeians themselves will be as ready as any to join in the cry, and run down their characters."[35]

The choice, as Adams saw it, was between the social balance he proposed, with class differences hardwired somehow into the constitutional system, and plain anarchy that would quickly lead to despotism enforced by military power: "Where the people have a voice, and there is no balance, there will be everlasting fluctuations, revolutions, and horrors, until a standing army, with a general at its head, commands the peace, or the necessity of an equilibrium is made [to] appear to all, and is adopted by all." Thus the lack of a republican monarchy would inevitably lead back to an old-fashioned one. But the equally inevitable conclusion, when reading John Adams, was that monarchy and aristocracy of some sort were permanent features of the political world, even in America, and that this was just fine with him. It was not at all fine with millions of other Americans who thought the point of the new nation was leaving such relics of barbarism, to use an Enlightenment phrase, behind.

Taken in context, Adams's arguments were part of a subtle defense of "balanced government" as necessary to ensure the stability of a republic and protect the people against the depredations of both their superiors and themselves. However, the argument Adams made really did involve his vindicating the utility of monarchical and aristocratic (as opposed to democratic) elements in government, a position that most Americans did not hold and that the initial constitutional system did not incorporate, with the single exception of the presidential veto—and that had not been part of the British system since the seventeenth century. In crucial ways, Adams's detractors were simply taking his writings seriously. As a writer signing himself "Safety" put it, there was no way around the simple fact that by their published works, "Mr. Adams has thus immortalized himself as an advocate for hereditary Governments," while "Mr. Jefferson, on the other hand, has distinguished himself by his writings in and out of office, as a true Republican and favourer of pure Elective Governments."[36]

In the final analysis, calling John Adams a monarchist based on reading the *Defence of the American Constitutions* was a smear, but only in the narrowest sense. As metaphorical shorthand for the basic thrust of his thought, intended to communicate with those likely to disagree with Adams's conservative premises, the monarchy charge was accurate enough and effective negative campaigning. If Democratic-Republicans had had the chance to go to the voters in New York and New Jersey with this theme, the outcome of the whole election might have been different.[37]

The *Defence*'s mixing of monarchical and aristocratic principles into republicanism forced some of Adams's opponents to consider updating their own terminology, in ways that pointed toward the future evolution of American party labels. An *Aurora* correspondent noted in early November that it had "become a trite custom" among the Federalists "to call friends of liberty *Democrats*" as a put-down and to dispute the opposition's exclusive claim to the label "Republican." Many moderate members of the opposition, especially those of elite backgrounds, still shrank from the term. Given the definition of democracy that advocates of mixed government such as Adams and Montesquieu seemed to use—"when the body of the people is possessed of the supreme power"—why did supporters of "a popular government" not simply embrace "democrat" as an "honorable appellation"? Plenty of citations could be found, like the ones John Adams used in the *Defence*, of historical republics (such as Venice) and theories of republicanism in which republics operated as aristocratic oligarchies or near monarchies. As far as this writer was concerned, republics and republicans "fashioned according to Adams's model" could keep the term "Republican": "*Democrat* in future shall be my political name, in contradiction to men who support John Adams, the unequivocal friend to hereditary power and civil distinctions. . . . *Republican, aristocrat, or Monocrat* [monarchist] then, being synonymous terms in the vocabulary of Adams, the British faction may take their choice of them."[38]

THE BLEEDING EDGE: TRANSATLANTIC RADICAL CULTURE AND THE DEMOCRATIC-REPUBLICAN CAMPAIGN

Accusations of monarchism are a strikingly eighteenth-century aspect of the eighteenth century's one American presidential campaign, but not perhaps the most striking difference from the presidential politics of later eras. It is axiomatic that general election candidates run to the middle and second nature that campaigns are a time for grandiose patriotism. Yet the campaign the pro-Jefferson forces ran in 1796 marks the rare case in American political history where the rhetoric of a major presidential campaign was directed by the radical left wing of a party, a proper term considering the origins of "left" and "right" in the seating arrangements of the French National Assembly. With no real national direction from the candidate or even his close circle, the initiative for pushing Jefferson fell to the local nests of activists in places like Philadelphia and Boston, the same men who had been the prime movers behind the Democratic-Republican Societies and the Jay Treaty protests and who did most of the writing for the *Aurora* and *Independent Chronicle* newspapers. And while they were loud and fervent patriots, as seen in their rage against the "British treaty," they had a broad, internationalist approach to patriotism, shaped and freed by what historian Seth Cotlar calls the "popular cosmopolitanism" of Tom Paine and the French

Revolution. They considered themselves "citizens of the world" as well as citizens of their states, and the United States, with their highest fealty pledged to the cause of mankind itself. This attitude led to rhetoric and behavior that did not always comport with more conventional and parochial notions of loyalty and taste, then or now.[39]

Some of the seeming contradictions of the fall campaign were not only prefigured but more or less announced in the Fourth of July toasts that the Philadelphia radicals drank while planning it the previous summer. The "memory of those Heroes" who sacrificed their lives to make the country free was saluted. The radicals raised their glasses to "Independence as established in 1776" and "Uniform Patriotism" and even expressed the wish that only good patriots would get to make time with the ladies: "The American Fair—May their charms be enjoyed by Patriots only." They shook their fists at "every Administration" who violated the nation's principles or tried to "barter its Rights to a Foreign Power." Any such would "be held in detestation by the Sons of Columbia" and "sink into Infamy." But then there was a left turn. The ultra-Americanism was followed by a long series of shout-outs to several foreign nations in succession, though not the British: "The Magnanimous French Nation"; "The Republic of Holland"; the navies of France, Spain, and Holland; and "The People of Poland" all took their turn. (Feeling sorry for the Poles and their dismembered republic was actually a bit of a competition between the parties, as we will see below.) While focusing on the upcoming American elections in hopes that all local, state, and national officials would be "cast in a pure Democratic Mould," the radicals were willing to share their hopes with the world: "Mankind—May all their Powers be united for the destruction of Tyranny." Lest this be mistaken as a messianic call for imperial conquest, the celebrants added that the goal was "equal Liberty" for all nations, not any imposing of America's will on others and not growing wealthy and powerful at the expense of others: "May all the Nations of the Earth be bro't to a level, live within the compass of Justice and square their actions by the Golden Rule."[40]

The writers of these sentiments and drinkers of these drinks were believers and practitioners of the school of political thought that intellectual historian Jonathan Israel has dubbed the Radical Enlightenment. Other less admiring scholars have gone with "low Enlightenment" to connote the prevalence of this style among a relatively down-market crowd of printers, pamphleteers, publicists, and occasional pornographers. This new-wave Enlightenment developed out of the revolutionary intellectual and political movements on the European continent in the decades leading up to the fall of the Bastille in 1789. This was a generation or more after the heyday of moderate Enlightenment figures such as Montesquieu and Voltaire, who tended to be advocates of mixed rather than democratic government as well as aristocrats or recipients of aristocratic patronage themselves. Radical Enlightenment figures in Europe factored in later French thought, along with the rather checkered experiences of liberal reformers in places like the Dutch Republic and the German states. The transatlantic radicals often looked to America for their explicit inspiration through the Toms—Jefferson and Paine—and their friend Benjamin Franklin. Via *The Rights of Man* and the French Revolution, their ideas then flowered in the "Jacobins" of Great Britain and regerminated in America, as we saw in chapter 2. Adherents of the Radical Enlightenment in 1796 considered themselves part of an international movement from monarchical tyranny and social hierarchy to republican liberty and social mobility, one that had begun in America and then progressed into Europe; its embattled vanguard was located in revolutionary France and the movements sympathetic to it across the rest of the European continent.[41]

The connections from the sources of the Radical Enlightenment to the people writing articles for the Democratic-Republican press in 1796, and reading them, were often painfully direct. Many of the writers and printers at the *Aurora* and allied publications, especially in Philadelphia, had experienced life in the vanguard directly and gotten themselves thrown out of their European homes for it. In the year or so before 1796, Benjamin Franklin Bache and the *Aurora* had received reinforcements from a wave of seasoned radical journalists who had become political refugees because of the British crackdown on supporters of the French Revolution. They were transatlantic radicals by necessity. In many cases, their main cause was not supporting France but reforming the corrupt and unequal institutions of Great Britain. James Thomson Callender had written Scotland's only radical pamphlet during the era of the French Revolution but had to flee the country for his trouble, informed on by friends and with the sheriff of Glasgow in pursuit. William Duane, born in the colony of New York but raised in Clonmel, Ireland, was a printer who emigrated to India and ended up in the Black Hole of Calcutta for criticizing the British East India Company. Deported back to England, Duane became involved in the working-class parliamentary reform group the London Corresponding Society but was soon forced to emigrate again, this time to Philadelphia. The Bache family and a number of other Philadelphians, usually liberals, immigrants, or both, were known for taking in political refugees, so Callender, Duane, and others naturally wound up in the *Aurora* circle, doing the only job that had been left to them, radical journalism. Duane would take over both Bache's newspaper and his family after Bache died in 1798.[42]

The crucial and immediate role of the refugees indicates that, while not the arm of an ocean-spanning French conspiracy as painted by the Federalists, the American exponents of the Radical Enlightenment really were "citizens of the world" in the sense of being part of an international movement that was fully engaged with their overseas confreres. The ardor for France's revolutionary leaders had cooled somewhat since the fall of the Girondins, but the American radicals still followed France's military struggles against Europe's monarchies with breathless interest. By 1796, this included Napoleon Bonaparte's conquest of northern Italy, which climaxed in mid-November with his defeat of the Austrians near Verona and launched the general's rise to imperial power. Reports on the "Army of Italy" actually took more space than the 1796 campaign in many American newspapers, and in the radical journals where that was not true, such as the *Aurora*, the Italian campaign was just one part of a broader struggle being played out across Europe: in France, a royalist rebellion had recently been dispersed; in the Netherlands, the French-inspired Batavian Republic was struggling to hold itself together; and in Poland, another rejuvenated republic had recently disappeared thanks to the machinations of neighboring monarchies, exactly what might have happened to France. Just two days before the presidential election, "Columbus" in the *Aurora* saluted the fact that it had "graciously pleased Almighty God to frustrate all of their [the anti-French monarchies'] schemes, save only the instance of the much lamented Poles."[43]

Federalists and other conservatives looked at French activities in Europe with horror, seeing the conquest and dictatorship they feared might be the future that France planned for America. Three of Europe's longest-running republics—the Netherlands, Genoa, and Venice—had been snuffed out by French armies and influence. These were aristocratically controlled republics, however, that the Radical Enlightenment was glad to see go, with elected rulers who were monarchs in practical effect. Radical Enlightenment thought had indeed been fashioned partly by Dutch writers responding to the autocratic power of the theoretically elective "stadtholder" regime. Over the previous centuries, the House of Orange had turned the Dutch Republic into not only a monarchy, but an adjunct of the British monarchy (through repeated intermarriage). The radicals saw George Washington and his chosen successor Adams as exactly this sort of creeping monarch. The comment about the Netherlands in the Fourth of July toasts cited above was directed as much at the president as anyone in the Low Countries: "May the Popularity of no Man render him dangerous to Liberty." William Duane was actually kinder to Washington than many radicals, treating him as a fallen hero who had given in to "*Machiavelian policy*" rather than a finished villain. The day of infamy was the moment Washington chose "state secrecy" over democracy by refusing to let the House of Representatives see the papers on the Jay Treaty, electing to "treat your country as an enemy [to be] overcome by stratagem." It was "from that fatal moment, when you listened to the seductions of your deadliest enemies, in opposition to the voice of Freedom" that "the enemies of Liberty and your Country called you *their own*, and the name of WASHINGTON sunk from the rank of the SOLONS and LYCURGUSES to the insignificance of a *Venetian Doge* or a *Dutch Stadtolder!*"[44]

The American democrats who worked for Jefferson did not see anything contradictory about having these foreign connections and enthusiasms. Their Enlightenment-based approach to patriotism allowed them to be loudly American and ultrapartisan, but also multilateral and internationalist at the same time. Ultimately aimed more at realizing a state of universal liberty, rationality, and equality everywhere than at promoting a particular state's interests, their patriotism could overspread the world, bring peace rather than war, and ultimately make itself unnecessary. Some remarkably expansive statements of these ideas were made at a Boston "Ox Feast" held a few weeks before the election for visiting French minister Pierre Adet. "Volunteers" at the end of the event toasted "the American, French, and Batavian Republics: May they, by the virtues which they practice, and the happiness which they exhibit, attach all nations to the cause of social Liberty." The democrats firmly believed that enlightened peoples with democratic governments following the principles of benevolence, and the *rational* self-interest that reason dictated, would never need to fight each other unless they were corrupted or usurped. Thus while patriotism—love of one's country and the willingness to defend its liberties—was a good thing, the need for patriotism would fade once the "General Revolution" had finished. The last toast at Adet's feast struck this note: "All Mankind—May the exalted virtue of Patriotism itself be finally lost in universal Philanthropy."[45]

As accustomed as we may be to thinking of strenuous political campaigning as an essentially cynical and self-interested activity, this was not the self-conception that devotees of the Radical Enlightenment had, though many of them were certainly not averse to helping themselves in the process. Like the Democratic-Republican Societies that many of these same men had joined, the radicals were committed, as a matter of ideology, to peaceful but rhetorically and tactically aggressive political activity. One of the objections to John Adams's thought that was distinctive of the *Aurora*'s writers was their opposition to the narrow, inert role Adams envisioned for the common American citizen. "A Friend to Equal Rights" quoted Adams from his chapter on Montesquieu, defining liberty as each person having "a tranquility of mind" that arose from being reasonably assured of their "safety." Liberty for Adams did not, then, the writer noted, "consist in the *Exercise* of *Equal Rights*." Without such active exercise, political rights had little meaning for the radicals. The ethic of active citizenship through bitter political criticism led some radicals to self-defeating and potentially cause-defeating behavior. Radical émigré and future *Aurora* editor William Duane decided that what he ought to do as his introduction to his new country was to boldly issue a rebuttal, pseudonymous but not very secret, to George Washington's Farewell Address.[46]

The combined imperatives toward General Revolution and electoral democracy also made for some moments of cognitive and rhetorical stress in which the radicals did not seem to realize how quasi-treasonous their rhetoric and actions could appear. The day before the election, the *Aurora* addressed the "People of America" on their need to "exercise the power of choosing the First Officer of your Federal Government." There was no need to tell Americans that theirs was a "Democratic Republic, founded on the principles of Liberty and Equality." Americans loved the French nation "as men and politicians . . . but they would not surrender one atom of their political rights to the French any more than to Mr. Pitt." The import of this remark, in the *Aurora* context, was that French pressure was nothing to worry about, so full hostility should be directed toward the British.[47]

What we need to realize before simply condemning the seeming disloyalty of the radicals' attitudes and tactics is that the American people did not necessarily object. With only the youngest adults having been born in the United States and new immigrants arriving every day, there were many ways in which even ordinary Americans of this era conducted themselves as "citizens of the world." Foreign news teemed through American newspapers, and foreign goods, travelers, and workers through the port towns. Frontier Americans of this era lived on or near international borders and were well accustomed to the idea of working with or living under adjacent foreign governments when required. As David Waldstreicher has pointed out, it was one of the great strengths of American nationalism that it could be so flexible and protean: almost crazily strident but able to fit itself to any situation.[48]

TOM PAINE VS. THE COLD HERMAPHRODITE FACULTY

For much of 1796, Bache had been plotting what he thought would be one of the masterstrokes of the fall campaign, a public letter against the Washington administration and John Adams from the pen of a figure who had the revolutionary credibility to be put up against Washington and Adams. This was the Philadelphia radicals' role model and favorite Founder of 1776 (after Jefferson and Franklin), Thomas Paine. Deploying Paine against his old colleagues Washington and Adams was an effort to draw on a less conservative well of historical prestige than the ones Washington and Adams provided. Never one to be shy regarding his own importance, Paine had no qualms about pitting his revolutionary credentials against Washington's: "Mr. Washington has not served America with greater Zeal, nor with more disinterestedness than myself, and I know not that he has done so with better effect." By the summer of 1796, he was eager to intervene. "It is necessary to speak out," Paine wrote to Benjamin Franklin Bache, covering the manuscript for a new pamphlet; "the American character is so much sunk in Europe that it is necessary to distinguish between the Government and the Country."[49]

Paine's reappearance in American politics resulted from a convergence of events in his career and in the adopted country he left behind. Considering himself a "citizen of the world," Paine had been willing to follow the General Revolution wherever it would lead. So in 1789 he went to observe the events in France, then moved back home to England to defend the French Revolution and spread the wave of political change by writing *The Rights of Man* and setting off the great controversy. In 1792, Paine was granted French citizenship by the National Assembly

The Founding Radical's Revenge: Common Sense *and* Rights of Man *author Thomas Paine felt the Washington administration had left him to rot in a French prison during the Reign of Terror. In return, the professional pamphleteer intervened in the 1796 campaign with a venomous open* Letter to George Washington. *(Engraving by James Shury, 1836, Library of Congress.)*

and then elected a deputy for Calais, just as the British government was preparing to make him an outlaw. Despite knowing very little of the language, he became an important figure in French politics upon arrival, only to have the whole situation go bad. In the French context, Paine found himself a moderate, voting against the execution of Louis XVI, and then a political prisoner after his allies the Girondins fell from power and the Reign of Terror began in 1793.

Paine came to blame his near-death experience in the Luxembourg Palace prison on Washington's administration, and not without justice.

Robespierre got the idea that Paine was somehow behind the troubles between Girondist French minister Edmond Genet and the Washington administration and decided that throwing Paine in prison might be a way to improve relations. It is not clear that Washington himself understood Paine's situation or how powerfully some friendly signal from him might have affected it, but in any case the signal was never going to come from Washington's envoy to France at the time, Gouverneur Morris, a Federalist who was an old enemy of Paine's from American revolutionary politics. With Paine growing ill in prison, the continued U.S. silence was construed by Robespierre as approval of the detention and as authorization for a death sentence that was only interrupted by the Jacobin dictator's fall from power a few days before it could be carried out. It took another four months for Paine to finally be released, into the care of a new and much more friendly American minister, James Monroe.[50]

Monroe's solicitude did little to mollify Paine's seething anger at his abandonment. His feelings were intensified by the fact that he had once had a fairly close personal relationship with Washington. As, respectively, the chief propagandist and the military leader of the American revolutionary cause, Paine and Washington had spent much time together socially and professionally during the war. Despite this, Paine believed, the "cold blooded traitor" Washington had tried to sacrifice him for political purposes, either "to gratify the English government" or else to provide another excuse to complain about the bloodthirstiness of revolutionary France.[51]

Paine conceived the idea of an open letter to President Washington airing his feelings and telling the story of his imprisonment, a project that took a more and more political direction as it developed through multiple versions. It was originally completed in February 1795 but not sent due to the entreaties of James Monroe. A revised version was actually delivered to James Madison and Washington himself in September 1795, and while Madison and Jefferson both loved it, Madison would have preferred to keep the incendiary missive unpublished. It was great for encouraging Jefferson not to suddenly announce his noncandidacy, but too intense to be welcomed in most Virginia drawing rooms.[52]

Given that the delivery vehicle was *Aurora* editor Benjamin Franklin Bache, publication was likely always the plan. As the grandson of Paine's original American benefactor, Benjamin Franklin, Bache had been a friend and admirer of Paine's since childhood and had already become his primary American publisher. Paine greatly expanded the letter for the campaign, incorporating large chunks of what he had written to Monroe from prison. Bache held the letter on reserve for just before the election. When the first excerpt appeared in an issue of the *Aurora* in mid-October 1796, Bache let the reader assume that the letter had recently arrived, though he had been seeing versions of it for over a year. He could assure readers with great accuracy, however, that the *Aurora* editor knew what Paine's handwriting looked like and could therefore vouch for its authenticity.[53]

The basic trope of the text itself was that of a respected authority on the American Revolution speaking up to corroborate the arguments that the *Aurora* had been making about the Washington administration. Paine's opinion would bolster what had already been written with the eyewitness countertestimony of a fellow Founder of the United States. Through Paine, history would provide guidance for the upcoming election. Speaking what he claimed was "the undisguised language of historical truth," the great pamphleteer of 1776 sided publicly with the Democratic-Republican opposition, describing Washington, Adams, and their supporters flatly as "the disguised traitors that call themselves Federalists."[54]

Contrary to Adams and most moderate Enlightenment thinkers, Paine still held to his original opinion that any kind of single executive was too monarchical for a republic: "It is necessary to the manly mind of a republic that it loses the debasing idea of obeying an individual." Then, setting aside this ideological opposition to the American presidency, Paine expressed outrage at the way Washington had abused the position that had been created for him: "Elevated to the chair of the Presidency, you assumed the merit of every thing to yourself, and the natural ingratitude of your constitution began to appear. You commenced your Presidential career by encouraging and swallowing the grossest adulation, and you travelled America from one end to the other to put yourself in the way of receiving it. You have as many addresses in your chest as James the II." Paine threw in some psychoanalysis for good measure, rendering a devastating judgment on the president's aloof personality and suggesting that Washington had gathered so much power to himself and stayed above the fray out of pure narcissism. Washington was "incapable of forming any" real friendships, his former compatriot concluded: "It is this cold hermaphrodite faculty that imposed itself upon the world, and was credited for a while by enemies as by friends, for prudence, moderation and impartiality." Washington's air of dignity and disinterestedness, Paine believed, was designed to mask his lack of interest in anyone but himself.[55]

For Bache, the money quote was Paine's endorsement of the monarchy charge against John Adams. He revealed the existence of Paine's letter with an extract labeled "IMPORTANT" on October 17. In the passage, Paine seemed to give his personal impressions of Adams, "always a speller after places and offices" who "never thought his little services were highly enough paid." Paine reported the rumor that Adams was so devoted to the idea of an American king that he had proposed making the presidency hereditary in the family of George Washington's cousin (and former Mount Vernon resident) Lund Washington, since the Father of His Country had fathered no heir. While also attacking Adams's "ignorant" political philosophy, Paine treated the Lund Washington proposal as chiefly self-interested. If the presidency became a hereditary office, the vice presidency would have to be made one, too; on the ground "that one good turn deserves another . . . John might then have counted upon some sinecure for himself and a provision for his descendants." While not one of Paine's more perceptive observations by a long shot—he actually devoted a whole paragraph to the argument that John Adams, of all people, "was one of those men who never contemplated the origin of government"—it did highlight the unbecoming nature of some of Adams's arguments, extolling a natural aristocracy of which his own sons were among the highest-placed members. Bache and friends thought the Lund Washington passage striking enough to include Paine's comments on the sample tickets that were distributed as flyers before the Pennsylvania presidential election.[56]

What was equally striking was that the Paine tactic seemed to work, at least among his old Pennsylvania fan base. The radical-led campaign would sweep the Jefferson electors to victory in Pennsylvania, even with Paine outed as a near atheist. Federalists took notice; more vitriolic and dismissive assaults on Paine began to appear literally alongside reports of the voting results. Paine's letter was "the most extraordinary composition of abuse, petulance, falsehood, and boyish vanity, that ever came from Grub-Street, a prison or a garret." Paine had "ridiculed Jesus Christ" and "blackguarded the Bible," but now that he had "vilified George Washington," he had finally gone too far. Several opposition journals printed an item purporting to recount a drawing room conversation in which a Federalist gentleman denounced Paine's criticism of Washington. A young lady replied, "When the Age of Reason appeared, you were not offended with the freedom with which Paine treated Jesus-Christ; but you are so good a man you cannot bear the least reflection on George Washington." William Loughton Smith and other Federalist writers also suddenly began attributing Paine's religious views to all Democratic-Republicans. According to the Hartford *Connecticut Courant*, Tom Paine was a religious teacher "whom Jefferson and his disciples exalt above Moses or Jesus."[57]

Motivated as much by politics as religion, Federalists made absolutely certain that Tom Paine's reputation was never the same again, and the 1796 campaign was only the beginning. Over the next few years, drawing heavily from the British press's onslaught against Paine, the Federalist press converted the author of *Common Sense* into a laughable yet dangerous figure whose views fell far outside the imagined mainstream of American political thought and tarred anyone or anything he supported or allied himself with, even implicitly. Just a few years later, merely allowing Paine to return to the United States was controversial, and he found he could not move around the country without attracting glares, snubs, and even mobs. He actually did stay at the Jefferson White House, fulfilling at least one of William Loughton Smith's prophecies.[58]

Turning onetime junior Founder Tom Paine into a fit subject for guilt-by-association attacks was part of a larger process of ideological narrowing in the cultural memory of the American Revolution that began in 1796 and continued apace thereafter. Retroactively, Paine's freethinking religious writings and the cosmopolitan notions of citizenship he represented were made to seem deeply troubling departures from American norms. Along with Paine, the figure of the political radical was read out of the public memory of the Revolution—Samuel Adams went with him—in favor of military leaders and a general conflation of the political revolution with national independence and the Revolutionary War. Washington and his supporters built the image of patriotic statesmanship around him too well. American political movements would continue to invoke the Revolution as a precedent for their demands, but they were able to do so much less effectively and convincingly once the memory of it had been narrowed to General Washington, the Minutemen, and the Tea Party—symbols of the right and sometimes the extreme right.[59]

TAKING THE ELECTORAL COLLEGE TO SCHOOL

HOW PRESIDENTIAL ELECTORS HELPED CREATE THE NATIONAL PRESIDENTIAL ELECTION RATHER THAN PREVENTING IT

The patchiness of the campaign and voting would seem to make 1796 almost the textbook example of what historian Ronald Formisano calls the "deferential-participant" model of politics of the Early American Republic. In this view, much or most of the campaigning and voting that took place was dominated not by grass-roots democracy or party machinery, but by a group he refers to as the "local notables."[1]

This is a term Formisano and others seem to have borrowed from European history. In that literature, the notables are the wealthy landowners, business owners, and officials who controlled eighteenth- and nineteenth-century European communities, the local ruling classes whose political power came from their family connections and the dependence of their common neighbors on them for work, money, and favors from church and government. The essential idea is that truly modern democratic opinion formation, representation, and governance cannot be said to have existed as long as the notables held sway.[2]

The term comes in closest proximity to the American Founders on the eve of the French Revolution. Just as the Americans were writing their new Constitution in 1787, King Louis XVI called together an Assembly of Notables from across France to try and solve his tottering realm's financial problems. While all but ten of the notables were still nobles (including thirty-six dukes), the idea was to reach a bit beyond the usual suspects, the higher nobility and clergy clustered in Paris who controlled the *ancien régime*'s weak national institutions, down to some of the local magistrates and administrators in the provinces. As "People of weight" in their communities, it was hoped that the notables' approval of the royal government's reforms "would powerfully influence general public opinion" back home; the common people would inevitably defer to their judgment and follow their leadership. Of course, the Assembly of Notables failed badly, but the analogy to the collections of regional bigwigs who created the United States is not inapt. By dubbing the lawyers, merchants, and planters who led the American Revolution and framed the U.S. Constitution "notables," Formisano and similarly minded scholars meant to convey that the Founders and their social peers were a similar sort of Lite Aristocracy themselves, a group whose continued prestige and authority precluded the advent of democracy and "modern politics" almost by definition.[3]

The larger message, and one shared even by many historians who do not use the "notables" terminology, is that the politics of the 1790s should be seen more as part of the colonial past than as the beginning of something new. For Formisano and other quantitative political historians, this approach helps wall off a messy political era unsuited to the statistical methodologies of social science. (The voting data series that such scholars relied on did not begin until 1824.) For the much more influential group of historians working in the twenty-first-century Founder Studies market, this distancing keeps the subjects up on their pedestals and allows writers to keep the focus where they and the reading public seem to prefer, on the personal dramas and deep thoughts of great men.[4]

The unfortunate effect of the "notables" approach has been to consign the details of early American campaigns and elections to the realm of trivia or prehistory. We might do better by embracing a term often used to dismiss historical events: "transitional." The election of 1796 was transitional in the true sense of the word, marking a transition from one national political culture to another, away from a politics of elites and "Continental Characters" acting independently of parties, to a new, more competitive and democratic system, the final form of which was yet unknown. To ignore the details of a transitional politics is to avert our eyes from the actual forces and processes by which America's national democracy came to be. It was not set up in the Constitution nor intended by its Framers; neither did it spring full-grown from the heads of Andrew Jackson or Martin Van Buren. It was an uneven process that may not be finished to this day, but it started almost as soon as the constitutional machinery was actually required to make a decision.[5]

ENROLLING IN THE ELECTORAL COLLEGE

To grapple with the details of this process, we must delve into the workings of America's murkiest political institution, the indirect system of presidential elections now known as the Electoral College. If ever there were a constitutionally defined role for America's local notables, the Electoral College was it.[6]

The national "college" never met, acting instead as a filtering mechanism to concentrate the large pool of names that bubbled up from below. The guiding logic was that the country was too big, and even most of its locally prominent men too parochial, to ever coalesce around a single candidate other than General George Washington. Most would vote for someone from their own state or region, argued Connecticut's Roger Sherman, generating a list too large and miscellaneous to be useful. At the same time, it was considered too dangerous to have a single body like Congress choose the chief magistrate all on its own: that could lead to "cabal faction & violence" as in the elective monarchy of Poland, where nobles and foreign governments battled it out to name a new king. So Article II, Section 1 of the Constitution provided for each state legislature to designate, by whatever method it chose, a number of electors equal to the size of its congressional delegation (the number of House members plus two for each state's equal number of senators). Each state's electors were then to gather simultaneously, in their own state, to prevent said cabals. Each elector would then vote for two men, including at least one man who was not from the elector's home state. Next the electors were to send their certified lists to Congress, where the votes would be compiled and the two top vote getters named president and vice president if they were selected by a majority of the electors. If not, then Congress would make the decision, according to complex rules that need not detain us here, choosing from the top five candidates the electors had voted for. At no point in any step of the process was anyone bound to vote a certain way (except for Congress choosing from the top five), and no provision was made, as we have seen, for running mates or party tickets. Instead, individual electors were to exercise their independent judgment of individual candidates.[7]

The format was a compromise hammered out in the last weeks of the Federal Convention in 1787 by the Committee on Postponed Parts, a working group made up of one member from each state delegation. The major issue the Electoral College settled was the summer-long dispute over how and by whom the new office of president would be filled. Given that one of the chief impulses behind the movement for a new Constitution was the creation of a government insulated from the excessive democracy and localism of the state governments, popular election of the president was a nonstarter at the Convention. A few of the large-state delegates made self-interested pitches for it, but most rejected the idea as impractical if not downright dangerous. George Mason of Virginia argued that "it would be as unnatural to refer the choice of a proper character for chief Magistrate to the people, as it would, to refer a trial of colours to a blind man. The extent of the Country renders it impossible that the people can have the requisite capacity to judge of the respective pretensions of the Candidates." The other major option, selection of the president by Congress, had more proponents than nationwide democracy, but it reminded too many of what Americans considered the corrupt British parliamentary system with its unseparated powers (the prime minister controlling Parliament and the executive functions of government). A legislative election would also be a playground for conspirators and party-builders. Said Gouverneur Morris, "It will be the work of intrigue, of cabal, and of faction: it will be like the election of a pope by a conclave of cardinals."[8]

The idea of a secondary popular election, with the people choosing the choosers, was originally suggested by nationalist James Wilson of Pennsylvania, who was trying to preserve some advantage for the large states but also some element of democracy in the presidential selection process. Wilson did not do this because he was any great lover of the common man—common Philadelphians had tried to kill him in the "Fort Wilson" riots in 1779 because of his alleged softness toward Loyalists. Wilson's attitude was more of a healthy fear; he had learned the hard way that in a free country, the common people needed to at least feel that their views were respected. Wilson's suggestion was ignored until John Dickinson of Delaware, arriving late to the deliberations of the Committee on Postponed Parts, challenged his colleagues over the legitimacy problems that a completely unelected president would face. Shocked that the Convention was still leaning toward a president selected by Congress, Dickinson wrote, "I observed, that the Powers which we had agreed to vest in the President, were so many and so great, that I did not think, the people would be willing to deposit them with him, unless they themselves would be more immediately concerned in his Election." In response, James Madison immediately sketched out a version of Wilson's idea on a piece of paper, and the Electoral College was born.[9]

On paper, the Electoral College served well as a way to steer theoretically between the large and small states and between oligarchy and democracy. What the Framers never discussed was how the thing was supposed to work in practice, or why it would be effective in meeting their goal of a chief magistrate who felt like the people's choice without being beholden to parties, parochial interests, or popular opinion. Excesses of democracy were still a far bigger worry for most of the Framers, who filled the Constitution with firebreaks against the potential depredations of the mob. Foreign policy and government appointments were kept in the hands of the nonpopularly elected Senate, property was protected from taking without compensation, and so on. They needed to get this new president elected while affording "as little opportunity as possible to tumult and disorder" and party organization. What emerged in their defenses of the Constitution during the ratification debates was a role for local notables.[10]

At least as seen in the *Federalist Papers* of Alexander Hamilton, James Madison, and John Jay, what the Constitution's supporters hoped was that the filtering layers of the indirect electoral system would strain out and diffuse the worst aspects of democracy and the most undesirable politicians. "Talents for low intrigue, and the little arts of popularity, may alone suffice to elevate a man to the first honors in a single State," Alexander Hamilton wrote hopefully in *Federalist* 68, "but it will require other talents and a different kind of merit to establish him in the esteem and confidence of the whole union." The Electoral College system would allow some participation by ordinary voters, but the temporary and isolated nature of individual state voting conclaves—"detached and divided" from any other institution—would make the elector positions unappealing to ambitious state-level demagogues, the ones good at the low intrigue and little arts.[11]

Instead, the *Federalist* essays implied, the honorific but obscure and temporary nature of the elector positions would allow old patterns of local social deference to reassert themselves. Those most apt to come forward as electors would be regionally prominent men of wealth, education, and refinement, secure in their positions and without sordid ambitions to climb the social or political ladder. Notables like these were the men most likely to be selected in the low-key, low-publicity process the *Federalist* essays envisioned, and they would also be the local citizens "most capable of analyzing the qualities adapted to the station [the presidency], and . . . be most likely to possess the information and discernment requisite to so complicated an investigation." Free to cast their votes for the presidential candidates of their own choice, these substantial men would be able to filter the worst of their neighbors' selfish political impulses while still representing their general attitudes and preferences.[12]

With no little irony considering his role in the creation of the party press, the "Father of the Constitution," James Madison, like many other Framers, placed great stress on the sheer size of the new national unit and how difficult it would be for even these relatively prominent citizens to transcend the boundaries of time and space. The country was so large, and the experience of most of its ordinary citizens so limited, Madison assumed, that it would be nearly impossible for large numbers of them to develop loyalties and knowledge that reached much beyond their home region. As men of great influence in their communities, the local notables were theoretically better known to their constituents than the presidential candidates themselves. Ordinary citizens would go along with whatever their local big shots said, and while these notables would make better choices than the common people, they would be local and isolated enough themselves not to be easily organized around a single national candidate. While the expectations were never fully outlined because the universally popular Washington was available as a candidate, the scenario likely envisioned was for the notables-as-electors to produce a relatively long list of respected regional figures, from which the collective wisdom of the country's best-informed leaders, sitting in Congress, would get to make the final choices. With all the layers, the geographical obstacles, and the local notables standing guard, anyone who tried to organize a national party or interest group or "any other improper or wicked project" would find the effort far too much to handle. In keeping with this approach, when it came time to implement the presidential electoral system, most of the states installed yet another layer between the people and the presidency by assigning the choice of the presidential electors to the state legislature. The states that allowed popular voting from the beginning kept the presidential election process opaque and ad hoc, holding the elector elections on a different day from all others and reorganizing the local process each cycle. Even the Framers who advocated for popular elections at the Federal Convention were hardly out to create a quadrennial nationwide electoral donnybrook.[13]

The problem for the *Federalist Papers* view of the presidential election process, and the idea of local notables as restraints on democratization, is that in practice real notables tended to open doors to popular partisanship and seek to mobilize the people as often they restrained them. They might be "opinion leaders" in the sense of educating ordinary citizens about national issues, candidates, and party alignments, but their role was more often to bring the national and the local together than to stand as buffers between them. An alternative model of the electors' role had existed from the beginning, or so some politicians in the more democratized state of Pennsylvania claimed in hindsight. Looking back on the Federal Convention fifteen years later, John Dickinson insisted that it was always intended that "the President should entirely owe his Elevation to the will of the people directly declared through" what Dickinson called the people's "Organs the Electors." According to Dickinson, the Electoral College was never meant to be a "Cloud interposed between [the president] and the people, to Obscure Objects," but he acknowledged that the Federalists, both the original supporters of the Constitution and the later party, had created such a cloud with their rhetoric and the procedure they had set up. Electors who were not officially pledged to a candidate, bindable by the people, or necessarily even selected by the people were hardly guaranteed to be mere organs.[14]

It was true enough that most Americans knew little of the country beyond a few square miles from the place they were born, but many local electors along with national leaders made it their business to counteract this isolation once they were engaged by a major conflict. As we will see below, one of the most important tools the electors used, and were used by, was the press. With the creation of the *National Gazette*, James Madison had put himself in the forefront of the drive to create fictive shared ideas and experiences where concrete local ones were lacking. Perhaps he was not contradicting the analysis given in the *Federalist Papers* he had coauthored so much as he was acting against the problems of parochialism and geographic isolation that he and the other Framers had identified. Newspapers easily breached the Constitution's geographic barriers, and the mail system that carried newspapers between printers also allowed private letters to fulfill some of the same duty of carrying political messages around the country. Newspapers, and publicity more generally, became the means by which electors could be brought to their democratic duty. The Philadelphia *Aurora* flatly offered a simple, limited, and easy-to-understand role for the electors to play in the presidential election: so "that our next President may be the man of the People and the object of their enlightened choice, and not merely the creature . . . of accommodation or intrigue among the electors," it was crucial that rather than independent deal-makers, the electors "should be the faithful agents of the people in this important business." The people also needed to do their part: "act with the eyes open" about the presidential candidates and make sure they voted for electors "with a view to the ultimate choice." Faithful agency was where the future of presidential electors lay. The filtering aspect of the constitutional electoral system turned out to be so weak, and many of the assumptions behind it so erroneous, that even the relatively nascent partisan press and the most rudimentary sort of party organizations were more than enough to take the Electoral College to school.[15]

This chapter considers the role of the so-called notables who became presidential electors in 1796. They were never able to act as independent buffers to or filters of popular political opinion and national political alignments. Instead, the activities of the notables in 1796 generally served to *stimulate* popular political opinion and *promote* national political alignments in their local communities. Perhaps some local elites still sought and received deference, but if so, they used their influence to begin to break down the political quiescence that usually goes along with deference. In effect, the members of the Electoral College did an end run around themselves, driven by democratic forces and ideological conflicts that not even the social and economic elect wanted to contain when they were competing for the nation's future.

ELECTING ELECTORS IN THE UPPER SOUTH

Since the eighteenth century, those who actually choose the president, the presidential electors, have become the lost men of American politics (lost people, eventually, but still lost). Not so in 1796. With no clear guidance on what they were supposed to do, the would-be electors took center stage. The major candidates kept completely silent, literally back on their respective farms, leaving it for others to work out the details of electing them. This played out differently in different localities. In small and oligarchic states such as South Carolina, Connecticut, and Delaware, the legislatures held on to the right to choose the electors themselves, and little outside campaigning was needed. In many cases, the legislatures simply designated some of their own leaders to serve as electors and left it at that. In South Carolina, legislative leader Edward Rutledge, reigning patriarch of the political family that included shadow presidential candidate Thomas Pinckney, was named a presidential elector almost automatically and essentially got to decide where the state votes went on his own, creating a temptation to ignore or game the national candidacies. We will see how this worked out below. At the other end of the spectrum, more politically developed states such as Pennsylvania and Massachusetts selected electors by popular vote. In Philadelphia and Boston, partisan slates of electors were ratified by town meetings in advance of full-scale campaigns led by party activists.[16]

The larger Upper South states stood halfway between the two extremes. Virginia, Maryland, and North Carolina all opted for popular elector elections, but in those predominantly rural places, it was the elector candidates who had to do both the standing for office and much of the campaigning. Rather than sitting back and making decisions for the people of their neighborhoods, the electors had to appeal to their neighbors for votes, trying to persuade them about national candidates and issues. Since Virginia, Maryland, and North Carolina together cast more than 30 percent of the total electoral vote, these campaigning electors would be no minor factor in the eventual outcome.

The political culture in which the Upper South electors had to do this was a deeply paradoxical one, democratic in form and stated values, but often highly productive of conformity and deference in practice. The most important local offices, on the county court and vestry, were unelected, and the few offices that were elected were commonly passed around or down the generations among the wealthy landowning families of the area. This paradox was reflected in election customs that exposed both voter and candidate to the scrutiny of their neighbors. The majority of adult white men probably met the property requirement that enfranchised them in Virginia, but the best lands and most of the enslaved work force were controlled by a few families, and the lack of publicly available transportation and banking facilities meant that small farmers often had to depend on large planters to market their crops or borrow money, in addition to living under their political control. Elections in Virginia and the rest of the South were *viva voce*: voters had to personally appear at the polling place and state their preference out loud before the sheriff, the assembled justices of the county court, and the candidates themselves, who often paid their own clerks to take down the names of supporters. Indeed, it seems to have been common for the candidate or designated friends to go through the neighborhood (often a very large area in Virginia) and bring his voters to the poll as a group. Quiet coercion and peer pressure weighed heavily on any voter's individual decision in such cases, as the whole procedure amounted to a public enactment of the local social order.[17]

Sometimes the coercion was not so quiet. In one sensational contested election case from 1794 (which southern congressmen yawned at as commonplace), Virginia Representative Francis Preston's military officer brother marched sixty or seventy of his men to the courthouse and refused to let avowed supporters of Preston's opponent through the door. "Altercations" between the soldiers and the local freeholders ensued. Even when troops did not get involved, Virginia elections could sometimes be little more than gang fights where opposing leaders and their bands of toughs tried to intimidate each other and whoever else happened to get in the way. Elections were often just another arena for manly competition like such typical southern amusements as the cockfight and the horse race.[18]

While displaying the planter elite's place at the top of Virginia's social hierarchy, elections also put candidates in the voters' power, if only temporarily. Edmund Morgan, Andrew Robertson, and other historians have argued that Virginia elections functioned as an "inversion ritual" much like the carnival seasons of peasant Europe, in which common people temporarily switched places with the wealthy and well-born, demanding food, drink, and service from their betters. While scholarly opinion has varied as to whether such periodic inversion rituals reinforced or undermined the social orders that fostered them, Virginia elections clearly required a more sustained egalitarian pretense on the part of office-seekers. Voters might only be choosing which local nabob would represent them, but as some of the wealthiest and most self-consciously aristocratic candidates discovered, they tended to choose the nabob with the less high-handed, more "friendly" approach. It was expected that a candidate would make some effort to personally acquaint himself with the men whose votes he sought, traveling through the neighborhood in the weeks before the election, visiting his constituents, buying them drinks at taverns, and often throwing court day "barbecues" at which the local freeholders (along with the rest of the population at hand) would be "treated" to copious helpings of meat and drink. This was an expensive proposition for candidates, many of whom went along only reluctantly.[19]

While treating voters has been a more common theme for historians writing about colonial Virginia than for those writing about southern politics after the Revolution, the evidence suggests that such practices did not fade away after independence but rather expanded and to some degree became institutionalized as tavern keepers and provisioners took to putting on the barbecues and sticking politicians with the bills. Virginia legislative leader Edmund Pendleton had hoped that the postrevolutionary regime would put an end to all forms of electoral corruption, but found himself disappointed as more candidates than ever doled out "frequent and expensive treats, a species of bribery the more dangerous, since it is masqued, and appears not in its plain shape as a piece of offered gold would."[20]

In Virginia, Maryland, and North Carolina, these mixed electoral practices would be in full effect during the popular elector elections of 1796. With no established precedents about how to act in such a situation, the elector candidates had to feel their way through the process. Their uncertainty about how to proceed resulted in one of the distinctive features of the early presidential elections: published statements from prospective Electoral College members explaining their intentions. Parsing a few of these statements reveals that while many of the elector candidates tried to project the idea that they were independent actors playing the role of discerning local notables, few of them were genuinely uncommitted, and a number of them were the opposite of uncommitted, essentially acting as agents of the national party divisions in their local communities.

A few candidates tried to appear to be standing above partisanship and not committing themselves in advance. Georgetown merchant William Deakins, Jr. published a notice in the Baltimore *Federal Gazette* in which he promised to "spare no pains to acquire the best information . . . of the characters" of all the conceivable candidates and pledged "to my fellow citizens, to vote for that man, who, to my judgment, after all the information I can obtain, shall appear best qualified, and most likely to support the honor, and to preserve and promote the freedom, the tranquility, and the prosperity of our common country." But constituents should not ask their would-be elector to surrender his judgment any further: "I expect to be urged . . . to be more explicit in favor of some one of the candidates, before the election takes place. But I am not, nor will I be made a party man."[21]

In practice, Deakins's independent stance was neither tenable nor completely honest. His real problem was not any lack of certainty about his position, but instead the fear that it would be unpopular with the electorate. Deakins was reputed to be a Federalist and an Adams man, and the intent of his statement was to respond to "*eloquent* harangues" against his candidacy on those grounds. His strategy was to play it coy. While still refusing to pledge himself or praise Adams, Deakins admitted that it was not "an empty boast to say that I have ever been a warm, and steady friend to our present happy government" and went on to repeat typical Federalist charges against Jefferson. An announcement was published in the local newspaper to the effect that Deakins and his opponent were withdrawing from the contest in favor of a Colonel Crawford who pledged his votes to both Adams *and* Jefferson. But apparently that independent arrangement of notables would not fly either: the people demanded a clear choice. So William Deakins's more forthrightly Federalist relative Francis Deakins entered the lists against the arch-Jeffersonian John Thomson Mason and won a handy victory for Adams, nearly 3-to-1 in Montgomery County.[22]

Northern Virginia elector candidate Charles Simms split the difference between a notable's independence and a democratic representative's responsibility to his constituency a little more elegantly. A wealthy Alexandria lawyer who was a friend and business partner of President Washington and had been rewarded with a job as the local port's customs collector, Simms opened his address with an unusually frank statement of the dilemma that a good classical republican elector found himself in: "The suffrages of freemen . . . ought to be given in the most free and unbiased manner," so "personal applications to individuals for their votes. . . . ought to be discountenanced in a republican government." On the other hand, Simms admitted, transparency was *also* a requirement of republicanism, and as such, "the political sentiments of every man who offers himself as a candidate for any office ought to be well-known and understood." Therefore he was constrained to devote two columns to explaining his preference for Patrick Henry or John Adams over Jefferson.[23]

Other elector candidates were eager for voters and neighbors to know whom they were for, assuming that the qualifications of the *presidential* candidates were of much greater interest and import than their own. Candidate William Munford announced his allegiance to the "virtuous and philosophic Jefferson" as early as May 1796, but he must have been unsuccessful in using Jefferson to boost his own popularity, as there was no Munford among the final victors. Waiting more appropriately until the fall but leaving aside the elaborate apologies and indirections of other candidates' publications, planter Daniel Carroll Brent of Stafford County, Virginia, announced in the first paragraph of a lengthy address to the freeholders of his district that his vote would "*certainly* be given" to Thomas Jefferson. Brent explained that he held off publishing such an address until he could get enough "authentic information" to refute the charges that other elector candidates had made against Jefferson. Brent was acting more as a campaigner for Jefferson than himself, ironically using classical republican modesty about his own "present pretentions" to defend and promote his party's candidate instead.[24]

A much more famous Virginia notable who helped Brent respond to Federalist charges against Jefferson and buttress Republican critiques of John Adams was John Taylor of Caroline, a former Virginia senator who went on to become a widely quoted philosopher of southern "agrarianism" and state's rights. Though probably the Early American Republic's most rigid classical republican, Taylor also stood for elector himself, not only making his allegiance to Jefferson clear in his announcement but also grounding it expressly in partisan principle: "The current of my political opinions is unfriendly to the chief measures of the federal government. . . . My wish is to see the government in the hands of administrators, who will bring it back to the republican ground, from which it has widely wandered."[25]

Few of the elector candidates who published addresses gave much indication that they expected voters to defer to their personal judgment as local notables—quite the contrary. Taylor explicitly declared, "I wish every man to vote in pursuance of his uninfluenced judgment," admittedly an easy thing when no recorded opponent seems to have materialized in his electoral district. (But of course Taylor's statement was sent out far beyond his district.) The resort to printed statements of electors' intentions signaled both this attitude and the belief that it would be useless, counterproductive, and improper to *assume* that voters would follow. Taylor's fellow Jefferson supporter Albert Russell, standing for elector in Virginia's far northeastern district, specifically abjured "any personal claims" upon the voters and presumed in his own letter that voters would "extend [their] views beyond the personal merits" of the men standing for elector "to the more important consideration of the fitness of those characters proposed to fill the office of President of the United States." Perhaps unconsciously, Russell echoed James Madison's language in *Federalist* 10 about the need to "extend the sphere" of politics, but to the opposite effect: he was connecting local public opinion to national politics rather than putting the latter out of reach.[26]

As for the Federalists, their desire for deference and misgivings about democracy were strong and sincere: "To *abler* heads leave state affairs, / . . . With politics ne'er break your sleep," went a Federalist poet's "Advice to Country Politicians." Yet when these friends of the existing order were faced with actual political competition, their response was to dive into partisan campaigning and join their opponents in promoting the democratic practice of voting for electors on the basis of presidential preference—at least when they thought they could win. Winchester, Virginia, Federalist "A. B." gave a matter-of-fact explanation for this apparent paradox. Since significant political differences were already abroad in the land, promoted by what the writer called "parties," the Electoral College filter simply had to be ignored or bypassed by any citizen who actually cared about his country: "In this election, tho' the people are not the immediate voters, yet, being choosers of the Electors who are, it concerns them highly to be well acquainted with the political principles of those to whom they confide a trust so important. That parties prevail amongst us is much to be lamented, but their existence renders caution the more necessary. Much depends upon the citizens at large." Lamentations notwithstanding, A. B.'s recommended solution to the rise of partisanship was more partisanship, though as was typical he preferred to construct his partisanship as a patriotic duty: "The choice of Federal Electors will secure the election of a Federal President, and with that the continuance of our present free and happy government."[27]

Though explicitly standing for the maintenance of the existing social order, Federalists in Jefferson's Virginia had to compete against Republican gentlemen and so urged voters *not* to simply follow a local notable's political example because of his respectable social position. "A Farmer" saw the election as a choice between "the existing order and harmony . . . plenty and abundance" and "the lately threatened anarchy and strife" as well as "the accumulated calamities of foreign war and domestic division." It might be more traditional and socially acceptable to pretend that all the available gentlemen were "highly respectable" and blameless in private life, but "this, however, [was] far from being the case." Voters should inquire carefully and specifically about whether the candidates supported the policies of the Washington administration and the congressional Federalists or their opponents. The candidate who could not answer all those questions in the correct Federalist manner should be deemed "unfit to be trusted" with the presidential choice, "whatever may be his private virtues."[28]

Here we face a basic problem with the argument that a politics driven by local notables represented a pre-partisan stage of political development. Deference kept partisan democratic politics in check when the notables of a locality were all unified, but what if they weren't? What happened when notables did not agree on policy issues or competed with each other for power and influence? Notables in power or in the majority might continue to wish for deference or try to filter out partisanship, but notables who disagreed naturally tried to do the opposite, injecting partisanship into elections and seeking to mobilize voters. The divided, multitiered electoral structure set up by the Framers actually made this strategy more tempting rather than less, as it was quite possible to be both "out" and "in" at the same time, depending on the political unit or level at issue. For example, the dominant landowner of some local community might be deferred to in his own home area, and allied with the men controlling the national government, but still be part of a minority faction in the state as a whole. This was the position that Virginia Federalists such as Charles Simms and future Chief Justice John Marshall found themselves in during 1796, with strong enough bases of support in the Tidewater and Northern Neck regions to provide at least a chance of victory in local or regional races but far outnumbered statewide. Virginia Republicans were in the opposite position: overwhelmingly dominant statewide and in most individual regions, but in opposition nationally. So there were incentives to use both strategies, with candidates expecting deference on some occasions and in some places and seeking partisan mobilization in others. Virginia's system of popular voting for electors by districts set up a situation where in most districts Jefferson electors won without much fuss or departure from traditional Virginia methods, but where in a few eastern districts, Federalist and Republican notables competed fiercely. Hence, the process of national party divisions seeping into local communities and reorganizing their politics was an uneven one. When this kind of change did come, the "local notables" were likely to be the agents of the change rather than bulwarks against it.

VIRGINIANS AGAINST JEFFERSON: COLONEL LEVEN POWELL AND NORTHERN VIRGINIA'S FEDERALIST STRONGHOLD

A situation just like this helped decide the whole election of 1796. Thomas Jefferson would eventually lose by only three electoral votes, and one-third of the margin of failure came from his home state. The problem locality was President Washington's stomping grounds along the Potomac, the twenty-first district of Loudoun and Fauquier Counties in Virginia's far northeast, and to a lesser extent the adjacent fifteenth district comprising Fairfax, Prince William, and Stafford Counties along with the city of Alexandria. In keeping with the area's modern-day reputation as upscale suburbia for Washington elites, but out of step with historians' stereotypes about Virginia (and Jeffersonian) politics, the Potomac region became a relative Federalist stronghold. A closer look at this area will help us be clearer about who we talk about when we talk about the Federalists, and more to the immediate point, zero in on a case where an individual elector may have made all the difference in a presidential race.

While the base of support for Alexander Hamilton's policies and the John Adams candidacy was distinctly urban and northeastern, certain regions of the South provided key Federalist leaders and the electoral votes that tipped the balance against Jefferson. The reasons why seem fairly clear. The Federalists were the party of the wealthy and the traditionally minded in the northeast, and so too in the South, except that southern commercial and financial elites looked a little different. Simply put, while slave country as a whole tilted toward Jefferson and the Republicans, the richest and most commercialized sections of slave country, in possession of the most slaves and other productive resources, did not. Political scientist Manning Dauer observed in his pioneering study of the *Adams Federalists* that the Federalist vote in the South tended to be cast in the areas where the land values were highest and the slave population was most concentrated, features characteristic of the coastal regions that had been longest and most thoroughly developed.

In Virginia that meant the Tidewater and Northern Neck regions that stretched along the western shore of Chesapeake Bay. Back in early colonial times, the region's various small rivers and Chesapeake Bay inlets provided water access that enabled shipping of crops (especially tobacco) directly from planters' docks, fostering the growth of both Virginia's wealthiest plantations and over time its most sophisticated society, refined by travel and frequent contact with the outside world. The stagnation of the old tobacco economy in the later eighteenth century actually promoted further development in the area. Large landowners had the capital to invest in new crops (especially wheat) and new enterprises, leading to the growth of Virginia's first two major port towns at Alexandria and Norfolk.

As inherited wealth built up over the generations, the Tidewater region also became the most self-consciously conservative and aristocratic area of the state. The coastal elites jealously guarded Virginia traditions such as slavery, the established church, and the malapportioned legislature that gave the coastal areas proportionally more voting power than the newly settled areas in the interior. The wartime defense of Virginia turned some of the area planters into revolutionary firebrands as they faced down British threats to their power and wealth, threats capped off by Lord Dunmore's Proclamation in 1774 freeing slaves who fled to the British lines. By the 1790s, however, names like Washington, Henry, and Lee again stood for conservative values, in defense of an orderly society dominated by commercial plantation-based agriculture.[29]

The region that actually voted against Jefferson was more newly settled than the Tidewater but still an extension of the Tidewater elite's domain. The Northern Neck area between the Rappahannock and Potomac Rivers—including George Washington's Mount Vernon and Loudoun County on its far northern edge—was literally aristocratic its origins, a center of what Rowland Berthoff and John Murrin have termed America's late colonial "feudal revival." In the mid-eighteenth century, for the first time since the beginning of the colonies, some landowners were successfully establishing the rentier lifestyle of the European aristocracy, where instead of managing a working farm or plantation, as was typical in North America, the landowner lived by leasing land to tenant farmers. One of the very few members of the British nobility to actually reside in America, Lord Thomas Fairfax, owned several counties' worth of land in northern Virginia as part of a royal grant and later sold it off in large chunks to members of well-connected Virginia families, including

George Washington's brother Lawrence. This settlement process made the Northern Neck a region with "an unusual number of great plantations," an exceptionally large concentration of slaves, and unusually low levels of land ownership (and hence eligible voters) among whites. "Society was in short more aristocratic," writes historian Jackson Turner Main.[30]

The feudal revival carried on in northern Virginia even outside the plantation belt proper and even after the Revolution, though on a less grand scale than with Lord Fairfax. The hilly terrain of Loudoun County could not support large-scale tobacco culture, but during the revolutionary era the Tidewater and Northern Neck planters began to colonize it anyway. They used their money to build "far more pretentious houses" than the area had seen before, including such still-standing horse country estates as Oatlands, Raspberry Plain, and Foxcroft. A number of the landowners recruited German, Quaker, and Scots-Irish settlers from nearby Pennsylvania and Maryland to rent and farm their land.[31]

One of the paradoxes of this eighteenth-century trend toward aristocracy-building, and a connection to the peculiarities of Federalist party ideology, is that the backward-looking yen for a hierarchical society was mixed with a forward-looking interest in economic modernization. Along with its feudal revival, northern Virginia was also undergoing what Norman Risjord calls an "agricultural revolution." Tobacco exhausted Loudoun County's lands so quickly that area farmers, led by planter John Alexander Binns, became some of Virginia's leading exponents of more scientific farming methods such as crop rotation, deep plowing, and fertilization. Virginia landowners in general began switching to wheat and corn, and in northern Virginia the search for a more diversified economy led some of the planters to start making more directly commercial investments, including in small-scale manufacturing, agricultural processing (milling the wheat into flour for export), and real estate development. To facilitate this diversification, the Northern Neck planter elite, led by George Washington, pushed for roads, canals, and other transportation improvements and became a center of support in the state for a stronger national government and the new Constitution.[32]

Much like the Washington administration's mix of progressive fiscal policy and regal trappings, Federalist real estate development combined old school paternalism with new school entrepreneurialism. The best-documented examples are found in the work of Alan Taylor and Alfred Young on Federalist districts in western New York and Maine. Not just out to sell land, many of the men who became rural Federalist leaders tried to set themselves up as lordly, superintending figures in the communities they created—"fathers of the people" in the way George Washington was Father of His Country. James Fenimore Cooper's father William developed the Cooperstown, New York, area by laying out the town, building a mansion in the middle of it, establishing necessary services like a newspaper, and then selling the adjacent town lots and farm lands. Not content to simply make money off the venture, Cooper also assumed political leadership over the community, becoming a Federalist congressman, controlling lower-level officials (or trying to), and making himself an overbearing presence to many of his neighbors. Washington's Secretary of War Henry Knox was one of the "great proprietors" who helped people the mid-Maine region through a series of land grants.[33]

Cooper and Knox eventually found their paternalism rejected by their communities, but a "father of the people" who largely succeeded was Colonel Leven Powell, founder of "the Federal party in Loudoun county" (according to his descendants) and the elector who did more than any other to deny Thomas Jefferson the presidency in 1796. In the process of building the community of Middleburg, Powell actively worked to bring a national political agenda into Virginia and made a crucial contribution to the culture war against Jefferson by providing eyewitness testimony and local credibility.[34]

Leven Powell was a local notable if there ever were such a thing. A "gentleman of long-tailed family" from neighboring Prince William County, he married into an even longer-tailed Tidewater family, the Harrisons of presidential fame, and got in on the ground floor of Loudoun County when it was created in 1757. Staked with "a few slaves" and the money to buy five hundred acres of land, he bought property athwart the Ashby's Gap Road, the main trade route from the new port of Alexandria on the Potomac to the Shenandoah Valley and points west. His friends and relatives on the county court—in Virginia an all-purpose, unelected ruling council—ordered major improvements to the roads through his lands, including what would become, with Powell's investment and political help, one of America's first turnpikes.[35]

Powell also got busy commercially. Over the revolutionary years, he built a small business empire by hook and by crook. Around 1770, Powell acquired a mill at a fire-sale price from an absentee owner. Then when the original location turned out to be inadequate, probably because of an insufficient water supply, he got the county court to condemn an acre of someone else's land and moved his mill to the site. Powell's new mill was so successful that he actually trademarked his "Sally" brand flour, named after his wife Sarah, at a time when branded consumer food products were a rarity. At the same time, Powell dealt in a wide variety of agricultural commodities, dry goods, and slaves, often using his political pull and family connections to get government aid and contracts, especially for supplying the military. Though Powell acquired his sobriquet "Colonel" during the Revolutionary War and even served at Valley Forge, he managed to find time to profit from a little wartime convict labor, sending two British POWs who happened to be skilled weavers back home to fill some contracts. Later a convenient medical discharge from General Washington allowed the retired colonel to get elected to the General Assembly, vote in land bounties for veterans, become an official of the state land office, and then travel west to Kentucky to locate six thousand acres of bounty land for himself, even as the war still raged.[36]

The capstone of Powell's entrepreneurial edifice was the creation of his own town, in which his family was set up semiofficially as the permanent aristocracy. In 1787, just as the new Constitution was being formed, Powell and a fellow military contractor, Samuel Love, opened a retail store on the Ashby's Gap Road. Powell laid out the new town of Middleburg around the site and recruited a group of Pennsylvanians as the first residents. Middleburg was organized feudal revival–style, with the Powell family remaining owners of the land even after it was divided up and transferred to others. Powell's lots were to be rented perpetually rather than sold outright in fee simple, establishing the neofeudal institution known as "ground rents." Land and buildings could move from hand to hand, but whoever controlled a property had to pay a yearly fee to the Powell family. Powell's mansion, "The Shades," lorded over Middleburg from a hill on the north edge of town, and other family members and neighbors would build more impressive manor houses all around the area. Political power came along with the wealth and social position. Even before the founding of Middleburg, Powell filled all the important local offices virtually at will, including the two key positions of justice of the Loudoun County court and vestryman of the local Anglican parish, along with multiple terms in the colonial and state legislatures and eventually a term in Congress (after 1796). All of Leven's power and status were passed on to his children, who married into other leading families and established their own countryseats in the area. Leven's son

Cuthbert Powell married the daughter of Charles Simms, Powell's fellow Federalist elector candidate and collector of the port of Alexandria, and built the notable estate Llangollan, later owned by twentieth-century tycoon John Hay "Jock" Whitney. A leading Whig in the next generation along with his brothers, Cuthbert filled his father's congressional seat for a term in the 1840s.[37]

As a former army officer, wealthy landowner, and businessman, Leven Powell naturally gravitated to the Federalists. The streets of Middleburg acquired the names of Federalist heroes: Hamilton, Jay, Pickering, Marshall, Pinckney, and even Madison (for his advocacy of the Constitution). It became a matter of great controversy later on as to whether Powell's political views matched his practical interest in aristocracy. Powell was known to harbor and express misgivings about democracy, especially any reliance on public opinion as a guide to government policy. He warned one of his sons that the "unsteady temper and disposition of the people I fear will prove destructive as it always has done to free Government." Despite these misgivings, which were possibly allayed by the small eligible voting population in the tenancy-ridden Northern Neck, Powell did not hesitate to enter partisan politics when faced with competing local aristocrats who had very different political tastes and interests.[38]

Powell's rivals were the Mason family, especially flamboyant young orator "General" Stevens Thomson (S. T.) Mason, nephew of leading antifederalist George Mason. Powell first came into national politics during the elections to the state ratification convention in 1788 when it looked as though S. T. Mason and an ally might throw Loudoun County's votes against the Constitution. Powell entered the race and, after what was remembered as a very bitter campaign, won the election as a delegate alongside Mason, ensuring that the members of the Loudoun delegation would at least cancel each other out in the Virginia convention. Powell's political métier became developing and using the small bloc of Federalist votes he controlled to shave off little pieces of the Virginia Republican majority whenever he could. As the party divisions developed in the 1790s, his local target was the Masons, and vice versa, personal rivalries dovetailing with highly divergent ideological sympathies. The Masons emerged as warm supporters of the French Revolution and opponents of the national administration and the Jay Treaty. In 1794, the Virginia state legislature chose the thirty-five-year-old S. T. Mason to serve in the U.S. Senate seat being vacated as James Monroe resigned to represent the country in Paris. Colonel Powell must have fumed at this, and perhaps he was not surprised when young General Mason immediately became embroiled in radical Philadelphia political circles.[39]

Early in his term, the hotheaded and cash-strapped Mason became the toast of the democratic radical world when he leaked the text of the Jay Treaty as the Senate was considering it in closed session, setting off the protests and year-long congressional battle discussed in chapter 3 of this book. The evidence suggests that Mason was paid for the document by the French minister, Pierre Adet. Mason hardly needed financial motivation to sink the Jay Treaty, but his "Raspberry Plain" estate in Loudoun was likely not paying for itself at that point. (General Mason and his younger brother were quietly making plans to move to Kentucky, and Mason's heirs would lose the place in the early nineteenth century.) Fourth of July revelers in New York toasted Mason's "manly patriotism" and hoped that "every honest representative" would imitate his example: "His disdain of dark proceedings entitle him to the plaudits of every true friend to liberty." One man's manly patriotism was another man's treason, though, and it seems a good surmise that Mason's moment of notoriety helped spark the proactive approach that Leven Powell and his friends took to the following year's elector elections.[40]

THE 1796 CAMPAIGN IN NORTHERN VIRGINIA

While the 1796 Virginia campaign clearly took place in physical settings—in parlors, in taverns, and on court-day stumps—as well as in print, its major venue was northern Virginia's one port town newspaper, the *Columbian Mirror and Alexandria Gazette*, a triweekly that was as close as the Old Dominion was going to come to city journalism for quite some time. The state had never had a daily newspaper, and even three times a week was a bold experiment. The *Columbian Mirror*'s printer, Ellis Price, had the only press in town and, in keeping with colonial practice, largely kept himself out of its pages and printed material from all political viewpoints. From shortly before the publication of Washington's Farewell Address through the middle of November, many of the triweekly paper's nonadvertising pages were filled with addresses and counteraddresses from the elector candidates for the two presidential elector districts in its local market area, the fifteenth, which Alexandria was actually located in, and the twenty-first, which included Leven Powell's Loudoun.[41]

Powell and his son's father-in-law, Charles Simms, both offered themselves as candidates for elector in a coordinated effort using language, themes, and anecdotes that meshed perfectly with what William Loughton Smith was writing nationally as "Phocion." Together, Powell and Simms set out to win Senator Mason's home region out from under him and made a signal contribution to the national Federalist campaign while bringing national politics to their local community.

They did not do this in so many words. Like most Federalists, Powell and Simms considered their opponents the partisans rather than themselves. Powell proclaimed that what he most dearly wanted was "to put an end to the party spirit which is growing in this country and threatens the destruction of our government and tranquility." He presented it as scandalous information that Senator Aaron Burr of New York— "as violent an opposer to the present . . . administration as any in the country"—had been to Jefferson's house in October 1795 and possibly discussed strategy against the Jay Treaty or the presidential election.[42]

Leven Powell deftly maneuvered northern Virginia into line with national partisan divisions by beginning from the required position of extreme reluctance to do anything of the sort. Almost certainly aware that his former commander and Simms's neighbor Washington was about to step down, Powell announced his candidacy the first week of September, slightly ahead of the Farewell Address's publication. This allowed for a bit of political Kabuki theater before the voters; he explained his supposed decision process in carefully loaded language that set up some of his later attacks on Jefferson. In the first of a series of addresses, Powell disingenuously named "GEORGE WASHINGTON" as his choice for president, with John Adams "to act with him." The prospective elector had "no wish to make experiments" and hoped Washington would stay on until peace was declared in Europe, though his language suggested that he or Simms had already read a draft of the Farewell Address. Admitting that reports were circulating about Washington's retirement, Powell then pretended to consider two other southern options: Patrick Henry, who had already refused to be a candidate, and Thomas Pinckney, whom Powell claimed not to know enough about. In making his final decision, the prospective elector promised windily that he would "weigh well the characters of the different Candidates" and "vote for no person, who cannot safely be trusted with the precious deposit of our happiness" and to "preserve the *peace* . . . of our country and the *government* under which we live." Powell's language was decidedly anti-Jeffersonian, from the rejection of "experiments" to a later reference to "firmness," but Powell nevertheless kept up the charade of indecision, obfuscating his well-known Federalist commitments.[43]

At the same time, nationally affiliated opponents were mobilizing against Powell. Following the strategy being used against Adams, Senator Mason and his allies put out the word that his old antagonist Powell was "a friend to Monarchy." Two weeks after the Powell announcement, Mason's cohort Albert Russell was in the paper announcing his candidacy for elector, in support of Thomas Jefferson. He set up Powell and friends as monarchical straw men: "Mr. Adams's well known predilection for Monarchy may have endeared him to some few amongst us, but [it] forms, in my mind, an insuperable objection to him." Russell also blatantly invoked the local interests of the Potomac, calling attention to the North-South compromise in 1790 that had selected the location for the new capital. Russell theorized that while Congress might well pass a bill revoking the decision, such a measure would be unlikely to survive a presidential veto. In Jefferson's hands, "I think we can more safely trust the interests of the Potomac than with a northern President." While it may be tempting to conclude from this that the campaign was only about local issues and local identity, this was primarily a tactic; it was far better locally to have concerned Virginia slaveholders think of Jefferson as one of themselves rather than as America's chief Jacobin and most famous public detractor of slavery.[44]

The next stage of the Federalist campaign was not attributed to Powell or Simms but was carefully crafted to fit in with the sequence of statements they did release. In the last week of September, in the issue of the *Columbian Mirror* that directly followed the publication of Washington's Farewell Address, "A Farmer" challenged the assumption that the elector election was an "immaterial" matter that only concerned the gentlemen directly involved, and even then only as a personal honor: on the contrary, "the Public Good is deeply involved in the event." The "Farmer" also took issue with the genteel avoidance of partisanship modeled in Powell's address. Following the example of James Madison's and Philip Freneau's seminal writings in the *National Gazette*, "A Farmer" argued that "there were two parties unfortunately existing in the United States, totally opposite in their political opinions" and tried to define for readers who they were and what they stood for: "In a few words, they may be defined to be the '*Friends*' and the '*Enemies*' of the government under which we live with such unequalled comfort and prosperity." He proposed four questions for voters to ask the elector candidates, largely designed to flush out former opponents of the Constitution. The specific examples of "Friend" and "Enemy" that the "Farmer" had in mind were, respectively, Charles Simms and Stafford County planter Daniel Carroll Brent, whose candidacies for elector had been announced and pronounced equally acceptable in the Dumfries newspaper two weeks earlier based on social standing alone. A debate was unnecessary, the paper had opined: "The MERITS and CHARACTERS of these Gentlemen" were too well known to even need description. "A Farmer," however, begged to differ: "Never were political opinions more fairly brought before the public than in the persons of Mr. SIMMS and Mr. BRENT; the former gentleman having been as uniform a friend to our constitution, and its administration, as the latter has been decidedly opposed to *both*."[45]

The ground having thus been prepared for the open taking of sides in the contest, Charles Simms and Leven Powell soon came out with long, pointed, and signed statements in the paper's next two issues. Simms went first, opening with the call for candidate disclosure of "political sentiments" quoted above and proceeding to a three-column defense of John Adams that mocked the idea of him as a monarchist—could his esteemed revolutionary colleagues, such as Franklin and Washington, really have been deceived for so long? Simms also tried to reassure northern Virginians that Adams's election would not lead to some northern city stealing back the U.S. capital from the Potomac. Turning to other candidates, Simms tried to shore up his Virginia bona fides with some bootless praise of already-withdrawn Patrick Henry, largely to set up the most significant news item in his address. Henry was the Virginian to support, Simms said, because the leading Virginia candidate in the race, Thomas Jefferson, had a record that proved him "to want firmness" and "not fit to be trusted," using language soon to be heavily featured in William Loughton Smith's "Phocion" series. Simms's address was the first major campaign publication to directly air the charge that Governor Jefferson had abandoned his post in 1781.[46]

Three days later, Leven Powell launched his own much more detailed attack on Jefferson. Powell never quite came all the way out for John Adams, preserving a bit of southern identity and an above-party stance for himself that Simms had largely thrown away. Instead, Powell decided to buttress his own preference for strong government by deflecting attention to the weakness of Thomas Jefferson. He considered "firmness of mind in the President of the United States, as one of the most essential qualifications" and offered his own supposedly firsthand impressions about how Jefferson had proved "deficient" in this area. Here Powell supplied the account of Jefferson the cowardly war governor that went viral around the country and ended up in William Loughton Smith's pamphlet: how Governor Jefferson had "discovered such a want of firmness" in himself as to leave the state records for the enemy to destroy and scampered from his home and out of office when threatened by "a few light-horse." And "this, too was at 'a time that tried men's souls.'" Powell's charge gained more credibility from the fact that it came from a fellow Virginian, someone casual readers might assume to be possessed of eyewitness knowledge and a natural inclination to support him. Even a Virginian thought Jefferson was a weak butterfly.[47]

This is not to say that Simms and Powell's charges were only a political stratagem. Clearly there was a significant segment of the Virginia planter elite that was genuinely disgusted with Jefferson's performance as governor, his style of leadership, and the dishonor they felt he had brought on the state. The point was at least saleable that a leader who had "abandoned the helm in the hour of danger or at the appearance of a tempest" might be "not fit to be trusted in better times, for no one can know how soon or from whence a storm may come." Much nastier but less well circulated than Leven Powell's address was a piece that appeared in a Fredericksburg newspaper publishing an anonymous letter written in 1788. It expressed the feelings of emasculation some Virginia gentlemen had been venting for years with exaggerated complaints and unrealistic scenarios about the handling of the British invasion. The complaint was that no attempt had been made to resist the British incursion even by some token force or to "punish the temerity of this invasion by preventing the retreat, and retrieve and vindicate the insulted honor" of Virginia. "If a baby in the cradle had been Governor and Commander in Chief, could it have done less [than Jefferson]? Certainly not." There were plenty of older Virginia gentlemen with rougher and more martial educations, including Colonel Powell, who had little reason to sympathize with a cultured college boy like Jefferson.[48]

The Simms and Powell addresses set off one of the most furious local campaigns of 1796.[49] Only two weeks in, "A Young Columbian" complained about how quickly the "busy hum of electioneering" came to "resound through our districts," and was able to distill the essence of the two campaign messages in one sentence: "Already do the advocates of ADAMS brand JEFFERSON with *want of firmness*; and *vice versa*, the friends of JEFFERSON tax ADAMS with *favouring principles inimical to republicanism.*" Local notables had brought the national campaign down to the local level with remarkable speed and effectiveness, while also (in the cases of Powell and Simms) making a powerful contribution of their own to the national message. That each main charge "proceeds from party spirit, not love of country, must be evident to the most superficial observer," complained "A Young Columbian." "Each [partisan] wishes to establish his favourite's fame on the imaginary vices of his opposer." Negative campaigning had arrived on the Potomac.[50]

Multiple counteraddresses and rejoinders flooded the *Columbian Mirror* in October and November. Daniel Carroll Brent's response to Charles Simms was delayed a few weeks, but only to give the elector candidate time to gather "incontrovertible evidence" refuting the charges of Simms and Powell, chiefly by consulting his fellow elector candidate, John Taylor of Caroline. Taylor wrote a long letter with direct testimony about Virginia's military and political situation in 1781, and explained in unfriendly terms the ideas of John Adams as expressed in his writings and his performance as vice president. When Brent's address did arrive, it spilled over seven columns and three pages of the four-page *Columbian Mirror* and tried to document his position on both major issues at hand. The article contained extracts from John Adams's writings exposing "his poisonous doctrines" (essentially another of the reading guides discussed in chapter 6), along with Brent's own exonerating account of Governor Jefferson's performance during the 1781 invasion and a full reprint of the delayed resolution of thanks Jefferson received from the Virginia legislature. The Virginia commendation was relied on by Republicans around the country as their main shield from the "want of firmness" meme. An unusual local nugget in Brent's lengthy discourse was his take on Jefferson's early retirement as governor, which was heavily influenced by Taylor. In Brent and Taylor's interpretation, the second-guessing and political infighting Governor Jefferson had suffered from the forces of his competitor Patrick Henry had rendered the atmosphere around the Virginia state government so toxic that retirement had seemed the most responsible and indeed the only feasible option. "So general was the mistaken resentment at that moment," Brent noted, that Jefferson could not have been reelected even if he had wanted to be.[51]

Having inserted themselves into the campaign, the electors themselves then became a major issue, though always in ways that highlighted the larger party conflict. The most successful argument that Virginia Federalists could make in favor of John Adams was that electing him represented a continuation of and a vote of confidence in George Washington's policies and approach to governing. Thus "A Citizen of Loudoun" queried Jefferson elector candidate Albert Russell about whether he and his candidate really shared that confidence when they had been so critical of the Washington administration: "When speaking of Mr. Jefferson, do you mean by his 'steady and uniform attachment to republican government,' that form of republican government which so happily exists in our country, or some Utopian and visionary scheme of his or your own, which you hope to introduce?" Of course "Utopian and visionary" schemes in the southern context conjured up thoughts of abolition even if the word "slavery" was not mentioned.[52]

With Leven Powell's and Charles Simms's charges against Jefferson taking flight across the country, northern Virginia's Republicans worked hard to both rebut them and impeach the sources of the information, and found themselves rebutted in turn. Senator Stevens T. Mason had accused Leven Powell of having monarchical tendencies himself, so Powell publicly challenged Mason to "furnish the grounds" for his insinuations, the sort of request for an explanation between gentlemen that was often prefatory to a duel. Mason responded with the much more categorical statement that he could produce "proof of Powell's uniform and steady attachment to monarchy" going back twenty years. He rejected Powell's implicit appeal to the code of honor and claimed it was "the right of every elector [voter]" to speak freely of a candidate's political tenets, as he admitted doing about Powell's.

The only proof Mason actually produced was friend-of-a-friend hearsay: he had heard George Hite say in Martinsburg that his relative Isaac Hite had heard Powell express the opinion that "Monarchy was the form of government best suited to this country," probably an oversimplification of the Adams-like views that Powell had already described himself. The next issues of the Alexandria paper hit harder, as Jefferson supporters tried to turn the tables on their candidate's accusers. A writer signing himself "Firmness" (to tweak the Federalist campaign message) suggested, in a rare headline, that "Men Who Live in a Glass House Should Not Begin to Throw Stones." It was with particularly bad grace, "Firmness" wrote, that Colonels Powell and Simms had indicted Jefferson for resigning in the middle of the Revolutionary War. Their war records showed that both of them had done the same thing, and that they had done so for a less than admirable reason: to make money off the war. Simms and Powell had both applied for leave in the midst of a campaign in 1779, and in Simms's case the application had generated a lengthy congressional resolution refusing it on the grounds of maintaining the officer corps. After all, if Simms got a leave, all the rest of the Virginians would want one, too. General Washington quietly let his neighbor's leave go through despite what Congress had said. Both Powell and Simms used their time off to secure their personal fortunes by consolidating the status of various lands they claimed. By the left-leaning lights of Stevens T. Mason and other Jeffersonians, the cupidity of Powell and Simms was a far more damning motive than whatever caused Jefferson to step down as governor: "the years 1778 and 1779 were *times that tried men's souls*; BUT SOME MEN'S SOULS ARE IN THEIR POCKETS." This was just the sort of behavior Republicans expected of greedy "paper-men" who loved Hamiltonian finance.[53]

The term "document dump" was unknown in 1796, but the political instinct to flood out scandal with a cascade of information was already in evidence. Both electors answered the countercharges in copious detail, though not always to helpful effect. The pompous Charles Simms dug himself in deeper, immediately publishing an exchange of letters between himself and Washington that looked even worse than what "Firmness" had alleged. The general had praised Simms as an officer, begged him to stay, and rejected his leave request as "inconsistent with the public interest." Simms had responded by petulantly insisting that he would leave the army anyway, explaining in some detail the rather sordid business he had needed to attend to: getting title to some Indian land in Pennsylvania he had purchased in a sketchy 1775 deal with frontier land jobber George Croghan and the Iroquois. The Virginia legislature had just ruled this deal illegal, so clearly Simms had a problem. Later, trying to answer Daniel Brent's defense of Jefferson, Simms issued a tedious handbill logic-chopping the legislative resolution of thanks Governor Jefferson had received and dwelling on the most illogical of the complaints about Jefferson's "want of firmness": his departure from the Washington administration after he had been exposed as an opponent of Hamiltonian policy. Did Federalists truly believe it would have been better for Jefferson to stay? Leven Powell did much better by playing the victim of "dark insinuation and glaring falsehood."[54]

The dive into the electors' personal lives took nothing away from the intensity of the partisan divisions being exposed. The personal stories of

Powell and Simms connected directly to the approaches to government being debated. "Jeffersonians" (the term was actually used) accused John Adams of favoring "that most despotic and dangerous principle, of bestowing all affairs of government upon the *Rich and Well-born!*" and the local Federalists seemed to have enacted that principle in their own lives, treating government as their personal property.[55]

The personal turn also did not prevent the campaign from raising larger issues of democracy, authority, and the social order, even though few of these were followed up afterward. "A Mechanic" wrote in to argue for more equal representation within the state of Virginia, including an end to the property requirement, and a searching mini-debate broke out over religious freedom. William Loughton Smith–like attacks on Jefferson's religious views seem to have been relatively rare in the Virginia press, but apparently they were being made orally, "in a more private and insinuating manner," using the Virginia Statute for Religious Freedom as their foundation. "A Dissenter from the Established Church" ventured to predict that "instead of wounding" him politically, the law would "immortalize the name of Jefferson." Writing in the fervent language of the Baptists and other evangelical Protestant groups, who provided a major base of support for Jefferson's program of religious liberalization, "A Dissenter" enthused that citizens who actually read the law would find it "expressed in terms of the most profound reverence for the great Majesty of Heaven." Of greatest political importance was the way that the "Dissenter" moved to make Jefferson's reputation as philosopher and reformer into something that could win votes. Evangelical Protestants and Catholics who no longer had to pay for the support of Anglican (Episcopal) churches or suffer political discrimination because of their faith should look on Jefferson "as the instrument of your relief from this oppression."[56]

The "Dissenter" also offered a sprightly, patriotic take on church and state that defined the choice of one's own religious beliefs as the essential American freedom: "Civil and religious liberty; let this be our theme, may this be our family pride." While reverent in his own tone, the "Dissenter" issued an interpretation of this liberty that was both far more thorough and more practical than the legalistic church-state debates of modern times: "Politics have nothing to do with religion . . . keep them separate; true religion can exist without legislative support or assistance; and false religion cannot deserve it." There was no stark, binary vision of a future world where either state and society forced Christianity and good behavior on all, or all religious requirements and restraints were lifted and the world fell into anarchy. The latter was the darker timeline envisioned by the New England clergy and many other Federalists (following the polemics against the Enlightenment and the French Revolution). By electing Jefferson electors, the "Dissenter" told readers, "you may continue to enjoy your native, your special privilege of judging for yourselves, respectively, in matters of religion."[57]

The Federalist response tried to have it both ways, belittling Jefferson like Powell, Simms, and Smith, while presaging the hysteria that the issue of Jefferson's religion would generate later in a decade. "A Freeholder" began his response with a pedantic quibble that the religious freedom law was not nearly so important as Jefferson supporters believed. The Virginia Declaration of Rights and the "good sense, virtue, and Christian forbearance of our fellow-citizens" had done the job. To credit one individual was "a sentiment too degrading to be broached or cherished by such a people as the citizens of America." Of course, this was a point Republicans had made about the deification of George Washington, but here a Federalist was turning the idea around. Then the writer who had pooh-poohed Jefferson's importance suddenly escalated in contradictory fashion to a full-scale freak-out about Jefferson's possible impact on the country, its religion, and morals. "Is it of no moment to you whether your Chief Magistrate be a follower of *Mahomet*, a *Deist*, or an *Atheist*?" If the government were to end up in the hands of Jefferson, the American people's "worship of Christ" would be switched to "the *Goddess of Reason*" and "their *Liberty* into *Licentiousness*."[58]

Though taking place in only one relatively rural local area, the northern Virginia electoral district race was being watched nationally as the epicenter of the Federalists' best Jefferson scandal and as a potentially devastating chink in his Virginia base. The same decentralized newspaper exchange system that brought the Philadelphia and Boston papers to Alexandria meant that the *Columbian Mirror* and other now less well-preserved Virginia papers could be read wherever politicians gathered. Colonels Powell and Simms were being cited everywhere, so it was a logical (if still a little shocking) development to have national figures suddenly intervene in their local political debate. John Taylor of Caroline's letter announcing his elector candidacy in another Virginia district was published "by request" in the *Columbian Mirror* in late October, and soon "Phocion" himself, William Loughton Smith, responded to it directly. Taylor had avowed himself an opponent of the "chief measures" of the Washington administration and an advocate of seeing the government in other hands. Staying the course "threaten[ed] to result in a revolution." It is possible that it was a Federalist who requested the publication, because "Phocion" pounced immediately on Taylor's frank language as proof of the Federalist argument that a vote for Jefferson would be an expression of disrespect for George Washington and the signal for radical change in a successful and popular new form of government. According to Smith, Taylor's letter was "full disclosure of the design and expectation" of the pro-Jefferson elector candidates, and more honest than the statements of the others who pretended to regret Washington's retirement.[59]

In terms of the printed debate, this dropping of the mask was clearly a turning point. The *Columbian Mirror*'s editor and printer, Ellis Price, had previously avoided any hint of favoritism, balancing the Federalist and Jeffersonian material in each individual issue. The last edition before the voting, however, suddenly seemed to tilt toward the Powell-Simms-Adams side of the battle, or at least arrange the material in a way that favored the Federalists. As an Alexandria community leader, Simms was probably a heavy influence. The preelection issue featured a reprint from the *Gazette of the United States* that decried the latest attempt at "Foreign Influence" (i.e., the French minister's threat of war if Adams were elected), and while the two local essays were paired as usual, one of each political persuasion, the overall effect was to make a Federalist vote seem by far the safer course. The Republican "Brutus" followed by the Federalist "A Friend to the Present Administration of the Government" presented a stark contrast between overheated political distrust and anodyne nationalism. "Brutus" (probably Stevens T. Mason or a surrogate) struck an uncomfortably menacing tone, arguing that the principles of John Adams would "in time reduce the country to a confirmed aristocracy, which must end in a dissolution of the union, if not the dreadful alternative of a civil war." While "Brutus" wrote in a language of class rather than region, the specter of sectionalism was thus duly raised. The pro-Adams essay that followed emphasized the fact that Adams was "highly esteemed" in his home state and all the others north and east of Pennsylvania, and assured Virginians that "those states are unquestionably as republican as we are" and feel "as great an abhorrence to the establishment of monarchy." It was churlish and parochial to assume that the people of New York, New Jersey, and especially New England had been so easily seduced or deluded away from the principles of a revolution they had been so instrumental in starting.[60]

In the end, the northeast of Virginia declined to throw out the revolutionary alliance on this particular occasion. Powell swamped Albert Russell more than 3-to-1 in his home county of Loudoun and just barely trailed him in the more lightly voting Fauquier, for an overall win of 592 votes to 313 in the district. At least one crucial Virginia electoral vote was not going to Thomas Jefferson. Moreover, this heavily publicized campaign quite likely had some influence in other slaveholding areas lost by the slaveholding candidate in Maryland, North Carolina, and Delaware.

The raw vote totals do not look particularly impressive, and indeed an ordinary estimate of the total voting against the adult white male population yields an estimate of only about 18 percent voter turnout. Yet this represents a much higher level of participation than first meets the eye. This was a completely novel type of election that did not coincide with any other election or geographic unit. And using the total adult white male population overstates the potential electorate because of Virginia's property requirement for voting. The usual rule of thumb figure cited is that property requirements disfranchised something like 40 percent of the adult white males in early America, with that figure decreasing a bit during the Revolution.[61] However, the franchise could vary sharply by locality because it depended on the distribution of landownership. It was much narrower than usual in a stratified area like northeastern Virginia. A petition from Loudoun County during the War of 1812 indicated that only *one-sixth* of the men called out for militia service were eligible to vote based on their property holdings. Some number of others must have just cleared the fifty-acre freehold requirement.[62] Leven Powell could not have been less interested in the democratization of anything, but he and Simms really did manage to leverage every available vote.

While the one electoral vote did not sink Jefferson by itself, it was a crucial one, and his stand for "firmness" established Powell and his authoritarian politics as pillars of patriotic southern manliness while throwing Jefferson and liberalism into a submissive position that would forever need to be explained away. A testosterone-laden anecdote was published about an incident in a Richmond theater at the end of the campaign. A Jefferson supporter named Isham Randolph, "supposing himself surrounded by birds of a feather," shouted to the orchestra to play "God Save the King" "for Leven Powell!" Randolph did not realize that Colonel Powell was sitting there in the audience. Challenged to explain his jest to Powell's face or retract it and apologize, Randolph humiliated himself and brightened the day of many a Federalist reader by taking the latter course. Powell went into the Adams administration as a national Federalist celebrity. The 1796 elector campaign became his calling card: "Wherever I went I was known as the person who voted singly for Adams." The new patriotic fervor spawned by the XYZ Affair and preparations for war with France propelled Powell into Congress in the 1798 elections, where he served one term and then retired back to his new Federalist stronghold and development projects.[63]

The year 1796 did not turn out quite as well for Charles Simms. He edged out Daniel C. Brent in the city of Alexandria and Fairfax County, but got crushed (receiving only six votes) in rural Stafford and Prince William Counties. Unperturbed, Simms applied to the new Adams administration for the very substantial reward of a Supreme Court seat, but had to settle for continued civic involvement in Alexandria. A comment or two may have been made about Simm's own firmness when, as Alexandria's mayor during the second British invasion of Virginia in 1814, he surrendered the city to the enemy without a shot. While other cities in the region, such as Baltimore, heroically resisted the invaders, Alexandria sent a delegation out to meet the British squadron before it arrived and agreed to humiliating peace terms that gave the British the run of the town and all its goods in exchange for leaving its people and buildings unmolested. The incident was immortalized in an early political cartoon, with a group of Alexandria dignitaries kneeling before John Bull, their hair standing up firmly in fright.[64]

SAMUEL ADAMS: BREWER, PATRIOT, ELECTOR, GOAT

Colonels Powell and Simms were individually important in short-circuiting the Constitution's deferential presidential selection process, but little of this kind of heavy campaigning by electors can be detected north of the Mason-Dixon line. It was regarded in some quarters as a southern peculiarity. Noah Webster took note of the Simms and Brent announcements in his New York newspaper and complained that the two had "*offered themselves*" as candidates: "This is the *modest* republicanism of Virginia."[65]

Modesty did not mean that the Electoral College system was any more effective in colder climates. The futility of relying on deference to local notables was demonstrated by one of the most spectacular Democratic-

Republican flops of the 1796 presidential campaign, in the electoral district that included Boston, Massachusetts. Like Virginia, Massachusetts held its presidential election by districts, but unlike Virginia, these were the same districts from which congressman were elected. Indeed, unlike any other state in 1796, the Massachusetts presidential election was actually held on the same day as other elections.[66] While John Adams was certainly expected to get the bulk of the votes from his home state and region, Republicans had some hope that an Adams vote or two might be stolen away. There was popular voting for electors in Massachusetts, and the district system seemed to offer at least one competitive slice. Almost all of the state was staunchly Federalist and pro-Adams, but "all the seditious and desperate" seemed to be concentrated in Boston.[67]

The principals here were the intense knot of democrats led by merchant Benjamin Austin Jr. and Dr. Charles Jarvis. The direct heirs of Samuel Adams's Boston political organization, they spoke out on the streets of Boston and in the pages of the *Independent Chronicle* newspaper. Their public meetings were held in Sam's favorite watering hole, the Green Dragon Tavern, and many of the older members of the group were Sam's old revolutionary cronies, such as former town clerk and "old Baboon" William Cooper. Seeing themselves as the saving remnant of Boston revolutionary principles, Austin, Jarvis, and their friends took to the French Revolution with great enthusiasm, forming the Massachusetts Constitutional Society as their local affiliate of the Democratic-Republican Society movement and holding "Civic Feasts" to celebrate French successes. The feasts were as edgy as those anywhere in the nation; in one instance, an ox they called "Aristocracy" was slaughtered and served "as a 'PEACE OFFERING TO LIBERTY AND EQUALITY.'" Contemptuous Boston Federalists called the local Jacobin hangouts "Equality Alley" and oscillated between fearing a guillotine would be set up and plotting to somehow silence the embarrassing noises being made in their backyards. Most horrifying of all to the Boston Federalist elite was the fact that the denizens of Equality Alley had real influence. Austin and Jarvis had both represented Boston in the state legislature, and one of the two of them had run against Fisher Ames for Congress at every election, winning a higher percentage each time out. Governor Samuel Adams headlined their civic feasts and other events—whenever he could sit up straight.[68]

Sam Adams also happened to be New England's only major

officeholder known to be sympathetic to the Republican opposition, and indeed one of the few other major figures from the independence struggle, along with Tom Paine, to side with Jefferson in the 1790s. Democratic radicalism was a natural fit for an old agitator like Sam, who lived and dressed the same as he had back when he was a poor tax collector making trouble for the British with the South End mob thirty years earlier. He seems never to have felt more at home than in a political club making fiery speeches.[69]

The political standing of the Equality Alley boys in 1796 is difficult to gauge, but the signs were clearly mixed. In November, the manic-depressive Fisher Ames found "the influence of the Boston Chronicle and the orations in the market" to be "most pestiferous" and potentially overwhelming. He and other Federalist gentlemen had gotten "routed" at the Dedham town meeting, and "a rower against the stream grows weak and weary." Yet by other measures, the power of the Boston Jacobins was on the downswing. The *Independent Chronicle* was as strident as ever, but improved Federalist organization and backlash from the Jay Treaty debate seem to have taken a toll. In 1795, the word went out that Boston would "not be represented . . . by a single *Jacobin!*" in the Massachusetts state senate, and Ben Austin was ousted from his habitual seat. The next year, prospects looked so dark and divisions were so deep that Dr. Jarvis declined to stand for reelection in a rather hollow bid for unity. The result was the lower-house half of the Boston legislative delegation getting swept by the Federalists as well. The *Independent Chronicle* printers were promptly removed from their longtime slot as state printers. On the bright side, Governor Sam Adams was reelected handily despite a determined bid to replace him with Judge Increase Sumner.[70]

Governor Sam's continued electability coupled with the decline of Democratic-Republican fortunes suggested a bold but rather hypocritical ploy, at least for professed radical democrats: they would try to use an elector candidate's local prestige and popularity to trump the voters' likely presidential and policy preferences. Sam Adams himself would be put up as an elector likely to vote against his cousin John. Opponents fingered visiting Aaron Burr as the likely source of the idea.[71]

The Sam Adams gambit proved to be as awkward as it was clever for the Republicans. The Federalist newspapers raised some plausible though erroneous questions about the constitutionality of a state governor serving in the Electoral College—a misprision of the constitutional provision banning any "Person holding an Office of Trust or Profit under the United States" from serving as an elector—and pounded the old patriot for embarrassing himself and the commonwealth by dallying so openly with French radicalism: "Let *him* blush, and resign forever *his* boasted pretentions to the gratitude of his countrymen" for "being made a handle of by faction" and used against a fellow "Massachusetts man." The newly appointed state printers at the *Massachusetts Mercury* went much further with the idea that Sam was "not the man he was" and a traitor to his New England home and revolutionary principles. Jefferson was a "southern-man," making him, from the righteous viewpoint of many Boston Federalists, one of those "men, whose Souls are ten fold blacker, than the faces of their stolen slaves." New Englanders should vote only for men who would battle against the "southern *Patriots*, who from pure democratic principles conceive themselves justified in holding a part of our fellow Creatures in Slavery." Since no one in the 1790s used democratic or egalitarian ideas to justify slavery—quite the opposite—the chief function of this rhetoric was to convince Yankee readers that democracy was an alien idea and southerners an alien people rather than to help any slaves.[72]

Provocative as those comments were, identification with the Federalist party seems to have been a stronger local selling point than antislavery. "The people of *New-England*, almost to a man, are federal," wrote "Humanitas" in the *Mercury*, so Sam Adams had no business supporting Jefferson on that ground alone. The *Columbian Centinel*'s Ben Russell had been trying to concentrate his readers' minds on "the choice of *Federal Electors*" since mid-September, and in the last few weeks he began publishing elector nomination notices that quietly certified the "uniform Federalism" of the named men and their loyalty to *John* Adams. Russell and his correspondents worked to firm up the Federalist identity of Sam's opponent in the elector race, Massachusetts senate president Thomas Dawes. Dawes had been the moderator of the huge anti–Jay Treaty meeting set off by Benjamin Franklin Bache and Stevens T. Mason's leaked text the previous summer, so in some Federalists' eyes, Dawes had some explaining to do. The *Centinel* assured readers that "no man" could "doubt of Col. Dawes's federalism" or "how he will vote for president" because he had been a Washington-Adams elector in 1792. A local builder who employed many in the Boston artisan community, Dawes may have been selected because he had as much influence on the street as Austin and Jarvis. Dawes' economic power and anti-British credentials probably helped counteract whatever advantage Sam may have had over "Jack Adams" among Boston workers. The *Centinel* covered the other end of the spectrum by coupling Dawes's candidacy with that of the arch-Federalist Harrison Gray Otis, a powerful speaker but confirmed nativist and elitist who was particularly worried about "wild Irishmen" and government by the "wrong" people. Otis was running for Congress to replace the retiring Fisher Ames with more of the same. It was a particularly bad occasion to get voters to overlook party and issues to honor the service of old Sam Adams.[73]

Meanwhile the *Independent Chronicle* flailed wildly trying to show the necessity of making Governor Adams an elector. Just days before Sam's candidacy was announced, the paper had suggested hesitantly that perhaps elector candidates ought to tell voters whom they would vote for. *Chronicle* writers remained far more engaged by the stakes of the national presidential battle, which the paper repeatedly couched as a stark choice between "MONARCHY or REPUBLICANISM" rather than as a local choice between Adamses. Regarding the local elector race, the *Independent Chronicle* tried to sell the trickle-down logic of the Electoral College, arguing that Samuel Adams could vouch for the presumably unknown out-of-stater Thomas Jefferson. Adams had a *"personal knowledge* of the political principles of the candidates" and an "intimate acquaintance with Mr. Jefferson" that should reassure suspicious Bostonians. On one level, the Boston democrats were trying to cancel out parochial impulses by offering Sam Adams as a local "friend of the people" who was well matched with Jefferson ideologically. Yet the implicit request that voters not focus their attention on the man who would actually be holding the highest national office conflicted with the stirring and nationally partisan appeals encountered elsewhere in the *Chronicle*, in its rival the *Centinel*, and in the streets and taverns of Boston.[74]

On the night before the election, Republicans caucused at the Green Dragon Tavern, while the Federalists met at the "Concert-Hall." Both groups trooped to Faneuil Hall the next morning to vote. That day's *Chronicle* barely mentioned Jefferson but practically dared Bostonians to ungratefully cast aside their "long-tried friend" and "blast the laurels" of an "intrepid political warrior," betting it all on Sam Adam's personal prestige and local hero status. *Chronicle* writers even showed a bit of concern for how John Adams and his supporters would take the defeat, pointing out that John would still likely be vice president, and therefore would lose nothing from losing their votes.[75]

Unfortunately, that was not enough for the well-informed voters of the First Middle District, almost 60 percent of whom selected Dawes and John Adams. Harrison Gray Otis's tally ran slightly ahead of John Adams's, underscoring the fact that this was a partisan Federalist vote. The result was doubly embarrassing for Governor Samuel Adams, a politician whose base had always been the streets of Boston. In most of the other Massachusetts electoral districts, there had been little campaigning and so many local men vying for elector that no one had been able to win a majority. They were all for John Adams in any case. Thus the Dawes landslide seemed a particular repudiation of Sam himself, though probably even more so of Thomas Jefferson. Deeply embittered, the old revolutionary warhorse carped about illegal voting and announced his retirement from politics a few weeks later. The Federalists would not have Sam Adams to kick around anymore.[76]

Sam need not have taken his defeat so personally. It was the presidential choice and the rising tide of Massachusetts Federalism that doomed his elector campaign, not anything to do with his own standing. Adams was not alone as a major revolutionary figure who got crushed when his name was pitted against the partisan tenor of the times. In Maryland, Jefferson supporter Gabriel Duvall embarrassed one of the grand old men of Maryland politics, Charles Carroll of Carrollton, with 70 percent of the vote. Carroll was a notable's notable: patriarch of one of the state's oldest and richest families, a signer of the Declaration, and the Catholic faith's primary contributor to the ranks of the Founding Fathers. Carroll was "not a little mortified" by his loss, but younger and more attentive politicians knew he never had a chance. His local notability—like Sam Adams's—just did not matter that much in the face of much larger concerns: national policy, partisan identity, and the presidency. On Maryland's Federalist Eastern Shore, "great party principles" went in the other direction, for John Adams, but trumped local notability even more sharply. Pro-Adams elector John Eccleston rolled to a massive 7-to-1 landslide victory despite being so "obnoxious to about one-half the county" that he was facing trouble in a sheriff's election. Clearly a presidential elector race was decided on completely different grounds than local popularity.[77]

Table 1. The 1796 Electoral Calendar

States are listed in chronological order by "decision point" (marked with an asterisk), the election that seems to have determined where its presidential electoral votes would go. All but three of the legislative election states are listed according to their legislative election times. The other three, South Carolina, Rhode Island, and Vermont, are listed like the popular election states, by the date of their elector elections. South Carolina held its decision until the last possible minute, pursuing an all-southern ticket, while no one seems to have known what Rhode Island would do, and questions were raised about Vermont. The disposition of the second votes in many of the states was not clear until the Electoral College meetings the first week of December.

State	Number of Electors	People or Legislature	Districts (with number) or Statewide	Legislative Elections	Elector Elections
New York	12	L	S	April–May*	Nov. 7
Tennessee	3	L	D-3	Aug.*	Nov. 2
Connecticut	9	L	S	Sept.*	Nov. 4
New Jersey	7	L	S	Oct.*.	Nov. 3
Delaware	3	L	S	Oct.*	Nov.10
Rhode Island	4	L	S	Aug.	Oct. 31*
Pennsylvania	15	P	S	Oct.	Nov. 4*
Vermont	4	L	S	Sept.	Nov. 4*
Georgia	4	P	S	Oct.	Nov. 7*
Massachusetts	16	P-7, L-9[1]	D-14, S-2	April–May	Nov. 7*
New Hampshire	6	P-5, L-16[2]	S	March	Nov. 7*
North Carolina	12	P	D-12	Aug.	Nov. 7*
Virginia	21	P	D-21	April	Nov. 7*
Maryland	20	P	D-10	Sept.–Oct.	Nov. 9-12*
Kentucky	4	P	D-4	Aug.	Dec. 3*
South Carolina	8	L	S	Oct.	Dec. 6*

1. In Massachusetts, the state legislature chose two electors at large and also filled any district elector slots where no candidate won a majority (not a plurality) of the votes cast. Because of this rule, only seven of sixteen electors finally chosen in Massachusetts were elected by the people.

2. In New Hampshire, like Massachusetts, the popular elections for elector required a majority of the votes cast to win, and the legislature filled slots where no majority was obtained. Five electors received enough votes to be chosen directly by the people, and one slot was filled by the legislature. (Thanks to Philip J. Lampi of the New Navigation Votes project for checking this fact.)

Table 2. Vice-Presidential Scenarios

Scenario	Candidates	States (Votes for Ticket)
Federalist Ticket	John Adams (Mass.) Thomas Pinckney (S.C.)	Mass. (13 of 16), Md. (4 of 10), N.C. (1 of 12), Va. (1 of 24)
Hamilton's "Pinckney Plot" (equal or extra votes for Pinckney)	Thomas Pinckney (S.C.) John Adams (Mass.)	Del., N.J., N.Y., Pa. (1 extra vote for Pinckney), Vt.
Republican Ticket	Thomas Jefferson (Va.) Aaron Burr (N.Y.)	Ky., Md. (3 of 10), N.C. (6 of 12), Pa. (13 of 15), Tenn., Va. (1 of 24)
Jonathan Dayton's Burr Gambit	Aaron Burr (N.Y.) John Adams (Mass.)	Md. (3 of 10)
Edward Rutledge's Southern Dream Team	Thomas Jefferson (Va.) Thomas Pinckney (S.C.)	N.C. (1 of 12), Pa. (1 of 15), S.C.
Final Results (states that cast some votes for both, though not necessarily by the same elector)	John Adams (Mass.) Thomas Jefferson (Va.)	Md. (4), N.C. (1), Pa. (1), Va. (1)

THE PARTY RACERS
VOTING FOR PRESIDENT IN 1796

The actual voting presents a severe problem for any effort to turn the election of 1796 into a spine-tingling
narrative. There was no national vote for president in
1796 and nothing that can even be artificially aggregated
as a national vote, despite what one may find on presidential history websites. There were sixteen different
processes operating under sixteen different sets of rules
and conditions; most of the states were using the same
procedures under the same laws they had set up for the
noncompetitive contests of 1789 and 1792. Only seven
of sixteen states allowed the people to vote directly even
for presidential electors, and only three—Pennsylvania,
Georgia, and New Hampshire—featured the statewide
vote that would become the norm for later presidential
elections. The other popular voting states—Virginia,
Massachusetts, Maryland, and North Carolina—all divided themselves into special electoral districts, most
of which were heavily tilted toward one party or the
other. This was more by geographic happenstance than
design, but it still limited the potential for widespread
competition, as did the nonsimultaneous timing of the
elections (see table 1, "The 1796 Electoral Calendar," at
the end of chapter 8). While the majority of the popular
elections were held in early November, a key legislative
election that would help determine the outcome (as we
have already seen in the case of New York, as detailed in
chapter 4) was held the previous spring.

Even though the electoral process can only be described state by state, and much less information exists

than we would like, what is striking is how quickly certain tendencies and patterns of the country's democratic electoral system emerge, long before there was an institutionalized national election or party system to organize them. Public opinion and voting were the determinative factors, even if only at a kind of prospective or theoretical level in some places. In *almost* every case, local candidacies and issues were shunted aside or used in the service of national ones. At the same time, the two great axes of American politics, party and region, were already very much in operation.

It must be admitted that on the national and even on a statewide level, the results of the 1796 campaigns did not always bear out the intensity expressed in the published statements we have covered in previous chapters. Then as now, many or most particular locations were obviously in one camp or the other, generating little reason to contest the elector elections. Where the possibility of swaying votes existed, however, "party racers" did indeed swing into action. John Beckley, clerk of the House of Representatives, has been named the mastermind of the ground-level campaigning in 1796, even "Jefferson's campaign manager," and while this is a little strong, in mid-September Beckley did sketch an electoral map that seems to have guided Republican efforts. He expected a unanimous vote for Jefferson from the lower southern and western states and Virginia, half of the votes in the other two Chesapeake slave states (Delaware and Maryland), plus a few extra votes from New Jersey or perhaps even shaved off from the Federalists' New England base. Perpetual loose cannon Rhode Island would come over to Jefferson, Beckley predicted very wrongly, perhaps joined by a vote or two from Vermont or Connecticut, the last idea a pure fantasy that must have been spun by Aaron Burr. (There was no more locked-in Federalist state than the Land of Steady Habits.) Yet even Beckley's most optimistic scenario recognized that New York was off the table and that Massachusetts and Virginia were likely to fall in behind their own candidates. This led him inexorably to the sound conclusion that Pennsylvania was crucial to Jefferson's chances: "If Pennsylvania stirs the business is safe," Beckley wrote. Or at least safer.[1]

PENNSYLVANIA 1796: AMERICA'S FIRST PRESIDENTIAL CAMPAIGN

A perennial battleground state to this day, Pennsylvania was where the one full-scale, statewide campaign of 1796 took place. While well known to historians and covered in most accounts of the 1790s, it deserves re-emphasis here in that it was in many ways the first "real" presidential campaign in American history.[2]

The Keystone State was an ideal setting for a political fight. Between crowded, diverse Philadelphia, the restive western mountain region, and a quiescent, heavily German farm belt, the state was evenly divided between areas and groups that were at least potentially outraged at the administration policies of the previous four years and those that were at least tacitly supportive. It was one of the two states that allowed its voters to choose all its presidential electors by statewide vote, and it also had the broadest suffrage of any state, conferring the right to vote on any adult male (of any race) who had paid or been assessed for taxes or whose father had met the requirements. Furthermore, Pennsylvania had party leaders who were willing and able to mount such a campaign. Philadelphia, the state's and the country's largest city, was the home base of the nation's most active and radical group of democratic activists. Led by Beckley, *Aurora* editor Benjamin Franklin Bache, and other veterans of the Democratic Society of Pennsylvania, the Philadelphia Democratic-Republicans had spearheaded the Jay Treaty protests and the attack on Washington. Many of them had marched west with the militia against the Whiskey rebels, even though they basically agreed with the rebels about the excise tax, just to prove the power and peacefulness of democratic politics: speaking, writing, and voting as opposed to drunken thuggery in the woods. Now they were determined to use those peaceful methods to punish the Washington administration at last by winning their state for Jefferson and possibly giving him the presidency in the process.

The *Aurora* launched the campaign a few days in advance of the publication of Washington's Farewell Address. Finally able to confirm "unqualifiedly" that the president would resign, the paper lamented the fact that this decision was well known "in the circle of those who seem to think themselves exclusively concerned in affairs of state" while "the public generally" was kept "in the dark." Bache's paper welcomed the opportunity for an open, democratic debate over the choice facing the country, and it named names: "It requires no talent at divination to decide who will be candidates for the chair. Thomas Jefferson & John Adams will be the men." The statement also introduced the Philadelphia democrats' preferred framing of the campaign, which was republicanism and democracy versus monarchism and aristocracy, straight up.[3]

While the "hat" may have been dropped in mid-September, presidentially speaking the party racers began with more of a quiet walk even in Pennsylvania. When the law setting up the state's presidential election had been written the previous April, in the teeth of the Federalist counteroffensive for the Jay Treaty, the Democratic-Republican opposition had actually tried to hold out for district elections, apparently fearing that a statewide election could not be won. The pattern had been for commercial towns (including the city of Philadelphia) to vote Federalist, driven by what many rural-minded Republicans chose to see as corruption by self-interested merchants and creditors. Federalists in the state legislature had not only forced a statewide race for presidential electors, but also implemented an array of voter and party suppression tactics. They scheduled the presidential election weeks after the state elections that people were more accustomed to participating in. Just getting to the polls in Republican-leaning rural areas often involved extensive travel by foot or horseback, a hardship that poorer voters would be unlikely to be able to afford twice in a month. The Federalist election law also banned the use of preprinted tickets. Presidential election voters were required to present a handwritten ballot with the names of fifteen electors, raising obvious barriers to voters with less access to information and poorer literacy skills, and hampering the propagation of party slates. The Federalist election plans seem to have been designed to create a low turnout election in which the wealthier and better educated who had easy access to polling places—Federalist townsmen, in other words—would predominate. Democratic-Republicans in the legislature complained about "the inconvenience of the mode adopted," but what they did not realize at the time was that the statewide election format actually gave Jefferson supporters the key to winning the election by allowing their strength in the working-class wards of outlying Philadelphia to just barely outweigh the "rotten towns."[4]

While the 1796 election in Pennsylvania may have developed into the first real presidential campaign, the structure of the election forced the Democratic-Republican opposition to use the fairly traditionalist strategy of relying on the reputations—or, more properly speaking, the name recognition—of various prominent men to guide the voters. The same fifteen elector names were going to have to be written on pieces of paper throughout the state, so the names had to be familiar enough to remember and spell correctly. This was hardly the same thing as the personal influence of "local notables" dominating the voter's choice, but then again, random people off the streets, or even ordinary political activists, were not going to do. At the end of the spring legislative session, Federalist and Republican legislators and other leaders gathered to frame competing slates of electors. The Republicans loaded their ticket with the best-known political names in the state, starting with sitting Chief Justice Thomas McKean; Revolutionary War general William Irvine; David Rittenhouse, the country's most famous living scientist; and several once-and-future members of Congress, many of whom also carried prominent family names: Peter Muhlenberg (the Speaker's brother), former U.S. senator and John Adams antagonist William Maclay, future governor Joseph Hiester, the appealingly named John Smilie, and so on. It was a notable crew even by Federalist standards, though John Adams with his usual measured judgment dismissed them as "the lowest dreggs of the mob of Philadelphia."[5]

A surprising element was the fact that the ticket's very existence was kept quiet until the fall. Writing his central Pennsylvania ally General William Irvine, strategist John Beckley seemed to be planning a colonial-style campaign of personal influence in which country gentlemen would circulate and bring in their neighbors: "A little exertion by a few good active republicans in each *county* would bring the people out, and defeat the influence of your little rotten towns such as Carlisle, Lancaster, York &c. A Silent, but Certain cooperation among the country people may do much."[6]

There were several reasons to keep the early presidential campaigning low-profile. The use of tickets and printed ballots had become controversial in previous elections—they were perceived as conspiratorial attempts to illegitimately manipulate and control voters, and few outside of Philadelphia radical circles embraced party loyalty or active campaigning as positive goods. Beyond this, with no precedent for a full-out presidential campaign, no one knew whether or how voters would react to a national election campaign or even if they would know what to do. The opposition's goal was to educate the electorate as thoroughly as possible without being so heavy-handed as to alienate them.

In late September, Beckley and his allies made preparations to take their Jefferson campaign to new and much more public levels. "Silent and certain" may have been the watchwords earlier, but things were going to get loud quickly, though not necessarily about the presidency at first. As the Federalists well knew, right in the middle of the period between Washington's retirement announcement and the presidential elector elections was the traditional high point of Pennsylvania's political calendar, the October 11 elections of the state legislature, the governor, and other major offices. There were hotly contested state and local races that Jefferson's chief partisans could not ignore or divert their energies from. In the *Aurora* crowd's home city alone, democratic tribune John Swanwick faced a fight for reelection to Congress, and Blair "Kick the Treaty to Hell" McClenachan was running to represent the Philadelphia suburbs. At the same time, a new Philadelphia charter had opened the city council to popular elections, and a raft of street-level democrats were trying for seats, included printers Benjamin Franklin Bache and Mathew Carey. Both Bache and Carey placed near the bottom of the list, but the over eleven hundred votes that the two men and other democratic activists had garnered suggest there was at least a strong base in the city for radical politics, even if it was not the majority. The failure of their candidacies also suggests that while voters may have been willing to take political guidance from the press, actually being represented by journalists was another matter: one could be influenced by partisan vitriol without necessarily admiring it.[7]

Concentrating on these state and local races first, Pennsylvania Republicans found their popularity reviving in ways that caused the presidential strategy to rapidly evolve toward more public methods. Swanwick was reelected despite determined opposition, and the fiery McClenachan was chosen to replace former Speaker Frederick Muhlenberg, whose vote had saved the Jay Treaty. "The great victory obtained" in Philadelphia "against the most violent exertions ever made in this City" predicted good things for the presidential election, Beckley hoped. In western Pennsylvania, congressmen Albert Gallatin and William Findley, implicated in the Whiskey Rebellion and the targets of heavy Federalist invective, won reelection with 61 percent and 79 percent of the vote, respectively.[8]

Next the radicals prepared for the presidential election. The Philadelphia-based committee of correspondence, led by Dr. Michael Leib, created and printed a late September circular letter aimed at local Republican activists around the state. It began with a message from Leib that explained the rules and circumstances of the election, apologizing for the failure of the state legislature's Republican delegation ("the advocates for fair election") to win a more manageable and rational mode of voting for presidential electors. The Federalists had forced the statewide election on them, Leib wrote, rallying the troops, so "let us defeat their designs by union and activity." He offered a new name for the elector ticket to replace the recently deceased David Rittenhouse and then set out the basic message of the campaign. This was a document aimed at instructing party leaders rather than keying up voters. Pennsylvania had to decide "between two men of very dissimilar politics, indeed— THOMAS JEFFERSON and JOHN ADAMS . . . the uniform advocate of equal rights among citizens, or the champion of rank, titles, and hereditary distinctions;—the steady supporter of our present republican constitution; or the warm panegyrist of the British Monarchical form of Government, one who has unqualifiedly declared as *hazardous* and *dangerous*, our departure from his model of excellence, the British constitution."

Only one Adams page reference was included with this first circular, but the Philadelphians were hard at work on a series of campaign flyers intended for public distribution and pitched much higher, both emotionally and ideologically. The next release, dated October 3, appended the full list of paraphrases from Adams's *Defence of the Constitutions* (discussed in chapter 7) to a document that summarized the résumés of both candidates and gave the bluntest version of the Democratic-Republican message yet printed: "Thomas Jefferson is a firm REPUBLICAN,—John Adams is an avowed MONARCHIST. . . . *Thomas Jefferson* first drew the declaration of American independence;—he first framed the sacred political sentence, that all men are *born* equal. *John Adams* says this is all a farce and a falsehood. . . . Which of those, freemen of Pennsylvania, will you have for your President?" Dated a week before the state elections, and likely handed out to the voters not only during the preceding week but while the voting was going on, the handbill tried to impress on readers the need to care about the presidential election: "Will you, by neglectfully staying at home," or rather by not coming out a second time, "permit others to saddle you with Political Slavery?"[9]

As an extra incentive, the handbill tried to revive old animosities between Pennsylvania and New England over claims in the state's Wyoming Valley. Just before the Revolution, settlers and speculators from New England had tried to make good on Connecticut's colonial claims to the northern half of Pennsylvania by selling land and taking up residence in the valley. This vicious conflict had been settled by the federal government, but some Connecticut claimants were still trying to press their case in 1796, and the pro-Jefferson handbill warned that Adams would side with his home region. "Federal New Englandmen" had been hot to send troops to put down the Whiskey Rebellion, but their real game was to further "their wicked and unjust pretensions" against Pennsylvania and "reduce her to become a dependant [sic] province of New England." Go ahead, voters were told sarcastically, vote for a Yankee chief justice and a Yankee president: "Your property is safe, and your rights secure—provided, you are silly enough to think them not worth the having." In the end, the actual voting in the affected area seemed to reflect the old fault lines. The Wyoming Valley county of Luzerne would vote its Yankee heritage and give 98 percent of its votes to Adams electors. The rebellious western counties would go almost as heavily for Jefferson.[10]

After the state elections, a new wave of handbills got down to the more basic project of spreading the information necessary to vote for president and motivating people to turn out. The new flyers, two versions of which have survived, amounted to voter guides, printed copies of the Republican elector ticket with voting instructions and a short campaign message attached. The upper half of each sheet provided the date and format of the election, followed by the names and home counties of the Republican elector candidates: "Subjoined is a list of fifteen good Republicans, friends of the people, who love Liberty, hate Monarchy, and will vote for a Republican President. Remember Friday the Fourth of November!" The bottom half of each handbill presented some quick documentation supporting the idea that the election was a contest between monarchism and republicanism. The physically larger of the two editions included another page-referenced guide to Adams's *Defence*. The other, a pocket-sized item reminiscent of a modern index card, carried the infamous passage from Tom Paine's *Letter to George Washington* alleging an Adams proposal to turn the Washingtons into a royal family (see chapter 7). Readers were invited to apply to the editor of the *Aurora* if they wanted to see the original. The Philadelphians were staking everything on fear of the Vice President Who Would Be King and their own energy in spreading the message.[11]

No figures exist on the number of handbills printed, but Federalists were aghast at how widely they seemed to circulate. "Whence this extraordinary exertion in favor of Mr. Jefferson?" the *Gazette of the United States* wondered. The Federalists preferred to blame outside agitators. It must all have been cooked up at a "congress" at Jefferson's house, where all this "bullock was preconcerted, and all the lies invented." Who could be paying for all of it? What could be the motivation? Were they looking for "foreign gold" as a reward? There may well have been some French

PUBLIC NOTICE.

FRIDAY THE FOURTH DAY OF NOVEMBER NEXT,

IS the day appointed by law, for the People to meet at their respective places of Election, to choose by WRITTEN TICKETS,* Fifteen Electors on behalf of this State, of a President and Vice-President of the United States. Citizens attend! On that day the important question is to be decided, whether the Republican JEFFERSON, or the Royalist ADAMS, shall be President of the United States. Subjoined is a list of fifteen good Republicans, friends of the people, who love Liberty, hate Monarchy, and will vote for a Republican President. Remember Friday the fourth of November!

* *Judges of Elections to reject printed Tickets. See Election Law of 1785.*

ELECTORS.

Thomas M'Kean, Philadelphia City.
Jacob Morgan, do. County.
James Boyd. Chester.
Jonas Hartzel, Northampton.
Peter Muhlenberg, Montgomery.
Joseph Heister, Berks.
William M'Clay, Dauphin.
James Hanna, Bucks.

John Whitehill, Lancaster County.
William Irwin, Cumberland.
Abraham Smith, Franklin.
William Brown, Mifflin.
John Piper, Bedford.
John Smilie, Fayette.
James Edgar, Washington.

CITIZENS OF PENNSYLVANIA!

THE following Maxims and Opinions are taken from Mr. ADAMS's Defence of the American Constitutions, and by them you will be able to judge for yourselves whether the man that holds such doctrines is a fit person to be elected President of the United States.

Page 8,=Vol. 1. It is no objection to monarchy that it is supported by Nobles, and a subordination of ranks, for the most democratic governments are supported by a subordination of offices and of ranks.

22, —— A limited Monarchy may be justly denominated a Republic.

70, —— English Constitution best, and most deserving of American imitation, and I confess that it is very much to my mortification, that the Constitution of the United States has not given to its Executive, an absolute negative on its laws, as in England.

110, —— Wealth, Birth, Family Pride respected by all People.

116, —— Wealth, Birth and Virtue, form the the best men.

159, —— A Commonwealth can no more consist of a people without gentry, than of a gentry without people.

206, —— Kingly government best, Tyranny worst. No city is more wretched than that under Tyranny, nor any more happy than that under Regal power.

Page 294,—Vol. 1. If the power of negotiation and of treaty, be in one man, there can be no intrigue.

321, —— Had Epaminandos lived to display his talents as Legislator, the world might have been blessed with an English Constitution, two or three thousand years sooner than it was.

324 —— Limited Monarchy the best government, superior to Republicanism.

360 —— Distinctions of poor and rich as necessary as labor and good government. Poor are destined to labor; the Rich, by advantages of education, independence and leisure, to superior stations.

373 —— Men of property and family, fittest for public service.

375 —— Rich well-born, well educated, must be preferred to Office, otherwise the people themselves will despise them.

479 —— Ministers of the Executive, only ought to be responsible.

(Besides innumerable others)

A REPUBLICAN.

Ticket and Talking Points: Handbill distributed throughout Pennsylvania in the fall of 1796, listing the pro-Jefferson electors and appending a list of damning passages from Adams's Defence of the Constitutions. *(Broadside from the collections of the Historical Society of Pennsylvania.)*

funding involved, but Beckley and Bache also had the backing of a handful of wealthy immigrant businessmen in Philadelphia who felt shut out by Federalists from the higher ramparts of social acceptance. French-born financier Étienne (Stephen) Girard and Irish tobacconist Thomas Leiper were two of the most active.[12]

For voters who might have difficulties making out their own ballots, Beckley planned help that went far beyond supplying them with information and ideological guidance. Apparently there was no requirement that the written tickets be created at the polls, or even in the voters' own handwriting, so he dug into his long clerical experience and mounted a ticket drive. Beckley and the other four members of his Philadelphia committee of correspondence all pitched in. As the clock ticked down to the election, Beckley hired eleven additional clerks to help, and dragooned his own family, urging other Republicans to do likewise. All in all, Beckley claimed, they scribbled out fifty thousand tickets to distribute around the state. Since this was around four times the number of Republican votes cast, this may be an exaggeration, but possibly not: 25 percent would be a remarkably high hit rate for political spam under any circumstances.[13]

Beckley's campaign material was distributed through agents sent out directly from Philadelphia to avoid the prying eyes of Federalist postmasters and conceal the intensity of Republican campaigning. Beckley planned to have copies spread through the countryside first and appear in the city later, closer to the day of the election. The Philadelphians consulted with local supporters in the regions they visited about the most suitable "districts & characters" to visit. The most remarkable of Beckley's agents was Major John Smith of Philadelphia. A hatter by trade, Smith had been a leading member of Philadelphia's Democratic Society, and served as an officer in the city's heavily politicized militia. In the fall of 1796, Smith campaigned on horseback through the Pennsylvania counties east of the Alleghenies, holding meetings, making speeches, and distributing tens of thousands of Beckley's tickets and handbills, even to children at schoolhouses. In one of his forays, Smith reported:

> I undertook and performed a journey of [more than] 600 miles . . . the object I had solely in view was to make Mr. Jefferson President . . . for upwards of three weeks that I was out, there was not one day I was not on horse back before the sun rose, nor put up at night till after it set. In that time, I held 18 public meetings making it a practice at

night to pay some person i[m]mediately to go through the neighborhood and notify the people to attend that night—at which respective
meetings I addressed myself to them in a zealous language.

Major Smith stopped to harangue the voters wherever he could find people gathered. Making his way through Northampton County, he heard
that a well-attended funeral was taking place at a nearby church. Arriving "at the moment they were about to be dismissed," Smith got up
in front of the congregation and launched into a political speech. Nor
was the major above a dirty trick or two. In Northumberland County,
he trailed two Federalist riders for sixty miles, picking up their tickets a
few minutes after they had passed them out. He kept a few samples for
purposes of opposition research and burned the rest. In Beckley's opinion, Smith acted "with a zeal, activity, intelligence, and exertion, seldom
equalled, but never exceeded" in American politics up to that time, unless by Beckley himself.[14]

The other major step that the Democratic-Republicans took was holding a series of public meetings in as many different towns and neighborhoods as possible, especially the sympathetic ones. Attendees would
hear an address, vote on any resolutions that might be offered, then approve the pro-Jefferson elector slate and send the notice to a newspaper.
Nominating meetings like these were already something of a Philadelphia and Pennsylvania tradition, a cross between a local party convention and a campaign rally. The format allowed local people to participate
in the nomination process, but for the most part, unless something
went wrong, no open-ended decisions were being made. Instead, the
local party activists were essentially ratifying the decision that the state
legislative delegation had made earlier.

If that took away from the democratic credibility of the meetings,
the sheer number and exposed nature of them added much of it back.
Just in the week before the election, there was a Monday meeting in a
wealthy area of Philadelphia at "Capt. Nelson's," chaired by Princeton-
ian Jonathan Bayard Smith. More modest groups of citizens gathered
at John Poor's School Room in the less fashionable South Mulberry
Ward on successive Wednesdays. At the second of these meetings, tavern keeper Israel Israel was in the chair and Benjamin Franklin Bache
himself acted as secretary. Perhaps unsurprisingly, both meetings went
"UNIANIMOUSLY" for the Jefferson electors. On the Saturday before
the election, citizens gathered at the "town-house" (local government

building) of the working-class and immigrant Northern Liberties neighborhood, just outside the then city limits in Philadelphia County, and at Ogden's tavern in the New Market Ward in a similar area to the south.

One of the more elaborate such meetings took place at Mr. Little's School-house. Chaired by popular militia officer Colonel John Barker, this meeting adopted a fulsome address containing some of the most lyrical praise of Jefferson published anywhere, using his enlightened reputation to suggest that his election might put an end to the distressing divisions that had generated this very meeting and campaign. Rationality and benevolence would triumph over all, and this first presidential campaign might be the last:

> Thomas Jefferson is the man on whom the friends of republican government cast their eyes.—A man of such enlightened views, such pure patriotism, such unsullied integrity, and such zeal for human happiness, can alone make our country flourishing, tranquil and happy. He will be the cement of discordant interests and of jarring passions.—Of no party but the great party of human benefactors, he will allay the heats of our country, heal its divisions, and calm the boisterous elements of political controversy.

The antipartyism and faith in the power of reason were no doubt sincere enough, but in this case they served chiefly as an appeal to the worried swing voter in the middle, probably Quakers worried that Adams's election might spark a war with France. But even this high-minded, above-partisanship rhetoric was still part of a strenuously Democratic-Republican campaign that chiefly sought to clarify voters' partisanship. The Barker address included a warning that Adams supporters had been mislabeling their slate of electors "a Jefferson ticket and have palmed it upon numbers of Republicans under that treacherous garb."[15]

While the amount of treachery is unknown, the Federalists were out actively campaigning, too. The two riders Major John Smith nobbled may have been the "Mountebank Doctor" and "Pettifogger" reported in the *Aurora* to have "travelled thro' every township" in York County and "speechified from rotten stumps." Perhaps what doomed the Federalist effort in Philadelphia was its decided lack of transparency, from intentionally misleading nomenclature to a flirtation with the secret plot to deliver the presidency to Thomas Pinckney. The main Federalist nominating meetings in Philadelphia, including one at Ogden's tavern on October 29 and at Dunwoody's tavern on November 2, presented what they called a "Federal and Republican" ticket "framed and recommended . . . by the friends of *Order and good Government.*" The only commitment made for this slate of elector candidates, led by Israel Whelen and Samuel Miles of Philadelphia, was that, approving of George Washington and his policies, the electors would "be expected to give their suffrages in favor of men who will probably continue the same system of wise and patriotic policy." Poor John Adams was not even mentioned.

With the city awash in John Beckley's handbills calumniating the vice president, Philadelphia Federalists were either deep in the Pinckney plot or so craven about affirming Adams's (and their own) political views as to be fearful of associating with his name. The *Aurora* taunted its opponents mercilessly for their cowardice, perfidy, and obvious unwillingness to practice even the most basic form of democracy, giving the voters some clue about what they were voting for: "These friends of order and good government have not condescended to inform '*the herd*' what man is their object as President of the United States." Perhaps they were afraid that by associating with Adams, "instead of being federalists and republicans, . . . they will be accounted royalists and aristocrats." Whatever they were up to, the Barker address observed, the local Federalists surely must have known that their cause was a bad one: "Such a cause, like the bird of night, skulks from the light of the sun." John Fenno's editorial column at least deigned to mention Adams, quoting from a Boston paper, but the item's conclusion conveyed well the deeply lukewarm feelings for the Federalist candidate that seemed to be abroad in silk-stocking Philadelphia: "Can we do better? May we not do worse? Think of these things, and think of JOHN ADAMS."[16]

The day of the presidential election, November 4, was hazy and pleasantly warm in Philadelphia. The word had gotten across even to the city's nonvoting population that "a matter of great moment" was at stake, and the streets were full of people. Quaker matron Elizabeth Drinker noted that her son William "gave his vote for electors" in the afternoon, but she well knew that the identity of the electors was not the point: "this is the day of Election for a President." Voting may have been limited to adult men, but engaging with partisan politics by reading and talking about it, and attending some of the public events, was not. No political or patriotic banquet was complete without a salute to the "American Fair," and the congressional lobby that gave its name to the political activity lobbying was heavily populated with women. More relevant to the election of 1796, the hectic political households of the

Aurora circle included several women, notably Maria Beckley and Margaret Markoe Bache, who pitched in directly with their husbands' ongoing campaign, in addition to supporting it emotionally and domestically. Several known and likely many more unknown women participated in politics by writing for the press under pseudonyms, though not necessarily during this election. "Female politicians" were a known-enough phenomenon in the 1790s, especially in Philadelphia, for a satirical play to be written about it and occasional controversies to arise.[17]

As was normal for early American elections, the polls did not present a sedate scene of citizens quietly making their private choices: the tumultuousness and publicity of the process were elements of the argument against female voting. Even with written ballots, voting took time and stamina, and the bars generally stayed open to keep the electorate well lubricated, if libations were not supplied directly. Crowds gathered early, lingered, and loudly made their prejudices known. According to Federalist observers, sixty "rioters" had been arrested and jailed the night before. On the day of the presidential voting, the "election ground" was filled by a "Mob" that paraded a flag with the French and American republics linked together, and shouted the opposition campaign's message: "JEFFERSON, and NO KING." The French tricolor was everywhere, especially in the emblem or "cockade" pinned to the men's tricorn hats. In working-class Kensington, William Loughton Smith heard, no one without a French cockade had been allowed to vote. The Federalists were equally active by this time, but not nearly as effective, weighed down by a lack of enthusiasm for their own candidate. There were no Philadelphia crowds shouting for John Adams.[18]

Measuring by the highest vote-getter in each slate (there were fifteen electors on each ticket, and the totals of each varied slightly), the Democratic-Republicans carried the city of Philadelphia 1,733 to 1,091 and their Philadelphia County base with more than 82 percent of the vote (1,400 to 399). The John Adams electors ran significantly behind the Federalist totals of a few weeks before in the state elections, even in the city's wealthiest neighborhoods. The assembly candidate who chaired the city Federalist meeting on the presidential election, George Latimer, had polled six hundred votes higher in the October election than the Adams electors would. With the Philadelphia region in their pocket, the Jefferson forces were able, just barely, to overcome lopsided Federalist votes in several northeastern and southeastern counties with "rotten towns." In York, the Adams supporters swamped the Jefferson supporters with more than twenty times their number of votes. Lancaster County voted Federalist by more than 3-to-1. The Jefferson forces scored better in the central Carlisle area (Cumberland County), where Beckley's friend General William Irvine had helped lead the campaign, and they expected and received heavy majorities in the western counties still angry with the Federalists because of issues arising from the Whiskey Rebellion. Washington County in the far southwest delivered the Jefferson electors 98 percent of its votes. Statewide, the Jefferson ticket electors all won by a clear but razor-thin majority that topped out at 12,516 votes for Thomas McKean to 12,229 for Israel Whelen, or something on the order of a 50.5 percent Jefferson victory.[19]

Beckley's campaign had not generated a landslide, but it had accomplished a "political revolution" nonetheless, shifting large numbers of votes in Philadelphia to Jefferson. There was no massive increase in voting, but it was a major accomplishment to maintain the level of participation seen in the hotly contested assembly elections just a few weeks prior, but this time for a novel, indirect, partly nontransparent election using an arcane and labor-intensive voting procedure. The turnout rate has been estimated at around 40 percent of the eligible voters, and while this was not yet the mass participation of ten, twenty, or fifty years later, it was hardly the "apathy" that some historians have claimed. Just this level of popular support for the opposition was more than enough to frighten Federalists into grabbing for more coercive and repressive responses early in the Adams administration—sedition laws, court orders, and armed occupation of the streets were coming. Suppressing the opposition press and party was more or less the avowed purpose of the Alien and Sedition Acts of 1798.[20]

Not that the Pennsylvania election was fully resolved by the popular vote. Close elections remain problematic to this day, but they were even more so in a manual voting system where returns still had to travel over the mountains by horseback. In what may or may not have been another clever vote-suppression move by legislative Federalists, the Pennsylvania election law gave the governor only fourteen days before he had to declare the winners in the presidential elector race, giving the chosen electors little time to get to Harrisburg for the state electoral college meeting on December 7, 1796. By the third week of November, the Democratic-Republicans of Philadelphia were getting nervous. The *Gazette of the United States* still gave a "Federal majority" of 1,064 because the heavily Republican western counties of Westmoreland, Greene, and

Fayette had not reported yet. John Fenno charged corruption, that the votes were being held until Jeffersonian officials out west decided how many votes were needed to carry the state. The *Aurora* had an opposing tale of incompetence that left open the possibility of conspiracy. The packet containing the returns had safely reached the Greensburg post office the week after the election, Bache reported, but then it had been mysteriously diverted during its journey to Philadelphia, turning back west to Pittsburgh. The strictest interpretation of the election law demanded that the governor proclaim the winners without the missing returns, even though the final result would undoubtedly be different. Governor Thomas Mifflin and Secretary of the Commonwealth Alexander J. Dallas, both Republican sympathizers but much more sensitive to their own reputations, decided to submit the problem to a panel of judges and other legal officials. The referees decided to wait a week.[21]

By the time the week was up, the Westmoreland and Fayette returns had appeared in Philadelphia. The former was a narrow Jefferson victory and the latter a Jefferson blowout; however, there was just enough variation in the individual totals, with a few voters making their selections based on name recognition or local or ethnic solidarity instead of presidential choice, to produce a divided result. When Mifflin declared the winners on November 24, only thirteen of the fifteen Jefferson electors had risen to the top of the standings. The other two, James Edgar of Washington County and Jonas Hartzell of Northampton County, were left out, while two electors from the Federalist "Federal and Republican" slate, Robert Coleman and Samuel Miles, were in. The Greene County returns eventually showed up, too, with a strong Jefferson vote that would have brought Edgar and Hartzell into the top fifteen, but it was too late. The two losers went to Harrisburg and demanded to vote, but to only partial avail. Pressure ran high for all the electors to fulfill the will of the majority, and Philadelphian Samuel Miles cracked and cast a Jefferson vote. Robert Coleman from Lancaster, where the Adams electors had taken 75 percent, stood firm, and cast one sorely needed Pennsylvania electoral vote for John Adams. Nevertheless, the Pennsylvania campaign was crucial on both sides. Jefferson would never have come so close to winning or have ever sustained his reputation as the man of the people and a national candidate without the fourteen northern electoral votes he received in Pennsylvania, and the one for Adams gave him one-third of his eventual margin over Jefferson for the presidency.[22]

"A POLISH ELECTION": AN AMERICAN EXPERIENCE WITH FOREIGN INTERVENTION

Following their usual pattern, the Federalists blamed their Pennsylvania disaster on the moral failings of others, and the French. Specifically, they contended that Philadelphia's rich, but pacifist, Quakers had been frightened away from their usual establishment allegiances by the implicit threats that had been made in a public letter by the current French minister to the U.S., Pierre-Auguste Adet, in which he said that there would be war in the event that American foreign policy did not change swiftly after the ongoing election. "If Mr. Jefferson is elected it will be owing entirely to the influence of this paper," grimaced Treasury Secretary Oliver Wolcott Jr. If so, John Adams might have become collateral damage of the peace offensive that the Federalists had mounted so successfully to save the Jay Treaty.

The impact of Adet's actions was somewhat more equivocal than the Federalists believed, but there is no question that he and his government intended to influence the results of the 1796 presidential election in Pennsylvania, making it the most open and flagrant foreign interference ever in the internal politics of the United States. While the French actions were weak and cuddly compared to the actions of colonial powers in other times and places (including both the United States and France), it was and is shocking for Americans to consider that their elections had been given a significant nudge through foreign intervention.[23]

The French Republic's foreign ministers were notable carriers—perhaps the original sufferers—of the diplomatic disease that also afflicted the United States. This was the delusion that the high political ideals and self-perceived moral superiority of a foreign government could inspire a colonial people to rise up against their own rulers. (Almost the first action the brand-new United States had taken in 1775 was invading Quebec in hopes that the French *habitants* would join the tiny invading force against the British.) French leaders were convinced that the American people were fundamentally sympathetic to the French Republic in their political beliefs and emotional attachments, despite the official antipathy to revolutionary France evinced ever more clearly since Jefferson had left the government. By the fall of 1796, regime change in America had long been the explicit, though not publicly admitted, policy of the French government. Like the United States in its days as a colonial power, the French believed that their aims were not colonial, that they did not intend to take self-determination away from the American people. Instead they meant to rekindle popular self-determination by inspiring the American people to get their government to "return to itself." One of the many problems with such anti-imperial imperial thought was (and is) the self-interested wishful thinking involved. The French far overestimated both their own ability to guide American events and the depth of their appeal.[24]

Despite its professions of love for Americans and their liberties, the French government continued to show little more respect for U.S. independence than the British had. By 1796, the Directory, as the group dictatorship then governing France was called, was clearly more concerned about reclaiming lost colonial possessions than about anything to do with the Rights of Man. Perhaps most egregiously, in March 1796 French minister Adet hired the ex-governor of Guadeloupe, General Victor Collot, to case out the western United States for possible pro-French secessionist conspirators. Collot toured through the old French western territory from Pittsburgh to St. Louis and New Orleans, speaking far too freely to many prominent citizens. The French hoped for a new breakaway republic that might cooperate better with French policy and aid both the fight against the British and the acquisition of Spanish territory with its ports, crops, and manpower. Collot was none too successful—he discovered that the British had gotten there first, in the form of the Blount conspiracy, and accidentally acquired a Federalist mole among his traveling companions who sent lurid reports back to Oliver Wolcott. The French had assumed that the machinations of a sister republic would be more successful in fomenting western conspiracies than the Spanish and British monarchs had been, not seeing that it simply brought them down to the level of the other colonial powers.[25]

Adet had more success with his political interference, gaining the cooperation of key American leaders and full access to the press through the *Aurora*. Adet had been battling with the highly undiplomatic new Secretary of State Timothy Pickering all summer over the Jay Treaty, the American acceptance of which the French saw as contradicting not only the old alliance but any pretense of neutrality. Far outmatched by the British on the high seas, France badly needed its former right to have privateers bring captured ships to American ports. Adet protested that there was nothing balanced or neutral about denying France what the British did not need and submitting to British commercial regulations while refusing any cooperation with France while the two nations were at war.[26]

In late summer 1796, the French minister traveled north to vacation, gauge public opinion, and encourage French supporters outside of Philadelphia, while seemingly taking pains to force Federalist dignitaries to pay him the required civilities. Adet was entertained in Albany by officials of the John Jay administration, visited Lake George, and then proceeded to Boston. In the "Metropolis of Massachusetts," Adet hobnobbed with the "Equality Alley" democrats, but also received an official tribute from the town selectmen and an "Ox Feast" in which Federalists (to the scandal of some of their confreres) participated along with the local "Jacobins." The Bostonians saluted the French Republic for "the energy of her councils—The liberality of her policy, and the unparalleled splendor of her arms," while the Boston selectmen hoped officially that "amity and friendship" between the two republics would last "until the end of time." Adet was visibly impressed by the show of support. At the feast, the guest of honor jumped up to reply when he had been toasted, giving a speech that he bragged to Paris had "reanimated the hopes" of France's beleaguered Boston supporters ("*j'ai reanimé leurs espérances*"). Gesturing toward Governor Sam Adams and General Benjamin Lincoln seated next to him ("those citizens who first raised the standard of liberty on this Continent, and who have known so well how to defend it"), Adet promised the audience his and the French Republic's continued affection for the United States, having thus been "assured that the Americans will exert every effort to cement with the people of France an union, formed under the auspices of victory . . . and the blessings of liberty." With this, the French minister more or less openly announced the hope that the American people would join his government in trying to change the policy of their own.[27]

Emboldened by the warm feelings for France that Americans had shown even on John Adams's home turf, Adet returned to Philadelphia ready to fight and just in time to be disgusted by Washington's Farewell Address. Sending a copy home to the French foreign minister Charles Delacroix, Adet called the great message a tissue of "insolence" and "immorality" that obviously reflected Hamilton's principles and would not fool the American people: "It would be useless to speak to you about it." Instead, Adet prepared to unload some addresses of his own, three open letters to Secretary of State Timothy Pickering that were directed equally to the American people, and translated and published in the *Aurora* before Pickering even had a chance to translate the official copies. Probably encouraged by the Philadelphia radicals, Adet and his government were convinced that Americans would never choose war with their sister republic and decided to make it absolutely clear that this was indeed the choice they faced.[28]

Adet's opening salvo appeared on the last day of October, the Monday before the Pennsylvania elector election, under the heading "AUTHEN-TIC." It was a cover letter enclosing a decree that the French Directory had issued over the summer stating that henceforth American ships would be treated, in terms of being searched or captured for carrying militarily or economically significant goods, "in the same manner as they shall suffer the English to treat them." The Jay Treaty had accepted British rights to search neutral American ships and confiscate as enemy property any goods, including food, they found if British officers believed that they might end up in France. In other words, the United States had given up any rights to neutral trade vis-à-vis the British. If the Americans were going to allow the British that kind of freedom with American ships, in violation of treaties with France, then they had better expect some similar liberties to be taken by French ships in return. As in his Boston appearance, Adet rehearsed the whole controversy with great feeling, like a wounded lover, pledging that France would respect the United States' neutrality if it even *tried* to remain virtuous with the British, made just some *appearance* of nonsubmission. But addressing Pickering and the now decidedly Federalist Washington administration, Adet held out little hope of this. If "thro' weakness, partiality, or other motives" (a reference to the charges of British corruption swirling in the pro-French camp) the United States government allowed "the English to sport with that neutrality, and turn it to their advantage," then the French would have to be allowed to take the same advantages, or else the United States would cross "the line of neutrality" with France and instead "become its enemy." This meant war, in other words, if the Washington administration's policies did not change. The owlish Pickering seemed to think war was a fine idea; he responded to Adet the next day with sarcastic insults and demands for proof. Putting popular cosmopolitanism on notice, Pickering complained that only the United States government had the right to communicate the policies of foreign governments to the American people.[29]

The voting took place on Friday, November 4, and the exchange between Adet and Pickering helped create the tense atmosphere and rollicking, cockade-color-coded election-day scene Federalists complained about. Advance word of Adet's next move must have leaked out of the

Bache home (also the *Aurora* office), Cordner's tavern, or other democratic haunts. On Saturday morning, with the local voting just completed and the returns yet to come in, the *Aurora* carried Adet's second blast, the so-called "cockade proclamation" demanding that Frenchmen abroad actively display their support for the republic. Following orders from home, Adet withdrew "the national protection" from Frenchmen who were such "contemptible beings" with such "unfeeling hearts" that they did not constantly "take a pride in wearing" the national colors, specifically the circular blue, white, and red cockade, or emblem in their hats. By wearing this "distinctive mark" and thus making themselves known, Adet wrote in a passage that did not seem aimed at Frenchmen at all, citizens of the French Republic living elsewhere would secure themselves "the protection and reciprocal respect guaranteed by our treaties." In other words, those who showed support for France could expect to conduct their business, including international trade, free of the interference from French ships and troops that other Americans would be suffering now that they had become de facto British allies. The proclamation fueled a fad for wearing the tricolor cockade among supporters of the French Republic as well as its actual citizens.[30]

The "cockade proclamation" and its predecessor made its way around the country just as voters in most of the popular vote states were going to the polls in early November, but Adet saved his most populist and devastating barrage for last, when it was too late to affect the hearts and minds in a way that might change the outcome. His third and final letter was released on November 15, just after voters in all the popular vote states but one had already cast their ballots (see table 2, at the end of chapter 8). Not quite understanding how it all worked, Adet seems to have based his timing more on the letter of the constitutional process, focusing on the Electoral College meetings in early December rather than the popular voting for electors. Or perhaps Adet just took the Constitution too literally and assumed that because the Adams electors were not officially committed or instructed to vote for Adams, they could be intimidated and flipped to Jefferson.

Adet's third letter announced that the French Republic was essentially taking a break from its relationship with the United States. Normal diplomatic relations were being suspended, and Adet was being called home, until such time as the U.S. government's "sentiments" and behavior changed. "The name of America still excites sweet emotions" in "the heart of Frenchmen," Adet wrote. The diplomat then tried to woo back the American people with what may be the most heartfelt, tear-jerking diplomatic communiqué ever penned. He asked Americans to try to remember the kind of September when France's embrace had saved them from British fire, sword, and rapine. The reminders were all around them:

Alas! time has not yet demolished the fortifications with which the English roughened this country, nor those the Americans raised for their defence; their half rounded summits still appear in every quarter; amidst plains—on the tops of mountains. The traveller need not search for the ditch which served to encompass them; it is still open under his feet. Scattered ruins of houses laid waste, which the fire had partly respected, in order to leave monuments of British fury, are still to be found. Men still exist who can say, here a ferocious Englishman slaughtered my father; there my wife tore her bleeding daughter from the hands of an unbridled Englishman. Alas! the soldiers who fell under the sword of the Britons are not yet reduced to dust; the laborer, in turning up his field, still draws from the bosom of the earth their whitened bones; while the ploughman, with tears of tenderness and gratitude, still recollects that his fields, now covered with rich harvests, have been moistened with French blood.[31]

Then came the tragic twist in the Franco-American love story. When the new French Republic found itself menaced by all the monarchies of Europe, and its ships hunted by Britain's maritime might, French "thoughts turned toward America. . . . In America, they saw friends . . . they expected to find in the ports of the United States an asylum as sure as at home, they thought, if I may use the expression, there to find a second country." But the American government had proven fickle: "Oh hope, worthy of a faithful people, how hast thou been deceived!" Adet seethed that

While every thing around the inhabitants of this country animates them to speak of the tyranny of Great Britain, and of the generosity of Frenchmen; when England has declared a war of death to that nation, to avenge herself for its having cemented with its blood the independence of the United States. It was at this moment their Government made a treaty of amity with their ancient tyrant, the implacable enemy of their ancient ally. O! Americans, covered with noble scars! O! you who have so often flown to death and to victory with French soldiers! You who know those generous sentiments which distinguish the true warrior! Whose hearts have always vibrated with those of your companions in arms! Consult them to-day, to know what they experience.

Thus a foreign diplomat delivered what was certainly the most emotional election appeal Americans received in 1796. Of course, while plucking the heartstrings, Adet had still managed to send a distinctly threatening message, announcing the "resolution of a Government terrible to its enemies," no matter how sweet the sentiments of its heart. The American people would face war unless they took their government back from the Federalists. Vote the right way and all would be forgiven: "Recollect, at the same time, that, if magnanimous souls with liveliness resent an affront, they also know how to forget one. Let your Government return to itself, and you will still find in Frenchmen faithful friends and generous allies."[32]

Federalists were understandably outraged at a foreign government menacing their country over election results. The firing of Adet's "Diplomatic Blunderbuss" exposed new wells of belligerent national pride in Federalist hearts that had been missing from the Jay Treaty debates of six months earlier. William Loughton Smith wrote his father-in-law back in Charleston that "there was never so barefaced and disgraceful an interference of a foreign power in any free country," warning South Carolinians that it was all driven by the "wishes" of the French, Jefferson, and the Philadelphia Quakers to free the slaves. To Oliver Wolcott Sr., the treasury secretary's father, it bid fair to render the relatively democratic if indirect presidential selection process little better than "a Polish election."[33]

Federalists became much enamored with this analogy of the young United States to the recently partitioned and dissolved Polish Republic. Poland had been an antimodel for many of the Founders during the constitutional debates of the 1780s, and its final fate was recent news in 1796, heavily featured in the American press. The Polish-Lithuanian Union had used an electoral system in which, theoretically, the country's entire "mass" nobility (comprising twenty-five thousand families and 6.6 percent of the population) assembled, armed and mounted, on a field outside Warsaw, and the armed camps jockeyed with each other until a new king was acclaimed. The election was over when everyone raised their swords and yelled the same name; only thirteen electors dead in the election of 1764 was considered a calm, peaceful contest.

With any individual noble enjoying the "Golden Freedom" to become king, block an election, or veto legislation in the *sejm*, Polish politics was proverbial for anarchic dysfunction. As a result of these constitutional defects and the geographical accident of its location, Poland was also crippled by interference from the Russian, Prussian, and Austrian monarchies that surrounded it. Able to paralyze the entire Polish Republic by keeping just a handful of nobles on retainer to use their vetoes when necessary, the Russians and their competitors prevented the development of a strong Polish state and sent their troops into the country at will, especially around the time of royal elections. In 1793, the Russians and Prussians had jointly coerced the king and *sejm* into reversing constitutional reforms and ceding the eastern and western ends of the country. "Just such were the elections" with which Adet was trying to "ripen" the United States for dismemberment, according to the Federalists.[34]

Their fears were sincere enough, but the analogy got more than a little ridiculous when contrasted with the bloodbath that Russia and Prussia had visited on the Polish Republic when the Poles tried to resist foreign interference. Before Adet, Poland was more often cited by Democratic-Republicans as an example of the evils of European monarchy. In the most recent events that were well known in America before 1796, Revolutionary War hero Tadeusz Kościuszko's nationalist uprising in 1794 had been savagely put down; the remaining Polish lands were divided among Russia, Prussia, and Austria; and the Polish Republic was wiped from the map. An item widely reprinted in the American press reported that fifteen thousand people had been killed in the Poles' last stand in the Warsaw suburb of Praga and the subsequent Russian rampage.[35]

Though hardly agreeing that Adet's newspaper letters had "polandized" the United States, high-ranking Republican leaders were none too pleased with the French minister either. James Madison knew that Citizen Adet had planned to visit Thomas Jefferson at Monticello that summer, and he did not see anything wrong with that. What he took great umbrage at was the charge that Adet's letters were just an "electioneering maneuver." The betrayal of the old alliance was as serious an issue for Madison and Jefferson as it was for the French. They thought Adet's arguments had much merit on substantive grounds, but as a campaign tactic the letters seemed ridiculously misjudged, providing ammunition to the very forces the French wanted to see defeated. Adet's publicity campaign was "working all the evil with which it is pregnant," Madison wrote to Jefferson, and "those who rejoice in its indiscretions" were "taking advantage of them" as aggressively as possible, chiefly by reclaiming the warlike, nationalist identity that the Federalists had lost during their brief, Jay Treaty–driven fling with pacifism. Though more freelance reactionary and patriotic Briton than Federalist partisan, journalist William "Peter Porcupine" Cobbett was almost as quick to publish "these arrogant effusions of upstart tyranny" as his least favorite competitor, Benjamin Franklin Bache, was. Appending a seventy-eight-page rejoinder, Cobbett, in his edition of Adet's letters, *The Gros Mousqueton Diplomatique,* reflected a view of the incident actually quite similar to Madison's, seeing it as an embarrassment for the French that would likely be counterproductive. Hence the metaphor of his title: "For all the long list of fire arms, none is so difficult to adjust, or makes so much noise and smoke, with so little execution, as a *Blunderbuss.*" Another metaphor was "bully," someone who tries "by means of a big look . . . and a thundering voice, to terrify peaceable men into a compliance with what he has neither a right to demand, nor power nor courage to enforce."[36]

By contrast, John Adams saw the Adet letters as a serious blow to Federalist prospects that had doomed him to return to private life. ("Mortifications. Humiliation," he moaned to Abigail.) The common New England Federalist interpretation, imbibed by Adams, was that Adet's threats had scared Philadelphia's rich Quakers out of their usual establishmentarian voting habits. As pacifists, they hated war; as merchants, they did not want to see businesses interrupted or taxes increased. It was galling for Federalists to think that their own peace message, applied so successfully in defense of the Jay Treaty earlier in the year, was going to be turned against them. Out in the countryside, Federalist campaigners were allegedly still telling the people that a vote for Adams was a vote for peace and a vote for Jefferson was a vote for war, but that message was already out of date. The French minister had switched the Jay Treaty–era calculus around and perhaps cracked some of the Quakers. "The conduct of the city fills me with chagrin and indignation," wrote Oliver Wolcott. "Many men who have been considered as friends to the government, yielded on this occasion, and publicly assigned as their reason, THAT THE ELECTION OF MR. JEFFERSON WAS NECESSARY TO PREVENT A RUPTURE WITH FRANCE!!!" While no Philadelphia Quakers admitted to this on paper, there was a notable shift in Philadelphia voting patterns that might be partly attributable to "frightened Quakers." Two silk-stocking wards, Dock and Chestnut, with the highest populations of merchants in the city, changed sides from the earlier state elections, supporting the Federalist congressional candidate Edward Tilghman by large majorities in October then swinging to the Jefferson ticket in November. Quantitative political historian Richard G. Miller calculated that the pro-Jefferson electors drew votes most heavily from both the city's poorest *and* wealthiest areas.[37]

Historians have generally been nearly as scandalized about the French intervention as the Federalists were, but what makes historical interpretation of the intervention difficult is that modern ethnonationalism was not yet in place in 1796, especially not in the United States. This very incident may have sparked the growth of a more exclusive, inward-looking style of nationalism, but there were still other alternatives. The American Revolution had inspired the French, and the French had inspired revolutions themselves in the Netherlands and elsewhere. It was not that far-fetched, or even that illegitimate, to think that they might be able to bring about *l'heureuse Révolution* in the United States. Though foreign minister Delacroix back in Paris had instructed Adet to "raise up the people and at the same time conceal the lever by which we do so," Adet had not bothered with the concealment part. William Loughton Smith was not wrong about the "barefaced" nature of Adet's messages, but a nicer and just as accurate word would be "transparent." Communicating with foreign publics might not have been part of proper diplomacy in 1796, but it certainly was part of the French Republic's new popular political culture.[38]

However one chooses to evaluate the incident morally, one aspect that is easy to overlook is that the idea for French interference in the election may have come from within the United States, specifically from Equality Alley in Boston. The smoking gun document is Adet's dispatch to Paris about his New England trip, in which he reported that it was the Bostonian Democratic-Republicans who suggested the strategy of public and threatening messages to the U.S. government. Frustrated with John Adams's strength in New England, Dr. Charles Jarvis, Ben Austin, or someone else in Boston told Adet that the only way to influence Federalist merchants was to use fear and greed the way Republicans believed the pro–Jay Treaty forces had done. The French should do something to fill the merchants with *"la crainte"* (fear or dread) about their property. In return for this help, the Bostonians promised Adet that they would work *"avec activité"* to elect Jefferson and drop John Adams. Perhaps the Sam Adams gambit described in the previous chapter was born at this meeting. This was an American suggestion of how to go about influencing American politics, but there was no question that some Democratic-Republicans hoped Adet might deliver a November surprise that would tip the election.[39]

Of course, Federalists suspected much more illicit French involvement with the American "Jacobins" than mere strategic consultation. There is no way to know whether or not Adet contributed money to help fund the Jefferson campaign, but if he did, it was not enough: the indications are that Bache, Beckley, and the others were bankrupting themselves to get Jefferson elected rather than wallowing in French largess. Federalists muttered darkly about mass bribery of voters, but French funds were far too limited for that, and in Philadelphia it seems to have been the wealthier voters who switched.[40]

Perhaps the most judicious interpretation of Adet's gambit is that, like many another imperial intervention, it worked well as a short-term tactic but proved highly counterproductive in the long run. The letters set off the beginnings of an emotional backlash that may have saved the presidency for Adams and doomed the "sister republic" relationship more surely than even the Reign of Terror. John Adams made a comment about this phenomenon that was more insightful than his electoral predictions. The French, Adams thought, were making the same mistake the British had if they thought that Americans would accept open, long-term clientage to a European power; threats would inspire a resistance that might push Americans to a sense of independence and levels of national feeling they had never experienced before: "If I have looked with any Accuracy into the Hearts of my Fellow Citizens, The French will find as the English have found, that Feelings may be Stirred which they never expected to find there, and that Perhaps the American People themselves are not Sensible are within them." It was the kickoff of a new, more exclusive kind of nationalism, built on raw self-love and self-interest rather than the principles of the Radical Enlightenment or finding a place in the world trading system. The new approach demanded military self-sufficiency and rendered the involvement of any foreigners in American politics, to say nothing of foreign governments, highly suspect. Alexander Hamilton explained the reaction as part of a long-term project of his: "We are labouring hard to establish in this country principles more and more *national* and free from all *foreign ingredients*—so that we may be neither *'Greeks nor Trojans'* but truly Americans." This was probably a necessary step in the development of a great nation, but it also predicted the nativism, isolationism, and imperialism that would often propel American nationalism and U.S. foreign policy in the future.[41]

More important for our purposes is the immediate aftermath of Adet's intervention. More popular voting and the actual Electoral College meetings were still to come. The French may have helped Jefferson get Pennsylvania, but they also clearly damaged his chances of picking up the freer-swinging votes that were still out there and solidified the Federalists behind John Adams. In postcolonial nations, it has often been the kiss of death for a domestic politician or party to be seen as sponsored by a colonial power. Adet had administered the kiss to Jefferson, raising fundamental questions of emotional and political independence for the young nation that were impossible to completely ignore. He had greatly strengthened the Federalist argument that "the election of Mr. Jefferson" should be considered "as fatal to our independence, now that interference of a foreign nation in our affairs is no longer disguised."[42]

LATE YANKEE RALLY: PROVINCIALISM OVER INTRIGUE IN NEW ENGLAND

One of the strangest results of the nationalistic reaction to Adet was the increase in sectional feeling that it seemed to promote. As the weakness of Adams's candidacy, and the strength of Jefferson's, was revealed, various Federalists and Federalist leaners among the political elite went scurrying to their own corners, their own interests, and their own schemes.

New Englanders recoiled from what they thought the Philadelphians had done and seemed to circle the wagons against any further French, democratic, or southern intrusion. After the Jay Treaty period of finding themselves on the less patriotic and belligerent side of foreign policy debates, New England Federalists relished the chance to let the eagle soar in response to Adet. One of the toughest statements came from Hartford's *Connecticut Courant*, which published "*THE PEOPLE'S ANSWER*," signed "The People" just to make sure the message was clear. Now that the French had made their preference for Jefferson known, "there is not an elector on this side of the Delaware that would not be sooner shot than vote for him." Governor Oliver Wolcott used nearly the same line in a letter to his son, so the newspaper sentiment came straight from the top. To the Wolcotts, the fact that Jefferson had not completely abjured his candidacy after receiving a foreign assist confirmed his reprehensible character and sordid ambition, not surprising for a postcolonial leader perceived to have an outside benefactor.[43]

Adet had also given New England Federalists an extra chance to play the religion card against Jefferson where it mattered most. "The People" turned French complaints that the United States had broken faith with their alliance into a bitter joke. Wasn't a nation "three times *regenerated* by Tom Paine, whom Jefferson and his disciples exalt above Moses or Jesus" also "*absolved from the faith of treaties*"? If the godless French were going to lay aside "the law of God," they might as well forget "*the law of nations*" while they were at it. This was all perfectly in keeping with the Federalist commitment to the old idea that neither law nor society could maintain order without divine sanction—a "future state of rewards and punishments" to back up human authority. This fed an anything-goes attitude when Yankees dealt with or wrote about the French or anyone perceived as their minions.[44]

New England Federalists perceived themselves as defending the nation and Christianity rather than a sectional interest. A New Hampshire writer bragged in rebuttal to an anti-Adams writer that George Washington had over time "discovered more virtue and integrity in New-England men, than in the precious confessing gentlemen of the Southern States," but hastened to add, "away with those 'geographical distinctions' of New-England and Southern—it is sufficient that Washington has recommended to the People to explode them."

Among Connecticut's presidential electors, the argument was made that "no southern character" could possibly expect the North's full support in case of a war, a remarkable statement. Governor and elector Oliver Wolcott pondered the question of which prospective president would allow New England to "retire with more ease . . . if the phrenzy of the southern states" made disunion necessary. In this case, Wolcott was referring to the alleged "phrenzy" for French Jacobinism, but in Connecticut they were nursing other regional grudges, in particular a sense of gloom about New England's seemingly shrinking influence in the union. Connecticut delegates had led the small-state forces at the Federal Convention in 1787, but by 1796 many in the state regretted some of the compromises that had been made there, seeing the rise of Jefferson and the Republicans as the by-product of unfair southern advantages. "We shall not be satisfied to have a President appointed by a negro representation only," referring to the extra votes that the Constitution allowed the southern states by counting three-fifths of their enslaved population for purposes of representation. This was not quite the killer argument that angry New Englanders imagined—white nonvoters (women, children, resident aliens, and men who could not meet property requirements) were fully counted everywhere, and also had their vote wielded by others. In any case, the lingering New England anger over the Three-Fifths Compromise was not primarily about the morality of slavery, though that was certainly involved. It had much more to do with the sectional balance of power and even racism. New Englanders chafed at the idea that they were being put on the same level as southern blacks; they referred to southern electoral votes as "Negro votes" and constantly compared the idea of counting slaves for purposes of representation with counting New England horses and cattle. Wolcott admitted to his son that the bitterness over "negro representation" was "perhaps a vulgar prejudice . . . but still it is mortifying one."[45]

The intensity of the sectional feelings in Connecticut, at least among the state's Standing Order of Federalist politicians and clergy, was something that neither Hamilton nor many other outsiders seem to have reckoned with. Some in the future host state of the Hartford Convention of 1814, organized to consider disunion in opposition to the War of 1812, were already considering that ultimate option in 1796. Just as the electors were gathering to cast their votes, the state's most widely circulated and virulent newspaper, the Hartford *Connecticut Courant*, ran a pair of articles over the signature "Pelham" that unleashed the full measure of Connecticut Federalist fear and loathing. "Pelham" asked the rhetorical question whether the "the moral and political sentiments and habits of the citizens of the southern states" did not conflict so badly with those of their northern brethren that the United States had "already approached near to the era, WHEN THEY MUST BE DIVIDED." No one in the North "whose heart is not thoroughly Democratic" could possibly disagree. "Reason yielded to fear" when the constitutional union was created, and the North would never get anything from the relationship except "contention, discord, jealousy, and animosity." "Pelham" attacked the moral evil of slavery, "the extreme wickedness of holding our fellow men in chains, merely to serve our own interested plans," but also evinced palpable disgust for *both* the enslaved people who "blackened" the land they lived on and the whites who claimed to own them. The "Pelham" articles deployed the livestock analogy mentioned above, but coarsened the insult with the comment that southern whites would probably eat their slaves if they tasted as good as cattle.[46]

What seemed to raise "Pelham's" ire most of all—and this was typical, if not always as harshly expressed, throughout New England Federalism—was the effrontery and hypocrisy of slaveholders spouting "reverential ideas of liberty and equality" while upbraiding northerners for their lack of fealty to republicanism. In truth, there had been relatively few blanket sectional indictments of this kind, but "Pelham" chose to resent the charges of monarchism against John Adams as attacks on the "northern states" as a whole, depicting the region where the American Revolution started as "filled with people, not merely in love with Aristocracy, but panting for Monarchy." Presaging sectional rhetoric that would be much more common during the Civil War era, "Pelham" thundered back with an image of a northern people who had cornered the market on the capitalist work ethic, Protestant morality, and the ability to live quietly and harmoniously under republican government:

> The character of the people of the northern states, is that of a sober, industrious, punctual, peaceable, and pious people. The great body of our citizens are temperate, free from dissipation, debauchery, gaming, drinking, &c, they mind their own peculiar business, till their farms, work at their trades, *pay their debts*, and taxes, submit to the governance of the laws, without murmuring, or repining, and pay a serious and devout attention to the duties of religion. Need it be asked, if there is not a total contrast in every particular in the southern states?

Not in Connecticut, apparently.[47]

Interestingly, "Pelham" set the dividing line between the good and evil halves of the nation at the Potomac River, not the Mason-Dixon line, leaving the Federalist-leaning slave states of Maryland, Delaware, and New Jersey on the side of light and thrift. In the "North," "Pelham" was content to see abolition sentiment "steadily gaining ground." The crux was politics. To New England Federalists like "Pelham," democracy was a symptom of the same deep-dyed sinfulness that allowed southerners to fight, drink, gamble, shirk debts, and avoid work, as well as hold slaves; in their self-indulgence, they coveted the labor and property of others. Lovers of social and political order who held slaves had at least not given themselves over to total depravity and might yet be redeemed.

(Another way to put it is that good Federalists got a temporary pass.) As for "the Democrats," they should keep silent or go away, because "the machinations of Pandemonium are outstripped in the career of guilt, by the plots of our Democratic fellow citizens." With no respect for order themselves, they would never be able to keep "a system so inhuman and discordant, so violent and bloody, as that of Slavery" in check for very long. New England did not need to be around when the South descended into a Haitian-style servile revolution.[48]

The "Pelham" essays do not seem to have been widely reprinted even in the Federalist press, but they give some sense of the antipathies squirming beneath or just above the surface of the New England mind in 1796, seemingly stirred up by the wounding of the Adams candidacy. Pennsylvania had concentrated the minds and stiffened the spines of New England's Federalist leadership just in time for the December Electoral College meetings. Earlier there had been at least some suggestion that John Adams might lose a vote here or there. At least two obvious Democratic-Republicans had been elected to Congress in recent times, Joseph Varnum in Massachusetts and, more alarmingly, the obstreperous Irishman Matthew Lyon. One of Ethan Allen's old Green Mountain Boys and an enthusiast of the local Democratic Society, Lyon had been a thorn in the side of Vermont's elites for years, raising his son to be a printer and setting him up with a newspaper to further his own causes. In late 1796, Lyon finally succeeded in a four-year crusade to reach Congress, and a Federalist newspaper in nearby New Hampshire wailed to the heavens over the result: "*Cannot* some *good thing* come out of that *Nazareth* of *antifederalism*," western Vermont? In Connecticut, Federalists eyed the slate of electors that Vermont had chosen with suspicion. Among them were Oliver Gallup, reputed to be a "vociferous anti-treaty tavern keeper," and Elisha Sheldon, "a compound of folly and knavery" from the Democratic-leaning area in the far northwest of the state. At the end of the day, however, Vermont proved as ready to close ranks against outsiders as the rest of rural New England.[49]

The prospect of their region being next in line for the presidency and then having it stolen from them spurred the Yankees to rally behind John Adams. A notice in the Boston *Columbian Centinel* assured the "friends of our country" that they "need not be alarmed" at the various efforts "to wound the interest of *America* by injuring the illustrious JOHN ADAMS—Like the immortal WASHINGTON, his fame will rise in spite of ignorance or envy, and his labours will bless his country." To lose the presidency for Adams now, to *any* other candidate, wrote Governor Oliver Wolcott of Connecticut, "would be a partial triumph of the French and their traitorous American partisans."[50]

Pennsylvania focused the New England mind not just on the dangers from Jefferson and the French, but also on the threat from some of their own political brethren. While John Adams had his detractors even at home, Alexander Hamilton and Rufus King's Pinckney plot began to seem like an unacceptable risk. Personally and through intermediaries like Oliver Wolcott Jr. and Theodore Sedgwick, Hamilton was pressuring northern Federalists to vote equally for Adams and his putative understudy Thomas Pinckney, gambling that by picking up a few extra southern votes in Jefferson states, Pinckney might "accidentally" finish ahead of Jefferson and Adams. Though Massachusetts influentials such as Sedgwick and King were secret supporters of the Pinckney plot, most of the region's electors seem to have innocently accepted the Hamilton line that equal Pinckney votes were needed to block out Thomas Jefferson from finishing second. At the same time, rumors of the truth were spreading through the Democratic-Republican press and more conventional means. A certain little senator whispered into the ear of his uncle in Connecticut that everything might not be as it seemed: "If the Eastern States should be unanimous for Pinkney [*sic*]," Aaron Burr warned Pierpont Edwards, a Republican, but one with numerous social and political contacts throughout New England's Federalist elite: "he will undoubtedly have more votes than Adams & be Pres[iden]t. . . . Can your people intend this—would they be satisfied with the result?"[51]

The answer for many New England electors seemed to be no. They got cold feet about the idea of strategic voting without knowing anything about Hamilton's true intentions. Confusion and uncertainty reigned regarding the ramifications of the lack of priority in the voting (i.e., the fact that two votes would be cast rather than one vote each for president and vice president), and the whole process was the subject of "general anxiety," reported the *Vermont Gazette*. It began to dawn that with Pennsylvania in the enemy's bag, any votes that took away from Adams's total would in effect be votes for Jefferson. Since Pinckney had southern support and Adams (apparently) did not, a match in their New England vote totals might leave Adams and New England out of the top two and out of the elected executive branch. Trying to vote equally for both Federalist candidates "on very conjectural grounds" would put New England and Adams at a "very considerable risk" that many were not willing to run, concluded Governor Wolcott. The logic of a two-party system was taking hold whether the participants wanted it to or not. "Party discipline" might seem to have dictated an Adams and Pinckney vote, as claimed by a classic study of the 1796 election, but in fact New Englanders were responding better than Hamilton to the exigencies of a two-sided partisan battle they were unwilling to see lost because of a factional plot to game a rough new system.[52]

At any rate, key local figures in New England Federalism simply refused to allow their region to let John Adams down. The bedrock of the Yankee rally in defense of John Adams was Connecticut, where the tightly knit political class had extensive inside knowledge courtesy of Treasury Secretary Oliver Wolcott Jr., son of the incumbent governor and Alexander Hamilton's former deputy. Oliver Jr. was a devoted Hamiltonian but clearly suffered in late 1796 from the strain of doubt and divided loyalties. His letters to the folks back home tried to sell them on Hamilton's plan while conveying lots of information that did anything but. The treasury secretary admitted just how "painful" and damaging a last-minute Adams loss would be for the region's prestige, especially if it came about because New Englanders had failed to fully support their favorite son—"it would betray levity and ingratitude." As Oliver Jr. did the math, if all of the New England votes were cast for both the top two Federalist candidates, Adams would be president and Pinckney would be his vice president, no funny business. If the New Englanders dropped too many Pinckney votes, then Jefferson was liable to come in second, landing in the spot where, Wolcott argued, he would be most dangerous. As president, Jefferson would have to act carefully and responsibly, while as vice president, his name would gain prominence without the burdens and restraints of command. Jefferson would become "a rallying point for faction," while the job itself would leave him nothing to do but "divide, undermine, and finally subvert the rival administration." This was not a bad prediction of Jefferson's eventual role as vice president, but it was also faintly ludicrous to pretend that understudy was the most crucial position to worry about. It hardly built confidence with genuine Adams supporters that Hamilton and his proxies were so solicitous about his running mate and so eager to put Adams at risk.[53]

In December, when Oliver's father and the other Connecticut electors actually gathered in Hartford to vote, they found they simply could not bring themselves to follow Hamilton's plan. Governor Wolcott went into the meeting intending to support Adams and Pinckney, although with a "strong repugnance" toward accidentally making a southerner like Pinckney president. "Such was the delirium of the times," the intense partisanship of this first contested presidential election, that he was even willing to take such a chance. Wolcott was sobered up by a discussion with his fellow electors. Connecticut 1796 offers a rare recorded case of an actual discussion at an Electoral College meeting; politics in the state were so lopsidedly Federalist and uncompetitive that the electors felt as free from democratic pressures as any of the Framers might have wished. The electors seemed to have convened as part of a more general convocation of the state's political elite, with Supreme Court Chief Justice Oliver Ellsworth (back from Philadelphia) sitting in. The only pull they felt was between the national Federalist leadership and the intense parochialism of their own state and especially of its small, tight-knit ruling class of Yale College graduates. Ellsworth convinced the others that securing John Adams as president had to be Connecticut's main goal; the group decided to hold off the vote until after the mail arrived that evening, hoping for new information that might relieve their minds about the possibility of Pinckney tying or passing Adams.[54]

None came, so they took it upon themselves to take Pinckney and the "anti-federalism of South Carolina" down a few notches, or five exactly, the number of electoral votes they decided to confer on noncontender John Jay. Besides underlining their intransigent support of everything that Democratic hearts complained about, this guaranteed Adams a five-vote lead over Pinckney, at least where their state was concerned. Rhode Island and New Hampshire ignored Pinckney as well, each giving all of their second votes to none other than Chief Justice Ellsworth, just as the man himself was lowering the boom on Pinckney in Connecticut. That put Pinckney fifteen votes behind Adams in New England. Oliver Wolcott Sr. explained the abandonment of Pinckney in terms of regional antipathy, but it would be wrong to read the failure of the Federalist ticket as wholly a failure of partisanship. New Englanders were also rejecting Hamilton's triangulating backroom ploy. Pinckney was an unknown in partisan terms whose principles could only be guessed at from his South Carolina origin and his close personal connection to some of the country's most outspoken defenders of slavery and particular southern interests. Certain commitment to Federalist principles would have been greatly preferable.[55]

Perhaps surprisingly—or perhaps not, given the candidate's stubborn independence and overbearing personality—the Federalists of John Adams's home state were the New England leaders who seemed least concerned about protecting their region's favorite son. Adams's relations with the Brahmin elites had rarely been comfortable, and the Boston merchant princes George Cabot and Stephen Higginson were either willing to throw Adams under the carriage or unwilling to risk their necks to save him. They seem to have been stopped short only by fear of the personal unpleasantness sure to result if they crossed Adams, whose "egotism" and bad temper would cause him "to break with every one who preferred the public to him." Abigail Adams was disgusted with the Bostonians' insincerity: they "pretend to be very Angry" with the designs for Pinckney, but "Massachusetts . . . seems to have been a dupe."[56]

Fortunately for Adams, Massachusetts had popular voting for presidential electors and happened to be one place where John Adams enjoyed a strong core of grassroots supporters and some popularity with ordinary voters. Fueled by a contract to print for the federal government in New England, Major Ben Russell of the Boston *Columbian Centinel* had done more to seriously promote the Adams candidacy than anyone, and during the 1796 campaign Russell showed himself to be one of the few Federalist editors who understood the power of parties and other democratic organizational tactics. The *Columbian Centinel* cheerled incessantly for "consistent federalism," and celebrated whatever Russell considered good for the Federalists. The writings of then thuggishly right-wing pamphleteer William Cobbett might "partake too much of the gall of bitterness," a *Centinel* item remarked, but they had "done much service to the cause of federalism, good order, and tranquility," so therefore would be featured in its pages. On a more practical level, the *Centinel* carried election-time notices trying to whip up voter enthusiasm and turnout that would not have been out of place in the heyday of American party politics half a century later: "A kind Providence has appeared to intervene, and Federal men have always been elected to Federal offices. But our exertions ought not to slacken; we must endeavor to 'conquer again, and again.' Let us unite, and by the 'LONG PULL, the STRONG PULL, and the PULL ALL TOGETHER,' continue to our country the blessings she enjoys."[57]

As the Massachusetts electors gathered, Russell ran a letter signed "A True American" decrying the Pinckney plot and calling for the selection of Adams because he was the people's choice, at least of the people of New England. It seemed that the one issue the *Aurora* and

Columbian Centinel.

Printed and published on Wednesdays and Saturdays, by BENJAMIN RUSSELL, PRINTER to the UNITED STATES, for the NORTHERN STATES—State-Street, BOSTON, (Massachusetts.)

Whole No. 2118,—No. 18, of VOL. XXVI.]   SATURDAY, NOVEMBER 5, 1796.   [Price THREE DOLLARS, per Annum

Rallying the Federalist Base: John Adam's most loyal and effective supporter was Major Benjamin Russell, Massachusetts state printer and editor of Boston's leading Federalist newspaper, the Columbian Centinel. *Russell criticized democracy, but knew how to use democratic tactics like getting out the vote. (Boston* Columbian Centinel, *5 November 1796, nameplate and clipping.)*

the *Columbian Centinel* could agree on was the role they envisioned for the Electoral College and independent elite judgment in selecting presidents, and that role was none.

> It will become the electors to consider that the voice of the people at large ought to be their guide. If we mean to make our constitution respectable in the eyes of Europeans, if we mean to prove that a republican government signifies the expression of the public voice, we must make it appear that the public voice designates the man who is to fill the first office in our government. If this is not the case, we had better at once trust all to the benevolence of Providence, for ours will become a government of chance, and of the worst kind of chance. Not only our national dignity, but all of our essential interests depend upon our respective offices being filled by the men contemplated by the people; and if ever this great principle is done away, the loss of our liberty must soon follow.

Democracy had to be the rule in presidential voting, despite the terrible things the *Centinel* printed about the "bloody Democrats." (These included in one item from late 1795 declaring the American Democrat "the vilest of human beings—far worse than a felon or a murderer.")[58]

The *Centinel* was specifically addressing a last-minute Hamilton gambit to spook a few more electoral votes to Pinckney. Hamilton had spread word of a rumor picked up from Vermont senator Isaac Tichenor that his state's elector election might not be valid because of the lack of a specific statute authorizing it. The idea seems to have been to frighten New England electors into sticking closely to the whole Federalist ticket so as to avoid Jefferson's sneaking in, thereby boosting Pinckney's total in the process. Some less duplicitous Vermont Federalist shot down this rumor in a note to the *Centinel*, and the "True American" called the Hamiltonians' bluff: "Shall a momentary pusillanimity in MR. ADAMS's friends put MR. PINCKNEY in the presidential chair? . . . No, MR. RUSSELL, firmness is expected in the electors, and from their characters we may fairly presume they will not disappoint the public." In the end, at least three electors protected John Adams, one by casting a vote for Oliver Ellsworth and two for Governor Samuel Johnston of North Carolina, a choice that provided a way of not insulting the South as Connecticut was so eager to do. One of the protective electors was John Adams's close friend Elbridge Gerry, who claimed it was an accident: he had not been told about the Pinckney plot until receiving a letter from Aaron Burr after the voting. Hamilton's plans explained quite a bit about how strangely some of the Federalist electors were acting, Gerry told the seething Adamses later.[59]

The other presidential game afoot in New England during the fall of 1796 was the mysterious campaign of Aaron Burr. Burr was there "electioneering" for some six weeks in September and October, working his many relatives and other connections around the region. His aims were unclear, and his success apparently very limited. John Beckley was certain that Burr was mostly out for himself rather than the Republican ticket, but what is certain is that neither Jefferson nor Burr got a single New England electoral vote. The whole exercise was so puzzling and suspicious that it led Beckley to strongly suggest that Virginia electors might want to give their second votes to someone else, in case Burr was cooking up some kind of self-interested surprise.[60]

They need not have worried. The one accession to his cause that Burr seemed to make on his New England sojourn was a short-lived Boston newspaper, the *Polar Star*. Boston's first attempted daily, the journal's principals were refugee Irish revolutionist and playwright John Daly Burk as editor and Alexander Martin as printer. Burk and Martin both had lively careers in the opposition press ahead of them, but they tried to keep the *Polar Star* on a high, largely nonpartisan plain, emphasizing thoughtful coverage of theater, literature, and foreign news. It was very striking when, at around the time of Burr's trip and with the publishers running short of money, the *Polar Star* suddenly dropped Aaron Burr's name for president out of nowhere: "If a strong mind and extensive erudition, a long and intimate acquaintance with the history, the views, the interest and policy of nations be considered as qualifications, he appears to us . . . qualified to fill any office in a republican government." Bostonians were not buying it, but Burk would follow Burr back to New York, edit a partisan newspaper there, and end up as one of the Sedition Act's first victims for his trouble.[61]

After the failure of the relatively public politics of his New England trip, Burr seems to have begun pursuing other arrangements through back channels. His close friend Jonathan Dayton of New Jersey, speaker of the House of Representatives and a heavy influence on his state's electoral vote, wrote north suggesting Burr as the understudy or replacement for *Adams*, not Pinckney. (See table 2 at the end of chapter 8 for a listing of the various vice-presidential scenarios and how they turned out.) Dayton (and doubtless Burr) believed the New Yorker would sweep the second votes in the South and West and Pennsylvania as part of Jefferson's ticket; then, if Dayton threw him New Jersey's vote, only a little New England support would make Burr president, and one New England Federalists knew better and could work with much more easily than any of the other candidates. Dayton's Massachusetts contact Theodore Sedgwick did not disagree about Burr's appropriateness for the role of turncoat. The Republicans had "not the smallest confidence in his hearty union to their cause. . . . They know, in short, he is not one of them." But Sedgwick advised Dayton that it was safer to stick with party loyalty and national unity and "not deviate from the course which the federalism of the country is pursuing." That included choosing a second candidate from the South, particularly South Carolina; to do otherwise would betray an intersectional, intraparty trust that would sow "incurable jealousy and hatred" between leaders who needed to stick together if they were going to keep the union intact and out of Jacobin hands. Just to make sure of this, Sedgwick turned the Dayton letters over to Hamilton himself. The whole complicated morass points us to the severe drawbacks of both undifferentiated votes and the indirect electoral system, as it did for many of the participants. The situation was a virtual invitation to the sort of "cabals" the Framers of the Constitution had been so worried about.[62]

Virginia Republicans were way ahead of Burr and Dayton in any case. They gave most of their second electoral votes to their favorite New

Englander, Sam Adams, punching Burr's ticket to fourth place and a temporary exit from public office. Burr and his Little Band regarded this as a gross betrayal and used it as motivation for a much more public and intense vice-presidential campaign in 1800, which resulted in an Electoral College tie and gave Federalists one more opportunity to try to make Burr president.[63]

In 1796, New England formed a solid base for Adams and got him slightly more than halfway to the total needed to win the election. New York and New Jersey stuck to Hamilton's script and gave equal votes to Adams and Pinckney, pushing the vice president all the way up to fifty-eight electoral votes, which were drawn only from the banks of the Hudson east. But a few more votes would have to come from somewhere—the constitutional requirement to get a majority of the electoral vote meant that any coalition had to be a somewhat national one. Connecticut's animus notwithstanding, New England's candidate would have to get some votes from slave states besides New Jersey.

SLAVEHOLDERS FOR ADAMS (AND JEFFERSON)

All the Federalist scenarios for victory actually hinged on the South, and especially South Carolina. William Loughton Smith had hoped all along to bring in his state against Jefferson and sincerely supported Adams. Hamilton's original scheme was built on the premise that Federalist electors could drop a few John Adams votes without looking faithless to their constituents and then let the likely wider support for Thomas Pinckney in the South edge him over the top. That would keep Adams safely in second place and Jefferson out of the money. Pennsylvania and New England changed the dynamic completely. With a month to go before South Carolina would even choose its electors, it looked increasingly like Jefferson would be one of the top vote-getters, and the Federalist ticket lay in tatters.

The surprising lower backbone of John Adams's strength turned out to be in the plantation counties of the two northernmost southern states, Delaware and Maryland, both of which chose their electors a week after Pennsylvania. In both states, rather stagnant countrysides faced off politically against rapidly growing, vibrant, and diverse port towns (Wilmington and Baltimore) with plenty of sailors, immigrants, artisans, and nascent manufacturing industries. State governments dominated by rural Federalist magnates were challenged by urban

Democratic-Republicans. Since the Revolution, Baltimore had grown up almost overnight as a flour-milling center fed by the wheat belt that then stretched down from Pennsylvania. In the 1790s, it was the fastest-growing city in the nation, the third largest by the end of the decade, even though it had yet to acquire a proper city government. Especially south and east of Baltimore, along the Potomac and the Eastern Shore of the Chesapeake Bay, rural Maryland and Delaware were character-ized by a mature colonial economy, with slave-owning planters growing tobacco and wheat for export overseas. Wealthy and suspicious of politi-cal and social change but not wedded to the financial interests behind Hamiltonian economics, these "tidewater agrarians" formed the south-ern base of pro-Adams Federalism, as political scientist Manning Dauer showed in his pioneering but largely forgotten work. (Leven Powell and Charles Simms in adjacent northern Virginia were ideological cousins, though those two were considerably more commercial and less "agrar-ian" in their outlook.)[64]

The transitional and divided nature of these Chesapeake states (be-tween north and south, rural and urban) provided an ideal political bat-tleground, especially in Maryland. The state's long, narrow geography, stretching from the central Appalachians all the way to the ocean with the Chesapeake Bay cutting down the middle, added the element of east and west. Hardscrabble mountaineers had to inhabit the same politi-cal space as prosperous family farmers, city-dwelling strivers, and blue-blooded planters. With its Catholic heritage, Maryland also had greater religious diversity, or least wider, than almost any other state. No one could be sure of an election's outcome, and the result was that strenuous campaigning and high interest in elections had become habits by 1796. Historians have singled out Maryland, especially among the slave states, for the precocity of its political development, including stable patterns of two-party voting and high voter participation. Studies of Maryland have shown that as early as 1790, more than 50 percent of eligible voters (free adult white males) were participating in most elections in most locali-ties, a far higher figure than almost anywhere else in the country and impressive even today.[65]

The high turnouts fed and were fed by a competitive political culture shaped by the close elections and the mix of contrasting regional styles. In Maryland, an urban associational style like Philadelphia's combined with the flamboyant competitive rituals of southern politics: stump speeches, bonfires, "treating" the voters with food and drink, and, last but not least, betting on election outcomes as though they were horse races. Debating a contested Virginia election in which the supporters of one candidate had skirmished with the federal troops brought by another, Baltimore congressman Samuel Smith warned the New England members of the House not to be squeamish: "They ought to be informed that a Southern election [a category in which he seemed to include the elections of his own state] is quite a different sort of transaction from one of theirs."[66]

Especially in the post-independence years, Smith's city and state (much more than Virginia) was the kind of place where a man could "make a trade of electioneering" if he was tough and aggressive enough. Maryland's leading conservative jurist, Samuel Chase, had made his political bones as a revolutionary mob leader, "a foul-mouthed and inflaming son of discord" who kept up his rabble-rousing right through the time of constitutional ratification. Chase's career as an elected official had come to an end after he sent a crew of drunken sailors to the polls, with a flag and a model boat, causing a minor riot when they confronted the *other* candidate's drunken sailors. Chase was then immediately appointed chief judge of the criminal court, an only-in-Baltimore turn of events. In Maryland and Delaware, the southern penchant for boisterous competition combined with a northern frankness and zest for association made for a political culture that participants actually enjoyed. There were fewer mute tribunes and ritual apologies than were customary across the Potomac in Virginia. William Vans Murray, a Federalist congressman from Cambridge, Maryland, admitted to finding political debate a "mental enjoyment of a masculine & energetic Kind." In the summer of 1796, having given up his seat in Congress and returned to his country law practice, Murray eagerly looked forward to relieving his rural boredom with a good campaign.[67]

Delaware played out in microcosm the Philadelphia story we have been following off and on throughout this book, from the Democratic-Republican Societies to the presidential challenge. The "Patriotic Society of Newcastle County" had formed in 1794 with the conviction that it was for republican citizens, whether individually or associated, "both OUR RIGHT AND OUR DUTY . . . TO REGARD with attention, and DISCUSS with freedom, the conduct of the Public Servants." In 1795, fiery meetings denounced the Jay Treaty, including one in Wilmington led by venerable patriot John Dickinson, *Delaware Gazette* editor and public education advocate Robert Coram, and Caesar A. Rodney, who would

Adams's Man in Maryland: William Vans Murray was a former diplomatic protégé of John Adams who became a Federalist congressman and helped Adams win some crucial slave state electoral votes. (Portrait by Mather Brown, 1787, National Gallery of Art.)

go on to be attorney general under President Jefferson. In 1796, Rodney won election to the state legislature, and he and his allies tried to push through a bill providing for elector selection by popular vote. The "high powers and important trusts" granted to the president by the Constitution, they argued, made it imperative to connect the office as closely with the people as possible, making presidential selection "dependent on them alone." Despite these efforts, the Democratic-Republicans of

Wilmington's New Castle County in the north of Delaware found them-selves overwhelmed by the two rural Federalist counties to the south. This was partly thanks to artificial advantages that the more thinly popu-lated countryside enjoyed in the structure of the legislature: represen-tation was apportioned equally among the three counties even though Wilmington's was growing far more rapidly than the other two. The leg-islature voted to appoint presidential electors and immediately picked three Federalists, who gave their votes to Adams and Pinckney despite Jefferson's support in the towns. Delaware was a case where legislative selection of electors was a patently oligarchic institution.[68]

The situation in Maryland was more complicated. In certain respects and on many occasions, the local Republicans could be a match for those in any state, including the keystone of the opposition party in Pennsylva-nia. Taking his campaign cues from Philadelphia, pro-Jefferson elector candidate Gabriel Duvall, another former congressman, rode the coun-tryside around Annapolis with a copy of Adams's *Defence of the American Constitutions*, orally "misinterpreting it to the people," especially to peo-ple who could not or would not read it (or so one Federalist complained). One of the most economical and effective pro-Jefferson texts produced anywhere in 1796 came out of the Eastern Shore town of Easton. This was a catechism that succinctly taught the gospel of Thomas Jefferson as it would be passed down for generations, starting with the sacred text that up until this time had been only sporadically presented as a na-tional mission statement and had not even been widely credited to Jef-ferson. "Who drew the declaration of independence, that great charter of our infranchisement [sic]? *Ans.* Thomas Jefferson." The text went on to provide quick answers to the most prevalent Federal attacks and tried to secure Jefferson's place in the founding pantheon by claiming that he had been George Washington's first "prime Minister." (Note the slight dig at Washington's kingly stance.) It ended by lumping the major Fed-eralists together, asking, who "planned the form of government" Hamil-ton advocated, with "a King, Lords, and Commons? *Ans.* John Adams."[69]

On the other hand, the Maryland Republicans could be somewhat primal in their organizational methods and resistant to national agenda-setting, at least in 1796. Baltimore was so overwhelmingly Republican that the various opposition sympathizers could fight among themselves over local issues without concern about a national contest. The town had an array of sympathetic associations, including the Mechanical Society and the Republican Society, but it lacked a strong central rallying point like the Philadelphia *Aurora* and the more sophisticated partisan leadership that the veterans of the old Democratic Society of Pennsylvania provided. The town's two major newspapers, the *Maryland Journal* and the *Federal Gazette*, were flush with ship advertisements and printed both Federalist and Republican material, when they had space for any politics at all. (Newspapers were invariably four pages long in this period—one large folded over sheet.) William Loughton Smith's "Phocion" series was declared "entirely too lengthy" for the *Federal Gazette*, and everyone else was asked to keep their ebullitions to half a column. On the opposition side, the message was sometimes confused, cutting against political lines that were fairly well established. A pro-Jefferson writer signing himself "Safety" violated the usual pattern and pitched *his* candidate as the logical successor to Washington, who would see that "things . . . proceed on smoothly and quietly in their present channels without risquing a departure from the system that has been adopted." John Adams, "Safety" spun, opposed Washington (based on his criticism of the general back during the Revolutionary War) and was being intentionally confused with Samuel Adams, the "staunch Anti-British republican."[70]

In terms of leadership, General Samuel Smith and his allies acted a bit more like gang leaders than party operatives, using Baltimore workers (especially sailors) to build personal power bases and fend off challenges. The Jay Treaty had riven Baltimore with marching groups of armed men, and a mob of workers had tarred and feathered a ship captain and sailor over a reversed (and thus disrespected) American flag. In 1796, Representatives Smith and Duvall had come under severe pressure from the merchant community over the treaty appropriations bill and caved, with Duvall resigning and Smith marshalling his nautical shock troops and the Baltimore Mechanical Society to beat back an effort to formally "instruct" him how to vote. Engineering a public memorial that denounced the merchants but expressed "ENTIRE CONFIDENCE" in him, Smith managed to go along with the treaty but still come out looking defiant. By the fall, Baltimore-area Republicans were so firmly in command there was hardly any need to build an organization that could carry the whole state. Smith ran for reelection unopposed, while Duvall announced his allegiance to Jefferson and won 70 percent of the vote. In the adjacent district, Jefferson man Dr. John Archer crushed John Eager Howard, a former governor and Revolutionary War hero who was about to be named to the U.S. Senate by the Federalist-controlled legislature.[71]

Yet thanks to Maryland's geographic divisions and districted electoral system, these locked-up Baltimore-area votes for Jefferson did not necessarily bode that ill for John Adams. Adams benefited from the fact that Maryland was one of the few states outside New England where he had real friends. Especially with the disaster unfolding just a state north, his press notices in the Free State were the most fulsome he received anywhere. "No man stands higher as a Moralist and a Christian," enthused a correspondent to the Baltimore *Federal Gazette*, "and he is known to be a decided, firm and tried patriot, from the 4th of July, 1776, to the present hour." Adams's biggest local fan was young congressman William Vans Murray, the lover of campaigning mentioned above. Murray had just returned home to Cambridge, Maryland, after deciding not to seek a third term. He had been an admirer of Adams since the 1780s, when he had been a law student in London and a frequent visitor to the American diplomat's house. Murray had earned Adams's "peculiar kindness" by treating him as a political guru, seeking out his guidance at a time when Adams felt even more abused and ignored than usual, and engaging in the kind of garrulous philosophical discussions he loved: "From 1785 I have been, as it were, his pupil, always indeed at the same time enjoying a great freedom of argumentation with him on hundreds of questions." Murray even published a pamphlet in London, *Political Sketches*, that he dedicated to John Adams. Thus a crucial swing elector district happened to have a very able politician on the scene who was also unquestionably one of John Adams's biggest fans.[72]

For obvious reasons, Adams's Federalist detractors had kept Murray out of the loop as to their plans, and he was puzzled to hear rumors from Annapolis that other candidates against Jefferson were even being considered: "I understood that Mr. A. was the man, if they divide the Friends of the Govt., the State of Virginia will again have a President." Bored in his rural seclusion, and concerned for his old mentor, Murray got busy speaking, organizing, and writing and urged others to do the same. At his local poll in Dorchester County, Murray exulted in the fact that Jefferson elector William Whitely got one vote to General John Eccleston's 582. He celebrated the performance as a model example of rational public opinion in action, sounding much like the *Aurora* in praising "an election so much of *principles*," and "party principles" even. There were "no riots—noise or seduction. The farmers came in without leaders to support government, they said, by voting for a Fedl. Man as Presdt."[73]

Whether the farmers also came in without drinks or snacks is another

EASTON, Nov. 8.

Attention.

Who drew the declaration of independence, that great charter of our infranchisement?

Anf. Thomas Jefferson.

Who was the first prime Minister under the federal government?

Anf. Thomas Jefferson.

Who appointed Thomas Jefferson to that office?

Anf. The patriot Washington.

Who advised the proclamation of neutrality?

Anf. Thomas Jefferson.

Who defended our government against the interference of Genet, on this attempt to draw us into the European war? ...

Anf. Thomas Jefferson.

Then must not. the " Federalists,' who charge Thomas Jefferson with being the leader of a faction against our goverment adopt that signature from being a subject of one of the despots of the confederacy at Pilnitz?

Anf. Undoubtedly.

Who are the proper judges of the propriety of Thomas Jefferson's resignation of the government of Virginia?

Anf. The legislature of Virginia, who unanimously applauded his conduct in a vote of thanks.

Will not the same miscreants who now abuse Thomas Jefferson for his resignation of the office of secretary, by and by abuse the President for quitting the government?

Anf. Yes, when it answers their purpose.

Who planned the form of government submitted to the convention by Alexander Hamilton, proposing a king, lords and commons?

Anf. John Adams.

REPUBLICAN·

Maryland Catechism: Pro-Jefferson newspaper item that borrowed its format from the Christian religion and promoted him as the author of the nation's founding document, a less well-known fact than it is today. ("Who Drew the Declaration of Independence?," reprinted from Hagerstown Washington Spy, *30 November 1796.)*

question. Rationality in Maryland politics either was not as universal as Murray supposed or existed in the eye of the beholder. The polls were open four days to allow time for travel and plenty of chicanery. "British electioneering bribery and corrupt influence never exceeded that lately in this place by both parties," a newspaper letter reported from Washington City, then still electorally part of Maryland. There were charges of illegal voting, which may have meant fraudulently helping voters meet the property qualification or bringing in ringers from the neighboring states. Jefferson carried Prince George's County in light voting, but the town of Georgetown and nearby Montgomery County went heavily for Adams elector Francis Deakins. In the first district on the Western Shore (south of Washington), Federalist John R. Plater won and wasted his second vote on Jefferson in order to reduce the Pinckney total. In mountainous western Maryland, an expected Jefferson win, Federalists surprised the opposition with their ruthlessness. The polls closed in Washington County when the approximate number of eligible voters was reached, but in smaller, Federalist-dominated Allegany, the sheriff kept the polling place open until nearly midnight on Saturday, just long enough for Adams elector John Lynn to get 204 additional votes, four over the number he needed to win the district. The local Jefferson supporters claimed that the Federalists had "brought over a crowd from Pennsylvania and Virginia," a plausible scenario in a region of thirsty hill people living where three states came close together.[74]

The best-documented campaign activity in Maryland was the sudden flurry of pro-Adams words from the pen of William Vans Murray. Embarrassed by the lukewarm support Adams received even from the *Aurora*'s direct opposite number, the *Gazette of the United States*, Murray took full advantage of the privileges of pseudonymous writing, appearing in more than one place at a time. He sent off pieces to the Georgetown and Baltimore papers while thoroughly monopolizing the pages of the Easton *Maryland Herald*, the only newspaper published anywhere between Chesapeake Bay and the ocean. Murray used several different pen names that emphasized the need for Federalists to stick together—"Union," "Union among Federalists," "A Federal American," and "Eastern Shore," among others—and put his long study of Adams to good use.[75]

Murray's most widely distributed effort was a "Short Vindication" of Adams's *Defence of the American Constitutions*; it was considered so superior to anything William Loughton Smith and other national Federalists had to offer that it was appended to the end of the later editions of Smith's *Pretensions of Thomas Jefferson*. Having read Adams's books so carefully and talked them over with the author, Murray was able to explain Adams's ideas with an ease, accuracy, and sympathy that eluded many of his peers. He was able to call out many of the quotations from older works that Adams had marked so poorly himself and to explain the context of the *Defence* clearly: "This was in 1786," when "the French Revolution was not even *thought* of" but the American state governments had almost all adopted "the division into *three branches* [as] the form," with the intent to set up checks and balances; "Mr. Adams wrote his work to vindicate the balanced constitutions of his beloved, and distant country, at a time when they were being attacked in Europe.—*These were Republican Governments*, in our genuine sense of the term" and "since then his work has stood the test of American good sense—the best test of practical politics now on earth." This was Murray's own cheerful spin on John Adams rather than the finger-wagging and dark truth-telling of the man himself, but it seems to have been effective in setting patriotic minds to rest, at least in rural Maryland where Murray's most extensive writings were being read.[76]

The charges of Jeffersonian cowardice brought by Leven Powell and Charles Simms of Virginia cut just as deeply in this adjacent southern state. To Maryland Federalists, Jefferson's failure to protect even the landlocked region where *he* lived spoke volumes about his deficiencies as a potential defender of their state's extensive exposed shores. A Jeffersonian future looked grim: "Could it be possible to conceive a more gloomy prospect than what the United States must exhibit" with someone like Jefferson "at its head"? Why, his "whole conduct may be a sacrifice of sentiment to pusillanimity." This was a fancy way of saying that Jefferson would not have the moral strength to withstand the pressures he would face as president. Here the Adet incident played into the Maryland Federalists' hands. Just days before word of Adet's letter had arrived, Maryland readers had been warned, possibly by Oliver Wolcott Jr., that poor, hapless Jefferson would be overwhelmed by the skullduggery afoot in the capital city:

> You that live at a distance can have no idea of the intrigues, both foreign and domestic, which perpetually surround the executive. . . . Factious men . . . become powerful and would invariably compel a timid president to adopt their politics. . . . Be assured that unless a pure

and manly spirit shall dwell in the breast of your first magistrate, this country will be ruled . . . by the most powerful faction at the seat of government, or what is infinitely more degrading, by the threats of a foreign minister.

Naturally, Maryland Federalists then jumped into the window Adet provided to prove the potential dangers of a Jeffersonian presidency. Murray warned that "a President of Experiments" would see the country "polandized." A writer professing to represent "a large group of Maryland farmers" pledged they would "appeal to our RIFLES" against French pressure if necessary.[77]

As in Massachusetts, also a popular vote state, a crucial element in the Federalists' electoral success in Maryland was their determination to practice democratic politics rather than arguing against it as some Federalists were prone to do. "No effort however ought to be omitted let what will come of it," William Vans Murray wrote. "No man ever Saved himself from drowning if instead of swimming he stopt stroke & trusted to the tide." The problem with Jefferson's alleged fainthearted-ness was that it might allow something or somebody to rule other than "the sentiments of [the] people at large." Murray also worked to get supporters of Washington's and Hamilton's policies in Maryland to identify specifically with the Federalist *party* and its nominee. "I appeal to federal men," Murray wrote, to see the misreading of Adams's work as an attack on "the federal party" ("lovers of the constitution" and "friends to the measures of our government") and "a continuation of that hostile spirit" that stretched back through all the previous controversies to the opponents of the Constitution. Not that lack of party identification seems to have been a problem among Maryland's Federalist politicians: Representative William Hindman prayed, "God send us a Federal Successor," after just barely surviving a reelection challenge. Maryland Federalists did not celebrate partisanship per se, but they did see it as an exceedingly necessary evil. It seemed to Murray that parties were better than the chaotic personal competition among notables that was the apparent alternative: "The language is, our choice is a party question, not a personal matter—this, for a Southern election, is a pleasing feature of the People's goodness."[78]

The final results were a disappointment to Murray. He lamented that after all his work, the state was going to end up divided "half and half— a punster would say quite drunk." Murray need not have worried so much. With the one suspicious western vote falling his way, Adams was able to get seven electoral votes out of Maryland, three ahead of Jefferson and Pinckney's four, opening the lead that would eventually stand up and win him the presidency. Adams himself realized a little glumly that he was "more indebted to the southern states for this Election than to Massachusetts," at least when it came to foiling the Pinckney plot.[79]

All but one of the Maryland votes for Adams came from the Eastern Shore and the then-rural area in and around present-day Washington, D.C., adjacent to Leven Powell's Federalist section of Virginia. In a pattern that held true in every slave state where John Adams received electoral votes, these were also the counties with the largest concentrations of slaves. Adams owed his margin of victory to a certain kind of established plantation district, and any reckoning of the impact of the Three-Fifths clause on the outcomes of his two presidential elections needs to take that fact into account. Northern Federalists commonly argued, and many historians have agreed, that Jefferson would never have been elected to any national office without the "extra" votes, but similar calculations are not usually applied to John Adams. Not that it is hard to see how historians could get confused. The feats of mental projection and displacement slave-state Federalists could sometimes perform when talking about slavery were truly remarkable. While cooperating in the meme that Jefferson the philosopher was dangerous to slavery, they rejected the southern label and tried to pin it on Democratic-Republicans, including a number of recent immigrant politicians and editors who had probably only traveled as far down south as South Philadelphia. William Vans Murray, living in an area considerably below Washington, D.C., where the land was worked by thousands of slaves, still inveighed against "the southern party," while congratulating himself on how unusually calm and thoughtful his local "southern election" had been.[80]

NATIONALISM, SECTIONALISM, AND THE PRESIDENTIAL ELECTION IN THE CAROLINAS

John Adams also got some surprise help from the next state south, North Carolina—it was only one electoral vote, but with a margin of three, every single vote counted heavily. As a slave state populated largely by small farmers, closely connected economically and politically to Virginia, the Tar Heel State was natural Jefferson territory where the voters proved highly resistant to Federalist appeals despite the ministrations of several Federalist politicians from the other Carolina. William Loughton Smith circulated his pamphlets across the border, to dubious effect. In Martinville, a public meeting had *The Pretensions of Thomas Jefferson* read out loud "for the information and consideration" of the assembled citizens, some of whom may not have been able to read all that well. The Martinville crowd declared the pamphlet "insidious, illiberal, and unmanly" and voted to have it burned. By a process of which we no longer have any records, eleven of the twelve North Carolina electoral districts chose Jefferson electors by popular vote, but without much recorded discussion that has survived. The only published advance elector commitment located was from John Hamilton of Edenton, who pledged himself to Jefferson to prevent "the introduction of foreign and *aristocratic* principles" by John Adams. In addition, there may have been a few alarming words from pamphlet-burning farmers said in favor of Jefferson or against Adams in person at the courthouse gatherings where voters had to appear to make their choices. Other North Carolina electors who considered themselves Federalists or strong Washington administration supporters seem to have kept their suffrages in the South, voting for Jefferson and scattering their second votes on other southerners, including Supreme Court Justice James Iredell, who hailed from North Carolina. One of these was former governor Richard Dobbs Spaight of Edenton, who voted for Jefferson even after having just lost a challenge to Republican congressman Nathan Bryan. North Carolina Federalists registered plenty of partisan consciousness and contempt for their opponents—"the family of the *Wrong-heads*," one of them called Jefferson's supporters—but in most of the state they were seemingly unable to do much about it in 1796.[81]

The gap in North Carolina's solid wall of Jeffersonianism was the piney, swampy southeastern area that includes the Cape Fear River valley and the towns of Wilmington and Fayetteville. This impoverished region had been heavily settled by Scots before the Revolution and became a hotbed of Loyalism and the seat of a bloody civil conflict during the Revolutionary War itself. Much of the adult male population had fought on the side of the British. Still dependent economically on the export of wood products to Britain (especially the naval stores that put the tar in Tar Heel), the Cape Fear Scots had had little reason to abandon their staunch loyalty to the crown and bitter hatred of the French and the local Patriots, many of whose leaders had gone on to become Republican politicians. At the same time, North Carolina had a surprisingly

Federalist-slanted press, led by Abraham Hodge's *North Carolina Journal* out of Fayetteville. State printer throughout the 1790s, Hodge published defenses of John Adams and increasingly dire information from Phila-delphia, sent perhaps by Justice Iredell, that included reports of mass arrests and open French bribery during the elections at Philadelphia: "Great God, if this is the fruit of French fraternity, deliver us from such a cause." Adet's intervention and the Quasi-War that followed it gave Cape Fear's old Tories a bridge to strident nationalism. The district's voters chose Adams supporter William Martin as their elector, and soon after the sailors at the port of Wilmington were brawling with the crew of a French privateer and discovering unknown depths of American pa-triotism. Like Leven Powell's northern Virginia, Cape Fear had delivered one-third of John Adams's three-vote margin.[82]

The presidential voting in the Carolinas saw Alexander Hamilton's Pinckney plot ramifying in ways he could not have expected or desired. In North Carolina, partisanship and misinformation trumped but also mixed with southern parochialism, as the word went out not to vote for Thomas Pinckney because his candidacy was "*a Lure* by the East-ern states, to draw off votes from Jefferson." This story may have been planted in South Carolina by William Loughton Smith, who was des-perately trying to fight off a counterplot that had developed in his home state and threatened to blow the entire election for the Federalists.[83]

As in New England, Hamilton's nationalist-minded scheming for Pinckney inadvertently opened the door to sectionalism. The ever-watchful oligarchs of South Carolina, including some of the very same people who had insisted on constitutional protection for slavery in the first place, saw a chance for the South to sweep the top offices entirely. The key figures were the members of the Rutledge family. "Dictator John" Rutledge Sr. had been an important player at the Philadelphia Convention, chairing the Committee of Detail that actually drafted the full Constitution. The Rutledges and their close allies and relatives, the Pinckneys, had accepted the Three-Fifths Compromise as a weaker al-ternative to various even less egalitarian, more proslavery schemes of representation that had been proposed earlier. John Rutledge Sr. had wanted representatives to be apportioned in at least one house of Con-gress according to wealth, measured by taxes paid, and Charles Pinckney advocated that the *full* slave population (not just three-fifths) be included in the basis of representation. The South Carolinians were seeking con-stitutional advantages for the South and slavery, of course, but their larger goal was the perfectly Federalist and conservative one that men of property should be given sufficient weight in the government to ward off attacks on their property. The South Carolina Low Country rice planters were among the wealthiest men in the United States in terms of their property values, in addition to facing a huge black majority they were desperate to control.[84]

With "Dictator John" increasingly incapacitated, the Rutledge family had a new head in 1796, John's brother Edward. Edward Rutledge had been muttering darkly about the danger of "Eastern interests" since the summer, complaining about the attempt to block Tennessee statehood, and seeing the Jay Treaty as an antisouthern measure. Charleston's own William Loughton Smith had been deeply involved in harassing Tennessee, but within the context of South Carolina's incestuous political elite, the Rutledges were part of a different, less Hamilton-friendly faction. Yet the Rutledges also stood second to none in their admiration for Thomas Pinckney, the crux of Hamilton's plot. Indeed, Edward Rutledge had been left in charge of Thomas and Charles Cotesworth Pinckney's affairs while they were out of the country, which entailed watching over both their financial and political interests. Edward Rutledge had clashed with John Adams in the Continental Congress, but always admired Thomas Jefferson; he conceived that South Carolina should give its votes to the all-slaveholder ticket of Jefferson and Thomas Pinckney. If other southern states went along, they might be able to put both southerners over the top, with no particular preference as to which one became president. South Carolina ended up with competing tickets of electors, one labeled "Jefferson's" and one labeled "Adams'," even though both contained supporters of the national administration and both favored Thomas Pinckney.[85]

South Carolina had a strange campaign even for its politically solipsistic self. With two members of its congressional delegation pouring their hearts out for Adams and a significant artisan community in Charleston that leaned toward Philadelphia-style Democratic-Republicanism—Philip Freneau's brother Peter was a printer in town who owned the *City Gazette*—the state had some of the elements in place for a "normal" party politics. Yet sectional consciousness and the weight of the oligarchy were just too strong. The real stakes poked through in some of the rather skittish byplay over slavery and southern loyalty that took place in the South Carolina press. As seen above, William Loughton Smith had tried to stir southern fears about Jefferson's nominally antislavery views, but "Z" in the *City Gazette* called his bluff. Jefferson was also an ardent defender of the Constitution, "Z" wrote, and "the constitution guarantees to us" the right to hold slaves. Real southerners knew that Jefferson was one of them, period. (Clearly not all southerners agreed, but such was "Z's" implication.) "I believe there is not a man of the country, who will value his black property less, because the President is a friend of equal rights."[86]

An interesting sidelight on the South Carolina approach to "equal rights" was that even though the state had essentially blackmailed the Federal Convention to keep the international slave trade open back in 1787, the South Carolina legislature had repeatedly voted to ban slave imports at the state level ever since then, renewing the ban right around the time when the 1796 presidential electors were picked. Closing slave imports kept domestic slave trade prices up for planters in the economically stagnant Low Country, where there was a superabundance of laborers and sharp fears of slave rebellion. Legislative votes on the import bans pitted the slave-selling Low Country against the still-developing and thus slave-buying areas to the west. This particular alignment of interests helps explain why Edward Rutledge was free to shrug off the slavery issue in 1796 and throw his support to Thomas Jefferson despite the Virginian's being understood as an antislavery candidate.[87]

Whatever the intentions behind it, Rutledge's backroom power play backfired, keeping his friend, relative, and legal client Pinckney out of the money while helping Jefferson slip into the second spot. The oligarchy worked almost too smoothly: Edward Rutledge and his nephew John, leaders in the state legislature, got themselves chosen as presidential electors. Aligning with opponents of the national administration for this occasion only, Edward drew 113 legislative votes at the top of what was labeled the Jefferson slate, and none of the Adams electors got more than thirty-seven. In December, when the Electoral College met, the Rutledges and their Jeffersonian allies split the state electoral vote evenly between Jefferson and Thomas Pinckney, eight apiece. If Rutledge had been able to spare any of the votes for John Adams, or even if he had thrown a couple of the Jefferson votes away, Pinckney might at least have come in second nationally. As William Loughton Smith predicted, Thomas Pinckney was headed for the "very mortifying" experience of having been held up as presidential material, drawn national support, and ended up with nothing, "owing entirely to the ridiculous and wicked conduct of his own State & particular friends." On this one occasion, anyway, South Carolina did not get away with its sectional shenanigans.[88]

ALL OVER BUT THE VOTING

The omniscient approach this chapter has taken to the voting process of 1796 may give a false impression of how the national election unfolded to any given individual participant. Even among the high political elite and the most concerned newspaper editors, information about the results was maddeningly sketchy and slow to come in, even after the Electoral College meetings the first week of December. There were sixteen of them, most taking place in distant interior towns, so it was late in the year before the results were known. Even though many electors had pledged themselves to Jefferson or Adams, much was left to guesswork, especially as regards the second votes. Hence, election-related debates raged on for weeks, throughout November and December, over both the reaction to Adet and a disputed set of legislative farewells to George Washington. Federal revenue commissioner Tench Coxe, a Philadelphian concerned about his future employment prospects after Jefferson's victory in his state, rushed into print with a belated reply to William Loughton Smith's "Phocion" essays from the point of view of "A Federalist." (John Adams would fire Coxe in 1797.) Federalist John Marshall of Richmond, Virginia, having failed to preserve his district for Adams as Leven Powell had up in the north of the state, concentrated on trying to push his state and others off of "the crooked path of Virginia. . . . To what has America fallen?"[89]

By mid-December, both sides had nearly despaired of winning. Based on the early reports that trickled in, the Pinckney plot seemed to be working. John Adams was depressed to realize just how many of his old revolutionary comrades had turned against him—his cousin Sam's and Pennsylvania Chief Justice Thomas McKean's apostasy bothered him especially—and rather agape to learn the sheer extent of Hamilton's scheming. "There is an active Spirit, in the Union, who will fill it with his Politicks wherever he is," Adams wrote his wife. "He must be attended to and not Suffered to do too much." The Adams family depended on John's official salary and he had not practiced law in decades, so the outlook looked a little bleak if Hamilton succeeded in doing him in. In light of his own political thought, it stung that maneuverings among the natural aristocracy had turned out so poorly so soon. One of the checks and balances was threatening to tip over his own career and push out the candidates with the best claims to national leadership: "The whole system is utterly repugnant to my Judgment and Wishes. I wish Patrick Henry had 138 Votes and would Accept them. Pinckney has no Pretensions to any of them." Even popularity or foreign influence seemed like better ways of choosing a president than "Chance and Trick."[90]

Things looked even worse for Jefferson. A week before Christmas, with the totals of the far southern and western states yet to be recorded but the surprisingly Federalist results from Virginia, Maryland, and North Carolina in, John Adams had sixty-one electoral votes, and Thomas Jefferson trailed even Thomas Pinckney. "After all our Exertions I fear Jefferson will fail altogether," John Beckley wailed. James Madison was less panicky but nevertheless not very optimistic about his friend winning the presidency. Jefferson's best possibility, having lost so much of the North and upper South, was a three-way split that would send the election to the House of Representatives, where a Republican majority and the new western states would likely break for him. Madison turned to softening Jefferson up for the possibility of accepting the vice presidency. "You *must* reconcile yourself to the secondary as well as primary station," Madison urged on December 10, adding in the following weeks that Vice President Jefferson might be a good influence on his old friend: "Your neighbourhood to Adams may have a valuable effect on his councils." Whoever he was, the new president would "have much in his power and it is important to make as many circumstances as possible conspire to lead him to a right use of it." Jefferson seemed to sincerely agree. He still liked Adams personally and considered him his senior in revolutionary services. There was some appeal in the idea of influencing Adams without having to be responsible for the challenges that were coming. At any rate, Jefferson had already composed a letter for Madison to show around deferring to Adams on grounds of seniority, even if there was a tie in the Electoral College. If the "public will" seemed to support the two of them equally, Jefferson was genuinely happy for Adams to be the one to inherit the spiraling crisis and possible war with France: "Let those come to the helm who think they can steer clear of the difficulties."[91]

As the year 1796 wound down, Adams's pessimism became increasingly ritualistic. Pinckney needed to do far better in the late-reporting far-off states of Georgia, Tennessee, and Kentucky than the "best information" suggested he had any chance of doing. In fact, when the votes came in, Jefferson would sweep the entire frontier except Vermont, and move into second place (see table 3). Pinckney's Treaty may have been popular, but Jefferson and the Democratic-Republicans were apparently more so. Indeed, the West and South stuck more closely to the Republican "ticket" than any other region, almost universally giving equal votes to Aaron Burr where several eastern Jefferson states threw some of their second votes away. Indeed, Burr was probably the biggest beneficiary of the voting on the frontier, where the little senator had earned credit for his martial ways and his stout defense of Tennessee statehood. He did well enough to maintain national relevance for the next presidential contest.

The one outlying state that failed Burr was Georgia, which gave its second votes to retired Governor George Clinton of New York. Little is known about the election in Georgia, but circumstantial evidence suggests that some of Burr's business dealings may have caused trouble in what should have been a natural state for him. Georgia picked electors by popular vote, and one of the electors was the "Colossus" of Georgia politics, James Jackson, who had recently resigned from Congress and returned home to clean up the mess created by the infamous Yazoo land frauds: the fraudulent sale of thirty-five million acres of western land that the entire Georgia legislature had been bribed to approve. Jackson had swept in and gotten a new legislature elected that promptly rescinded the sales. Before the rescission, the Yazoo land companies had resold much of the land to northern speculators, including a business associate of Burr's named James Greenleaf and a whole network of northeastern-ers (numerous Republicans among them) who lobbied and litigated to have the federal government confirm their purchases. Jackson certainly knew Burr and Greenleaf in Philadelphia, and there must have been little appeal in casting Georgia electoral votes for a prominent "Yazoo-ist." The votes for George Clinton do not have any ready explanation, but there was a schooner called the *Governor Clinton* anchored at Savannah in November 1796, so at least the man had name recognition.[92]

Finally, two days after Christmas, John Adams allowed himself to conclude that his total of seventy-one electoral votes was the "*Ne Plus ultra*" (see table 3) and started shopping for presidential carriages. Because of the lack of priority in voting and the mutual canceling-out of the various strategic voting plots, Thomas Jefferson as second-place finisher would get to inherit the clinging, binding mantle of "Daddy Vice" (the Adamses' pet name for John's office). Soon Adams was positively swaggering in his letters home, referring to himself in the third person: "John Adams must be an intrepid to encounter the open Assaults of France and the Secret Plotts of England, in concert with all his treacherous Friends and open Enemies in his own Country. Yet I assure you he never felt more Serene in his Life." He was, however, a little worried that Jefferson and Madison and the other "Southern Politicians" might still have something up their sleeves. Adams's decade was made when Republican congressman John Smilie of Pennsylvania, suddenly full of friendship, reported that Madison was whipping out Jefferson's concession letter all over town. The electoral votes were not formally counted until February 8, 1797, but by that time Adams was mostly worried about whether Congress was going to provide and furnish a house, which he was quite sure they would find a way to make tattier than whatever Jefferson had. "Prepare yourself for honourable Tryals," he wrote Abigail, and "very moderate Furniture."[93]

Table 3. The 1796 Electoral Vote

Name of Candidate	CT	DE	GA	KY	MD	MA	NH	NJ	NY	NC	PA	RI	SC	TN	VT	VA	Total
John Adams, of Massachusetts	9	3	—	—	7	16	6	7	12	1	1	4	—	—	4	1	71
Thomas Jefferson, of Virginia	—	—	4	4	4	—	—	—	—	11	14	—	8	3	—	20	68
Thomas Pinckney, of South Carolina	4	3	—	—	4	13	—	7	12	1	2	—	8	—	4	1	59
Aaron Burr, of New York	—	—	—	4	3	—	—	—	—	6	13	—	—	3	—	1	30
Samuel Adams, of Massachusetts	—	—	—	—	—	—	—	—	—	—	—	—	—	—	—	15	15
Oliver Ellsworth, of Connecticut	—	—	—	—	—	1	6	—	—	—	—	4	—	—	—	—	11
John Jay, of New York	5	—	—	—	—	—	—	—	—	—	—	—	—	—	—	—	5
George Clinton, of New York	—	—	4	—	—	—	—	—	—	—	—	—	—	—	—	3	7
Samuel Johnston, of North Carolina	—	—	—	—	—	2	—	—	—	—	—	—	—	—	—	—	2
James Iredell, of North Carolina	—	—	—	—	—	—	—	—	—	3	—	—	—	—	—	—	3
George Washington, of Virginia	—	—	—	—	—	—	—	—	—	1	—	—	—	—	—	1	2
Charles C. Pinckney, of South Carolina	—	—	—	—	—	—	—	—	—	1	—	—	—	—	—	—	1
John Henry, of Maryland	—	—	—	—	2	—	—	—	—	—	—	—	—	—	—	—	2
Total Electoral Vote	18	6	8	8	20	32	12	14	24	24	30	8	16	6	8	42	276

Source: National Archives, www.archives.gov/federal-register/electoral-college/votes/1789_1821.html#1796

EPILOGUE
KISS MY ASS AND GO TO HELL

The conclusion of every presidential election sets off a scramble to influence the new chief executive, but the 1796 transition was quite distinctive. Not only was it the first transition to a new president, it was also the only case where the two main rivals had essentially *both* won and now had to move in to office together. "Supplications" for employment rolled in as usual; but instead of Federalists seeking to guide the incoming administration, it was Adams's erstwhile Republican opponents who suddenly rallied to his side. Jefferson readied multiple direct and indirect letters of deference and praise, trying to make overtures about rekindling their old association that Adams would believe. "I can particularly have no feelings which would revolt at a secondary position to Mr. Adams. I am his junior in life, was his junior in Congress, his junior in the diplomatic line, his junior lately in our civil government," Jefferson wrote, taking an attitude he and Madison hoped the prickly Adams would be "soothed" by. Another old colleague from the Continental Congress, Dr. Benjamin Rush, turned up at Adams's Philadelphia lodgings on New Year's Eve, full of "so many Compliments, so many old Anecdotes" and assurances that the election "had given vast Satisfaction in this City and State." (This was news after the pro-French election mobs of just a few weeks earlier.) Rush leaned heavily Republican in the politics of the 1790s and was also a confidant of John Beckley and some of the other radical Philadelphia Democrats. House Republican leader William Branch Giles paid the president-elect the ultimate compliment of endorsing a key Adams tenet as well as his tenancy of the chief executive office: "The old Man will make a good President . . . we shall have to *check* him a little now and then. That will be all."[1]

Perhaps most shocking of all, the Adams name was suddenly no longer monarchical mud in the *Aurora* and other opposition newspapers. On December 21, Benjamin Franklin Bache printed an item averring that while it might be "singular" for his journal to endorse "a professed aristocrat" under most circumstances, Adams would at least be preferable to Washington. Appealing to Adams's sense of himself and his isolation from most other Federalists, the *Aurora* saluted the new president for having too much "integrity" to "sacrifice his country's interests at the shrine of party." While it was awkward for the *Aurora* to suddenly switch to celebrating nonpartisanship after years of careful party-building, Bache had always emphasized policy issues and active citizenship rather than promoting a particular organization. The paper reminded readers that Adams and Jefferson actually did have some views in common: Adams, too, had been "an enemy to the corruptions . . . of funding and bank systems." Another element of consistency in supporting Adams could be found in the simple act of submitting to an adverse election result. Bache and his friends had marched against the Whiskey Rebels to prove the viability of peaceful but aggressive public criticism of government, and supporting Adams now showed how seriously they took this principle. By February, the *Aurora* and other opposition journals were celebrating Jefferson and Adams as republicanism's dream team: "Upon the whole, America has a right to rejoice in the prospect she has of wise and virtuous administration under two such distinguished patriots."[2]

In many cases, the new Democratic-Republican fans of Adams made up for the switch by doubling down on their animus against his soon-to-be predecessor, George Washington. The *Aurora* item that launched the courting of Adams pitched the opposition's new love strictly in terms of a contrast with the odious Washington. The country could be assured that Adams at least "would not be a *puppet*," as the *Aurora* contended Washington was, "that having an opinion and judgment of his own, [Adams] would act from his own impulses rather than the impulses of others," like Alexander Hamilton. Adams was to also be preferred because despite his allegedly monarchical opinions, he lived "with the simplicity of a republican" rather than "the ostentation of an eastern bashaw" and "holds none of his fellow men in slavery." In short, "Adams is an Aristocrat only in *theory*," but Washington "is one in *practice*." This was only the beginning of an epically nasty *Aurora* send-off that included biting pamphlets by William Duane and a truly extreme one by Bache himself that indulged in out-and-out conspiracy theories about Washington working for the British during the Revolutionary War.[3]

To a less extreme degree, "better Adams than Washington" was the misguided theme that many of Adams's Democratic-Republican friends took up even when schmoozing him personally. Adams had once been known to cast a jaundiced eye on Washington himself, so Jefferson, Dr. Rush, and others seemed to go out of their way to take potshots at the outgoing president when communicating with their old friend. This phenomenon greatly pained Adams, who was getting more sentimental about his predecessor by the day now that the hoped-for succession was really taking place.[4]

The Federalist press was bitterly skeptical about the new departure, especially as regards Bache, but the charm offensive was a tactical move rather than a flip-flop, and one based on some reasonably genuine motives as such things go. The Republicans' greatest fear was war between the French and American republics. "An awful scene appears to be opening upon us," Madison wrote from Philadelphia as angry messages continued to fly back and forth across the Atlantic. "The only chance to escape lies in the President-Elect." At Madison's urging, Jefferson rushed to Philadelphia in late January, weeks before he needed to. He had not been more than seven miles from home since retiring as secretary of state, but there was no time to waste in trying to get Jefferson's gravitational field around the incoming president.[5]

There was of course a strong element of political calculation to all this. Jefferson, Madison, and their followers were well aware of Adams's independence and estrangement from Hamilton and much of the rest of the Federalist leadership. They hoped to split the Federalists enough to stymie Hamilton and his policies, if not necessarily grab power themselves. Adams was "perhaps the only sure barrier against Hamilton's getting in," and Jefferson was even willing to consider coming "to a good understanding with him as to his future elections," essentially trying to recruit Adams into the opposition party. As long as Adams "could be induced to administer the government on it's [*sic*] true principles and to relinquish his bias for the English constitution," all would be well.[6]

Over the short and long term, the Republicans' judgment of Adams was dead on. Mr. and Mrs. Adams both were looking forward to renewing close relations with their former intimate Jefferson, and Adams had privately resolved before the election was even settled that there would be no war with France on his watch. His suspicion of both British foreign policy and Hamiltonian economics was only intermittently apparent during his presidency, but by the end of Jefferson's, both John and John Quincy Adams were in the Democratic-Republican camp, writing for their newspapers and supporting Jefferson's 1807–1809 embargo on foreign trade despite their previous differences. In the medium term, however, the press of events—especially the misbehavior of the French and the domestic war measures that Federalists took in response, often with Adams's enthusiastic cooperation—would bring the partisan thaw to a swift end.[7]

What about the Federalists themselves, the winners of the recent election at the congressional as well as the presidential level? They were in the awkward position of not rushing to take control of anything. The operating assumption from the president-elect on down was that the Adams administration was a continuation of Washington's, so there were essentially no vacant positions to fill. British parliamentary practice was for all cabinet ministers to tender their resignations after a new election or a change of prime ministers, but only Treasury Secretary Oliver Wolcott Jr. made any gestures of that nature, and his offer was rejected. John Adams had already made public statements against the principle of "rotation in office," so wholesale removals would have been a contradiction for him in any case. In point of fact, Adams was in no position to suddenly staff an entire administration. He had no personal secretaries or close advisors outside his family, and he had never been a chief executive or manager of any organization. Abigail managed the family farm and finances. Upon election, his only option was to go meet with each of Washington's existing department heads and hope they would stay on; otherwise "it would turn the World upside down" and put Adams in a position he feared, that of daring to remove one of Washington's men. The danger inherent in this timid approach should have become apparent when Secretary of State Timothy Pickering showed almost no loyalty to Washington, denouncing the old boss's grammar to the new boss. Adams might have guessed how well so conceited a man would treat him. The awkward result was that Adams more or less willingly inherited a cabinet and an administration that looked to his most inveterate foe, Alexander Hamilton, for leadership. Trying to govern without party, as even Washington had not been doing toward the end of his term, Adams stunned his cabinet into silence at one of their first meetings by announcing his desire to send opposition congressional leader James Madison on a diplomatic mission to France. "After some time," the secretaries "broke out in 'Mr. President, we are willing to resign.'" The Madison proposal would have been a great, subtle stratagem for easing the old cabinet out, except that it was not a stratagem. Adams dropped the Madison idea, and kept on every one of the old secretaries.[8]

For those who had hoped that bitter fights for the presidency would never develop, the behavior of the president-elect and vice president–elect on the eve of their administration was a hopeful sign—perhaps the partisanship had only been a temporary pathology. A Washington Birthday banquet in Federalist-leaning Chester County, Pennsylvania, toasted "Adams and Jefferson" as a pair of national bachelor uncles taking over guardianship from the departed Father of the Country: "May they, when the head of the family of the United States, go hand in hand in cherishing, protecting and instructing it." On March 4, 1797, Jefferson took his oath of office in the Senate chamber two hours before Adams took his over in the House of Representatives. When the president-elect entered the crowded chamber filled with "the principal inhabitants" of the nation's largets city, "loud and reiterated applause involuntarily burst from the audience." Both men had soothing words for the other. Jefferson said that the presidency had been "justly confided to the eminent" Adams, "whose talents and integrity have been known and revered by me thro' a long course of years" and formed "the foundation of a cordial and uninterrupted friendship between us," which was only a partial untruth. Adams's lengthy speech was by far the most conciliatory statement the opposition had heard from the executive branch since Washington's reelection, and it even made positive noises about the French nation, which Adams claimed to hold high in his "personal esteem." Despite the applause and mutual admiration, Adams found the atmosphere of his inauguration more funereal than festive. Power was being handed over peacefully after serious contention, and the executive authority shared by the two leading contenders, but no one seemed as happy about it as they might. "Stilness and silence" greeted his speech, and the new president was left to conclude that the dominant emotion was grief, "whether from the Loss of their beloved President, or from the Accession of an unbeloved one."[9]

The issues and emotions stirred up during the election of 1796 and the preceding troubles were not so easily cast aside for those more involved in the everyday political battles than Adams and Jefferson. "It is really to be regretted that these ideas had not occurred to the 'Friend of the People' a few weeks sooner," Massachusetts Senator Theodore Sedgwick quipped. Jefferson "might then have spared the good man [Adams], whom he so highly reveres, much unmerited abuse, and his friends much painful anxiety." Sedgwick and many other Federalists thought Adams was being far too soft on the French and the "Jacobin" opposition. The moment the Congress elected in 1796 gathered, a newly Federalist majority would purge House clerk and Democratic-Republican activist John Beckley from his office and replace him with a loyal Federalist.

The small number of true Adams partisans in the Federalist press had an equally hard time accepting the thaw, especially the editor who had done more than anyone to save Adams's candidacy, Ben Russell of the Boston *Columbian Centinel*. Having expended so much energy and ink delineating the differences between the two contending parties and candidates, Russell could hardly see how two opposites could suddenly harmonize so well together. When one of his correspondents compared Jefferson versus Adams to a medieval dynastic squabble that had no real meaning to it and could be resolved with a marriage between the two families, Russell snarled in response: "The correspondent who so sanguinely expects the union of '*the roses red and white*,' by the election of Messrs. ADAMS and JEFFERSON, to the Executive chairs, will assuredly be disappointed. Fire and frost are not more opposite in their natures than those characters are; and the prosperity, honor, and dignity of the United States, depend on an administration *perfectly* federal. That those gentlemen differ essentially on the leading principles of government is certain."[10]

Though Adams and Jefferson would reunite again in the long run, Russell was not wrong in finding the friendly words of the Adams inauguration more than a little chimerical. Alongside the opposition's effort to bring out the softer side of John Adams regarding the French, the bitter feelings of the previous eight years still lingered, not least in the new president himself. The Adams administration began with a chip firmly ensconced on the chief executive's shoulder. He felt "so Strangely Used in this Country, so belied and undefended."[11] In the same inaugural breath that Adams warned of "the danger to our liberties if anything partial or extraneous should infect the purity of our free, fair, virtuous, and independent elections," he made clear his own distrust of the process that had elected him and the basic loyalty of many of his opponents. If elections had to be decided by such narrow margins as his, it could "be procured by a party through artifice or corruption," and the government would "be the choice of a party for its own ends, not of the nation for the national good." The new president had not accepted the basic necessity of organized opposition. He went into his administration watching for a disturbingly long and flexible list of potentially treasonous actions, many of which he felt had already occurred and which were not at all limited to attempted overthrow of the government. "If that solitary suffrage" needed to make a president could be acquired "by flattery or menaces, by fraud or violence, by terror, intrigue, or venality, the Government may not be the choice of the American people, but of foreign nations. It may be foreign nations who govern us, and not we, the people, who govern ourselves," Adams warned in his inaugural address. He could have declared that the system had worked, that the nation had *not* elected a president brought in by corruption, violence, or foreign influence. Instead, following his antiparty and antidemocratic philosophy, Adams put the country on notice that close, hard-fought elections portended treason and disaster. With the "XYZ" scandal and Quasi-War with France waiting in the wings, the logic of domestic political repression was already in place.[12]

At the same time, some of those who campaigned for Jefferson more actively than the man himself felt betrayed to see their standard-bearer fawn over John Adams after all that had been said. More brusquely partisan types did not universally accept the logic of agreeing to serve under a political opponent, especially when no other Jeffersonians besides Jefferson had been brought along into the new administration. One such partisan was former Governor George Clinton of New York, John Beckley's choice for vice president over Adams in 1792 and Burr in 1796, and a future understudy for Jefferson himself. When asked to run as a Jefferson elector in 1800, Clinton exploded with rage over Jefferson's behavior in the aftermath of 1796. "What he did do?" Clinton ranted. "His first act in the Senate was, to make a *damned time serving* trimming speech, in which he declared, that it was a great pleasure to him, to have an opportunity of serving his country under such a tried patriot as John Adams, which was saying to his friends, 'I am in; kiss my ___ and go to H_ll.'" Clinton's party rival Aaron Burr and his supporters agreed completely, having been victimized (as they saw it) by Madison's and Jefferson's calculation much more personally.[13]

Clinton had only to wait. It would not be too many months before Adams was signing the Sedition Act, Timothy Pickering was throwing Jefferson supporters in jail, and Jefferson had turned the vice president's office into a nerve center of resistance to an Adams regime he came to see as "the reign of witches." Hope as the Founders might have for political peace and harmony, the 1797 inauguration was just a temporary breather for the American party conflict, not the end.[14]

NOTES

ABBREVIATIONS

AFP *Adams Family Papers: An Electronic Archive*, Massachusetts Historical Society, http://www.masshist.org/digitaladams

Aurora *Aurora General Advertiser* (Philadelphia)

CMAG *Columbian Mirror and Alexandria Gazette* (Alexandria, Va.)

GUS *Gazette of the United States* (New York, 1789–90; Philadelphia, 1790–1804)

NNV *A New Nation Votes: American Election Returns, 1787–1825*, American Antiquarian Society and Tufts University, http://elections.lib.tufts.edu/aas_portal/index.xq

PAH Harold C. Syrett and Jacob E. Cooke, eds., *The Papers of Alexander Hamilton* (New York: Columbia University Press, 1961–1987)

PJM William T. Hutchinson, et al., eds., *The Papers of James Madison*, vols. 1–10 (Chicago: University of Chicago Press, 1962–1977); vols. 11–17 (Charlottesville: University Press of Virginia, 1977–1991)

PTJ Julian P. Boyd, et al., eds., *The Papers of Thomas Jefferson* (Princeton: Princeton University Press, 1950–)

INTRODUCTION

1 Richard Hofstadter, *The Idea of a Party System: The Rise of Legitimate Opposition in the United States, 1780–1840* (Berkeley: University of California Press, 1969); Ralph Ketcham, *Presidents above Party: The First American Presidency, 1789–1829* (Chapel Hill: University of North Carolina Press for the Institute of Early American History and Culture, 1984).

2 Quotations from Thomas Jefferson to Francis Hopkinson, 13 March 1789, in *Writings*, ed. Merrill D. Peterson (New York: Literary Classics of the United States, 1984), 940–942; John Adams to Jonathan Jackson, 2 October 1780, in *The Works of John Adams, Second President of the United States*, ed. Charles Francis Adams (Boston: Little, Brown, 1856), 9:511; Adams to Jefferson, 6 December 1787, in *The Adams-Jefferson Letters: The Complete Correspondence between Thomas Jefferson and Abigail and John Adams*, ed. Lester J. Cappon (Chapel Hill: University of North Carolina Press for the Institute of Early American History and Culture, 1988), 214; "Historicus," Middletown *Middlesex Gazette*, 25 September 1786; "Mr. Spangler's Speech to His Fellow Students," Philadelphia *Pennsylvania Packet*, 18 July 1788.

3 Ketcham, *Presidents above Party*; Zoltán Haraszti, *John Adams and the Prophets of Progress* (Cambridge, Mass.: Harvard University Press, 1952), 49–64; Jefferson to Francis Eppes, 19 January 1821, in Jefferson, *Writings*, ed. Peterson, 1451; Henry St. John, Viscount Bolingbroke, *Political Writings*, ed. David Armitage (Cambridge: Cambridge University Press, 1997), 244, 271; Carl J. Richard, *The Founders and the Classics: Greece, Rome and the American Enlightenment* (Cambridge, Mass.: Harvard University Press, 1994), 57–60.

4 Gordon S. Wood, "Interests and Disinterestedness in the Making of the Constitution," in *Beyond Confederation: Origins of the Constitution and American National Identity*, ed. Richard Beeman, Stephen Botein, and Edward C. Carter II (Chapel Hill: University of North Carolina Press for the Institute of Early

American History and Culture, 1987), 69–109; Gordon S. Wood, *The Creation of the American Republic, 1776–1787* (New York: W. W. Norton, 1972), 393–429; James Madison, "Vices of the Political System of the United States," in *The Mind of the Founder: Sources of the Political Thought of James Madison*, ed. Marvin Meyers, rev. ed. (Hanover, N.H.: University Press of New England for Brandeis University Press, 1981), 57–69; Jack N. Rakove, *Original Meanings: Politics and Ideas in the Making of the Constitution* (New York: Vintage, 1997), 268.

5 Tadahisa Kuroda, *The Origins of the Twelfth Amendment: The Electoral College in the Early Republic, 1787–1804* (Westport, Conn.: Greenwood Press, 1994); James P. Pfiffner and Jason Hartke, "The Electoral College and the Framers' Distrust of Democracy," *White House Studies* 3 (2003): 261–271; Shlomo Slonim, "The Electoral College at Philadelphia: The Evolution of an Ad Hoc Congress for the Selection of a President," *Journal of American History* 73 (1986): 35–58.

6 Manning J. Dauer, *The Adams Federalists*, 2nd ed. (Baltimore: Johns Hopkins University Press, 1968); Stephen G. Kurtz, *The Presidency of John Adams: The Collapse of Federalism, 1795–1800* (New York: A. S. Barnes, 1961). Of course, the election also gets chapters, usually rather superficial, in all the major histories of the 1790s. These are far too numerous to pack into a footnote and will be addressed or drawn on as necessary in the pages below.

7 Ronald P. Formisano, "Deferential-Participant Politics: The Early Republic's Political Culture, 1789–1840," *American Political Science Review* 68 (1974): 473–487, quotation on 474. For other social science–based approaches to early parties, see William Nisbet Chambers, *Political Parties in a New Nation: The American Experience, 1776–1809* (New York: Oxford University Press, 1963); William Nisbet Chambers and Walter Dean Burnham, eds., *The American Party Systems: Stages of Political Development* (New York: Oxford University Press, 1967); Ronald P. Formisano, *The Transformation of Political Culture: Massachusetts Parties, 1790s–1840s* (New York: Oxford University Press, 1983); Paul Kleppner, Walter Dean Burnham, Ronald P. Formisano, Samuel P. Hays, Richard Jensen, and William G. Shade, *The Evolution of American Electoral Systems* (Westport, Conn.: Greenwood Press, 1981); Joel H. Silbey, Allan G. Bogue, and William H. Flanigan, eds., *The History of American Electoral Behavior* (Princeton: Princeton University Press, 1978). The 1980s were the last scholarly era when political history still retained much of its former preeminence in the discipline, and despite some efforts by myself and others, no new synthesis has emerged in political history since then. For the efforts, see Jeffrey L. Pasley, Andrew W. Robertson, and David Waldstreicher, eds., *Beyond the Founders: New Approaches to the Political History of the Early American Republic* (Chapel Hill: University of North Carolina Press, 2004).

8 David R. Mayhew, *Placing Parties in American Politics: Organizations, Electoral Settings, and Government in the Twentieth Century* (New Haven: Yale University Press, 1986); Martin Shefter, *Political Parties and the State: The American Historical Experience* (Princeton: Princeton University Press, 1994); Thomas E. Patterson, *Out of Order* (New York: Vintage, 1994); Martin P. Wattenberg, *The Rise of Candidate-Centered Politics: Presidential Elections of the 1980s* (Cambridge, Mass.: Harvard University Press, 1991).

9　For a thorough application of this idea, see Marty Cohen, David Karol, Hans Noel, and John R. Zaller, *The Party Decides: Presidential Nominations before and after Reform* (Chicago: University of Chicago Press, 2008).

10　A highly influential work among historians in this respect is Maurice Duverger, *Political Parties: Their Organization and Activity in the Modern State* (London: Methuen, 1964).

11　Benedict Anderson, *Imagined Communities: Reflections of the Origins and Spread of Nationalism*, 3rd ed. (London: Verso, 2006); Wilson Carey McWilliams, "Parties as Civic Associations," in *Party Renewal in America: Theory and Practice*, ed. Gerald M. Pomper (New York: Praeger, 1980), 51–68.

12　Catharine Maria Sedgwick, *Tales and Sketches* (Philadelphia: Carey, Lea, and Blanchard, 1835), 10, 23. For a similar argument, see Pasley, "The Cheese and the Words: Popular Political Culture and Participatory Democracy in the Early American Republic," in Pasley, Robertson, and Waldstreicher, *Beyond the Founders*, 31–56.

13　For instance, and especially, see Lee Benson, *The Concept of Jacksonian Democracy: New York as a Test Case* (Princeton: Princeton University Press, 1961).

14　Particularly good on the issue of modern parties reaching back to claim major figures are Merrill D. Peterson, *The Jefferson Image in the American Mind* (New York: Oxford University Press, 1960); Merrill D. Peterson, *Lincoln in American Memory* (New York: Oxford University Press, 1994). On Jefferson-Jackson Day dinners, see Ronald F. Stinnett, *Democrats, Dinners and Dollars: A History of the Democratic Party, Its Dinners, Its Ritual* (Ames: Iowa State University Press, 1967). On Abraham Lincoln's Whiggery, see Daniel Walker Howe, *The Political Culture of the American Whigs* (Chicago: University of Chicago Press, 1979), 263–298.

15　On the changing configuration of the American party system, see Chambers and Burnham, *American Party Systems*; Walter Dean Burnham, *Critical Elections and the Mainsprings of American Politics* (New York: W. W. Norton, 1970); and Paul Kleppner et al., *The Evolution of American Electoral Systems* (Westport, Conn.: Greenwood Press, 1981).

16　Quotation from Noble E. Cunningham Jr., *The Jeffersonian Republicans: The Formation of Party Organization, 1789–1801* (Chapel Hill: University of North Carolina Press for the Institute of Early American History and Culture, 1957), 114. On New Jersey, see *NNV*.

17　Ronald P. Formisano, "Federalists and Republicans: Parties, Yes—System, No," in Kleppner et al., *The Evolution of American Electoral Systems*, 33–76; Ronald P. Formisano, *The Birth of Mass Political Parties: Michigan, 1827–1861* (Princeton: Princeton University Press, 1971); Joel H. Silbey, *The American Political Nation, 1838–1893* (Stanford: Stanford University Press, 1991). On the pro-party side of the debate, really the targets of the debate, were such works as Cunningham, *Jeffersonian Republicans*; William Nisbet Chambers, *Political Parties in a New Nation: The American Experience, 1776–1809* (New York: Oxford University Press, 1963); Joseph Charles, *The Origins of the American Party System* (Chapel Hill: University of North Carolina Press for the Institute of Early American History and Culture, 1956); Carl E. Prince, *New Jersey's Jeffersonian Republicans: The Genesis of an Early Party Machine, 1789–1817* (Chapel Hill: University of North Carolina Press for the Institute of Early American History and Culture, 1967); Carl E. Prince, *The Federalists and the Origins of the U.S. Civil Service* (New York: New York University Press, 1977).

18 Joanne B. Freeman, "The Presidential Election of 1796," in *John Adams and the Founding of the Republic*, ed. Richard Alan Ryerson (Boston: Massachusetts Historical Society and Northeastern University Press, 2001), 142–167, quotations on 143.

19 James Roger Sharp, *American Politics in the Early Republic: The New Nation in Crisis* (New Haven: Yale University Press, 1993), 138; Abigail Adams to John Adams, 31 December 1796, *AFP*. Sharp himself takes the middle-of-the-road position, calling the Federalist and Republicans "proto-parties," but dismisses the 1796 election as merely "sectional."

20 George Lakoff, *Moral Politics: What Conservatives Know That Liberals Don't* (Chicago: University of Chicago Press, 1996); George Lakoff with Mark Johnson, *Metaphors We Live by* (Chicago: University of Chicago Press, 2003); Alan Taylor, "From Fathers to Friends of the People: Political Personas in the Early Republic," *Journal of the Early Republic* 11 (1991): 465–491; John Adams to Abigail Adams, 20, 27 December 1796, *AFP*.

21 [John Gardner], *A Brief Consideration of the Important Services, and Distinguished Virtues and Talents, Which Recommend Mr. Adams for the Presidency of the United States* (Boston: Manning & Loring, for Joseph Nancrede, 1796), quotations on 5, 13, 22, 23, 26–27.

22 Alexander Hamilton to James A. Bayard, April 1802, in *Writings*, ed. Joanne B. Freeman (New York: Literary Classics of the United States, 2001), 988. The problems of the "informed voter" model have been a persistent thread in political science over the years. For examples, see John R. Zaller, *The Nature and Origins of Mass Opinion* (New York: Cambridge University Press, 1992); Donald P. Green, Bradley Palmquist, and Eric Schickler, *Partisan Hearts and Minds: Political Parties and the Social Identities of Voters* (New Haven: Yale University Press, 2002). For analogous arguments in history, see Andrew W. Robertson, " 'Look on This Picture . . . And on This!': Nationalism, Localism, and Partisan Images of Otherness in the United States, 1787–1820," *American Historical Review* 106 (2001): 1263–1280; and Michael E. McGerr, *The Decline of Popular Politics: The American North, 1865–1928* (New York: Oxford University Press, 1986).

23 Lynn Hunt, *The Family Romance of the French Revolution* (Berkeley: University of California Press, 1993); Francois Furstenberg, *In the Name of the Father: Washington's Legacy, Slavery, and the Making of a Nation* (New York: Penguin, 2006), esp. 21, 34–36, 74–78; Lakoff, *Moral Politics*, 153ff.; Mark E. Kann, *The Gendering of American Politics: Founding Mothers, Founding Fathers, and Political Patriarchy* (Westport, Conn.: Praeger, 1999), 96–105; Mark E. Kann, *A Republic of Men: The American Founders, Gendered Language, and Patriarchal Politics* (New York: New York University Press, 1998); George B. Forgie, *Patricide in the House Divided: A Psychological Interpretation of Lincoln and His Age* (New York: W. W. Norton, 1979).

24 *Maryland Journal*, quoted in Richmond *Virginia Gazette, and General Advertiser*, extraordinary ed., 28 September 1796; and Norfolk *Virginia Herald*, 26 September 1796; St. John Honeywood, *A Poem on Reading President Washington's Address, Declining a Re-Election to the Presidency. [Written in October*

1796] By S. J. H. Esquire, One of the Federal Electors of the State of New-York (Albany: Charles R. and George Webster, 1796). A more famous example from the Early Republic is the election of 1828 when Andrew Jackson's marriage became a major issue: Norma Basch, "Marriage, Morals, and Politics in the Election of 1828," *Journal of American History* 80 (1993): 890–918.

25 For some examples of the relatively small band of scholars who have argued in favor of long-term continuities in American politics, though almost all in different ways, see Charles Maurice Wiltse, *The Jeffersonian Tradition in American Democracy* (New York: Hill & Wang, 1960); Albert Fried, ed., *The Jeffersonian and Hamiltonian Traditions in American Politics* (Garden City, N.Y.: Anchor Books, 1968); Robert Kelley, *The Cultural Pattern in American Politics: The First Century* (New York: Alfred A. Knopf, 1979); Jo Freeman, "The Political Culture of the Democratic and Republican Parties," *Political Science Quarterly* 101 (1986): 327–356; Saul Cornell, *The Other Founders: Anti-Federalism and the Dissenting Tradition in America, 1788–1828* (Chapel Hill: University of North Carolina Press for the Omohundro Institute of Early American History and Culture, 1999); and most promisingly but controversially, Corey Robin, *The Reactionary Mind: Conservatism from Edmund Burke to Sarah Palin* (New York: Oxford University Press, 2011).

26 Pasley, Robertson, and Waldstreicher, *Beyond the Founders*. On the emergence of the Founder Studies movement, see Evan Thomas, "Founders Chic: Live from Philadelphia," *Newsweek*, 9 July 2001, 48–49, and the following critiques: Sean Wilentz, "America Made Easy: McCullough, Adams, and the Decline of Popular History," *New Republic*, 2 July 2001, 35–40; Jeffrey L. Pasley, "Publick Occurrences: Federalist Chic," *Common-Place* 2 (2002), http://www.common-place.org/publick/200202.shtml; David Waldstreicher, "Founders Chic as Culture War," *Radical History Review* 84 (2002): 185–194; Allan Kulikoff, "The Founding Fathers: Best Sellers! TV Stars! Punctual Plumbers!," *Journal of the Historical Society* 5 (2005): 155–187.

CHAPTER 1. A NEW REPUBLIC AND ITS DISCONTENTS

1 Gordon S. Wood, *The Creation of the American Republic, 1776–1787*, 2nd ed. (New York: W. W. Norton, 1969); Mark D. Kaplanoff, "The Federal Convention and the Constitution," in *The Blackwell Encyclopedia of the American Revolution*, ed. Jack P. Greene and J. R. Pole (Cambridge, Mass.: Blackwell, 1991), 457–470; Richard R. Beeman, *Plain, Honest Men: The Making of the American Constitution* (New York: Random House, 2009), 64–68; Robert Middlekauff, *The Glorious Cause: The American Revolution, 1763–1789* (New York: Oxford University Press, 1985), 624; Forrest McDonald, *We the People: The Economic Origins of the Constitution* (Chicago: University of Chicago Press, 1958), 90; James Madison, "Vices of the Political System of the United States, April 1787," in *The Mind of the Founder: Sources of the Political Thought of James Madison*, ed. Marvin Meyers (Hanover, N.H.: University Press of New England for Brandeis University Press, 1981), 63; Richard B. Bernstein with Kym S. Rice, *Are We to Be a Nation? The Making of the Constitution* (Cambridge, Mass.: Harvard University Press, 1987), 149–150; Margaret C. S. Christman, *The First Federal Congress, 1789–1791* (New York: Smithsonian Institution Press for the National Portrait Gallery and the United States Congress, 1989).

2 Ralph Ketcham, *Presidents above Party: The First American Presidency,*

1789–1829 (Chapel Hill: University of North Carolina Press for the Institute of Early American History and Culture, 1984), 89–90; Paul K. Longmore, *The Invention of George Washington* (Berkeley: University of California Press, 1988), 208–209.

3 Thomas A. Lewis, *For King and Country: George Washington, The Early Years* (New York: John Wiley & Sons, 1993); Longmore, *Invention of George Washington*, esp. 179–183.

4 Douglass Adair, *Fame and the Founding Fathers* (New York: W. W. Norton for the Institute of Early American History and Culture, 1974), 3–26; Longmore, *Invention of George Washington*, 170; William M. Fowler Jr., *American Crisis: George Washington and the Dangerous Two Years after Yorktown, 1781–1783* (New York: Walker, 2011), 159–188; Richard H. Kohn, *Eagle and Sword: The Beginnings of the Military Establishment in America* (New York: Free Press, 1975), 17–39.

5 Longmore, *Invention of George Washington*, 173–174; Carl J. Richard, *The Founders and the Classics: Greece, Rome and the American Enlightenment* (Cambridge, Mass.: Harvard University Press, 1994), 55–74; Garry Wills, *Cincinnatus: George Washington and the Enlightenment* (New York: Doubleday, 1984); Fowler, *American Crisis*, 2.

6 Beeman, *Plain, Honest Men*, 56, 128; Bernstein, *Are We to Be a Nation?*, 154–155; Forrest McDonald, *The American Presidency: An Intellectual History* (Lawrence: University Press of Kansas, 1994), 149–153, 212–218.

7 Quotation from Boston *Massachusetts Centinel*, 29 April 1789.

8 John Ferling, *John Adams: A Life* (New York: Henry Holt, 1996), 9–26.

9 Quotations from John Adams autobiography, part 1, sheet 23, *AFP*; Ferling, *John Adams*, 155–157.

10 "Thoughts on Government," in *The Works of John Adams, Second President of the United States*, ed. Charles Francis Adams (Boston: Little, Brown, 1856), 4:200; R. B. Bernstein, "'Let Us Dare to Read, Think, Speak, and Write': John Adams's Use of Reading as Political and Constitutional Armory," in *The Libraries, Leadership, and Legacy of John Adams and Thomas Jefferson*, ed. Robert C. Baron and Conrad Edick Wright (Golden, Colo.: Fulcrum Publishing and Massachusetts Historical Society, 2010), 81–93; Ferling, *John Adams*, 155–158.

11 Franklin B. Sawvel, ed., *The Complete Anas of Thomas Jefferson* (New York: Round Table Press, 1903), 37.

12 "Thoughts on Government," in Adams, *Works of John Adams*, 4:193; John Adams to James Sullivan, 26 May 1776, in Adams, *Works of John Adams*, 9:377–378. For readings of John Adams as a conservative, see Corey Robin, *The Reactionary Mind: Conservatism from Edmund Burke to Sarah Palin* (New York: Oxford University Press, 2011), 14, 15, 33–34; Peter Shaw, *The Character of John Adams* (Chapel Hill: University of North Carolina Press for the Institute of Early American History and Culture, 1976); Joseph J. Ellis, *Passionate Sage: The Character and Legacy of John Adams* (New York: W. W. Norton, 1993), 143–173; Patrick Allitt, *The Conservatives: Ideas and Personalities throughout American History* (New Haven: Yale University Press, 2010), 6, 11–12; John Patrick Diggins, *John Adams* (New York: Times Books, 2003); Daniel I. O'Neill, "John Adams versus Mary Wollstonecraft on the French Revolution and Democracy," *Journal of the History of Ideas* 68 (2007): 451–476.

13 Ferling, *John Adams*, chaps. 11–12.

14 Edith B. Gelles, "The Abigail Industry," *William and Mary Quarterly*, 3rd ser., 45 (1988): 656–683.

15 Alexander Hamilton to James Wilson, 25 January 1789, *PAH*, 5:247–249; John Adams to Benjamin Rush, 17 May 1789, in *Old Family Letters*, Series A, ed. Alexander Biddle (Philadelphia: J. B. Lippincott, 1892), 36; Ferling, *John Adams*, 298–299.

16 Fowler, *American Crisis*, 171–173, 206–207.

17 Forrest McDonald, *Alexander Hamilton: A Biography* (New York: W. W. Norton, 1982), 6–14; Alexander Hamilton to Edward Stevens, 11 November 1769, *PAH*, 1:4–5.

18 Alexander Hamilton to George Clinton, 13 February 1778, in *Writings*, ed. Joanne B. Freeman (New York: Literary Classics of the United States, 2001), 48–49; McDonald, *Alexander Hamilton*, 10–25.

19 E. James Ferguson, *The Power of the Purse: A History of American Public Finance, 1776–1790* (Chapel Hill: University of North Carolina Press for the Institute of Early American History and Culture, 1961); the quotation is from John Lamberton Harper, *American Machiavelli: Alexander Hamilton and the Origins of U.S. Foreign Policy* (New York: Cambridge University Press, 2004), 33.

20 Alexander Hamilton to Rufus King, 2 October 1798, *PAH*, 22:192; Max Farrand, ed., *The Records of the Federal Convention of 1787* (New Haven: Yale University Press, 1937), 1:287; Jacob E. Cooke, ed., *The Federalist* (Middletown, Conn.: Wesleyan University Press, 1961), 5–6.

21 Farrand, *Records of the Federal Convention*, 1:284–301; Stanley Elkins and Eric McKitrick, "The Founding Fathers: Young Men of the Revolution," *Political Science Quarterly* 76 (1961): 181–216; Wood, *Creation of the American Republic*, 391–464.

22 Sawvel, *Complete Anas of Thomas Jefferson*, 37; J. H. Plumb, *The Growth of Political Stability in England, 1675–1725* (London: Macmillan, 1967). On the republican commitments that animated and somewhat constrained Hamilton's statecraft, see Max M. Edling, *A Revolution in Favor of Government: Origins of the U.S. Constitution and the Making of the American State* (Oxford: Oxford University Press, 2003); and Karl-Friedrich Walling, *Republican Empire: Alexander Hamilton on War and Free Government* (Lawrence: University Press of Kansas, 1999).

23 This side of Hamilton emerges throughout Joanne B. Freeman, *Affairs of Honor: National Politics in the New Republic* (New Haven: Yale University Press, 2001), and can also be seen in the sheer mass of the *PAH* volumes taken up with newspaper essays and pamphlets. Volume 12 (July–October 1792) features Hamilton writing under ten different pseudonyms.

24 The most widely read work on this theme in recent times is Joseph J. Ellis, *American Sphinx: The Character of Thomas Jefferson* (New York: Alfred A. Knopf, 1997).

25 Declaration text from National Archives, www.archives.gov/exhibits/charters/declaration_transcript.html. For a survey of the Declaration's impact, see David Armitage, *The Declaration of Independence: A Global History* (Cambridge, Mass.: Harvard University Press, 2007).

26 Thomas Jefferson to Henry Lee, 8 May 1825, in *Writings*, ed. Merrill D.

Peterson (New York: Literary Classics of the United States, 1984), 1500–1501; Gordon S. Wood, *Revolutionary Characters: What Made the Founders Different* (New York: Penguin, 2006), 100–101.

27 Wood, *Revolutionary Characters*, 102.

28 Ibid., 101–103; Jefferson to Giovanni Fabbroni, 8 June 1778, in Jefferson, *Writings*, ed. Peterson, 760. Postwar historians typically emphasized Jefferson as a figure of the Enlightenment: Daniel J. Boorstin, *The Lost World of Thomas Jefferson* (Chicago: University of Chicago Press, 1981); Henry Steele Commager, *Jefferson, Nationalism, and the Enlightenment* (New York: G. Braziller, 1975); Noble E. Cunningham Jr., *In Pursuit of Reason: The Life of Thomas Jefferson* (New York: Ballantine Books, 1988). On Monticello and architecture, see William Howard Adams, ed., *The Eye of Thomas Jefferson* (Charlottesville, Va. and Columbia, Mo.: Thomas Jefferson Memorial Foundation and University of Missouri Press, 1992); Talbot Hamlin, *Greek Revival Architecture in America* (New York: Dover, 1964); Roger G. Kennedy, *Greek Revival America* (New York: Stewart Tabori & Chang, 1989); Pamela Scott, *Temple of Liberty: Building the Capitol for a New Nation* (New York: Oxford University Press, 1995); Susan R. Stein, *The Worlds of Thomas Jefferson at Monticello* (New York: H. N. Abrams, in association with the Thomas Jefferson Memorial Foundation, 1993).

29 Jefferson to William Green Munford, 18 June 1799, in Jefferson, *Writings*, ed. Peterson, 1064.

30 New York *GUS*, 27 March 1790.

31 Andrew Burstein and Nancy Isenberg, *Madison and Jefferson* (New York: Random House, 2010), esp. 186–192; Adams to Rush, 17 May 1789, in Biddle, *Old Family Letters*, 38.

32 Bernard Bailyn, *Ideological Origins of the American Revolution*, 2nd ed. (Cambridge, Mass.: Belknap Press of Harvard University Press, 1992), chap. 6.

33 Duncan J. MacLeod, *Slavery, Race and the American Revolution* (Cambridge: Cambridge University Press, 1974); David Waldstreicher, *Slavery's Constitution: From Revolution to Ratification* (New York: Hill & Wang, 2009), 57–61; Winthrop D. Jordan, *White over Black: American Attitudes toward the Negro, 1550–1812* (New York: W. W. Norton, 1977), 342–349.

34 John Fea, *Was America Founded as a Christian Nation? A Historical Introduction* (Louisville: Westminster John Knox Press, 2011), 169–227; Leonard W. Levy and Dennis J. Mahoney, eds., *The Framing and Ratification of the Constitution* (New York: Macmillan, 1987), 151, 174–194.

35 The contrast comes out strongly in Richard J. Purcell, *Connecticut in Transition, 1775–1818* (Middletown, Conn.: Wesleyan University Press, 1963) read against Rhys Isaac, *The Transformation of Virginia, 1740–1790* (Chapel Hill: University of North Carolina Press for the Institute of Early American History and Culture, 1982). On the Charlottesville church, see Adams, *Eye of Thomas Jefferson*, 265.

36 Jefferson, *Writings*, ed. Peterson, 346–347; Burstein and Isenberg, *Madison and Jefferson*, 117–119; Ralph Ketcham, *James Madison: A Biography* (Charlottesville: University Press of Virginia, 1990), 162–168; Thomas Buckley, *Church and State in Revolutionary Virginia, 1776–1787* (Charlottesville: University Press of Virginia, 1977), 71–76, 157–166; Purcell, *Connecticut in Transition*, 11, 55. For aspects of the long-term conflict, see Vera Brodsky Lawrence, *Music for Patriots,*

Politicians, and Presidents: Harmonies and Discords of the First Hundred Years (New York: Macmillan, 1975), 165–167; Robert J. Imholt, "Timothy Dwight, Federalist Pope of Connecticut," *New England Quarterly* 73 (2000): 386–411; Alan V. Briceland, "The Philadelphia Aurora, the New England Illuminati, and the Election of 1800," *Pennsylvania Magazine of History and Biography* 50 (1976): 3–36; Vernon Stauffer, *New England and the Bavarian Illuminati* (New York: Columbia University Press, 1918).

37 Waldstreicher, *Slavery's Constitution*, 61–101; Drew R. McCoy, "James Madison and Visions of American Nationality in the Confederation Period: A Regional Perspective," in *Beyond Confederation: Origins of the Constitution and American National Identity*, ed. Richard Beeman, Stephen Botein, and Edward C. Carter II (Chapel Hill: University of North Carolina Press for the Institute of Early American History and Culture, 1987), 226–258. On the social and political origins of South Carolina's proslavery belligerence, see S. Max Edelson, *Plantation Enterprise in Colonial South Carolina* (Cambridge, Mass.: Harvard University Press, 2006); Philip D. Morgan, *Slave Counterpoint: Black Culture in the Eighteenth-Century Chesapeake and Low Country* (Chapel Hill: University of North Carolina Press for the Omohundro Institute of Early American History and Culture, 1998); Rachel N. Klein, *Unification of a Slave State: The Rise of the Planter Class in the South Carolina Backcountry, 1760–1808* (Chapel Hill: University of North Carolina Press for the Institute of Early American History and Culture, 1990); George C. Rogers, *Charleston in the Age of the Pinckneys*, 2nd ed. (Columbia: University of South Carolina Press, 1984); Robert M. Weir, "The South Carolinian as Extremist," *South Atlantic Quarterly* 74 (1975): 86–103; Peter H. Wood, *Black Majority: Negroes in Colonial South Carolina from 1670 through the Stono Rebellion* (New York: W. W. Norton, 1974); Robert M. Weir, " 'The Harmony We Were Famous for': An Interpretation of Pre-Revolutionary South Carolina Politics," *William and Mary Quarterly*, 3rd ser., 26, no. 4 (1969): 473–501.

38 Hamilton to Washington, 14 April 1794, Hamilton to Rufus King, 2 October 1798, *PAH*, 16:272, 22:192.

39 John Adams to James Sullivan, 26 May 1776, in *Papers of John Adams*, Series 3, ed. Robert J. Taylor, Mary-Jo Kline, and Gregg L. Lint (Cambridge, Mass.: Belknap Press of Harvard University Press, 1977–), 4:208–212; Ferling, *John Adams*, 301–316.

40 Drew R. McCoy, *The Elusive Republic: Political Economy in Jeffersonian America* (New York: W. W. Norton, 1982).

41 On the term, and the British example, see John Brewer, *The Sinews of Power: War, Money, and the English State, 1688–1783* (New York: Alfred A. Knopf, 1988).

42 On Hamilton's financial system, see E. James Ferguson, *The Power of the Purse: A History of American Public Finance, 1776–1790* (Chapel Hill: University of North Carolina Press for the Institute of Early American History and Culture, 1961), chaps. 12–15; McDonald, *Alexander Hamilton*; Stanley Elkins and Eric McKitrick, *The Age of Federalism* (New York: Oxford University Press, 1993), chap. 2, 242–244; Robert F. Jones, *"The King of the Alley": William Duer, Politician, Entrepreneur, and Speculator, 1768–1799* (Philadelphia: American Philosophical Society, 1992).

43 Jefferson quotations from letters to George Washington, 23 May 1792, and to Lafayette, 16 June 1792, in Jefferson, *Writings*, ed. Peterson, 986–987, 988, 990; and Jefferson to Madison, 2 October 1792, *PJM*, 14:375.

44 "Opinion on the Constitutionality of a National Bank," and Jefferson to Washington, 23 May 1792, in Jefferson, *Writings*, ed. Peterson, 416, 988.

45 Alexander Hamilton, "Opinion on the Constitutionality of a National Bank," 23 February 1791, *PAH*, 8:97–106. For a sober view that makes a good case for what constitutional limitations Hamilton did believe in, see Edling, *Revolution in Favor of Government*.

46 Hamilton to Charles Cotesworth Pinckney, 10 October 1792, *PAH*, 12:543–544.

47 James Hart, *The American Presidency in Action, 1789: A Study in Constitutional History* (New York: Macmillan, 1948), 10–54. Quotations from Kenneth R. Bowling and Helen E. Veit, eds., *The Diary of William Maclay and Other Notes on Senate Debates* (Baltimore: Johns Hopkins University Press, 1988), 27; "To the Noblesse and Courtiers of the United States," Philadelphia *National Gazette*, 5 January 1793, in *The Prose of Philip Freneau*, ed. Philip M. Marsh (New Brunswick, N.J.: Scarecrow Press, 1955), 294–295.

48 John Adams to Benjamin Rush, 9 June 1789, in Biddle, *Old Family Letters*, 37.

49 Jack D. Warren Jr., "In the Shadow of Washington: John Adams as Vice President," in *John Adams and the Founding of the Republic*, ed. Richard Alan Ryerson (Boston: Massachusetts Historical Society and Northeastern University Press, 2001), 117–141; James H. Hutson, "John Adams' Title Campaign," *New England Quarterly* 41 (1968): 30–39; Richard Alan Ryerson, "'Like a Hare before the Hunters': John Adams and the Idea of Republican Monarchy," *Proceedings of the Massachusetts Historical Society* 107 (1995): 16–29. Quotations from Bowling and Veit, *Diary of William Maclay*, 31–33. On monarchy as the keystone to all forms of inequality in colonial America, see Richard L. Bushman, *King and People in Provincial Massachusetts* (Chapel Hill: University of North Carolina Press for the Institute of Early American History and Culture, 1992); Brendan McConville, *The King's Three Faces: The Rise and Fall of Royal America* (Chapel Hill: University of North Carolina Press for the Omohundro Institute of Early American History and Culture, 2006); Gordon S. Wood, *The Radicalism of the American Revolution* (New York: Alfred A. Knopf, 1992).

50 Adams, *Works of John Adams*, 6:280; Ferling, *John Adams*, 306–309; Zoltán Haraszti, *John Adams and the Prophets of Progress* (Cambridge, Mass.: Harvard University Press, 1952), 165–179.

51 The fullest account is "*Rights of Man*: The Contest of Burke and Paine . . . in America," *PTJ*, 20:268–313. The original publication of the "preface" was Thomas Paine, *Rights of Man: Being an Answer to Mr. Burke's Attack on the French Revolution*, 2nd ed. (Philadelphia: Samuel Harrison Smith, 1791), Evans 23664, p. 4. The "Evans number" given in the citations for some pre-1800 published works refers to the item's location in Readex-Newsbank's *Early American Imprints, Series 1, Evans, 1639–1800* database and microform set, available in or through most academic libraries. See the bibliographic essay at the end of this book for an explanation.

52 Boston *Columbian Centinel*, 8 June 1791, *PTJ*, 20:280–283.

53 "Agricola," Boston *Independent Chronicle*, 23 June 1791; "The Northern Journey of Jefferson and Madison," *PTJ*, 20:434–473; Merrill D. Peterson, *Thomas*

Jefferson and the New Nation (New York: Oxford University Press, 1970), 439–440.

54 Quotations from Jacob E. Cooke, ed., *The Federalist* (Middletown, Conn.: Wesleyan University Press, 1961), 460, 458; and James Madison, "Vices of the Political System of the United States: April 1787," 62–63.

55 Jefferson to Edward Carrington, 16 January 1787, *PTJ*, 11:49. On newspapers in the American Revolution, see Philip Davidson, *Propaganda and the American Revolution, 1763–1783* (1941; New York: W. W. Norton, 1973); Arthur M. Schlesinger, *Prelude to Independence: The Newspaper War on Britain, 1764–1776* (1958; Boston: Northeastern University Press, 1980); Bernard Bailyn and John B. Hench, eds., *The Press and the American Revolution* (Boston: Northeastern University Press, 1981); Jeffrey L. Pasley, *"The Tyranny of Printers": Newspaper Politics in the Early American Republic* (Charlottesville: University Press of Virginia, 2001), chap. 2.

56 Jefferson to Paine, 19 June 1792, *PTJ*, 20:312; Jefferson to William Short, 28 July 1791, *PTJ*, 20:691n–692n; Charles Downer Hazen, *Contemporary American Opinion of the French Revolution* (Baltimore: Johns Hopkins University Press, 1897), 159.

57 Madison, "Public Opinion," Philadelphia *National Gazette*, 19 December 1791, *PJM*, 14:170.

58 On the *National Gazette* episode, see "Jefferson, Freneau, and the Founding of the *National Gazette*," *PTJ*, 20:718–759; Pasley, *Tyranny of Printers*, chap. 3; Jeffrey L. Pasley, "The Two National Gazettes: Newspapers and the Embodiment of American Political Parties," *Early American Literature* 35 (2000): 51–86. The following passages draw on a longer original draft of my updated account of the incident written for Greil Marcus and Werner Sollors, eds., *A New Literary History of America* (Cambridge, Mass.: Belknap Press of Harvard University Press, 2009), 117–122. Only quotations have been cited below.

59 The idea that political loyalties and affiliations were built through print-based "communities" was most influentially developed, with regard to nations, in Benedict Anderson, *Imagined Communities*, rev. ed. (London: Verso, 1991). I have made the full argument sketched above in Pasley, *Tyranny of Printers*, chap. 1.

60 *PJM*, 14:370–373, 426–427.

61 Quotations from "To Mr. George Latimer, Chairman of the Committee of Correspondence," *National Gazette*, 25 August 1792; "Rules," part 2 (see below), *National Gazette*, 7 July 1792, in Marsh, *Prose of Philip Freneau*, 290, 284.

62 The original "Rules" can be found in *National Gazette*, 4, 7 July 1792; and Marsh, *Prose of Philip Freneau*, 281–287.

63 Pasley, *Tyranny of Printers*, chaps. 1, 9–14; Gerald J. Baldasty, "The Press and Politics in the Age of Jackson," *Journalism Monographs* 89 (1984): 1–28; Gerald J. Baldasty, *The Commercialization of News in the Nineteenth Century* (Madison: University of Wisconsin Press, 1992), chap. 1; Culver H. Smith, *The Press, Politics, and Patronage: The American Government's Use of Newspapers, 1789–1875* (Athens: University of Georgia Press, 1977); Mark Wahlgren Summers, *The Press Gang: Newspapers and Politics, 1863–1878* (Chapel Hill: University of North Carolina Press, 1994). For a list of the major printers in each party network, Republican and Federalist, on the eve of the 1796 election, and the

proposals for publishing "Anecdotes of Democrats," see Boston *Columbian Centinel*, 5 December 1795.

64 Quotations from *PAH*, 12:192, 194, 163–164.

65 Hamilton to Charles Cotesworth Pinckney, 10 October 1792, *PAH*, 12:543–544; Carl E. Prince, "The Federalist Party and Creation of a Court Press, 1789–1801," *Journalism Quarterly* 53 (1976): 238–241; Carl E. Prince, *The Federalists and the Origins of the U.S. Civil Service* (New York: New York University Press, 1977).

66 Philadelphia *Dunlap's American Daily Advertiser*, 22 September, 20 October 1792; *National Gazette*, 26 September, 4, 13 October 1792; *PJM*, 14:368–370, 387–392; *GUS*, 24 October 1792; *PAH*, 12:613.

67 Robert M. S. McDonald, "The Hamiltonian Invention of Thomas Jefferson," in *The Many Faces of Alexander Hamilton: The Life and Legacy of America's Most Elusive Founding Father*, ed. Douglas Ambrose and Robert W. T. Martin (New York: New York University Press, 2007), 54–76. See chapter 6 below for much more on Smith and his writings, during the 1792 and 1796 campaigns.

68 Quotations from *PJM*, 14:368. On the larger theme, see Pasley, *Tyranny of Printers*; and Jeffrey L. Pasley, "Thomas Greenleaf: Printers and the Struggle for Democratic Politics and Freedom of the Press," in *Revolutionary Founders: Rebels, Radicals, and Reformers in the Making of the Nation*, ed. Alfred F. Young, Gary B. Nash, and Ray Raphael (New York: Alfred A. Knopf, 2011), 357–375, 428–429.

CHAPTER 2. POPULAR POLITICS IN A POSTCOLONIAL NATION

1 Jefferson to Madison, 20 December 1787, in *Writings*, ed. Merrill D. Peterson (New York: Literary Classics of the United States, 1984), 916–917.

2 On Sheffield and the American response to him, see Jacob E. Cooke, *Tench Coxe and the Early Republic* (Chapel Hill: University of North Carolina Press for the Institute of Early American History and Culture, 1978), 202–208; Stanley Elkins and Eric McKitrick, *The Age of Federalism* (New York: Oxford University Press, 1993), 69–70.

3 Quotations from *The Columbian Tragedy* (Boston: Russell for Bassett, 1791), broadside, Massachusetts Historical Society, Evans 23268; Wiley Sword, *President Washington's Indian War: The Struggle for the Old Northwest, 1790–1795* (Norman: University of Oklahoma Press, 1985), 160–195; Colin G. Calloway, *Crown and Calumet: British-Indian Relations, 1783–1815* (Norman: University of Oklahoma Press, 1987); Francis S. Philbrick, *The Rise of the West, 1754–1830* (New York: Harper & Row, 1965), chap. 6; Richard White, *The Middle Ground: Indians, Empires, and Republics in the Great Lakes Region, 1650–1815* (Cambridge: Cambridge University Press, 1991), chap. 10.

4 Philbrick, *Rise of the West*, chap. 7; Arthur P. Whitaker, *The Mississippi Question, 1795–1803: A Study in Trade, Politics, and Diplomacy* (Gloucester, Mass.: Peter Smith, 1962); John Mack Faragher, *Daniel Boone: The Life and Legend of an American Pioneer* (New York: Henry Holt, 1992).

5 Seth Cotlar, *Tom Paine's America: The Rise and Fall of Transatlantic Radicalism in the Early Republic* (Charlottesville: University of Virginia Press, 2011), 49–97.

6 The French Revolution has generated perhaps the most extensive and intricate historical literature of any topic in world history, at least for this period,

and the relationship between the United States and the French Revolution forms its own luxuriant subliterature. Therefore no attempts at comprehensive citation will be made. In addition to the works in diplomatic history cited elsewhere, see the following on the French Revolution's impact in the Americas, and the relationship of the two republics: Elkins and McKitrick, *Age of Federalism*, 303–373; R. R. Palmer, *The Age of Democratic Revolution: A Political History of Europe and America, 1760–1800*, 2 vols. (Princeton: Princeton University Press, 1959–1964); David Brion Davis, *Revolutions: Reflections on American Equality and Foreign Liberations* (Cambridge, Mass.: Harvard University Press, 1990); Susan Branson, *These Fiery Frenchified Dames: Women and Political Culture in Early National Philadelphia* (Philadelphia: University of Pennsylvania Press, 2001); Patrice L. R. Higonnet, *Sister Republics: The Origins of French and American Republicanism* (Cambridge, Mass.: Harvard University Press, 1988); Rachel Hope Cleves, *The Reign of Terror in America: Visions of Violence From Anti-Jacobinism to Antislavery* (New York: Cambridge University Press, 2009); Matthew Rainbow Hale, "Neither Britons Nor Frenchmen: The French Revolution and American National Identity" (Ph.D. diss., Brandeis University, 2002); Gary B. Nash, "The American Clergy and the French Revolution," *William and Mary Quarterly*, 3rd ser., 22 (1965): 392–412; Laurent Dubois, *Avengers of the New World: The Story of the Haitian Revolution* (Cambridge, Mass.: Harvard University Press, 2004); Laurent Dubois, *A Colony of Citizens: Revolution and Slave Emancipation in the French Caribbean, 1787–1804* (Chapel Hill: University of North Carolina Press for the Omohundro Institute of Early American History and Culture, 2004); Stauffer, *New England and the Bavarian Illuminati*. My understanding of the French Revolution itself has also been shaped by: Keith Michael Baker, *Inventing the French Revolution: Essays on French Political Culture in the Eighteenth Century* (Cambridge: Cambridge University Press, 1990); Charles Breunig, *The Age of Revolution and Reaction, 1789–1850* (New York: W. W. Norton, 1977); Roger Chartier, *The Cultural Origins of the French Revolution* (Durham: Duke University Press, 1991); Robert Darnton and Daniel Roche, eds., *Revolution in Print: The Press in France, 1775–1800* (Berkeley: University of California Press, 1989); Marianne Elliott, *Partners in Revolution: The United Irishmen and France* (New Haven: Yale University Press, 1982); Eric Hobsbawm, *The Age of Revolution, 1789–1848* (New York: Vintage, 1996); Lynn Hunt, *The Family Romance of the French Revolution* (Berkeley: University of California Press, 1993); Jeremy D. Popkin, *Revolutionary News: The Press in France, 1789–1799* (Durham: Duke University Press, 1990); François Furet and Mona Ozouf, eds., *A Critical Dictionary of the French Revolution* (Cambridge, Mass.: Belknap Press of Harvard University Press, 1989).

7　Dumas Malone, *Jefferson and the Rights of Man* (Boston: Little, Brown, 1951), 222–225.

8　Davis, *Revolutions*, 20–47; Paul R. Hanson, *Historical Dictionary of the French Revolution* (Lanham, Md.: Scarecrow Press, 2004), 171–172.

9　Philadelphia *National Gazette*, 5 December 1791.

10　A special edition of Barlow's writings in support of the French Revolution was published in Philadelphia during the election year of 1796. These included the philosophical work *Advice to the Privileged Orders* as well as his *Letter Addressed to the People of Piedmont* advising the population of northern Italy to embrace the coming French invasion and the revolution it brought. Quotations from Joel Barlow, *The Political Writings of Joel Barlow*, new corrected ed. (New York: Mott & Lyon, 1796), 241, 249; Jefferson to James Madison, 19 May 1793, in Jefferson, *Writings*, ed. Peterson, 1009.

11 Marshall Smelser, "The Jacobin Phrenzy: Federalism and the Menace of Liberty, Equality, and Fraternity," *Review of Politics* 13 (1951): 457–482.

12 Elkins and McKitrick, *Age of Federalism*, 310–311; Philadelphia *National Gazette*, 19 December 1792; Philadelphia *General Advertiser*, 1 January 1793; Charles Downer Hazen, *Contemporary American Opinion of the French Revolution* (Baltimore: Johns Hopkins University Press, 1897), 166–169; Abigail Adams to John Adams, 22 January, 1 February 1793, *AFP*.

13 Jefferson to William Short, 3 January 1793, in Jefferson, *Writings*, ed. Peterson, 1004–1005. For what can only be described as a screed against Jefferson on this point, see Conor Cruise O'Brien, *The Long Affair: Thomas Jefferson and the French Revolution, 1785–1800* (Chicago: University Of Chicago Press, 1998).

14 "Paris, Jan. 22," Boston *Massachusetts Mercury*, 29 March 1793; "Guillotine" (and rest of p. 2), New York *Daily Advertiser*, 8 April 1793; *New-York Journal, & Patriotic Register*, 10 April 1793, p. 3; "Guillotine," *National Gazette*, 13 April 1793; "London, Feb. 14," *National Gazette*, 17 April 1793. For background on the guillotine, see Hanson, *Historical Dictionary of the French Revolution*, 151–153.

15 Harry Ammon, *The Genet Mission* (New York: W. W. Norton, 1973), 38–42; Hamilton to Edward Carrington, *PAH*, 11:438–439.

16 Hazen, *Contemporary Opinion of the French Revolution*, 182.

17 *Hough's Concord Herald*, 14 February 1793.

18 The Genet affair has its own vast, bewildering literature, which again I have cited below only as needed. My major references have been Alexander DeConde, *Entangling Alliance: Politics and Diplomacy under George Washington* (Durham: Duke University Press, 1958); Albert Hall Bowman, *The Struggle for Neutrality: Franco-American Diplomacy during the Federalist Era* (Knoxville: University of Tennessee Press, 1974); Harry Ammon, "The Genet Mission and the Development of American Political Parties," *Journal of American History* 52 (1966): 725–741; Ammon, *Genet Mission*; Eugene R. Sheridan, "The Recall of Edmond Charles Genet: A Study in Transatlantic Politics and Diplomacy," *Diplomatic History* 18 (1994): 463–488; Marco Sioli, "Citizen Genet and Political Struggle in the Early American Republic," *Revue Francaise d'Etudes Americaines* (1995): 259–267; Elkins and McKitrick, *Age of Federalism*, 330–373.

19 Ammon, *Genet Mission*, 25–29; Sheridan, "Recall of Edmond Charles Genet," 466–467; Frederick Jackson Turner, ed., *Correspondence of the French Ministers to the United States, 1791–1797* (Washington, D.C.: Government Printing Office, 1904), 203–205.

20 Elkins and McKitrick, *Age of Federalism*, 334–335; Bowman, *Struggle for Neutrality*, 56–57; Sheridan, "Recall of Genet," 467–468.

21 Charleston *City Gazette and Daily Advertiser*, 16, 20 April 1793.

22 *National Gazette*, 10 April ("Pennsylvanian"), 4 May 1793.

23 Joyce Appleby, *Capitalism and a New Social Order: The Republican Vision of the 1790s* (New York: New York University Press, 1984). For insight into the Democratic-Republicans of Philadelphia, see Roland M. Baumann, "John Swanwick: Spokesman for 'Merchant Republicanism' in Philadelphia, 1790–98," *Pennsylvania Magazine of History and Biography* 97 (1973): 131–182;

Roland M. Baumann, "Philadelphia's Manufacturers and the Excise Taxes of 1794: The Forging of the Jeffersonian Coalition," *Pennsylvania Magazine of History and Biography* 106 (1982): 3–39; Richard G. Miller, *Philadelphia—The Federalist City: A Study of Urban Politics, 1789–1801* (Port Washington, N.Y.: Kennikat Press, 1976); Raymond Walters Jr., *Alexander James Dallas: Lawyer—Politician—Financier, 1759–1817* (Philadelphia: University of Pennsylvania Press, 1943).

24 *National Gazette*, 18, 22 May 1793; Hazen, *Contemporary American Opinion*, 176–178.

25 Jefferson to Madison, 19 May 1793, *PTJ*, 26:61–62.

26 Philadelphia *General Advertiser*, 21 May 1793; Hazen, *Contemporary American Opinion*, 181–182.

27 Turner, "Correspondence of the French Ministers," 214–216.

28 Simon P. Newman, *Parades and the Politics of the Street: Festive Culture in the Early American Republic* (Philadelphia: University of Pennsylvania Press, 1997); David Waldstreicher, *In the Midst of Perpetual Fetes: The Making of American Nationalism, 1776–1820* (Chapel Hill: University of North Carolina Press for the Omohundro Institute of Early American History and Culture, 1997); Len Travers, *Celebrating the Fourth: Independence Day and the Rites of Nationalism in the Early Republic* (Amherst: University of Massachusetts Press, 1997); Albrecht Koschnik, "Political Conflict and Public Contest: Rituals of National Celebration in Philadelphia, 1788–1815," *Pennsylvania Magazine of History and Biography* 118 (1994): 209–248; Brooks McNamara, *Days of Jubilee: The Great Age of Public Celebrations in New York, 1788–1909* (New Brunswick, N.J.: Rutgers University Press, 1997).

29 On the politicization of the St. Tammany Societies, see Jerome Mushkat, *Tammany: The Evolution of a Political Machine, 1789–1865* (Syracuse: Syracuse University Press, 1971), chap. 1; and Jerome Mushkat, "Matthew Livingston Davis and the Political Legacy of Aaron Burr," *New-York Historical Society Quarterly* 59 (1975): 123–148. On the conservative Federalist bent of the Cincinnati, see Minor Myers Jr., *Liberty without Anarchy: A History of the Society of the Cincinnati* (Charlottesville: University Press of Virginia, 1983).

30 Quotations from Philadelphia *General Advertiser*, 6, 8 July 1793. On the Feast of Reason, see David Houpt, "Critical Masses: Celebratory Politics and Mobilization in Philadelphia's Congressional Election of 1794," unpublished paper presented at the annual meeting of Society for Historians of the Early American Republic, 16 July 2011.

31 DeConde, *Entangling Alliance*, 204–234. Quotations from Jefferson to Madison, 13 May, 7 July 1793, *PTJ*, 26:25–26, 444; "Memorandum of a Conversation with Edmond Charles Genet," *PTJ*, 26:463–466; Genet to Jefferson, 8, 9 July 1793, in *American State Papers*, vol. 1, *Foreign Relations*, ed. Walter Lowrie and Matthew St. Clair Clarke (Washington, D.C.: Gales and Seaton, 1833), 163.

32 Adams to Jefferson, 30 June 1813, in *The Adams-Jefferson Letters: The Complete Correspondence between Thomas Jefferson and Abigail and John Adams*, ed. Lester J. Cappon (Chapel Hill: University of North Carolina Press for the Institute of Early American History and Culture, 1988), 346–347; Martin S. Pernick, "Politics, Parties, and Pestilence: Epidemic Yellow Fever in Philadelphia and the Rise of the First Party System," *William and Mary Quarterly*, 3rd ser., 29 (1972): 559–586; J. H. Powell, *Bring Out Your Dead: The Great Plague of Yellow Fever in 1793* (New York: Time, 1965).

33 Jefferson to Madison, 19 May 1793, in Jefferson, *Writings*, ed. Peterson, 1008; Donald S. Spencer, "Appeals to the People: The Later Genet Affair," *New-York Historical Society Quarterly* 54 (1970): 241–267; Sheridan, "Recall of Genet," 473–488; Philadelphia *Dunlap's American Daily Advertiser*, 31 July 1793.

34 Edmund Burke, *Reflections on the Revolution in France: A Critical Edition*, ed. J. C. D. Clark (Stanford: Stanford University Press, 2001), 56; Michael Durey, *Transatlantic Radicals and the Early American Republic* (Lawrence: University Press of Kansas, 1997), chap. 1; Mary Thale, ed., *Selections From the Papers of the London Corresponding Society, 1792–1799* (Cambridge: Cambridge University Press, 1983).

35 By far the most useful works on political clubs and associations in the Early Republic are John L. Brooke, "Ancient Lodges and Self-Created Societies: Voluntary Association and the Public Sphere in the Early Republic," in *Launching the "Extended Republic": The Federalist Era*, ed. Ronald Hoffman and Peter J. Albert (Charlottesville: University of Virginia Press, 1996), 273–377; Albrecht Koschnik, *"Let a Common Interest Bind Us Together": Associations, Partisanship, and Culture in Philadelphia, 1775–1840* (Charlottesville: University of Virginia Press, 2007); Philip S. Foner, ed., *The Democratic-Republican Societies, 1790–1800: A Documentary Sourcebook of Constitutions, Declarations, Addresses, Resolutions, and Toasts* (Westport, Conn.: Greenwood Press, 1976); Albrecht Koschnik, "The Democratic Societies of Philadelphia and the Limits of the American Public Sphere, Circa 1793–1795," *William and Mary Quarterly*, 3rd ser., 58 (2001): 615–636; Judah Adelson, "The Vermont Democratic-Republican Societies and the French Revolution," *Vermont History* 32 (1964): 3–23; Jeffrey A. Davis, "Guarding the Republican Interest: The Western Pennsylvania Democratic Societies and the Excise Tax," *Pennsylvania History* 67 (2000): 43–62; Eugene Perry Link, *Democratic-Republican Societies, 1790–1800* (New York: Octagon Books, 1973); William Miller, "The Democratic Societies and the Whiskey Insurrection," *Pennsylvania Magazine of History and Biography* 62 (1938): 324–349; William Miller, "First Fruits of Republican Organization: Political Aspects of the Congressional Election of 1794," *Pennsylvania Magazine of History and Biography* 63 (1939): 118–143; Matthew Schoenbachler, "Republicanism in the Age of Democratic Revolution: The Democratic-Republican Societies of the 1790s," *Journal of the Early Republic* 18 (1998): 237–261; Marco M. Sioli, "The Democratic Republican Societies at the End of the Eighteenth Century: The Western Pennsylvania Experience," *Pennsylvania History* 60 (1993): 288–304.

36 *National Gazette*, 4 July 1792, 13 April 1792; Foner, *Democratic-Republican Societies*, 53.

37 Foner, *Democratic-Republican Societies*, 64–66.

38 Jonathan Israel, *A Revolution of the Mind: Radical Enlightenment and the Intellectual Origins of Modern Democracy* (Princeton: Princeton University Press, 2010), 38, 47, 62–65. Even more recently, Israel has expounded these themes in far greater detail in the third volume of his magnum opus: Jonathan I. Israel, *Democratic Enlightenment: Philosophy, Revolution, and Human Rights, 1750–1790* (Oxford: Oxford University Press, 2011). Israel's use of the term "Radical Enlightenment" is different from that of Margaret Jacob, who applies it to an earlier period and a group whose radicalism was much more cultural than directly political. See Margaret C. Jacob, *The Radical Enlightenment:*

Pantheists, Freemasons, and Republicans (London: Allen & Unwin, 1981). Other scholars seem to prefer Robert Darnton's term "low Enlightenment" to denote the legions of sketchy, vulgar popularizers and exploiters of Enlightenment thought who teemed in France before and during the Revolution. See Robert Darnton, *The Literary Underground of the Old Regime* (Cambridge, Mass.: Harvard University Press, 1985); Darrin M. McMahon, "Edmund Burke and the Literary Cabal: A Tale of Two Enlightenments," in *Reflections on the Revolution in France* by Edmund Burke, ed. Frank M. Turner (New Haven: Yale University Press, 2003), 233–247; and Darrin M. McMahon, "The Enlightenment's True Radicals," *New York Times*, Sunday Book Review, 25 December 2011. (My thanks to David Houpt for calling my attention to the McMahon piece.) Yet other terms suggested for the English-speaking followers of what Israel calls the Radical Enlightenment are "transatlantic radicals" or "Jacobins" or "Paineites": Michael Durey, "Thomas Paine's Apostles: Radical Emigrés and the Triumph of Jeffersonian Republicanism," *William and Mary Quarterly*, 3rd ser., 44 (1987): 661–688; Durey, *Transatlantic Radicals*; Richard J. Twomey, *Jacobins and Jeffersonians: Anglo-American Radicalism in the United States, 1790–1820* (New York: Garland Publishing, 1989); Cotlar, *Tom Paine's America*.

39 On Bache, Leib, and their political base in the working-class and immigrant neighborhoods of Philadelphia, see James D. Tagg, *Benjamin Franklin Bache and the Philadelphia "Aurora"* (Philadelphia: University of Pennsylvania Press, 1991), chap. 8; Marcus Daniel, *Scandal and Civility: Journalism and the Birth of American Democracy* (New York: Oxford University Press, 2009), chap. 3; Kim Tousley Phillips, *William Duane: Radical Journalist in the Age of Jefferson* (New York: Garland Publishing, 1989), 104–107; Kim T. Phillips, "William Duane, Philadelphia's Democratic Republicans, and the Origins of Modern Politics," *Pennsylvania Magazine of History and Biography* 101 (1977): 365–387; Jeffrey L. Pasley, *"The Tyranny of Printers": Newspaper Politics in the Early American Republic* (Charlottesville: University Press of Virginia, 2001), 90–91 and passim. Probably the best work on Bache's outlook is Jeffery A. Smith, *Franklin and Bache: Envisioning the Enlightened Republic* (New York: Oxford University Press, 1990).

40 For the nineteenth-century political culture of participation, followed by three concerned modern analyses of its decline, see William E. Gienapp, " 'Politics Seem to Enter into Everything': Political Culture in the North, 1840–1860," in *Essays on American Antebellum Politics, 1840–1860*, ed. Stephen E. Maizlish and John J. Kushma (College Station: Texas A & M University Press, 1982), 14–69; Michael E. McGerr, *The Decline of Popular Politics: The American North, 1865–1928* (New York: Oxford University Press, 1986); Nina Eliasoph, *Avoiding Politics: How Americans Produce Apathy in Everyday Life* (Cambridge: Cambridge University Press, 1998); Robert D. Putnam, *Bowling Alone: The Collapse and Revival of American Community* (New York: Simon & Schuster, 2000).

41 Foner, *Democratic-Republican Societies*, 53–54.

42 Ibid., 54, 151.

43 Ibid., 7; Link, *Democratic-Republican Societies*, 8–16.

44 Foner, *Democratic-Republican Societies*, 54, 151, 154.

45 Ibid., 64.

46 David R. Hoth and Carol S. Ebel, eds., *The Papers of George Washington: Presidential Series*, vol. 16, *1 May–30 September 1794* (Charlottesville: University of Virginia Press, 2011), 520–529; [Edmund Randolph], *Vindication of Mr. Randolph's Resignation* (Philadelphia: Samuel H. Smith, 1795), Evans 29384, p. 102. Sword, *President Washington's Indian War*, 272–321; Andrew R. L. Cayton, "'Noble Actors' upon the 'Theatre of Honour': Power and Civility in the Treaty of Greenville," in *Contact Points: American Frontiers from the Mohawk Valley to the Mississippi, 1750–1830*, ed. Andrew R. L. Cayton and Fredrika J. Teute (Chapel Hill: University of North Carolina Press for the Omohundro Institute of Early American History and Culture, 1998), 235–269.

47 Leland D. Baldwin, *Whiskey Rebels: The Story of a Frontier Uprising* (Pittsburgh: University of Pittsburgh Press, 1992); William Hogeland, *The Whiskey Rebellion: George Washington, Alexander Hamilton, and the Frontier Rebels Who Challenged America's Newfound Sovereignty* (New York: Simon & Schuster, 2006); Thomas P. Slaughter, *The Whiskey Rebellion: Frontier Epilogue to the American Revolution* (New York: Oxford University Press, 1986).

48 Paul A. Gilje, *Rioting in America* (Bloomington: Indiana University Press, 1999); William Pencak, Matthew Dennis, and Simon P. Newman, eds., *Riot and Revelry in Early America* (University Park: Pennsylvania State University Press, 2002); Pauline Maier, *From Resistance to Revolution: Colonial Radicals and the Development of American Opposition to Britain, 1765–1776* (New York: Vintage, 1974).

49 This is the main thesis of Slaughter, *Whiskey Rebellion*.

50 On John Neville's role in sparking the violence, see Jacob E. Cooke, "The Whiskey Insurrection: A Reevaluation," *Pennsylvania History* 30 (1963): 316–346; and Chadwick Allen Harp, "The Tax Collector of Bower Hill," *Pennsylvania Heritage* 18 (1992): 24–29; and Slaughter, *Whiskey Rebellion*. Quotation from Samuel Hodgdon to Isaac Craig, 26 July 1794, in "'Such Disorders Can Only Be Cured by Copious Bleedings': The Correspondence of Isaac Craig during the Whiskey Rebellion," ed. Kenneth A. White, *Western Pennsylvania Historical Magazine* 67 (1984): 220. According to Pennsylvania's official state history, there were only five to six deaths, all but one a rebel. See Randall M. Miller and William Pencak, eds., *Pennsylvania: A History of the Commonwealth* (University Park and Harrisburg: Pennsylvania State University Press and Pennsylvania Historical and Museum Commission, 2002), 147–148.

51 "Conference Concerning the Insurrection in Western Pennsylvania," 2 August 1794, *PAH*, 17:9–13; Richard H. Kohn, "The Washington Administration's Decision to Crush the Whiskey Rebellion," *Journal of American History* 59 (1972): 567–584; Randolph, *Vindication*, 83.

52 Robert Goodloe Harper, "A Letter Containing a Short View of the Political Principles and System of the Federalists, and the Situation in Which They Found and Left the Government," 5 March 1801, in *Select Works of Robert Goodloe Harper* (Baltimore: O. H. Neilson, 1814), 338; Richard H. Kohn, *Eagle and Sword: The Beginnings of the Military Establishment in America* (New York: Free Press, 1975), 138.

53 Jerry Clouse, "The Whiskey Boys versus the Watermelon Army," *Pennsylvania Heritage* 17 (1991): 22–29.

54 For works framing Shays' Rebellion as relatively successful traditionalist popular resistance, see Robert A. Gross, ed., *In Debt to Shays: The Bicentennial of*

an *Agrarian Rebellion* (Charlottesville: University Press of Virginia, 1993); and David P. Szatmary, *Shays' Rebellion: The Making of an Agrarian Insurrection* (Amherst: University of Massachusetts Press, 1980).

55 Elkins and McKitrick, *Age of Federalism*, 484–485; Harper, "A Letter Containing a Short View," 338; Johann N. Neem, "Freedom of Association in the Early Republic: The Republican Party, the Whiskey Rebellion, and the Philadelphia and New York Cordwainers' Cases," *Pennsylvania Magazine of History and Biography* 127 (2003): 259–290, quotation on 272. See also Miller, "The Democratic Societies and the Whiskey Insurrection."

56 Israel, *Revolution of the Mind*, esp. 62–65. While Jonathan Israel's "Radical Enlightenment" is a not universally accepted doctrine among intellectual historians in terms of explaining all of Enlightenment thought, it does provide a convincing intellectual framework for understanding an issue intellectual historians have tended to ignore: what many American democrats and the transatlantic radicals who joined or influenced them thought was at stake in their strenuous promotion of competitive elections and public criticism as positive goods. That in turn helps clarify the origins of the Democratic Society's hostile response to the Whiskey Rebellion.

57 Maier, *From Resistance to Revolution*. On the Paxton Boys episode, see Kevin Kenny, *Peaceable Kingdom Lost: The Paxton Boys and the Destruction of William Penn's Holy Experiment* (New York: Oxford University Press, 2009); James Kirby Martin, "The Return of the Paxton Boys and the Historical State of the Pennsylvania Frontier, 1764–1774," *Pennsylvania History* 38 (1971): 117–133; Alison Olson, "The Pamphlet War over the Paxton Boys," *Pennsylvania Magazine of History and Biography* 123 (1999): 31–55; Edwin Thomas Schock Jr., "The 'Cloven Foot' Rediscovered: The Historiography of the Conestoga Massacre through Three Centuries of Scholarship," *Journal of the Lancaster County Historical Society* 96 (1994): 99–112.

58 Quotations from Philadelphia *General Advertiser*, 26 July 1794; and Foner, *Democratic-Republican Societies*, 88.

59 "Excise," Philadelphia *General Advertiser*, 2 August 1794.

60 "A Democrat," Philadelphia *General Advertiser*, 4 August 1794.

61 Democratic Society of Pennsylvania Minutes, 4 September 1794, in Foner, *Democratic-Republican Societies*, 90–91; Philadelphia *General Advertiser*, 26 July 1794.

62 Philadelphia *General Advertiser*, 26 July 1794.

63 Ibid.

64 Quotations from "Franklin," Philadelphia *General Advertiser*, 22 August 1794. On the Swanwick election, see Roland M. Baumann, "John Swanwick: Spokesman for 'Merchant Republicanism' in Philadelphia, 1790–98," *Pennsylvania Magazine of History and Biography* 97 (1973): 131–182; Roland M. Baumann, "Philadelphia's Manufacturers and the Excise Taxes of 1794: The Forging of the Jeffersonian Coalition," *Pennsylvania Magazine of History and Biography* 106 (1982): 3–39.

65 Philadelphia *General Advertiser*, 26 July 1794. The original text uses the spelling "burdins," which has been corrected for intelligibility.

66 Philadelphia *General Advertiser*, 26 July 1794; Foner, *Democratic-Republican Societies*, 94; "A Democrat," Philadelphia *General Advertiser*, 12 August 1794.

67 Foner, *Democratic-Republican Societies*, 88, 91–92.

68 Tagg, *Benjamin Franklin Bache*, 218–219; Phillips, *William Duane*, 104–105. Quotations from George Mifflin Dallas, ed., *Life and Writings of Alexander James Dallas* (Philadelphia: J. B. Lippincott, 1871), 30–31, 151–152.

69 Minutes of the Democratic Society of Pennsylvania (typescript of mss.), 11 September 1794, Historical Society of Pennsylvania, 142; Foner, *Democratic-Republican Societies*, 30, 92; Miller, "Democratic Societies and the Whiskey Insurrection," 330–332; Elkins and McKitrick, *Age of Federalism*, 481; Koschnik, "Democratic Societies of Philadelphia," 634; Phillips, *William Duane*, 104–107; Frederick B. Tolles, *George Logan of Philadelphia* (New York: Oxford University Press, 1953), 141–142. Some differences were patched up later, but in many ways the rift in the Democratic Society in Philadelphia persisted as factions in the Philadelphia Democratic Party through the Age of Jackson. See Kim T. Phillips, "Democrats of the Old School in the Era of Good Feelings," *Pennsylvania Magazine of History and Biography* 95 (1971): 363–382; Kim T. Phillips, "The Pennsylvania Origins of the Jackson Movement," *Political Science Quarterly* 91 (1976): 489–508.

70 Phillips, *William Duane*, 106; Foner, *Democratic-Republican Societies*, 62; Elkins and McKitrick, *Age of Federalism*, 481–482; Koschnik, "Democratic Societies of Philadelphia," 634n71; Michael Leib to Lydia Leib, 5 October 1794, Society Collection, Historical Society of Pennsylvania.

71 Foner, *Democratic-Republican Societies*, 31–32, 339; *Annals of Congress*, House of Representatives, 3rd Congress, 2nd session, 25 November 1794, 908–909; Frank A. Cassell, *Merchant Congressman in the Young Republic: Samuel Smith of Maryland, 1752–1839* (Madison: University of Wisconsin Press, 1971), 58–60; Libero M. Renzulli Jr., *Maryland: The Federalist Years* (Madison, N.J.: Fairleigh Dickinson University Press, 1972), 169–171. Smith quotation from J. Thomas Scharf, *History of Maryland from the Earliest Period to the Present Day* (Baltimore: John B. Piet, 1879), 2:585.

72 Elkins and McKitrick, *Age of Federalism*, 484–485; George Washington, "Sixth Annual Message," in *George Washington: A Collection*, ed. W. B. Allen (Indianapolis: Liberty Fund, 1988), 492.

73 Foner, *Democratic-Republican Societies*, 98–102; Jefferson, "First Inaugural Address," in Jefferson, *Writings*, ed. Peterson, 493.

CHAPTER 3. THE JAY TREATY CRISIS AND THE ORIGINS OF THE 1796 CAMPAIGN

1 This point is made in many works, but my immediate influences are Joseph Charles, *The Origins of the American Party System: Three Essays* (New York: Harper & Row, 1961), chap. 3; and Paul Goodman, *The Democratic-Republicans of Massachusetts: Politics in a Young Republic* (Cambridge, Mass.: Harvard University Press, 1964), 57–59.

2 On the Jay Treaty and the politics surrounding it, see (among a vast literature) Samuel Flagg Bemis, *Jay's Treaty: A Study in Commerce and Diplomacy* (New Haven: Yale University Press, 1962); Jerald A. Combs, *The Jay Treaty: Political Battleground of the Founding Fathers* (Berkeley: University of California Press, 1970); Charles R. Ritcheson, *Aftermath of Revolution: British Policy toward the United States, 1783–1795* (New York: W. W. Norton, 1971); James Roger Sharp, *American Politics in the Early Republic: The New Nation in Crisis* (New Haven:

Yale University Press, 1993), 113–137; Stanley Elkins and Eric McKitrick, *The Age of Federalism* (New York: Oxford University Press, 1993), 375–449; and most recently, Todd Estes, *The Jay Treaty Debate, Public Opinion, and the Evolution of Early American Political Culture* (Amherst: University of Massachusetts Press, 2006).

3 "From the PITTSBURG GAZETTE," Elizabethtown *New-Jersey Journal,* 7 May 1794; "From Correspondents," *Boston Gazette,* 12 May 1794; Philadelphia *General Advertiser,* 15 April 1794.

4 Phineas Hedges, *An Oration Delivered before the Republican Society of Ulster County, and Other Citizens* (Goshen, N.Y.: David M. Westcott, 1795), 12–15; Philip S. Foner, ed., *The Democratic-Republican Societies, 1790–1800: A Documentary Sourcebook of Constitutions, Declarations, Addresses, Resolutions, and Toasts* (Westport, Conn.: Greenwood Press, 1976), 352; Philadelphia *General Advertiser,* 21 June 1794; John Jay to Alexander Hamilton, in *PAH,* 17:97–98.

5 For the first report of Dorchester's speech, see Philadelphia *General Advertiser,* 27 March 1794. On the events in the northwest, see Wiley Sword, *President Washington's Indian War: The Struggle for the Old Northwest, 1790–1795* (Norman: University of Oklahoma Press, 1985), 258–271.

6 Philadelphia *General Advertiser,* 16 April 1794; *Boston Gazette,* 12 May 1794; Combs, *Jay Treaty,* 121.

7 Philadelphia *General Advertiser,* 15 April 1794.

8 Philadelphia *General Advertiser,* 16–17 April 1794; Philadelphia *Gazette of the United States,* 14 April 1794; the quotation is from New York *Diary or Loudon's Register,* 16 April 1794.

9 *Annals of Congress,* House of Representatives, 3rd Congress, 1st Session, 14 April 1794, 587, 588–589; Philadelphia *General Advertiser,* 16 April 1794.

10 Newburyport *Impartial Herald,* 18 April 1794; "Communications," Boston *Columbian Centinel,* 24 June 1795; Oliver Wolcott Jr. to Oliver Wolcott Sr., 18 January 1794, in *Memoirs of the Administration of Washington and John Adams, Edited From the Papers of Oliver Wolcott, Secretary of the Treasury,* ed. George Gibbs (New York: William Van Norden, 1846), 1:127; Hamilton to Washington, 14 April 1794, *PAH,* 16:275.

11 George Cabot to Samuel Phillips, 8 March 1794, in *Life and Letters of George Cabot,* ed. Henry Cabot Lodge (Boston: Little, Brown, 1878), 78; Oliver Wolcott Jr. to Oliver Wolcott Sr., 14 April 1794, in Gibbs, *Memoirs,* 1:133–134.

12 On the Jay-Gardoqui affair, see Drew R. McCoy, "James Madison and Visions of American Nationality in the Confederation Period: A Regional Perspective," in *Beyond Confederation: Origins of the Constitution and American National Identity,* ed. Richard Beeman, Stephen Botein, and Edward C. Carter II (Chapel Hill: University of North Carolina Press for the Institute of Early American History and Culture, 1987), 239–243.

13 "Resolutions Adopted on the Appointment of John Jay as Envoy to Great Britain," 8 May 1794, in Foner, *Democratic-Republican Societies,* 105–106; "Democratic Society," Philadelphia *Independent Gazetteer,* 14 May 1794; Arthur P. Whitaker, *The Mississippi Question, 1795–1803: A Study in Trade, Politics, and Diplomacy* (1934; Gloucester, Mass.: Peter Smith, 1962), 23–24; Sharp, *American Politics in the Early Republic,* 116; *PAH,* 16: 264; Elkins and McKitrick, *Age of Federalism,* 395.

14 Combs, *Jay Treaty,* 134–135; *Aurora,* 4 July 1795; Alexander Hamilton to Angelica Church, 8 December 1794, Hamilton to George Washington, 11 November 1794, *PAH,* 17:429, 366.

15 New York *American Minerva,* 5 July 1794; *Greenleaf's New York Journal,* 9 July 1794; Portland *Eastern Herald,* 5 July 1794; Philadelphia *General Advertiser,* 5, 8, 9 July 1794; Len Travers, *Celebrating the Fourth: Independence Day and the Rites of Nationalism in the Early Republic* (Amherst: University of Massachusetts Press, 1997), 95–96.

16 Bradford Perkins, *The Cambridge History of American Foreign Relations,* vol. 1, *The Creation of a Republican Empire, 1776–1865* (New York: Cambridge University Press, 1993), 97–99.

17 Samuel Flagg Bemis, *Jay's Treaty: A Study in Commerce and Diplomacy* (New Haven: Yale University Press, 1962), 368–370, 337–340, 343–344; "Conversation with George Hammond," 1–10 July 1794, *PAH,* 16:548–549; Reginald Horsman, *The Diplomacy of the New Republic, 1776–1815* (Arlington Heights, Ill.: Harlan Davidson, 1985), 58–59.

18 "London, Jan. 7. PUBLIC DINNER," *Philadelphia Gazette & Universal Daily Advertiser,* 21 February 1795; "British Friendship for America," Portsmouth *Oracle of the Day,* 18 February 1795; Charleston *City Gazette,* 23 March 1795; *Aurora,* 4, 30 March 1795; Philadelphia *Gazette of the United States,* 25 February 1795; "The President's Birth Day," Boston *Federal Orrery,* 9 March 1795; Combs, *Jay Treaty,* 160.

19 "The Editor's Address to the Public," New York *Argus & Greenleaf's New Daily Advertiser* (hereafter *Argus*), 2 June 1795. For background on Greenleaf and his prominent role in New York City politics, see Alfred F. Young, *The Democratic Republicans of New York: The Origins, 1763–1797* (Chapel Hill: University of North Carolina Press for the Institute of Early American History and Culture, 1967); and Jeffrey L. Pasley, "Thomas Greenleaf: Printers and the Struggle for Democratic Politics and Freedom of the Press," in *Revolutionary Founders: Rebels, Radicals, and Reformers in the Making of the Nation,* ed. Alfred F. Young, Gary B. Nash, and Ray Raphael (New York: Alfred A. Knopf, 2011), 357–375, 428–429.

20 *Aurora,* 8 November 1794. The present author's take on Bache is presented at length in Jeffrey L. Pasley, *"The Tyranny of Printers": Newspaper Politics in the Early American Republic* (Charlottesville: University Press of Virginia, 2001), chap. 4, which this paragraph draws on.

21 *Aurora,* 31 January, 2, 3, 4, 5, 6 (quoted), 7, 9, 10, 11 February 1795.

22 Elkins and McKitrick, *Age of Federalism,* 416–417; Eleazer Oswald, ed., *Letters of Franklin, on the Conduct of the Executive and the Treaty Negociated by the Chief Justice of the United States with the Court of Great Britain* (Philadelphia: E. Oswald, 1795), Evans 29256. "Franklin" was fifty-six pages long in pamphlet form. One of the more highly regarded series of the 1790s, "Old South" in the Boston *Independent Chronicle,* stretched to seventy-five essays and appeared later as a 317-page book: Benjamin Austin Jr., *Constitutional Republicanism, in Opposition to Fallacious Federalism as Published Occasionally in the Independent Chronicle, under the Signature of Old-South: to Which Is Added, a Prefatory Address to the Citizens of the United States, Never before Published* (Boston: Printed for Adams & Rhoades, editors of the *Independent Chronicle,* 1803).

23 Oswald, *Letters of Franklin*, 4, 7.

24 James J. Kirschke, *Gouverneur Morris: Author, Statesman, and Man of the World* (New York: Thomas Dunne Books, 2005), 169–171.

25 Lance Banning, "Republican Ideology and the Triumph of the Constitution, 1789 to 1793," *William and Mary Quarterly*, 3rd ser., 31 (1974): 167–188.

26 "Sidney, No. II," *Aurora*, 19 June 1795.

27 Oswald, *Letters of Franklin*, 13; *Aurora*, 16, 18, 23 June, 30 March 1795; Elkins and McKitrick, *Age of Federalism*, 418.

28 "To the People," *Greenleaf's New-York Journal*, 8 April 1795; Oswald, *Letters of Franklin*, 22, 11; "From a Correspondent," *Aurora*, 4 March 1795.

29 Combs, *Jay Treaty*, 163–166; David L. Sterling, "A Federalist Opposes the Jay Treaty: The Letters of Samuel Bayard," *William and Mary Quarterly*, 3rd ser., 18 (1961): 408–424, quotation on 415; Oliver Wolcott Jr. to Oliver Wolcott Sr., 27 June 1795, in Gibbs, *Memoirs*, 1: 201; "Mr. Jay's Treaty," Boston *Columbian Centinel*, 24 June 1795.

30 George Washington to Alexander Hamilton, 3 July 1795, *PAH*, 18:398–399; Oswald, *Letters of Franklin*, 22. On the changing style of political leaders that Republican victories would eventually bring in, see Alan Taylor, "From Fathers to Friends of the People: Political Personas in the Early Republic," *Journal of the Early Republic* 11 (1991): 465–491; Jeffrey L. Pasley, "The Cheese and the Words: Popular Political Culture and Participatory Democracy in the Early American Republic," in *Beyond the Founders: New Approaches to the Political History of the Early American Republic*, ed. Jeffrey L. Pasley, Andrew W. Robertson, and David Waldstreicher (Chapel Hill: University of North Carolina Press, 2004), 31–56.

31 "To the Free Electors of the State of New-York," *Greenleaf's New-York Journal*, 15 April 1795.

32 On this "celebratory politics," see Simon P. Newman, *Parades and the Politics of the Street: Festive Culture in the Early American Republic* (Philadelphia: University of Pennsylvania Press, 1997); David Waldstreicher, *In the Midst of Perpetual Fetes: The Making of American Nationalism, 1776–1820* (Chapel Hill: University of North Carolina Press for the Omohundro Institute of Early American History and Culture, 1997); Pasley, Robertson, and Waldstreicher, *Beyond the Founders*.

33 Elkins and McKitrick, *Age of Federalism*, 420–421; "Norfolk, June 9," New York *Argus*, 22 June 1795; "To the Lovers and Supporters of Monarchy and Aristocracy," reprinted in *Aurora*, 13 April 1795; Paul A. Gilje, *Liberty on the Waterfront: American Maritime Culture in the Age of Revolution* (Philadelphia: University of Pennsylvania Press, 2004), 142–143.

34 "Original Handbill, Published in Boston . . . ," New York *Argus*, 30 June 1795; "Il-'legal' and Hasty 'Adjudication,'" *Aurora*, 27 June 1795; "Unwarrantable Proceedings," reprinted in Philadelphia *Gazette of the United States*, 29 June 1795; Gilje, *Liberty on the Waterfront*, 142.

35 "Expected Riot," reprinted in *Aurora*, 3 July 1795; "Communication," reprinted in *Aurora*, 4 July 1795; Boston *Columbian Centinel*, 27 June, 2 July 1795; Travers, *Celebrating the Fourth*, 95–96.

36 *Aurora*, 26, 27 June 1795; Daniel N. Hoffman, *Governmental Secrecy and the Founding Fathers: A Study in Constitutional Controls* (Westport, Conn.:

Greenwood Press, 1981), esp. chap. 5; "Letter I. To the Freemen of the United States," Philadelphia *Independent Gazetteer,* 8 July 1795; Pasley, *Tyranny of Printers,* 98–101.

37 On Adet's role, see Alexander DeConde, *Entangling Alliance: Politics and Diplomacy under George Washington* (Durham: Duke University Press, 1958), 427.

38 Margaret Bache to Benjamin Franklin Bache, 2, 4 July 1795; Benjamin Franklin Bache to Margaret Bache, 3, 5, 8, 10 July 1795, Bache Papers, Castle Collection, American Philosophical Society; Pasley, *Tyranny of Printers,* 91–92; Albrecht Koschnik, "Political Conflict and Public Contest: Rituals of National Celebration in Philadelphia, 1788–1815," *Pennsylvania Magazine of History and Biography* 118 (1994): 228–229.

39 The story of the 1795 Philadelphia Fourth of July celebration has been told many times, but never quite the same way twice: For the most recent accounts, see Gilje, *Liberty on the Waterfront,* 142–143; Travers, *Celebrating the Fourth,* 97–99; and Koschnik, "Political Conflict and Public Contest," 229–233. These and other accounts conflict on certain points, so I have gone back to the original newspaper reports in constructing the following account.

40 Margaret Bache to Benjamin Franklin Bache, 2, 4 July 1795, Bache Papers, Castle Collection, American Philosophical Society; *Aurora,* 4, 7 July 1795; Philadelphia *Independent Gazetteer,* 4 July 1795.

41 Philadelphia *Independent Gazetteer,* 8 July 1795; "Extract of Letter from a Gentleman at Philadelphia, to His Friend in this City," New York *Argus,* 15 July 1795.

42 Boston *Columbian Centinel,* 15 July 1795; Travers, *Celebrating the Fourth,* 98.

43 "To the Militia of Philadelphia" and "GENERAL ORDERS," *Aurora,* 3 July 1795. On the politics of the Philadelphia militia, see Steven Rosswurm, *Arms, Country, and Class: The Philadelphia Militia and the "Lower Sort" during the American Revolution* (New Brunswick, N.J.: Rutgers University Press, 1987); Kim Tousley Phillips, "William Duane, Revolutionary Editor" (Ph.D. diss., University of California, Berkeley, 1968); Kim T. Phillips, "William Duane, Philadelphia's Democratic Republicans, and the Origins of Modern Politics," *Pennsylvania Magazine of History and Biography* 101 (1977): 365–387; and most relevant to the events of 1795, Koschnik, "Political Conflict and Public Contest," 223–226.

44 Philadelphia *Independent Gazetteer,* 8 July 1795; New York *Argus,* 15 July 1795; Boston *Columbian Centinel,* 15 July 1795.

45 Baltimore *Federal Intelligencer,* 7 July 1795; Libero M. Renzulli Jr., *Maryland: The Federalist Years* (Madison, N.J.: Fairleigh Dickinson University Press, 1972), 168; Elizabethtown, Md. *Washington Spy,* 14 July 1795.

46 Baltimore *Federal Intelligencer,* 7 July 1795.

47 Benjamin Franklin Bache to Margaret Bache, 3 July 1795, Bache Papers, Castle Collection, American Philosophical Society; New York *Argus,* 6, 7, 8 July 1795; Young, *Democratic Republicans of New York,* 446–448.

48 New York *Argus,* 7, 8 July 1795; Elizabethtown *New-Jersey Journal,* 15 July 1795.

49 Benjamin Franklin Bache to Margaret Bache, 15 July 1795, Bache Papers, Castle Collection, American Philosophical Society.

50 George Blake, *An Oration Pronounced July 4, 1795, at the Request of the Inhabitants of the Town of Boston, in Commemoration of the Anniversary of American Independence* (Boston: Benjamin Edes, 1795), Evans 28307, 13, 22, 26–27; *Boston Gazette,* 6 July 1795; Boston *Columbian Centinel,* 8 July 1795, reprinted in *GUS,* 13 July 1795.

51 Quotations in this paragraph and the following one are from Benjamin Franklin Bache to Margaret Bache, 8 July 1795, Bache Papers, Castle Collection, American Philosophical Society. Useful accounts of the July 1795 mass meetings appear in Estes, *Jay Treaty Debate*, 70–78; James D. Tagg, *Benjamin Franklin Bache and the Philadelphia "Aurora"* (Philadelphia: University of Pennsylvania Press, 1991), 247–250; and William Bruce Wheeler, "Urban Politics in Nature's Republic: The Development of Political Parties in the Seaport Cities in the Federalist Era" (Ph.D. diss., University of Virginia, 1967). On the *Independent Chronicle*, see John B. Hench, "The Newspaper in a Republic: Boston's 'Centinel' and 'Chronicle,' 1784–1801" (Ph.D. diss., Clark University, 1979); and Joseph T. Buckingham, *Specimens of Newspaper Literature: With Personal Memoirs, Anecdotes, and Reminiscences* (Boston: Charles C. Little and James Brown, 1850), 1:248–287.

52 On the uses of the town meeting in the coming of the Revolution, see John C. Miller, *Sam Adams: Pioneer in Propaganda* (Stanford: Stanford University Press, 1960); and Richard D. Brown, *Revolutionary Politics in Massachusetts: The Boston Committee of Correspondence and the Towns, 1772–1774* (New York: W. W. Norton, 1976). The rules for calling a town meeting in Boston are explained in *GUS*, 16 July 1795.

53 Fisher Ames to Oliver Wolcott, 9 July 1795, in *Works of Fisher Ames, as Published by Seth Ames*, ed. W. B. Allen (Indianapolis: LibertyClassics, 1983), 2:1107; "Citizens of Boston, ATTEND!," Boston *Columbian Centinel*, 8 July 1795; *GUS*, 15 July 1795; Benjamin Franklin Bache to Margaret Bache, 15 July 1795, Bache Papers, Castle Collection, American Philosophical Association.

54 On the proceedings of the Boston meetings, see *GUS*, 15 July 1795; Benjamin Franklin Bache to Margaret Bache, 15 July 1795, Bache Papers, Castle Collection, American Philosophical Association; Boston *Independent Chronicle*, reprinted in Philadelphia *Independent Gazetteer*, 18 July 1795; New York *Herald*, 22 July 1795; Estes, *Jay Treaty Debate*, 73–75; Wheeler, "Urban Politics," 367–369.

55 Benjamin Franklin Bache to Margaret Bache, 15 July 1795, Bache Papers, Castle Collection, American Philosophical Association; Tagg, *Benjamin Franklin Bache*, 248–249. On the language of sensibility, see Sarah Knott, *Sensibility and the American Revolution* (Chapel Hill: University of North Carolina Press for the Omohundro Institute of Early American History and Culture, 2009).

56 Wheeler, "Urban Politics," 369. For demonstrations in cities besides Boston, New York, and Philadelphia, see (among others) *Aurora*, 25, 27 July 1795; *Boston Gazette*, 27 July 1795.

57 This paragraph and the next two draw heavily on the very thorough account of the New York meetings in Young, *Democratic Republicans of New York*, 449–454. For local newspaper reports, see *PAH*, 18:485n–488n; and New York *Argus*, 20 July 1795.

58 "Extract of a Letter from New-York, Dated July 20th, 1795," *Aurora*, 22 July 1795; Young, *Democratic Republicans of New York*, 451.

59 Young, *Democratic Republicans of New York*, 452–453; *PAH*, 18:471–472n1; "Seventy-Six," New York *Argus*, 22 July 1795.

60 Young, *Democratic Republicans of New York*, 451–452; New York *Argus*, 21 July 1795; the quotation is from Benjamin Franklin Bache to Margaret Bache, 21 July 1795, Bache Papers, Castle Collection, American Philosophical Society.

61 New York *Argus*, 21 July 1795; Young, *Democratic Republicans of New York*, 454–455; Estes, *Jay Treaty Debate*, 78–79.

62 Alexander Hamilton to Robert Troup, 25 July 1795, *PAH*, 18:503–507; Hamilton to Oliver Wolcott Jr., 28 July 1795, *PAH*, 18:512.

63 John Beckley to De Witt Clinton, 24 July 1795, in *Justifying Jefferson: The Political Writings of John James Beckley*, ed. Gerard Gawalt (Washington, D.C.: Library of Congress, 1995), 95; "Hypocrite," New York *Argus*, 21 July 1795.

64 Secondary accounts of the Philadelphia Jay Treaty meetings abound, including Richard G. Miller, *Philadelphia—The Federalist City: A Study of Urban Politics, 1789–1801* (Port Washington, N.Y.: Kennikat Press, 1976), 71–73; Tagg, *Benjamin Franklin Bache*, 249–250; and Wheeler, "Urban Politics," 97–99. Local news reports of the first meeting, including the text of the resolutions, appear in Philadelphia *Gazette of the United States*, 24 July 1795; and *Aurora*, 24, 29 July 1795. The handbill was reprinted in *Kline's Carlisle Weekly Gazette*, 29 July 1795.

65 *Aurora*, 24, 25 July 1795; John Beckley to De Witt Clinton, 24 July 1795, in Gawalt, *Justifying Jefferson*, 95.

66 *Aurora*, 25, 27, 29 July 1795; Philadelphia *Gazette of the United States*, 27, 29 July 1795; Miller, *Philadelphia—The Federalist City*, 72–73; Wheeler, "Urban Politics," 97–99.

67 *Aurora*, 27, 29 July 1795; Philadelphia *Gazette of the United States*, 27, 29 July 1795; Tagg, *Benjamin Franklin Bache*, 249–250. On Federalist nativism, see Edward C. Carter II, "A 'Wild Irishman' under Every Federalist's Bed: Naturalization in Philadelphia, 1789–1906," *Pennsylvania Magazine of History and Biography* 94 (1970): 331–346.

68 John Jay to Reverend Richard Price, 27 September 1785, in *The Life of John Jay: With Selections from His Correspondence and Miscellaneous Papers*, by William Jay (New York: Harper, 1833), 2:174; George Cabot to Rufus King, 14 August 1795, in Lodge, *Life and Letters of George Cabot*, 85.

69 Estes, *Jay Treaty Debate*, 78–79.

70 Beckley to Clinton, 24 July 1795, in Gawalt, *Justifying Jefferson*, 96.

71 For judicious discussions of this often-rehashed incident, see Andrew Burstein and Nancy Isenberg, *Madison and Jefferson* (New York: Random House, 2010), 296–300; Elkins and McKitrick, *Age of Federalism*, 422–431. For Randolph's side of the story, see John J. Reardon, *Edmund Randolph: A Biography* (New York: Macmillan, 1974), 307–334.

CHAPTER 4. FROM MEASURES TO "THAT MAN"

1 "Hancock," Philadelphia *Aurora General Advertiser*, 21 August 1795; Richard R. Beeman, *Plain, Honest Men: The Making of the American Constitution* (New York: Random House, 2009), 345–346.

2 The cult of Washington and the subsequent attacks on it have been covered by countless scholars, but perhaps the most useful treatments for present purposes are Donald H. Stewart, *The Opposition Press of the Federalist Period* (Albany: State University of New York Press, 1969), 519–536; James D. Tagg, "Benjamin Franklin Bache's Attack on George Washington," *Pennsylvania Magazine of History and Biography* 100 (1976): 191–230; Simon P. Newman, "Principles or Men? George Washington and the Political Culture of National Leadership, 1776–1801," *Journal of the Early Republic* 12 (1992): 477–507;

Alexander DeConde, *Entangling Alliance: Politics and Diplomacy under George Washington* (Durham: Duke University Press, 1958), 459–467; and Barry Schwartz, *George Washington: The Making of an American Symbol* (New York: Free Press, 1987), 13–80.

3 DeConde, *Entangling Alliance*, 459–463.

4 Quotations from New York *Argus*, 23 June 1795.

5 "Hancock," *Aurora*, 21 August 1795.

6 Newman, "Principles or Men?"; Schwartz, *George Washington*, 73–89. Quotations from Alexander Hamilton to Tobias Lear, 2 January 1800, *PAH*, 24:155; "Portius," *Aurora*, 21 October 1795; "The Contrast," Charleston *Columbian Herald*, 19 November 1795.

7 David Tappan, *Christian Thankfulness Explained and Enforced: A Sermon, Delivered at Charlestown, in the Afternoon of February 19, 1795: The Day of General Thanksgiving through the United States* (Boston: Samuel Hall, 1795), 7–8, 21–22, 19.

8 Samuel Stanhope Smith, *The Divine Goodness to the United States of America: A Discourse, on the Subjects of National Gratitude*, 2nd ed. (Philadelphia: William Young, 1795), 19.

9 "Belisarius, No. II," *Aurora*, 15 September 1795; "A Fragment," Boston *Columbian Centinel*, 21 October 1795, also reprinted in Brookfield, Mass., *Moral and Political Telegraphe or Brookfield Advertiser*, 28 October 1795; Portsmouth *New Hampshire Gazette*, 3 November 1795; *The Eagle, or Dartmouth Centinel*, 23 November 1795; Keene, N.H., *Rising Sun*, 8 December 1795. On the passive obedience of subordinates as a central ideal of conservative politics, going back to the Federalists, see Corey Robin, *The Reactionary Mind: Conservatism from Edmund Burke to Sarah Palin* (New York: Oxford University Press, 2011), 3–17.

10 "A Correspondent," "Valerius," and "Belisarius," *Aurora*, 22 August, 9, 15 September 1795.

11 George Washington to Ezekiel Price, Thomas Walley, et al., 28 July 1795, in *Writings of George Washington*, ed. Worthington C. Ford (New York: G. P. Putnam's Sons, 1892), 13:74–75; Stewart, *Opposition Press*, 522; "Belisarius," *Aurora*, 22 September, 3 October 1795.

12 *Aurora*, 22 August, 14 September 1795; Stewart, *Opposition Press*, 525.

13 "A Correspondent," *Aurora*, 22 August 1795; "Valerius," *Aurora*, 9 September 1795; Jeffrey L. Pasley, *"The Tyranny of Printers": Newspaper Politics in the Early American Republic* (Charlottesville: University Press of Virginia, 2001), chap. 5.

14 Stewart, *Opposition Press*, 522–525; Carl J. Richard, *The Founders and the Classics: Greece, Rome and the American Enlightenment* (Cambridge, Mass.: Harvard University Press, 1994), 41, 208; Jona Lendering, "Publius Valerius Publicola," http://www.livius.org/va-vh/valerius/publicola.html; Titus Livius, *History of Rome: The First Eight Books*, trans. D. Spillan, book 2, http://www.gutenberg.org/files/19725/19725-h/19725-h.htm#b7; "Valerius," *Aurora*, 1, 9 September 1795.

15 Advertisement for Faugeres play, New York *Daily Advertiser*, 27 April 1795; Douglas L. Wilson, "Thomas Jefferson's Library and the French Connection," *Eighteenth-Century Studies* 26 (1993): 675–676.

16 *Aurora*, 11, 15 September 1795.

17 "Portius," *Aurora*, 24 September, 12 October 1795; Stewart, *Opposition Press*, 526.

18 Elizabethtown *New-Jersey Journal*, 30 September 1795. The "Calm Observer" series appeared in the *Aurora*, 23, 27, 29 October, 2 November 1795, and is reprinted in *Justifying Jefferson: The Political Writings of John James Beckley*, ed. Gerard Gawalt (Washington, D.C.: Library of Congress, 1995), 102–113.

19 On John Beckley, see Edmund Berkeley and Dorothy Smith Berkeley, *John Beckley: Zealous Partisan in a Nation Divided* (Philadelphia: American Philosophical Society, 1973); Noble E. Cunningham Jr., "John Beckley: An Early American Party Manager," *William and Mary Quarterly*, 3rd ser., 13 (1956): 40–52; Jeffrey L. Pasley, "'A Journeyman, Either in Law or Politics': John Beckley and the Social Origins of Political Campaigning," *Journal of the Early Republic* 16 (1996): 531–569.

20 The most complete account of the "Calm Observer" controversy can be found in Berkeley and Berkeley, *John Beckley*, 120–129.

21 Gawalt, *Justifying Jefferson*, 104–105.

22 George Gibbs, ed., *Memoirs of the Administration of Washington and John Adams, Edited From the Papers of Oliver Wolcott, Secretary of the Treasury* (New York: William Van Norden, 1846), 1:259–261; *PAH*, 19:364.

23 *Aurora*, 2 November 1795; Berkeley and Berkeley, *John Beckley*, 128; Boston *Columbian Centinel*, 7 November 1795; "Advertisement Extraordinary," Philadelphia *Gazette of the United States*, 27 October 1795.

24 *PAH*, 19:350–354, 400–426; Tagg, "Bache's Attack on George Washington," 214–215.

25 "The Political Creed of 1795," *Aurora*, 23 November 1795; also reprinted in New York *American Minerva*, 25 November 1795; Mount Pleasant *Jersey Chronicle*, 12 December 1795; and others. For similar items, from different viewpoints, see "Political Catechism of a True Blue Demagogue," Columbia *South Carolina State Gazette*, 14 August 1796, reprinted in New York *American Minerva*, 29 September 1796; "A Political Creed," Mount Pleasant *Jersey Chronicle*, 5 December 1795; "The Political Creed of a Western American," reprinted in *Aurora*, 3 November 1795; "Political Creed," Boston *Massachusetts Mercury*, 20 May 1796; "Political Catechism," *NY Journal*, 5 April 1796.

26 For 1790s examples, see Alan V. Briceland, "The Philadelphia Aurora, the New England Illuminati, and the Election of 1800," *Pennsylvania Magazine of History and Biography* 50 (1976): 3–36; Robert J. Imholt, "Timothy Dwight, Federalist Pope of Connecticut," *New England Quarterly* 73 (2000): 386–411.

27 "To the President of the United States," *Aurora*, 20 November 1795; John Adams to Abigail Adams, 1 March 1796, *AFP*; Tagg, "Bache's Attack on George Washington," 211.

28 Stephen G. Kurtz, *The Presidency of John Adams: The Collapse of Federalism, 1795–1800* (New York: A. S. Barnes, 1961), 34–35.

29 "Scipio," *Aurora*, 20 November 1795.

30 Philip B. Kurland and Ralph Lerner, eds., *The Founders' Constitution*, Internet ed. (Chicago: University of Chicago Press, 2000), http://press-pubs.uchicago.edu/founders/documents/a2_2_2-3s1.html; Madison to Jefferson, 13 December 1795, *PJM*, 16:163–164; Jack N. Rakove, *Original Meanings: Politics and Ideas in the Making of the Constitution* (New York: Vintage, 1997), 355–365; Andrew Burstein and Nancy Isenberg, *Madison and Jefferson* (New York: Random House, 2010), 307–309.

31 Madison to Jefferson, 13, 27 December 1795, 10 January 1796, *PJM*, 16:163–164, 173, 180–181.

32 Alfred F. Young, *The Democratic Republicans of New York: The Origins, 1763–1797* (Chapel Hill: University of North Carolina Press for the Institute of Early American History and Culture, 1967), 420–421; William B. Hatcher, *Edward Livingston, Jeffersonian Republican and Jacksonian Democrat* (Baton Rouge: Louisiana State University Press, 1940); George Dangerfield, *Chancellor Robert R. Livingston of New York, 1746–1813* (New York: Harcourt Brace, 1960), 278–280; *PJM*, 16:144, 248n5; Jerald A. Combs, *The Jay Treaty: Political Battleground of the Founding Fathers* (Berkeley: University of California Press, 1970), 174–176.

33 Daniel N. Hoffman, *Governmental Secrecy and the Founding Fathers: A Study in Constitutional Controls* (Westport, Conn.: Greenwood Press, 1981), 152–153; *Annals of Congress*, House of Representatives, 4th Congress, 1st Session, 7 March 1796, 426.

34 Hoffman, *Governmental Secrecy and the Founding Fathers*, 153–158; Elizabeth-Town *New-Jersey Journal*, 16 March 1796.

35 On the Anglo-American tradition of popular constitutionalism, see Pauline Maier, *From Resistance to Revolution: Colonial Radicals and the Development of American Opposition to Britain, 1765–1776* (New York: Vintage, 1974), chap. 1; Larry Kramer, *The People Themselves: Popular Constitutionalism and Judicial Review* (New York: Oxford University Press, 2004); Christian G. Fritz, *American Sovereigns: The People and America's Constitutional Tradition before the Civil War* (New York: Cambridge University Press, 2008); Jeffrey L. Pasley, "Popular Constitutionalism in Philadelphia: How Freedom of Expression Was Secured by Two Fearless Newspaper Editors," *Pennsylvania Legacies* 8 (May 2008): 6–11.

36 Combs, *Jay Treaty*, 176; Oliver Wolcott Sr. to Jonathan Trumbull, 14 March 1796, in Gibbs, *Memoirs*, 1:322.

37 *Annals of Congress*, House of Representatives, 4th Congress, 1st Session, 7 March 1796, 427–428; Louis Fisher, *The Politics of Executive Privilege* (Durham: Carolina Academic Press, 2004), 6–33; Hoffman, *Governmental Secrecy and the Founding Fathers*, 150–158.

38 Leonard D. White, *The Federalists: A Study in Administrative History* (New York: Macmillan, 1948), 63; Washington to Hamilton, 29, 31 March 1796, *PAH*, 20:90, 103–104; Hoffman, *Governmental Secrecy and the Founding Fathers*, 158–165; *PAH*, 20:81–105.

39 Hoffman, *Governmental Secrecy and the Founding Fathers*, 165–169; George Washington to the House of Representatives, 30 March 1796, in *The Writings of George Washington from the Original Manuscript Sources*, ed. John C. Fitzpatrick (Washington, D.C.: Government Printing Office, 1940), 35:2–5.

40 Madison to Monroe, 18 April 1796, Madison to Jefferson, *PJM*, 16:285–286, 333; Hamilton to Rufus King, 15 April 1796, *PAH*, 20:112–113; Beckley to Monroe, 2 April 1796, in Gawalt, *Justifying Jefferson*, 114; Noble E. Cunningham Jr., *The Jeffersonian Republicans: The Formation of Party Organization, 1789–1801* (Chapel Hill: University of North Carolina Press for the Institute of Early American History and Culture, 1957), 81–83.

41 Quotations from Madison to Monroe, 26 February, 18 April 1796, *PJM*, 16:232, 333. My understanding of Hamilton has been most shaped by Kurtz, *Presidency of John Adams*, esp. 204–207; Max M. Edling, *A Revolution in Favor*

of Government: Origins of the U.S. Constitution and the Making of the American State (Oxford: Oxford University Press, 2003); Joanne B. Freeman, *Affairs of Honor: National Politics in the New Republic* (New Haven: Yale University Press, 2001); Forrest McDonald, *Alexander Hamilton: A Biography* (New York: W. W. Norton, 1982); John C. Miller, *Alexander Hamilton and the Growth of the New Nation* (New York: Harper & Row, 1964); and Karl-Friedrich Walling, *Republican Empire: Alexander Hamilton on War and Free Government* (Lawrence: University Press of Kansas, 1999), but it does not exactly reflect the views of any of these authors.

42 Chauncey Goodrich to Oliver Wolcott Sr., 6 May 1796, in Gibbs, *Memoirs*, 1:337.

43 Hamilton to King, 15 April 1796, *PAH*, 20:112–115; Alexander Hamilton, "To the Citizens Who Shall Be Convened This Day in the Fields in the City of New York," *PAH*, 20:131–134. The best discussion of the Federalist counterattack is still probably Stephen Kurtz's chapter on "Popular Federalism" in *Presidency of John Adams*, 52–77, but the most recent and thorough discussion of the petition campaign is Todd Estes, *The Jay Treaty Debate, Public Opinion, and the Evolution of Early American Political Culture* (Amherst: University of Massachusetts Press, 2006), 160–178.

44 Estes, *Jay Treaty Debate*, 160–178; Philadelphia *Claypoole's American Daily Advertiser*, 16, 18 April 1796; King to Hamilton, 17–18, 20 April 1796, and editorial notes, *PAH*, 20:121–126.

45 On Thomas Fitzsimons, see David Hackett Fischer, *The Revolution of American Conservatism: The Federalist Party in the Era of Jeffersonian Democracy* (New York: Harper & Row, 1965), 337; Estes, *Jay Treaty Debate*, 166–167; *Providence Gazette*, 23 April 1796. The "astroturf" petition is found in *To the Honorable the House of Representatives of the United States: The Memorial of the Subscribers, Merchants and Traders of [blank]*, Broadside (Boston?, 1796), Evans 31304. On the Evans copy, the blank has been filled by the handwritten words "Mechanics and others, Citizens of Boston."

46 On McHenry, Smith, and the Baltimore events, see Bernard C. Steiner, "Maryland Politics in 1796—McHenry Letters," *Publications of the Southern Historical Association* 9 (1905): 374–378; Frank A. Cassell, *Merchant Congressman in the Young Republic: Samuel Smith of Maryland, 1752–1839* (Madison: University of Wisconsin Press, 1971), 66–68; DeConde, *Entangling Alliance*, 137.

47 Edmund Randolph to James Madison, 22, 26 April 1796, *PJM*, 16:334–335, 338–339.

48 Hamilton to King, 20 April 1796, Hamilton, "To the Citizens," *PAH*, 20:126–128, 131–134; Young, *Democratic Republicans of New York*, 465.

49 King to Hamilton, 17–18, 20 April 1796, Hamilton to King, 20, 23, 24 April 1796, and editorial notes, *PAH*, 20:121–128, 135–137. Philip Schuyler to Hamilton, 25 April 1796, *PAH*, 20:138–140. Schuyler's form letter is reprinted in Allan McLane Hamilton, ed., *The Intimate Life of Alexander Hamilton* (New York: Charles Scribner's Sons, 1910), between 292 and 293; Young, *Democratic Republicans of New York*, 465.

50 Estes, *Jay Treaty Debate*, 164–165. On newspapers and politics in 1790s Boston, see Hench, "Newspaper in a Republic."

51 Boston *Columbian Centinel*, 28 April 1796. On Federalist nativism and reactionary populism, see Robert Ernst, *Rufus King: American Federalist* (Chapel Hill: University of North Carolina Press for the Institute of Early American

History and Culture, 1968), 214; Edward C. Carter II, "A 'Wild Irishman' under Every Federalist's Bed: Naturalization in Philadelphia, 1789–1906," *Pennsylvania Magazine of History and Biography* 94 (1970): 331–346; and Fischer, *Revolution of American Conservatism*.

52 Boston *Columbian Centinel*, 28 April 1796; Alexander Hamilton to George Washington, 11 November 1794, *PAH*, 17:366. Max Edling has argued convincingly that Hamilton carefully calibrated (and restrained) his financial system to be acceptable to American public opinion. See Edling, *Revolution in Favor of Government*.

53 New York *American Minerva*, 19 April 1796; *The Petition of the Freemen of the Town of Hartford in the State of Connecticut*, Evans 47798 [Hartford: n.p. 1796]; Philadelphia *Claypoole's American Daily Advertiser*, 18 April 1796; *Greenleaf's New-York Journal & Patriotic Register*, 19 April 1796.

54 "Old Moe Sarcasm," *Greenleaf's New York Journal*, 19 April 1796; Philadelphia *Claypoole's American Daily Advertiser*, 18 April 1796; *To the Honourable the House of Representatives of the United States: The Memorial of the Subscribers, Citizens of [blank] in Massachusetts*, Broadside (Boston?, 1796), Evans 31305; *The Petition of the Town of Hartford in the State of Connecticut*, Broadside (Hartford, 1796), Evans 47798.

55 On merchant petitioning and lobbying, see Michael G. Kammen, *A Rope of Sand: The Colonial Agents, British Politics, and the American Revolution* (New York: Vintage, 1974); Rebecca Starr, *A School for Politics: Commercial Lobbying and Political Culture in Early South Carolina* (Baltimore: Johns Hopkins University Press, 1998), 24, 114–117, 141–142; Alison Gilbert Olson, *Making the Empire Work: London and American Interest Groups, 1690–1790* (Cambridge, Mass.: Harvard University Press, 1992); Thomas M. Doerflinger, *A Vigorous Spirit of Enterprise: Merchants and Economic Development in Revolutionary Philadelphia* (New York: W. W. Norton, 1987); Jeffrey L. Pasley, "Private Access and Public Power: Gentility and Lobbying in the Early Congress," in *The House and Senate in the 1790s: Petitioning, Lobbying, and Institutional Development*, ed. Kenneth R. Bowling and Donald R. Kennon (Athens: Ohio University Press for the United States Capitol Historical Society, 2002), 59–64.

56 Boston *Massachusetts Mercury*, 26 April 1796; Boston *Columbian Centinel*, 28 April 1796. The New England town studies of the 1960s generally dispelled the myth of town-meeting democracy, most classically in Michael Zuckerman, *Peaceable Kingdoms: New England Towns in the Eighteenth Century* (New York: Alfred A. Knopf, 1970); Bruce C. Daniels, *The Connecticut Town: Growth and Development, 1635–1790* (Middletown, Conn.: Wesleyan University Press, 1979); and Kenneth A. Lockridge, *A New England Town: The First Hundred Years* (New York: W. W. Norton, 1970), 37–49.

57 James Madison to Thomas Jefferson, 23 April 1796, *PJM*, 16:335.

58 "Important Information," *GUS*, 8 April 1796; "At a Meeting of Committees Appointed by the New-York and United Insurance Companies," *GUS*, 20 April 1796; *GUS*, 13 April 1796; "Extract of Letter from Philadelphia, Dated April 15," *Providence* Gazette, 23 April 1796; Young, *Democratic Republicans of New York*, 464.

59 John Langdon to James Madison, 28 April 1796, *PJM*, 16:340–341; Kurtz, *Presidency of John Adams*, 56.

60 "Dramaticus," *Greenleaf's New-York Journal*, 19 April 1796.

61 Richard C. Knopf, ed., *Anthony Wayne, a Name in Arms: Soldier, Diplomat, Defender of Expansion Westward of a Nation: The Wayne-Knox-Pickering-McHenry Correspondence* (Pittsburgh: University of Pittsburgh Press, 1960), 466–469, 477; Wiley Sword, *President Washington's Indian War: The Struggle for the Old Northwest, 1790–1795* (Norman: University of Oklahoma Press, 1985), 312–321, 334–335.

62 Winifred E. A. Bernhard, *Fisher Ames: Federalist and Statesman, 1758–1808* (Chapel Hill: University of North Carolina Press for the Institute of Early American History and Culture, 1965), esp. 238–240; Ames to Thomas Dwight, 16 April 1791, in *Works of Fisher Ames, as Published by Seth Ames*, ed. W. B. Allen (Indianapolis: LibertyClassics, 1983), 2:866; Michael J. Dubin, *United States Congressional Elections, 1788–1997: The Official Results* (Jefferson, N.C.: McFarland, 1998), 7, 10.

63 The literature on these topics is too vast to cite here, but the particular points made in this paragraph were influenced by, among others works, Roy Harvey Pearce, "The Significances of the Captivity Narrative," *American Literature* 19 (1947): 1–20; David L. Minter, "By Dens of Lions: Notes on Stylization in Early Puritan Captivity Narratives," *American Literature* 54 (1973): 335–347; Richard Slotkin, *Regeneration through Violence: The Mythology of the American Frontier, 1600–1860* (Middletown, Conn.: Wesleyan University Press, 1973); Carter, "'Wild Irishman,'" 331–346; Jared Gardner, "Alien Nation: Edgar Huntly's Savage Awakening," *American Literature* 66 (1994): 429–461; and W. M. Verhoeven, "Gothic Logic: Charles Brockden Brown and the Science of Sensationalism," *European Journal of American Culture* 20 (2001): 91–99, quotation on 99.

64 Bernhard, *Fisher Ames*, 267–268; "Life of Fisher Ames," Philadelphia *Port-Folio*, January 1813, 2, 13 (quoted). On the origins of "lobby" and "lobbying," see Pasley, "Private Access and Public Power," 57–99.

65 John Adams to Abigail Adams, 30 April 1796, *AFP*; "Life of Fisher Ames," 13; Keene, N. H., *Rising Sun*, 10 May 1796.

66 For scholarly analyses of the speech, see James M. Farrell, "Fisher Ames and Political Judgment: Reason, Passion, and Vehement Style in the Jay Treaty Speech," *Quarterly Journal of Speech* 76 (1990): 415–434; Beth Innocenti Manolescu, "Style and Spectator Judgment in Fisher Ames's Jay Treaty Speech," *Quarterly Journal of Speech* 84 (1998): 62–79; Todd Estes, "'The Most Bewitching Piece of Parliamentary Oratory': Fisher Ames' Jay Treaty Speech Reconsidered," *Historical Journal of Massachusetts* 28 (2000): 1–22. Reprintings of the speech included Fisher Ames, *The Speech of Mr. Ames, in the House of Representatives of the United States* (Philadelphia: John Fenno, 1796), Evans 29985, plus one other Philadelphia edition (Evans 47701) and three more in Boston (Evans 29983, 29984, and 31734). The later, more famous sections of the speech are available on Internet at http://www.bartelby.com/268/8/22 .html, a text taken from an anthology of great American speeches edited by William Jennings Bryan. The complete speech appears as "Speech on the Jay Treaty," 28 April 1796, in Allen, *Works of Fisher Ames*, 1142–1182.

67 While a much-contested phenomenon in terms of both its desirability and the degree of adherence it was ever given, it seems undeniable at this point that rational debate in the bourgeois public sphere was a reigning ideal in late eighteenth-century America. My understanding is most influenced by:

Jürgen Habermas, *The Structural Transformation of the Public Sphere: An Inquiry into a Category of Bourgeois Society* (Cambridge, Mass.: MIT Press, 1991); Michael Warner, *The Letters of the Republic: Publication and the Public Sphere in Eighteenth-Century America* (Cambridge, Mass.: Harvard University Press, 1990); Michael Warner, *Publics and Counterpublics* (New York: Zone Books, 2005); Craig Calhoun, ed., *Habermas and the Public Sphere* (Cambridge, Mass.: MIT Press, 1992); John L. Brooke, "Reason and Passion the Public Sphere: Habermas and the Cultural Historians," *Journal of Interdisciplinary History* 29 (1998): 43–67; John L. Brooke, "Consent, Civil Society, and the Public Sphere in the Age of Revolution and the Early American Republic," in *Beyond the Founders: New Approaches to the Political History of the Early American Republic*, ed. Jeffrey L. Pasley, Andrew W. Robertson, and David Waldstreicher (Chapel Hill: University of North Carolina Press, 2004), 207–250; John Ehrenberg, *Civil Society: The Critical History of an Idea* (New York: New York University Press, 1999); Michael Schudson, *The Good Citizen: A History of American Civic Life* (New York: Free Press, 1998); Harold Mah, "Phantasies of the Public Sphere: Rethinking the Habermas of Historians," *Journal of Modern History* 72 (2000): 153–182.

68 Ames, "Speech on the Jay Treaty," 1144.

69 There is a vast and growing literature on sensibility stretching across several disciplines and subfields. Most influential on my account are: Andrew Burstein, *Sentimental Democracy: The Evolution of America's Romantic Self-Image* (New York: Hill & Wang, 1999); Sarah Knott, *Sensibility and the American Revolution* (Chapel Hill: University of North Carolina Press for the Omohundro Institute of Early American History and Culture, 2009); G. J. Barker-Benfield, *The Culture of Sensibility: Sex and Society in Eighteenth-Century Britain* (Chicago: University of Chicago Press, 1992); Bruce Burgett, *Sentimental Bodies: Sex, Gender, and Citizenship in the Early American Republic* (Princeton: Princeton University Press, 1998); Mary Chapman and Glenn Hendler, eds., *Sentimental Men: Masculinity and the Politics of Affect in American Culture* (Berkeley: University of California Press, 1999); Elizabeth B. Clark, " 'The Sacred Rights of the Weak': Pain, Sympathy, and the Culture of Individual Rights in Antebellum America," *Journal of American History* 82 (1995): 463–493; Elizabeth Maddock Dillon, "Sentimental Aesthetics," *American Literature* 76 (2004): 495–523; Julie Ellison, *Cato's Tears and the Making of Anglo-American Emotion* (Chicago: University of Chicago Press, 1999); Gareth Evans, "Rakes, Coquettes and Republican Patriarchs: Class, Gender and Nation in Early American Sentimental Fiction," *Canadian Review of American Studies* 25 (1995): 41–62; Joseph Fichtelberg, *Critical Fictions: Sentiment and the American Market, 1780–1870* (Athens: University of Georgia Press, 2003); June Howard, "What Is Sentimentality?," *American Literary History* 11 (1999): 63–81; Lynn Hunt, *Inventing Human Rights: A History* (New York: W. W. Norton, 2007); Sarah Knott, "Sensibility and the American War for Independence," *American Historical Review* 109 (2004): 19–40; Paul Langford, *A Polite and Commercial People: England, 1727–1783* (Oxford: Oxford University Press, 1992); John Phillips Resch, *Suffering Soldiers: Revolutionary War Veterans, Moral Sentiment, and Political Culture in the Early Republic* (Amherst: University of Massachusetts Press, 1999); Jessica Riskin, *Science in the Age of Sensibility: The Sentimental Empiricists of the French Enlightenment* (Chicago: University of Chicago Press,

2002); Jane Tompkins, *Sensational Designs: The Cultural Work of American Fiction, 1790–1860* (New York: Oxford University Press, 1985); Verhoeven, "Gothic Logic."

70 On the shift to "hortatory" rhetoric in the 1790s, see Andrew W. Robertson, *The Language of Democracy: Political Rhetoric in the United States and Britain, 1790–1900* (Ithaca: Cornell University Press, 1995), esp. 11–14.

71 Burstein, *Sentimental Democracy*, 181–199; Knott, *Sensibility and the American Revolution*, 282–285; Rachel Hope Cleves, *The Reign of Terror in America: Visions of Violence From Anti-Jacobinism to Antislavery* (New York: Cambridge University Press, 2009); Vernon Stauffer, *New England and the Bavarian Illuminati* (New York: Columbia University, 1918).

72 Ames, "Speech on the Jay Treaty," 1144–1145.

73 Ibid., 1145–1148.

74 New York *Argus*, 2 May 1796.

75 Marshall Smelser, "The Jacobin Phrenzy: Federalism and the Menace of Liberty, Equality, and Fraternity," *Review of Politics* 13 (1951): 457–482; Pasley, *Tyranny of Printers*, 239–240; Burstein, *Sentimental Democracy*, 148; [Lemuel Hopkins], *The Guillotina, or A Democratic Dirge* (Philadelphia: The Political Book-Store, 1796), 7; Jay Fliegelman, *Prodigals and Pilgrims: The American Revolution against Patriarchal Authority, 1750–1800* (Cambridge: Cambridge University Press, 1982), 236–237.

76 Ames, "Speech on the Jay Treaty," 1152, 1170, 1166.

77 Barbara Graymont, *The Iroquois in the American Revolution* (Syracuse: Syracuse University Press, 1972); Francis Jennings, *Empire of Fortune: Crowns, Colonies and Tribes in the Seven Years War in America* (New York: W. W. Norton, 1988); Patrick M. Malone, *The Skulking Way of War: Technology and Tactics among the New England Indians* (Lanham, Md.: Madison Books, 2000); Daniel K. Richter, *The Ordeal of the Longhouse: The Peoples of the Iroquois League in the Era of European Colonization* (Chapel Hill: University of North Carolina Press for the Institute of Early American History and Culture, 1992); Richard White, *The Middle Ground: Indians, Empires, and Republics in the Great Lakes Region, 1650–1815* (Cambridge: Cambridge University Press, 1991).

78 Ames, "Speech on the Jay Treaty," 1174–1176.

79 Ibid., 1176.

80 New York *Argus*, 2 May 1796; John Adams to Abigail Adams, 30 April 1796, AFP.

81 Portsmouth *Oracle of the Day*, 26 May 1796; Philadelphia *Gazette of the United States*, reprinted in Portland *Eastern Herald*, 16 May 1796; "Hancock," Boston *Independent Chronicle*, 10 October 1796.

82 *Annals of Congress*, House of Representatives, 4th Congress, 1st Session, 28 April 1796, 1263–1264.

83 *Annals of Congress*, House of Representatives, 4th Congress, 1st Session, 29 April 1796, 1264–1280, quotations on 1274 and 1276. On Dayton's role as speaker, see Norman K. Risjord, "Partisanship and Power: House Committees and the Powers of the Speaker, 1789–1801," *William and Mary Quarterly*, 3rd ser., 49 (1992): 628–651.

84 *Annals of Congress*, House of Representatives, 4th Congress, 1st Session, 29 April 1796, 1280; Kurtz, *Presidency of John Adams*, 71. The Federalist *Pittsburgh*

Gazette (9 July 1796), on the other hand, found the trunk-mailing to be only a "trifling indiscretion."

85 Paul A. W. Wallace, *The Muhlenbergs of Pennsylvania* (Philadelphia: University of Pennsylvania Press, 1950), 285–288; Combs, *Jay Treaty*, 184–185.

86 Noble E. Cunningham Jr., ed., *Circular Letters of Congressmen to Their Constituents, 1789–1829* (Chapel Hill: University of North Carolina Press for the Institute of Early American History and Culture, 1978), 59–60.

87 John Beckley to De Witt Clinton, 11, 21 April 1796, in Gawalt, *Justifying Jefferson*, 115–117.

88 Michael Kammen, *Colonial New York: A History* (Millwood, N.Y.: KTO Press, 1975), 304–375; Milton M. Klein, ed., *The Empire State: A History of New York* (Ithaca: Cornell University Press, with the New York State Historical Association, 2001), 257–268.

89 On "Frontier Federalism," see Young, *Democratic Republicans of New York*, chaps. 12, 23. For an introduction to the context for New Yorkers' fears, see Barbara Graymont, *The Iroquois in the American Revolution* (Syracuse: Syracuse University Press, 1972); Isabel Thompson Kelsay, *Joseph Brant: Man of Two Worlds* (Syracuse: Syracuse University Press, 1984); and Anthony F. C. Wallace, *The Death and Rebirth of the Seneca* (New York: Vintage, 1972).

90 Young, *Democratic Republicans of New York*, 460–463; *Annals of Congress*, House of Representatives, 4th Congress, 1st Session, 21 March, 19 April 1796, 642–650, 1065–1078, quotations on 1068, 1075. Williams is listed as a Federalist in various reference works, but this would seem to be based on his Jay Treaty vote rather than a positive party identification.

91 Lawrence M. Hauptman, *A Conspiracy of Interests: Iroquois Dispossession and the Rise of New York State* (Syracuse: Syracuse University Press, 1999), 88–97; Walter Lowrie and Matthew St. Clair Clarke, eds., *American State Papers*, vol. 1, *Foreign Relations* (Washington, D.C.: Gales and Seaton, 1833), 484; Orsamus Turner, *Pioneer History of the Holland Purchase of Western New York* (Buffalo: Jewett, Thomas and Geo. H. Derby, 1850), 337–349, 393–394.

92 John Beckley to De Witt Clinton, 11, 21 April 1796, in Gawalt, *Justifying Jefferson*, 115–118; Young, *Democratic Republicans of New York*, 461–464; *Annals of Congress*, House of Representatives, 4th Congress, 1st Session, 19 April 1796, quotations on 1077, 1075, 1069.

93 Beckley to Clinton, 11, 21 April 1796, in Gawalt, *Justifying Jefferson*, 115–118; Young, *Democratic Republicans of New York*, 463–465.

94 By far the most complete account of the Keteltas case and the events and conditions that led to it appears in Young, *Democratic Republicans of New York*, 468–495. See also Graham Russell Hodges, *New York City Cartmen, 1667–1850* (New York: New York University Press, 1986), 95–99; Sidney I. Pomerantz, *New York, an American City, 1783–1803: A Study of Urban Life*, 2nd ed. (Port Washington, N.Y.: Ira J. Friedman, 1965), 263–267.

95 Hamilton to King, [4 May 1796], *PAH*, 20:158.

96 "To the Electors of the State of New-York," New York *Argus*, 22 April 1796.

97 *Let Every True Whig Read This with Attention: To the Electors of the City and County of New-York* (New York: n.p., 1796), Evans 46239 (misdated); Young, *Democratic Republicans of New York*, 465–466.

98 *Let Every True Whig.*

99 *Greenleaf's New York Journal*, 3 May 1796; Wheeler, "Urban Politics in Nature's Republic," 281–282.

100 *Greenleaf's New York Journal*, 7 June 1796; Young, *Democratic Republicans of New York*, 490–491; Howard B. Rock, "The Artisan and the State in the 1790s: A Comparison of New York and London," in *New York in the Age of the Constitution, 1775–1800*, ed. Paul A. Gilje and William Pencak (Madison, N.J.: Fairleigh Dickinson University Press, 1992), 74–97. Not even all the lawyers necessarily qualified to vote. In 1800, a group of aspiring young attorney-politicians, including future Vice President Daniel D. Tompkins, purchased a city residence together as a "tontine" to qualify them all for the suffrage. It was only through such electorate-expansion tactics that the Republicans ever started to carry certain New York City wards. See Ray W. Irwin, *Daniel D. Tompkins: Governor of New York and Vice President of the United States* (New York: New-York Historical Society, 1968), 43–44.

101 Jabez D. Hammond, *The History of Political Parties in the State of New-York, from the Ratification of the Federal Constitution to December, 1840* (Buffalo: Phinney, 1850), 100–101; Young, *Democratic Republicans of New York*, 466–467; Boston *Columbian Centinel*, 11 June 1796.

102 James Madison to Thomas Jefferson, 22 May 1796, *PJM*, 16:364.

103 William Smith to Rufus King, 23 July 1796, in *The Life and Correspondence of Rufus King; Comprising His Letters, Private and Official, His Public Documents, and His Speeches*, ed. Charles R. King (New York: G. P. Putnam's Sons, 1894–1900), 2:66.

CHAPTER 5. THE LONG GOODBYE

1 Boston *Columbian Centinel*, 24 February 1796.

2 Stephen G. Kurtz, *The Presidency of John Adams: The Collapse of Federalism, 1795–1800* (New York: A. S. Barnes, 1961), 80–81; John Adams to Abigail Adams, 15 February 1796, Abigail Adams to John Adams, 3 February 1796, *AFP*.

3 George Washington, "Circular to the States," 14 June 1783, in *George Washington: A Collection*, ed. W. B. Allen (Indianapolis: Liberty Fund, 1988), 239; William M. Fowler Jr., *American Crisis: George Washington and the Dangerous Two Years after Yorktown, 1781–1783* (New York: Walker, 2011), 186; Richard H. Kohn, *Eagle and Sword: The Beginnings of the Military Establishment in America* (New York: Free Press, 1975), 39; Paul K. Longmore, *The Invention of George Washington* (Berkeley: University of California Press, 1988); Carl J. Richard, *The Founders and the Classics: Greece, Rome and the American Enlightenment* (Cambridge, Mass.: Harvard University Press, 1994).

4 Washington to Madison, 20 May 1791, *PJM*, 14: 310–311.

5 Alexander DeConde, *Entangling Alliance: Politics and Diplomacy under George Washington* (Durham: Duke University Press, 1958), 459–460; Philadelphia *Aurora*, 3 November 1795.

6 John Adams to Abigail Adams, 24 December 1795, 12 (quoted), 20 (quoted) January 1796, Abigail to John, 10 January 1796, *AFP*.

7 Margaret A. Hogan and C. James Taylor, eds., *My Dearest Friend: Letters of Abigail and John Adams* (Cambridge, Mass.: Harvard University Press, 2007), 401, 403–404.

8 Kurtz, *Presidency of John Adams*, 81–85. Quotations from *Ode on the Birthday of the President of the United States* (Philadelphia, 1796), Evans 30924; Boston

Columbian Centinel, 24, 27 February 1796; John Adams to Abigail Adams, 1 March 1796, *AFP*.

9 Washington to Hamilton, 26 June 1796, Hamilton to Washington, 10 May, 5 July 1796, *PAH*, 20:169, 173, 176, 239–240, 246–247.

10 Samuel Flagg Bemis, "Washington's Farewell Address: A Foreign Policy of Independence," *American Historical Review* 39 (1934): 257–258.

11 James Madison to James Monroe, 26 February 1796, *PJM*, 16:232–233.

12 DeConde, *Entangling Alliance*, 456–457.

13 Gil Troy, *See How They Ran: The Changing Role of the Presidential Candidate* (New York: Free Press, 1991), 7–11; Ralph Ketcham, *Presidents above Party: The First American Presidency, 1789–1829* (Chapel Hill: University of North Carolina Press for the Institute of Early American History and Culture, 1984).

14 On the candidates' lack of involvement in the 1796 campaign, see Joanne B. Freeman, "The Presidential Election of 1796," in *John Adams and the Founding of the Republic*, ed. Richard Alan Ryerson (Boston: Massachusetts Historical Society and Northeastern University Press, 2001), 144–145. The John Adams quotation appears in John Adams to Abigail Adams, 20 January 1796, *AFP*.

15 On letters and other private contacts as a primary means of political communication, see Joanne B. Freeman, *Affairs of Honor: National Politics in the New Republic* (New Haven: Yale University Press, 2001); Freeman, "Presidential Election of 1796"; and Nathan Perl-Rosenthal, "Private Letters and Public Diplomacy: The Adams Network and the Quasi-War, 1797–1798," *Journal of the Early Republic* 31 (2011): 283–311. I am less convinced by Perl-Rosenthal's assertion, and Freeman's assumption, that the Founders and other high-level politicians "relied on private epistolary networks" to get their political information. They lavished too much attention on newspapers for that to be completely true. On private letters as a means of communication in early America more generally, with considerably more attention to issues of class and power, see Richard D. Brown, *Knowledge Is Power: The Diffusion of Information in Early America, 1700–1865* (New York: Oxford University Press, 1990).

16 Robert R. Livingston to James Madison, 16 November 1795, *PJM*, 16: 126–127.

17 Noble E. Cunningham Jr., *The Jeffersonian Republicans: The Formation of Party Organization, 1789–1801* (Chapel Hill: University of North Carolina Press for the Institute of Early American History and Culture, 1957), 85–86; Andrew Burstein and Nancy Isenberg, *Madison and Jefferson* (New York: Random House, 2010), 284, 311.

18 Cunningham, *Jeffersonian Republicans*, 85–88; Dumas Malone, *Jefferson and the Ordeal of Liberty* (Boston: Little, Brown, 1962), 167–242; Burstein and Isenberg, *Madison and Jefferson*, 284; Annette Gordon-Reed, *The Hemingses of Monticello: An American Family* (W. W. Norton, 2009), 505–510, 517.

19 Lucia C. Stanton, " 'Those Who Labor for My Happiness': Thomas Jefferson and His Slaves," in *Jeffersonian Legacies*, ed. Peter S. Onuf (Charlottesville: University Press of Virginia, 1993), 147–180; Annette Gordon-Reed, *Thomas Jefferson and Sally Hemings: An American Controversy* (Charlottesville: University Press of Virginia, 1997); Gordon-Reed, *Hemingses of Monticello*, 11, 516–530, and passim. A good, short, balanced statement of the facts in the case, including the birthdates of Sally's children, has been posted by the Monticello staff at www.monticello.org/plantation/hemingscontro/hemings-jefferson_contro.html.

20 James Madison to James Monroe, 26 February 1796, *PJM*, 16:232–233.

21 Jefferson to William Branch Giles, 31 December 1795, *PTJ*, 28:566; Burstein and Isenberg, *Madison and Jefferson*, 298. On the circulation of private letters in politics, see Freeman, *Affairs of Honor*.

22 Thomas Jefferson to Philip Mazzei, 24 April 1796, *PTJ*, 29:82; and accompanying editorial note, *PTJ*, 29:73–81.

23 Matthew Livingston Davis Memorandum Book, Rufus King Papers, Vol. 57, New-York Historical Society, 19–20, 23; [William Loughton Smith], *The Politicks and Views of a Certain Party, Displayed* ([Philadelphia]: n.p., 1792), 29–30.

24 Freeman, *Affairs of Honor*; Paul Goodman, *The Democratic-Republicans of Massachusetts: Politics in a Young Republic* (Cambridge, Mass.: Harvard University Press, 1964); Daniel P. Jordan, *Political Leadership in Jefferson's Virginia* (Charlottesville: University Press of Virginia, 1983); Alan Taylor, "'The Art of Hook and Snivey': Political Culture in Upstate New York during the 1790s," *Journal of American History* 79 (1993): 1371–1396.

25 Troy, *See How They Ran*, 20–81, 116; Robert J. Dinkin, *Campaigning in America: A History of Electoral Practices*, Contributions in American History (Westport, Conn.: Greenwood Press, 1989), 66–68; M. J. Heale, *The Presidential Quest: Candidates and Images in American Political Culture, 1787–1852* (London: Longman, 1982), 1–22.

26 Boston *Columbian Centinel*, 27 February, 21 May 1796; John Adams to Abigail Adams, 24 December 1795, 12 (quoted), 20 (quoted) January 1796, Abigail to John, 10 January 1796, *AFP*.

27 "Anniversary of American Independence," *Aurora*, 7 July 1795.

28 Boston *Columbian Centinel*, 24 February 1796; Abigail Adams to John Adams, 28 February 1796, *AFP*; Hogan and Taylor, *My Dearest Friend*, 408.

29 The "Great Mentioner" concept originated with Russell Baker's "Observer" column in the *New York Times*, 12 December 1963, 38. Robert M. S. McDonald, "The Hamiltonian Invention of Thomas Jefferson," in *The Many Faces of Alexander Hamilton: The Life and Legacy of America's Most Elusive Founding Father*, ed. Douglas Ambrose and Robert W. T. Martin (New York: New York University Press, 2007), 54–76.

30 "The Defence No. 1," 22 July 1795, *PAH*, 18:482–483; *American Minerva and New-York Advertiser*, 30 November 1795. The toasts Hamilton was complaining about seemed to be those published in the New York *Argus*, 6, 7, 8 July 1795.

31 *PAH*, 18:482.

32 "Cinna, No. II," reprinted in Albany *Register*, 7 September 1795; "From the Newburgh Packet," New York *Argus & Greenleaf's New Daily Advertiser*, 17 November 1795; "Valerius, No. IX," Philadelphia *Aurora*, 11 November 1795.

33 Milton Lomask, *Aaron Burr: The Years from Princeton to Vice President, 1756–1805* (New York: Farrar, Straus Giroux, 1979), 168–188; Nancy Isenberg, *Fallen Founder: The Life of Aaron Burr* (New York: Viking Penguin, 2007), 131–138; Pierce Butler to James Madison, 26 June 1795, *PJM*, 16:24–27.

34 *The Democratiad, a Poem in Relation for the "Philadelphia Jockey Club,"* 3rd ed. (Philadelphia: Thomas Bradford, 1796), 6–7, 10–11. On the Connecticut Wits, see Vernon Louis Parrington, ed., *The Connecticut Wits*, Apollo ed. (New York: Thomas Y. Crowell, 1969). On Burr's surprisingly extensive career as a literary

character, see Isenberg, *Fallen Founder*, 138–141; and Charles J. Nolan, *Aaron Burr and the American Literary Imagination* (Westport, Conn.: Greenwood Press, 1980).

35 Richard P. McCormick, *The Presidential Game: The Origins of American Presidential Politics* (New York: Oxford University Press, 1982), 46–48; Isenberg, *Fallen Founder*, 144–147; Lomask, *Aaron Burr*, 173–177, 187–188.

36 William Smith to Ralph Izard, 18 May 1796, in Ulrich B. Phillips, "South Carolina Federalist Correspondence, 1789–1797," *American Historical Review* 14 (1909): 780; Hamilton to ?, *PAH*, 12:480; Lomask, *Aaron Burr*, 173–174.

37 Thomas Jefferson to Wilson Cary Nicholas, 19 October 1795, *PTJ*, 28:512; "Certificate of Joseph Jones Monroe and Thomas Bell," 17 October 1796, *PTJ*, 29:198. On the Burrites and their misunderstandings with Jefferson, see Noble E. Cunningham Jr., *The Jeffersonian Republicans in Power: Party Operations, 1801–1809* (Chapel Hill: University of North Carolina Press for the Institute of Early American History and Culture, 1963); Jerome Mushkat, "Matthew Livingston Davis and the Political Legacy of Aaron Burr," *New-York Historical Society Quarterly* 59 (1975): 123–148; and Jeffrey L. Pasley, "Matthew Livingston Davis's Notes From the Political Underground: The Conflict of Political Values in the Early American Republic" (unpublished essay, May 2000), http://jeff.pasleybrothers.com/writings/davisv2.htm.

38 James Monroe to James Madison, 5 August 1795, *PJM*, 16:43–44.

39 Timothy J. Gilfoyle, *City of Eros: New York City, Prostitution, and the Commercialization of Sex, 1790–1820* (New York: W. W. Norton, 1992). On Mrs. Jumel, see pp. 23–26, 70.

40 The most honest account of Burr's marriage appears in Isenberg, *Fallen Founder*, 55–79.

41 Matthew L. Davis, *Memoirs of Aaron Burr: With Miscellaneous Selections From His Correspondence* (1836; Freeport, N.Y.: Books for Libraries Press, 1970), 1:iv–vi, 87–92. Davis was a notorious whorehouse investor and reprobate himself, so he may have protested a bit too much. On Davis, see Gilfoyle, *City of Eros*, 45; Mushkat, "Matthew Livingston Davis"; and Jeffrey L. Pasley, "Minnows, Spies, and Aristocrats: The Social Crisis of Congress in the Age of Martin Van Buren," *Journal of the Early Republic* 27 (2007): 599–653.

42 Isenberg, *Fallen Founder*, esp. 55–83.

43 James S. Chase, *The Emergence of the Presidential Nominating Convention, 1789–1832* (Urbana: University of Illinois Press, 1973), 1–15; William G. Morgan, "The Origin and Development of the Congressional Nominating Caucus," *Proceedings of the American Philosophical Society* 113, no. 2 (1969): 184–196.

44 James Monroe to James Madison, 14 May 1796, *PJM*, 16:358; Cunningham, *Jeffersonian Republicans*, 91–92.

45 William Smith to Ralph Izard, 18 May 1796, in Phillips, "South Carolina Federalist Correspondence," 780; John Adams Diary 46, 17 July 1796, *AFP*; William Nisbet Chambers, *Political Parties in a New Nation: The American Experience, 1776–1809* (New York: Oxford University Press, 1963), 116–117; John Beckley to James Madison, 20 June 1796, *PJM*, 16:371.

46 Abigail Adams to John Adams, 31 December 1796, *AFP*; "An Extract from a Letter from a Member in Congress, to His Friend in the Country," Stockbridge

Western Star, 24 May 1796; "The Cadets," Brookfield, Mass., *Moral and Political Telegraphe*, 1 June 1796; Portsmouth *Oracle of the Day*, 16 June 1796; Boston *Columbian Centinel*, 25, 28 May, 11 June 1796.

47 Quotations from Alexander Hamilton, *Letter from Alexander Hamilton, Concerning the Public Conduct and Character of John Adams, Esq., President of the United States* (New York: John Lang, 1800), 5, 7, 9.

48 Manning J. Dauer, *The Adams Federalists*, 2nd ed. (Baltimore: Johns Hopkins University Press, 1968), 19; James H. Broussard, *The Southern Federalists, 1800–1816* (Baton Rouge: Louisiana State University Press, 1978), 3–13; David Hackett Fischer, *The Revolution of American Conservatism: The Federalist Party in the Era of Jeffersonian Democracy* (New York: Harper & Row, 1965), 353–412. For judicious accounts of historians' growing tendency to treat the Federalists as a northern, antislavery party, see Rachel Hope Cleves, " 'Hurtful to the State': The Political Morality of Federalist Antislavery," in *Contesting Slavery: The Politics of Bondage and Freedom in the New American Nation*, ed. John Craig Hammond and Matthew Mason (Charlottesville: University of Virginia Press, 2011), 207–208, 221–222; Matthew Mason, "Federalists, Abolitionists, and the Problem of Influence," *American Nineteenth Century History* 10, no. 1 (2009): 1–27.

49 Fischer, *Revolution of American Conservatism*, 374–375; Richard R. Beeman, *Patrick Henry: A Biography* (New York: McGraw-Hill, 1974), 110–120; Norman K. Risjord, *Chesapeake Politics, 1781–1800* (New York: Columbia University Press, 1978), 464–467.

50 Rufus King to Alexander Hamilton, 2 May 1796, enclosing John Marshall to King, 19 April 1796, *PAH*, 20:151–153; John Marshall to Hamilton, 25 April 1796, 20:137–138; Robert Ernst, *Rufus King: American Federalist* (Chapel Hill: University of North Carolina Press for the Institute of Early American History and Culture, 1968), 214–215.

51 Hamilton to King, 4 May 1796, *PAH*, 20:158; Ernst, *Rufus King*, 215n71; Hamilton, *Letter from Alexander Hamilton*, 10–12.

52 Francis Leigh Williams, *A Founding Family: The Pinckneys of South Carolinia* (New York: Harcourt Brace Jovanovich, 1978); Samuel Flagg Bemis, *Pinckney's Treaty: America's Advantage from Europe's Distress, 1783–1800* (New Haven: Yale University Press, 1960); Arthur Scherr, "The Significance of Thomas Pinckney's Candidacy in the Election of 1796," *South Carolina Historical Magazine* 76 (1975): 51–59.

53 Harper to Ralph Izard, 4 November 1796, in Phillips, "South Carolina Federalist Correspondence," 782–783; Lisle A. Rose, *Prologue to Democracy: The Federalists in the South, 1789–1800* (Lexington: University of Kentucky Press, 1968), 125–127; George C. Rogers Jr., *Evolution of a Federalist: William Loughton Smith of Charleston, 1758–1812* (Columbia: University of South Carolina Press, 1962), 290; *Letter from Alexander Hamilton*, 11.

54 Maurie D. McInnis, *The Politics of Taste in Antebellum Charleston* (Chapel Hill: University of North Carolina Press, 2005), 75. On the antislavery image of the Federalists, see note 48 above. By far the two most widely read renditions of the Federalists-as-abolitionists in the early twenty-first century are Garry Wills, *Negro President: Jefferson and the Slave Power* (Boston: Houghton Mifflin, 2003); and Ron Chernow, *Alexander Hamilton* (New York: Penguin, 2004), which heavily influenced a PBS documentary.

55 For just a few examples, to vastly different effects, see John D. Barnhart, "The Tennessee Constitution of 1796: A Product of the Old West," *Journal of Southern History* 9 (1943): 532–548; John D. Barnhart, *Valley of Democracy: The Frontier versus the Plantation in the Ohio Valley, 1775–1818* (Lincoln: University of Nebraska Press, 1970); Leonard L. Richards, *The Slave Power: The Free North and Southern Domination, 1780–1860* (Baton Rouge: Louisiana State University Press, 2000); Robin L. Einhorn, *American Taxation, American Slavery* (Chicago: University of Chicago Press, 2006); and Wills, *Negro President*.

56 François Furstenberg, "The Significance of the Trans-Appalachian Frontier in Atlantic History," *American Historical Review* 113 (2008): 668n40. As Furstenberg acknowledges, this is probably a minority opinion among historians, but for other works that demonstrate the Federalist commitment to ordering the frontier, see (in addition to the works cited in the following two notes), Wiley Sword, *President Washington's Indian War: The Struggle for the Old Northwest, 1790–1795* (Norman: University of Oklahoma Press, 1985); Francis Paul Prucha, *The Sword of the Republic: The United States Army on the Frontier, 1783–1846* (Bloomington: Indiana University Press, 1969); Richard H. Kohn, *Eagle and Sword: The Beginnings of the Military Establishment in America* (New York: Free Press, 1975); Alan Taylor, *Liberty Men and Great Proprietors: The Revolutionary Settlement on the Maine Frontier, 1760–1820* (Chapel Hill: University of North Carolina Press for the Institute of Early American History and Culture, 1990); Alan Taylor, *William Cooper's Town: Power and Persuasion on the Frontier of the Early American Republic* (New York: Alfred A. Knopf, 1995); Alfred F. Young, "The Rise of Frontier Federalism, 1788–1792," in *The Democratic Republicans of New York: The Origins, 1763–1797* (Chapel Hill: University of North Carolina Press for the Institute of Early American History and Culture, 1967), 257–276; Andrew R. L. Cayton, *The Frontier Republic: Ideology and Politics in the Ohio Country, 1780–1825* (Kent, Ohio: Kent State University Press, 1986); Patrick Griffin, "Reconsidering the Ideological Origins of Indian Removal: The Case of the Big Bottom 'Massacre,'" in *The Center of a Great Empire: The Ohio Country in the Early American Republic*, ed. Andrew R. L. Cayton and Stuart D. Hobbs (Athens: Ohio University Press, 2005); David A. Nichols, *Red Gentleman and White Savages: Indians, Federalists, and the Search for Order on the American Frontier* (Charlottesville: University of Virginia Press, 2008); Donald R. Hickey, "Federalist Defense Policy in the Age of Jefferson, 1801–1812," *Military Affairs* 45 (1981): 63–70; Jeffrey L. Pasley, "Midget on Horseback: American Indians and the History of the American State," *Common-Place* 9, no. 1 (October 2008), http://www.common-place.org/vol-09/no-01/pasley/; Kristopher Maulden, "The Arts of Conquest: The Rise of Federal Authority in Ohio, 1783–1795" (M.A. thesis, University of Missouri, 2005).

57 Nichols, *Red Gentleman and White Savages*, 180–181; Andrew R. L. Cayton, "'When Shall We Cease to Have Judases?': The Blount Conspiracy and the Limits of the 'Extended Republic,'" in *Launching the "Extended Republic": The Federalist Era*, ed. Ronald Hoffman and Peter J. Albert (Charlottesville: University Press of Virginia, 1996), 156–189; Thomas Perkins Abernethy, *From Frontier to Plantation in Tennessee: A Study in Frontier Democracy* (Chapel Hill: University of North Carolina Press, 1932), 142–143; *Knoxville Gazette*, 13, 27 March 1794, quoted in Walter T. Durham, *Before Tennessee: The Southwest Territory, 1790–1796* (Piney Flats, Tenn.: Mount Historical Association, 1990),

167. For the prominence of Federalist officials on another part of the frontier, see Thomas P. Slaughter, *The Whiskey Rebellion: Frontier Epilogue to the American Revolution* (New York: Oxford University Press, 1986). For another western state dominated by large landowners by 1796, see Stephen Aron, *How the West Was Lost: The Transformation of Kentucky from Daniel Boone to Henry Clay* (Baltimore: Johns Hopkins University Press, 1996).

58 Abernethy, *From Frontier to Plantation in Tennessee*, 142–143; Cayton, "When Shall We Cease to Have Judases?," 177–178.

59 John R. Finger, *Tennessee Frontiers: Three Regions in Transition* (Bloomington: Indiana University Press, 2001), 125–144; quotation from Paul H. Bergeron, Stephen V. Ash, and Jeanette Keith, *Tennesseans and Their History* (Knoxville: University of Tennessee Press, 1999), 63. On Pickering, see Gerard H. Clarfield, *Timothy Pickering and the American Republic* (Pittsburgh: University of Pittsburgh Press, 1980); Wills, *Negro President*; and Nichols, *White Gentlemen and Red Savages*.

60 Finger, *Tennessee Frontiers*, 145–149; Jo Tice Bloom, "Establishing Precedents: Dr. James White and the Southwest Territory," *Tennessee Historical Quarterly* 54 (1995): 325–335.

61 Goodrich to Oliver Wolcott Sr., 13 May 1796, in *Memoirs of the Administration of Washington and John Adams, Edited From the Papers of Oliver Wolcott, Secretary of the Treasury*, ed. George Gibbs (New York: William Van Norden, 1846), 338–339. On New England Federalist fears about cultural degradation on the frontier, Nichols, *Red Gentleman and White Savages*.

62 *Annals of Congress*, Senate, 4th Congress, 92–94; *Annals of Congress*, House of Representatives, 4th Congress, 916; Charlotte Williams, "Congressional Action on the Admission of Tennessee into the Union," *Tennessee Historical Quarterly* 2 (1943): 291–315, quotation on 291. Perhaps the most succinct and useful account of the Tennessee statehood debate appears in Mary-Jo Kline, "Editorial Note: Tennessee Statehood," in *Political Correspondence and Public Papers of Aaron Burr* (Princeton: Princeton University Press, 1983), 257–263.

63 Blount and Cocke letter quoted in Williams, "Congressional Action on the Admission of Tennessee," 291; *GUS*, 20 May 1796.

64 *Annals of Congress*, House of Representatives, 4th Congress, 5 May 1796, 1299–1312. On the widespread violations of the ban on slavery in the Northwest Territory, see Paul Finkelman, *Slavery and the Founders: Race and Liberty in the Age of Jefferson* (Armonk, N.Y.: M. E. Sharpe, 1996); and Peter S. Onuf, *Statehood and Union: A History of the Northwest Ordinance* (Bloomington: Indiana University Press, 1992), 109–132.

65 Williams, "Congressional Action"; *PJM*, 16:349–350; Kline, "Tennessee Statehood," 261–263.

66 Kline, "Tennessee Statehood," 262–263; "Extract of a Letter from Major Wm. C. Claiborn [W.C.C. Claiborne], of Tennessee, to his Friend in Richmond, dated Knoxville, Aug. 25," reprinted in Newfield, Conn., *American Telegraphe & Fairfield County Gazette*, 25 August 1796.

67 *Aurora*, 6 July 1796.

68 Philadelphia *Daily Advertiser*, 11 July 1796; Cooperstown *Otsego Herald*, 7 July 1796; *Greenleaf's New-York Journal*, 8, 12 July 1796; Boston *Columbian Centinel*, 6 July 1796; Stockbridge *Western Star*, 12 July 1796.

69 Hamilton to Washington, 5 July 1796, *PAH*, 20:246–247; Hamilton to Tobias Lear, 2 January 1800, *PAH*, 24:155.

70 Felix Gilbert, *To the Farewell Address: Ideas of Early American Foreign Policy* (Princeton: Princeton University Press, 1961). Gilbert even links the form of the Farewell Address to the tradition of "political testament" practiced by the empire-building monarchs who created the nation-state, such as Frederick the Great of Prussia.

71 John Lamberton Harper, *American Machiavelli: Alexander Hamilton and the Origins of U.S. Foreign Policy* (New York: Cambridge University Press, 2004); Forrest McDonald, *Alexander Hamilton: A Biography* (New York: W. W. Norton, 1982); Karl-Friedrich Walling, *Republican Empire: Alexander Hamilton on War and Free Government* (Lawrence: University Press of Kansas, 1999); Chernow, *Alexander Hamilton*. For a response to the Hamilton boom, see Mike Wallace, "Business-Class Hero," Gotham Center for New York City History website, November 2004, www.gothamcenter.org/hamilton/businessclasshero/bch.pdf.

72 Washington's Farewell Address is one of the more frequently commented-on topics in American historiography, as detailed in Arthur A. Markowitz, "Washington's Farewell and the Historians: A Critical Review," *Pennsylvania Magazine of History and Biography* 94 (1970): 173–191; and Burton Ira Kaufman, ed., *Washington's Farewell Address: The View From the 20th Century* (Chicago: Quadrangle Books, 1969), among other places. Most discussions focus on the authorship of the address or ruminate on its long-term influence on American foreign policy, with particular concern over whether George Washington is to blame for the isolationism that so exercised mid-twentieth-century historians. See, e.g., Samuel Flagg Bemis, "Washington's Farewell Address: A Foreign Policy of Independence," *American Historical Review* 39 (1934): 250–268; Gilbert, *To the Farewell Address*; and Edward Pessen, "George Washington's Farewell Address, the Cold War, and the Timeless National Interest," *Journal of the Early Republic* 7 (1987): 1–25. For the relatively rare interpretation that sets the Farewell Address in its immediate political context, and hence has much more relevance for the present work, see Alexander DeConde, "Washington's Farewell, the French Alliance, and the Election of 1796," *Mississippi Valley Historical Review* 43 (1957): 641–658. Stanley Elkins and Eric McKitrick have it both ways in *The Age of Federalism* (New York: Oxford University Press, 1993), 492–494.

73 Washington, "Abstract of Points to Form an Address," May 1796, *PAH*, 20:178–183; and Hamilton to Washington, 10 August 1796, *PAH*, 20:300. Washington cannot be completely absolved of partisan feeling. He signed the final version of the Farewell Address, after all, and also rejected some final changes from Hamilton that would have made some of the complaints a bit more evenhanded.

74 For convenient, accurate texts of the final Farewell Address, see James D. Richardson, ed., *A Compilation of the Messages and Papers of the Presidents* (Washington, D.C.: Bureau of National Literature and Art, 1908), 213–224; and Allen, *George Washington*, 512–527.

75 Quotations from Richardson, *Messages and Papers of the Presidents*, 1:217–219.

76 Ibid., 216, 222; Elkins and McKitrick, *Age of Federalism*, 496–497.

77 See chapter 6 for more on Smith's pamphlet, published in 1792: William

Loughton Smith, *The Politicks and Views of a Certain Party, Displayed* ([Philadelphia]: n.p., 1792).

78 Richardson, *Messages and Papers of the Presidents*, 1:220–221; John Fea, *Was America Founded as a Christian Nation? A Historical Introduction* (Louisville: Westminster John Knox Press, 2011), 171–190; Douglass Adair, "Was Alexander Hamilton a Christian Statesman?," in *Fame and the Founding Fathers* (New York: W. W. Norton for the Institute of Early American History and Culture, 1974), 141–159.

79 Philadelphia *Daily Advertiser*, 7 November 1796; Rose, *Prologue to Democracy*, 134–138; Rogers, *Evolution of a Federalist*, 290–291; James Haw, *John and Edward Rutledge of South Carolina* (Athens: University of Georgia Press, 1997), 248–256.

80 *PAH*, 20:170–172.

81 Madison to Monroe, 29 September 1796, *PJM*, 16:403; Fisher Ames to Oliver Wolcott, 26 September 1796, in *Works of Fisher Ames, as Published by Seth Ames*, ed. W. B. Allen (Indianapolis: LibertyClassics, 1983), 1192

CHAPTER 6. THE FIRST CULTURE WAR

1 *Aurora*, 13 September 1796, as reprinted in *Boston Gazette and Weekly Republican Journal*, 26 September 1796.

2 James Roger Sharp, *American Politics in the Early Republic: The New Nation in Crisis* (New Haven: Yale University Press, 1993), quotations on 158 and 138. Noble E. Cunningham Jr., *The Jeffersonian Republicans: The Formation of Party Organization, 1789–1801* (Chapel Hill: University of North Carolina Press for the Institute of Early American History and Culture, 1957), 97.

3 For accounts of late-twentieth- and early-twenty-first-century political campaigning that emphasize the central role of character-driven narratives that still communicate policy positions and party ideology, see John Gray Geer, *In Defense of Negativity: Attack Ads in Presidential Campaigns* (Chicago: University of Chicago Press, 2006); Thomas A. Hollihan, *Uncivil Wars: Political Campaigns in a Media Age*, 2nd ed. (Boston: Bedford/St. Martin's, 2008), 8–20. For a lighter application of the idea of presidential campaign narratives that ranges further back in American history, see Evan Cornog, *The Power and the Story: How the Crafted Presidential Narrative Has Determined Presidential Success from George Washington to George W. Bush* (New York: Penguin, 2004). For a similar but much more serious approach focusing specifically on the Early American Republic, chiefly in the Jacksonian era, see M. J. Heale, *The Presidential Quest: Candidates and Images in American Political Culture, 1787–1852* (London: Longman, 1982).

4 "Hampden," *Richmond Virginia Gazette and General Advertiser*, 12 October 1796; Chastellux to Jefferson, 27 December 1784, *PTJ*, 7:585n–586n; "Characters," *Columbian Magazine* (Philadelphia), July 1787, 555; Jefferson to Chastellux, 2 September 1785, *PTJ*, 8:467; Andrew Burstein, *The Inner Jefferson: Portrait of a Grieving Optimist* (Charlottesville: University Press of Virginia, 1995), 35.

5 "Extracts from the Diary of Ezra Stiles," [8 June 1784], *PTJ*, 7:303; "Antiquity. Letter III. From Mr. N. Webster to the Rev. Dr. Ezra Stiles, President of Yale College, on the Remains of the Fortifications in the Western Country," *American Magazine*, February 1788, 151; "Essay on American Genius," reprinted in *United States Chronicle*, 1 March 1787. Magazine citations are drawn from

ProQuest's American Periodical Series Online database, where a search for "Jefferson" before 1792 reveals that excerpts from the *Notes on the State of Virginia* were widely republished, especially in the *Columbian Magazine*.

6 David Waldstreicher, *Slavery's Constitution: From Revolution to Ratification* (New York: Hill & Wang, 2009), 37–38, 46–48, 58–60, 64–67.

7 Quotations from "To the Editors of the Massachusetts Magazine," *Massachusetts Magazine, or Monthly Museum of Knowledge and Rational Entertainment*, September 1789, 567; and Thomas Jefferson, *Writings*, ed. Merrill D. Peterson (New York: Literary Classics of the United States, 1984), 288–289. One of the best discussions of Jefferson's racial views, especially in terms of his relations with the antislavery movement of the time, remains Winthrop D. Jordan, *White over Black: American Attitudes toward the Negro, 1550–1812* (New York: W. W. Norton, 1977), 429–481. Less forgiving and nuanced views can be found in Paul Finkelman, *Slavery and the Founders: Race and Liberty in the Age of Jefferson* (Armonk, N.Y.: M. E. Sharpe, 1996); Garry Wills, *Negro President: Jefferson and the Slave Power* (Boston: Houghton Mifflin, 2003); Henry Wiencek, *Master of the Mountain: Thomas Jefferson and His Slaves* (Farrar, Straus and Giroux, 2012).

8 Robert M. S. McDonald, "Thomas Jefferson's Changing Reputation as Author of the Declaration of Independence: The First Fifty Years," *Journal of the Early Republic* 19 (1999): 169–195; Philip F. Detweiler, "The Changing Reputation of the Declaration of Independence: The First Fifty Years," *William and Mary Quarterly*, 3rd ser., 19 (1962): 557–565; Pauline Maier, *American Scripture: Making the Declaration of Independence* (New York: Alfred A. Knopf, 1997). Quotation from "Thomas Jefferson," *New-York Diary*, 1796, reprinted in *Washington Spy*, Md., 30 November 1796.

9 "To the Author of Plain Truth," *Maryland Journal and Baltimore Advertiser*, 22 March 1791, partially quoted in *PTJ*, 19:545.

10 The clearest discussion of the 1792 vice-presidential "race" appears in John P. Kaminski, *George Clinton: Yeoman Politician of the New Republic* (Madison, Wis.: Madison House, 1993), 229–236.

11 Dumas Malone, *Jefferson and the Rights of Man* (Boston: Little, Brown, 1951), 469–474; George C. Rogers Jr., *Evolution of a Federalist: William Loughton Smith of Charleston, 1758–1812* (Columbia: University of South Carolina Press, 1962). Much of what follows in the next few pages draws freely on Rogers's old-fashioned but authoritative biography of Smith. Readers should note that William Loughton Smith was known simply as William Smith before he officially added a middle name to honor his mother's family in 1804. I have used the longer name throughout this book to match Smith's designation in most reference books and databases and to distinguish him from several other William Smiths who were active in the politics of the Early Republic.

12 On the Federalists as an antislavery party, see Linda K. Kerber, "Anti-Virginia and Anti-Slavery," in *Federalists in Dissent: Imagery and Ideology in Jeffersonian America* (Ithaca: Cornell University Press, 1970), 23–66; Paul Finkelman, "The Problem of Slavery in the Age of Revolution," in *Federalists Reconsidered*, ed. Doron Ben-Atar and Barbara B. Oberg (Charlottesville: University Press of Virginia, 1998), 135–156; Marc M. Arkin, "The Federalist Trope: Power and Passion in Abolitionist Rhetoric," *Journal of American History* 88 (June 2001): 75–98; Wills, *Negro President*; Rachel Hope Cleves, *The Reign of Terror*

in America: Visions of Violence from Anti-Jacobinism to Antislavery (New York: Cambridge University Press, 2009); Matthew Mason, "Federalists, Abolitionists, and the Problem of Influence," *American Nineteenth Century History* 10 (2009): 1–27; Rachel Hope Cleves, "'Hurtful to the State': The Political Morality of Federalist Antislavery," in *Contesting Slavery: The Politics of Bondage and Freedom in the New American Nation*, ed. John Craig Hammond and Matthew Mason (Charlottesville: University of Virginia Press, 2011), 207–226.

13 George C. Rogers Jr., "South Carolina Federalists and the Origins of the Nullification Movement," *South Carolina Historical Magazine* 101 (2000): 53–67.

14 Quotation from "*PUBLIC NOTICE EXTRAORDINARY*," Martinsburg *Potomak Guardian*, 5 May 1796. On the French refugees in Charleston, see Rogers, *Evolution of a Federalist*, 248–250. For alternative views and questions regarding the antislavery image of the Federalists, see Mason, "Federalists, Abolitionists, and the Problem of Influence"; Cleves, "'Hurtful to the State,'" 207–208, 221–222; John Kyle Day, "The Federalist Press and Slavery in the Age Of Jefferson," *Historian* 65 (2003): 1303–1329; Simon Newman, "The World Turned Upside Down: Revolutionary Politics, Fries' and Gabriel's Rebellions, and the Fears of the Federalists," *Pennsylvania History* 67 (2000): 5–20; and Arthur Scherr, "'Sambos' and 'Black Cut-Throats': Peter Porcupine on Slavery and Race in the 1790's," *American Periodicals* 13 (2003): 3–30.

15 On the South Carolina planter oligarchy and its defense of slavery, see Robert M. Weir, "'The Harmony We Were Famous for': An Interpretation of Pre-Revolutionary South Carolina Politics," *William and Mary Quarterly*, 3rd ser., 26 (1969): 473–501; Robert M. Weir, "The South Carolinian as Extremist," *South Atlantic Quarterly* 74, no. 1 (1975): 86–103; George C. Rogers Jr., *Charleston in the Age of the Pinckneys*, 2nd ed. (Columbia: University of South Carolina Press, 1984); Rogers, "South Carolina Federalists"; William W. Freehling, *Prelude to Civil War: The Nullification Controversy in South Carolina, 1816–1836* (New York: Harper & Row, 1968); Francis Leigh Williams, *A Founding Family: The Pinckneys of South Carolina* (New York: Harcourt Brace Jovanovich, 1978); John Niven, *John C. Calhoun and the Price of Union* (Baton Rouge: Louisiana State University Press, 1988); Rachel N. Klein, *Unification of a Slave State: The Rise of the Planter Class in the South Carolina Backcountry, 1760–1808* (Chapel Hill: University of North Carolina Press for the Institute of Early American History and Culture, 1990); Marty D. Matthews, *Forgotten Founder: The Life and Times of Charles Pinckney* (Columbia: University of South Carolina Press, 2004); S. Max Edelson, *Plantation Enterprise in Colonial South Carolina* (Cambridge, Mass.: Harvard University Press, 2006).

16 Rogers, *Evolution of a Federalist*, 162–167, 237, 197; *Annals of Congress*, 1st Congress, 2nd Session, House of Representatives, 17 March 1790, 1503–1514. On Smith's leading role in ridiculing and rejecting the Quaker antislavery petitions, see William C. diGiacomantonio, "'For the Gratification of a Volunteering Society': Antislavery and Pressure Group Politics in the First Federal Congress," *Journal of the Early Republic* 15 (1995): 169–197.

17 Rogers, *Evolution of a Federalist*, 8–17, 56–96. Thomas Jefferson's infamous "Mazzei letter" characterized Federalists as, among other things, "British merchants and Americans trading on British capitals." See Jefferson to Philip Mazzei, 24 April 1796, *PTJ*, 29:82. Probably the best comparison of Virginia and Low Country South Carolina plantation culture can be found in Philip

D. Morgan, *Slave Counterpoint: Black Culture in the Eighteenth-Century Chesa-peake and Low Country* (Chapel Hill: University of North Carolina Press for the Omohundro Institute of Early American History and Culture, 1998).

18 Rogers, *Evolution of a Federalist*, 112–134, 159–167, 225–237; Charles Cotes-worth Pinckney to Thomas Pinckney, 5 October 1794, Pinckney Papers, Library of Congress, quoted in ibid., 266. Smith personally does not seem to have invested as heavily or directly in plantation land and slaves as other members of the Low Country elite, though his family certainly did, and his other interests depended on slavery.

19 Rogers, *Evolution of a Federalist*, 159–241, quotation on 237.

20 Ibid., 219–237.

21 [William Loughton Smith], *The Politicks and Views of a Certain Party, Displayed* ([Philadelphia]: n.p., 1792), 2–3 and passim. Although attributed to Hamilton in some bibliographies, the pamphlet seems to be Smith's work. Many of its particular points probably originated in Hamilton's own 1792 newspaper es-says attacking Jefferson over the *National Gazette* (see chapter 1).

22 On the Federalist turn against the Enlightenment, see Henry F. May, *The En-lightenment in America* (New York: Oxford University Press, 1978), 252–277; Kerber, *Federalists in Dissent*, 1–22; Vernon Stauffer, *New England and the Ba-varian Illuminati* (New York: Columbia University Press, 1918).

23 Christopher Grasso, *A Speaking Aristocracy: Transforming Public Discourse in Eighteenth-Century Connecticut* (Chapel Hill: University of North Carolina Press for the Omohundro Institute of Early American History and Culture, 1999), 230–234, 240–242, 327–385, 444–447; Richard J. Purcell, *Connecticut in Transition: 1775–1818*, 2nd ed. (Middletown, Conn.: Wesleyan University Press, 1963), 8–17; Peter S. Field, *The Crisis of the Standing Order: Clerical Intel-lectuals and Cultural Authority in Massachusetts, 1780–1833* (Amherst: University of Massachusetts Press, 1998); Jonathan D. Sassi, *A Republic of Righteousness: The Public Christianity of the Post-Revolutionary New England Clergy* (New York: Oxford University Press, 2001). Quotations from *The Diary or Loudon's Regis-ter* (New York), 1 June 1793.

24 Edmund Burke, *Reflections on the Revolution in France*, ed. Frank M. Turner (New Haven: Yale University Press, 2003), 44, 30, 73–74; William Cobbett, *Peter Porcupine in America: Pamphlets on Republicanism and Revolution*, ed. David A. Wilson (Ithaca: Cornell University Press, 1994), 25–27, 130–131. On Cobbett, see Marcus Daniel, *Scandal & Civility: Journalism and the Birth of American Democracy* (New York: Oxford University Press, 2009), 187–230. A future British radical hero, the thuggish Cobbett does not feature much in this book, because while bitterly partisan in his reporting and commentary, his relationship with American party politics was actually quite distant. Cobbett rarely mentioned Jefferson or Adams, and many Federalists found him far too abrasive to be embraced or reprinted, though others appreciated him for being a vocal enemy of their enemies, the French and the Democratic-Repub-lican press. Most telling, however, was the fact that while Cobbett's works sold very well, they were most popular in Republican rather than Federalist areas. He was probably read for titillation more than political guidance. See David A. Wilson's introduction to *Peter Porcupine in America*, 35–38, on Cobbett's American reception. For more Federalist antipathy to feminists, see Chan-dos Michael Brown, "Mary Wollstonecraft, Or, The Female Illuminati: The

Campaign against Women and 'Modern Philosophy' in The Early Republic," *Journal of the Early Republic* 15 (1995): 389–424; Daniel I. O'Neill, "John Adams versus Mary Wollstonecraft on the French Revolution and Democracy," *Journal of the History of Ideas* 68, no. 3 (July 1, 2007): 451–476.

25 "Catullus, No. III," *GUS*, 29 September 1792, *PAH*, 12:504.

26 Darrin M. McMahon, "Edmund Burke and the Literary Cabal: A Tale of Two Enlightenments," in Burke, *Reflections on the Revolution in France*, ed. Turner, 233–247.

27 Darren Staloff, *Hamilton, Adams, Jefferson: The Politics of Enlightenment and the American Founding* (New York: Farrar, Straus and Giroux, 2005), esp. 78–79; Peter Gay, *The Enlightenment: The Science of Freedom* (New York: W. W. Norton, 1996), 454–455, 555–568. For another reading of Adams as enlightened and modern, see C. Bradley Thompson, *John Adams and the Spirit of Liberty*, ed. Wilson Carey McWilliams and Lance Banning (Lawrence: University Press of Kansas, 2002).

28 On the "rhetoric of reaction" over the centuries, see Albert O. Hirschman, *The Rhetoric of Reaction: Perversity, Futility, Jeopardy* (Cambridge, Mass.: Harvard University Press, 1991); James Schmidt, "What Enlightenment Project?," *Political Theory* 28 (2000): 734–757; Philip J. Cook and James A. Leitzel, " 'Perversity, Futility, Jeopardy': An Economic Analysis of the Attack on Gun Control," *Law and Contemporary Problems* 59 (1996): 91–118.

29 *Annals of Congress*, 1st Congress, 2nd Session, House of Representatives, 17 March 1790, 1510–1511.

30 Burke, *Reflections on the Revolution in France*, ed. Turner, 68, 105; Daniel, *Scandal & Civility*, 46–47, 304n76; Joseph J. Ellis, *Passionate Sage: The Character and Legacy of John Adams* (New York: W. W. Norton, 1993), 146. For three among the innumerable references to the "swinish multitude" in the Democratic-Republican press, see Philadelphia *National Gazette*, 25 August 1792; Philadelphia *General Advertiser*, 17 January 1794; NY *Journal*, 9 April 1794. For Burke's influence on Federalists and other American conservatives, see Wilson, *Peter Porcupine in America*, 35; Patrick Allitt, *The Conservatives: Ideas and Personalities throughout American History* (New Haven: Yale University Press, 2010), 12, 50–51, 71, 168; Russell Kirk, ed., *The Portable Conservative Reader* (New York: Viking Penguin, 1982), 3–112; Corey Robin, *The Reactionary Mind: Conservatism from Edmund Burke to Sarah Palin* (New York: Oxford University Press, 2011).

31 Burke, *Reflections on the Revolution in France*, ed. Turner, 7, 20, 35, 36, 49, 52, 190, 75, 89; 10, 54, 91.

32 Smith, *Politicks and Views of a Certain Party*, 8, 28–29, 32; McDonald, "Thomas Jefferson's Changing Reputation." On Federalist satire as a genre, see Kerber, *Federalists in Dissent*, chap. 1. An emblematic and unusually funny example of the genre is David Daggett, *Sun-Beams May Be Extracted from Cucumbers, but the Process Is Tedious; An Oration, Pronounced on the Fourth of July, 1799. At the Request of the Citizens of New-Haven* (New-Haven: Printed by Thomas Green and Son, 1799). Certain Loyalist and antifederalist writers earlier used the rhetoric of reaction, too, but for present purposes I am sticking to the realm of national politics under the Constitution.

33 Smith, *Politicks and Views of a Certain Party*, 35.

34 Ibid., 29–30; Burke, *Reflections on the Revolutions in France*, ed. Turner, 88–89;

Michael Knox Beran, *Jefferson's Demons: Portrait of a Restless Mind* (New York: Free Press, 2003), 122; Andrew Burstein, *Jefferson's Secrets: Death and Desire at Monticello* (New York: Basic Books, 2005), 51. Here is a modern example that came across the Internet just as I was originally writing this paragraph. The conservative radio commentator Rush Limbaugh attacked President Barack Obama, as he did almost daily, as "Barry Obama," insinuating that the president was both too black and too white, a "race-baiter" prejudiced against white people *and* inauthentic because he was raised by white grandparents. See " 'Barry Obama' Comes from a 'Very White' Background—'He's Not From Da 'Hood,'" *Media Matters for America*, 3 March 2011, http://mediamatters.org/mmtv/201103030022.

35 Sassi, *Republic of Righteousness*; John Fea, *Was America Founded as a Christian Nation? A Historical Introduction* (Louisville: Westminster John Knox Press, 2011).

36 Hamilton to Bayard, April 1802, in *Writings*, ed. Joanne B. Freeman (New York: Literary Classics of the United States, 2001), 988; David Hackett Fischer, *The Revolution of American Conservatism: The Federalist Party in the Era of Jeffersonian Democracy* (New York: Harper & Row, 1965), 112–113; "From the National Gazette," *Baltimore Evening Post*, 29 December 1792; Douglass Adair, "Was Alexander Hamilton a Christian Statesman?," in *Fame and the Founding Fathers* (New York: W. W. Norton for the Institute of Early American History and Culture, 1974), 141–159.

37 Burke, *Reflections on the Revolution in France*, ed. Turner, 77, 234–235; Smith, *Politicks and Views of a Certain Party*, 32, 34–35.

38 George Lakoff, *Moral Politics: What Conservatives Know That Liberals Don't*, 2nd ed. (Chicago: University of Chicago Press, 1996), 65–107; Daniel Walker Howe, *The Political Culture of the American Whigs* (Chicago: University of Chicago Press, 1979), 29; and Sean Wilentz, *The Rise of American Democracy: Jefferson to Lincoln* (New York: W. W. Norton, 2005), 492–493. Of course, many historians (including Howe) would vigorously dispute my labeling of the Whigs as a "rightist" party, but the thread of Christian moral discipline and Wall Street–backed, probusiness policies runs quite clearly from the Federalists to the Whigs to the modern-day Republicans. Some northern Federalists and Whigs happened to be on the "left" side of the slavery issue, and most eagerly supported material progress (through finance, tariff protection of industry, and public economic development projects like canals and railroads), but this hardly outweighs the fundamentally rightist core qualities of politicized Christian piety, the protection of wealth, and tempering democracy though moral discipline. For two arguments in favor of the Whigs as the progressive party of their age, see Lee Benson, *The Concept of Jacksonian Democracy: New York as a Test Case* (Princeton: Princeton University Press, 1961); and Daniel Walker Howe, *What Hath God Wrought: The Transformation of America, 1815–1848* (New York: Oxford University Press, 2007).

39 Smith, *Politicks and Views of a Certain Party*, 28–29; Charles Granquist, "Thomas Jefferson's 'Whirligig' Chairs," *Magazine Antiques* 109 (1976): 1056–1060; Susan R. Stein, *The Worlds of Thomas Jefferson at Monticello* (New York: H. N. Abrams, in association with the Thomas Jefferson Memorial Foundation, 1993), 103–105, 267, 364–373. Ironically, George Washington had a whirligig chair, too.

40 Smith, *Politicks and Views of a Certain Party*, 28–29, 35.

41 On Monroe's near-duel with Hamilton over the "Reynolds Affair," see Harry Ammon, *James Monroe: The Quest for National Identity* (Charlottesville: University Press of Virginia, 1990), 158–160. On the competitive customs of southern men, see, among others, T. H. Breen, *Tobacco Culture: The Mentality of the Great Tidewater Planters on the Eve of Revolution* (Princeton: Princeton University Press, 1985); Rhys Isaac, *The Transformation of Virginia, 1740–1790* (Chapel Hill: University of North Carolina Press for the Institute of Early American History and Culture, 1982), 98–114, 317–320. On the code of honor in early American politics, see Joanne B. Freeman, *Affairs of Honor: National Politics in the New Republic* (New Haven: Yale University Press, 2001). On the Jeffersonian style, see Alan Taylor, "From Fathers to Friends of the People: Political Personas in the Early Republic," *Journal of the Early Republic* 11 (1991): 465–491; and Jeffrey L. Pasley, "1800 as a Revolution in Political Culture: Newspapers, Celebrations, Democratization, and Voting in the Early Republic," in *The Revolution of 1800: Democracy, Race, and the New Republic*, ed. James Horn, Jan Ellen Lewis, and Peter S. Onuf (Charlottesville: University of Virginia Press, 2002), 121–152.

42 Smith, *Politicks and Views of a Certain Party*, 3, 29.

43 Rogers, *Evolution of a Federalist*, 266–268; Charleston *City Gazette & Daily Advertiser*, 8, 10 October 1794. On the creaky, reform-resistant electoral system in South Carolina, see Rebecca Starr, "Parity without Equality: Representation 'Reform' in the South Carolina Legislature in the Early Republic, 1783–94," *Parliaments, Estates and Representation* 17 (1997): 89–109.

44 Rogers, *Evolution of a Federalist*, 266–279.

45 Ibid., 304–305; "A Correspondent," *Aurora*, 3 November 1796.

46 Rogers, *Evolution of a Federalist*, 286–287; William Smith, *An Oration, Delivered in St. Philip's Church, before the Inhabitants of Charleston, South-Carolina, on the Fourth of July, 1796, in Commemoration of American Independence* (Charleston: W. P. Young, 1796), 10, 11, 12–13, 15, 21.

47 Ibid., 12, 15; Burke, *Reflections on the Revolution in France*, ed. Turner, 49. For a variety of historical interpretations of the Antifederalists, none of which treats them as Enlightenment speculatists, see Cecelia M. Kenyon, "Men of Little Faith: The Anti-Federalists on the Nature of Representative Government," *William and Mary Quarterly*, 3rd ser., 12 (1955): 3–43; Robert Allen Rutland, *The Ordeal of the Constitution: The Antifederalists and the Ratification Struggle of 1787–1788* (Boston: Northeastern University Press, 1966); Jackson Turner Main, *The Antifederalists* (New York: W. W. Norton, 1974); Herbert J. Storing, *What the Anti-Federalists Were for* (Chicago: University of Chicago Press, 1981); John P. Kaminski, *George Clinton: Yeoman Politician of the New Republic* (Madison, Wis.: Madison House, 1993); Eric Robert Papenfuse, "Unleashing the 'Wildness': The Mobilization of Grassroots Antifederalism in Maryland," *Journal of the Early Republic* 16 (1996): 73–106; Saul Cornell, *The Other Founders: Anti-Federalism and the Dissenting Tradition in America, 1788–1828* (Chapel Hill: University of North Carolina Press for the Omohundro Institute of Early American History and Culture, 1999); Jeff Broadwater, *George Mason: Forgotten Founder* (Chapel Hill: University of North Carolina Press, 2006).

48 Smith, *Oration*, 11–12.

49 Rogers, *Evolution of a Federalist*, 288, 290–291; Jefferson to Edward Rutledge, *PTJ*, 29:231–233.

50 "Thomas Jefferson," *New-York Diary*, 1796, reprinted in *Washington Spy*, Md., 30 November 1796; "From the Chronicle," New York *Argus*, 10 October 1796; *President II. Being Observations on the Late Official Address of George Washington: Designed to Promote the Interest of a Certain Candidate for the Executive, and to Explode the Pretensions of Others* (Philadelphia: n.p., 1796), Evans 31042, p. 5; "Extract of a Letter from Major Wm. C. Claiborn [W. C. C. Claiborne], of Tennessee, to his friend in Richmond, dated Knoxville, Aug. 25," reprinted in Newfield, Conn., *American Telegraphe & Fairfield County Gazette*, 25 August 1796; "Death," *New York Magazine, or Literary Repository*, October 1796, 553; Arthur Scherr, "The 'Republican Experiment' and the Election of 1796 in Virginia," *West Virginia History* 37 (1976): 89–90.

51 Richmond *Virginia Gazette and General Advertiser*, 12 October 1796.

52 [William Loughton Smith], *The Pretensions of Thomas Jefferson to the Presidency Examined*, 2 vols. (Philadelphia: [John Fenno], 1796), Evans 31212 and 31213; Philadelphia *Gazette of the United States*, 14 October–24 November 1796.

53 Quotations from Smith, *Pretensions of Thomas Jefferson*, 1:16n; Stein, *Worlds of Thomas Jefferson at Monticello*, 267.

54 Smith, *Pretensions of Thomas Jefferson*, 1:4; Noble E. Cunningham Jr., ed., *Circular Letters of Congressmen to Their Constituents, 1789–1829* (Chapel Hill: University of North Carolina Press for the Institute of Early American History and Culture, 1978), 1:63.

55 Burke, *Reflections on the Revolution in France*, ed. Turner, 68.

56 Burke, *Reflections on the Revolution in France*, ed. Turner, 208; Richard Hofstadter, *Anti-Intellectualism in American Life* (New York: Vintage, 1963), 146–148; "Catullus No. VI," 22 December 1792, *PAH*, 13:355. On early American intellectuals and artists, see, among many others, Joseph J. Ellis, *After the Revolution: Profiles of Early American Culture* (New York: W. W. Norton, 1979); Robert A. Ferguson, *Law and Letters in American Culture* (Cambridge, Mass.: Harvard University Press, 1984); Perry Miller, *The Life of the Mind in America: From the Revolution to the Civil War* (San Diego: Harcourt Brace Jovanovich, 1965).

57 Ibid., 5–6; *Annals of Congress*, 1st Congress, 2nd Session, House of Representatives, 17 March 1790, 1505–1506; Smith, *Pretensions of Thomas Jefferson*, 1:5–6.

58 Ibid.

59 Ibid., 1:7; Jordan, *White over Black*, 452, 464.

60 Smith, *Pretensions of Thomas Jefferson*, 1:5.

61 Banneker to Jefferson, 19 August 1791, *PTJ*, 22:49–54, including editorial notes; Jordan, *White over Black*, 444–452.

62 Thomas Jefferson to Benjamin Banneker, 30 August 1791, *PTJ*, 22:97–98; Jefferson to Condorcet, 30 August 1791, *PTJ*, 22:98; Silvio A. Bedini, *The Life of Benjamin Banneker* (New York: Charles Scribner's Sons, 1972), 137–190; Richard S. Newman, " 'Good Communications Corrects Bad Manners': The Banneker-Jefferson Dialogue and the Project of White Uplift," in Hammond and Mason, *Contesting Slavery*, 69–93.

63 Jordan, *White over Black*, 451–457; Silvio A. Bedini, "The Survey of the Federal Territory: Andrew Ellicott and Benjamin Banneker," *Washington History*

3 (1991): 76–95; Annette Gordon-Reed, "Engaging Jefferson: Blacks and the Founding Father," *William and Mary Quarterly*, 3rd ser., 57 (2000): 171–182.

64 Smith, *Pretensions of Thomas Jefferson*, 1:13–14.

65 Ibid., 1:8–10.

66 Ibid., 1:16–17; *PTJ*, 22:98.

67 Ibid., 16–17. On the "epidemical contagion," see Jordan, *White over Black*, 386–391. On Condorcet and slavery, see Laurent Dubois, *Avengers of the New World: The Story of the Haitian Revolution* (Cambridge, Mass.: Harvard University Press, 2004), 71–73.

68 Smith, *Pretensions of Thomas Jefferson*, 1:13.

69 Smith, *Pretensions of Thomas Jefferson*, 1:15, 36, 39.

70 Ibid., 1: 37; *GUS*, 27 October 1796; Charles B. Sanford, *The Religious Life of Thomas Jefferson* (Charlottesville: University Press of Virginia, 1984), 1–15, 102–140; Fea, *Was America Founded a Christian Nation?*, 203–215.

71 Smith, *Pretensions of Thomas Jefferson*, 1:36–38, 40; Jefferson, *Writings*, ed. Peterson, 290; "A Friend of the Union," Reading *Weekly Advertiser*, 29 October 1796. Phocion X was first published in *GUS*, 27 October 1796.

72 Eric Foner, *Tom Paine and Revolutionary America* (New York: Oxford University Press, 1976), 245–249.

73 New York *American Minerva*, 5 January 1796; "Character of Thomas Paine," Leominster *Rural Repository*, 28 January 1796; Smith, *Pretensions of Thomas Jefferson*, 1:36. For the argument that Paine-style religious skepticism actually did have a popular following in America, see Mark A. Lause, "The 'Unwashed Infidelity': Thomas Paine and Early New York City Labor History," *Labor History* 27 (1986): 385–409; Cotlar, *Tom Paine's America*.

74 Smith, *Pretensions of Thomas Jefferson*, 1:36–40; Charles O. Lerche Jr., "Jefferson and the Election of 1800: A Case Study in the Political Smear," *William and Mary Quarterly*, 3rd ser., 5 (1948): 467–469. In fact, the years of the Jefferson presidency saw a wave of religious revivals in strongly Democratic-Republican areas like Kentucky that helped create the southern and Midwestern Bible Belt. It turned out that Jeffersonian democracy and Tom Paine's visits to the White House went together perfectly well with enthusiastic Christianity. On religious revivals under Jeffersonian rule, see Nathan O. Hatch, *The Democratization of American Christianity* (New Haven: Yale University Press, 1989).

75 Lance Banning, "Republican Ideology and the Triumph of the Constitution, 1789 to 1793," *William and Mary Quarterly*, 3rd ser., 31 (1974): 167–188.

76 Quotations from Hamilton, "Report on Public Credit," in *Writings*, ed. Freeman, 533–534; and Smith, *Pretensions of Thomas Jefferson*, 2:4. On the French debt mini-scandal, see Herbert E. Sloan, *Principle and Interest: Thomas Jefferson and the Problem of Debt* (New York: Oxford University Press, 1995), 45–46, 274n202; Malone, *Jefferson and the Rights of Man*, 470–471.

77 Smith, *Pretension of Thomas Jefferson*, 1:18, 33.

78 Ibid., 1:34.

79 Ibid.

80 The account of Jefferson's term as governor and the Virginia invasion of 1781 presented here draws primarily on John E. Selby, *The Revolution in Virginia, 1775–1783* (Williamsburg: Colonial Williamsburg Foundation, 1988), 204–285; Dumas Malone, *Jefferson the Virginian* (Boston: Little, Brown, 1948),

301–369; and *PTJ*, 4:256–278, 6:88–109. See also Michael Kranish, *Flight from Monticello: Thomas Jefferson at War* (New York: Oxford University Press, 2010).

81 Smith, *Pretensions of Thomas Jefferson*, 1:34.

82 "Another Freeholder," *Virginia Herald and Fredericksburg and Falmouth Advertiser*, 25 October 1796.

83 Jefferson, "Diary of Arnold's Invasion," *PTJ*, 4:265–266.

84 *PTJ*, 6:135–136.

85 Reading *Weekly Advertiser*, 29 October 1796; Halifax *North Carolina Journal*, 28 November 1796.

86 Eric Slauter, *The State as a Work of Art: The Cultural Origins of the Constitution* (Chicago: University of Chicago Press, 2009), 59–88; Kirk Savage, "The Self-Made Monument: George Washington and the Fight to Erect a National Memorial," *Winterthur Portfolio* 22 (1987): 225–242; John Seelye, *Memory's Nation: The Place of Plymouth Rock* (Chapel Hill: University of North Carolina Press, 1998), 46–47; Thomas Paine, "The Rights of Man: Part First," in *The Life and Major Writings of Thomas Paine*, ed. Philip S. Foner (New York: Citadel Press, 1993), 338; Smith, *Pretensions of Thomas Jefferson*, 1:34.

87 Halifax *North Carolina Journal*, 28 November 1796; "To the Democrats and Jacobins of the United States," *Columbian Mirror and Alexandria Gazette*, 4 October 1796; "Amicus," No. VI, Boston *Columbian Centinel*, 5 November 1796.

88 Smith, *Pretensions of Thomas Jefferson*, 2:39.

89 "Depositions Taken in 1796 Respecting Jefferson's Conduct during Arnold's Invasion," *PTJ*, 4:271–273.

90 Ibid.; *Columbian Mirror and Alexandria Gazette*, 22 October 1796 and passim (October-November); "A Subscriber," reprinted Gerard W. Gawalt, ed., *Justifying Jefferson: The Political Writings of John James Beckley* (Washington, D.C.: Library of Congress, 1995), 130–133.

91 "Z," Charleston *City Gazette and Daily Advertiser*, 10 November 1796.

92 "To the People of the United States," *Virginia Gazette and Petersburg Intelligencer*, 21 October 1796.

93 See Beckley's *Address to the People of the United States, with an Epitome and Vindication of the Public Life and Character of Thomas Jefferson* (Philadelphia: James Carey, 1800), reprinted in Gawalt, *Justifying Jefferson*, 166–189.

CHAPTER 7. HIS ROTUNDITY

1 On Adams's eclipse, see Zoltán Haraszti, *John Adams and the Prophets of Progress* (Cambridge, Mass.: Harvard University Press, 1952), 1–13. Adams was the first major beneficiary of the "Founder Chic" trend in publishing that arose around the turn of the twenty-first century. See Joseph J. Ellis, *Founding Brothers: The Revolutionary Generation* (New York: Alfred A. Knopf, 2001); David McCullough, *John Adams* (New York: Simon & Schuster, 2001); and my critique Jeffrey L. Pasley, "Publick Occurrences: Federalist Chic," *Common-Place* 2 (2002), www.common-place.org/publick/200202.shtml.

2 The literature on John Adams is vast, but my primary references have been, in addition to those already cited, Richard Alan Ryerson, ed., *John Adams and the Founding of the Republic* (Boston: Massachusetts Historical Society and Northeastern University Press, 2001); Peter Shaw, *The Character of John Adams* (Chapel Hill: University of North Carolina Press for the Institute of Early American

History and Culture, 1976); Gordon S. Wood, *The Creation of the American Republic, 1776–1787* (New York: W. W. Norton, 1972), 567–587; Page Smith, *John Adams* (Garden City, N.Y.: Doubleday, 1962); John Ferling, *John Adams: A Life* (New York: Henry Holt, 1996); Joseph J. Ellis, *Passionate Sage: The Character and Legacy of John Adams* (New York: W. W. Norton, 1993); John R. Howe Jr., *The Changing Political Thought of John Adams* (Princeton: Princeton University Press, 1966). On Adams as an insider leader, see Ryerson's introduction, pp. 5–7.

3 [John Gardner], *A Brief Consideration of the Important Services, and Distinguished Virtues and Talents, Which Recommend Mr. Adams for the Presidency of the United States* (Boston: Manning & Loring, for Joseph Nancrede, 1796), 7–8.

4 *CMAG*, 18 October 1796.

5 Sidney, "To the People of the United States," reprinted in *Greenleaf's New York Journal and Patriotic Register*, 25 October 1796.

6 Except where noted, page citations are to John Adams, *A Defence of the Constitutions of Government of the United States of America, against the Attack of M. Turgot, in His Letter to Dr. Price, Dated the Twenty-Second Day of March, 1778*, 3 vols. (London: John Stockdale, 1794), available on Google Books. This was the edition most widely cited in 1796. Note that the pagination of this edition is slightly different from the now more commonly cited 1797 edition published by William Cobbett after the election. On the publication history of the *Defence*, see Smith, *John Adams*, 2:689–701. Quotation from John Adams to Samuel Perley, 19 June 1809, in *The Works of John Adams, Second President of the United States*, ed. Charles Francis Adams (Boston: Little, Brown, 1856), 9:622–624.

7 Adams, *Defence*, 1:vii; A. Owen Aldridge, "John Adams Confronts Turgot," *Studies in Eighteenth-Century Culture* 30 (2001): 91–104; Haraszti, *John Adams and the Prophets of Progress*, 139–154. Turgot felt that the Americans had unthinkingly copied the British system of a king, house of lords, and house of commons, and he wished that the Americans had picked a system that better reflected their own society.

8 Adams to Perley, 19 June 1809, in *Works of John Adams*, 9:622–624.

9 R. B. Bernstein, "'Let Us Dare to Read, Think, Speak, and Write': John Adams's Use of Reading as Political and Constitutional Armory," in *The Libraries, Leadership, & Legacy of John Adams and Thomas Jefferson*, ed. Robert C. Baron and Conrad Edick Wright (Golden, Colo.: Fulcrum Publishing and Massachusetts Historical Society, 2010), 81–93.

10 Haraszti, *Adams and the Prophets of Progress*, 155–164 and passim; Adams, *Defence*, 1:viii–ix.

11 Bernstein, "Let Us Dare to Read, Think, Speak, and Write"; Haraszti, *John Adams and the Prophets of Progress*, 155–164.

12 Smith, *John Adams*, 2:698–701; *GUS*, 8 September 1796 (also New York *Minerva*, 10 September 1796, and Stockbridge *Western Star*, 19 September 1796). For uses of "Dr. Adams," see Boston *Argus*, 5 August 1791; Worcester *American Herald*, 1–8 January 1789.

13 For instance, see Robert L. Brunhouse, *The Counter-Revolution in Pennsylvania, 1776–1790* (Harrisburg: Pennsylvania Historical and Museum Commission, 1971).

14 Adams, *Defence*, 1:70–71, 321.

15 Boston *Massachusetts Mercury*, 4 July 1794; "BOSTON, 24 Sept. 1796," broadside, Library Company of Philadelphia, Evans 29982. Other published lists of page references from the *Defence* include "Citizens of New Jersey!," Elizabethtown *New-Jersey Journal*, 2 November 1796; "Fellow Citizens!," broadside dated 3 October 1796, Historical Society of Pennsylvania, Evans 30411; "Public Notice, Friday the Fourth Day of November Next. . . . ," broadside, Historical Society of Pennsylvania, Evans 30984. For a version that used full quotations instead of paraphrases, see "Citizens of America," *Aurora*, 1 November 1796.

16 "BOSTON, 24 Sept. 1796," Evans 29982, p. 3.

17 Adams, *Defence*, 1:xxv, 3:296; Adams to Jefferson, 6 December 1787, in *The Adams-Jefferson Letters: The Complete Correspondence between Thomas Jefferson and Abigail and John Adams*, ed. Lester J. Cappon (Chapel Hill: University of North Carolina Press for the Institute of Early American History and Culture, 1988), 214.

18 Adams as quoted in New York *Argus*, 3 November 1796, and many other places. The quotations direct from Adams himself can be found in *Defence*, 1:70, vii, 321, xxiv.

19 Thomas Jefferson to Philip Mazzei, 24 April 1796, *PTJ*, 29:82.

20 Adams, *Defence*, 1:xiv.

21 Ibid., 1:xi.

22 *Aurora*, 4 November 1796.

23 Adams, *Defence*, 1:108; Adams to Jefferson, 6 December 1787, in Cappon, *Adams-Jefferson Letters*, 213.

24 Adams, *Defence*, 1:xxvi–xxvii; Aldridge, "John Adams Confronts Turgot," 93.

25 Joyce Appleby, *Capitalism and a New Social Order: The Republican Vision of the 1790s* (New York: New York University Press, 1984); "Sidney No. III," *Aurora*, reprinted in the *Greenleaf's New York Journal and Patriotic Register*, 1 November 1796.

26 Adams, *Defence*, 1:110–116.

27 Adams, *Defence*, 1:116–117, 164; "Citizens of America," *Aurora*, 1 November 1796. On the shared but different ideas of "natural aristocracy" in the thought of Adams, Jefferson, and other Founders, see (among many, many others) Cappon, *Adams-Jefferson Letters*, chap. 10; Ellis, *Passionate Sage*, chap. 5; and Gordon S. Wood, *The Radicalism of the American Revolution* (New York: Alfred A. Knopf, 1992).

28 Adams, *Defence*, 1:116, 114–115.

29 "Communication Third," Philadelphia *New World*, reprinted in New York *Argus*, 13 October 1796. Some states did have property requirements (really, wealth requirements) for voting and holding certain offices. New York and Rhode Island were both notable in this regard.

30 Adams, *Defence*, 1:ix.

31 "Sidney," *Aurora*, reprinted in *Greenleaf's New York Journal and Patriotic Register*, 25, 28 October, 1 November 1796.

32 Ibid.; Boston *Independent Chronicle*, 20 October 1796.

33 "Fellow Citizens!"; "Safety," Boston *Independent Chronicle*, reprinted in New York *Argus*, 8 November 1796; Samuel Flagg Bemis, *John Quincy Adams and the Foundations of American Foreign Policy* (New York: Alfred A. Knopf, 1949), 50–51, 85.

34 Gardner, *Brief Consideration*, 7; "Fair Play," *Aurora*, 1 November 1796; Richard

Alan Ryerson, "'Like a Hare before the Hunters': John Adams and the Idea of Republican Monarchy," *Proceedings of the Massachusetts Historical Society* 107 (1995): 16–29; James H. Hutson, "John Adams' Title Campaign," *New England Quarterly* 41 (1968): 30–39.

35 Adams, *Defence*, 1:375.

36 Ibid., 1:382; "Polybius, I," New York *Argus*, 3, 8 November 1796.

37 Adams, *Defence*, 1:390.

38 *Aurora*, 9 November 1796.

39 Seth Cotlar, *Tom Paine's America: The Rise and Fall of Transatlantic Radicalism in the Early Republic* (Charlottesville: University of Virginia Press, 2011), 49–114.

40 *Aurora*, 6 July 1796.

41 Jonathan Israel, *A Revolution of the Mind: Radical Enlightenment and the Intellectual Origins of Modern Democracy* (Princeton: Princeton University Press, 2010), 38, 47, 62–65. More recently, Israel has released the third volume of his magnum opus: Jonathan I. Israel, *Democratic Enlightenment: Philosophy, Revolution, and Human Rights, 1750–1790* (Oxford: Oxford University Press, 2011).

42 Michael Durey, "Thomas Paine's Apostles: Radical Emigrés and the Triumph of Jeffersonian Republicanism," *William and Mary Quarterly*, 3rd ser., 44 (1987): 661–688; Kim Tousley Phillips, *William Duane, Radical Journalist in the Age of Jefferson* (New York: Garland, 1989); Michael Durey, *"With the Hammer of Truth": James Thomson Callender and America's Early National Heroes* (Charlottesville: University Press of Virginia, 1990); Michael Durey, *Transatlantic Radicals and the Early American Republic* (Lawrence: University Press of Kansas, 1997); Jeffrey L. Pasley, *"The Tyranny of Printers": Newspaper Politics in the Early American Republic* (Charlottesville: University Press of Virginia, 2001); Marcus Daniel, *Scandal and Civility: Journalism and the Birth of American Democracy* (New York: Oxford University Press, 2009).

43 *Aurora*, 2 November 1796; Daniel, *Scandal and Civility*, 119–120. On democratic radicals as "citizens of the world," see Cotlar, *Tom Paine's America*.

44 *Aurora*, 6 July 1796; Jasper Dwight [William Duane], *A Letter to George Washington, President of the United States: Containing Strictures on His Address of the Seventeenth of September, 1796, Notifying His Relinquishment of the Presidential Office* (Philadelphia: Printed for George Keatinge's Book-Store, 1796), 10–11.

45 Boston *Columbian Centinel*, 24 September 1796.

46 "Citizens of America," *Aurora*, 1 November 1796; Adams, *Defence*, 1:153; Dwight [Duane], *Letter to Washington*.

47 "People of America," *Aurora*, 3 November 1796.

48 David Waldstreicher, *In the Midst of Perpetual Fetes: The Making of American Nationalism, 1776–1820* (Chapel Hill: University of North Carolina Press for the Omohundro Institute of Early American History and Culture, 1997).

49 Paine to Bache, 7 August 1796, Bache Papers, Castle Collection, American Philosophical Society. On Paine as a Founder that common folk could emulate rather than worship from below, see Cotlar, *Tom Paine's America*, 39–41. On Paine's intervention in the election of 1796, see Jeffrey L. Pasley, "Thomas Paine and the U.S. Election of 1796: In Which It Is Discovered That George Washington Was More Popular Than Jesus," *Publick Occurrences 2.0*, July 2009, http://www.common-place.org/pasley/wp-content/uploads/2009/07/pasley_paine1796.pdf.

50 Thomas Paine to James Madison, 24 September 1795, *PJM*, 16:89–93; John Keane, *Tom Paine: A Political Life* (Boston: Little, Brown, 1995), 382–419, 429–430. The campaign edition of Paine's letter was Thomas Paine, *Letter to George Washington, President of the United States of America, on Affairs Public and Private* (Philadelphia: Benjamin Franklin Bache, 1796).

51 Paine to Madison, 24 September 1795, *PJM*, 16:92; Keane, *Tom Paine*, 429.

52 Thomas Paine to James Madison, 24 September 1795, *PJM*, 16:91–92.

53 James D. Tagg, *Benjamin Franklin Bache and the Philadelphia "Aurora"* (Philadelphia: University of Pennsylvania Press, 1991), 124–127, 282–283.

54 Thomas Paine, "Letter to George Washington," in *The Writings of Thomas Paine*, ed. Moncure Daniel Conway (New York: G. P. Putnam's Sons, 1895), 3:213, 214n, 217–218.

55 Ibid., 3:220.

56 *Aurora*, 17 October 1796; "Public Notice, Friday the Fourth Day of November Next. . . . ," broadside, Historical Society of Pennsylvania, Evans 30983.

57 "The People's Answer," reprinted in Worcester *Massachusetts Spy*, 23 November 1796; "From a George-Town Paper," Newark *Centinel of Freedom*, 25 January 1797; *GUS*, 27 October 1796; New York *Herald*, 28 December 1796; Baltimore *Federal Gazette*, 3 January 1797; Boston *Columbian Centinel*, 14, 18 January 1797.

58 Keane, *Tom Paine*, 479–482.

59 Cotlar, *Tom Paine's America*, makes a number of similar and compatible points in a somewhat different way. On Tom Paine's problematic place in American historical memory, see Paul Collins, *The Trouble with Tom: The Strange Afterlife and Times of Thomas Paine* (New York: Bloomsbury, 2005); Frederick Voss, "Honoring a Scorned Hero: America's Monument to Thomas Paine," *New York History* 68 (1987): 132–150. On the problematic nature and conservative uses of revolutionary memory in early-twenty-first-century politics, see Jill Lepore, *The Whites of Their Eyes: The Tea Party's Revolution and the Battle over American History* (Princeton: Princeton University Press, 2010).

CHAPTER 8. TAKING THE ELECTORAL COLLEGE TO SCHOOL

1 Ronald P. Formisano, "Deferential-Participant Politics: The Early Republic's Political Culture, 1789–1840," *American Political Science Review* 68 (1974): 473–487; Ronald P. Formisano, "Federalists and Republicans: Parties, Yes—System, No," in Paul Kleppner, Walter Dean Burnham, Ronald P. Formisano, Samuel P. Hays, Richard Jensen, and William G. Shade, *The Evolution of American Electoral Systems* (Westport, Conn.: Greenwood Press, 1981), 33–76. Gordon Wood has offered the fullest development of the idea of the Founding generation as an aristocratically minded "natural aristocracy" in Gordon S. Wood, *The Radicalism of the American Revolution* (New York: Alfred A. Knopf, 1992). Two other broad interpretations of the Early Republic's politics that hinge on the trope of democracy only flowering once the Founders' generation had passed are Robert H. Wiebe, *The Opening of American Society* (New York: Vintage, 1985); and Ronald P. Formisano, *The Transformation of Political Culture: Massachusetts Parties, 1790s–1840s* (New York: Oxford University Press, 1983), 57–170.

2 For a helpful survey of these issues ranging across Europe in time and space, and including several applications of the "notables" concept, see Simona

Piattoni, ed., *Clientelism, Interests, and Democratic Representation: The European Experience in Historical and Comparative Perspective* (New York: Cambridge University Press, 2001).

3 On the Assembly of Notables, see William Doyle, *The Oxford History of the French Revolution*, 2nd ed. (New York: Oxford University Press, 2003), 70–75.

4 The lucrative Founder Studies market emerged at the turn of the twenty-first century with the rise of what is called "Founder Chic." The three most prominent books in the first wave were David McCullough, *John Adams* (New York: Simon & Schuster, 2001); Joseph J. Ellis, *Founding Brothers: The Revolutionary Generation* (New York: Alfred A. Knopf, 2001); and the book that strongly influenced Ellis even though his manuscript made it to print first, Joanne B. Freeman, *Affairs of Honor: National Politics in the New Republic* (New Haven: Yale University Press, 2001). For a critique, see David Waldstreicher, "Founders Chic as Culture War," *Radical History Review* 84 (2002): 185–194.

5 Quotations from Shlomo Slonim, "The Electoral College at Philadelphia: The Evolution of an Ad Hoc Congress for the Selection of a President," *Journal of American History* 73 (1986): 35–58.

6 The history of the Electoral College specifically is an understudied subject. See Tadahisa Kuroda, *The Origins of the Twelfth Amendment: The Electoral College in the Early Republic, 1787–1804* (Westport, Conn.: Greenwood Press, 1994); and Slonim, "Electoral College at Philadelphia." For considerations by political scientists, see Robert A. Dahl, *How Democratic Is the American Constitution?* (New Haven: Yale University Press, 2003); Samuel Issacharoff, "Law, Rules, and Presidential Selection," *Political Science Quarterly* 120 (2005): 113–129; and James P. Pfiffner and Jason Hartke, "The Electoral College and the Framers' Distrust of Democracy," *White House Studies* 3 (2003): 261–271.

7 The constitutional text and the key passages of the Records of the Federal Convention concerning the creation of the Electoral College are conveniently gathered in the online edition of Philip B. Kurland and Ralph Lerner, eds., *The Founder's Constitution* (Chicago: University of Chicago Press, 2000), http://press-pubs.uchicago.edu/founders, at the page for Article 2, Section 1, Clauses 2 and 3. Quotations from Max Fernand, ed., *The Records of the Federal Convention of 1787* (New Haven: Yale University Press, 1937), 2:501.

8 Richard R. Beeman, *Plain, Honest Men: The Making of the American Constitution* (New York: Random House, 2009), 131–135, 297–301; Farrand, ed., *Records of the Federal Convention*, 2:29–31.

9 Beeman, *Plain, Honest Men*, 131–135, 299–300; Farrand, *Records of the Federal Convention*, 1:80; John Dickinson to George Logan, 16 January 1802, in *Supplement to Max Farrand's "The Records of the Federal Convention of 1787,"* ed. James H. Hutson (New Haven: Yale University Press, 1987), 300–301.

10 Quotations from Jacob E. Cooke, ed., *The Federalist* (Middletown, Conn.: Wesleyan University Press, 1961), 458.

11 Ibid., 459–460.

12 Ibid., 458.

13 Ibid., 64–65; Jack N. Rakove, *Original Meanings: Politics and Ideas in the Making of the Constitution* (New York: Vintage, 1997), 89–90, 266.

14 Dickinson to Logan, 16 January 1802, in Hutson, *Supplement to Farrand's Records*, 300–301.

15 *PJM*, 14:100–112, 371, 170; "Sidney," *Aurora*, reprinted in *NY Journal*, 25 October, 1 November 1796; Richard R. John, *Spreading the News: The American Postal System from Franklin to Morse* (Cambridge, Mass.: Harvard University Press, 1995).

16 James Haw, *John and Edward Rutledge of South Carolina* (Athens: University of Georgia Press, 1997), 264–266; Lisle A. Rose, *Prologue to Democracy: The Federalists in the South, 1789–1800* (Lexington: University of Kentucky Press, 1968), 134–138.

17 The classic account of eighteenth-century Virginia elections is Charles S. Sydnor, *Gentlemen Freeholders: Political Practices in Washington's Virginia* (Chapel Hill: University of North Carolina Press for the Institute of Early American History and Culture, 1952), but it should be supplemented with Daniel P. Jordan, *Political Leadership in Jefferson's Virginia* (Charlottesville: University Press of Virginia, 1983); and John Gilman Kolp, *Gentlemen and Freeholders: Electoral Politics in Colonial Virginia* (Baltimore: Johns Hopkins University Press, 1998).

18 On the Preston incident, see Edmund S. Morgan, *Inventing the People: The Rise of Popular Sovereignty in England and America* (New York: W. W. Norton, 1988), 186–189. On Virginia election violence in general, see Sydnor, *Gentlemen Freeholders*. On macho, competitive displays of power and prowess as the key to Virginia culture, and its social hierarchy, see T. H. Breen, *Tobacco Culture: The Mentality of the Great Tidewater Planters on the Eve of Revolution* (Princeton: Princeton University Press, 1985); Rhys Isaac, *The Transformation of Virginia, 1740–1790* (Chapel Hill: University of North Carolina Press for the Institute of Early American History and Culture, 1982).

19 Kolp, *Gentlemen and Freeholders*, 28–32; Sydnor, *Gentlemen Freeholders*, 38–59; Edmund S. Morgan, *Inventing the People*), 202–207; Andrew W. Robertson, "Voting Rites and Voting Acts: Electioneering Ritual, 1790–1820," in *Beyond the Founders: New Approaches to the Political History of the Early American Republic*, ed. Jeffrey L. Pasley, Andrew W. Robertson, and David Waldstreicher (Chapel Hill: University of North Carolina Press, 2004), 57–78.

20 Daniel Dupre, "Barbecues and Pledges: Electioneering and the Rise of Democratic Politics in Antebellum Alabama," *Journal of Southern History* 60 (1994): 479–512; Robert J. Dinkin, *Voting in Revolutionary America: A Study of Elections in the Original Thirteen Colonies, 1776–1789* (Westport, Conn.: Greenwood Press, 1982), 81–83.

21 Noble E. Cunningham Jr., *The Jeffersonian Republicans: The Formation of Party Organization, 1789–1801* (Chapel Hill: University of North Carolina Press for the Institute of Early American History and Culture, 1957), 96; William Deakins, "An Address to the Freemen of Prince George's and Montgomery," Baltimore *Federal Gazette*, 20 October 1796.

22 Baltimore *Federal Gazette*, 20 October 1796; NNV; John T. Willis, *Presidential Elections in Maryland* (Mt. Airy, Md.: Lomond, 1984), 161.

23 Charles Simms, "To the Freeholders of the Counties of Prince William, Stafford and Fairfax," *CMAG*, 29 September 1796, reprinted in Charleston *Columbian Herald*, 27 October 1796; Philadelphia *Claypoole's American Daily Advertiser*, 14 November 1796; *NY Journal*, 18 November 1796. On Simms, see Carl E. Prince, *The Federalists and the Origins of the U.S. Civil Service* (New York: New York University Press, 1977), 113–114, 311n12; Corra Bacon-Foster, *Early Chapters in the Development of the Potomac Route to the West* (Washington,

D.C.: Columbia Historical Society, 1912), 235–267; and John W. Herndon, "Applications of Virginians for Office during the Presidency of George Washington, 1789–1797," *William and Mary Quarterly Historical Magazine*, 2nd ser., 23 (1943): 185, 192n34.

24 *CMAG*, 18 October 1796. Munford quoted in Richard R. Beeman, *The Old Dominion and the New Nation, 1788–1801* (Lexington: University Press of Kentucky, 1972), 159–160.

25 Taylor announcement dated 11 July 1796, published in *CMAG*, 25 October 1796. Taylor's other contribution to the campaign has been published as John Taylor to Daniel Carroll Brent, 9 October 1796, in William E. Dodd, ed., "Letters of John Taylor of Caroline County, Virginia," *John P. Branch Historical Papers of Randolph-Macon College* 2 (June 1908): 260–268.

26 *CMAG*, 8, 20 September, 1, 25 October 1796; Cook, *Federalist*, 64.

27 *CMAG*, 20, 25 August 1796; "From the Winchester Centinel," Elizabethtown, Md., *Washington Spy*, 12 October 1796.

28 "Political Miscellany," *CMAG*, 27 September 1796.

29 Manning J. Dauer, *The Adams Federalists*, 2nd ed. (Baltimore: Johns Hopkins University Press, 1968); Breen, *Tobacco Culture*; J. R. Pole, "Representation and Authority in Virginia from the Revolution to Reform," *Journal of Southern History* 24 (1958): 16–50; Stevenson, *Life in Black and White*.

30 Jackson Turner Main, *Political Parties before the Constitution* (New York: W. W. Norton, 1974), 248; Rowland Berthoff and John M. Murrin, "Feudalism, Communalism, and the Yeomen Freeholder: The American Revolution Considered as a Social Accident," in *Essays on the American Revolution*, ed. Stephen G. Kurtz and James H. Hutson (New York: W. W. Norton, 1973), 256–288.

31 Harrison Williams, *Legends of Loudoun: An Account of the History and Homes of a Border County in Virginia's Northern Neck* (Richmond: Garrett and Massie, 1938), 168.

32 Norman K. Risjord, "The Virginia Federalists," *Journal of Southern History* 33 (1967): 486–517, quotation on 496; Brenda E. Stevenson, *Life in Black and White: Family and Community in the Slave South* (New York: Oxford University Press, 1996), 10–29; Charles Preston Poland Jr., *From Frontier to Suburbia* (Marceline, Mo.: Walsworth, 1976), 62–75.

33 For instance, see Alfred F. Young, *The Democratic Republicans of New York: The Origins, 1763–1797* (Chapel Hill: University of North Carolina Press of the Institute of Early American History and Culture, 1967), 257–276; Alan Taylor, *Liberty Men and Great Proprietors: The Revolutionary Settlement on the Maine Frontier, 1760–1820* (Chapel Hill: University of North Carolina Press for the Institute of Early American History and Culture, 1990); Alan Taylor, *William Cooper's Town: Power and Persuasion on the Frontier of the Early American Republic* (New York: Alfred A. Knopf, 1995).

34 On Leven Powell, see Stevenson, *Life in Black and White*, 34–35; Robert C. Powell, *A Biographical Sketch of Colonel Leven Powell, Including His Correspondence during the Revolutionary War* (Alexandria, Va.: G. H. Ramey & Son, 1877), 4–7; Williams, *Legends of Loudoun*, 81–82, 166–181; 56–58; Eugene M. Scheel, *The History of Middleburg and Vicinity* (Middleburg, Va.: Middleburg Bicentennial Committee, 1987), 7–56; and Richard J. Brownell, "Virginia Federalist: The Business and Political Career of Leven Powell, 1737–1810" (M.A. thesis,

College of William and Mary, 1983). While not presented as such, Stevenson's book is a social history of antebellum Loudoun County, much of it centering on and sourced to Leven Powell's family.

35 Scheel, *History of Middleburg*, 11–14.

36 "Men Who Live in a Glass House Should Not Begin to Throw Stones," *CMAG*, 27 October 1796; Powell's response, *CMAG*, 3 November 1796.

37 Scheel, *History of Middleburg*, 16–18, 21–23; Powell, *Biographical Sketch*, 7–8; Harrison, *Legends of Loudoun*, 168–181.

38 Leven Powell to Burr Powell, 12 February 1798, in Powell, *Biographical Sketch*, 32–33; Scheel, *History of Middleburg*, 23–25, 30.

39 Powell, *Biographical Sketch*, 6–7.

40 On the Masons, see Lyon Gardiner Tyler, ed., *Encyclopedia of Virginia Biography* (New York: Lewis Historical Publishing, 1915), 2:87–88; Harrison, *Legends of Loudon*, 170–171; Kent Sagendorph, *Stevens Thomson Mason: Misunderstood Patriot* (New York: E. P. Dutton, 1947), 15–37. Quotations from "Volunteers," *Aurora*, 7 July 1795.

41 A short history of the paper and a guide to the highlights of its contents can be found in Nelson Nichols, "An Early Newspaper of Alexandria, Va.," *Bulletin of the New York Public Library* 25 (1921): 663–669.

42 *CMAG*, 1 October 1796.

43 *CMAG*, 8 September, 20 October 1796.

44 Albert Russell, "To the Freeholders of the Counties of Loudoun and Fauquier," *CMAG*, 20 September 1796.

45 *CMAG*, 27 September 1796; "Civis," *Republican Journal and Dumfries Weekly Advertiser*, 25 August 1796.

46 Charles Simms, "To the Freeholders of the Counties of Prince William, Stafford, and Fairfax," *CMAG*, 29 September 1796. Simms was cited and quoted in "Phocion—No. IX,"*GUS*, 25 October 1796.

47 Leven Powell, "To the Freeholders of the Counties of Loudoun and Fauquier," *CMAG*, 1 Oct. 1796. Here is just a sample of the newspapers that reprinted Powell's address: *GUS*, 7 October 1796; *Federal Gazette & Baltimore Daily Advertiser*, 29 October 1796; *Albany Gazette*, 5 December 1796; Boston *Polar Star*, 14 December 1796.

48 Simms, *CMAG*, 29 September 1796; "Another Freeholder," *Virginia Herald and Fredericksburg and Falmouth Advertiser*, 25 October 1796.

49 The Virginia campaign of 1796 has been covered briefly in previous studies, but almost always without a sense of the contest's national importance and often with the explicit interpretation that the campaign was merely a sectional and personal contest rather than a partisan battle of ideologies. For example, see Beeman, *Old Dominion and the New Nation*, 165–168. A partial exception is Arthur Scherr, "The 'Republican Experiment' and the Election of 1796 in Virginia," *West Virginia History* 37 (1976): 89–108.

50 "A Young Columbian," *CMAG*, 20 October 1796.

51 Daniel C. Brent, "To the Freeholders of Prince William, Stafford, and Fairfax," *CMAG*, 18 October 1796; Taylor to Brent, 9 October 1796, in Dodd, "Letters of John Taylor," 263–265.

52 "To the Freeholders of Loudoun and Fauquier," *CMAG*, 20 October 1796.

53 *CMAG*, 25, 27 October, 3 November 1796.

54 *CMAG*, 29 October, 3 November 1796.

55 "Brutus," *CMAG*, 1 November 1796.

56 *CMAG*, 27, 29 October 1796.

57 *CMAG*, 29 October 1796.

58 *CMAG*, 5 November 1796. "A Freeholder" was following the patterns described in Albert O. Hirschman, *The Rhetoric of Reaction: Perversity, Futility, Jeopardy* (Cambridge, Mass.: Harvard University Press, 1991), attacking Jefferson as both unimportant ("futility") and dangerous. On the religion issue in the election of 1800, see Charles O. Lerche Jr., "Jefferson and the Election of 1800: A Case Study in the Political Smear," *William and Mary Quarterly*, 3rd ser., 5 (1948): 467–491.

59 *CMAG*, 25, 27 October 1796.

60 *CMAG*, 1 November 1796.

61 Alexander Keyssar's survey estimates that around 40 percent of adult white men could not vote across all of late colonial America, with that figure decreasing during the Revolution: Alexander Keyssar, *The Right to Vote: The Contested History of Democracy in the United States* (New York: Basic Books, 2000), 7.

62 J. R. Pole, "Representation and Authority in Virginia from the Revolution to Reform," *Journal of Southern History* 24 (1958): 34.

63 *GUS*, 20 December 1796; *Kline's Carlisle Weekly Gazette*, 28 December 1796; Leven Powell to Burr Powell, 12 February 1798, in Powell, *Biographical Sketch*, 32–33.

64 On Alexandria and the British invasion, see Donald Shomette, *Maritime Alexandria: The Rise and Fall of an American Entrepôt* (Bowie, Md.: Heritage Books, 2003), 96–103.

65 New York *Minerva & Mercantile Evening Advertiser*, 6 September 1796.

66 Michael J. Dubin, *United States Congressional Elections, 1788–1997: The Official Results* (Jefferson, N.C.: McFarland, 1998), 14–15.

67 John Beckley to James Madison, 15 October 1796, *PJM*, 16:409; and Charles Warren, *Jacobin and Junto, or Early American Politics as Viewed in the Diary of Dr. Nathaniel Ames, 1758–1822* (Cambridge, Mass.: Harvard University Press, 1931), 51.

68 Joseph T. Buckingham, *Specimens of Newspaper Literature: With Personal Memoirs, Anecdotes, and Reminiscences* (Boston: Charles C. Little and James Brown, 1850), 1:268–274; Paul Goodman, *The Democratic-Republicans of Massachusetts: Politics in a Young Republic* (Cambridge, Mass.: Harvard University Press, 1964), 50–51, 70–73; Anson Ely Morse, *The Federalist Party in Massachusetts to the Year 1800* (Princeton: Princeton University Library, 1909), 145–147; Dubin, *United States Congressional Elections*, 1–14.

69 John C. Miller, *Sam Adams: Pioneer in Propaganda* (Stanford: Stanford University Press, 1960), 391–395.

70 Warren, *Jacobin and Junto*, 66–67, 72–73; W. B. Allen, ed., *Works of Fisher Ames, as Published by Seth Ames* (Indianapolis: LibertyClassics, 1983), 2:1201–1202; Miller, *Sam Adams*, 397; Boston *Federal Orrery*, 6, 10 April 1796; Jerome V. C. Smith, ed., *Bowen's Boston News-Letter and City Record* (Boston: Abel Bowen, 1826), 2:134; NNV.

71 Miller, *Sam Adams*, 398–399; Boston *Columbian Centinel*, 2, 5 November 1796.

72 Boston *Columbian Centinel*, 5 November 1796, esp. "Hancock" and "Facts"; Boston *Massachusetts Mercury*, 4 November 1796.

73 Ibid.; Boston *Columbian Centinel*, 14 September, 8, 12, 19, 26 October, 5 November 1796. On Dawes and Otis, see Goodman, *Democratic-Republicans of Massachusetts*, 51; and Samuel Eliot Morison, *Harrison Gray Otis, 1765–1848: The Urbane Federalist* (Boston: Houghton Mifflin, 1969), 92–96, 107–109.

74 Miller, *Sam Adams*, 398; Boston *Independent Chronicle*, 31 October 3, 7 November 1796; Boston *Columbian Centinel*, 5, 9 November 1796.

75 Ibid.

76 Miller, *Sam Adams*, 399; *Greenleaf's New-York Journal*, 11, 15, 29 November 1796.

77 Malcolm C. Clark, "Federalism at High Tide: The Election of 1796 in Maryland," *Maryland Historical Magazine* 61 (1966): 227; Charles G. Steffen, *The Mechanics of Baltimore: Workers and Politics in the Age of Revolution, 1763–1812* (Urbana: University of Illinois Press, 1984), 158; Bernard C. Steiner, ed., "Maryland Politics in 1796—McHenry Letters," *Publications of the Southern History Association* 9 (1905): 381–385.

CHAPTER 9. THE PARTY RACERS

1 John Beckley to William Irvine, 15, 30 September 1796, in *Justifying Jefferson: The Political Writings of John James Beckley*, ed. Gerard W. Gawalt (Washington, D.C.: Library of Congress, 1995), 122, 124; Noble E. Cunningham Jr., "John Beckley: An Early American Party Manager," *William and Mary Quarterly*, 3rd ser., 13 (1956): 40–52; Gloria Jahoda, "John Beckley: Jefferson's Campaign Manager," *Bulletin of the New York Public Library* 64 (1960): 247–260.

2 The most detailed accounts of the 1796 Pennsylvania campaign appear in Harry Marlin Tinkcom, *The Republicans and the Federalists in Pennsylvania, 1790–1801: A Study in National Stimulus and Local Response* (Harrisburg: Pennsylvania Historical and Museum Commission, 1950), 159–174; and Richard G. Miller, *Philadelphia—The Federalist City: A Study of Urban Politics, 1789–1801* (Port Washington, N.Y.: Kennikat Press, 1976), 79–90, but it also gets heavy play in Stephen G. Kurtz, *The Presidency of John Adams: The Collapse of Federalism, 1795–1800* (New York: A. S. Barnes, 1961), chap. 8, "A Political Revolution in Pennsylvania"; and Noble E. Cunningham Jr., *The Jeffersonian Republicans: The Formation of Party Organization, 1789–1801* (Chapel Hill: University of North Carolina Press for the Institute of Early American History and Culture, 1957), 97–106, among many other works. This section also draws on my own article, Jeffrey L. Pasley, "'A Journeyman, Either in Law or Politics': John Beckley and the Social Origins of Political Campaigning," *Journal of the Early Republic* 16 (1996): 531–569.

3 *Aurora*, 13 September 1796.

4 Circular, 25 September 1796, reprinted in Cunningham, *Jeffersonian Republicans*, 112; John Beckley to William Irvine, 15, 22, 30 September 1796, in Gawalt, *Justifying Jefferson*, 122–124; "Rotten towns" seems to be a reference to the British institution of rotten boroughs, parliamentary constituencies that the prime minister controlled by means of corrupting very small electorates in malapportioned constituencies. Supposedly the merchants and local officials had been able to do that in Pennsylvania, buying off enough votes to make the towns vote Federalist.

5 Ibid.; Miller, *Philadelphia—The Federalist City*, 89–90.

6 Beckley to Irvine, 15 September 1796, in Gawalt, *Justifying Jefferson*, 122.

7 *Aurora*, 15 October 1796; NNV.

8   Beckley to Irvine, 17 October 1796, in Gawalt, *Justifying Jefferson*, 128.

9   Circular, 25 September 1796; "Fellow Citizens!," broadside dated 3 October 1796, Historical Society of Pennsylvania, Evans 30411.

10 "Fellow Citizens!"; Randall M. Miller and William Pencak, eds., *Pennsylvania: A History of the Commonwealth* (University Park and Harrisburg: Pennsylvania State University Press and Pennsylvania Historical and Museum Commission, 2002), 130–132; NNV.

11 Cunningham, *Jeffersonian Republicans*, 94–109; "Public Notice, Friday the Fourth Day of November Next. . . . ," broadsides, Historical Society of Pennsylvania, Evans 30983 (Paine quote), 30984 (Adams paraphrases).

12 *GUS*, 26 October 1796.

13 John Beckley to Thomas Jefferson, 10 March 1801, RG59-NA, John Smith file; Beckley to Irvine, 17 October 1796, in Gawalt, *Justifying Jefferson*, 128; Cunningham, *Jeffersonian Republicans*, 106; Edmund Berkeley and Dorothy Smith Berkeley, *John Beckley: Zealous Partisan in a Nation Divided* (Philadelphia: American Philosophical Society, 1973), 148.

14 Beckley to Jefferson, 10 March 1801, John Smith file, Letters of Application 1801–1809, National Archives; and John Smith to Tench Coxe, Philadelphia, 5 December 1800, Tench Coxe Papers, Historical Society of Pennsylvania. On Smith's background and early career, see Thomas Leiper to Thomas Jefferson, Philadelphia, 11 February 1801, Jefferson Papers, Library of Congress; *Pennsylvania Archives*, 6th ser., 4:413; Philip S. Foner, ed., *The Democratic-Republican Societies, 1790–1800: A Documentary Sourcebook of Constitutions, Declarations, Addresses, Resolutions, and Toasts* (Westport, Conn.: Greenwood Press, 1976), 44, 68, 79, 90, 102, 106; Minutes of the Democratic Society of Pennsylvania, typescript, 51, 139, 140, 142, 171, Historical Society of Pennsylvania.

15 *Aurora*, 26, 28, 31 October, 1, 4 November 1796; Philadelphia *Claypoole's American Daily Advertiser*, 1 November 1796.

16 *Aurora*, 1, 2, 10 November 1796; Philadelphia *Claypoole's American Daily Advertiser*, 1, 4 November 1796; *GUS*, 4 November 1796; 26 October, Miller, *Philadelphia—The Federalist City*, 88.

17 Elaine Forman Crane, ed., *The Diary of Elizabeth Drinker* (Boston: Northeastern University Press, 1991), 2:851, 858 (quoted), entries for 11 October and 4 November 1796; Rosemarie Zagarri, *Revolutionary Backlash: Women and Politics in the Early American Republic* (Philadelphia: University of Pennsylvania Press, 2007); Susan Branson, *These Fiery Frenchified Dames: Women and Political Culture in Early National Philadelphia* (Philadelphia: University of Pennsylvania Press, 2001); John Murdock, *The Politicians; or, A State of Things* (Philadelphia: For the author, 1798), Evans 34160; Jeffrey L. Pasley, "Private Access and Public Power: Gentility and Lobbying in the Early Congress," in *The House and Senate in the 1790s: Petitioning, Lobbying, and Institutional Development*, ed. Kenneth R. Bowling and Donald R. Kennon (Athens: Ohio University Press for the United States Capitol Historical Society, 2002), 57–99; Jeffrey L. Pasley, *"The Tyranny of Printers": Newspaper Politics in the Early American Republic* (Charlottesville: University Press of Virginia, 2001), chap. 4; Berkeley and Berkeley, *Beckley*, passim. For Fourth of July 1796 toasts to women from the opposite points of view, see *Aurora*, 6 July 1796; and Charleston *Daily Advertiser*, 29 July 1796.

18 "Extract of Another Letter from Philadelphia," Halifax *North Carolina Journal*, 14 November 1796; William Smith to Ralph Izard, 8 November 1796, in Ulrich B. Phillips, ed., "South Carolina Federalist Correspondence, 1789–1797," *American Historical Review* 14 (1909): 784–785. On the conditions at polling places more generally, see Zagarri, *Revolutionary Backlash*, 36–37, 117–118; Andrew W. Robertson, "Voting Rites and Voting Acts: Electioneering Ritual, 1790–1820," in *Beyond the Founders: New Approaches to the Political History of the Early American Republic*, ed. Jeffrey L. Pasley, Andrew W. Robertson, and David Waldstreicher (Chapel Hill: University of North Carolina Press, 2004), 57–78; and Richard Franklin Bensel, *The American Ballot Box in the Mid-Nineteenth Century* (New York: Cambridge University Press, 2004).

19 NNV, Pennsylvania, Presidential electors, 1796; see note 1 for this entry on the NNV website for the total result including Greene County.

20 NNV; Miller, *Philadelphia—The Federalist City*, 87–90; Kurtz, *Presidency of Adams*, 186–187; Tinkcom, *The Republicans and the Federalists*, 173–174; James Morton Smith, *Freedom's Fetters: The Alien and Sedition Laws and American Civil Liberties* (Ithaca: Cornell University Press, 1956).

21 NNV; *GUS*, 18 November 1796; Tinkcom, *The Republicans and the Federalists*, 169–172.

22 Tinkcom, *The Republicans and the Federalists*, 170–172. Unfortunately for Adams, Thomas Pinckney got two votes from other Pennsylvania electors, making it a net loss for him vis-à-vis other Federalists.

23 Quotation from Oliver Wolcott Jr. to Oliver Wolcott Sr., 19 November 1796, in *Memoirs of the Administration of Washington and John Adams, Edited From the Papers of Oliver Wolcott, Secretary of the Treasury*, ed. George Gibbs (New York: William Van Norden, 1846), 1:396.

24 Alexander DeConde, *Entangling Alliance: Politics and Diplomacy under George Washington* (Durham: Duke University Press, 1958), 428–429, 440, 456–457; George W. Kyte, "A Spy on the Western Waters: The Military Intelligence Mission of General Collot in 1796," *Mississippi Valley Historical Review* 34 (1947): 427–442; Durand Echeverria, trans., "General Collot's Plan for a Reconnaissance of the Ohio and Mississippi Valleys, 1796," *William and Mary Quarterly*, 3d ser. 9 (1952): 512–520.

25 DeConde, *Entangling Alliance*, 446–455.

26 Albert Hall Bowman, *The Struggle for Neutrality: Franco-American Diplomacy during the Federalist Era* (Knoxville: University of Tennessee Press, 1974), 264–265.

27 *Albany Gazette*, 5, 12 September 1796; "Municipal Civility," Portland *Eastern Herald*, 5 October 1796; Boston *Columbian Centinel*, 24 September 1796; DeConde, *Entangling Alliance*, 472–473; Frederick Jackson Turner, ed., *Correspondence of the French Ministers to the United States, 1791–1797*, Annual Report of the American Historical Association for 1903, vol. 2 (Washington, D.C.: Government Printing Office, 1904), 947–948.

28 DeConde, *Entangling Alliance*, 470–471, 473; Bowman, *Struggle for Neutrality*, 268–269.

29 *Aurora*, 31 October 1796; DeConde, *Entangling Alliance*, 473–474; Walter Lowrie and Matthew St. Clair Clarke, eds., *American State Papers*, vol. 1, *Foreign Relations* (Washington, D.C.: Gales and Seaton, 1833), 578.

30 DeConde, *Entangling Alliance*, 474; Philadelphia *Claypoole's American Daily Advertiser*, 7 November 1796.

31 Lowrie and Clark, *American State Papers*, 1:579–583.

32 Lowrie and Clark, *American State Papers*, 1:579, 583.

33 William Loughton Smith to Ralph Izard, 8 November 1796, in Phillips, "South Carolina Federalist Correspondence," 785; Oliver Wolcott Sr. to Oliver Wolcott Jr., 21 November 1796, in Gibbs, *Memoirs*, 1:398.

34 Norman Davies, *God's Playground: A History of Poland* (New York: Columbia University Press, 1982), 1:214–215, 331–336, 537–542; "An American," Hartford *Connecticut Courant*, reprinted in *GUS*, 26 November 1796.

35 Davies, *God's Playground*, 1:537–542. For American reports, see, e.g., *Salem Gazette*, 30 June 1795.

36 Beckley to Madison, 20 June 1796, Madison to Jefferson, 5 December 1796, *PJM*, 16:372–373, 422–423; William Cobbett, *Porcupine's Works* (London: Cobbett and Morgan, 1801), 4:211; William Cobbett, ed., *The Gros Mousqueton Diplomatique; or Diplomatic Blunderbuss. Containing, Citizen Adet's Notes to the Secretary of State. As Also His Cockade Proclamation. With a Preface, by Peter Porcupine* (Philadelphia: William Cobbett, 1796), v–vi, iii.

37 John Adams to Abigail Adams, 27 November, 4, 7 December 1796, *AFP*; Oliver Wolcott Jr. to Oliver Wolcott Sr., 19, 27 November 1796, in Gibbs, *Memoirs*, 1:396–397, 400–401; Miller, *Philadelphia—The Federalist City*, 88–90; DeConde, *Entangling Alliance*, 473; *Aurora*, 10 November 1796.

38 DeConde, *Entangling Alliance*, 457.

39 Adet to Minister of Foreign Relations, 3 Vendemiaire, Ann. V, in Turner, *Correspondence of the French Ministers*, 947–949; Kurtz, *Presidency of Adams*, 125–127, 142–143.

40 The Democratic-Republican masterminds' extensive financial troubles can be followed in James D. Tagg, *Benjamin Franklin Bache and the Philadelphia "Aurora"* (Philadelphia: University of Pennsylvania Press, 1991); Berkeley and Berkeley, *John Beckley*; Pasley, "Journeyman, Either in Law or Politics"; Pasley, *Tyranny of Printers*, chap. 4

41 John Adams to Abigail Adams, 27 November, 4, 7 December 1796, *AFP*; Alexander Hamilton to Rufus King, 16 December 1796, *PAH*, 20:446. From a somewhat different angle, not mentioning the Adet intervention, Seth Cotlar has described the narrowing of American nationalism in the mid-1790s in *Tom Paine's America: The Rise and Fall of Transatlantic Radicalism in the Early Republic* (Charlottesville: University of Virginia Press, 2011). I am not as convinced as Cotlar that popular cosmopolitanism disappeared in America after 1796, but party politicians certainly learned to be more careful around it.

42 Quotation from Oliver Wolcott Jr. to Oliver Wolcott Sr., 19 November 1796, in Gibbs, *Memoirs*, 1:397.

43 "The People's Answer," Hartford *Connecticut Courant*, 14 November 1796; Oliver Wolcott Sr. to Oliver Wolcott Jr., 21 November 1796, in Gibbs, *Memoirs*, 1:398.

44 "People's Answer"; James Hutson, *Forgotten Features of the Founding: The Recovery of Religious Themes in the Early Republic* (Lanham, MD.: Lexington Books, 2003), chapter 1.

45 "Concord, December 6," reprinted in Hanover, N.H., *Eagle or Dartmouth Centinel*, 12–19 December 1796; Oliver Wolcott Sr. to Oliver Wolcott Jr., 12 December 1796, in Gibbs, *Memoirs*, 1:409.

46 Hartford *Connecticut Courant*, 21 November, 12 December 1796; Manning J. Dauer, *The Adams Federalists* (Baltimore: Johns Hopkins University Press,

1953), 102–103. The earliest use of the cattle analogy I have found is actually by Samuel Chase of Maryland, during a debate in the Continental Congress on the Articles of Confederation. At that point it was a relatively matter-of-fact discussion about the basis of taxation. Chase was a vociferous Federalist by 1796. Thomas Jefferson, *Writings*, ed. Merrill D. Peterson (New York: Literary Classics of the United States, 1984), 25.

47 Hartford *Connecticut Courant*, 21 November, 12 December 1796. This northern image of the South seems fairly typical of what many scholars have described in works covering the northern and southern stereotypes of each other that helped produce the sectional crisis, though they are not usually seen as fully developed as this so early in U.S. history. See, e.g., Anne Norton, *Alternative Americas: A Reading of Antebellum American Political Culture* (Chicago: University of Chicago Press, 1986); William R. Taylor, *Cavalier and Yankee: The Old South and American National Character*, new ed. (Cambridge, Mass.: Harvard University Press, 1979).

48 Hartford *Connecticut Courant*, 21 November, 12 December 1796.

49 James Truslow Adams, *New England in the Republic, 1776–1850* (Boston: Little, Brown, 1926), 215–216; Aleine Austin, *Matthew Lyon: "New Man" of the Democratic Revolution, 1749–1822* (University Park: Pennsylvania State University Press, 1981), 64–87. Quotations from Hanover, N.H., *Eagle, or Dartmouth Centinel*, 31 October 1796; Oliver Wolcott Sr. to Oliver Wolcott Jr., 28 November 1796, in Gibbs, *Memoirs*, 1:403.

50 Boston *Columbian Centinel*, 26 October 1796; Oliver Wolcott Sr. to Oliver Wolcott Jr., 12 December 1796, in Gibbs, *Memoirs*, 1:409.

51 Aaron Burr to Pierpont Edwards, 30 November 1796, in *Political Correspondence and Public Papers of Aaron Burr*, ed. Mary-Jo Kline (Princeton: Princeton University Press, 1983), 1:276–277. The stratagems and counterstratagems between Burr and Hamilton are a bit dizzying to contemplate. By wounding the Pinckney plot in New England, Burr actually helped both Adams *and* Jefferson, but the one person he was thwarting for certain was his once and future New York rival.

52 Bennington *Vermont Gazette*, 22 December 1796; Oliver Wolcott Sr. to Oliver Wolcott Jr., 12 December 1796, in Gibbs, *Memoirs*, 1:409; Kurtz, *Presidency of Adams*, 194–196.

53 Oliver Wolcott Jr. to Oliver Wolcott Sr., 19, 27 November 1796, in Gibbs, *Memoirs*, 1:397, 402.

54 Oliver Wolcott Sr. to Oliver Wolcott Jr., 12 December 1796, in Gibbs, *Memoirs*, 1:408–409. On Connecticut's political system, see Richard J. Purcell, *Connecticut in Transition: 1775–1818*, 2nd ed. (Middletown, Conn.: Wesleyan University Press, 1963), 113–145.

55 Oliver Wolcott Sr. to Oliver Wolcott Jr., 12 December 1796, in Gibbs, *Memoirs*, 1:408–409.

56 George Cabot to Oliver Wolcott Jr., 30 November 1796, in *Life and Letters of George Cabot*, ed. Henry Cabot Lodge (Boston: Little, Brown, 1878), 112; George Cabot to Oliver Wolcott Jr., 3 April 1797, in Gibbs, *Memoirs*, 1:488; Stephen Higginson to Alexander Hamilton, 9 December 1796, *PAH*, 20:437–438; Abigail Adams to John Adams, 31 December 1796, *AFP*; Dauer, *Adams Federalists*, 103.

57 "PETER PORCUPINE—AGAIN," Boston *Columbian Centinel*, 10 August 1796; "THE PULL," Boston *Columbian Centinel*, 5 November 1796. Russell's masthead

proudly trumpeted his federal printing contract. On the importance of public printing contracts for maintaining party newspapers, see Culver H. Smith, *The Press, Politics, and Patronage: The American Government's Use of Newspapers, 1789–1875* (Athens: University of Georgia Press, 1977).

58 Boston *Columbian Centinel,* 7 December, 10 August 1796, 5 December 1795; Dauer, *Adams Federalists,* 103–104.

59 Dauer, *Adams Federalists,* 103–104; Hamilton to Jeremiah Wadsworth, 1 December 1796, *PAH,* 20:418–419; Boston *Columbian Centinel,* 7 December 1796; "Editorial Note: The 1796 Presidential Election," and Burr to Gerry, 30 November 1796, in Kline, *Political Correspondence and Public Papers of Aaron Burr,* 1:266–270, 278–279.

60 Beckley to James Madison, 15 October 1796, *PJM,* 16:409.

61 Joseph I. Shulim, *John Daly Burk: Irish Revolutionist and American Patriot* (Philadelphia: American Philosophical Society, 1964), 13–23. Quotation from Boston *Polar Star,* 18 October 1796.

62 Jonathan Dayton to Theodore Sedgwick, 12, 13, 19 November 1796, enclosures in Sedgwick to Alexander Hamilton, 19 November 1796, *PAH,* 20:402–407.

63 Risjord, *Chesapeake Politics,* 509.

64 Dauer, *Adams Federalists,* 4–7, 18–25.

65 J. R. Pole, "Suffrage and Representation in Maryland From 1776 to 1810: A Statistical Note and Some Reflections," *Journal of Southern History* 24 (1958): 218–225; Robert J. Brugger, *Maryland: A Middle Temperament, 1634–1980* (Baltimore: Johns Hopkins University Press and the Maryland Historical Society, 1988), 165–166; David A. Bohmer, "The Maryland Electorate and the Concept of a Party System in the Early National Period," in *The History of American Electoral Behavior,* ed. Joel H. Silbey, Allan G. Bogue, and William H. Flanigan (Princeton: Princeton University Press, 1978), 146–173; David A. Bohmer, "Stability and Change in Early National Politics: The Maryland Voter and the Election of 1800," *William and Mary Quarterly,* 3rd ser., 36 (1979): 27–50; Eric Robert Papenfuse, "Unleashing the 'Wildness': The Mobilization of Grassroots Antifederalism in Maryland," *Journal of the Early Republic* 16 (1996): 73–106.

66 Edmund S. Morgan, *Inventing the People: The Rise of Popular Sovereignty in England and America* (New York: W. W. Norton, 1988), 186–188.

67 Charles G. Steffen, *The Mechanics of Baltimore: Workers and Politics in the Age of Revolution, 1763–1812* (Urbana: University of Illinois Press, 1984), 94–98; Murray to James McHenry, 21 August 1796, in *The Life and Correspondence of James McHenry: Secretary of War under Washington and Adams,* ed. Bernard C. Steiner (Cleveland: Burrows Brothers, 1907), 196; Allen Johnson and Dumas Malone, eds., *Dictionary of American Biography* (New York: Charles Scribner's Sons, 1943), 4:34–37; John A. Munroe, *Federalist Delaware, 1775–1815* (New Brunswick, N.J.: Rutgers University Press, 1954), 195–196, 206.

68 Munroe, *Federalist Delaware,* 147, 200–202, 238–241; Philip S. Foner, ed., *The Democratic-Republican Societies, 1790–1800: A Documentary Sourcebook of Constitutions, Declarations, Addresses, Resolutions, and Toasts* (Westport, Conn.: Greenwood Press, 1976), 319; David P. Peltier, "Party Development and Voter Participation in Delaware, 1792–1811," *Delaware History* 14 (1970): 80–81; H. Clay Reed, "Presidential Electors in Delaware, 1789–1829," *Delaware History* 14 (1970): 8–9.

69 The catechism originated with the Easton *Maryland Herald and Eastern Shore*

Intelligencer, 8 November 1796, and was reprinted in *Washington Spy*, 30 November 1796; Portsmouth *New Hampshire Gazette*, 10 December 1796; and Charleston *City Gazette*, 3 December 1796, doubtless among others. On Duvall, see Malcolm C. Clark, "Federalism at High Tide: The Election of 1796 in Maryland," *Maryland Historical Magazine* 61 (1966): 223; and William Vans Murray to James McHenry, 23 November 1796, in Bernard C. Steiner, "Maryland Politics in 1796—McHenry Letters," *Publications of the Southern History Association* 9 (1905): 385.

70 William Bruce Wheeler, "The Baltimore Jeffersonians, 1788–1800: A Profile of Intra-Factional Conflict," *Maryland Historical Magazine* 66 (1971): 153–168; Steffen, *Mechanics of Baltimore*, 121–142; Clark, "Federalism at High Tide," 219; *Federal Gazette and Baltimore Daily Advertiser*, 24 October, 1 November 1796. There was a more radical Democratic-Republican journal called the *Baltimore Telegraphe*, but few copies have survived from the election and almost no one seems to have quoted, reprinted, or mentioned it.

71 Steffen, *Mechanics of Baltimore*, 154–158; Clark, "Federalism at High Tide," 227–228; Libero M. Renzulli Jr., *Maryland: The Federalist Years* (Madison, N.J.: Fairleigh Dickinson University Press, 1972), 186–187; Frank A. Cassell, *Merchant Congressman in the Young Republic: Samuel Smith of Maryland, 1752–1839* (Madison: University of Wisconsin Press, 1971).

72 Peter P. Hill, *William Vans Murray, Federalist Diplomat: The Shaping of Peace with France, 1797–1801* (Syracuse: Syracuse University Press, 1971), 4–5; Murray to John Quincy Adams, 16 April 1799, in Worthington Chauncey Ford, "Letters of William Vans Murray to John Quincy Adams, 1797–1803," in *Annual Report of the American Historical Association for the Year 1912* (Washington, D.C.: [American Historical Association], 1914), 539; *Federal Gazette & Baltimore Daily Advertiser*, 25 October 1796.

73 Murray to James McHenry, 2, 15 November 1796, in Steiner, "Maryland Politics in 1796," 382–385; Hill, *William Vans Murray*, 36–37; Steiner, *Life and Correspondence of McHenry*, 198–202.

74 Clark, "Federalism at High Tide," 225–226; Charleston *City Gazette and Daily Advertiser*, 5 December 1796.

75 Hill, *William Vans Murray*, 37–39.

76 *GUS*, 5 November 1796; [William Loughton Smith], *The Pretensions of Thomas Jefferson to the Presidency Examined; and the Charges against John Adams Refuted . . . Part the Second* ([Philadelphia: John Fenno,] November 1796), 39–42; Baltimore *Federal Gazette*, 25 October 1796; Easton *Maryland Herald*, 1, 8 November 1796.

77 "To the Citizens of Maryland," Baltimore *Federal Gazette*, 25 October 1796; Hill, *William Vans Murray*, 38–39; Baltimore *Maryland Journal*, 23 November 1796, quoted in Clark, "Federalism at High Tide," 221.

78 Murray to James McHenry, 2, 15 November 1796, in Steiner, "Maryland Politics in 1796," 382–384; Baltimore *Federal Gazette*, 3 November 1796; *GUS*, 5 November 1796; Hindman to James McHenry, 13 October 1796, Steiner, *Life and Correspondence of McHenry*, 199.

79 Steiner, *Life and Correspondence of McHenry*, 201; John Adams to Abigail Adams, 18 December 1796, *AFP*.

80 Dauer, *Adams Federalists*, 18–19; Murray to James McHenry, 24 June 1796, in Steiner, "Maryland Politics in 1796," 377.

81 Delbert Harold Gilpatrick, *Jeffersonian Democracy in North Carolina, 1789–1816* (1931; New York: Octagon Books, 1967), 74–76; Halifax *North-Carolina Journal*, 12 December 1796; Edenton *State Gazette of North Carolina*, 20 October 1796; Griffith J. McRee, ed., *Life and Correspondence of James Iredell, One of the Associate Justices of the Supreme Court* (New York: D. Appleton, 1858), 2:480–482.

82 Gilpatrick, *Jeffersonian Democracy in North Carolina*, 74–76, 83; Halifax *North-Carolina Journal*, 14 November 1796; Leonard L. Richards, "John Adams and the Moderate Federalists: The Cape Fear Valley as a Test Case," *North Carolina Historical Review* 43 (1966): 14–30.

83 Edenton *State Gazette of North Carolina*, 20 October 1796.

84 James Haw, *John and Edward Rutledge of South Carolina* (Athens: University of Georgia Press, 1997), 206–212; Richard R. Beeman, *Plain, Honest Men: The Making of the American Constitution* (New York: Random House, 2009), 246, 266–269.

85 Lisle A. Rose, *Prologue to Democracy: The Federalists in the South, 1789–1800* (Lexington: University of Kentucky Press, 1968), 136–138; George C. Rogers Jr., *Evolution of a Federalist: William Loughton Smith of Charleston, 1758–1812* (Columbia: University of South Carolina Press, 1962), 290–293; Haw, *John and Edward Rutledge*, 264–266.

86 Charleston *City Gazette and Daily Advertiser*, 10 November 1796; Richard B. Davis and Milledge B. Seigler, "Peter Freneau, Carolina Republican," *Journal of Southern History* 13 (1947): 395–405.

87 Patrick S. Brady, "The Slave Trade and Sectionalism in South Carolina, 1787–1808," *Journal of Southern History* 38 (1972): 601–620.

88 Haw, *John and Edward Rutledge*, 265–266; Rogers, *Evolution of a Federalist*, 294.

89 John Marshall to James Iredell, 15 December 1796, in *The Papers of John Marshall*, ed. Herbert Alan Johnson, Charles T. Cullen, and Charles F. Hobson (Chapel Hill: University of North Carolina Press for the Institute of Early American History and Culture, 1974–2006), 3:58–59; Jacob E. Cooke, *Tench Coxe and the Early Republic* (Chapel Hill: University of North Carolina Press for the Institute of Early American History and Culture, 1978), 286–290, 307.

90 John Adams to Abigail Adams, 12, 16 December 1796, *AFP*; Page Smith, *John Adams* (Garden City, N.Y.: Doubleday, 1962), 2:906–908.

91 Beckley to William Irvine, 16 December 1796, in Gawalt, *Justifying Jefferson*, 134; *Aurora*, 17 December 1796; Madison to Jefferson, 10, 19, 25 December 1796, *PTJ*, 29:218, 226–228; Jefferson to Madison, 17 December 1796, *PTJ*, 29:223.

92 *Augusta Chronicle*, 10 December 1796; George R. Lamplugh, " 'Oh the Colossus! The Colossus!': James Jackson and the Jeffersonian Republican Party in Georgia, 1796–1806," *Journal of the Early Republic* 9 (1989): 315–334; C. Peter Magrath, *Yazoo: Law and Politics in the New Republic—the Case of "Fletcher V. Peck"* (New York: W. W. Norton, 1967); Kline, *Political Correspondence and Public Papers of Aaron Burr*, 1:244–245, 293–295; *Columbian Museum & Savannah Advertiser*, 18 November 1796.

93 John Adams to Abigail Adams, 27, 30 December 1796, 1 January, 9 February 1797, *AFP*.

1 Jefferson to Adams, 28 December 1796, Jefferson to Madison, 1 January 1797, *PTJ*, 29: 235–236, 248; Madison to Jefferson, 19 December 1796, *PTJ*, 29:226; Page Smith, *John Adams* (Garden City, N.Y.: Doubleday, 1962), 2:906, 922; John Adams to Abigail Adams, 12 December 1796, 1 January 1797, *AFP*.

2 "From a Correspondent," *Aurora*, 21 December 1796; "Let the People Judge," Boston *Columbian Centinel*, 31 December 1796; *Aurora*, 22 February 1797; James D. Tagg, *Benjamin Franklin Bache and the Philadelphia "Aurora"* (Philadelphia: University of Pennsylvania Press, 1991), 296–297; Arthur Scherr, "Inventing the Patriot President: Bache's Aurora and John Adams," *Pennsylvania Magazine of History and Biography* 119 (1995): 369–399.

3 *Aurora*, 21 December 1796; James D. Tagg, "Benjamin Franklin Bache's Attack on George Washington," *Pennsylvania Magazine of History and Biography* 100 (1976): 191–230.

4 John to Abigail Adams, 1 January 1797, *AFP*; Smith, *John Adams*, 2:909–910.

5 Madison to Jefferson, 8, 22 January 1797, *PTJ*, 29:255–256, 272–273.

6 Jefferson to Madison, 1 January 1797, *PTJ*, 29:248.

7 Smith, *John Adams*, 2:922; Manning J. Dauer, *The Adams Federalists* (Baltimore: Johns Hopkins University Press, 1953), 260–262.

8 John Adams to Benjamin Rush, 22 April 1812, in *The Spur of Fame: Dialogues of John Adams and Benjamin Rush, 1805–1813*, ed. John A. Schutz and Douglass Adair (San Marino: Huntington Library, 1980), 213–214; John Ferling, *John Adams: A Life* (New York: Henry Holt, 1996), 333; John Adams, *Correspondence of John Adams, Esquire, Late President of the United States . . . Originally Published in the Boston Patriot* (Baltimore: H. Niles, 1809), 54–55.

9 "Chester County, February 24," *GUS*, 4 March 1797; Thomas Jefferson, "Address to the Senate," 4 March 1797, *PTJ*, 29:310–311; *GUS*, 6 March 1797; John Adams to Abigail Adams, 9 March 1797, *AFP*.

10 Sedgwick to Rufus King, 12 March 1797, in *The Life and Correspondence of Rufus King; Comprising His Letters, Private and Official, His Public Documents, and His Speeches*, ed. Charles R. King (New York: G. P. Putnam's Sons, 1894–1900), 2:157; Boston *Columbian Centinel*, 18 January 1797.

11 John Adams to Abigail Adams, 9 March 1797, *AFP*.

12 For the text of Adams's Inaugural Address as it would have been read at the time, see *Philadelphia Gazette & Universal Daily Advertiser*, extraordinary ed., 5 March (dated 4 March) 1797.

13 *Aurora*, 7 March 1797; Matthew Livingston Davis Memorandum Book, Rufus King Papers, New-York Historical Society, 57:10.

14 Thomas Jefferson to John Taylor, 4 June 1798, in *Writings*, ed. Merrill D. Peterson (New York: Literary Classics of the United States, 1984), 1050.

BIBLIOGRAPHIC ESSAY

Despite being the first contested presidential election, the election of 1796 has never attracted a study of more than article length, although it is a focus of several works with a somewhat broader focus. The basic literature includes: Stephen G. Kurtz, *The Presidency of John Adams: The Collapse of Federalism, 1795–1800* (New York: A. S. Barnes, 1961); Manning J. Dauer, *The Adams Federalists*, 2nd ed. (Baltimore: Johns Hopkins University Press, 1968); John Ferling, "1796: The First Real Election," *American History* 31 (1996): 24–28, 66–68; Joanne B. Freeman, "The Presidential Election of 1796," in *John Adams and the Founding of the Republic*, ed. Richard Alan Ryerson (Boston: Massachusetts Historical Society and Northeastern University Press, 2001), 142–167; Malcolm C. Clark, "Federalism at High Tide: The Election of 1796 in Maryland," *Maryland Historical Magazine* 61 (1966): 210–230; Arthur Scherr, "The Significance of Thomas Pinckney's Candidacy in the Election of 1796," *South Carolina Historical Magazine* 76 (1975): 51–59; Arthur Scherr, "The 'Republican Experiment' and the Election of 1796 in Virginia," *West Virginia History* 37 (1976): 89–108. Of course, 1796 also comes up in every survey of the politics of the Early Republic, though typically such books rush over the event on the way to more decisive events like the election of 1800: Stanley Elkins and Eric McKitrick, *The Age of Federalism* (New York: Oxford University Press, 1993); John C. Miller, *The Federalist Era, 1789–1801* (New York: Harper & Row, 1960); James Roger Sharp, *American Politics in the Early Republic: The New Nation in Crisis* (New Haven: Yale University Press, 1993); Gordon S. Wood, *Empire of Liberty: A History of the Early Republic, 1789–1815* (New York: Oxford University Press, 2011); Sean Wilentz, *The Rise of American Democracy: Jefferson to Lincoln* (New York: W. W. Norton, 2005); William Nisbet Chambers, *Political Parties in a New Nation: The American Experience, 1776–1809* (New York: Oxford University Press, 1963); Noble E. Cunningham Jr., *The Jeffersonian Republicans: The Formation of Party Organization, 1789–1801* (Chapel Hill: University of North Carolina Press for the Institute of Early American History and Culture, 1957).

THE FOUNDERS

Because the election of 1796 falls into the Founding era of American history, research on the topic is both easy and unimaginably daunting. The sheer mass of available materials, and their increasing ease of availability, presents the scholar with an infinite vista, much of which can be accessed without leaving one's desk or the local university library. The starting place for any serious research and writing on the Founding era has to be the "Papers of" projects that aim to gather and publish, in book form, virtually all the significant correspondence of the personage in question, incoming and outgoing, with explanatory footnotes. In effect, the goal is one-stop shopping for research on that particular figure, though the one stop involves stacks and stacks of books and access to a research library. This still makes the primary sources on the Founders much more accessible than they were when the only way to read them was to go through hundreds of rolls of microfilm or spend months traveling to archives scattered around the country as well as many weeks at the Library of Congress manuscript division. Probably the most ambitious documentary editing and publishing project in the field of U.S. history, the "Papers of" projects have been starved for funding in recent years because of cutbacks to the National Historical Publications and Records Commission (NHPRC) budget as well as the redirection of funding to digital projects. Given how often Americans turn to the Founders for wisdom, guidance, and legal precedents, the completion and continued use of these projects really ought to be regarded as a patriotic duty.

"Papers of" projects exist for all of the frontline Founders and quite a few of the secondary figures. A list of "Founder Era" projects funded by the NHPRC appears at www.archives.gov/nhprc/projects/publishing/projects-era.html, which also serves as a portal to the Internet offerings of the various projects. The project websites include guides to their organization and current status (such as volumes published) as well as page images of some manuscripts and other added features. The oldest and most elaborate of the "Papers of" projects is Julian P. Boyd's *The Papers of Thomas Jefferson* (Princeton: Princeton University Press, 1950–) at Princeton University, which in its early decades included "Editorial Notes" so comprehensive that they amounted to installments in the world's longest biography of Jefferson, in addition to printing all the sources. Boyd died in 1980 after twenty volumes, which had only reached August 1791, so later editors, especially Barbara Oberg, have sped up the process and streamlined the "Editorial Notes." The project finally made it to the election of 1796 in 2001 and at the time of this writing (2012) has reached thirty-six volumes and 1802, in the middle of Jefferson's first term as president. Following a trend among the "Papers of" projects, part of the effort has been spun off. In this case, Jefferson's postpresidential papers are being published by the Thomas Jefferson Memorial Foundation (Monticello) as a separate series: J. Jefferson Looney, et al., eds., *The Papers of Thomas Jefferson: Retirement Series*, 8 vols. to date (Princeton: Princeton University Press, 2004–). Of course, Jefferson's general lack of involvement in his own first presidential campaign limited the utility of *The Papers of Thomas Jefferson* for the present work, but they are beyond authoritative on everything that did directly involve him. For easier access to Jefferson's state papers, published works, and best-known letters, Merrill D. Peterson's Jefferson volume in the Library of America series is hard to beat: Thomas Jefferson, *Writings*, ed. Merrill D. Peterson (New York: Literary Classics of the United States, 1984). Most of the rest of the Jefferson manuscripts are available on microfilm from the Library of Congress and the University of Virginia. Searchable page images of the Library of Congress collection are available at the Library of Congress's American Memory site: http://memory.loc.gov/ammem/collections/jefferson_papers/.

Like their crisply efficient, focused subjects, the "Papers of" projects devoted to Jefferson's greatest enemy and his closest lieutenant proceeded much more rapidly. Aided by the subject's short life as well as much more limited documentary ambitions, Alexander Hamilton's manuscripts are presented in Harold C. Syrett and Jacob E. Cooke, eds., *The Papers of Alexander Hamilton*, 27 vols. (New York: Columbia University Press, 1961–1987). The papers covering James Madison's career before he became secretary of state were also completed relatively rapidly, despite switching publishers midstream: William T. Hutchinson, et al., eds., *The Papers of James Madison*, vols. 1–10 (Chicago: University of Chicago Press, 1962–1977); vols. 11–17 (Charlottesville: University Press of Virginia, 1977–1991). *The Papers of James Madison* are still working on separate series that cover his time as secretary of state and president and his retirement. A notable feature of the Hamilton and Madison volumes are their inclusion of the two men's voluminous newspaper essays.

George Washington's "Papers of" is ironically the youngest of the projects devoted to the major Founders, having only been launched, at the University of Virginia, in 1968. It is divided into six different series, and the most relevant for this book is Dorothy Twohig, ed., *The Papers of George Washington: Presidential Series* (Charlottesville: University Press of Virginia, 1987–), which has reached September 1794 (and sixteen volumes) as of the time of this writing. The Library of Congress holds the largest collection of Washington manuscripts, and they are available on microfilm and as searchable page images at the Library of Congress's American Memory site: http://memory.loc.gov/ammem/gwhtml/gwhome.html.

The winner of the 1796 election has the "Papers of" project that seems furthest from completion. The massive Adams Family Papers at the Massachusetts Historical Society, covering many generations of a large political family, are being published in six different series, including L. H. Butterfield, et al., eds., *The Adams Family Correspondence* (Cambridge, Mass.: Harvard University Press, 1963–), which has reached 1795 in ten volumes; and the more directly relevant Robert J. Taylor, et al., eds., *Papers of John Adams* (Cambridge, Mass.: Harvard University Press, 1977–), which has taken sixteen volumes to reach only 1785. Of course, John Adams emitted prodigious amounts of verbiage. One day, researchers on the Adams vice presidency and the election of 1796 will have everything at their fingertips, but the day has not yet arrived. Fortunately, the Adams Family Papers project has provided highly useful versions of several jewels in their collection online at http://www.masshist.org/adams/: John Adams's autobiography, the diaries of John and John Quincy Adams, and especially the "Correspondence between John and Abigail Adams," which is at http://www.masshist.org/digitaladams/aea/ letter/, an important source for this study. Presenting page images along with very accurate and searchable transcribed text, this is one of the better online presentations of early American manuscripts available. The rest of the Adams manuscripts are available on microfilm from the Massachusetts Historical Society.

Most of the Founders' own letters were published previously, often by their descendants, in the nineteenth century. In the case of John Adams, the most convenient way to access some of his materials is still Charles Francis Adams, ed., *The Works of John Adams, Second President of the United States*, 10 vols. (Boston: Little, Brown, 1856), available through libraries and Google Books. An essential edition of Adams letters that goes beyond other presently available collections is Lester J. Cappon, ed., *The Adams-Jefferson Letters: The Complete Correspondence between Thomas Jefferson and Abigail and John Adams* (Chapel Hill: University of North Carolina Press for the Institute of Early American History and Culture, 1988). The correspondence between John Adams and his good friend Benjamin Rush can be found in Alexander Biddle, ed., *Old Family Letters* (Philadelphia: J. B. Lippincott, 1892); and John A. Schutz and Douglass Adair, eds., *The Spur of Fame: Dialogues of John Adams and Benjamin Rush, 1805–1813* (San Marino: Huntington Library, 1980).

The letters and writings of other major Federalists have been published in older but still useful editions: Charles R. King, ed., *The Life and Correspondence of Rufus King; Comprising His Letters, Private and Official, His Public Documents, and His Speeches*, 6 vols. (New York: G. P. Putnam's Sons, 1894–1900); W. B. Allen, ed., *Works of Fisher Ames, As Published by Seth Ames* (Indianapolis: LibertyClassics,

1983), largely a reprint of a nineteenth-century edition; and George Gibbs, ed., *Memoirs of the Administration of Washington and John Adams, Edited from the Papers of Oliver Wolcott, Secretary of the Treasury*, 2 vols. (New York: William Van Norden, 1846).

Jefferson's "running mate" is covered by a selective "Papers of" collection: Mary-Jo Kline, ed., *Political Correspondence and Public Papers of Aaron Burr* (Princeton: Princeton University Press, 1983).

To adequately notice the vast panoply of biographies and other studies of the major Founders would be another book in itself. One has to contend with scholars in multiple fields as well as popular authors and television personalities pouring out new works weekly. Despite the high literary quality of such recent best sellers as David McCullough, *John Adams* (New York: Simon & Schuster, 2001) and Ron Chernow, *Alexander Hamilton* (New York: Penguin, 2004), I have largely relied on academic scholarly studies in the writing of this book. Popular biographies have their place, but tend to repeat information presented more contextually and with better documentation in scholarly works. I saw no reason to abandon standard works just because they do not carry them at the local Barnes & Noble. For works on the Founders as a group, which tend to emphasize them as men apart from the rest of humanity, see Douglass Adair, *Fame and the Founding Fathers* (New York: W. W. Norton for the Institute of Early American History and Culture, 1974); Bernard Bailyn, *Faces of Revolution: Personalities and Themes in the Struggle for American Independence* (New York: Alfred A. Knopf, 1990); Robert C. Baron and Conrad Edick Wright, eds., *The Libraries, Leadership, and Legacy of John Adams and Thomas Jefferson* (Golden, Colo.: Fulcrum Publishing and Massachusetts Historical Society, 2010); Richard D. Brown, "The Founding Fathers of 1776 and 1787: A Collective View," *William and Mary Quarterly*, 3rd ser., 33 (1976): 465–480; Stanley Elkins and Eric McKitrick, "The Founding Fathers: Young Men of the Revolution," *Political Science Quarterly* 76 (1961): 181–216; Joseph J. Ellis, *Founding Brothers: The Revolutionary Generation* (New York: Alfred A. Knopf, 2001); Ralph Ketcham, *Presidents above Party: The First American Presidency, 1789–1829* (Chapel Hill: University of North Carolina Press for the Institute of Early American History and Culture, 1984); Darren Staloff, *Hamilton, Adams, Jefferson: The Politics of Enlightenment and the American Founding* (New York: Farrar, Straus and Giroux, 2005); Gordon S. Wood, *Revolutionary Characters: What Made the Founders Different* (New York: Penguin, 2006); and Gordon S. Wood, *The Radicalism of the American Revolution* (New York: Alfred A. Knopf, 1992).

All one writer can do is pick out a fraction of the Founder literature that seems most useful. For Thomas Jefferson and James Madison, mine were (in alphabetical order): Richard B. Bernstein, *Thomas Jefferson* (New York: Oxford University Press, 2003); Daniel J. Boorstin, *The Lost World of Thomas Jefferson* (Chicago: University of Chicago Press, 1981); Andrew Burstein, *The Inner Jefferson: Portrait of a Grieving Optimist* (Charlottesville: University Press of Virginia, 1995); Andrew Burstein, *Jefferson's Secrets: Death and Desire at Monticello* (New York: Basic Books, 2005); Andrew Burstein and Nancy Isenberg, *Madison and Jefferson* (New York: Random House, 2010); Noble E. Cunningham Jr., *In Pursuit of Reason: The Life of Thomas Jefferson* (New York: Ballantine Books, 1988); Annette Gordon-Reed, *Thomas Jefferson and Sally Hemings: An American Controversy* (Charlottesville: University Press of Virginia, 1997); Joseph J. Ellis, *American Sphinx: The Character of Thomas Jefferson* (New York: Alfred A. Knopf, 1997); Ralph Ketcham, *James Madison: A*

Biography (Charlottesville: University Press of Virginia, 1990); Dumas Malone, *Jefferson and His Time* (Boston: Little, Brown, 1948–1981); Peter S. Onuf, ed., *Jeffersonian Legacies* (Charlottesville: University Press of Virginia, 1993); Merrill D. Peterson, *The Jefferson Image in the American Mind* (New York: Oxford University Press, 1960); Merrill D. Peterson, *Thomas Jefferson and the New Nation* (New York: Oxford University Press, 1970); and Susan R. Stein, *The Worlds of Thomas Jefferson at Monticello* (New York: H. N. Abrams, in association with the Thomas Jefferson Memorial Foundation, 1993).

On John Adams, I have relied on Joseph J. Ellis, *Passionate Sage: The Character and Legacy of John Adams* (New York: W. W. Norton, 1993); John Ferling, *John Adams: A Life* (New York: Henry Holt, 1996); Zoltán Haraszti, *John Adams and the Prophets of Progress* (Cambridge, Mass.: Harvard University Press, 1952); Richard Alan Ryerson, ed., *John Adams and the Founding of the Republic* (Boston: Massachusetts Historical Society and Northeastern University Press, 2001); Peter Shaw, *The Character of John Adams* (Chapel Hill: University of North Carolina Press for the Institute of Early American History and Culture, 1976); John R. Howe Jr., *The Changing Political Thought of John Adams* (Princeton: Princeton University Press, 1966); James H. Hutson, "John Adams' Title Campaign," *New England Quarterly* 41 (1968): 30–39; Richard Alan Ryerson, ed., *John Adams and the Founding of the Republic* (Boston: Massachusetts Historical Society and Northeastern University Press, 2001); Richard Alan Ryerson, "'Like a Hare before the Hunters': John Adams and the Idea of Republican Monarchy," *Proceedings of the Massachusetts Historical Society* 107 (1995): 16–29; Peter Shaw, *The Character of John Adams* (Chapel Hill: University of North Carolina Press for the Institute of Early American History and Culture, 1976); and especially the encyclopedic Page Smith, *John Adams*, 2 vols. (Garden City, N.Y.: Doubleday, 1962). Abigail Adams has a whole literature to herself, but what I found useful were the following: Edith Gelles, *Portia: The World of Abigail Adams* (Bloomington: Indiana University Press, 1992); and Woody Holton, "Abigail Adams, Bond Speculator," *William and Mary Quarterly*, 3rd ser., 64 (2007): 821–838. On women's relations with early American politics and ideology, see Susan Branson, *These Fiery Frenchified Dames: Women and Political Culture in Early National Philadelphia* (Philadelphia: University of Pennsylvania Press, 2001); Linda K. Kerber, *Women of the Republic: Intellect and Ideology in Revolutionary America* (New York: W. W. Norton, 1986); Mary Beth Norton, *Liberty's Daughters: The Revolutionary Experience of American Women, 1750–1800* (New York: HarperCollins, 1980); and Rosemarie Zagarri, *Revolutionary Backlash: Women and Politics in the Early American Republic* (Philadelphia: University of Pennsylvania Press, 2007).

On Alexander Hamilton, I used Douglas Ambrose and Robert W. T. Martin, ed., *The Many Faces of Alexander Hamilton: The Life and Legacy of America's Most Elusive Founding Father* (New York: New York University Press, 2007); Jacob E. Cooke, *Alexander Hamilton* (New York: Charles Scribner's Sons, 1982); Max M. Edling, *A Revolution in Favor of Government: Origins of the U.S. Constitution and the Making of the American State* (New York: Oxford University Press, 2003); Max M. Edling and Mark D. Kaplanoff, "Alexander Hamilton's Fiscal Reform: Transforming the Structure of Taxation in the Early Republic," *William and Mary Quarterly*, 3rd ser., 61 (2004): 713–744; John Lamberton Harper, *American Machiavelli: Alexander Hamilton and the Origins of U.S. Foreign Policy* (New York: Cambridge University Press, 2004); Forrest McDonald, *Alexander Hamilton: A Biography* (New

York: W. W. Norton, 1982); John C. Miller, *Alexander Hamilton and the Growth of the New Nation* (New York: Harper & Row, 1964); and Karl-Friedrich Walling, *Republican Empire: Alexander Hamilton on War and Free Government* (Lawrence: University Press of Kansas, 1999).

On the other 1796 candidates or shadow candidates, see Nancy Isenberg, *Fallen Founder: The Life of Aaron Burr* (New York: Viking Penguin, 2007), the first true scholarly biography of Burr ever; Milton Lomask, *Aaron Burr: The Years from Princeton to Vice President, 1756–1805* (New York: Farrar, Straus Giroux, 1979); Francis Leigh Williams, *A Founding Family: The Pinckneys of South Carolinia* (New York: Harcourt Brace Jovanovich, 1978); John P. Kaminski, *George Clinton: Yeoman Politician of the New Republic* (Madison, Wis.: Madison House, 1993); Richard R. Beeman, *Patrick Henry: A Biography* (New York: McGraw-Hill, 1974); William M. Fowler Jr., *Samuel Adams: Radical Puritan* (New York: Longman, 1997); and John C. Miller, *Sam Adams: Pioneer in Propaganda* (Stanford: Stanford University Press, 1960).

Thomas Paine certainly should count as one of the frontline Founders, but tends not to because his occupation was slashing pamphleteer rather than statesman or general. Most helpful on Paine for me were Eric Foner, *Tom Paine and Revolutionary America* (New York: Oxford University Press, 1976); John Keane, *Tom Paine: A Political Life* (Boston: Little, Brown, 1995); Philip S. Foner, ed., *The Life and Major Writings of Thomas Paine* (New York: Citadel Press, Carol Publishing Group, 1993); Jack P. Greene, "Paine, America, and the 'Modernization' of Political Consciousness," *Political Science Quarterly* 93 (1978): 73–92; Winthrop D. Jordan, "Familial Politics: Thomas Paine and the Killing of the King, 1776," *Journal of American History* 60 (1973): 294–308; and Craig Nelson, *Thomas Paine: Enlightenment, Revolution, and the Birth of Modern Nations* (New York: Penguin, 2006).

Biographies on major Democratic-Republican officeholders besides Jefferson, Burr, and Madison are relatively few and far between, but a few that do exist are Raymond Walters Jr., *Albert Gallatin: Jeffersonian Financier and Diplomat* (New York: Macmillan, 1957); George Dangerfield, *Chancellor Robert R. Livingston of New York, 1746–1813* (New York: Harcourt Brace, 1960); Harry Ammon, *James Monroe: The Quest for National Identity* (Charlottesville: University Press of Virginia, 1990); Frederick B. Tolles, *George Logan of Philadelphia* (New York: Oxford University Press, 1953); and Paul A. W. Wallace, *The Muhlenbergs of Pennsylvania* (Philadelphia: University of Pennsylvania Press, 1950).

The Federalists are much better served by biographers. On the southern Federalists: George C. Rogers Jr., *Evolution of a Federalist: William Loughton Smith of Charleston, 1758–1812* (Columbia: University of South Carolina Press, 1962); Peter P. Hill, *William Vans Murray, Federalist Diplomat: The Shaping of Peace with France, 1797–1801* (Syracuse: Syracuse University Press, 1971); Joseph W. Cox, *Champion of Southern Federalism: Robert Goodloe Harper of South Carolina* (Port Washington, N.Y.: Kennikat Press, 1972); James Haw, *John and Edward Rutledge of South Carolina* (Athens: University of Georgia Press, 1997). For their colleagues up north and down east, see Robert Ernst, *Rufus King: American Federalist* (Chapel Hill: University of North Carolina Press for the Institute of Early American History and Culture, 1968); Winifred E. A. Bernhard, *Fisher Ames: Federalist and Statesman, 1758–1808* (Chapel Hill: University of North Carolina Press for the Institute of Early American History and Culture, 1965); Richard E. Welch Jr., *Theodore Sedgwick, Federalist: A Political Portrait* (Middletown, Conn.: Wesleyan University Press,

1965); Samuel Eliot Morison, *Harrison Gray Otis, 1765–1848: The Urbane Federalist* (Boston: Houghton Mifflin, 1969); and Alan Taylor, *William Cooper's Town: Power and Persuasion on the Frontier of the Early American Republic* (New York: Alfred A. Knopf, 1995).

Of course, one of the points of this book is that there were other people besides or instead of the frontline Founders involved in the election of 1796. The House of Representatives clerk John Beckley has attracted several biographical studies: Edmund Berkeley and Dorothy Smith Berkeley, *John Beckley: Zealous Partisan in a Nation Divided* (Philadelphia: American Philosophical Society, 1973); Noble E. Cunningham Jr., "John Beckley: An Early American Party Manager," *William and Mary Quarterly*, 3rd ser., 13 (1956): 40–52; Jeffrey L. Pasley, " 'A Journeyman, Either in Law or Politics': John Beckley and the Social Origins of Political Campaigning," *Journal of the Early Republic* 16 (1996): 531–569. Beckley even has his own mini "Papers of" volume: Gerard W. Gawalt, ed., *Justifying Jefferson: The Political Writings of John James Beckley* (Washington, D.C.: Library of Congress, 1995).

On the street-level radicals, many of them refugees from British oppression, who were so important in driving forward the politics of the 1790s, see Seth Cotlar, *Tom Paine's America: The Rise and Fall of Transatlantic Radicalism in the Early Republic* (Charlottesville: University of Virginia Press, 2011); Michael Durey, "Thomas Paine's Apostles: Radical Emigrés and the Triumph of Jeffersonian Republicanism," *William and Mary Quarterly*, 3rd ser., 44 (1987): 661–688; Michael Durey, *"With the Hammer of Truth": James Thomson Callender and America's Early National Heroes* (Charlottesville: University Press of Virginia, 1990); Michael Durey, *Transatlantic Radicals and the Early American Republic* (Lawrence: University Press of Kansas, 1997); Philip S. Foner, ed., *The Democratic-Republican Societies, 1790–1800: A Documentary Sourcebook of Constitutions, Declarations, Addresses, Resolutions, and Toasts* (Westport, Conn.: Greenwood Press, 1976); Eugene Perry Link, *Democratic-Republican Societies, 1790–1800* (New York: Octagon Books, 1973); Kim Tousley Phillips, *William Duane, Radical Journalist in the Age of Jefferson* (New York: Garland Publishing, 1989); Richard J. Twomey, *Jacobins and Jeffersonians: Anglo-American Radicalism in the United States, 1790–1820* (New York: Garland Publishing, 1989); and Alfred F. Young, Gary B. Nash, and Ray Raphael, eds., *Revolutionary Founders: Rebels, Radicals, and Reformers in the Making of the Nation* (New York: Alfred A. Knopf, 2011).

BEYOND THE FOUNDERS

In the early stages of this project, I had hoped to be able to go further "beyond the Founders" and deal with this first presidential election almost entirely in terms of popular politics, but the limitations of the source material on grassroots electoral politics, especially at the presidential level, proved too great to carry through fully on my original intentions. The *New Nation Votes* project, sponsored by the American Antiquarian Society and Tufts University, and funded by the National Endowment for the Humanities, is engaged in collecting, digitizing, and presenting all available election records up to 1825 at http://elections.lib.tufts.edu/aas_portal/index.xq. Thanks to the Herculean efforts of Philip Lampi, Andrew Robertson, and the *New Nation Votes* staff, our knowledge of early American electoral politics is being revolutionized. More voting data is available on the election of 1796 than ever before, even if not quite enough for the study I initially planned. One of the inspirations behind *New Nation Votes* were the voting studies of J. R. Pole: J. R.

Pole, "Suffrage and Representation in Massachusetts: A Statistical Note," *William and Mary Quarterly*, 3d ser., 14 (1957): 560–596; J. R. Pole, "Representation and Authority in Virginia from the Revolution to Reform," *Journal of Southern History* 24 (1958): 16–50; J. R. Pole, "Suffrage and Representation in Maryland from 1776 to 1810: A Statistical Note and Some Reflections," *Journal of Southern History* 24 (1958): 218–225; J. R. Pole, "Election Statistics in North Carolina to 1861," *Journal of Southern History* 24 (1958): 225–228; J. R. Pole, "Constitutional Reform and Election Statistics in Maryland, 1790–1812," *Maryland Historical Magazine* 55 (1960): 275–292; all of which contributed to J. R. Pole, *Political Representation in England and the Origins of the American Republic* (Berkeley: University of California Press, 1971).

On the case for doing political history of this period that goes "beyond the Founders," see David Waldstreicher, "Founders Chic as Culture War," *Radical History Review* 84 (2002): 185–194; Jeffrey L. Pasley, Andrew W. Robertson, and David Waldstreicher, eds., *Beyond the Founders: New Approaches to the Political History of the Early American Republic* (Chapel Hill: University of North Carolina Press, 2004); Jeffrey L. Pasley, "1800 as a Revolution in Political Culture: Newspapers, Celebrations, Democratization, and Voting in the Early Republic," in *The Revolution of 1800: Democracy, Race, and the New Republic*, ed. James Horn, Jan Ellen Lewis, and Peter S. Onuf (Charlottesville: University of Virginia Press, 2002), 121–152; Jeffrey L. Pasley and Edward G. Gray, eds., *Beyond the Valley of the Founders: Democracy in Early America, and after*, The *Common-Place* Politics Issue 2008, *Common-Place* 9 (October 2008), issue 1, http://www.common-place.org/vol-09/no-01/. This was accompanied by "Myths of the Lost Atlantis: A Blog Series Dedicated to Phil Lampi," http://www.common-place.org/pasley/?cat=135, which includes a post that I wrote introducing the *New Nation Votes* project.

If a study of popular voting in 1796 faces some challenges, there are many fewer problems studying the efforts that the Founders and especially many other smaller fries made to influence popular opinion as they campaigned for or against their preferred policies and candidates. Print defined the public sphere of 1796, and an astonishingly high percentage of the printed materials that were released that year are still available to us. Essentially *every* book or pamphlet published in the present United States before 1800 is available in Readex-Newsbank's *Early American Imprints, Series 1, Evans, 1639–1800* database, produced in conjunction with and chiefly out of the collections of the American Antiquarian Society in Worcester, Massachusetts. (Another series, Shaw-Shoemaker, covers everything published from 1800 to 1820.) Most research libraries now provide access to this database, and some still hold its original incarnation, published using a long-defunct technology called the "microcard," literally tiny page images printed on cards. *Early American Imprints, Series 1* collects all the extant materials (except newspapers) listed in Charles Evans, *American Bibliography: A Chronological Dictionary of All Books, Pamphlets, and Periodical Publications Printed in the United States of America from the Genesis of Printing in 1639 Down to and Including the Year 1820*, 14 vols. (New York: Peter Smith, 1941–1959). While searchable down to the text, making allowances for eighteenth-century typographical irregularities, *Early American Imprints* items are easiest to find and distinguish from each other (because of the lengthy, opaque, and overlapping titles that were common and the typical lack of author attribution) using the "Evans number" they were given in *American Bibliography*. Citations should always include that number.

As I argue in my book *"The Tyranny of Printers": Newspaper Politics in the Early American Republic* (Charlottesville: University Press of Virginia, 2001), newspapers were perhaps the most important vehicles for partisan politics in this period, and they are a bit less easily and much less comprehensively available than books and pamphlets. Readex's *America's Historical Newspapers* database, especially *Early American Newspapers, Series 1, 1690–1876*, is indispensable despite having some frustrating gaps. The press was extremely decentralized in 1796, so there were important newspapers all up and down the country. For the fullest views of the Federalist viewpoint, researchers should consult the Boston *Columbian Centinel*, the Hartford *Connecticut Courant*, the Philadelphia *Gazette of the United States*, and Noah Webster's New York *American Minerva*. The Portsmouth *New Hampshire Gazette* was not as political as the others but very well covered by the *Early American Newspapers* database. The leading Democratic-Republican newspapers were the Philadelphia *Aurora General Advertiser*, *Greenleaf's New York Journal* (and its alternate daily edition, the New York *Argus*), and the Boston *Independent Chronicle*. The Elizabethtown (Elizabeth) *New-Jersey Journal* was less important but has a very full run available in *Early American Newspapers*. Newspapers were much rarer in the South, and many that did exist are difficult to obtain now electronically or on microfilm. One southern newspaper that was full of the 1796 campaign was the Alexandria *Columbian Mirror*. The Charleston, South Carolina, *City Gazette* was generally Democratic-Republican, but did not print as much political material as major papers in other cities. For guides to all the early American newspapers available anywhere, see Clarence S. Brigham, *History and Bibliography of American Newspapers, 1690–1820*, 2 vols. (Worcester, Mass.: American Antiquarian Society, 1947); and the derivative Edward Connery Lathem, *Chronological Tables of American Newspapers, 1690–1820* (Barre, Mass.: American Antiquarian Society and Barre Publishers, 1972). Other key secondary works on the press of 1796 include Marcus Daniel, *Scandal and Civility: Journalism and the Birth of American Democracy* (New York: Oxford University Press, 2009); James D. Tagg, *Benjamin Franklin Bache and the Philadelphia "Aurora"* (Philadelphia: University of Pennsylvania Press, 1991); John B. Hench, "The Newspaper in a Republic: Boston's 'Centinel' and 'Chronicle,' 1784–1801" (Ph.D. diss., Clark University, 1979); William David Sloan, "The Early Party Press: The Newspaper Role in American Politics, 1788–1812," *Journalism History* 9 (1982): 18–24; William David Sloan, " 'Purse and Pen': Party-Press Relationships, 1789–1816," *American Journalism* 6 (1989): 103–127; and Donald H. Stewart, *The Opposition Press of the Federalist Period* (Albany: State University of New York Press, 1969). On the printing trade, which controlled and produced early American newspapers, see Milton W. Hamilton, *The Country Printer: New York State, 1785–1830* (New York: Columbia University Press, 1964); W. J. Rorabaugh, *The Craft Apprentice: From Franklin to the Machine Age in America* (New York: Oxford University Press, 1986); and Rollo G. Silver, *The American Printer, 1787–1825* (Charlottesville: University Press of Virginia, 1967). On the communications system that allowed newspaper items to circulate so far and wide despite the small circulations of individual newspapers, see Richard R. John, *Spreading the News: The American Postal System from Franklin to Morse* (Cambridge, Mass.: Harvard University Press, 1995).

The press is only one aspect of the expanded notion of what counts as politics that is a hallmark of the new "new political history" that *Beyond the Founders* was trying to propagate. Parades, celebrations, songs, and especially toasts were also central to politics in the 1790s, and have been the subject of a wave of scholarship that began in the late 1980s: Susan G. Davis, *Parades and Power: Street Theatre in Nineteenth-Century Philadelphia* (Philadelphia: Temple University Press, 1986); Albrecht Koschnik, "Political Conflict and Public Contest: Rituals of National Celebration in Philadelphia, 1788–1815," *Pennsylvania Magazine of History and Biography* 118 (1994): 209–248; Simon P. Newman, *Parades and the Politics of the Street: Festive Culture in the Early American Republic* (Philadelphia: University of Pennsylvania Press, 1997); William Pencak, Matthew Dennis, and Simon P. Newman, eds., *Riot and Revelry in Early America* (University Park: Pennsylvania State University Press, 2002); Len Travers, *Celebrating the Fourth: Independence Day and the Rites of Nationalism in the Early Republic* (Amherst: University of Massachusetts Press, 1997); David Waldstreicher, *In the Midst of Perpetual Fetes: The Making of American Nationalism, 1776–1820* (Chapel Hill: University of North Carolina Press for the Omohundro Institute of Early American History and Culture, 1997); Sean Wilentz, "Artisan Republican Festivals and the Rise of Class Conflict in New York City, 1788–1837," in *Working-Class America: Essays on Labor, Community, and American Society*, ed. Michael Frisch and Daniel J. Walkowitz (Urbana: University of Illinois Press, 1983), 37–77. Just as important were dueling and other rituals associated with the culture of the eighteenth-century gentleman: Joanne B. Freeman, *Affairs of Honor: National Politics in the New Republic* (New Haven: Yale University Press, 2001). For suggestive studies of American political culture in the 1790s, see Alan Taylor, "From Fathers to Friends of the People: Political Personas in the Early Republic," *Journal of the Early Republic* 11 (1991): 465–491; and Alan Taylor, "'The Art of Hook and Snivey': Political Culture in Upstate New York during the 1790s," *Journal of American History* 79 (1993): 1371–1396.

Party politics in this early era has risen and fallen as a subject of historical interest. William Nisbet Chambers and Walter Dean Burnham, eds., *The American Party Systems: Stages of Political Development* (New York: Oxford University Press, 1967) proposed the notion of the Federalists and Republicans as constituting a "First Party System," the first stage of a series of paradigm shifts in the American political universe punctuated by critical realignments that brought on different party systems later. Other works that fed into or supported this approach were Walter Dean Burnham, *Critical Elections and the Mainsprings of American Politics* (New York: W. W. Norton, 1970); Joseph Charles, *The Origins of the American Party System* (Chapel Hill: University of North Carolina Press for the Institute of Early American History and Culture, 1956); and the books by Chambers and Cunningham cited above. This led to a wave of state and regional studies that are highly useful for following the details of the election of 1796: Paul Goodman, *The Democratic-Republicans of Massachusetts: Politics in a Young Republic* (Westport, Conn.: Greenwood Press, 1986); Carl E. Prince, *New Jersey's Jeffersonian Republicans: The Genesis of an Early Party Machine, 1789–1817* (Chapel Hill: University of North Carolina Press for the Institute of Early American History and Culture, 1967); Libero M. Renzulli Jr., *Maryland: The Federalist Years* (Madison, N.J.: Fairleigh Dickinson University Press, 1972); Norman K. Risjord, *Chesapeake Politics, 1781–1800* (New York: Columbia University Press, 1978); Alfred F. Young, *The Democratic Republicans of New York: The Origins, 1763–1797* (Chapel Hill: University of North Carolina Press for the Institute of Early American History and Culture, 1967); Richard G. Miller, *Philadelphia—The Federalist City: A Study of*

Urban Politics, 1789–1801 (Port Washington, N.Y.: Kennikat Press, 1976); and William Bruce Wheeler, "Urban Politics in Nature's Republic: The Development of Political Parties in the Seaport Cities in the Federalist Era" (Ph.D. diss., University of Virginia, 1967); and William Bruce Wheeler, "The Baltimore Jeffersonians, 1788–1800: A Profile of Intra-Factional Conflict," *Maryland Historical Magazine* 66 (1971): 153–168. Older state studies are also useful, including Delbert Harold Gilpatrick, *Jeffersonian Democracy in North Carolina, 1789–1816* (New York: Octagon Books, 1967); Richard J. Purcell, *Connecticut in Transition, 1775–1818* (Middletown, Conn.: Wesleyan University Press, 1963); William A. Robinson, *Jeffersonian Democracy in New England* (New York: Greenwood Press, 1968); Harry Marlin Tinkcom, *The Republicans and the Federalists in Pennsylvania, 1790–1801: A Study in National Stimulus and Local Response* (Harrisburg: Pennsylvania Historical and Museum Commission, 1950); and John A. Munroe, *Federalist Delaware, 1775–1815* (New Brunswick, N.J.: Rutgers University Press, 1954). A brand-new, ultramagisterial local study of political culture and society in New York State is John L. Brooke, *Columbia Rising: Civil Life on the Upper Hudson from the Revolution to the Age of Jackson* (Chapel Hill: University of North Carolina Press for the Omohundro Institute of Early American History and Culture, 2010).

A number of studies of the Democratic-Republican party have already been cited, but the famous dueling interpretations of the ideologies of the two major parties should also be consulted: Lance Banning, *The Jeffersonian Persuasion: Evolution of a Party Ideology* (Ithaca: Cornell University Press, 1978); and Joyce Appleby, *Capitalism and a New Social Order: The Republican Vision of the 1790s* (New York: New York University Press, 1984). The Federalists attracted comparatively fewer "First Party System" scholars, but there are some useful works on the Federalists: David Hackett Fischer, *The Revolution of American Conservatism: The Federalist Party in the Era of Jeffersonian Democracy* (New York: Harper & Row, 1965); James M. Banner Jr., *To the Hartford Convention: The Federalists and the Origins of Party Politics in Massachusetts* (New York: Alfred A. Knopf, 1970); Linda K. Kerber, *Federalists in Dissent: Imagery and Ideology in Jeffersonian America* (Ithaca: Cornell University Press, 1970); and James H. Broussard, *The Southern Federalists, 1800–1816* (Baton Rouge: Louisiana State University Press, 1978). Federalist studies have enjoyed a boom since the publication of Elkins and McKitrick's *Age of Federalism*, though not always by name: Marc M. Arkin, "The Federalist Trope: Power and Passion in Abolitionist Rhetoric," *Journal of American History* 88 (2001): 75–98; Doron Ben-Atar and Barbara B. Oberg, eds., *Federalists Reconsidered* (Charlottesville: University Press of Virginia, 1998); Rachel Hope Cleves, *The Reign of Terror in America: Visions of Violence from Anti-Jacobinism to Antislavery* (New York: Cambridge University Press, 2009); William C. Dowling, *Poetry and Ideology in Revolutionary Connecticut* (Athens: University of Georgia Press, 1990); William C. Dowling, *Literary Federalism in the Age of Jefferson: Joseph Dennie and "The Port Folio," 1801–1811* (Columbia: University of South Carolina Press, 1999); Todd Estes, *The Jay Treaty Debate, Public Opinion, and the Evolution of Early American Political Culture* (Amherst: University of Massachusetts Press, 2006); Marshall Foletta, *Coming to Terms with Democracy: Federalist Intellectuals and the Shaping of an American Culture* (Charlottesville: University Press of Virginia, 2001); Catherine O'Donnell Kaplan, *Men of Letters in the Early Republic: Cultivating Forms of Citizenship* (Chapel Hill: University of North Carolina Press for the Omohundro Institute of Early American History and Culture, 2008); and Jonathan D. Sassi, *A Republic of Righteousness: The Public Christianity of the Post-Revolutionary New England Clergy* (New York: Oxford University Press, 2001).

Ronald Formisano's attacks on the concept of a "first party system" on behalf of the quantitative New Political History of the 1960s and 1970s virtually ended the study of party politics in this period for twenty-five years: Ronald P. Formisano, "Deferential-Participant Politics: The Early Republic's Political Culture, 1789–1840," *American Political Science Review* 68 (1974): 473–487; Ronald P. Formisano, "Federalists and Republicans: Parties, Yes—System, No," in Paul Kleppner, Walter Dean Burnham, Ronald P. Formisano, Samuel P. Hays, Richard Jensen, and William G. Shade, *The Evolution of American Electoral Systems* (Westport, Conn.: Greenwood Press, 1981), 33–76; and Ronald P. Formisano, *The Transformation of Political Culture: Massachusetts Parties, 1790s–1840s* (New York: Oxford University Press, 1983).

Besides *Beyond the Founders* itself, the most effective answers to the nonparty view of early American political history are found in the works of the *New Nation Votes* mastermind Andrew W. Robertson: *The Language of Democracy: Political Rhetoric in the United States and Britain, 1790–1900* (Ithaca: Cornell University Press, 1995); and "'Look on This Picture . . . And on This!': Nationalism, Localism, and Partisan Images of Otherness in the United States, 1787–1820," *American Historical Review* 106 (2001): 1263–1280. Two lonely early challenges to Formisano were David A. Bohmer, "The Maryland Electorate and the Concept of a Party System in the Early National Period," in *The History of American Electoral Behavior*, ed. Joel H. Silbey, Allan G. Bogue, and William H. Flanigan (Princeton: Princeton University Press, 1978), 146–173; and David A. Bohmer, "Stability and Change in Early National Politics: The Maryland Voter and the Election of 1800," *William and Mary Quarterly*, 3rd ser., 36 (1979): 27–50.

Finally, let me make a note about sourcing and citations in the text of this book. To avoid exhausting all reader (and writer) patience, I have not tried to cite every scholar who has ever previously used a certain piece of information or quotation or who has ever written on a certain topic and beg my fellow scholars' patience if some obvious reference has been left out. The overlaps and redundancies across the entire corpus of Early Republic political historiography are innumerable, meaning in many cases that there are an almost infinite number of paths available to the same points. Striving to present my own interpretation of these events, I have limited myself to citing the particular texts in front of me that inspired particular arguments.

Index

abolitionism, 93, 210, 233, 234, 258, 259, 261, 334, 378

Adams, Abigail, 10, 25–26, 36, 59, 120, 185, 194, 203, 383, 410

Adams, Henry, 107–108

Adams, John, 1, 20–26, 42, 49, 120–121, 193, 194, 206, 207, 208, 403–404, 405–406; and Adet letters, 372, 374–375; on aristocracy, 284–286; and balanced government, 23–24, 277, 278; and British constitution, 23–24, 354, 409; campaign, noninvolvement in, 10, 188, 203, 226, 230; campaigning on behalf of, 194, 203–204, 250–251, 331, 338, 383, 393; and democratic politics, 23, 278, 283; electoral votes for, 26, 387, 390, 398, 404, 405; "firmness" of asserted, 11, 194, 276, 392; and Fisher Ames speech, 164, 167, 170; Hamilton's plotting against, 204–208, 222, 252; historiography of, 291; image of, 11, 20, 226, 290; inherits cabinet loyal to Hamilton, 410–411; as lesser-known Founder, 275–276; monarchical impulses of, 48–49, 285; monarchism, charged with, 292–293, 295, 330, 354, 378; named as presidential candidate, 204, 350; New England sectionalism, 378, 379–382, 387; "poisonous doctrines" of, 277, 281–283, 289, 290, 291–292, 333; on political opposition, 413; portrait of, 21; on social equality, 24, 49; sons of, 13, 26, 225, 292; South, owes presidential victory to, 398; Southern support for, 387–388, 390, 393, 395–398, 400; status consciousness of, 25, 185, 204, 285, 407; on term of presidency, 283, 286, 292; titles, campaign for, 48–49, 230, 285, 293, 354; and Washington's retirement, 183, 184–185, 203, 204; See also *Defence of the American Constitutions; Thoughts on Government*

Adams, John Quincy, 26, 50, 292, 410

Adams, Samuel, 22, 115, 341–345, 366, 392

Adams Family Papers (Massachusetts Historical Society), 293, 489

Addison, Joseph, 2, 19

Adet, Pierre, 186, 299–300, 364, 365, 371–375, 396, 403; *Aurora*, access to, 365, 366, 368; Cockade Proclamation of, 368; and electoral interference of, 374–375; and Jay Treaty, 116, 328; Pickering, sends open letters to, 366–370; war, threatens U.S. with, 364, 367, 370, 372

Age of Reason (Thomas Paine), 237, 264, 305

Alexandria, Va., 37, 322, 323, 325, 327, 337, 338, 340. See also *Columbian Mirror and Alexandria Gazette*

Alien and Sedition Acts, 162–163, 220, 362, 386, 414; Farewell Address lays groundwork for, 219

American Philosophical Society, 75, 258

American Revolution. *See* Revolution, American

Ames, Fisher, 122, 162–171, 174, 180, 223, 224, 341, 342, 344; Jay Treaty speech of, 162, 164–170; portrait of, 163

Anglican Church. *See* Church of England

Annapolis, Md., 391, 393

Antifederalists, 26, 109, 110, 251, 266, 397

anti-intellectualism, 220, 242, 251, 254, 256

antipartyism, 1–2, 359

Archer, John, 392

aristocracy, 323, 338, 341, 350, 378; Adams and, 284–286; Adams and Jefferson, differing views of, 288–289; and balanced government, 23, 30, 84–85, 241, 285, 290, 294 (*see also* Adams, John; *Defence of the American Constitutions*); British, 17, 284–285 (*see also* Constitution,

aristocracy (*continued*)
British: House of Lords); French, 64, 66; and monarchy, 285–287; natural, 147, 288–289, 305, 308, 403–404; need for disputed, 23, 54–55, 83, 96–97, 255–256, 281, 287; New York manor lords as, 28, 29, 111, 126, 147, 235; titled, lack of in America, 93, 290; *See also* "feudal revival"; Fairfax, Thomas

Arnold, Benedict, 269

Articles of Confederation, 29, 30, 31, 278

Austin, Benjamin, Jr., 121, 159, 341, 342, 373

Bache, Benjamin Franklin, 75, 126, 343, 353, 357, 358; and Adams post-election, 408; background and education of, 85; democratic constitutionalism of, 94, 112; in Jay Treaty crisis, 116–117, 119–124, 126, 127, 128, 129, 350; and Paine's *A Letter to George Washington*, 301, 303–304; Radical Enlightenment, 85, 91, 93, 217; use of peaceful model of political opposition, 94–97, 104, 128, 408; Washington administration, attacks on, 144–145, 350; *See also* Democratic Society of Pennsylvania; Philadelphia *Aurora;* Philadelphia *General Advertiser*

Bache, Margaret Markoe, 116, 117, 361

Baltimore, Md., 98, 99–100, 119, 154, 340, 387–389, 391, 392–393

Baltimore *Federal Gazette*, 317–318, 392, 393

Baltimore *Maryland Journal*, 230, 392

Baltimore Mechanical Society, 391, 392

Baltimore Republican Society, 99, 391

Bank of the United States, 44, 45, 46, 236

Banneker, Benjamin, 258–261

Barlow, Joel, 67, 272, 427–428n10

Beckley, John, 59, 128, 130–131, 141–142, 151, 385, 412, 413; as "Calm Observer," 141, 142–143; electoral predictions of, 349; and Federalist charges against Jefferson, 273–274; and Jefferson letter, 49–50; and New York legislative election, 173, 176,

177–178; and Pennsylvania elector election, 352–353, 357–358, 362, 404; Pennsylvania electors election, 357

Beckley, Maria, 361

Bemis, Samuel Flagg, 108

Binns, John Alexander, 324

Blake, George, 121

Blount, Thomas, 151–152

Blount, William, 211–212, 213, 214, 216, 365

Boston, Mass., 295; anti-British demonstrations in, 115; anti–Jay Treaty meetings in, 122–123; Democratic-Republican activists in ("Equality Alley"), 341, 342, 343, 366, 373; election of presidential electors in, 341–345

Boston *Columbian Centinel*, 121, 180, 276, 412; Adams, promoted by, 204, 343, 379, 383, 384–385; defends Jay Treaty, 105, 122–123, 156, 159; democratic tactics in Boston presidential electors election, 343–344; nameplate of, 384; and Washington, 143, 193, 204

Boston *Independent Chronicle*, 156, 159, 162, 295; in Boston presidential electors election, 341, 342, 344; in Jay Treaty protests, 115, 121, 122, 123

Boston *Massachusetts Mercury*, 159, 343

Boston *Polar Star*, 385–386

Brent, Daniel Carroll, 277, 319, 331, 333, 335, 340

Brissot de Warville, Jacques Pierre, 260

British. *See* Great Britain

British Constitution. *See* Constitution, British

Brown, Charles Brockden, 162, 165

Burk, John Daly, 385–386

Burke, Edmund, 11, 70, 82, 162, 164, 238–239, 241, 251, 254–256; and rhetoric of reaction, 241; See also *Reflections on the Revolution in France*

Burr, Aaron, 120, 179, 196–202, 230, 247, 380, 413; electoral votes for, 385, 387, 405; Jay Treaty debate, role in, 196–197; Monticello, visited by, 188, 198, 199; New England machinations of, 385–386; open campaigning, draws fire for, 188, 198; political colleagues' distrust of,

199–200; and Tennessee statehood
battle, 212, 215, 216; women and,
200–202
Butler, Pierce, 203

Cabot, George, 105, 130, 383
Callender, James Thomson, 297–298
"Calm Observer" series. *See under*
Beckley, John
campaign, presidential (1796), 182, 225;
candidates' noninvolvement in, 10,
13, 188, 189, 203, 226, 295; public
images of candidates in, 11, 14, 226
campaigning, 191, 226, 300, 307, 315,
340, 345, 388; cultural illegitimacy
of, in Early Republic, 182, 187, 193,
194, 199; Democratic-Republican,
319, 333, 336, 349, 352–359; "dirty
tricks" in, 358, 359; Federalist, 194,
203–204, 250–251, 330–332, 334,
338, 359–360, 372, 383, 393; the
"gaffe" tactic in, 263; negative, 225,
294, 333; role of "friends" in, 192
campaign themes, Democratic-
Republican: Declaration of
Independence, Jefferson as author
of, 194, 217, 277, 354, 391, 394;
Defence of the American Constitutions,
"poisonous doctrines" of, 281–282,
283, 289, 291; Enlightenment
statesman, Jefferson as, 227–228,
252, 253, 274; equal rights, Jefferson
as avatar of, 287, 289, 300, 354;
hereditary government, Adams
as proponent of, 224, 294, 295,
305, 354, 355; "man of the people,"
Jefferson as, 179, 193, 196, 314, 363;
monarchist, Adams as, 292, 294,
295, 331, 350, 354; republicanism/
democracy vs. monarchy/aristocracy,
109–110, 299, 344, 350, 354, 356, 360
campaign themes, Federalist:
Christianity, Jefferson as danger to,
50, 221, 237, 244–246, 263–264;
Enlightenment dilettante, Jefferson
as, 220, 231, 248, 254, 270; slavery,
Jefferson as danger to, 257–258,
259–261, 398; "speculation" vs.
"experience," 241–242, 397; "want
of firmness," 225, 268, 271–272, 331,
332, 333, 335

Carey, Mathew, 353
Carroll, Charles, 345
Cato (Joseph Addison), 2, 19
caucuses, 5, 149, 151, 152, 202, 203,
206, 344; congressional nominating,
202–203, 206
celebratory politics, 69, 76–78, 104,
114, 118, 185, 316–317, 341, 361;
newspaper reporting of, 76, 77, 114;
partisanization of, 77–78; *See also*
Fourth of July celebrations; toasts
character attacks, 225, 275, 277, 285
Charleston, S.C., 74, 180, 208, 222, 233,
236, 249–250, 274
Charleston *City Gazette,* 401
Chase, Samuel, 389, 392
Chastellux, Marquis de, 227, 270
Cherokee and Chickamauga Indians,
211–212
Christianity: established (tax-supported)
churches, 42, 221, 323, 336 (*see
also* "Virginia Statute for Religious
Freedom"; religious freedom); and
Federalists, 245–246; Federalists
deploy in politics, 11, 135–137,
167–168, 231, 244–245, 262–266,
337, 376, 393, 463n38; French
Revolution's threat to, 66, 262;
government, role in, 39, 221;
Jefferson attacked for alleged
hostility to, 50, 221, 231, 244–246; in
postrevolutionary America, 39–41,
237–238, 466n74
Christie, Gabriel, 99, 171
Church of England, 31, 39, 40, 221, 323,
326, 336
Cincinnati, Society of, 77
classical models: Belisarius, 139–140;
Cato, 2, 19; Cincinnatus, 19, 139;
Publicola, 139; Publius, 31, 139;
Valerius, 139
Clay, Henry, 257
Claypoole, David C., 222–223
Clinton, De Witt, 128, 173, 178
Clinton, George, 28, 49, 120, 195, 198,
230, 405, 413–414
Cobbett, William, 238–239, 372, 383,
461n24, 468n6
Cocke, William, 214
Coleman, Robert, 363
Collot, Victor, 365

House of Representatives, U.S.: debate over role in foreign policy, 146, 147, 149, 152, 233; Jay Treaty debate in, 145–148; and Tennessee statehood battle, 214–215, 216
Howard, John Eager, 392
human perfectability, 35, 240
Hume, David, 238, 239–240
Hutchinson, James, 75

Illuminati, 237, 265
inequality, social, 42, 49, 69, 95, 286, 289, 424n49
Indians, American, 60–61, 62, 79–80, 102, 103, 174, 212; allied with British, 60, 62, 79–80, 102–103, 153, 161, 174–175, 209, 211; Ames on, in Jay Treaty speech, 163, 168–171; northwestern confederacy of, 62, 88, 162, 211; on southwestern frontier, 211–212; as target of Hamilton's military muscle flexing, 88; *See also* Cherokee and Chickamauga Indians; Iroquois Confederacy; Miamis; Mohawks; Northwest, Old; war
internationalism. *See* "popular cosmopolitanism"; Europe; "foreign influence"; foreign interference and intervention; toasts
Iredell, James, 164, 399, 400
Iroquois Confederacy, 156, 174–175, 335
Irvine, William, 352, 362
Isenberg, Nancy, 201–202
Israel, Israel, 75, 358
Israel, Jonathan, 84, 91, 296, 430–431n38, 433n56
Izard, Ralph, 235, 250

Jackson, Andrew, 9, 63, 99, 309
Jackson, James, 405
Jacobins, 66, 68, 71, 72, 82, 83, 91; as epithet for Democratic-Republicans, 7, 68, 122, 123, 124, 127, 198
Jarvis, Charles, 121, 123, 159, 162, 341, 342, 373
Jay, John, 106, 177, 209; appointment of and Democratic-Republicans, 106; Britain, mission to, 106–107, 108, 112–113, 281; and Hamilton's disclosures, 108
Jay Treaty, 101, 102, 108, 109, 139, 181; appropriations for, 147, 148, 151–152,

153, 163, 171–172, 187, 213, 392; corruption of alleged, 113; principal measures of, 107, 367; secrecy of condemned as unrepublican, 112; Washington and allies deeply embarrassed by, 113; Washington seals contents of, 108
Jay Treaty crisis, 112, 133, 137, 187, 197, 250, 295; Ames speech in, 162, 164–170, 174; antitreaty meetings, 124; Boston meetings on, 122–123; commercial interests and, 158; early Federalist counterdemonstrations, 126; Federalist counterattack in, 152–162; Federalists on *Independent Chronicle*, 115; "Franklin" series and, 110–112, 436n22; New York meetings on, 124–126; Philadelphia meetings on, 127–129
Jefferson, Thomas, 32–37, 173, 179, 186, 226, 242, 251, 253, 259; Adams, personal friendship with, 36, 50, 279, 404, 411; as antislavery figure, 228–229; Banneker, Benjamin, correspondence with, 258–261; campaign, noninvolvement in, 10, 189, 226, 295; campaigning on behalf of, 319, 333, 336, 349, 352–359; Christianity, attacked for alleged hostility to, 50, 221, 231, 244–246; "colonization" policy of, 257; Declaration of Independence, author of, 32, 194, 217, 229, 258, 276, 391, 394; electoral votes for, 398, 402, 404, 405; as Enlightenment dilettante, 11, 220, 225, 231, 248, 253–254; Enlightenment interests of, 34–36, 51, 227; France, minister to, 36–37, 64, 266; French Revolution, supporter of, 69–70, 205, 229; and Hamilton's financial system, 44–46; historiography of, 226, 229, 259, 274; image of, 11, 226, 228, 229, 269; inventions of ridiculed, 243, 247, 254, 255; investigation of by Virginia legislature, 271; manliness of attacked, 11, 246, 247, 272–273, 397; as "man of the people," 179, 193, 196, 314, 363; and Mazzei letter, 191–192, 284; named as presidential candidate, 188, 224, 350; *National Gazette* scandal, 57–58;

Jefferson "catechism," 391, 394 (fig.); political culture of, 388–389, 392

masculinity. *See* manliness

Mason, George, 251, 310, 327

Mason, John Thomson, 318

Mason, Stevens Thomson, 116, 128, 327–328, 343

Massachusetts, 38–39, 156, 159, 385; Electoral College meeting in, 383; end of slavery in, 39; religion in, 39, 40

Mazzei, Phillip, 191, 284

McClenachan, Blair, 129, 353

McHenry, James, 154, 209

McKean, Thomas, 92, 128, 352, 362, 403

memorials. *See* petitions

metaphors, political, 10, 12–13, 29, 167, 268, 277, 291, 294, 372; family model, 12–13, 168, 220, 240, 265, 270, 411; "fathers" of the people, 10, 220, 325; "firmness," 225, 271, 270–272, 332–334; "friends of the people," 10, 54, 83, 249, 316, 344, 355, 412; "strict father morality" (Lakoff), 10, 246; Washington as "Father of His Country," 12–13, 138–139, 142, 168, 184, 305, 411; *See also* manliness

Miamis, 62, 80, 88, 162

Mid-Atlantic states, 10, 41, 173, 202. *See also* New Jersey; New York; Pennsylvania

Mifflin, Thomas, 92, 97–98, 363

Miles, Samuel, 360, 363

militias, 74, 78, 98, 107, 115, 119, 127, 140, 269, 339, 350; politicization of in Philadelphia, 117–118, 357

Mississippi River, 62, 106, 206, 209, 211, 215

Mohawks, 174. *See also* Iroquois Confederacy

monarchy, 22, 424n49; Adams and charged with advocating, 285–287, 292–293, 295, 330, 354, 378; balanced government, as element in, 23, 24, 30, 84–85, 278, 279, 281, 285, 290, 293–294; British, 20, 30, 45, 47, 48, 242, 281, 291, 299; French, 64, 66–67, 68, 70, 71, 72, 91, 121, 302, 307–308; as hereditary rule, 49, 55, 224, 238, 241, 294,

295, 305; Polish, 309, 370–371; presidency as elective, 2, 20, 47–49, 56, 187, 193, 299; *See also* Great Britain: defends monarchy against French Revolution; metaphors, political: family model; presidency

Monroe, James, 58, 141, 186–187, 200, 247, 265, 303–304

Montesquieu, 84, 295, 297, 300

Monticello, 35, 37, 51, 189–190, 227, 243, 269, 270, 371; Burr's visit to, 188, 198–200

Morris, Gouverneur, 29, 111, 303, 310

Morris, Robert, 29–30

Muhlenberg, Frederick A. C., 172, 353

Munford, William, 319

Murray, William Vans, 104, 389, 393, 395–396, 397–398; democratic politics, use of, 397; partisanship, embrace of, 393, 397; portrait of, 390; pseudonymous writings by, 395; "Short Vindication" of Adams's *Defence*, author of, 395–396

Nashville, Tenn., 212

nationalism, 27, 41, 291, 301, 373, 374–375, 400

Native Americans. *See* Indians

Netherlands, 175, 186, 266–267, 296, 298–299, 373

Neville, John, 88, 89, 95

Newburgh conspiracy, 19–20, 27, 29, 183

New England: Adet's interference in presidential election, response to, 375–376; as "Bible belt" of early republic, 39, 40–41; clergy on religion, 237–238, 337; historiography of, 288; leadership in, 288; Pinckney plot, Federalist leaders grapple with, 380–385; slavery, end of in, 38–39; Standing Order in, 40, 262, 377; support for Adams, 378, 379–382, 387; Tennessee statehood, hostility of Federalists to, 213–214; and Three-Fifths Compromise, 377; town meetings in, 159; *See also* Christianity

New Hampshire, 71, 86, 160, 170–171, 198, 216, 348, 376, 379, 382

New Jersey, 28, 120, 148, 294, 349, 378, 386, 387

New Jersey Journal, 141

New Nation Votes database, 8–9, 493, 494, 498

newspapers: addresses in, 109, 218; business models of, 53, 56; as communities of opinion, 54, 313; exchange, 56, 337; geographic barriers, as breachers of, 52–53, 312, 313–314; network of, 56, 110, 139, 425n63; partisan, 54; as party-building mechanism, 56, 408; pseudonymous writings in, 50, 53, 110, 139–141, 218; as tool for managing public opinion, 52, 53

newspapers, Democratic-Republican: circulate quotes from *Defence of the American Constitutions,* 282–283; retooled for Jay Treaty fight, 109

newspapers, Federalist, 197, 271, 272; promote *Defence of the American Constitutions,* 280; on Democratic-Republicans and Adams, 409, 412

New York (state), 28–29, 41, 78, 114, 155–156, 172, 173–176, 230, 387; and Adams's election, 180; and Jay Treaty, 175; legislative election (1796) in, 172, 176, 177–180; western, 155–156, 173–175, 180, 324–325

New York *Argus,* 109, 126, 166–167, 170, 177

New York City, 107, 109, 119–120, 127, 155, 157, 160, 161; anti–Jay Treaty meetings in, 124–126; and Keteltas affair, 176–177

New York Democratic Society, 85, 147

Nicholas, Wilson Cary, 199

Nicholson, James, 126, 127

nominations, presidential, 187, 188, 202, 203, 206, 208; "Great Mentioner in Reverse" effect, 195, 196, 217; *See also* caucuses

Norfolk, Va., 114–115, 124, 323

North Carolina, 40, 102, 211, 280, 398; and Adams's election, 400; Cape Fear region, 399–400; partisanship in, 399; Pinckney plot, electors opt out of, 400

Northwest, Old, 61–62, 88, 103, 162; Northwest Ordinance, 212, 213, 214, 215; Northwest Territory, 62, 209, 213, 228; *See also* frontier; Indians, American; West

notables, local, 307–309, 311–313, 317, 318, 319, 320–322; Assembly of Notables (France), as origin of term, 307–308; Founders as, 308; and partisanship, 313, 314, 321–322, 333

Notes on the State of Virginia (Thomas Jefferson), 236, 243, 256–257, 258, 262, 263, 275, 279; as abolitionist work, 228–229; in Federalist campaign against Jefferson, 227, 256–257, 259, 260, 263; initial reception of, 227–228

opposition (concept), 1, 59, 89–90, 132, 209, 219, 222, 267, 304, 412

"Orders in Council," 102, 103; as blow to U.S. national pride, 102

Ordinance of 1787. *See* Northwest, Old: Northwest Ordinance

Ore, James, 212

Oswald, Eleazer, 110–111

Otis, Harrison Gray, 344, 345

Otis, Samuel A., 203, 214

"out of doors" politics, 80–81, 94, 104, 133, 157, 158, 219; Federalist fear of, 105; *See also* Democratic-Republican Societies; public opinion

Paine, Thomas, 52, 68, 70, 72, 92, 165, 263–265, 270, 272; in French Revolution, 301–303; imprisonment and near execution of, 302–303; *A Letter to George Washington,* author of, 303–306, 355; portrait of, 302; unicameral constitutional model of, 23, 92, 278; and Washington administration, 302–303; See also *Age of Reason; Common Sense; The Rights of Man*

parties, institutionalized, 4–5, 144, 349

parties, U.S. political: as communities of opinion, 6–7, 54, 425n59; constitutional discouragement of, 3, 5, 10, 16; continuity/lineages of, 7–8, 13, 156, 231, 246, 419n25, 463n38; formation of, 3; Founders' aversion to, 1–2, 182; informality of, early, 9; *See also* history, political; metaphors, political

partisanship, 5, 12, 349, 359; Boston presidential electors election in, 343, 345; embrace of, 109, 117,

Quasi-War, 237, 400, 413